PERCY BYSSHE SHELLEY

Selected Poems and Prose

Edited by
JACK DONOVAN *and* CIAN DUFFY

PENGUIN BOOKS

PENGUIN CLASSICS

UK | USA | Canada | Ireland | Australia
India | New Zealand | South Africa

Penguin Books is part of the Penguin Random House group of companies
whose addresses can be found at global.penguinrandomhouse.com.

This edition first published in Penguin Classics 2016

014

Set in 9.25/11 pt Adobe Sabon
Typeset by Jouve (UK), Milton Keynes
Printed in Great Britain by Clays Ltd, Elcograf S.p.A.

ISBN: 978-0-241-25306-9

www.greenpenguin.co.uk

Contents

THE PROSE

Chronology

1792 4 *August*: Percy Bysshe Shelley (hereafter PBS) born at Field Place, Warnham, near Horsham, Sussex; eldest child of Timothy Shelley, landowner and Whig MP (1790–92, 1802–18), and Elizabeth Shelley, née Pilfold, of a neighbouring family of landed gentry. Four younger sisters and one younger brother follow.

1793 21 *January*: Execution of King Louis XVI of France.

September: 'Reign of Terror' begins (continues until *July* 1794).

1798 *May–September*: United Irishmen rebel against British rule.

1800 *July–August*: Acts of Union between Great Britain and Ireland.

1802–4 PBS at Syon House Academy, Isleworth, near London; here and later at Eton attends lectures on general science by Adam Walker, author of *Analysis of a Course of Lectures on Natural and Experimental Philosophy* (1766).

1804–10 At Eton College, rebels against the 'fagging' system which required younger boys to perform menial tasks for older ones; befriended by the physician Dr James Lind, author of important research on typhus and scurvy.

1806 Grandfather becomes Sir Bysshe Shelley, Baronet.

1808 Opens correspondence with cousin, Harriet Grove; her family will put an end to their attachment in 1810.

1810 *Spring*: Publishes *Zastrozzi*, a Gothic romance.

September: *Original Poetry; by Victor and Cazire*, written together with sister Elizabeth, subsequently withdrawn when one of the poems is discovered to be a plagiarism.

October: Goes up to University College, Oxford; begins friendship with fellow undergraduate Thomas Jefferson Hogg.

November: Publishes *Posthumous Fragments of Margaret Nicholson*.

December: Publishes a second Gothic romance, *St. Irvyne* (dated 1811).

1811 *January*: First meeting with sixteen-year-old Harriet Westbrook. George III declared mentally incompetent; Prince of Wales becomes regent.

March: PBS publishes anonymously the political satire *Poetical Essay on the Existing State of Things*, to benefit imprisoned Irish journalist Peter Finnerty, and subscribes to a fund for Finnerty's support. Distributes a pamphlet, *The Necessity of Atheism* (written with Hogg early in the year).

25 March: Together with Hogg is expelled from University College after refusing to respond to questions about the authorship of the pamphlet at a disciplinary hearing.

June: Begins lengthy correspondence with Sussex schoolmistress Elizabeth Hitchener.

25–29 August: Elopes with Harriet Westbrook and marries her in Edinburgh.

Winter: Travels to Keswick and meets Robert Southey (*November–January* 1812).

1812 *January*: Introduces himself by letter to William Godwin, whose novels and *Enquiry Concerning Political Justice* (1793) he had long admired.

February–April: Travels with Harriet to Dublin, where he speaks in favour of Catholic emancipation and repeal of the Union and distributes two pamphlets: *An Address to the Irish People* and *Proposals for an Association of . . . Philanthropists*. *A Declaration of Rights* printed. PBS adopts a vegetarian diet.

April–August: Disillusioned with Irish politics, moves first to Wales (*April–June*), then to Lynmouth, Devon (*June–August*), where he writes *A Letter to Lord Ellenborough* to protest against the imprisonment of Daniel Isaac Eaton for selling the third part of Thomas Paine's *Age of Reason*, and is subject to government surveillance. His Irish servant is imprisoned for distributing *A Declaration of Rights* and a satirical poem, 'The Devil's Walk'.

May: British prime minister, Spencer Perceval, assassinated in the House of Commons; succeeded by Lord Liverpool.

September: PBS Moves to Tremadoc, north Wales, where he supports construction of embankment and model village.

October–November: Close association with William Godwin and first meeting with Thomas Love Peacock in London; meets for first time Mary, daughter of Godwin and Mary Wollstonecraft. Transcribes early poems into 'Esdaile Notebook' (from *November* to early 1813); most remain unpublished until 1964.

1813 *27 February*: Leaves Tremadoc suddenly, claiming that a nocturnal intruder had fired two shots at him at Tan-yr-Allt, the house where the Shelleys were staying.

March: Travels to Dublin and Killarney.

5 April: Returns to London.

May: Publishes *A Vindication of Natural Diet* (on the benefits of vegetarianism); *Queen Mab* printed and circulated privately.

23 June: Daughter, Eliza Ianthe, born.

July–October: PBS attains legal majority of twenty-one years (*4 August*). Moves to Bracknell, Berkshire, associates with a radical circle of supporters of the French Revolution, including the vegetarian and naturist John Frank Newton and his sister-in-law Harriet de Boinville.

1814 Divides time between Windsor, London and Bracknell, raising loans for his own and Godwin's benefit, avoiding creditors and regularly visiting the Godwin household. *A Refutation of Deism* printed and privately circulated early in the year.

April: French monarchy restored after Allied defeat of Napoleon.

26 June: Mary Godwin declares her love for PBS.

28 July: Elopes with Mary to France and Switzerland, accompanied by her stepsister, Claire Clairmont (hereafter CC).

25–26 August: Begins composition of the prose tale 'The Assassins'.

September: Returns to London (*13 September*); pursued by creditors, attempts to raise money over the following months.

Congress of Vienna convenes to determine the shape of post-Napoleonic Europe.

30 November: Son, Charles, born to Harriet.

December: PBS's review of Hogg's novel *Memoirs of Prince Alexy Haimatoff* published.

1815 *January–February*: Death of grandfather, Sir Bysshe Shelley (*5 January*). Meets with radical publisher George Cannon, editor of the *Theological Inquirer*, which will reprint *A Refutation of Deism* and large extracts from *Queen Mab*.

22 February: Mary gives birth to premature infant, who dies *6 March*.

26 February: Napoleon escapes from Elba.

May: Financial settlement with PBS's father allows PBS to pay debts, make gifts to Harriet and Godwin, and grants him an annual income of £1,000, £200 of which is allocated to Harriet.

18 June: Final defeat of Napoleon at Waterloo.

August–September: PBS moves with Mary to Bishopsgate, at the eastern entrance to Windsor Great Park. Ten days' excursion up the Thames with Mary, Peacock and CC's brother Charles.

26 September: Treaty of the Holy Alliance signed by Austria, Prussia and Russia.

Autumn: PBS composes *Alastor*.

1816 *24 January*: Son, William, born to Mary.
February: *Alastor* volume published.
3 May: PBS travels to Switzerland with Mary and CC.
27 May: Meets Byron in Geneva.
June: Mary conceives the idea for *Frankenstein*. PBS tours Lake Geneva with Byron; drafts 'Hymn to Intellectual Beauty'.
July: Visits Chamonix with Mary and CC; drafts 'Mont Blanc'.
September: Returns to England (*8 September*) and moves to Bath.
October: Mary's half-sister Fanny Imlay (daughter of Mary Wollstonecraft and her lover, Gilbert Imlay) commits suicide (*9 October*).
November: Harriet Shelley drowns herself in the Serpentine, London (her body is found *10 December*).
PBS frequents Leigh Hunt's social gatherings together with Keats, J. H. Reynolds and Horace Smith.
December: Learns of Harriet's death (*15 December*). Marries Mary (hereafter MWS) (*30 December*); marriage reconciles the couple with Godwin.

1817 *12 January*: Birth of Alba (later 'Allegra'), CC's daughter by Byron.
March: Habeas Corpus suspended in England until 1 February 1818 in response to agitation for reform (*4 March*).
PBS publishes the pamphlet *A Proposal for Putting Reform to the Vote* under the nom de plume 'The Hermit of Marlow'. The Shelleys, together with CC and her child, occupy Albion House, Great Marlow; Peacock is near neighbour.
27 March: PBS denied custody of the children of his first marriage in the Court of Chancery, on a decision of the Lord Chancellor, Lord Eldon.
Composes *Laon and Cythna* (*March–September*).
2 September: MWS gives birth to a daughter, Clara.
October: PBS detained briefly for debt.
November: Anonymous publication of *History of a Six Weeks' Tour* (which includes 'Mont Blanc'), co-authored with MWS. Death of the Princess Charlotte and execution of the 'Pentridge Martyrs' for leading an armed revolt in Derbyshire (*6–7 November*) – PBS composes pamphlet linking the two events, *An Address to the People on the Death of the Princess Charlotte* (*11–12 November*).
Drafts 'On Christianity' (late 1817).
December: Writes 'Ozymandias'; *Laon and Cythna* published and withdrawn from sale.

1818 *January*: Revised version of *Laon and Cythna*, its attack on religion toned down and incest theme removed, published as *The Revolt of Islam*.

March: MWS's *Frankenstein* published anonymously.

11 March: PBS departs for Italy, accompanied by MWS, CC, their children and two servants.

4 *April*: Arrives in Milan.

28 *April*: Allegra sent to Byron in Venice.

May: PBS meets Maria Gisborne and her family at Livorno.

June: Moves to Bagni di Lucca, where he translates Plato's *Symposium*, writes 'On Love' and completes title-poem of *Rosalind and Helen* volume.

August: Accompanies CC to Venice; visits Byron to discuss Allegra's future; stays in a villa (I Cappuccini), rented but not occupied by Byron, at Este, south-west of the city (until *November*).

September–October: Begins *Prometheus Unbound* and *Julian and Maddalo*.

24 *September*: One-year-old Clara Shelley dies in Venice.

October: PBS composes 'Lines Written among the Euganean Hills, October, 1818'.

November: The Shelley party visits Ferrara and Bologna en route for Rome, where PBS begins to write 'The Coliseum'.

December: Settles at Naples (*1 December–28 February*): with MWS and CC makes excursion to ascend Vesuvius; visits Herculaneum, various volcanic landscapes, Pompei, and other sites of Classical interest. Composes 'Stanzas Written in Dejection . . . near Naples'.

27 *December*: Elena Adelaide Shelley born; the birth will be registered on 27 *February* 1819 and the child declared his and MWS's legitimate offspring – her true parentage an abiding enigma for biographers.

1819 5 *March*: Family arrives back in Rome.

April: Acts I–III of *Prometheus Unbound* completed.

Rosalind and Helen, a Modern Eclogue; with Other Poems published (*spring*).

May: Begins to compose *The Cenci*.

7 *June*: Death of William Shelley, aged three and a half.

17 June: PBS relocates to Livorno.

August: Completes *The Cenci* and sends *Julian and Maddalo* to Leigh Hunt for anonymous publication (though it does not appear until 1824). Composes Act IV of *Prometheus Unbound* (*August–December*).

September: Writes *The Mask of Anarchy* in response to the 'Peterloo Massacre'.

October: Moves to Florence (2 *October*). Composes 'Ode to the West Wind' and *Peter Bell the Third*.

November–December: Drafts 'On Life' and begins *A Philosophical View of Reform*.

12 November: Son, Percy Florence, the Shelleys' only child to reach adulthood, born.

December: In an attempt to control dissent, Parliament passes the 'Six Acts', curtailing freedom of the press and freedom of assembly. PBS sends 'England in 1819' to Leigh Hunt.

1820 *January*: Death of George III; Prince Regent becomes George IV.

26 January: The Shelley household moves to Pisa.

February: Cato Street conspiracy to assassinate the British prime minister and cabinet detected (leaders executed *1 May*).

Spring: Constitutional monarchy re-established in Spain following rebellion of the armed forces (*March*).
PBS composes 'The Sensitive-Plant' and 'Ode to Liberty'.

Summer: The Shelleys occupy the Gisbornes' house at Livorno, while they are in England (*15 June–4 August*), where PBS writes 'Letter to Maria Gisborne' and 'To a Sky-Lark' (*June–July*).

July: Learns of the death (on *9 June*) of Elena Adelaide Shelley. Constitutional revolution begins in Naples.

August: The Shelleys move to the spa Bagni di San Giuliano (Bagni di Pisa) (staying there until *October*). PBS writes *The Witch of Atlas*, 'Ode to Naples' and *Oedipus Tyrannus; or, Swellfoot the Tyrant*, a burlesque Greek tragedy (on the political crisis over the claims of Caroline of Brunswick, estranged wife of George IV, to be crowned queen), which is published anonymously in London in *December* and immediately suppressed.

Prometheus Unbound . . . with Other Poems published.

20 October: CC moves to Florence.

29 October: The Shelleys return to Pisa.

November: First meeting of PBS with Teresa Viviani, to whom *Epipsychidion* will be addressed.

December: First meeting with Alexandros Mavrokordatos, Greek patriot and future president of Greece.

1821 *January–February*: Introduced to Edward and Jane Williams, newly arrived in Pisa (*13 January*). Writes *Epipsychidion*.

February–March: Writes *A Defence of Poetry* (published 1840); second edition of *The Cenci* published in London (*spring*).

March: Neapolitan revolutionaries defeated by Austrian troops acting on behalf of the Holy Alliance.

April: PBS learns (from Mavrokordatos) that an armed revolt has begun in Greece against Ottoman rule, and of the death in Rome (on *23 February*) of John Keats.

April–June: PBS composes *Adonais* (printed at Pisa in *July*).

May: Death of Napoleon (*5 May*; PBS probably receives the news in *July*).

The Shelleys return to Bagni di San Giuliano (*8 May*). *Epipsychidion* published anonymously in London.

July: Drafts 'Written on hearing the news of the death of Napoleon' (published with *Hellas* in 1822).

August: Visits Byron at Ravenna.

Late September–November: Composes *Hellas*.

25 October: Returns from Bagni di San Giuliano to Pisa.

1 November: Byron moves to Pisa.

1822 *January*: PBS writes scenes for drama *Charles the First*, which is left unfinished.

14 January: Meets Edward Trelawny, who joins the Byron–Shelley circle in Pisa. Increasing attachment to Jane Williams, to whom he addresses a number of poems (*January–July*).

February–April: Translates passages from Goethe and Calderón, and works on 'Unfinished Drama'.

20 April: Death of Allegra.

30 April: The Shelleys and the Williamses move to San Terenzo, on the Bay of Spezia near Lerici.

May–June: PBS drafts the unfinished *The Triumph of Life*.

12 May: His sailing boat, the *Don Juan*, is delivered.

16 June: MWS miscarries dangerously, crediting her recovery to PBS's prompt attention.

1 July: Accompanied by Edward Williams, PBS sails to Livorno to meet Leigh Hunt and his family, who have come to Italy.

8 July: Drowns during a squall on the return voyage, along with Williams and the young seaman Charles Vivian.

Mid July: Bodies of PBS and Williams recovered.

15–16 August: Bodies cremated on the beach near Viareggio, with Hunt, Byron, Trelawny and others in attendance; ashes interred in the Protestant Cemetery, Rome, in 1823.

1823 *July*: MWS returns to England.

1824 *June*: MWS publishes *Posthumous Poems of Percy Bysshe Shelley*; edition suppressed at the insistence of Sir Timothy Shelley.

1839 MWS publishes *The Poetical Works of Percy Bysshe Shelley*, in four volumes, and late in the year a revised *Poetical Works* in one volume dated 1840.

1840 MWS publishes *Essays, Letters from Abroad, Translations and Fragments* in two volumes.

Introduction

I

When Percy Bysshe Shelley drowned off the north-west coast of Italy in July 1822, just a month short of his thirtieth birthday, he left behind a quantity of poetry and prose as remarkable for substance and scope as for intellectual range and formal diversity. In a literary career of little more than a dozen years, Shelley produced some 450 finished poems and verse fragments. These extend across virtually the entire spectrum of genres and modes practised in the Romantic period: dream vision and epic-romance, tragic and comic verse drama, political ballad, satirical squib, popular song, funeral elegy, allegory, confessional autobiography, ode and hymn; occasional pieces on both private and public themes; sentimental, mythological and symbolic narratives; conversation poems, meditative and topical sonnets – as well as the exquisitely crafted brief lyrics for which he is mostly remembered. Shelley also made a number of verse translations – from Greek and Latin, Italian, Spanish and German, including a number of the *Homeric Hymns* and passages of Virgil, Dante, Calderón and Goethe. His work in prose includes two Gothic novels and several shorter fictional narratives; political pamphlets; metaphysical and psychological speculation; translations of Platonic dialogues; critical essays on subjects as varied as religious belief, vegetarianism, sexuality, the Devil and diabolism, and brief considerations of several others – as well as the classic of English literary theory, *A Defence of Poetry*.

Shelley's extraordinary output has come to be recognized as one of the major literary contributions to the English Romantic Movement, and his poetry in particular as boldly original, technically accomplished and critically challenging – altogether a brilliantly distinctive reinterpretation of the European poetic tradition. Such was not the case in Shelley's lifetime, however, when a number of factors combined to deny him the audience that he persisted in seeking in the face of both widespread disregard and outright hostility. Both material and cultural factors account for the neglect of his writing by his contemporaries. Much of the verse and prose that now forms the basis of his reputation was not published until after his death. *The Mask of Anarchy*, for example, written in autumn 1819 as a response to the 'Peterloo Massacre' in Manchester, was withheld for fear of prosecution until 1832. *Julian and Maddalo*, *The Witch of Atlas*, *Peter Bell the Third*, 'Letter to Maria Gisborne' and *A Defence of Poetry* did not appear until Mary Shelley's editions of her late husband's work in 1824, 1839 and 1840. Other examples of posthumous publication, including most of Shelley's lyric poetry, could be cited. The dozen volumes of his verse that did appear in his lifetime, almost all of them at his own expense (the usual practice at the time for an author untried in the marketplace), sold poorly, and that in an age when poetry could and did earn both critical esteem and commercial success for lesser talents than his – setting aside the remarkable status attained by major figures like Thomas Moore, Walter Scott and Lord Byron.[1] The highly controversial subject matter of several of Shelley's most ambitious works was another obstacle to recognition, established booksellers being averse to the financial and legal risk of publishing them. The firm that did bring out most of his published volumes, C. and J. Ollier, was a small, impecunious and inexperienced operation lacking the resources to promote a little-known author. Shelley came to regret his connection with the Olliers, whose dealings with him and his poetry were certainly less than assiduous and largely ineffective.[2]

Partisan literary politics also played its part. Shelley's *Queen Mab* (1813) and *Laon and Cythna* (1817), revised and reissued as *The Revolt of Islam* (1818), made outright attacks on monarchy and institutional religion as principal sources of the injustice and oppression which had continued to blight the world since first kings and priests leagued together in mutual interest. Both poems also frankly denied the existence of God and (in the unrevised *Laon and Cythna*) celebrated the incestuous love of a brother and sister as liberation from arbitrary moral proscription. Polemical and openly belligerent, these substantial works attracted the animosity, and on occasion the malevolence, of the conservative press, instances of which are considered below. Shelley's association with the liberal weekly *The Examiner* and its editor, the poet and man of letters Leigh Hunt (1784–1859), gave rise to further contention. Hunt had introduced Shelley in his newspaper as a rising talent, published some of his poems and defended his literary gifts and personal integrity. To some, Shelley was tarnished by association with what *Blackwood's Magazine* lampooned as an impudent and subversive coterie gathered round Hunt, the 'Cockney School', which included John Keats and William Hazlitt.[3] And, as if all this were not enough to nourish suspicion and provoke censure, a few notorious events in Shelley's personal life served as a basis on which to construct a sensational history of impiety and moral depravity.

In March 1811 Shelley had been expelled from University College, Oxford, for diffusing, and then refusing to deny his joint authorship (with his fellow undergraduate Thomas Jefferson Hogg) of, the rationalist pamphlet *The Necessity of Atheism*.[4] For this, together with the two long poems mentioned above, he was in orthodox quarters caricatured as impious, not to say demonic. Additional opprobrium (as well as prurient interest) was attracted by the tangled involvements of his private life. In July 1814 he had eloped with the then Mary Godwin, abandoning Harriet, his wife of three years, and their two children – an act which acquired a tragic dimension when Harriet committed suicide in autumn 1816. Mary's stepsister, Claire Clairmont, had accompanied her and Shelley to France and Switzerland in summer 1814 and lived with them for long periods thereafter. Claire (then pregnant by Byron) again made one of their party in summer 1816 in Switzerland, giving rise to rumours of a 'league of incest' involving herself, Mary, Byron and Shelley.[5] From early 1817 the presence of Claire's child Alba (later 'Allegra') in the Shelley household inspired further rumours of promiscuity. The imputations of sexual licence combined with his reputation for atheism to prepossess opinion against Shelley as both irreligious and dissolute, the latter condition seeming to follow as a matter of course from the former. As if in official validation of these charges, in March 1817 the Court of Chancery denied him custody of his two children by his first wife, in order, the court ruled, to prevent the principles that governed his behaviour being communicated to his offspring.

And then many of Shelley's major poems, among them several on which he himself set great store, are (in the words of his friend Edward Williams) 'far above the level of common apprehension'.[6] Ambitious in scope, sophisticated in their procedures, they ask for close and sustained attention from readers as well as an alert receptiveness to literary experiment. Shelley himself repeatedly acknowledged that such poetry could only ever be of limited appeal, qualifying the audience he addressed as 'enlightened and refined' (*Laon and Cythna*) or (in Greek) 'the discerning' (*Epipsychidion*) or consisting of no 'more than 5 or 6 persons' (*Prometheus Unbound*).[7] The figures gathered by William St Clair confirm the truth of the publisher Charles Ollier's remark in 1823, that 'the sale, in every instance, of Mr Shelley's works has been very confined'.[8]

This set of circumstances prevented Shelley's poetry from reaching any considerable number of readers in his lifetime. The one, modest, exception was the tragedy *The Cenci* (1819), 250 copies of which he had printed in Italy and sent to London, where a second edition was published in 1821, although this did not itself sell well. For a poet determined to write for his times, as Shelley was, this signal failure to find an audience was deeply dispiriting. His growing persuasion that Byron's recent poetry, especially *Don Juan* (1819–24) and *Cain* (1821), had consolidated his status as the pre-eminent writer of the age added to the disappointment that appears over and again in Shelley's letters during the last year or so of his life. 'I despair of rivalling Lord Byron, as well I may: and there is no other with whom it is worth contending,' he wrote to Mary in August 1821. And to his friend the novelist and poet Thomas Love Peacock (1785–1866) in January 1822: 'I wish I had something better to do than furnish this jingling food for the hunger of oblivion, called *verse*.'[9]

Such a signal absence of contemporary success might seem the inevitable consequence of Shelley's nature as other-worldly dreamer, an idea of him which has proved remarkably persistent, and which appears to be borne out by some picturesque incidents in his early life. His first wife, Harriet, reported to a friend that she was 'ready to die of laughter' when, in Dublin, they threw Shelley's political pamphlets out of the window, handed them to passers-by in the street, even 'put one into a woman's hood of a cloak'.[10] The Romantic gestures celebrated in his two sonnets of August 1812, 'On launching some bottles filled with *Knowledge* into the Bristol Channel' and 'To a balloon, laden with *Knowledge*', seem to confirm the portrait of the young Shelley as high-minded but naïve, and feckless at delivering a message he considered of benefit to humanity.[11] The truth is quite another matter. From the time of his earliest literary efforts, Shelley displays a practical awareness of the readers he means particularly to address among the various strands of the increasing and increasingly diverse reading public of the early nineteenth century.[12] The second of his two Gothic romances, *St. Irvyne; or, The Rosicrucian* was, he wrote to the publisher in November 1810, 'a thing which almost *mechanically* sells to circulating libraries, &c'.[13] In March 1813 he advised a prospective publisher to have printed no more than 250 copies of the aggressively radical *Queen Mab* as a 'small neat Quarto, on fine paper & so as to catch the aristocrats: They will not read it, but their sons & daughters may'.[14] The self-deprecatory Advertisement to his volume *Rosalind and Helen* (1819) specifies the object of the title-poem, as no more than 'interesting the affections and amusing the imagination', thereby signalling the broad popular readership he means to address in this sentimental domestic tale.[15] He evokes the 'highly refined imagination of the more select classes of poetical readers' in the Preface to *Prometheus Unbound* (1820), having forewarned the publisher Charles Ollier that this 'lyrical drama' was unlikely to sell 'beyond twenty copies'.[16] *The Cenci* (1820), on the other hand, was 'written for the multitude', an audience of metropolitan theatre-goers for whom he had taken care to produce 'the greatest degree of popular effect' by presenting historical characters as naturally as possible and in unadorned language.[17] Following the Peterloo Massacre he tried in spring 1820 to enlist Leigh Hunt's help in publishing 'a little volume of *popular songs*, wholly political, & destined to awaken & direct the imagination of the reformers', a project which never came to fruition, no doubt owing to Hunt's prudence; while his long and incomplete prose essay *A Philosophical View of Reform* he conceived as a kind of textbook for 'the philosophical [i.e. educated and thoughtful] reformers', the appeal of which would be 'from the passions to the reason of men'.[18] Another sort of appeal (to those potential supporters acquainted with Greek history and culture) was made in autumn 1821 in favour of a current cause in urgent need of assistance, the incipient Greek revolution against Ottoman rule, which required the '*immediate* publication' (Shelley wrote to Ollier) of his topical drama *Hellas*.[19]

II

Remarkably, for a writer whose works did not enjoy wide circulation, Shelley's volumes of verse were regularly reviewed in contemporary literary periodicals.[20] These notices encompass a more extreme range of opinion than that provoked by any major English poet of the Romantic period. The Shelley that emerges from them is not a single figure but several, usually portrayed in striking colours, not infrequently from the garish quarter of the palette. The most egregious instance of this kind is the vain, sour, querulous, ignorant and vicious individual who is sketched in a review of *Laon and Cythna/The Revolt of Islam* in the April 1819 number of the *Quarterly Review*.[21] To this image of moral deformity even blacker traits might be added, the reviewer (Shelley's Eton contemporary J. T. Coleridge, nephew of the poet) assures readers, were he inclined to 'withdraw the veil of private life'. Years later T. L. Peacock recalled this review as a 'malignant' example of '*odium theologicum*', exhibiting all the venomous animosity of religious dispute.[22] The same might be said more emphatically of an article in *The Investigator* for 1822, which serves as both an obituary notice of Shelley and a repudiation 'with unmingled horror and disgust' of *Queen Mab* as 'nine cantos of blasphemy and impiety, such as we never thought that any one, on the outside of Bedlam, could have uttered', before going on to imagine the spirit of the drowned atheist trembling before the throne of God, to be judged for infidelity, seduction and incest.[23] As against the paternalistic severity of the Tory *Quarterly Review*, administering necessary chastisement to one of its own class who has gone astray, while allowing that he just might still be redeemed, and the evangelical and moralistic *Investigator*'s unmingled revulsion, may be set the liberal Leigh Hunt's sustained defence of his friend Shelley in a series of reviews and articles in *The Examiner*, as a benevolent reformer, tolerant, philanthropic and, although a philosophical non-believer, a truer Christian, because more charitable, than his self-righteous detractors. Hunt's admiration found an unexpected echo when, in 1821, relatively cheap pirated editions of *Queen Mab* began to appear. Ironically, the poem that Shelley originally imagined as influencing aristocratic youth circulated widely right through the nineteenth century among the labouring classes, in particular Chartists, socialists and freethinkers – acquiring the popular epithet of 'the Chartists' Bible'.[24]

Opinions considered subversive of the established order and a supposedly licentious biography were not the focus of all contemporary reviews, however; a not inconsiderable number avoid any comment on the political stance and moral character of the man to deliver what can be nuanced and subtly appreciative responses to the poetry. To be sure, there are reservations. The representation of incestuous rape and parricide in *The Cenci* provokes shock and revulsion, for example, and the peculiarly concentrated imagery of *Prometheus Unbound* is condemned by several critics as muddled and incomprehensible – 'absolutely and intrinsically unintelligible' and displaying a 'total want of meaning', according to the *Quarterly Review*.[25] Such judgements notwithstanding, there is a large consensus that Shelley possesses poetic and dramatic powers that are considerable, even exceptional, and that they promise well for future development. Shelley himself insisted in *A Defence of Poetry* on the distinction between the imperfections of the poet as a man and the poet 'inasmuch as he is a poet' and as such 'the happiest, the best, the wisest and the most illustrious of men' (p. 676). In fact this idea of the poet as a divided being, though in another key, was a leading theme of criticism of Shelley in his lifetime and continued in various forms through the nineteenth century and beyond as an opposition between the reprehensible opinions and behaviour of the man and his exceptional gifts and accomplishments as an author. A conspicuous example appears in the May 1820 issue of the *London Magazine*, then under the editorship of the liberal John Scott, which delivers a long and scathing verdict on Shelley as one of those modern writers who, out of self-absorbed vanity, claim as morally liberating what is in fact indecent, weak and corrupted. In particular, the plot, characters and tendency of *The Cenci* are judged to fail utterly of their declared object of 'teaching the human heart . . . the knowledge of itself' (see Preface: p. 275). For all that, the reviewer considers that the tragedy, together with his other works, amply demonstrates that Shelley the poet displays 'real power of intellect, great vivacity of fancy, and a quick, deep, serious feeling, responding readily and harmoniously, to every call made on the sensibility by the imagery and incidents of this variegated world'.[26]

The majority of contemporary reviews were based on Shelley's long poems, the vehicles of his most contentious views. It was not until the appearance in 1824 of Mary Shelley's edition of *Posthumous Poems of Percy Bysshe Shelley* that a substantial quantity of his medium-length and shorter verse, including a large number of personal lyrics, became available. This landmark volume, containing eighty-three completed poems, fragments and verse translations, most of them not previously published, aimed to win the readers that Shelley's poetry had failed to find while he was alive. In addition, Mary's brief Preface represented her first efforts to counter her late husband's reputation as depraved and profligate, instead recalling him as a wise, brave and gentle companion and friend, selflessly devoted to 'the improvement of the moral and physical state of mankind'.[27] Within two months *Posthumous Poems* had been withdrawn from sale, following the intervention of the poet's father, after little more than 300 of the 500 copies that were printed had been sold. Sir Timothy Shelley did not wish the works of his late scandalous son to be given an afterlife during his own lifetime, and made the suppression of the *Posthumous Poems* and the destruction of all remaining copies a condition of maintaining the allowance he provided to Mary and her son Percy.[28] But an interest in Shelley's poetry had been stimulated, and a number of unauthorized editions appeared before Mary published the enlarged *Poetical Works of Percy Bysshe Shelley* in four volumes in 1839. Later that year she reissued the *Poetical Works* as a single volume with additions. Together these supplemented *Posthumous Poems* with more than forty further titles. The publication of Shelley's *Essays, Letters from Abroad, Translations and Fragments* (1840) completed Mary's editorial labours, which brought before the public almost all his verse and an important selection of his prose, including *A Defence of Poetry*.

Mary Shelley's editions were remarkable achievements in the recovery of Shelley's texts, especially those that she derived from his often untidy and tangled manuscripts. But they were neither complete nor completely accurate. As the considerable mass of the surviving manuscripts gradually became available for examination in the course of the nineteenth and twentieth centuries, a series of individual publications and editions were able to supplement and correct the foundations she had laid down in 1824 and 1839–40. They also provided more ample information on Shelley's life and the circumstances in which his texts were published, as did the substantial scholarly biography by the Victorian academic Edward Dowden.[29] The critical editions of the complete poetry by W. M. Rossetti (1870, 1878) and (especially) by Harry Buxton Forman (1876–7) confirmed Shelley's position as one of the major poets of the nineteenth century, and the inclusion of his poetry in the Oxford Standard Authors series (1904) might be said to have sealed his canonical status. For bibliographical details of ongoing twentieth-century editions of the complete poetry and prose, see Abbreviations (p. 679) and Further Reading (p. xxxvii).

As the nature and extent of Shelley's poetry became more widely known, it gradually secured its place in the mainstream of English literary tradition, though still regularly provoking controversy. Some important waymarks along this route to acceptance were the advocacy for Shelley of the Cambridge Apostles, a group of undergraduates which included Alfred Tennyson and Arthur Hallam and which bore the cost of a facsimile of the first edition of *Adonais* in 1829. The most widely read and influential Victorian anthology of verse, Francis Turner Palgrave's *The Golden Treasury of the Best Songs and Lyrical Poems in the English Language* (1861), included twenty-two titles by Shelley, the third largest number after William Wordsworth (forty-one) and Shakespeare (thirty-two). Palgrave's selection of Shelley's verse consisted exclusively of lyrics, largely of those first published by Mary in *Posthumous Poems*, half of these on the subject of love – thus setting the terms of popular appreciation of the poet through to the end of the century and into the twentieth. But as Shelley's reputation as a lyricist of intimate feeling grew, the radical poet continued to live a parallel existence, though in a different social sphere. *Queen Mab* enjoyed phenomenal circulation in cheap pirated texts following the unauthorized editions of 1821, for one of which the nominal printer and publisher was prosecuted and imprisoned on an action brought by the Society for the Suppression of Vice.[30] The formation of the Shelley Society in 1885 by the scholar, Christian socialist and advocate for workers' education F. J. Furnivall marked yet another stage in the process of legitimization. The society, which counted George Bernard Shaw among its members as well as several of the great Victorian Shelley specialists, arranged monthly lectures, supported reprints of rare Shelley texts and encouraged serious study of the poet's ideas and literary techniques. Its most celebrated undertaking was sponsoring the well-publicized first performance of *The Cenci* in 1886. Ostensibly a 'private' occasion – the Lord Chamberlain, exercising the office of censor, had refused to license a public production – the performance was attended by an audience of some 2,400. The society's achievement in mounting *The Cenci* was to situate Shelley's tragedy on the moral fringe of the lively Victorian theatrical world and test its suitability for the stage. The performance was extensively reviewed as a notable dramatic occasion – Oscar Wilde and Bernard Shaw were among the reviewers – attracting considered, and mixed, opinions on the tragedy itself, the production and the acting, rather than the outraged condemnation the play had attracted when first published.[31] Out of the Shelley Society's activities also emerged the committed political interpretations *Shelley's Socialism* (1888), by Eleanor Marx and Edward Aveling, and the social reformer and vegetarian Henry Salt's *A Shelley Primer* (1887), a tradition continued, and revised, for the twentieth century in Paul Foot's *Red Shelley* (1980).

III

In a letter of October 1819 to his publisher, Charles Ollier, Shelley evokes the example of the leading poets of the day, for him Wordsworth and Byron, who have drawn upon 'the new springs of thought and feeling, which the great events of our age have exposed to view'.[32] Born in 1792, three years after the outbreak of the French Revolution, Shelley lived in a time of 'great events' such as had never been experienced in the modern history of Europe. Pre-eminent among these was the grand narrative of the French Revolution. Its ideals and accomplishments, failings and atrocities, its experiment in republicanism, the emergence of Napoleon – the empire that rapidly succeeded, followed by the final collapse of the Napoleonic regime and the restoration of monarchy – constituted an overarching influence on Shelley's writing in verse and prose, as it did on the minds and expectations of his contemporaries. And if the French revolutionary and imperial experiments are viewed as encompassing not only an astonishing sequence of political initiatives and military actions but also the intellectual influences that underlay them – the philosophical and literary responses to them across Europe and in the wider world, the debates occasioned, the sense of possibility opened up and the impetus given to both reform and reaction – then we can appreciate the force of Shelley's remarks to Byron in letters of September 1816 on the Revolution as 'the master theme of the epoch in which we live' and its suitability for a literary work 'involving all that is best qualified to interest and to instruct mankind'.[33] The recent history of France inevitably recalled the establishment of the young American Republic, which itself had been achieved through a 'just and successful Revolt' (as Shelley puts it in *A Philosophical View of Reform*: p. 640) inspired by democratic ideals and with French assistance.[34] An associated conflict, the British–American War of 1812, continued from the middle of that year until the end of 1814.

The war with France, which lasted with brief interruptions from 1793 to 1815, occasioned significant hardship in Britain. Increased taxation and the scarcity of resources required by the war effort were felt most acutely by those of low or modest income, the continuing heavy impositions necessary to repay the increase in the national debt being a particular source of privation and resentment. The outdated and unequal system of parliamentary representation in Britain had long been the cause of popular discontent, and led to a post-war revival of organized agitation for electoral reform, which was harshly repressed by government. Following the first defeat of Napoleon, the European settlement agreed by the victorious powers at the Congress of Vienna (1814–15) represented a cruel disappointment for British liberals, who condemned it as reactionary; while the 'Holy Alliance' of September 1815 entered into by Austria, Russia and Prussia (but not Britain), which sought to lend religious sanction to the renewed order of absolutist governance and forestall any fresh revolutionary movements, appeared to European liberal opinion as no more than a cover of pious hypocrisy for the continued exercise of arbitrary political authority. Both at home and abroad the ideals of the Revolution seemed clearly to have given way to reaction.

As an intellectual heir of the European Enlightenment of the seventeenth and eighteenth centuries, Shelley viewed the momentous happenings and public debates of his time within an established tradition of critical thought. The leading ideas that shaped his outlook, evident in both his published works and his private correspondence, are rationalist, secular, progressive and egalitarian. He regularly evokes, to take important examples, the Roman poet Lucretius (98–*c*.55 BC), materialist critic of religious superstition; the scientific reformer Francis Bacon (1561–1626); the philosophical anarchist William Godwin (1756–1836), who would become his father-in-law in 1816; and the empirical philosopher and sceptic Sir William Drummond (?1770–1828). A summary definition of the modern liberal perspective, together with a history in outline of the major thinkers who have contributed to form it, is set out in the initial section of *A Philosophical View of Reform* (p. 636), which concludes:

> The result of the labours of the political philosophers has been the establishment of the principle of Utility [or 'general advantage'] as the substance, and liberty and equality as the forms, according to which the concerns of human life ought to be administered.

Shelley was persuaded that these ideals, conspicuously recalling the Revolutionary *Liberté, Égalité, Fraternité*, would inevitably be realized by a gradual dissemination of knowledge. Human well-being and lasting social improvement could be achieved only if they were preceded and directed by the necessary mental and moral enlightenment. This moderate gradualism he shared with many upper- and middle-class intellectuals of his time. In common with them, he struggled with the practical dilemma of how best to promote the durable reform of inequitable and oppressive political regimes in an age when established power had become deeply resistant to reform. In a postscript to his pamphlet *An Address to the Irish People* (1812), Shelley urges the need for a comprehensive moral and political regeneration of society which avoids equally 'the rapidity and danger of revolution' and the minor concessions and half measures that amount to no more than the 'time servingness of temporizing reform'.[35]

Religion, too, Shelley regarded from a rational and sceptical point of view. Although he maintained a deep admiration for the character and social teachings of Christ, he considered that the grand biblical scheme of Creation, Fall, Redemption and Last Judgement could not command belief in an enlightened age. He especially deplored what he considered the historical exploitation of the fictional narratives and prophecies of the Bible by the collusion of the Christian Church with dynastic and absolutist political systems in order that the 'cunning and selfish few' might consolidate their power over the fearful and ignorant many.[36] Nor could he accept the conclusions on the origin and governance of the universe arrived at solely by reasoning on the phenomena and operations of nature, the traditional ground of 'natural religion' or 'deism', subscribing instead to the sceptical conclusions of empirical philosophers such as David Hume, who held that certainty was unattainable in such matters. Nonetheless, in various contexts Shelley formulated his intuitive persuasion of the existence of a universal presiding and directing power that is immanent in nature. 'The interfused and overruling Spirit of all the energy and wisdom included within the circle of existing things' is how he puts it in 'On Christianity' (p. 614), where he explores the idea most fully. This Spirit he conceived of not as remote from human experience but as closely implicated with it. In his commentary on the beatitude 'Blessed are the pure in heart, for they shall see God' (Matthew 5:8) Shelley makes it clear that, for him, so far from being transcendent and impenetrable, the divine is experienced by the exercise of virtue at the highest reach of our human nature (p. 614).

IV

In the resonant concluding paragraph of *A Defence of Poetry* (p. 677), Shelley memorably articulates the relation between contemporary writers and what he calls 'the spirit of the age' which animates them. An epoch of great intellectual and artistic achievement is one in which revolutionary events, ideas and imagination energize each other. Such was the case in the England of the Renaissance, and so it is at the present moment:

> we live among such philosophers and poets as surpass beyond comparison any who have appeared since the last national struggle for civil and religious liberty . . . At such periods there is an accumulation of the power of communicating and receiving intense and impassioned conceptions respecting man and nature.

Within this atmosphere of creative interchange, the art of great poets such as Dante exhibits a vital relation to contemporary 'knowledge, and sentiment, and religion, and political condition', so shaping an indispensable representation of the epoch to itself and transmitting it to succeeding ages (p. 669). This high and serious office Shelley began to define in the Preface to *Laon and Cythna* and pursued in the Preface to *Prometheus Unbound*, where artists are said to be 'in one sense, the creators, and, in another, the creations, of their age' (p. 187). His exploration of this central idea of his poetics in *A Defence of Poetry* concludes that the artist must engage critically with contemporary realities if art is to remain relevant: his task is 'to create afresh the associations' that words and images and ideas have acquired over time if they are not to become 'dead to all the nobler purposes of human intercourse' (pp. 653–4). On this view, all imaginative creation, and poetry pre-eminently, is at once determined by and able to determine how we apprehend the world in which we live; it

> purges from our inward sight the film of familiarity which obscures from us the wonder of our being. It compels us to feel that which we perceive, and to imagine that which we know. It creates anew the universe after it has been annihilated in our minds by the recurrence of impressions blunted by re-iteration. (p. 675)

The primary task of poetry is to absorb and transform its sources in nature, art and thought, past and present, into instruments for knowing the world as it has become; in effect bringing a new reality into being. The corollary of these visionary, creative and ethical functions is Shelley's celebrated declaration that 'Poets are the unacknowledged legislators of the World' (p. 678).

Fundamental to this creative enterprise as he conceived it was an original engagement with poetic form. In this Shelley followed the example of the writers he regarded as having defined the age as one of exceptional imaginative power, for a distinguishing hallmark of the Romantic period was the extent of its experimentation with genre, style and versification. To deploy these effectively requires an alert awareness of decorum – that is, of the language, narrative structures, characters, prosody (and so on) which tradition had established as proper to a given literary kind. Not that these conventions simply dictate the attributes of a given Shelley poem: many of his most memorable effects involve the revision, even subversion, of received styles and stories, of genre itself. His awareness of traditional prescriptions always remains acute, however, and his characteristic impulse is to test the limits of the convention within which he works. Harold Bloom's contention that our reading of Shelley's verse ought above all to remain conscious of its relation to the history of poetry is pertinent here.[37] Shelley's handling of a traditional form both bears the impress of the age and functions as a searching means of exploring it.

His variations on the ballad form offer a signal example. Historically, a leading theme of the popular ballad was mockery of the great as a means of social protest, Shelley's object in 'The Monarch's funeral: An Anticipation' (1810), in which a contrast between the pomp and luxury of royalty and the obscure grave of the true patriot is developed. *The Mask of Anarchy*, written in the immediate aftermath of the Peterloo Massacre of August 1819, elicits a more variously nuanced response. It combines the simplicity of language and relaxed versification of the ballad style with elements of biblical dream vision, courtly masque and public pageant to form a generic hybrid in which those heterogeneous elements interact to mimic the discontinuities and dissonances of the socially fractured encounter they commemorate. Traditionally the ballad also served as vehicle for the narration of local events of an apparently supernatural character. Such was Wordsworth's tale, in a five-line expansion of the ballad stanza, of the conversion to an upright life of an itinerant seller of earthenware pots in *Peter Bell* (1819), whose imminent publication prompted Shelley to recast the tale in *Peter Bell the Third*, with a stricter rhyme scheme and a farcical caricature of Wordsworth himself as chief personage. In Shelley's reworking, the pedlar's conversion has been replaced with Wordsworth's passage from reformist to conservative politics, the consequent dullness of his poetry being his fitting recompense. Within a narrower compass, Shelley was a determined experimenter in the sonnet form. None of the nine sonnets included in the present selection follows the same rhyme scheme, and only the translation 'From the Italian of Dante' conforms to a major traditional pattern of rhyme – the Shakespearean (*abab cdcd efef gg*) – though not to its division into three quatrains and a concluding couplet. Nor do any of the sonnets respect the Petrarchan model's division into octave and sestet, rhyming *abba abba cdecde*. The distinctive effects that Shelley achieves through innovative rhyming and unexpected divisions of sense in his sonnets reward close attention.

So does his management of other, even more intricate forms. The poems that Shelley composed between 1809 and 1812, which include the first thirteen titles in this volume, display a remarkable spectrum of metres, stanzas and rhyme schemes, a prelude to the continued development in technical ingenuity and control throughout his career. The skill with which he negotiates the prosodic variations over forty lines on only three rhymes in 'Written on hearing the news of the death of Napoleon' represents a quite astonishing example, as if the masterly display of the poet's art carried through in the poem's five stanzas rendered homage to the prodigious existence of the subject that is recalled. As remarkable, in their different ways, are his sustained handling of the solemn fifteen-line stanzas of 'Ode to Liberty', and the rapid verbal music and lightness of rhythm he creates in 'The Cloud'. The interplay of the iambic pentameter couplets of *Julian and Maddalo* with what Shelley described as the poem's 'familiar style of language' is as exhilarating as the animated conversation of the two principals as they ride along the shore of the Venetian Lido through wind-blown sunny spray.[38] Exhilarating too, though in quite another mode, is the fanciful journey of the lady witch in *The Witch of Atlas*, in which the delighted play and gleeful mischief generated by the confrontation between the things of this world and the creative imagination are brilliantly adapted to the Italian comic measure of *ottava rima*.

Such experimentation and formal diversity are the principal medium through which Shelley constructs the substantial autobiographical dimension of his verse. In the course of his correspondence with his future father-in-law, William Godwin, in early 1812, he suggests that an account of the whole of a life from youth to age, recording successive intellectual and sentimental states when and as they are experienced, would possess a scientific value to rival that of systematic studies of mental phenomena:

> If any man would determine sincerely and cautiously at *every* period of his life to publish books which should contain the real state of his feelings and opinions, I am willing to suppose that this portraiture of his mind would be worth many metaphysical disquisitions.[39]

Shelley was acutely conscious of the obstacles in the way of carrying out such a scheme, as well as the related one of reconstituting a life through methodical recollection. In a series of notes on the science of mind, he writes that 'thought can with difficulty visit the intricate and winding chambers which it inhabits'.[40] And he was especially aware, both in the exercise of self-reflection and more generally, of the imperfections of language itself as an expressive instrument: 'These words inefficient & metaphorical—Most words so—No help—', as he put it in a manuscript footnote to 'On Love' (p. 618). Such caveats notwithstanding, self-portraiture forms a major strain in his verse and prose and one to which he returns at critical intervals. The poems that embody this continuing impulse range from the explicitly autobiographical first-person meditations of 'The Retrospect: Cwm Elan

1812' and the Dedication before *Laon and Cythna*, through the formal portraits of himself as Poet speaking to his public in the prefaces to *Laon and Cythna* and *Prometheus Unbound*, the imaginative working-through of an interval of personal grief in 'Lines Written among the Euganean Hills, October, 1818', or the lament from a moment of deep despondency in 'Stanzas Written in Dejection—December 1818, near Naples', to the highly wrought symbolic narratives of *Epipsychidion* (1821). A pivotal event in the construction of his life story as possessing significant shape and purpose is recounted in both 'Hymn to Intellectual Beauty' (1816) and the Dedication before *Laon and Cythna*. In each poem he recalls in quasi-religious terms, and with important variations, a conversion experience of dramatic suddenness and intensity which condenses the decisive change of direction that he described in his letters to Godwin in early 1812: from the life of privilege into which he had been born, and its accompanying restrictions, to an existence dedicated to free enquiry and general justice.

But the pre-eminent theme of his autobiographical narratives and lyrics is the quest for love. In exploring the – sometimes highly charged, entangled and painfully fraught – personal experiences that define its course, he represents himself both directly in the first person and in various fictional guises. The latter include the tragic figures of the revolutionary Laon in *Laon and Cythna*, the Maniac in *Julian and Maddalo* and the doomed patriot and lover Lionel in *Rosalind and Helen* (1818). The personal lyrics, many never intended for publication, include those addressed to his first wife, Harriet, in which love is invoked as incitement to virtue; those written to Mary in which love is the condition of mutual creative endeavour; the playful and flirtatious songs composed or recycled for Sophia Stacey (for whom see headnote to 'Love's Philosophy': p. 775); the passionate exaltation of *Epipsychidion*; the late lyrics taking Shelley's troubled attachment to Jane Williams as their subject; and those like 'On a Dead Violet: To ——' or 'When passion's trance is overpast', which frankly confront love's exhaustion and death. A technically accomplished and deeply unsettling example of this engagement with love's extinction is 'Time Long Past', one of three poems that Shelley inscribed in a pocket diary which he presented to Sophia Stacey on her departure from Florence for Rome at the end of December 1819. A mordant recasting of a familiar theme from the lyric repertoire, regret for the passing of a love that was too delightful to endure, these plangent verses (see also p. 402) are a tour de force of lyric craftsmanship.

Time Long Past

Like the ghost of a dear friend dead
Is Time long past.
A tone which is now forever fled,
A hope, which is now forever past,
A love, so sweet it could not last
Was Time long past.

There were sweet dreams in the night
Of Time long past;
And, was it sadness or delight,
Each day a shadow onward cast
Which made us wish it yet might last—
That Time long past.

There is regret, almost remorse
For Time long past.
'Tis like a child's beloved corse
A father watches, till at last
Beauty is like remembrance, cast
From Time long past.

A close reading of the three stanzas underscores the truth of Wordsworth's assertion – in a consideration of major contemporary poets, including Thomas Moore, Walter Scott and Byron – that 'Shelley is one of the best *artists* of us all: I mean in workmanship of style'.[41] The eighteen lines count only four rhymes, the title itself occurring six times in the body of the lyric, each occurrence subtly individualized by the addition of a single monosyllabic word. The strict economy of means and the formal patterning rein in the familiar conversational quality of both language and syntax by, as it were, compulsive returns to the three emphatic stresses of the title. Rhetorically, each stanza consists of two statements, both concluding with a variation on the title, the first expressing prosaically, and without strict adherence to any prosodic scheme, a condition for which 'time long past' functions simply as a temporal adverb; the second, rhythmically varied in each case, also leads back to the title-phrase, which echoes all previous instances of itself and yet is both grammatically distinct and significantly distinguished in meaning from them. The bitter and shocking image of the dead child and grieving father in the third stanza cruelly realizes the ominous suggestions in the 'dear friend dead' and 'shadow' of stanzas 1 and 2, jarring with the conventional idiom of erotic complaint that has governed the poem till then by introducing a detail borrowed from Shelley's personal life, the death of his three-year-old son, William, in June 1819. The sense of 'remembrance' in the penultimate line, an act of recollecting the dead, encompasses lost love and lost child as well as the process of memorializing them in the poem itself – an artful instance of carrying the tensions implicit in a traditional lyric topic to their limits and beyond, and of the power of lyric poetry at its best to create much from little. To read Shelley's poems on erotic themes in broadly chronological order, together with the rapturous celebration of both individual and cosmic love in Acts III and IV of *Prometheus Unbound*, is to follow one of the most distinctive and absorbing sequences on love in English poetry.

The finely tuned verbal music and masterful versification which Wordsworth admired, and which complement the copiousness and variety of Shelley's poetry, make an appropriate vehicle for the intensity and precision of his response to the things of the world. This 'animation of delight', in the phrase of the Earth regenerated by Love in *Prometheus Unbound* IV.322 (p. 265), is the expression of the sensual – at its highest pitch erotic – energy that quickens that response at its most memorable and characteristic. The resultant visionary quality of Shelley's verse typically remains anchored to its source in natural experience. In *The Witch of Atlas*, to take the example of that 'visionary rhyme' (as Shelley describes it in line 8: p. 448), the speaker interrupts the description of the hearth in the witch's cavern to reflect on a neglected source of loveliness:

> Men scarcely know how beautiful fire is—
> Each flame of it is as a precious stone
> Dissolved in ever moving light, and this
> Belongs to each and all who gaze upon.
> (p. 456)

The process of creative observation is unfolded before our eyes in a reciprocal movement from fire to gem and back again, from the fluidity of motion, to the brilliantly fixed, to dissolution – suggesting a perpetual negotiation between the flame and the jewel, between the natural and visionary planes of reality. One could hardly find a more appropriate guide to the creative reading of Shelley's poems than this display of the discovery of a beauty that is open to all.

NOTES

For bibliographical details of the abbreviated references *Letters*, *Poems*, *Complete Poetry*, *Prose Works* and *Prose*, see Abbreviations on pp. 679–82.

1 William St Clair, *The Reading Nation in the Romantic Period* (Cambridge: Cambridge University Press, 2004), pp. 649–51 and Appendix 9.
2 Stephen Behrendt, 'Shelley and His Publishers', in *The Oxford Handbook of Percy Bysshe Shelley*, ed. Michael O'Neill and Anthony Howe (Oxford: Oxford University Press, 2013), pp. 83–97; *Letters* II, pp. 372, 387–8, 395.
3 Leigh Hunt, 'Young Poets', *The Examiner* (1 December 1816, 19 January 1817), in *Shelley: The Critical Heritage*, ed. James E. Barcus (London and Boston: Routledge & Kegan Paul, 1975) – hereafter *Critical Heritage*; Jeffrey N. Cox, *Poetry and Politics in the Cockney School* (Cambridge: Cambridge University Press, 2004).
4 Reprinted with some modifications and additions as a note to *Queen Mab*, VII.13 (p. 94).
5 *Letters* I, p. 540, II, p. 326; *Byron's Letters and Journals*, ed. Leslie A. Marchand, 13 vols (London: John Murray, 1973–94), VI, p. 76.
6 *Maria Gisborne and Edward E. Williams, Shelley's Friends: Their Journals and Letters*, ed. F. L. Jones (Norman, Okla.: University of Oklahoma Press, 1951), p. 111.
7 *Poems* II, p. 32; *Letters* II, pp. 363, 388.
8 St Clair, *The Reading Nation*, pp. 649–51.
9 *Letters* II, pp. 323, 374.
10 *Letters* I, p. 265.
11 *Poems* I, pp. 238–9; *Complete Poetry* II, pp. 65–6.
12 Robin Jarvis, 'The Literary Marketplace', in his *The Romantic Period: The Intellectual and Cultural Context of English Literature, 1789–1830* (Harlow: Pearson Education, 2004), pp. 50–73; St Clair, *The Reading Nation*; Stephen C. Behrendt, *Shelley and His Audiences* (Lincoln, Nebr., and London: University of Nebraska Press, 1989).
13 *Letters* I, p. 20.
14 *Letters* I, p. 361.
15 *Poems* II, pp. 268–9.
16 *Letters* II, p. 174.
17 *Letters* II, p. 102; *Poems* II, pp. 733–4.
18 *Letters* II, pp. 191, 201, 164.
19 *Letters* II, p. 365.
20 See Newman Ivey White, *The Unextinguished Hearth: Shelley and His Contemporary Critics* (Durham, NC: Duke University Press, 1938; reprinted New York: Octagon Books, 1966); a broad selection of periodical criticism and opinion up to the mid nineteenth century is gathered in *Critical Heritage*; for a complete collection of contemporary reviews, see *The Romantics Reviewed: Contemporary Reviews of British Romantic Writers 1793–1830*, Part C: *Shelley, Keats, and London Radical Writers*, ed. Donald H. Reiman, 2 vols (New York: Garland, 1972).

21 *Critical Heritage*, pp. 124–35.
22 'Memoirs of Percy Bysshe Shelley, Part II', in *The Works of Thomas Love Peacock*, ed. H. F. B. Brett-Smith and C. E. Jones, 10 vols (New York: AMS Press, 1967; original edition 1927), VIII, p. 107.
23 *Critical Heritage*, pp. 87–94.
24 H. Buxton Forman, *Vicissitudes of Shelley's* Queen Mab*: A Chapter in the History of Reform* (London: privately printed, 1887); Bouthaina Shaaban, 'Shelley and the Chartists', in *Shelley: Poet and Legislator of the World*, ed. Betty T. Bennett and Stuart Curran (Baltimore: Johns Hopkins University Press, 1996), pp. 114–25; St Clair, *The Reading Nation*, pp. 318–22.
25 *Critical Heritage*, pp. 254–5.
26 *Critical Heritage*, p. 192.
27 *Posthumous Poems of Percy Bysshe Shelley* (London: John and Henry L. Hunt, 1824), p. iv.
28 *The Letters of Mary Wollstonecraft Shelley*, ed. Betty T. Bennett, vol. 1 (Baltimore and London: Johns Hopkins University Press, 1980), pp. 444–5; Roger Ingpen, *Shelley in England* (London: Kegan Paul, 1917), pp. 576–86; Michael Rossington, 'Editing Shelley', in *The Oxford Handbook*, pp. 645–56.
29 *The Life of Percy Bysshe Shelley*, 2 vols (London: Kegan Paul, Trench & Co., 1886).
30 St Clair, *The Reading Nation*, pp. 318–20, 680–82; *Complete Poetry*, II, pp. 509–10.
31 Stuart Curran, *Shelley's Cenci: Scorpions Ringed with Fire* (Princeton, NJ: Princeton University Press, 1970), pp. 183–97.
32 *Letters* II, p. 127.
33 *Letters* I, pp. 504, 507–8.
34 Shelley refers approvingly to the American experience in *Laon and Cythna*, ll. 4414–39, and in *Hellas*, ll. 66–71, 1027–30 (pp. 518, 547).
35 *Prose Works* I, p. 37.
36 *A Philosophical View of Reform* – see p. 637.
37 *The Visionary Company: A Reading of English Romantic Poetry*, revised edn (Ithaca, NY: Cornell University Press, 1971), p. 282.
38 *Letters* II, p. 108.
39 *Letters* I, p. 242.
40 *Prose*, pp. 185–6.
41 *The Prose Works of William Wordsworth*, ed. Reverend Alexander B. Grosart, 3 vols (London: Edward Moxon, Son and Co., 1876), III, pp. 462–3.

Further Reading

Collected and Selected Editions of the Poems

Two editions of Shelley's complete poetry are in progress. *The Poems of Shelley* – published by Longman (vol. 1), Pearson Education (vols 2–3) and Routledge (vol. 4) in the series Longman Annotated English Poets – presents poems and verse fragments in chronological order by date of composition. Four volumes of a projected five have so far been published: *Volume One: 1804–1817*, edited by Geoffrey Matthews and Kelvin Everest (1989); *Volume Two: 1817–1819*, edited by Kelvin Everest and Geoffrey Matthews with contributions by Jack Donovan, Ralph Pite and Michael Rossington (2000); *Volume Three: 1819–1820*, edited by Jack Donovan, Cian Duffy, Kelvin Everest and Michael Rossington (2011); *Volume Four: 1820–1821*, edited by Michael Rossington, Jack Donovan and Kelvin Everest (2013). *The Complete Poetry of Percy Bysshe Shelley*, published by Johns Hopkins University Press, which will run to eight volumes when complete, maintains the original order of those poems that appeared in early published volumes, presenting other poems according to the dates at which they were printed or privately circulated and treating incomplete or rejected drafts separately. Three volumes have so far appeared, covering the years 1809 to 1818: *Volume One* (2000) and *Volume Two* (2004), edited by Donald H. Reiman and Neil Fraistat; *Volume Three* (2012), edited by Donald H. Reiman, Neil Fraistat and Nora Crook with contributions by Stuart Curran, Michael J. Neth and Michael O'Neill. Earlier editions still worth consulting include: *The Poems of Percy Bysshe Shelley*, 2 vols, edited by C. D. Locock (London: Methuen, 1911); *Shelley: Poetical Works*, edited by Thomas Hutchinson (Oxford: Oxford University Press, 1905), corrected by G. M. Matthews (Oxford: Oxford University Press, 1970); see also under 'Collected Works and Editions of the Prose' below. Notable selections of Shelley's poems and prose include: *Shelley: Selected Poems and Prose*, edited by G. M. Matthews (Oxford: Oxford University Press, 1964); *The Esdaile Notebook*, edited by Kenneth Neill

Cameron (London: Faber and Faber, 1964) – a collection of Shelley's early poems, most of them published for the first time; *Percy Bysshe Shelley: Poems and Prose*, edited by Timothy Webb (London: J. M. Dent, 1995); *Shelley's Poetry and Prose*, second edition edited by Donald H. Reiman and Neil Fraistat (New York and London: W. W. Norton, 2002); and *Percy Bysshe Shelley: The Major Works*, edited by Zachary Leader and Michael O'Neill (Oxford: Oxford University Press, 2003).

Collected Works and Editions of the Prose

The Works of Percy Bysshe Shelley in Verse and Prose, edited by Harry Buxton Forman, 8 vols (London: Reeves and Turner, 1880) – the first four volumes, containing the verse, were published in 1876–7; *The Complete Works of Percy Bysshe Shelley*, edited by Roger Ingpen and Walter E. Peck, 10 vols (London: Ernest Benn, 1926–30); *Shelley's Prose; or, The Trumpet of a Prophecy*, corrected edition edited by David Lee Clark (London: Fourth Estate, 1988); *The Prose Works of Percy Bysshe Shelley*, edited by E. B. Murray, vol. 1 (1811–18) (Oxford: Clarendon Press, 1993) – a second volume is in preparation.

Manuscript Sources

Two series of facsimiles under the general editorship of Donald H. Reiman include almost all the surviving manuscripts of Shelley's verse and prose – personal letters apart – with annotation and commentary: *The Bodleian Shelley Manuscripts*, 23 vols (New York and London: Garland, 1986–2002), presents facsimiles of manuscripts in the Bodleian Library, University of Oxford. *The Manuscripts of the Younger Romantics: Shelley*, 9 vols (New York and London: Garland, 1985–96), presents facsimiles of Shelley's manuscripts in libraries other than the Bodleian. Most volumes in each series include transcriptions. *Shelley and His Circle 1773–1822*, 10 vols to date, edited (successively) by Kenneth Neill Cameron, Donald H. Reiman and Doucet Devin Fisher (Cambridge, Mass.: Harvard University Press, 1961–2002), is a continuing edition of the manuscripts of Shelley, Byron, Mary Shelley, Peacock, Leigh Hunt and others in the Carl H. Pforzheimer Collection, the New York Public Library, with extensive commentaries and related essays.

Letters and Journals

The Letters of Percy Bysshe Shelley, edited by F. L. Jones, 2 vols (Oxford: Clarendon Press, 1964); *The Letters of Mary Wollstonecraft Shelley*, edited by Betty T. Bennett, 3 vols (Baltimore and London: Johns Hopkins University Press, 1980–88); *The Journals of Mary Shelley 1814–1844*, edited by Paula R. Feldman and Diana Scott-Kilvert, 2 vols (Oxford: Oxford University Press, 1987; single-volume edition: Baltimore and London: Johns Hopkins University Press, 1995).

Biographies

Modern full-length critical biographies include Newman Ivey White, *Shelley*, 2 vols (New York: Alfred A. Knopf, 1940); Richard Holmes, *Shelley: The Pursuit* (London: Weidenfeld and Nicolson, 1974); James Bieri, *Percy Bysshe Shelley: A Biography*, 2 vols (Newark, Del.: University of Delaware Press, 2004, 2005). There are good brief accounts of Shelley's life in the generously illustrated *Shelley and His World* by Claire Tomalin (London: Thames and Hudson, 1980; revised Harmondsworth: Penguin Books, 1992) and in Michael O'Neill, *Shelley: A Literary Life* (London: Palgrave Macmillan, 1989), which stresses its subject's development as an author. *The Life of Percy Bysshe Shelley*, edited by Humbert Wolfe, 2 vols (London: J. M. Dent, 1933), gathers important accounts of Shelley by three of his friends: Thomas Jefferson Hogg's *The Life of Percy Bysshe Shelley* (1858); Thomas Love Peacock's *Memoirs of Percy Bysshe Shelley* (1858–62); and Edward John Trelawny's *Recollections of the Last Days of Shelley and Byron* (1858). *Lives of the Great Romantics: Volume 1: Shelley*, edited by John Mullan (London: William Pickering, 1996), includes excerpts from the three biographical works just mentioned as well as collecting several other nineteenth-century portraits and reminiscences of the poet.

Critical Sources

Early reviews are collected in *The Romantics Reviewed: Contemporary Reviews of British Romantic Writers 1793–1830*, Part C: *Shelley, Keats, and London Radical Writers*, edited by Donald H. Reiman, 2 vols (New York: Garland, 1972). Important reviews and selections from others published in Shelley's lifetime are given with commentary in Newman Ivey White, *The Unextinguished Hearth:*

Shelley and His Contemporary Critics (Durham, NC: Duke University Press, 1938; reprinted New York: Octagon Books, 1966). Karsten Klejs Engelberg considers further nineteenth-century estimates in *The Making of the Shelley Myth: An Annotated Bibliography of Criticism of Percy Bysshe Shelley 1822–1860* (London: Mansell Publishing, 1988). For later nineteenth- and early twentieth-century critical opinion, see James E. Barcus (ed.), *Shelley: The Critical Heritage* (London: Routledge, 1975), and Clement Dunbar, *A Bibliography of Shelley Studies, 1823–1950* (New York: Garland, 1976). Jerrold E. Hogle's chapter on Shelley in *Literature of the Romantic Period: A Bibliographical Guide*, edited by Michael O'Neill (Oxford: Clarendon Press, 1998), gives a brief overview of Shelley scholarship and criticism from the second half of the twentieth century. The annual bibliography in the *Keats-Shelley Journal* from 1952 lists scholarly and critical work on Shelley, Mary Shelley and their circle as well as on other Romantic-period authors and topics.

The following is a selection of important book-length critical appraisals post-1950. Shorter studies of relevance to particular works are referenced in the notes to individual poems.

Behrendt, Stephen C., *Shelley and His Audiences* (Lincoln, Nebr.: University of Nebraska Press, 1989)

Bennett, Betty T., and Stuart Curran (eds), *Shelley: Poet and Legislator of the World* (Baltimore: Johns Hopkins University Press, 1996)

Blank, G. Kim, *Wordsworth's Influence on Shelley* (London: Palgrave Macmillan, 1988)

Bloom, Harold, *Shelley's Mythmaking* (New Haven, Conn.: Yale University Press, 1959)

Brown, Nathaniel, *Sexuality and Feminism in Shelley* (Cambridge, Mass.: Harvard University Press, 1979)

Cameron, Kenneth Neill, *The Young Shelley: Genesis of a Radical* (London, Macmillan, 1950)

——, *Shelley: The Golden Years* (Cambridge, Mass.: Harvard University Press, 1974)

Chernaik, Judith, *The Lyrics of Shelley* (Cleveland, Ohio, and London: Press of Case Western Reserve University, 1972)

Clark, Timothy, *Embodying Revolution: The Figure of the Poet in Shelley* (Oxford: Clarendon Press, 1989)

Colbert, Benjamin, *Shelley's Eye: Travel Writing and Aesthetic Vision* (Burlington, Vt.: Ashgate, 2005)

Cronin, Richard, *Shelley's Poetic Thoughts* (London: Macmillan, 1981)
Crook, Nora, and Derek Guiton, *Shelley's Venomed Melody* (Cambridge: Cambridge University Press, 1986)
Curran, Stuart, *Shelley's Annus Mirabilis: The Maturing of an Epic Vision* (San Marino, Calif.: Huntington Library, 1975)
Dawson, P. M. S., *The Unacknowledged Legislator: Shelley and Politics* (Oxford: Clarendon Press, 1980)
Duff, David, *Romance and Revolution: Shelley and the Politics of a Genre* (Cambridge: Cambridge University Press, 1994)
Duffy, Cian, *Shelley and the Revolutionary Sublime* (Cambridge: Cambridge University Press, 2005)
Everest, Kelvin (ed.), *Shelley Revalued* (Leicester: Leicester University Press, 1983)
Foot, Paul, *Red Shelley* (London: Bookmarks, 1984)
Garrett, Martin, *The Palgrave Literary Dictionary of Shelley* (London: Palgrave, 2013)
Gelpi, Barbara, *Shelley's Goddess: Maternity, Language, Subjectivity* (Oxford: Oxford University Press, 1992)
Goslee, Nancy, *Shelley's Visual Imagination* (Cambridge: Cambridge University Press, 2011)
Hebron, Stephen, and Elizabeth C. Denlinger, *Shelley's Ghost: Reshaping the Image of a Literary Family* (Oxford: Bodleian Library Publishing, 2010), and at shelleysghost.bodleian.ox.ac.uk
Hoagwood, Terence Allan, *Skepticism & Ideology: Shelley's Political Prose and its Philosophical Context from Bacon to Marx* (Iowa City: University of Iowa Press, 1998)
Jones, Steven E., *Shelley's Satire: Violence, Exhortation, and Authority* (DeKalb, Ill.: Northern Illinois University Press, 1994)
Keach, William, *Shelley's Style* (New York and London: Methuen, 1984)
King-Hele, Desmond, *Shelley: His Thought and Work*, 2nd edn (London: Macmillan, 1971)
Matthews, Geoffrey, 'A Volcano's Voice in Shelley', *ELH* 24 (1957), pp. 191–228.
Morton, Timothy, *Shelley and the Revolution in Taste* (Cambridge: Cambridge University Press, 1994)
——, *The Cambridge Companion to Shelley* (Cambridge: Cambridge University Press, 2006)
Mulhallen, Jacqueline, *The Theatre of Shelley* (Cambridge: Open Book Publishers, 2010)
O'Brien, Paul, *Shelley and Revolutionary Ireland* (London: Redwords, 2002)

O'Neill, Michael, *The Human Mind's Imaginings: Conflict and Achievement in Shelley's Poetry* (Oxford: Clarendon Press, 1989)

—— and Antony Howe (eds), *The Oxford Handbook of Percy Bysshe Shelley* (Oxford: Oxford University Press, 2013)

Pulos, C. E., *The Deep Truth: A Study of Shelley's Skepticism* (Lincoln, Nebr.: University of Nebraska Press, 1962)

Reiman, Donald, *Shelley's 'The Triumph of Life': A Critical Study* (Champaign, Ill.: Illinois University Press, 1965)

Roberts, Hugh, *Shelley and the Chaos of History: A New Politics of Poetry* (University Park, Pa.: Pennsylvania State University Press, 1997)

Robinson, Charles E., *Shelley and Byron: The Snake and Eagle Wreathed in Fight* (Baltimore: Johns Hopkins University Press, 1976)

Ruston, Sharon, *Shelley and Vitality* (London: Palgrave Macmillan, 2005)

Schmid, Susanne, and Michael Rossington (eds), *The Reception of P. B. Shelley in Europe* (London: Continuum, 2008)

Scrivener, Michael Henry, *Radical Shelley* (Princeton, NJ: Princeton University Press, 1982)

Shelley, Bryan, *Shelley and Scripture: The Interpreting Angel* (Oxford: Clarendon Press, 1994)

Sperry, Stuart, *Shelley's Major Verse: The Narrative and Dramatic Poetry* (Cambridge, Mass.: Harvard University Press, 1988)

Stock, Paul, *The Shelley–Byron Circle and the Idea of Europe* (London: Palgrave, 2010)

Ulmer, William, *Shelleyan Eros* (Princeton, NJ: Princeton University Press, 1990)

Wasserman, Earl, *Shelley: A Critical Reading* (Baltimore: Johns Hopkins University Press, 1971)

Webb, Timothy, *The Violet in the Crucible: Shelley and Translation* (Oxford: Oxford University Press, 1976)

——, *Shelley: A Voice Not Understood* (Manchester: Manchester University Press, 1977)

Weinberg, Alan, *Shelley's Italian Experience* (London: Palgrave Macmillan, 1991)

—— and Timothy Webb (eds), *The Unfamiliar Shelley* (Farnham: Ashgate, 2009)

—— and Timothy Webb (eds), *The Neglected Shelley* (Farnham: Ashgate, 2015)

Weisman, Karen, *Imageless Truths: Shelley's Poetic Fictions* (Philadelphia: University of Pennsylvania Press, 1994)

Online Resources

www.bodleian.ox.ac.uk/bodley/news/2015/nov-10: Shelley's recently recovered early verse satire *Poetical Essay on the Existing State of Things* (see Chronology: March 1811) may be read online at this website.

www.rc.umd.edu: The *Romantic Circles* website provides a wide range of scholarly and pedagogical resources and comment on Percy Bysshe and Mary Shelley and their circle.

www.shelleygodwinarchive.org: The Shelley-Godwin Archive, now in progress, will eventually make available in digitized form some 90 per cent of the known manuscripts of Percy Bysshe and Mary Shelley, Mary Wollstonecraft and William Godwin.

Note on the Texts

The present selection aims to provide as generous and varied a representation of Shelley's poetry and prose as limitations of space allow. All of what have come to be regarded as his major poems have been included with the exception of the 4,818 lines of the epic-romance *Laon and Cythna* (1817), though the Dedication before that poem, addressed to Shelley's wife Mary and in some measure a separate work, has been retained. Within both 'The Poems' and 'The Prose' sections the texts are presented in chronological order of composition, inasmuch as that can be determined.

Because Shelley spent the final third or so of his writing life in Italy, he was not able to correct for the press those of his volumes that were printed and published in London during the years 1819–22, and a consequence of his sudden and untimely death was that a significant number of his works were left in manuscript notebooks and published posthumously without having received his final attention. As a result, the textual witnesses for Shelley's verse and prose, of very different kinds, have always posed correspondingly varied, and sometimes very difficult, problems for his editors. The most authoritative source of a given text may be a printed volume published in Shelley's lifetime for which he may or may not have seen proofs; one of the few manuscripts that he prepared for the press to have survived (for example, *The Mask of Anarchy* or *Peter Bell the Third*); a fair copy in his own hand or transcribed by another which he may have meant for safe-keeping, or for private circulation rather than regular publication; or one of his many surviving drafts, which range from clean and unambiguous at one extreme to untidy, unresolved, incomplete and barely legible at the other.

The copy-texts we have chosen for the present edition have been treated on the principle of minimal intervention. We have almost always retained their spelling and capitalization (even where these are inconsistent), and we have modified punctuation where we have judged it necessary to clarify a passage or to reduce what has appeared to us the excessive punctuation of some source-texts. Modern accents and breathings have been supplied where necessary for Greek epigraphs. In the endnotes on each title, we have indicated the source of our text and, for manuscript sources, have provided a reference to a facsimile of the manuscript where one exists in one of the three series, *The Bodleian Shelley Manuscripts*, *The Manuscripts of the Younger Romantics: Shelley* and *Shelley and His Circle 1773–1822*. For bibliographical details of these, see Abbreviations (p. 679) and Further Reading (p. xxxvii).

In both the Poems and Prose sections, a word or phrase within angle brackets <word> is cancelled in the manuscript source; space within square brackets [ ] signals a missing word or phrase; a question mark within square brackets [?] indicates an illegible word or phrase; a question mark and word(s) within square brackets [?word(s)] marks a conjectural reading. Word(s) within square brackets [word(s)] are missing in the manuscript source and have been supplied by the editors. Suspension points . . . in a text are present in the copy-text; an ellipsis within square brackets [. . .] signifies an editorial omission.

SELECTED POEMS AND PROSE

THE POEMS

The Irishman's Song

The stars may dissolve, and the fountain of light
May sink into ne'er ending chaos and night,
Our mansions must fall, and earth vanish away,
But thy courage O Erin! may never decay.

See! the wide wasting ruin extends all around,
Our ancestors' dwellings lie sunk on the ground,
Our foes ride in triumph throughout our domains,
And our mightiest heroes lie stretched on the plains.

Ah! dead is the harp which was wont to give pleasure,
Ah! sunk is our sweet country's rapturous measure,
But the war note is waked, and the clangor of spears,
The dread yell of Sloghan yet sounds in our ears.

Ah! where are the heroes! triumphant in death,
Convulsed they recline on the blood sprinkled heath,
Or the yelling ghosts ride on the blast that sweeps by,
And 'my countrymen! vengeance!' incessantly cry.

Song ('Fierce roars the midnight storm')

Fierce roars the midnight storm,
O'er the wild mountain,
Dark clouds the night deform,
Swift rolls the fountain—

See! o'er yon rocky height,
Dim mists are flying—
See by the moon's pale light,
Poor Laura's dying!

Shame and remorse shall howl,
By her false pillow—
Fiercer than storms that roll,
O'er the white billow;

No hand her eyes to close,
When life is flying,
But she will find repose,
For Laura's dying!

Then will I seek my love,
Then will I cheer her,
Then my esteem will prove,
When no friend is near her.

On her grave I will lie,
When life is parted,
On her grave I will die,
For the false hearted.

'How eloquent are eyes!'

How eloquent are eyes!
Not the rapt Poet's frenzied lay
When the soul's wildest feelings stray
Can speak so well as they.
How eloquent are eyes!
Not music's most impassioned note
On which love's warmest fervours float
Like they bid rapture rise.

Love! look thus again,
That your look may light a waste of years
Darting the beam that conquers cares
Thro' the cold shower of tears!
Love! look thus again,
That Time the victor as he flies
May pause to gaze upon thine eyes,
A victor then in vain!—

Yet no! arrest not Time,
For Time, to others dear, we spurn,
When Time shall *be* no more we burn,
When Love meets full return.
Ah no! arrest not Time,

Fast let him fly on eagle wing
Nor pause till Heaven's unfading spring
   Breathes round its holy clime.

   Yet quench that thrilling gaze
Which passionate Friendship arms with fire,
For what will eloquent eyes inspire
   But feverish, false desire?
   Quench then that thrilling gaze
For age may freeze the tremulous joy,
But age can never *love* destroy.
   It lives to better days.

   Age cannot love destroy.
Can perfidy then blight its flower
Even when in most unwary hour
   It blooms in fancy's bower?
   Age cannot love destroy.
Can slighted vows then rend the shrine
On which its chastened splendours shine
   Around a dream of joy?

Fragment, or The Triumph of Conscience

'Twas dead of the night, when I sat in my dwelling;
   One glimmering lamp was expiring and low;
Around, the dark tide of the tempest was swelling,
Along the wild mountains night-ravens were yelling,—
   They bodingly presag'd destruction and woe.

'Twas then that I started!—the wild storm was howling,
   Nought was seen, save the lightning, which danc'd in the sky;
Above me, the crash of the thunder was rolling,
   And low, chilling murmurs, the blast wafted by.

My heart sank within me—unheeded the war
   Of the battling clouds, on the mountain-tops, broke;—
Unheeded the thunder-peal crash'd in mine ear—
   This heart, hard as iron, is stranger to fear;
But conscience in low, noiseless whispering spoke.

'Twas then that her form on the whirlwind upholding,
The ghost of the murder'd Victoria strode;
In her right hand, a shadowy shroud she was holding,
She swiftly advanc'd to my lonesome abode.

I wildly then call'd on the tempest to bear me—

Song ('Ah! faint are her limbs')

I

Ah! faint are her limbs, and her footstep is weary,
Yet far must the desolate wanderer roam;
Though the tempest is stern, and the mountain is dreary,
She must quit at deep midnight her pitiless home.
I see her swift foot dash the dew from the whortle,
As she rapidly hastes to the green grove of myrtle;
And I hear, as she wraps round her figure the kirtle,
'Stay thy boat on the lake,—dearest Henry, I come.'

II

High swell'd in her bosom the throb of affection,
As lightly her form bounded over the lea,
And arose in her mind every dear recollection:
'I come, dearest Henry, and wait but for thee.'
How sad, when dear hope every sorrow is soothing,
When sympathy's swell the soft bosom is moving,
And the mind the mild joys of affection is proving,
Is the stern voice of fate that bids happiness flee!

III

Oh! dark lower'd the clouds on that horrible eve,
And the moon dimly gleam'd through the tempested air;
Oh! how could fond visions such softness deceive?
Oh! how could false hope rend a bosom so fair?
Thy love's pallid corse the wild surges are laving,
O'er his form the fierce swell of the tempest is raving;
But, fear not, parting spirit; thy goodness is saving,
In eternity's bowers, a seat for thee there.

The Monarch's funeral
An Anticipation

The growing gloom of eventide
  Has quenched the sunbeam's latest glow
And lowers upon the woe and pride
  That blasts the city's peace below.

At such an hour how sad the sight
  To mark a Monarch's funeral
When the dim shades of awful night
  Rest on the coffin's velvet pall;

To see the Gothic Arches shew
  A varied mass of light and shade
While to the torches' crimson glow
  A vast cathedral is displayed;

To see with what a silence deep
  The thousands o'er this death-scene brood
As tho' some wizard's charm did creep
  Upon the countless multitude;

To see this awful pomp of death
  For one frail mass of mouldering clay
When nobler men the tomb beneath
  Have sunk unwept, unseen away.

For who was he, the uncoffined slain,
  That fell in Erin's injured isle
Because his spirit dared disdain
  To light his country's funeral pile?

Shall he not ever live in lays
  The warmest that a Muse may sing
Whilst monumental marbles raise
  The fame of a departed King?

May not the Muse's darling theme
  Gather its glorious garland thence
Whilst some frail tombstone's Dotard dream
  Fades with a monarch's impotence?

—Yet, 'tis a scene of wondrous awe
  To see a coffined Monarch lay,
That the wide grave's insatiate maw
  Be glutted with a regal prey!

Who *now* shall public councils guide?
  Who rack the poor on gold to dine?
Who waste the means of regal pride
  For which a million wretches pine?

It is a child of earthly breath,
  A being perishing as he,
Who throned in yonder pomp of death
  Hath now fulfilled his destiny.

Now dust to dust restore! . . . O Pride,
  Unmindful of thy fleeting power,
Whose empty confidence has vied
  With human life's most treacherous hour,

One moment feel that in the breast
  With regal crimes and troubles vext
The pampered Earthworms soon will rest,
  One moment feel . . . and die the next.

Yet deem not in the tomb's control
  The vital lamp of life can fail,
Deem not that e'er the Patriot's soul
  Is wasted by the withering gale.

The dross which forms the *King* is gone
  And reproductive Earth supplies
As senseless as the clay and stone
  In which the kindred body lies.

The soul which makes the *Man* doth soar,
And love alone survives to shed
All that its tide of bliss can pour
Of Heaven upon the blessed dead.

So shall the Sun forever burn,
So shall the midnight lightnings die,
And joy that glows at Nature's bourn
Outlive terrestrial misery.

And will the crowd who silent stoop
Around the lifeless Monarch's bier,
A mournful and dejected group,
Breathe not one sigh, or shed one tear?

Ah! no. 'Tis wonder, 'tis not woe;
Even royalists might groan to see
The *Father of the People* so
Lost in the Sacred Majesty.

A Winter's Day

O! wintry day! that mockest spring
With hopes of the reviving year,
That sheddest softness from thy wing
And near the cascade's murmuring
Awakenest sounds so clear
That peals of vernal music swing
Thro' the balm atmosphere.

Why hast thou given, O year! to May
A birth so premature,
To live one incompleted day
That the mad whirlwind's sullen sway
May sweep it from the moor,
And winter reassume the sway
That shall so long endure?

Art thou like Genius's matin bloom,
  Unwelcome promise of its prime,
That scattereth its rich perfume
Around the portals of the tomb,
  Decking the scar of time
In mockery of the early doom?

Art thou like Passion's rapturous dream
  That o'er life's stormy dawn
Doth dart its wild and flamy beam
Yet like a fleeting flash doth seem
  When many chequered years are gone
And tell the illusion of its gleam
  Life's blasted springs alone?

Whate'er thou emblemest, I'll breathe
  Thy transitory sweetness now,
And whether Health with roseate wreathe
May bind mine head, or creeping Death
  Steal o'er my pulse's flow,
Struggling the wintry winds beneath
  I'll love thy vernal glow.

To the Republicans of North America

Brothers! between you and me
  Whirlwinds sweep and billows roar,
Yet in spirit oft I see
  On the wild and winding shore
Freedom's bloodless banner wave,
Feel the pulses of the brave
Unextinguished by the grave,
  See them drenched in sacred gore,
Catch the patriot's gasping breath
Murmuring 'Liberty' in death.

Shout aloud! let every slave
  Crouching at corruption's throne
Start into a man and brave
  Racks and chains without a groan!

Let the castle's heartless glow
And the hovel's vice and woe
Fade like gaudy flowers that blow,
  Weeds that peep and then are gone,
Whilst from misery's ashes risen
Love shall burst the Captive's prison.

Cotopaxi! bid the sound
  Thro' thy sister mountains ring
Till each valley smile around
  At the blissful welcoming,
And O! thou stern Ocean-deep
Whose eternal billows sweep
Shores where thousands wake to weep
  Whilst they curse some villain King,
On the winds that fan thy breast
Bear thou news of freedom's rest.

Earth's remotest bounds shall start;
  Every despot's bloated cheek,
Pallid as his bloodless heart,
  Frenzy, woe and dread shall speak . . .
Blood may fertilize the tree
Of new bursting Liberty;
Let the guiltiness then be
  On the slaves that ruin wreak,
On the unnatural tyrant brood
Slow to Peace and swift to blood.

Can the daystar dawn of love
  Where the flag of war unfurled
Floats with crimson stain above
  Such a desolated world? . . .
Never! but to vengeance driven
When the patriot's spirit shriven
Seeks in death its native Heaven,
  Then to speechless horror hurled
Widowed Earth may balm the bier
Of its memory with a tear.

On Robert Emmet's Tomb

May the tempests of Winter that sweep o'er thy tomb
  Disturb not a slumber so sacred as thine;
May the breezes of summer that breathe of perfume
  Waft their balmiest dews to so hallowed a shrine.

May the foot of the tyrant, the coward, the slave
  Be palsied with dread where thine ashes repose,
Where that undying shamrock still blooms on thy grave
  Which sprung when the dawnlight of Erin arose.

There oft have I marked the grey gravestones among,
  Where thy relics distinguished in lowliness lay,
The peasant boy pensively lingering long
  And silently weep as he passed away.

And how could he not pause if the blood of his sires
  Ever wakened one generous throb in his heart:
How could he inherit a spark of their fires
  If tearless and frigid he dared to depart?

Not the scrolls of a court could emblazon thy fame
  Like the silence that reigns in the palace of thee,
Like the whispers that pass of thy dearly loved name,
  Like the tears of the good, like the groans of the free.

No trump tells thy virtues—the grave where they rest
  With thy dust shall remain unpolluted by fame,
Till thy foes, by the world and by fortune caressed,
  Shall pass like a mist from the light of thy name.

When the storm cloud that lowers o'er the daybeam is gone,
  Unchanged, unextinguished its lifespring will shine;
When Erin has ceased with their memory to groan
  She will smile thro' the tears of revival on thine.

To Liberty

O let not Liberty
  Silently perish;
May the groan and the sigh
  Yet the flame cherish
Till the voice to Nature's bursting heart given,
  Ascending loud and high,
  A world's indignant cry,
  And startling on his throne
  The tyrant grim and lone,
Shall beat the deaf vault of Heaven.

Say, can the Tyrant's frown
  Daunt those who fear not
Or break the spirits down
  His badge that wear not?
Can chains or death or infamy subdue
  The pure and fearless soul
  That dreads not their control,
  Sees Paradise and Hell,
  Sees the Palace and the cell,
Yet bravely dares prefer the good and true?

Regal pomp and pride
  The Patriot falls in scorning,
The spot whereon he died
  Should be the despot's warning;
The voice of blood shall on his crimes call down
      Revenge!
  And the spirits of the brave
  Shall start from every grave
  Whilst from her Atlantic throne
  Freedom sanctifies the groan
That fans the glorious fires of its change.

Monarch! sure employer
  Of vice and want and woe,
Thou Conscienceless destroyer,
  Who and what are thou?—
The dark prison house that in the dust shall lie,

The pyramid which guilt
First planned, which man has built,
At whose footstone want and woe
With a ceaseless murmur flow
And whose peak attracts the tempests of the sky.

The pyramids shall fall . . .
And Monarchs! so shall ye,
Thrones shall rust in the hall
Of forgotten royalty
Whilst Virtue, Truth and Peace shall arise
And a Paradise on Earth
From your fall shall date its birth,
And human life shall seem
Like a short and happy dream
Ere we wake in the daybeam of the skies.

Written on a Beautiful Day in Spring

In that strange mental wandering when to live,
To breathe, to be, is undivided joy,
When the most woe-worn wretch would cease to grieve,
When satiation's self would fail to cloy;
When unpercipient of all other things
Than those that press around, the breathing Earth,
The gleaming sky and the fresh season's birth,
Sensation all its wondrous rapture brings,
And to itself not once the mind recurs—
Is it foretaste of Heaven?
So sweet as this the nerves it stirs,
And mingling in the vital tide
With gentle motion driven,
Cheers the sunk spirits, lifts the languid eye,
And scattering thro' the frame its influence wide
Revives the spirits when they droop and die.
The frozen blood with genial beaming warms,
And to a gorgeous fly the sluggish worm transforms.

'Dark Spirit of the desart rude'

Dark Spirit of the desart rude
That o'er this awful solitude,
Each tangled and untrodden wood,
Each dark and silent glen below
Where sunlight's gleamings never glow,
Whilst jetty, musical and still
In darkness speeds the mountain rill;
That o'er yon broken peaks sublime,
Wild shapes that mock the scythe of time,
And the pure Ellan's foamy course,
Wavest thy wand of magic force—
Art thou yon sooty and fearful fowl
  That flaps its wing o'er the leafless oak
That o'er the dismal scene doth scowl
  And mocketh music with its croak?

I've sought thee where day's beams decay
  On the peak of the lonely hill;
I've sought thee where they melt away
  By the wave of the pebbly rill;
I've strained to catch thy murky form
Bestride the rapid and gloomy storm;
Thy red and sullen eyeball's glare
Has shot, in a dream thro' the midnight air,
  But never did thy shape express
  Such an emphatic gloominess.

And where art thou, O thing of gloom? . . .
On Nature's unreviving tomb
Where sapless, blasted and alone
She mourns her blooming centuries gone!—
From the fresh sod the Violets peep,
The buds have burst their frozen sleep,
  Whilst every green and peopled tree
Is alive with Earth's sweet melody.
    But thou alone art here,
Thou desolate Oak, whose scathed head
For ages has never trembled,

Whose giant trunk dead lichens bind,
Moaningly sighing in the wind,
With huge loose rocks beneath thee spread—
Thou, Thou alone art here!
Remote from every living thing,
Tree, shrub or grass or flower,
Thou seemest of this spot the King,
And with a regal power
Suck like that race all sap away
And yet upon the spoil decay.

The Retrospect
Cwm Elan 1812

To trace Duration's lone career,
To check the chariot of the year
Whose burning wheels forever sweep
The boundaries of oblivion's deep . . .
To snatch from Time the monster's jaw
The children which she just had borne,
And ere entombed within her maw
To drag them to the light of morn
And mark each feature with an eye
Of cold and fearless scrutiny . . .
It asks a soul not formed to feel,
An eye of glass, a hand of steel;
Thoughts that have passed and thoughts that are
With truth and feeling to compare;
A scene which wildered fancy viewed
In the soul's coldest solitude,
With that same scene when peaceful love
Flings rapture's colour o'er the grove,
When mountain, meadow, wood and stream
With unalloying glory gleam
And to the spirit's ear and eye
Are unison and harmony.

The moonlight was my dearer day:—
Then would I wander far away
And lingering on the wild brook's shore
To hear its unremitting roar

Would lose in the ideal flow
All sense of overwhelming woe;
Or at the noiseless noon of night
Would climb some heathy mountain's height
And listen to the mystic sound
That stole in fitful gasps around.
I joyed to see the streaks of day
Above the purple peaks decay
And watch the latest line of light
Just mingling with the shades of night;
For day with me, was time of woe
When even tears refused to flow;
Then would I stretch my languid frame
Beneath the wild-wood's gloomiest shade
And try to quench the ceaseless flame
That on my withered vitals preyed;
Would close mine eyes and dream I were
On some remote and friendless plain
And long to leave existence there
If with it I might leave the pain
That with a finger cold and lean
Wrote madness on my withering mien.

It was not unrequited love
That bade my wildered spirit rove;
'Twas not the pride disdaining life,
That with this mortal world at strife
Would yield to the soul's inward sense,
Then groan in human impotence,
And weep, because it is not given
To taste on Earth the peace of Heaven.
'Twas not, that in the narrow sphere
Where Nature fixed my wayward fate
There was no friend or kindred dear
Formed to become that spirit's mate
Which searching on tired pinion found
Barren and cold repulse around . . .
Ah no! yet each one sorrow gave
New graces to the narrow grave:

For broken vows had early quelled
The stainless spirit's vestal flame.
Yes! whilst the faithful bosom swelled
Then the envenomed arrow came
And apathy's unaltering eye
Beamed coldness on the misery;
And early I had learned to scorn
The chains of clay that bound a soul
Panting to seize the wings of morn,
And where its vital fires were born
To soar, and spurn the cold control
Which the vile slaves of earthly night
Would twine around its struggling flight.
O many were the friends whom fame
Had linked with the unmeaning name
Whose magic marked among mankind
The casket of my unknown mind,
Which hidden from the vulgar glare
Imbibed no fleeting radiance there.
My darksome spirit sought. It found
A friendless solitude around.—
For who, that might undaunted stand
The saviour of a sinking land,
Would crawl its ruthless tyrant's slave
And fatten upon freedom's grave,
Tho' doomed with her to perish, where
The captive clasps abhorred despair?

They could not share the bosom's feeling
Which passion's every throb revealing
Dared force on the world's notice cold
Thoughts of unprofitable mould,
Who bask in Custom's fickle ray,
Fit sunshine of such wintry day!
They could not in a twilight walk
Weave an impassioned web of talk
Till mysteries the spirit press
In wild yet tender awfulness,
Then feel within our narrow sphere
How little yet how great we are!
But they might shine in courtly glare,
Attract the rabble's cheapest stare,

And might command where'er they move
A thing that bears the name of love;
They might be learned, witty, gay,
Foremost in fashion's gilt array,
On Fame's emblazoned pages shine,
Be princes' friends, but never mine!

Ye jagged peaks that frown sublime,
Mocking the blunted scythe of Time,
Whence I would watch its lustre pale
Steal from the moon o'er yonder vale!

Thou rock, whose bosom black and vast
Bared to the stream's unceasing flow,
Ever its giant shade doth cast
On the tumultuous surge below!

Woods to whose depth retires to die
The wounded echo's melody,
And whither this lone spirit bent
The footstep of a wild intent—

Meadows! whose green and spangled breast
These fevered limbs have often pressed
Until the watchful fiend Despair
Slept in the soothing coolness there!
Have not your varied beauties seen
The sunken eye, the withering mien,
Sad traces of the unuttered pain
That froze my heart and burned my brain?

How changed since nature's summer form
Had last the power my grief to charm,
Since last ye soothed my spirit's sadness,
Strange chaos of a mingled madness!
Changed!—not the loathsome worm that fed
In the dark mansions of the dead,
Now soaring thro' the fields of air
And gathering purest nectar there,
A butterfly whose million hues
The dazzled eye of wonder views
Long lingering on a work so strange,
Has undergone so bright a change!

How do I feel my happiness?
I cannot tell, but they may guess
Whose every gloomy feeling gone
Friendship and passion feel alone,
Who see mortality's dull clouds
Before affection's murmur fly,
Whilst the mild glances of her eye
Pierce the thin veil of flesh that shrouds
The spirit's radiant sanctuary.

O thou! whose virtues latest known
First in this heart yet claim'st a throne,
Whose downy sceptre still shall share
The gentle sway with virtue there,
Thou fair in form and pure in mind,
Whose ardent friendship rivets fast
The flowery band our fates that bind
Which incorruptible shall last
When duty's hard and cold control
Had thawed around the burning soul.
The gloomiest retrospects that bind
With crowns of thorn the bleeding mind,
The prospects of most doubtful hue
That rise on Fancy's shuddering view,
Are gilt by the reviving ray
Which thou hast flung upon my day.

QUEEN MAB;

A PHILOSOPHICAL POEM: WITH NOTES

ECRASEZ L'INFAME!

Correspondance de Voltaire.

Avia Pieridum peragro loca, nullius ante
Trita solo; juvat integros accedere fonteis;
Atque haurire: juvatque novos decerpere flores.

* * * * * * *

Unde prius nulli velarint tempora musae.
Primum quod magnis doceo de rebus; et arctis
Religionum animos nodis exsolvere pergo.

Lucret. lib. iv.

Δὸς που στῶ, καὶ κόσμον κινήσω.

Archimedes.

*To Harriet *****

Whose is the love that, gleaming through the world,
Wards off the poisonous arrow of its scorn?
  Whose is the warm and partial praise,
  Virtue's most sweet reward?

Beneath whose looks did my reviving soul
Riper in truth and virtuous daring grow?
  Whose eyes have I gazed fondly on,
  And loved mankind the more?

Harriet! on thine:—thou wert my purer mind;
Thou wert the inspiration of my song;
  Thine are these early wilding flowers,
  Though garlanded by me.

Then press unto thy breast this pledge of love;
And know, though time may change and years may roll,
Each flowret gathered in my heart
It consecrates to thine.

Queen Mab

I

How wonderful is Death,
Death, and his brother Sleep!
One, pale as yonder waning moon
With lips of lurid blue;
The other, rosy as the morn
When throned on ocean's wave
It blushes o'er the world:
Yet both so passing wonderful!

Hath then the gloomy Power
Whose reign is in the tainted sepulchres
Seized on her sinless soul?
Must then that peerless form
Which love and admiration cannot view
Without a beating heart, those azure veins
Which steal like streams along a field of snow,
That lovely outline, which is fair
As breathing marble, perish?
Must putrefaction's breath
Leave nothing of this heavenly sight
But loathsomeness and ruin?
Spare nothing but a gloomy theme,
On which the lightest heart might moralize?
Or is it only a sweet slumber
Stealing o'er sensation,
Which the breath of roseate morning
Chaseth into darkness?
Will Ianthe wake again,
And give that faithful bosom joy
Whose sleepless spirit waits to catch
Light, life and rapture from her smile?

Yes! she will wake again,
Although her glowing limbs are motionless,
And silent those sweet lips,
Once breathing eloquence,
That might have soothed a tyger's rage,
Or thawed the cold heart of a conqueror.
Her dewy eyes are closed,
And on their lids, whose texture fine
Scarce hides the dark blue orbs beneath,
The baby Sleep is pillowed:
Her golden tresses shade
The bosom's stainless pride,
Curling like tendrils of the parasite
Around a marble column.

Hark! whence that rushing sound?
'Tis like the wondrous strain
That round a lonely ruin swells,
Which, wandering on the echoing shore,
The enthusiast hears at evening:
'Tis softer than the west wind's sigh;
'Tis wilder than the unmeasured notes
Of that strange lyre whose strings
The genii of the breezes sweep:
Those lines of rainbow light
Are like the moonbeams when they fall
Through some cathedral window, but the teints
Are such as may not find
Comparison on earth.

Behold the chariot of the Fairy Queen!
Celestial coursers paw the unyielding air;
Their filmy pennons at her word they furl,
And stop obedient to the reins of light:
These the Queen of spells drew in,
She spread a charm around the spot,
And leaning graceful from the etherial car,
Long did she gaze, and silently,
Upon the slumbering maid.

Oh! not the visioned poet in his dreams,
When silvery clouds float through the wildered brain,
When every sight of lovely, wild and grand
  Astonishes, enraptures, elevates,
    When fancy at a glance combines
    The wondrous and the beautiful,—
  So bright, so fair, so wild a shape
    Hath ever yet beheld,
As that which reined the coursers of the air,
  And poured the magic of her gaze
    Upon the maiden's sleep.

    The broad and yellow moon
    Shone dimly through her form—
  That form of faultless symmetry;
  The pearly and pellucid car
    Moved not the moonlight's line:
    'Twas not an earthly pageant:
  Those who had looked upon the sight,
    Passing all human glory,
    Saw not the yellow moon,
    Saw not the mortal scene,
    Heard not the night-wind's rush,
    Heard not an earthly sound,
    Saw but the fairy pageant,
    Heard but the heavenly strains
    That filled the lonely dwelling.

The Fairy's frame was slight, yon fibrous cloud,
That catches but the palest tinge of even,
And which the straining eye can hardly seize
When melting into eastern twilight's shadow,
Were scarce so thin, so slight; but the fair star
That gems the glittering coronet of morn,
Sheds not a light so mild, so powerful,
As that which, bursting from the Fairy's form,
Spread a purpureal halo round the scene,
  Yet with an undulating motion,
  Swayed to her outline gracefully.

From her celestial car
The Fairy Queen descended,
And thrice she waved her wand
Circled with wreaths of amaranth:
Her thin and misty form
Moved with the moving air,
And the clear silver tones,
As thus she spoke, were such
As are unheard by all but gifted ear.

FAIRY

Stars! Your balmiest influence shed!
Elements! Your wrath suspend!
Sleep, Ocean, in the rocky bounds
That circle thy domain!
Let not a breath be seen to stir
Around yon grass-grown ruin's height,
Let even the restless gossamer
Sleep on the moveless air!
Soul of Ianthe! thou,
Judged alone worthy of the envied boon,
That waits the good and the sincere; that waits
Those who have struggled, and with resolute will
Vanquished earth's pride and meanness, burst the chains,
The icy chains of custom, and have shone
The day-stars of their age;—Soul of Ianthe!
Awake! arise!

Sudden arose
Ianthe's Soul; it stood
All beautiful in naked purity,
The perfect semblance of its bodily frame,
Instinct with inexpressible beauty and grace.
Each stain of earthliness
Had passed away, it reassumed
Its native dignity, and stood
Immortal amid ruin.

Upon the couch the body lay
Wrapt in the depth of slumber:
Its features were fixed and meaningless,
Yet animal life was there,

And every organ yet performed
Its natural functions: 'twas a sight
Of wonder to behold the body and soul.
The self-same lineaments, the same
Marks of identity were there:
Yet, oh, how different! One aspires to Heaven,
Pants for its sempiternal heritage,
And ever changing, ever rising still,
Wantons in endless being.
The other, for a time the unwilling sport
Of circumstance and passion, struggles on;
Fleets through its sad duration rapidly;
Then like an useless and worn-out machine,
Rots, perishes, and passes.

FAIRY

Spirit! who hast dived so deep;
Spirit! who hast soared so high;
Thou the fearless, thou the mild,
Accept the boon thy worth hath earned,
Ascend the car with me!

SPIRIT

Do I dream? is this new feeling
But a visioned ghost of slumber?
If indeed I am a soul,
A free, a disembodied soul,
Speak again to me.

FAIRY

I am the Fairy MAB: to me 'tis given
The wonders of the human world to keep:
The secrets of the immeasurable past,
In the unfailing consciences of men,
Those stern, unflattering chroniclers, I find:
The future, from the causes which arise
In each event, I gather: not the sting
Which retributive memory implants
In the hard bosom of the selfish man;
Nor that extatic and exulting throb
Which virtue's votary feels when he sums up
The thoughts and actions of a well-spent day,

Are unforeseen, unregistered by me:
And it is yet permitted me, to rend
The veil of mortal frailty, that the spirit
Clothed in its changeless purity, may know
How soonest to accomplish the great end
For which it hath its being, and may taste
That peace, which in the end all life will share.
This is the meed of virtue; happy Soul,
Ascend the car with me!

The chains of earth's immurement
Fell from Ianthe's spirit;
They shrank and brake like bandages of straw
Beneath a wakened giant's strength.
She knew her glorious change,
And felt in apprehension uncontrolled
New raptures opening round:
Each day-dream of her mortal life,
Each frenzied vision of the slumbers
That closed each well-spent day,
Seemed now to meet reality.

The Fairy and the Soul proceeded;
The silver clouds disparted;
And as the car of magic they ascended,
Again the speechless music swelled,
Again the coursers of the air
Unfurled their azure pennons, and the Queen
Shaking the beamy reins
Bade them pursue their way.

The magic car moved on.
The night was fair, and countless stars
Studded heaven's dark blue vault,—
Just o'er the eastern wave
Peeped the first faint smile of morn:—
The magic car moved on—
From the celestial hoofs
The atmosphere in flaming sparkles flew,
And where the burning wheels
Eddied above the mountain's loftiest peak,
Was traced a line of lightning.

Now it flew far above a rock,
The utmost verge of earth,
The rival of the Andes, whose dark brow
Lowered o'er the silver sea.

Far, far below the chariot's path,
Calm as a slumbering babe,
Tremendous Ocean lay.
The mirror of its stillness shewed
The pale and waning stars,
The chariot's fiery track,
And the grey light of morn
Tinging those fleecy clouds
That canopied the dawn.
Seemed it, that the chariot's way
Lay through the midst of an immense concave,
Radiant with million constellations, tinged
With shades of infinite colour,
And semicircled with a belt
Flashing incessant meteors.

The magic car moved on.
As they approached their goal
The coursers seemed to gather speed;
The sea no longer was distinguished; earth
Appeared a vast and shadowy sphere;
The sun's unclouded orb
Rolled through the black concave;
Its rays of rapid light
Parted around the chariot's swifter course,
And fell, like ocean's feathery spray
Dashed from the boiling surge
Before a vessel's prow.

The magic car moved on.
Earth's distant orb appeared
The smallest light that twinkles in the heaven;
Whilst round the chariot's way
Innumerable systems rolled,
And countless spheres diffused
An ever-varying glory.
It was a sight of wonder: some

Were horned like the crescent moon;
Some shed a mild and silver beam
Like Hesperus o'er the western sea;
Some dash'd athwart with trains of flame,
Like worlds to death and ruin driven;
Some shone like suns, and as the chariot passed,
Eclipsed all other light.

Spirit of Nature! here!
In this interminable wilderness
Of worlds, at whose immensity
Even soaring fancy staggers,
Here is thy fitting temple.
Yet not the lightest leaf
That quivers to the passing breeze
Is less instinct with thee:
Yet not the meanest worm
That lurks in graves and fattens on the dead
Less shares thy eternal breath.
Spirit of Nature! thou!
Imperishable as this scene,
Here is thy fitting temple.

II

If solitude hath ever led thy steps
To the wild ocean's echoing shore,
And thou hast lingered there,
Until the sun's broad orb
Seemed resting on the burnished wave,
Thou must have marked the lines
Of purple gold, that motionless
Hung o'er the sinking sphere:
Thou must have marked the billowy clouds
Edged with intolerable radiancy
Towering like rocks of jet
Crowned with a diamond wreath.
And yet there is a moment,
When the sun's highest point
Peeps like a star o'er ocean's western edge,
When those far clouds of feathery gold,
Shaded with deepest purple, gleam

Like islands on a dark blue sea;
Then has thy fancy soared above the earth,
And furled its wearied wing
Within the Fairy's fane.

Yet not the golden islands
Gleaming in yon flood of light,
Nor the feathery curtains
Stretching o'er the sun's bright couch,
Nor the burnished ocean waves
Paving that gorgeous dome,
So fair, so wonderful a sight
As Mab's etherial palace could afford.
Yet likest evening's vault, that faery Hall!
As Heaven, low resting on the wave, it spread
Its floors of flashing light,
Its vast and azure dome,
Its fertile golden islands
Floating on a silver sea;
Whilst suns their mingling beamings darted
Through clouds of circumambient darkness,
And pearly battlements around
Looked o'er the immense of Heaven.

The magic car no longer moved.
The Fairy and the Spirit
Entered the Hall of Spells:
Those golden clouds
That rolled in glittering billows
Beneath the azure canopy
With the etherial footsteps trembled not:
The light and crimson mists,
Floating to strains of thrilling melody
Through that unearthly dwelling,
Yielded to every movement of the will.
Upon their passive swell the Spirit leaned,
And, for the varied bliss that pressed around,
Used not the glorious privilege
Of virtue and of wisdom.

Spirit! the Fairy said,
And pointed to the gorgeous dome,
This is a wondrous sight
And mocks all human grandeur;
But, were it virtue's only meed, to dwell
In a celestial palace, all resigned
To pleasurable impulses, immured
Within the prison of itself, the will
Of changeless nature would be unfulfilled.
Learn to make others happy. Spirit, come!
This is thine high reward:—the past shall rise;
Thou shalt behold the present; I will teach
The secrets of the future.

The Fairy and the Spirit
Approached the overhanging battlement.—
Below lay stretched the universe!
There, far as the remotest line
That bounds imagination's flight,
Countless and unending orbs
In mazy motion intermingled,
Yet still fulfilled immutably
Eternal Nature's law.
Above, below, around
The circling systems formed
A wilderness of harmony;
Each with undeviating aim,
In eloquent silence, through the depths of space
Pursued its wondrous way.

There was a little light
That twinkled in the misty distance:
None but a spirit's eye
Might ken that rolling orb;
None but a spirit's eye,
And in no other place
But that celestial dwelling, might behold
Each action of this earth's inhabitants.
But matter, space and time
In those aërial mansions cease to act;

And all-prevailing wisdom, when it reaps
The harvest of its excellence, o'erbounds
Those obstacles, of which an earthly soul
Fears to attempt the conquest.

The Fairy pointed to the earth.
The Spirit's intellectual eye
Its kindred beings recognized.
The thronging thousands, to a passing view,
Seemed like an anthill's citizens.
How wonderful! that even
The passions, prejudices, interests,
That sway the meanest being, the weak touch
That moves the finest nerve,
And in one human brain
Causes the faintest thought, becomes a link
In the great chain of nature.

Behold, the Fairy cried,
Palmyra's ruined palaces!—
Behold! where grandeur frowned;
Behold! where pleasure smiled;
What now remains?—the memory
Of senselessness and shame—
What is immortal there?
Nothing—it stands to tell
A melancholy tale, to give
An awful warning: soon
Oblivion will steal silently
The remnant of its fame.
Monarchs and conquerors there
Proud o'er prostrate millions trod—
The earthquakes of the human race;
Like them, forgotten when the ruin
That marks their shock is past.

Beside the eternal Nile,
The Pyramids have risen.
Nile shall pursue his changeless way:
Those pyramids shall fall;

Yea! not a stone shall stand to tell
The spot whereon they stood;
Their very scite shall be forgotten,
As is their builder's name!

Behold yon sterile spot;
Where now the wandering Arab's tent
Flaps in the desart-blast.
There once old Salem's haughty fane
Reared high to heaven its thousand golden domes,
And in the blushing face of day
Exposed its shameful glory.
Oh! many a widow, many an orphan cursed
The building of that fane; and many a father,
Worn out with toil and slavery, implored
The poor man's God to sweep it from the earth,
And spare his children the detested task
Of piling stone on stone, and poisoning
The choicest days of life,
To soothe a dotard's vanity.
There an inhuman and uncultured race
Howled hideous praises to their Demon-God;
They rushed to war, tore from the mother's womb
The unborn child,—old age and infancy
Promiscuous perished; their victorious arms
Left not a soul to breathe. Oh! they were fiends:
But what was he who taught them that the God
Of nature and benevolence had given
A special sanction to the trade of blood?
His name and theirs are fading, and the tales
Of this barbarian nation, which imposture
Recites till terror credits, are pursuing
Itself into forgetfulness.

Where Athens, Rome, and Sparta stood,
There is a moral desart now:
The mean and miserable huts,
The yet more wretched palaces,
Contrasted with those antient fanes
Now crumbling to oblivion;
The long and lonely colonnades,
Through which the ghost of Freedom stalks,

Seem like a well-known tune,
Which, in some dear scene we have loved to hear,
Remembered now in sadness.
But, oh! how much more changed,
How gloomier is the contrast
Of human nature there!
Where Socrates expired, a tyrant's slave,
A coward and a fool, spreads death around—
Then, shuddering, meets his own.
Where Cicero and Antoninus lived,
A cowled and hypocritical monk
Prays, curses and deceives.

Spirit! ten thousand years
Have scarcely past away,
Since, in the waste where now the savage drinks
His enemy's blood, and aping Europe's sons,
Wakes the unholy song of war,
Arose a stately city,
Metropolis of the western continent:
There, now, the mossy column-stone,
Indented by time's unrelaxing grasp,
Which once appeared to brave
All, save its country's ruin;
There the wide forest scene,
Rude in the uncultivated loveliness
Of gardens long run wild,
Seems, to the unwilling sojourner, whose steps
Chance in that desart has delayed,
Thus to have stood since earth was what it is.
Yet once it was the busiest haunt,
Whither, as to a common centre, flocked
Strangers, and ships, and merchandize:
Once peace and freedom blest
The cultivated plain:
But wealth, that curse of man,
Blighted the bud of its prosperity:
Virtue and wisdom, truth and liberty,
Fled, to return not, until man shall know
That they alone can give the bliss
Worthy a soul that claims
Its kindred with eternity.

There's not one atom of yon earth
But once was living man;
Nor the minutest drop of rain,
That hangeth in its thinnest cloud,
But flowed in human veins:
And from the burning plains
Where Lybian monsters yell,
From the most gloomy glens
Of Greenland's sunless clime,
To where the golden fields
Of fertile England spread
Their harvest to the day,
Thou canst not find one spot
Whereon no city stood.

How strange is human pride!
I tell thee that those living things,
To whom the fragile blade of grass,
That springeth in the morn
And perisheth ere noon,
Is an unbounded world;
I tell thee that those viewless beings,
Whose mansion is the smallest particle
Of the impassive atmosphere,
Think, feel and live like man;
That their affections and antipathies,
Like his, produce the laws
Ruling their moral state;
And the minutest throb
That through their frame diffuses
The slightest, faintest motion,
Is fixed and indispensable
As the majestic laws
That rule yon rolling orbs.

The Fairy paused. The Spirit,
In extacy of admiration, felt
All knowledge of the past revived; the events
Of old and wondrous times,
Which dim tradition interruptedly
Teaches the credulous vulgar, were unfolded
In just perspective to the view;

Yet dim from their infinitude.
The Spirit seemed to stand
High on an isolated pinnacle;
The flood of ages combating below,
The depth of the unbounded universe
Above, and all around
Nature's unchanging harmony.

III

Fairy! the Spirit said,
And on the Queen of Spells
Fixed her etherial eyes,
I thank thee. Thou hast given
A boon which I will not resign, and taught
A lesson not to be unlearned. I know
The past, and thence I will essay to glean
A warning for the future, so that man
May profit by his errors, and derive
Experience from his folly:
For, when the power of imparting joy
Is equal to the will, the human soul
Requires no other heaven.

MAB

Turn thee, surpassing Spirit!
Much yet remains unscanned.
Thou knowest how great is man,
Thou knowest his imbecility:
Yet learn thou what he is;
Yet learn the lofty destiny
Which restless time prepares
For every living soul.

Behold a gorgeous palace, that, amid
Yon populous city, rears its thousand towers
And seems itself a city. Gloomy troops
Of centinels, in stern and silent ranks,
Encompass it around: the dweller there
Cannot be free and happy; hearest thou not
The curses of the fatherless, the groans
Of those who have no friend? He passes on:
The King, the wearer of a gilded chain

That binds his soul to abjectness, the fool
Whom courtiers nickname monarch, whilst a slave
Even to the basest appetites—that man
Heeds not the shriek of penury; he smiles
At the deep curses which the destitute
Mutter in secret, and a sullen joy
Pervades his bloodless heart when thousands groan
But for those morsels which his wantonness
Wastes in unjoyous revelry, to save
All that they love from famine: when he hears
The tale of horror, to some ready-made face
Of hypocritical assent he turns,
Smothering the glow of shame, that, spite of him,
Flushes his bloated cheek.
Now to the meal
Of silence, grandeur, and excess, he drags
His palled unwilling appetite. If gold,
Gleaming around, and numerous viands culled
From every clime, could force the loathing sense
To overcome satiety,—if wealth
The spring it draws from poisons not,—or vice,
Unfeeling, stubborn vice, converteth not
Its food to deadliest venom; then that king
Is happy; and the peasant who fulfills
His unforced task, when he returns at even,
And by the blazing faggot meets again
Her welcome for whom all his toil is sped,
Tastes not a sweeter meal.
Behold him now
Stretched on the gorgeous couch; his fevered brain
Reels dizzily awhile: but ah! too soon
The slumber of intemperance subsides,
And conscience, that undying serpent, calls
Her venomous brood to their nocturnal task.
Listen! he speaks! oh! mark that frenzied eye—
Oh! mark that deadly visage.

KING

No cessation!
Oh! must this last forever! Awful death,
I wish, yet fear to clasp thee!—Not one moment
Of dreamless sleep! O dear and blessed peace!

Why dost thou shroud thy vestal purity
In penury and dungeons? Wherefore lurkest
With danger, death, and solitude; yet shun'st
The palace I have built thee? Sacred peace!
Oh visit me but once, but pitying shed
One drop of balm upon my withered soul.

MAB

Vain man! that palace is the virtuous heart,
And peace defileth not her snowy robes
In such a shed as thine. Hark! yet he mutters;
His slumbers are but varied agonies,
They prey like scorpions on the springs of life.
There needeth not the hell that bigots frame
To punish those who err: earth in itself
Contains at once the evil and the cure;
And all-sufficing nature can chastise
Those who transgress her law,—she only knows
How justly to proportion to the fault
The punishment it merits.
Is it strange
That this poor wretch should pride him in his woe?
Take pleasure in his abjectness, and hug
The scorpion that consumes him? Is it strange
That, placed on a conspicuous throne of thorns,
Grasping an iron sceptre, and immured
Within a splendid prison, whose stern bounds
Shut him from all that's good or dear on earth,
His soul asserts not its humanity?
That man's mild nature rises not in war
Against a king's employ? No—'tis not strange.
He, like the vulgar, thinks, feels, acts and lives
Just as his father did; the unconquered powers
Of precedent and custom interpose
Between a *king* and virtue. Stranger yet,
To those who know not nature, nor deduce
The future from the present, it may seem,
That not one slave, who suffers from the crimes
Of this unnatural being; not one wretch,
Whose children famish, and whose nuptial bed
Is earth's unpitying bosom, rears an arm
To dash him from his throne!

Those gilded flies
That, basking in the sunshine of a court,
Fatten on its corruption!—what are they?
—The drones of the community; they feed
On the mechanic's labour: the starved hind
For them compels the stubborn glebe to yield
Its unshared harvests; and yon squalid form,
Leaner than fleshless misery, that wastes
A sunless life in the unwholesome mine,
Drags out in labour a protracted death,
To glut their grandeur; many faint with toil,
That few may know the cares and woe of sloth.

Whence, thinkest thou, kings and parasites arose?
Whence that unnatural line of drones, who heap
Toil and unvanquishable penury
On those who build their palaces, and bring
Their daily bread?—From vice, black loathsome vice;
From rapine, madness, treachery, and wrong;
From all that genders misery, and makes
Of earth this thorny wilderness; from lust,
Revenge, and murder . . . And when reason's voice,
Loud as the voice of nature, shall have waked
The nations; and mankind perceive that vice
Is discord, war, and misery; that virtue
Is peace, and happiness and harmony;
When man's maturer nature shall disdain
The playthings of its childhood;—kingly glare
Will lose its power to dazzle; its authority
Will silently pass by; the gorgeous throne
Shall stand unnoticed in the regal hall,
Fast falling to decay; whilst falsehood's trade
Shall be as hateful and unprofitable
As that of truth is now.
Where is the fame
Which the vain-glorious mighty of the earth
Seek to eternize? Oh! the faintest sound
From time's light footfall, the minutest wave
That swells the flood of ages, whelms in nothing
The unsubstantial bubble. Aye! to-day
Stern is the tyrant's mandate, red the gaze
That flashes desolation, strong the arm

That scatters multitudes. To-morrow comes!
That mandate is a thunder-peal that died
In ages past; that gaze, a transient flash
On which the midnight closed, and on that arm
The worm has made his meal.
The virtuous man,
Who, great in his humility, as kings
Are little in their grandeur; he who leads
Invincibly a life of resolute good,
And stands amid the silent dungeon-depths
More free and fearless than the trembling judge,
Who, clothed in venal power, vainly strove
To bind the impassive spirit;—when he falls,
His mild eye beams benevolence no more:
Withered the hand outstretched but to relieve;
Sunk reason's simple eloquence, that rolled
But to appal the guilty. Yes! the grave
Hath quenched that eye, and death's relentless frost
Withered that arm: but the unfading fame
Which virtue hangs upon its votary's tomb;
The deathless memory of that man, whom kings
Call to their mind and tremble; the remembrance
With which the happy spirit contemplates
Its well-spent pilgrimage on earth,
Shall never pass away.

Nature rejects the monarch, not the man;
The subject, not the citizen: for kings
And subjects, mutual foes, forever play
A losing game into each other's hands,
Whose stakes are vice and misery. The man
Of virtuous soul commands not, nor obeys.
Power, like a desolating pestilence,
Pollutes whate'er it touches; and obedience,
Bane of all genius, virtue, freedom, truth,
Makes slaves of men, and, of the human frame,
A mechanized automaton.
When Nero,
High over flaming Rome, with savage joy
Lowered like a fiend, drank with enraptured ear
The shrieks of agonizing death, beheld
The frightful desolation spread, and felt

A new created sense within his soul
Thrill to the sight, and vibrate to the sound;
Thinkest thou his grandeur had not overcome
The force of human kindness? And, when Rome,
With one stern blow, hurled not the tyrant down,
Crushed not the arm red with her dearest blood,
Had not submissive abjectness destroyed
Nature's suggestions?
                                        Look on yonder earth:
The golden harvests spring; the unfailing sun
Sheds light and life; the fruits, the flowers, the trees,
Arise in due succession; all things speak
Peace, harmony, and love. The universe,
In nature's silent eloquence, declares
That all fulfil the works of love and joy,—
All but the outcast, man. He fabricates
The sword which stabs his peace; he cherisheth
The snakes that gnaw his heart; he raiseth up
The tyrant, whose delight is in his woe,
Whose sport is in his agony. Yon sun,
Lights it the great alone? Yon silver beams,
Sleep they less sweetly on the cottage thatch
Than on the dome of kings? Is mother earth
A step-dame to her numerous sons, who earn
Her unshared gifts with unremitting toil;
A mother only to those puling babes
Who, nursed in ease and luxury, make men
The playthings of their babyhood, and mar,
In self-important childishness, that peace
Which men alone appreciate?

            Spirit of Nature! no.
The pure diffusion of thy essence throbs
   Alike in every human heart.
            Thou, aye, erectest there
   Thy throne of power unappealable:
   Thou art the judge beneath whose nod
   Man's brief and frail authority
            Is powerless as the wind
            That passeth idly by.
   Thine the tribunal which surpasseth
      The shew of human justice,
            As God surpasses man.

Spirit of Nature! thou
Life of interminable multitudes;
Soul of those mighty spheres
Whose changeless paths thro' Heaven's deep silence lie;
Soul of that smallest being,
The dwelling of whose life
Is one faint April sun-gleam;—
Man, like these passive things,
Thy will unconsciously fulfilleth:
Like theirs, his age of endless peace,
Which time is fast maturing,
Will swiftly, surely come;
And the unbounded frame, which thou pervadest,
Will be without a flaw
Marring its perfect symmetry.

IV

How beautiful this night! the balmiest sigh,
Which vernal zephyrs breathe in evening's ear,
Were discord to the speaking quietude
That wraps this moveless scene. Heaven's ebon vault,
Studded with stars unutterably bright,
Through which the moon's unclouded grandeur rolls,
Seems like a canopy which love had spread
To curtain her sleeping world. Yon gentle hills,
Robed in a garment of untrodden snow;
Yon darksome rocks, whence icicles depend,
So stainless, that their white and glittering spires
Tinge not the moon's pure beam; yon castled steep,
Whose banner hangeth o'er the time-worn tower
So idly, that rapt fancy deemeth it
A metaphor of peace;—all form a scene
Where musing solitude might love to lift
Her soul above this sphere of earthliness;
Where silence undisturbed might watch alone,
So cold, so bright, so still.
The orb of day,
In southern climes, o'er ocean's waveless field
Sinks sweetly smiling: not the faintest breath
Steals o'er the unruffled deep; the clouds of eve
Reflect unmoved the lingering beam of day;
And vesper's image on the western main

Is beautifully still. To-morrow comes:
Cloud upon cloud, in dark and deepening mass,
Roll o'er the blackened waters; the deep roar
Of distant thunder mutters awfully;
Tempest unfolds its pinion o'er the gloom
That shrouds the boiling surge; the pityless fiend,
With all his winds and lightnings, tracks his prey;
The torn deep yawns,—the vessel finds a grave
Beneath its jagged gulf.
                                        Ah! whence yon glare
That fires the arch of heaven?—that dark red smoke
Blotting the silver moon? The stars are quenched
In darkness, and the pure and spangling snow
Gleams faintly through the gloom that gathers round!
Hark to that roar, whose swift and deaf'ning peals
In countless echoes through the mountains ring,
Startling pale midnight on her starry throne!
Now swells the intermingling din; the jar
Frequent and frightful of the bursting bomb;
The falling beam, the shriek, the groan, the shout,
The ceaseless clangor, and the rush of men
Inebriate with rage:—loud, and more loud
The discord grows; till pale death shuts the scene,
And o'er the conqueror and the conquered draws
His cold and bloody shroud.—Of all the men
Whom day's departing beam saw blooming there,
In proud and vigorous health; of all the hearts
That beat with anxious life at sun-set there;
How few survive, how few are beating now!
All is deep silence, like the fearful calm
That slumbers in the storm's portentous pause;
Save when the frantic wail of widowed love
Comes shuddering on the blast, or the faint moan
With which some soul bursts from the frame of clay
Wrapt round its struggling powers.
                                                        The grey morn
Dawns on the mournful scene; the sulphurous smoke
Before the icy wind slow rolls away,
And the bright beams of frosty morning dance
Along the spangling snow. There tracks of blood
Even to the forest's depth, and scattered arms,
And lifeless warriors, whose hard lineaments

Death's self could change not, mark the dreadful path
Of the outsallying victors: far behind,
Black ashes note where their proud city stood.
Within yon forest is a gloomy glen—
Each tree which guards its darkness from the day,
Waves o'er a warrior's tomb.
I see thee shrink,
Surpassing Spirit!—wert thou human else?
I see a shade of doubt and horror fleet
Across thy stainless features: yet fear not;
This is no unconnected misery,
Nor stands uncaused, and irretrievable.
Man's evil nature, that apology
Which kings who rule, and cowards who crouch, set up
For their unnumbered crimes, sheds not the blood
Which desolates the discord-wasted land.
From kings, and priests, and statesmen, war arose,
Whose safety is man's deep unbettered woe,
Whose grandeur his debasement. Let the axe
Strike at the root, the poison-tree will fall;
And where its venomed exhalations spread
Ruin, and death, and woe, where millions lay
Quenching the serpent's famine, and their bones
Bleaching unburied in the putrid blast,
A garden shall arise, in loveliness
Surpassing fabled Eden.
Hath Nature's soul,
That formed this world so beautiful, that spread
Earth's lap with plenty, and life's smallest chord
Strung to unchanging unison, that gave
The happy birds their dwelling in the grove,
That yielded to the wanderers of the deep
The lovely silence of the unfathomed main,
And filled the meanest worm that crawls in dust
With spirit, thought, and love; on Man alone,
Partial in causeless malice, wantonly
Heaped ruin, vice, and slavery; his soul
Blasted with withering curses; placed afar
The meteor-happiness, that shuns his grasp,
But serving on the frightful gulph to glare
Rent wide beneath his footsteps?
Nature!—no!

Kings, priests, and statesmen, blast the human flower
Even in its tender bud; their influence darts
Like subtle poison through the bloodless veins
Of desolate society. The child,
Ere he can lisp his mother's sacred name,
Swells with the unnatural pride of crime, and lifts
His baby-sword even in a hero's mood.
This infant-arm becomes the bloodiest scourge
Of devastated earth; whilst specious names,
Learnt in soft childhood's unsuspecting hour,
Serve as the sophisms with which manhood dims
Bright reason's ray, and sanctifies the sword
Upraised to shed a brother's innocent blood.
Let priest-led slaves cease to proclaim that man
Inherits vice and misery, when force
And falshood hang even o'er the cradled babe,
Stifling with rudest grasp all natural good.

Ah! to the stranger-soul, when first it peeps
From its new tenement, and looks abroad
For happiness and sympathy, how stern
And desolate a tract is this wide world!
How withered all the buds of natural good!
No shade, no shelter from the sweeping storms
Of pityless power! On its wretched frame,
Poisoned, perchance, by the disease and woe
Heaped on the wretched parent whence it sprung
By morals, law, and custom, the pure winds
Of heaven, that renovate the insect tribes,
May breathe not. The untainting light of day
May visit not its longings. It is bound
Ere it has life: yea, all the chains are forged
Long ere its being: all liberty and love
And peace is torn from its defencelessness;
Cursed from its birth, even from its cradle doomed
To abjectness and bondage!

Throughout this varied and eternal world
Soul is the only element, the block
That for uncounted ages has remained
The moveless pillar of a mountain's weight
Is active, living spirit. Every grain

Is sentient both in unity and part,
And the minutest atom comprehends
A world of loves and hatreds; these beget
Evil and good: hence truth and falsehood spring;
Hence will and thought and action, all the germs
Of pain or pleasure, sympathy or hate,
That variegate the eternal universe.
Soul is not more polluted than the beams
Of heaven's pure orb, ere round their rapid lines
The taint of earth-born atmospheres arise.

Man is of soul and body, formed for deeds
Of high resolve, on fancy's boldest wing
To soar unwearied, fearlessly to turn
The keenest pangs to peacefulness, and taste
The joys which mingled sense and spirit yield.
Or he is formed for abjectness and woe,
To grovel on the dunghill of his fears,
To shrink at every sound, to quench the flame
Of natural love in sensualism, to know
That hour as blest when on his worthless days
The frozen hand of death shall set its seal,
Yet fear the cure, though hating the disease.
The one is man that shall hereafter be;
The other, man as vice has made him now.

War is the statesman's game, the priest's delight,
The lawyer's jest, the hired assassin's trade,
And, to those royal murderers, whose mean thrones
Are bought by crimes of treachery and gore,
The bread they eat, the staff on which they lean.
Guards, garbed in blood-red livery, surround
Their palaces, participate the crimes
That force defends, and from a nation's rage
Secure the crown, which all the curses reach
That famine, frenzy, woe and penury breathe.
These are the hired bravos who defend
The tyrant's throne—the bullies of his fear:
These are the sinks and channels of worst vice,
The refuse of society, the dregs
Of all that is most vile: their cold hearts blend

Deceit with sternness, ignorance with pride,
All that is mean and villainous, with rage
Which hopelessness of good, and self-contempt,
Alone might kindle; they are decked in wealth,
Honour and power, then are sent abroad
To do their work. The pestilence that stalks
In gloomy triumph through some eastern land
Is less destroying. They cajole with gold,
And promises of fame, the thoughtless youth
Already crushed with servitude: he knows
His wretchedness too late, and cherishes
Repentance for his ruin, when his doom
Is sealed in gold and blood!
Those too the tyrant serve, who, skilled to snare
The feet of justice in the toils of law,
Stand, ready to oppress the weaker still;
And, right or wrong, will vindicate for gold,
Sneering at public virtue, which beneath
Their pityless tread lies torn and trampled, where
Honour sits smiling at the sale of truth.

Then grave and hoary-headed hypocrites,
Without a hope, a passion, or a love,
Who, through a life of luxury and lies,
Have crept by flattery to the seats of power,
Support the system whence their honours flow . . .
They have three words:—well tyrants know their use,
Well pay them for the loan, with usury
Torn from a bleeding world!—God, Hell, and Heaven.
A vengeful, pityless, and almighty fiend,
Whose mercy is a nick-name for the rage
Of tameless tygers hungering for blood.
Hell, a red gulf of everlasting fire,
Where poisonous and undying worms prolong
Eternal misery to those hapless slaves
Whose life has been a penance for its crimes.
And Heaven, a meed for those who dare belie
Their human nature, quake, believe, and cringe
Before the mockeries of earthly power.

These tools the tyrant tempers to his work,
Wields in his wrath, and as he wills destroys,
Omnipotent in wickedness: the while
Youth springs, age moulders, manhood tamely does
His bidding, bribed by short-lived joys to lend
Force to the weakness of his trembling arm.

They rise, they fall; one generation comes
Yielding its harvest to destruction's scythe.
It fades, another blossoms: yet behold!
Red glows the tyrant's stamp-mark on its bloom,
Withering and cankering deep its passive prime.
He has invented lying words and modes,
Empty and vain as his own coreless heart;
Evasive meanings, nothings of much sound,
To lure the heedless victim to the toils
Spread round the valley of its paradise.

Look to thyself, priest, conqueror, or prince!
Whether thy trade is falsehood, and thy lusts
Deep wallow in the earnings of the poor,
With whom thy master was:—or thou delightst
In numbering o'er the myriads of thy slain,
All misery weighing nothing in the scale
Against thy short-lived fame: or thou dost load
With cowardice and crime the groaning land,
A pomp-fed king. Look to thy wretched self!
Aye, art thou not the veriest slave that e'er
Crawled on the loathing earth? Are not thy days
Days of unsatisfying listlessness?
Dost thou not cry, ere night's long rack is o'er,
'When will the morning come?' Is not thy youth
A vain and feverish dream of sensualism?
Thy manhood blighted with unripe disease?
Are not thy views of unregretted death
Drear, comfortless, and horrible? Thy mind,
Is it not morbid as thy nerveless frame,
Incapable of judgment, hope, or love?
And dost thou wish the errors to survive
That bar thee from all sympathies of good,
After the miserable interest
Thou holdst in their protraction? When the grave

Has swallowed up thy memory and thyself,
Dost thou desire the bane that poisons earth
To twine its roots around thy coffined clay,
Spring from thy bones, and blossom on thy tomb,
That of its fruit thy babes may eat and die?

V

Thus do the generations of the earth
Go to the grave, and issue from the womb,
Surviving still the imperishable change
That renovates the world; even as the leaves
Which the keen frost-wind of the waning year
Has scattered on the forest soil, and heaped
For many seasons there, though long they choke,
Loading with loathsome rottenness the land,
All germs of promise. Yet when the tall trees
From which they fell, shorn of their lovely shapes,
Lie level with the earth to moulder there,
They fertilize the land they long deformed,
Till from the breathing lawn a forest springs
Of youth, integrity, and loveliness,
Like that which gave it life, to spring and die.
Thus suicidal selfishness, that blights
The fairest feelings of the opening heart,
Is destined to decay, whilst from the soil
Shall spring all virtue, all delight, all love,
And judgment cease to wage unnatural war
With passion's unsubduable array.

Twin-sister of religion, selfishness!
Rival in crime and falshood, aping all
The wanton horrors of her bloody play;
Yet frozen, unimpassioned, spiritless,
Shunning the light, and owning not its name—
Compelled, by its deformity, to screen
With flimsy veil of justice and of right,
Its unattractive lineaments, that scare
All, save the brood of ignorance: at once
The cause and the effect of tyranny;
Unblushing, hardened, sensual, and vile;
Dead to all love but of its abjectness,

With heart impassive by more noble powers
Than unshared pleasure, sordid gain, or fame;
Despising its own miserable being,
Which still it longs, yet fears, to disenthrall.

Hence commerce springs, the venal interchange
Of all that human art or nature yield;
Which wealth should purchase not, but want demand,
And natural kindness hasten to supply
From the full fountain of its boundless love,
For ever stifled, drained, and tainted now.
Commerce! beneath whose poison-breathing shade
No solitary virtue dares to spring,
But poverty and wealth with equal hand
Scatter their withering curses, and unfold
The doors of premature and violent death,
To pining famine and full-fed disease,
To all that shares the lot of human life,
Which, poisoned body and soul, scarce drags the chain,
That lengthens as it goes and clanks behind.

Commerce has set the mark of selfishness,
The signet of its all-enslaving power
Upon a shining ore, and called it gold:
Before whose image bow the vulgar great,
The vainly rich, the miserable proud,
The mob of peasants, nobles, priests, and kings,
And with blind feelings reverence the power
That grinds them to the dust of misery.
But in the temple of their hireling hearts
Gold is a living god, and rules in scorn
All earthly things but virtue.

Since tyrants, by the sale of human life,
Heap luxuries to their sensualism, and fame
To their wide-wasting and insatiate pride,
Success has sanctioned to a credulous world
The ruin, the disgrace, the woe of war.
His hosts of blind and unresisting dupes
The despot numbers; from his cabinet
These puppets of his schemes he moves at will,
Even as the slaves by force or famine driven,

Beneath a vulgar master, to perform
A task of cold and brutal drudgery;—
Hardened to hope, insensible to fear,
Scarce living pullies of a dead machine,
Mere wheels of work and articles of trade,
That grace the proud and noisy pomp of wealth!

The harmony and happiness of man
Yields to the wealth of nations; that which lifts
His nature to the heaven of its pride,
Is bartered for the poison of his soul;
The weight that drags to earth his towering hopes,
Blighting all prospect but of selfish gain,
Withering all passion but of slavish fear,
Extinguishing all free and generous love
Of enterprize and daring, even the pulse
That fancy kindles in the beating heart
To mingle with sensation, it destroys,—
Leaves nothing but the sordid lust of self,
The groveling hope of interest and gold,
Unqualified, unmingled, unredeemed
Even by hypocrisy.
And statesmen boast
Of wealth! The wordy eloquence that lives
After the ruin of their hearts, can gild
The bitter poison of a nation's woe,
Can turn the worship of the servile mob
To their corrupt and glaring idol fame,
From virtue, trampled by its iron tread,
Although its dazzling pedestal be raised
Amid the horrors of a limb-strewn field,
With desolated dwellings smoking round.
The man of ease, who, by his warm fire-side,
To deeds of charitable intercourse
And bare fulfilment of the common laws
Of decency and prejudice, confines
The struggling nature of his human heart,
Is duped by their cold sophistry; he sheds
A passing tear perchance upon the wreck
Of earthly peace, when near his dwelling's door
The frightful waves are driven,—when his son
Is murdered by the tyrant, or religion

Drives his wife raving mad. But the poor man,
Whose life is misery, and fear, and care;
Whom the morn wakens but to fruitless toil;
Who ever hears his famished offsprings scream;
Whom their pale mother's uncomplaining gaze
Forever meets, and the proud rich man's eye
Flashing command, and the heart-breaking scene
Of thousands like himself;—he little heeds
The rhetoric of tyranny; his hate
Is quenchless as his wrongs; he laughs to scorn
The vain and bitter mockery of words,
Feeling the horror of the tyrant's deeds,
And unrestrained but by the arm of power,
That knows and dreads his enmity.

The iron rod of penury still compels
Her wretched slave to bow the knee to wealth,
And poison, with unprofitable toil,
A life too void of solace, to confirm
The very chains that bind him to his doom.
Nature, impartial in munificence,
Has gifted man with all-subduing will.
Matter, with all its transitory shapes,
Lies subjected and plastic at his feet,
That, weak from bondage, tremble as they tread.
How many a rustic Milton has passed by,
Stifling the speechless longings of his heart,
In unremitting drudgery and care!
How many a vulgar Cato has compelled
His energies, no longer tameless then,
To mould a pin, or fabricate a nail!
How many a Newton, to whose passive ken
Those mighty spheres that gem infinity
Were only specks of tinsel, fixed in heaven
To light the midnights of his native town!

Yet every heart contains perfection's germ:
The wisest of the sages of the earth,
That ever from the stores of reason drew
Science and truth, and virtue's dreadless tone,
Were but a weak and inexperienced boy,
Proud, sensual, unimpassioned, unimbued

With pure desire and universal love,
Compared to that high being, of cloudless brain,
Untainted passion, elevated will,
Which death (who even would linger long in awe
Within his noble presence, and beneath
His changeless eyebeam) might alone subdue.
Him, every slave now dragging through the filth
Of some corrupted city his sad life,
Pining with famine, swoln with luxury,
Blunting the keenness of his spiritual sense
With narrow schemings and unworthy cares,
Or madly rushing through all violent crime,
To move the deep stagnation of his soul,—
Might imitate and equal.
But mean lust
Has bound its chains so tight around the earth,
That all within it but the virtuous man
Is venal: gold or fame will surely reach
The price prefixed by selfishness, to all
But him of resolute and unchanging will;
Whom, nor the plaudits of a servile crowd,
Nor the vile joys of tainting luxury,
Can bribe to yield his elevated soul
To tyranny or falshood, though they wield
With blood-red hand the sceptre of the world.

All things are sold: the very light of heaven
Is venal; earth's unsparing gifts of love,
The smallest and most despicable things
That lurk in the abysses of the deep,
All objects of our life, even life itself,
And the poor pittance which the laws allow
Of liberty, the fellowship of man,
Those duties which his heart of human love
Should urge him to perform instinctively,
Are bought and sold as in a public mart
Of undisguising selfishness, that sets
On each its price, the stamp-mark of her reign.
Even love is sold; the solace of all woe
Is turned to deadliest agony, old age
Shivers in selfish beauty's loathing arms,
And youth's corrupted impulses prepare

A life of horror from the blighting bane
Of commerce; whilst the pestilence that springs
From unenjoying sensualism, has filled
All human life with hydra-headed woes.

Falshood demands but gold to pay the pangs
Of outraged conscience; for the slavish priest
Sets no great value on his hireling faith:
A little passing pomp, some servile souls,
Whom cowardice itself might safely chain,
Or the spare mite of avarice could bribe
To deck the triumph of their languid zeal,
Can make him minister to tyranny.
More daring crime requires a loftier meed:
Without a shudder, the slave-soldier lends
His arm to murderous deeds, and steels his heart,
When the dread eloquence of dying men,
Low mingling on the lonely field of fame,
Assails that nature, whose applause he sells
For the gross blessings of a patriot mob,
For the vile gratitude of heartless kings,
And for a cold world's good word,—viler still!

There is a nobler glory, which survives
Until our being fades, and, solacing
All human care, accompanies its change;
Deserts not virtue in the dungeon's gloom,
And, in the precincts of the palace, guides
Its footsteps through that labyrinth of crime;
Imbues his lineaments with dauntlessness,
Even when, from power's avenging hand, he takes
Its sweetest, last and noblest title—death;
—The consciousness of good, which neither gold,
Nor sordid fame, nor hope of heavenly bliss,
Can purchase; but a life of resolute good,
Unalterable will, quenchless desire
Of universal happiness, the heart
That beats with it in unison, the brain,
Whose ever wakeful wisdom toils to change
Reason's rich stores for its eternal weal.

This commerce of sincerest virtue needs
No mediative signs of selfishness,
No jealous intercourse of wretched gain,
No balancings of prudence, cold and long;
In just and equal measure all is weighed,
One scale contains the sum of human weal,
And one, the good man's heart.
How vainly seek
The selfish for that happiness denied
To aught but virtue! Blind and hardened, they,
Who hope for peace amid the storms of care,
Who covet power they know not how to use,
And sigh for pleasure they refuse to give,—
Madly they frustrate still their own designs;
And, where they hope that quiet to enjoy
Which virtue pictures, bitterness of soul,
Pining regrets, and vain repentances,
Disease, disgust, and lassitude, pervade
Their valueless and miserable lives.

But hoary-headed selfishness has felt
Its death-blow, and is tottering to the grave:
A brighter morn awaits the human day,
When every transfer of earth's natural gifts
Shall be a commerce of good words and works;
When poverty and wealth, the thirst of fame,
The fear of infamy, disease and woe,
War with its million horrors, and fierce hell
Shall live but in the memory of time,
Who, like a penitent libertine, shall start,
Look back, and shudder at his younger years.

VI

All touch, all eye, all ear,
The Spirit felt the Fairy's burning speech.
O'er the thin texture of its frame,
The varying periods painted changing glows,
As on a summer even,
When soul-enfolding music floats around,
The stainless mirror of the lake

Re-images the eastern gloom,
Mingling convulsively its purple hues
With sunset's burnished gold.

Then thus the Spirit spoke:
It is a wild and miserable world!
Thorny, and full of care,
Which every fiend can make his prey at will.
O Fairy! in the lapse of years,
Is there no hope in store?
Will yon vast suns roll on
Interminably, still illuming
The night of so many wretched souls,
And see no hope for them?
Will not the universal Spirit e'er
Revivify this withered limb of Heaven?

The Fairy calmly smiled
In comfort, and a kindling gleam of hope
Suffused the Spirit's lineaments.
Oh! rest thee tranquil; chase those fearful doubts,
Which ne'er could rack an everlasting soul,
That sees the chains which bind it to its doom.
Yes! crime and misery are in yonder earth,
Falshood, mistake, and lust;
But the eternal world
Contains at once the evil and the cure.
Some eminent in virtue shall start up,
Even in perversest time:
The truths of their pure lips, that never die,
Shall bind the scorpion falshood with a wreath
Of ever-living flame,
Until the monster sting itself to death.

How sweet a scene will earth become!
Of purest spirits, a pure dwelling-place,
Symphonious with the planetary spheres;
When man, with changeless nature coalescing,
Will undertake regeneration's work,
When its ungenial poles no longer point
To the red and baleful sun
That faintly twinkles there.

Spirit! on yonder earth,
Falshood now triumphs; deadly power
Has fixed its seal upon the lip of truth!
Madness and misery are there!
The happiest is most wretched! Yet confide,
Until pure health-drops, from the cup of joy,
Fall like a dew of balm upon the world.
Now, to the scene I shew, in silence turn,
And read the blood-stained charter of all woe,
Which nature soon, with recreating hand,
Will blot in mercy from the book of earth.
How bold the flight of passion's wandering wing,
How swift the step of reason's firmer tread,
How calm and sweet the victories of life,
How terrorless the triumph of the grave!
How powerless were the mightiest monarch's arm,
Vain his loud threat, and impotent his frown!
How ludicrous the priest's dogmatic roar!
The weight of his exterminating curse,
How light! and his affected charity,
To suit the pressure of the changing times,
What palpable deceit!—but for thy aid,
Religion! but for thee, prolific fiend,
Who peoplest earth with demons, hell with men,
And heaven with slaves!

Thou taintest all thou lookest upon!—the stars,
Which on thy cradle beamed so brightly sweet,
Were gods to the distempered playfulness
Of thy untutored infancy: the trees,
The grass, the clouds, the mountains, and the sea,
All living things that walk, swim, creep, or fly,
Were gods: the sun had homage, and the moon
Her worshipper. Then thou becamest, a boy,
More daring in thy frenzies: every shape,
Monstrous or vast, or beautifully wild,
Which, from sensation's relics, fancy culls;
The spirits of the air, the shuddering ghost,
The genii of the elements, the powers
That give a shape to nature's varied works,
Had life and place in the corrupt belief
Of thy blind heart: yet still thy youthful hands

Were pure of human blood. Then manhood gave
Its strength and ardour to thy frenzied brain;
Thine eager gaze scanned the stupendous scene,
Whose wonders mocked the knowledge of thy pride:
Their everlasting and unchanging laws
Reproached thine ignorance. Awhile thou stoodst
Baffled and gloomy; then thou didst sum up
The elements of all that thou didst know;
The changing seasons, winter's leafless reign,
The budding of the heaven-breathing trees,
The eternal orbs that beautify the night,
The sun-rise, and the setting of the moon,
Earthquakes and wars, and poisons and disease,
And all their causes, to an abstract point
Converging, thou didst bend, and called it GOD!
The self-sufficing, the omnipotent,
The merciful, and the avenging God!
Who, prototype of human misrule, sits
High in heaven's realm, upon a golden throne,
Even like an earthly king; and whose dread work,
Hell, gapes forever for the unhappy slaves
Of fate, whom he created in his sport,
To triumph in their torments when they fell!
Earth heard the name; earth trembled, as the smoke
Of his revenge ascended up to heaven,
Blotting the constellations; and the cries
Of millions, butchered in sweet confidence
And unsuspecting peace, even when the bonds
Of safety were confirmed by wordy oaths
Sworn in his dreadful name, rung through the land;
Whilst innocent babes writhed on thy stubborn spear,
And thou didst laugh to hear the mother's shriek
Of maniac gladness, as the sacred steel
Felt cold in her torn entrails!

Religion! thou wert then in manhood's prime:
But age crept on: one God would not suffice
For senile puerility; thou framedst
A tale to suit thy dotage, and to glut
Thy misery-thirsting soul, that the mad fiend
Thy wickedness had pictured, might afford
A plea for sating the unnatural thirst

For murder, rapine, violence, and crime,
That still consumed thy being, even when
Thou heardst the step of fate;—that flames might light
Thy funeral scene, and the shrill horrent shrieks
Of parents dying on the pile that burned
To light their children to thy paths, the roar
Of the encircling flames, the exulting cries
Of thine apostles, loud commingling there,
Might sate thine hungry ear
Even on the bed of death!

But now contempt is mocking thy grey hairs;
Thou art descending to the darksome grave,
Unhonored and unpitied, but by those
Whose pride is passing by like thine, and sheds,
Like thine, a glare that fades before the sun
Of truth, and shines but in the dreadful night
That long has lowered above the ruined world.

Throughout these infinite orbs of mingling light,
Of which yon earth is one, is wide diffused
A Spirit of activity and life,
That knows no term, cessation, or decay;
That fades not when the lamp of earthly life,
Extinguished in the dampness of the grave,
Awhile there slumbers, more than when the babe
In the dim newness of its being feels
The impulses of sublunary things,
And all is wonder to unpractised sense:
But, active, stedfast, and eternal, still
Guides the fierce whirlwind, in the tempest roars,
Cheers in the day, breathes in the balmy groves,
Strengthens in health, and poisons in disease;
And in the storm of change, that ceaselessly
Rolls round the eternal universe, and shakes
Its undecaying battlement, presides,
Apportioning with irresistible law
The place each spring of its machine shall fill;
So that, when waves on waves tumultuous heap
Confusion to the clouds, and fiercely driven
Heaven's lightnings scorch the uprooted ocean-fords,
Whilst, to the eye of shipwrecked mariner,

Lone sitting on the bare and shuddering rock,
All seems unlinked contingency and chance:
No atom of this turbulence fulfils
A vague and unnecessitated task,
Or acts but as it must and ought to act.
Even the minutest molecule of light,
That in an April sunbeam's fleeting glow
Fulfills its destined, though invisible work,
The universal Spirit guides; nor less,
When merciless ambition, or mad zeal,
Has led two hosts of dupes to battle-field,
That, blind, they there may dig each other's graves,
And call the sad work glory, does it rule
All passions: not a thought, a will, an act,
No working of the tyrant's moody mind,
Nor one misgiving of the slaves who boast
Their servitude, to hide the shame they feel,
Nor the events enchaining every will,
That from the depths of unrecorded time
Have drawn all-influencing virtue, pass
Unrecognized, or unforeseen by thee,
Soul of the Universe! eternal spring
Of life and death, of happiness and woe,
Of all that chequers the phantasmal scene
That floats before our eyes in wavering light,
Which gleams but on the darkness of our prison,
    Whose chains and massy walls
    We feel, but cannot see.

Spirit of Nature! all-sufficing Power,
Necessity! thou mother of the world!
Unlike the God of human error, thou
Requirest no prayers or praises; the caprice
Of man's weak will belongs no more to thee
Than do the changeful passions of his breast
To thy unvarying harmony: the slave,
Whose horrible lusts spread misery o'er the world,
And the good man, who lifts, with virtuous pride,
His being, in the sight of happiness,
That springs from his own works; the poison-tree,
Beneath whose shade all life is withered up,
And the fair oak, whose leafy dome affords

A temple where the vows of happy love
Are registered, are equal in thy sight:
No love, no hate thou cherishest; revenge
And favoritism, and worst desire of fame
Thou knowest not: all that the wide world contains
Are but thy passive instruments, and thou
Regardst them all with an impartial eye,
Whose joy or pain thy nature cannot feel,
  Because thou hast not human sense,
  Because thou art not human mind.

  Yes! when the sweeping storm of time
Has sung its death-dirge o'er the ruined fanes
And broken altars of the almighty fiend,
Whose name usurps thy honors, and the blood
Through centuries clotted there, has floated down
The tainted flood of ages, shalt thou live
Unchangeable! A shrine is raised to thee,
  Which, nor the tempest breath of time,
  Nor the interminable flood,
  Over earth's slight pageant rolling,
      Availeth to destroy,—
The sensitive extension of the world,
  That wonderous and eternal fane,
Where pain and pleasure, good and evil join,
To do the will of strong necessity,
  And life, in multitudinous shapes,
Still pressing forward where no term can be,
  Like hungry and unresting flame
Curls round the eternal columns of its strength.

VII

SPIRIT

I was an infant when my mother went
To see an atheist burned. She took me there:
The dark-robed priests were met around the pile;
The multitude was gazing silently;
And as the culprit passed with dauntless mien,
Tempered disdain in his unaltering eye,
Mixed with a quiet smile, shone calmly forth:
The thirsty fire crept round his manly limbs;

His resolute eyes were scorched to blindness soon;
His death-pang rent my heart! the insensate mob
Uttered a cry of triumph, and I wept.
Weep not, child! cried my mother, for that man
Has said, There is no God.

FAIRY

There is no God!
Nature confirms the faith his death-groan sealed:
Let heaven and earth, let man's revolving race,
His ceaseless generations tell their tale;
Let every part depending on the chain
That links it to the whole, point to the hand
That grasps its term! let every seed that falls
In silent eloquence unfold its store
Of argument: infinity within,
Infinity without, belie creation;
The exterminable spirit it contains
Is nature's only God; but human pride
Is skilful to invent most serious names
To hide its ignorance.
The name of God
Has fenced about all crime with holiness,
Himself the creature of his worshippers,
Whose names and attributes and passions change,
Seeva, Buddh, Foh, Jehovah, God, or Lord,
Even with the human dupes who build his shrines,
Still serving o'er the war-polluted world
For desolation's watchword; whether hosts
Stain his death-blushing chariot wheels, as on
Triumphantly they roll, whilst Brahmins raise
A sacred hymn to mingle with the groans;
Or countless partners of his power divide
His tyranny to weakness; or the smoke
Of burning towns, the cries of female helplessness,
Unarmed old age, and youth, and infancy,
Horribly massacred, ascend to heaven
In honor of his name; or, last and worst,
Earth groans beneath religion's iron age,
And priests dare babble of a God of peace, .

Even whilst their hands are red with guiltless blood,
Murdering the while, uprooting every germ
Of truth, exterminating, spoiling all,
Making the earth a slaughter-house!

O Spirit! through the sense
By which thy inner nature was apprised
Of outward shews, vague dreams have rolled,
And varied reminiscences have waked
Tablets that never fade;
All things have been imprinted there,
The stars, the sea, the earth, the sky,
Even the unshapeliest lineaments
Of wild and fleeting visions
Have left a record there
To testify of earth.

These are my empire, for to me is given
The wonders of the human world to keep,
And fancy's thin creations to endow
With manner, being, and reality;
Therefore a wondrous phantom, from the dreams
Of human error's dense and purblind faith,
I will evoke, to meet thy questioning.
Ahasuerus, rise!

A strange and woe-worn wight
Arose beside the battlement,
And stood unmoving there.
His inessential figure cast no shade
Upon the golden floor;
His port and mien bore mark of many years,
And chronicles of untold ancientness
Were legible within his beamless eye:
Yet his cheek bore the mark of youth;
Freshness and vigor knit his manly frame;
The wisdom of old age was mingled there
With youth's primaeval dauntlessness;
And inexpressible woe,
Chastened by fearless resignation, gave
An awful grace to his all-speaking brow.

SPIRIT

Is there a God?

AHASUERUS

Is there a God!—aye, an almighty God,
And vengeful as almighty! Once his voice
Was heard on earth: earth shuddered at the sound;
The fiery-visaged firmament expressed
Abhorrence, and the grave of nature yawned
To swallow all the dauntless and the good
That dared to hurl defiance at his throne,
Girt as it was with power. None but slaves
Survived,—cold-blooded slaves, who did the work
Of tyrannous omnipotence; whose souls
No honest indignation ever urged
To elevated daring, to one deed
Which gross and sensual self did not pollute.
These slaves built temples for the omnipotent fiend,
Gorgeous and vast: the costly altars smoked
With human blood, and hideous paeans rung
Through all the long-drawn aisles. A murderer heard
His voice in Egypt, one whose gifts and arts
Had raised him to his eminence in power,
Accomplice of omnipotence in crime,
And confidant of the all-knowing one.
These were Jehovah's words.

From an eternity of idleness
I, God, awoke; in seven days' toil made earth
From nothing; rested, and created man:
I placed him in a paradise, and there
Planted the tree of evil, so that he
Might eat and perish, and my soul procure
Wherewith to sate its malice, and to turn,
Even like a heartless conqueror of the earth,
All misery to my fame. The race of men
Chosen to my honor, with impunity
May sate the lusts I planted in their heart.
Here I command thee hence to lead them on,
Until, with hardened feet, their conquering troops
Wade on the promised soil through woman's blood,

And make my name be dreaded through the land.
Yet ever burning flame and ceaseless woe
Shall be the doom of their eternal souls,
With every soul on this ungrateful earth,
Virtuous or vicious, weak or strong,—even all
Shall perish, to fulfill the blind revenge
(Which you, to men, call justice) of their God.

The murderer's brow
Quivered with horror.
God omnipotent,
Is there no mercy? must our punishment
Be endless? will long ages roll away,
And see no term? Oh! wherefore hast thou made
In mockery and wrath this evil earth?
Mercy becomes the powerful—be but just:
O God! repent and save.
One way remains:
I will beget a son, and he shall bear
The sins of all the world; he shall arise
In an unnoticed corner of the earth,
And there shall die upon a cross, and purge
The universal crime; so that the few
On whom my grace descends, those who are marked
As vessels to the honor of their God,
May credit this strange sacrifice, and save
Their souls alive: millions shall live and die,
Who ne'er shall call upon their Saviour's name,
But, unredeemed, go to the gaping grave.
Thousands shall deem it an old woman's tale,
Such as the nurses frighten babes withal:
These in a gulph of anguish and of flame
Shall curse their reprobation endlessly,
Yet tenfold pangs shall force them to avow,
Even on their beds of torment, where they howl,
My honor, and the justice of their doom.
What then avail their virtuous deeds, their thoughts
Of purity, with radiant genius bright,
Or lit with human reason's earthly ray?
Many are called, but few will I elect.
Do thou my bidding, Moses!

Even the murderer's cheek
Was blanched with horror, and his quivering lips
Scarce faintly uttered—O almighty one,
I tremble and obey!

O Spirit! centuries have set their seal
On this heart of many wounds, and loaded brain,
Since the Incarnate came: humbly he came,
Veiling his horrible Godhead in the shape
Of man, scorned by the world, his name unheard,
Save by the rabble of his native town,
Even as a parish demagogue. He led
The crowd; he taught them justice, truth, and peace,
In semblance; but he lit within their souls
The quenchless flames of zeal, and blessed the sword
He brought on earth to satiate with the blood
Of truth and freedom his malignant soul.
At length his mortal frame was led to death.
I stood beside him: on the torturing cross
No pain assailed his unterrestrial sense;
And yet he groaned. Indignantly I summed
The massacres and miseries which his name
Had sanctioned in my country, and I cried,
Go! go! in mockery.
A smile of godlike malice reillumined
His fading lineaments.—I go, he cried,
But thou shalt wander o'er the unquiet earth
Eternally.——The dampness of the grave
Bathed my imperishable front. I fell,
And long lay tranced upon the charmed soil.
When I awoke hell burned within my brain,
Which staggered on its seat; for all around
The mouldering relics of my kindred lay,
Even as the Almighty's ire arrested them,
And in their various attitudes of death
My murdered children's mute and eyeless sculls
Glared ghastily upon me.
But my soul,
From sight and sense of the polluting woe
Of tyranny, had long learned to prefer
Hell's freedom to the servitude of heaven.
Therefore I rose, and dauntlessly began

My lonely and unending pilgrimage,
Resolved to wage unweariable war
With my almighty tyrant, and to hurl
Defiance at his impotence to harm
Beyond the curse I bore. The very hand
That barred my passage to the peaceful grave
Has crushed the earth to misery, and given
Its empire to the chosen of his slaves.
These I have seen, even from the earliest dawn
Of weak, unstable and precarious power;
Then preaching peace, as now they practise war;
So, when they turned but from the massacre
Of unoffending infidels, to quench
Their thirst for ruin in the very blood
That flowed in their own veins, and pityless zeal
Froze every human feeling, as the wife
Sheathed in her husband's heart the sacred steel,
Even whilst its hopes were dreaming of her love;
And friends to friends, brothers to brothers stood
Opposed in bloodiest battle-field, and war,
Scarce satiable by fate's last death-draught waged,
Drunk from the winepress of the Almighty's wrath;
Whilst the red cross, in mockery of peace,
Pointed to victory! When the fray was done,
No remnant of the exterminated faith
Survived to tell its ruin, but the flesh,
With putrid smoke poisoning the atmosphere,
That rotted on the half-extinguished pile.

Yes! I have seen God's worshippers unsheathe
The sword of his revenge, when grace descended,
Confirming all unnatural impulses,
To sanctify their desolating deeds;
And frantic priests waved the ill-omened cross
O'er the unhappy earth: then shone the sun
On showers of gore from the upflashing steel
Of safe assassination, and all crime
Made stingless by the spirits of the Lord,
And blood-red rainbows canopied the land.

Spirit! no year of my eventful being
Has passed unstained by crime and misery,
Which flows from God's own faith. I've marked his slaves
With tongues whose lies are venomous, beguile
The insensate mob, and, whilst one hand was red
With murder, feign to stretch the other out
For brotherhood and peace; and that they now
Babble of love and mercy, whilst their deeds
Are marked with all the narrowness and crime
That freedom's young arm dare not yet chastise,
Reason may claim our gratitude, who now
Establishing the imperishable throne
Of truth, and stubborn virtue, maketh vain
The unprevailing malice of my foe,
Whose bootless rage heaps torments for the brave,
Adds impotent eternities to pain,
Whilst keenest disappointment racks his breast
To see the smiles of peace around them play,
To frustrate or to sanctify their doom.

Thus have I stood,—through a wild waste of years
Struggling with whirlwinds of mad agony,
Yet peaceful, and serene, and self-enshrined,
Mocking my powerless tyrant's horrible curse
With stubborn and unalterable will,
Even as a giant oak, which heaven's fierce flame
Had scathed in the wilderness, to stand
A monument of fadeless ruin there;
Yet peacefully and movelessly it braves
The midnight conflict of the wintry storm,
  As in the sun-light's calm it spreads
  Its worn and withered arms on high
To meet the quiet of a summer's noon.

        The Fairy waved her wand:
        Ahasuerus fled
Fast as the shapes of mingled shade and mist,
That lurk in the glens of a twilight grove,
        Flee from the morning beam:

The matter of which dreams are made
Not more endowed with actual life
Than this phantasmal portraiture
Of wandering human thought.

VIII

The present and the past thou hast beheld:
It was a desolate sight. Now, Spirit, learn
The secrets of the future.—Time!
Unfold the brooding pinion of thy gloom,
Render thou up thy half-devoured babes,
And from the cradles of eternity,
Where millions lie lulled to their portioned sleep
By the deep murmuring stream of passing things,
Tear thou that gloomy shroud.—Spirit, behold
Thy glorious destiny!

Joy to the Spirit came.
Through the wide rent in Time's eternal veil,
Hope was seen beaming through the mists of fear:
Earth was no longer hell;
Love, freedom, health, had given
Their ripeness to the manhood of its prime,
And all its pulses beat
Symphonious to the planetary spheres:
Then dulcet music swelled
Concordant with the life-strings of the soul;
It throbbed in sweet and languid beatings there,
Catching new life from transitory death,—
Like the vague sighings of a wind at even,
That wakes the wavelets of the slumbering sea
And dies on the creation of its breath,
And sinks and rises, fails and swells by fits:
Was the pure stream of feeling
That sprung from these sweet notes,
And o'er the Spirit's human sympathies
With mild and gentle motion calmly flowed.

Joy to the Spirit came,—
Such joy as when a lover sees
The chosen of his soul in happiness,

And witnesses her peace
Whose woe to him were bitterer than death,
Sees her unfaded cheek
Glow mantling in first luxury of health,
Thrills with her lovely eyes,
Which like two stars amid the heaving main
Sparkle through liquid bliss.

Then in her triumph spoke the Fairy Queen:
I will not call the ghost of ages gone
To unfold the frightful secrets of its lore;
The present now is past,
And those events that desolate the earth
Have faded from the memory of Time,
Who dares not give reality to that
Whose being I annul. To me is given
The wonders of the human world to keep,
Space, matter, time, and mind. Futurity
Exposes now its treasure; let the sight
Renew and strengthen all thy failing hope.
O human Spirit! spur thee to the goal
Where virtue fixes universal peace,
And midst the ebb and flow of human things,
Shew somewhat stable, somewhat certain still,
A lighthouse o'er the wild of dreary waves.

The habitable earth is full of bliss;
Those wastes of frozen billows that were hurled
By everlasting snow-storms round the poles,
Where matter dared not vegetate or live,
But ceaseless frost round the vast solitude
Bound its broad zone of stillness, are unloosed;
And fragrant zephyrs there from spicy isles
Ruffle the placid ocean-deep, that rolls
Its broad, bright surges to the sloping sand,
Whose roar is wakened into echoings sweet
To murmur through the heaven-breathing groves
And melodize with man's blest nature there.

Those deserts of immeasurable sand,
Whose age-collected fervors scarce allowed
A bird to live, a blade of grass to spring,

Where the shrill chirp of the green lizard's love
Broke on the sultry silentness alone,
Now teem with countless rills and shady woods,
Corn-fields and pastures and white cottages;
And where the startled wilderness beheld
A savage conqueror stained in kindred blood,
A tygress sating with the flesh of lambs,
The unnatural famine of her toothless cubs,
Whilst shouts and howlings through the desert rang,
Sloping and smooth the daisy-spangled lawn,
Offering sweet incense to the sun-rise, smiles
To see a babe before his mother's door,
Sharing his morning's meal
With the green and golden basilisk
That comes to lick his feet.

Those trackless deeps, where many a weary sail
Has seen above the illimitable plain,
Morning on night, and night on morning rise,
Whilst still no land to greet the wanderer spread
Its shadowy mountains on the sun-bright sea,
Where the loud roarings of the tempest-waves
So long have mingled with the gusty wind
In melancholy loneliness, and swept
The desert of those ocean solitudes,
But vocal to the sea-bird's harrowing shriek,
The bellowing monster, and the rushing storm,
Now to the sweet and many-mingling sounds
Of kindliest human impulses respond.
Those lonely realms bright garden-isles begem,
With lightsome clouds and shining seas between,
And fertile vallies, resonant with bliss,
Whilst green woods overcanopy the wave,
Which like a toil-worn labourer leaps to shore,
To meet the kisses of the flowrets there.

All things are recreated, and the flame
Of consentaneous love inspires all life:
The fertile bosom of the earth gives suck
To myriads, who still grow beneath her care,
Rewarding her with their pure perfectness:
The balmy breathings of the wind inhale

Her virtues, and diffuse them all abroad:
Health floats amid the gentle atmosphere,
Glows in the fruits, and mantles on the stream:
No storms deform the beaming brow of heaven,
Nor scatter in the freshness of its pride
The foliage of the ever verdant trees;
But fruits are ever ripe, flowers ever fair,
And autumn proudly bears her matron grace,
Kindling a flush on the fair cheek of spring,
Whose virgin bloom beneath the ruddy fruit
Reflects its tint and blushes into love.
The lion now forgets to thirst for blood:
There might you see him sporting in the sun
Beside the dreadless kid; his claws are sheathed,
His teeth are harmless, custom's force has made
His nature as the nature of a lamb.
Like passion's fruit, the nightshade's tempting bane
Poisons no more the pleasure it bestows:
All bitterness is past; the cup of joy
Unmingled mantles to the goblet's brim,
And courts the thirsty lips it fled before.

But chief, ambiguous man, he that can know
More misery, and dream more joy than all;
Whose keen sensations thrill within his breast
To mingle with a loftier instinct there,
Lending their power to pleasure and to pain,
Yet raising, sharpening, and refining each;
Who stands amid the ever-varying world,
The burthen or the glory of the earth;
He chief perceives the change, his being notes
The gradual renovation, and defines
Each movement of its progress on his mind.

Man, where the gloom of the long polar night
Lowers o'er the snow-clad rocks and frozen soil,
Where scarce the hardiest herb that braves the frost
Basks in the moonlight's ineffectual glow,
Shrank with the plants, and darkened with the night;
His chilled and narrow energies, his heart,
Insensible to courage, truth, or love,
His stunted stature and imbecile frame,

Marked him for some abortion of the earth,
Fit compeer of the bears that roamed around,
Whose habits and enjoyments were his own:
His life a feverish dream of stagnant woe,
Whose meagre wants, but scantily fulfilled,
Apprised him ever of the joyless length
Which his short being's wretchedness had reached;
His death a pang which famine, cold and toil
Long on the mind, whilst yet the vital spark
Clung to the body stubbornly, had brought:
All was inflicted here that earth's revenge
Could wreak on the infringers of her law;
One curse alone was spared—the name of God.

Nor where the tropics bound the realms of day
With a broad belt of mingling cloud and flame,
Where blue mists through the unmoving atmosphere
Scattered the seeds of pestilence, and fed
Unnatural vegetation, where the land
Teemed with all earthquake, tempest and disease,
Was man a nobler being; slavery
Had crushed him to his country's bloodstained dust;
Or he was bartered for the fame of power,
Which all internal impulses destroying,
Makes human will an article of trade;
Or he was changed with Christians for their gold,
And dragged to distant isles, where to the sound
Of the flesh-mangling scourge, he does the work
Of all-polluting luxury and wealth,
Which doubly visits on the tyrants' heads
The long-protracted fulness of their woe;
Or he was led to legal butchery,
To turn to worms beneath that burning sun,
Where kings first leagued against the rights of men,
And priests first traded with the name of God.

Even where the milder zone afforded man
A seeming shelter, yet contagion there,
Blighting his being with unnumbered ills,
Spread like a quenchless fire; nor truth till late
Availed to arrest its progress, or create
That peace which first in bloodless victory waved

Her snowy standard o'er this favoured clime:
There man was long the train-bearer of slaves,
The mimic of surrounding misery,
The jackal of ambition's lion-rage,
The bloodhound of religion's hungry zeal.

Here now the human being stands adorning
This loveliest earth with taintless body and mind;
Blest from his birth with all bland impulses,
Which gently in his noble bosom wake
All kindly passions and all pure desires.
Him, still from hope to hope the bliss pursuing,
Which from the exhaustless lore of human weal
Draws on the virtuous mind, the thoughts that rise
In time-destroying infiniteness, gift
With self-enshrined eternity, that mocks
The unprevailing hoariness of age,
And man, once fleeting o'er the transient scene
Swift as an unremembered vision, stands
Immortal upon earth: no longer now
He slays the lamb that looks him in the face,
And horribly devours his mangled flesh,
Which still avenging nature's broken law,
Kindled all putrid humours in his frame,
All evil passions, and all vain belief,
Hatred, despair, and loathing in his mind,
The germs of misery, death, disease, and crime.
No longer now the winged habitants,
That in the woods their sweet lives sing away,
Flee from the form of man; but gather round,
And prune their sunny feathers on the hands
Which little children stretch in friendly sport
Towards these dreadless partners of their play.
All things are void of terror: man has lost
His terrible prerogative, and stands
An equal amidst equals: happiness
And science dawn though late upon the earth;
Peace cheers the mind, health renovates the frame;
Disease and pleasure cease to mingle here,
Reason and passion cease to combat there;
Whilst each unfettered o'er the earth extend
Their all-subduing energies, and wield

The sceptre of a vast dominion there;
Whilst every shape and mode of matter lends
Its force to the omnipotence of mind,
Which from its dark mine drags the gem of truth
To decorate its paradise of peace.

IX

O happy Earth! reality of Heaven!
To which those restless souls that ceaselessly
Throng through the human universe, aspire;
Thou consummation of all mortal hope!
Thou glorious prize of blindly-working will!
Whose rays, diffused throughout all space and time,
Verge to one point and blend forever there:
Of purest spirits thou pure dwelling-place!
Where care and sorrow, impotence and crime,
Languor, disease, and ignorance dare not come:
O happy Earth, reality of Heaven!

Genius has seen thee in her passionate dreams,
And dim forebodings of thy loveliness
Haunting the human heart, have there entwined
Those rooted hopes of some sweet place of bliss
Where friends and lovers meet to part no more.
Thou art the end of all desire and will,
The product of all action; and the souls
That by the paths of an aspiring change
Have reached thy haven of perpetual peace,
There rest from the eternity of toil
That framed the fabric of thy perfectness.

Even Time, the conqueror, fled thee in his fear;
That hoary giant, who, in lonely pride,
So long had ruled the world, that nations fell
Beneath his silent footstep. Pyramids,
That for milleniums had withstood the tide
Of human things, his storm-breath drove in sand
Across that desert where their stones survived
The name of him whose pride had heaped them there.
Yon monarch, in his solitary pomp,
Was but the mushroom of a summer day,

That his light-winged footstep pressed to dust:
Time was the king of earth: all things gave way
Before him, but the fixed and virtuous will,
The sacred sympathies of soul and sense,
That mocked his fury and prepared his fall.

Yet slow and gradual dawned the morn of love;
Long lay the clouds of darkness o'er the scene,
Till from its native heaven they rolled away:
First, crime triumphant o'er all hope careered
Unblushing, undisguising, bold and strong;
Whilst falshood, tricked in virtue's attributes,
Long sanctified all deeds of vice and woe,
Till done by her own venomous sting to death,
She left the moral world without a law,
No longer fettering passion's fearless wing,
Nor searing reason with the brand of God.
Then steadily the happy ferment worked;
Reason was free; and wild though passion went
Through tangled glens and wood-embosomed meads,
Gathering a garland of the strangest flowers,
Yet like the bee returning to her queen,
She bound the sweetest on her sister's brow,
Who meek and sober kissed the sportive child,
No longer trembling at the broken rod.

Mild was the slow necessity of death:
The tranquil spirit failed beneath its grasp,
Without a groan, almost without a fear,
Calm as a voyager to some distant land,
And full of wonder, full of hope as he.
The deadly germs of languor and disease
Died in the human frame, and purity
Blest with all gifts her earthly worshippers.
How vigorous then the athletic form of age!
How clear its open and unwrinkled brow!
Where neither avarice, cunning, pride, or care,
Had stamped the seal of grey deformity
On all the mingling lineaments of time.
How lovely the intrepid front of youth!
Which meek-eyed courage decked with freshest grace;
Courage of soul, that dreaded not a name,

And elevated will, that journeyed on
Through life's phantasmal scene in fearlessness,
With virtue, love, and pleasure, hand in hand.

Then, that sweet bondage which is freedom's self,
And rivets with sensation's softest tie
The kindred sympathies of human souls,
Needed no fetters of tyrannic law:
Those delicate and timid impulses
In nature's primal modesty arose,
And with undoubting confidence disclosed
The growing longings of its dawning love,
Unchecked by dull and selfish chastity,
That virtue of the cheaply virtuous,
Who pride themselves in senselessness and frost.
No longer prostitution's venomed bane
Poisoned the springs of happiness and life;
Woman and man, in confidence and love,
Equal and free and pure together trod
The mountain-paths of virtue, which no more
Were stained with blood from many a pilgrim's feet.

Then, where, through distant ages, long in pride
The palace of the monarch-slave had mocked
Famine's faint groan, and penury's silent tear,
A heap of crumbling ruins stood, and threw
Year after year their stones upon the field,
Wakening a lonely echo; and the leaves
Of the old thorn, that on the topmost tower
Usurped the royal ensign's grandeur, shook
In the stern storm that swayed the topmost tower
And whispered strange tales in the whirlwind's ear.

Low through the lone cathedral's roofless aisles
The melancholy winds a death-dirge sung:
It were a sight of awfulness to see
The works of faith and slavery, so vast,
So sumptuous, yet so perishing withal!
Even as the corpse that rests beneath its wall.
A thousand mourners deck the pomp of death
To-day, the breathing marble glows above
To decorate its memory, and tongues

Are busy of its life: to-morrow, worms
In silence and in darkness seize their prey.

Within the massy prison's mouldering courts,
Fearless and free the ruddy children played,
Weaving gay chaplets for their innocent brows
With the green ivy and the red wall-flower,
That mock the dungeon's unavailing gloom;
The ponderous chains, and gratings of strong iron,
There rusted amid heaps of broken stone
That mingled slowly with their native earth:
There the broad beam of day, which feebly once
Lighted the cheek of lean captivity
With a pale and sickly glare, then freely shone
On the pure smiles of infant playfulness:
No more the shuddering voice of hoarse despair
Pealed through the echoing vaults, but soothing notes
Of ivy-fingered winds and gladsome birds
And merriment were resonant around.

These ruins soon left not a wreck behind:
Their elements, wide-scattered o'er the globe,
To happier shapes were moulded, and became
Ministrant to all blissful impulses:
Thus human things were perfected, and earth,
Even as a child beneath its mother's love,
Was strengthened in all excellence, and grew
Fairer and nobler with each passing year.

Now Time his dusky pennons o'er the scene
Closes in stedfast darkness, and the past
Fades from our charmed sight. My task is done:
Thy lore is learned. Earth's wonders are thine own,
With all the fear and all the hope they bring.
My spells are past: the present now recurs.
Ah me! a pathless wilderness remains
Yet unsubdued by man's reclaiming hand.

Yet, human Spirit, bravely hold thy course,
Let virtue teach thee firmly to pursue
The gradual paths of an aspiring change:
For birth and life and death, and that strange state

Before the naked soul has found its home,
All tend to perfect happiness, and urge
The restless wheels of being on their way,
Whose flashing spokes, instinct with infinite life,
Bicker and burn to gain their destined goal:
For birth but wakes the spirit to the sense
Of outward shews, whose unexperienced shape
New modes of passion to its frame may lend;
Life is its state of action, and the store
Of all events is aggregated there
That variegate the eternal universe;
Death is a gate of dreariness and gloom,
That leads to azure isles and beaming skies
And happy regions of eternal hope.
Therefore, O Spirit! fearlessly bear on:
Though storms may break the primrose on its stalk,
Though frosts may blight the freshness of its bloom,
Yet spring's awakening breath will woo the earth,
To feed with kindliest dews its favorite flower,
That blooms in mossy banks and darksome glens,
Lighting the green wood with its sunny smile.

Fear not then, Spirit, death's disrobing hand,
So welcome when the tyrant is awake,
So welcome when the bigot's hell-torch burns;
'Tis but the voyage of a darksome hour,
The transient gulph-dream of a startling sleep.
Death is no foe to virtue: earth has seen
Love's brightest roses on the scaffold bloom,
Mingling with freedom's fadeless laurels there,
And presaging the truth of visioned bliss.
Are there not hopes within thee, which this scene
Of linked and gradual being has confirmed?
Whose stingings bade thy heart look further still,
When to the moonlight walk by Henry led,
Sweetly and sadly thou didst talk of death?
And wilt thou rudely tear them from thy breast,
Listening supinely to a bigot's creed,
Or tamely crouching to the tyrant's rod,
Whose iron thongs are red with human gore?
Never: but bravely bearing on, thy will
Is destined an eternal war to wage

With tyranny and falshood, and uproot
The germs of misery from the human heart.
Thine is the hand whose piety would soothe
The thorny pillow of unhappy crime,
Whose impotence an easy pardon gains,
Watching its wanderings as a friend's disease:
Thine is the brow whose mildness would defy
Its fiercest rage, and brave its sternest will,
When fenced by power and master of the world.
Thou art sincere and good; of resolute mind,
Free from heart-withering custom's cold control,
Of passion lofty, pure and unsubdued.
Earth's pride and meanness could not vanquish thee,
And therefore art thou worthy of the boon
Which thou hast now received: virtue shall keep
Thy footsteps in the path that thou hast trod,
And many days of beaming hope shall bless
Thy spotless life of sweet and sacred love.
Go, happy one, and give that bosom joy
  Whose sleepless spirit waits to catch
  Light, life and rapture from thy smile.

  The fairy waves her wand of charm.
Speechless with bliss the Spirit mounts the car,
  That rolled beside the battlement,
Bending her beamy eyes in thankfulness.
  Again the enchanted steeds were yoked,
  Again the burning wheels inflame
The steep descent of heaven's untrodden way.
  Fast and far the chariot flew:
  The vast and fiery globes that rolled
  Around the Fairy's palace-gate
Lessened by slow degrees, and soon appeared
Such tiny twinklers as the planet orbs
That there attendant on the solar power
With borrowed light pursued their narrower way.

    Earth floated then below:
  The chariot paused a moment there;
    The Spirit then descended:
The restless coursers pawed the ungenial soil,
Snuffed the gross air, and then, their errand done,
Unfurled their pinions to the winds of heaven.

The Body and the Soul united then,
A gentle start convulsed Ianthe's frame:
Her veiny eyelids quietly unclosed;
Moveless awhile the dark blue orbs remained:
She looked around in wonder and beheld
Henry, who kneeled in silence by her couch,
Watching her sleep with looks of speechless love,
And the bright beaming stars
That through the casement shone.

[SHELLEY'S] NOTES

[1] I.242–3

The sun's unclouded orb
Rolled through the black concave.

Beyond our atmosphere the sun would appear a rayless orb of fire in the midst of a black concave. The equal diffusion of its light on earth is owing to the refraction of the rays by the atmosphere, and their reflection from other bodies. Light consists either of vibrations propagated through a subtle medium, or of numerous minute particles repelled in all directions from the luminous body. Its velocity greatly exceeds that of any substance with which we are acquainted: observations on the eclipses of Jupiter's satellites have demonstrated that light takes up no more than 8' 7" in passing from the sun to the earth, a distance of 95,000,000 miles.—Some idea may be gained of the immense distance of the fixed stars, when it is computed that many years would elapse before light could reach this earth from the nearest of them; yet in one year light travels 5,422,400,000,000 miles, which is a distance 5,707,600 times greater than that of the sun from the earth.

[2] I.252–3

Whilst round the chariot's way
Innumerable systems rolled.

The plurality of worlds,—the indefinite immensity of the universe is a most awful subject of contemplation. He who rightly feels its mystery and grandeur, is in no danger of seduction from the falshoods of religious systems, or of deifying the principle of the universe. It is impossible to believe that the Spirit that pervades this infinite machine, begat a son upon the body of a Jewish woman; or is angered at the consequences of that necessity, which is a synonime of itself. All that miserable tale of the Devil, and Eve, and an Intercessor, with the childish mummeries of the God of the Jews, is irreconcileable with the knowledge of the stars. The works of his fingers have borne witness against him.

The nearest of the fixed stars is inconceivably distant from the earth, and they are probably proportionably distant from each other. By a calculation of the velocity of light, Sirius is supposed to be at least 54,224,000,000,000 miles from the earth.* That which appears only like a thin and silvery cloud streaking the heaven, is in effect composed of innumerable clusters of suns, each shining with its own light, and illuminating numbers of planets that revolve around them. Millions and millions of suns are ranged around us, all attended by innumerable worlds, yet calm, regular, and harmonious, all keeping the paths of immutable necessity.

[3] IV.178–9

These are the hired bravos who defend
The tyrant's throne.

To employ murder as a means of justice, is an idea which a man of an enlightened mind will not dwell upon with pleasure. To march forth in rank and file, and all the pomp of streamers and trumpets, for the purpose of shooting at our fellow-men as a mark; to inflict upon them all the variety of wound and anguish; to leave them weltering in their blood; to wander over the field of desolation, and count the number of the dying and the dead,—are employments which in thesis we may maintain to be necessary, but which no good man will contemplate with gratulation and delight. A battle we suppose is won:—thus truth is established, thus the cause of justice is confirmed! It surely requires no common sagacity to discern the connection between this immense heap of calamities and the assertion of truth or the maintenance of justice.

Kings, and ministers of state, the real authors of the calamity, sit unmolested in their cabinet, while those against whom the fury of the storm is directed are, for the most part, persons who have been trepanned into the service, or who are dragged unwillingly from their peaceful homes into the field of battle. A soldier is a man whose

* See Nicholson's Encyclopedia, art. Light. [Shelley's note]

business it is to kill those who never offended him, and who are the innocent martyrs of other men's iniquities. Whatever may become of the abstract question of the justifiableness of war, it seems impossible that the soldier should not be a depraved and unnatural being.

To these more serious and momentous considerations it may be proper to add a recollection of the ridiculousness of the military character. Its first constituent is obedience: a soldier is, of all descriptions of men, the most completely a machine; yet his profession inevitably teaches him something of dogmatism, swaggering, and self-consequence: he is like the puppet of a showman, who, at the very time he is made to strut and swell and display the most farcical airs, we perfectly know cannot assume the most insignificant gesture, advance either to the right or the left, but as he is moved by his exhibitor.—*Godwin's Enquirer, Essay V.*

I will here subjoin a little poem, so strongly expressive of my abhorrence of despotism and falshood, that I fear lest it never again may be depictured so vividly. This opportunity is perhaps the only one that ever will occur of rescuing it from oblivion.

FALSHOOD AND VICE:
A DIALOGUE

Whilst monarchs laughed upon their thrones
To hear a famished nation's groans,
And hugged the wealth wrung from the woe
That makes its eyes and veins o'erflow,—
Those thrones, high built upon the heaps
Of bones where frenzied famine sleeps,
Where slavery wields her scourge of iron,
Red with mankind's unheeded gore,
And war's mad fiends the scene environ,
Mingling with shrieks a drunken roar,
There Vice and Falshood took their stand,
High raised above the unhappy land.

FALSHOOD

Brother! arise from the dainty fare,
Which thousands have toiled and bled to bestow;
A finer feast for thy hungry ear
Is the news that I bring of human woe.

VICE

And, secret one, what hast thou done,
To compare, in thy tumid pride, with me?
I, whose career, through the blasted year,
Has been tracked by despair and agony.

FALSHOOD

What have I done!—I have torn the robe
From baby truth's unsheltered form,
And round the desolated globe
Borne safely the bewildering charm:
My tyrant-slaves to a dungeon-floor
Have bound the fearless innocent,
And streams of fertilizing gore
Flow from her bosom's hideous rent,
Which this unfailing dagger gave . . .
I dread that blood!—no more—this day
Is ours, though her eternal ray
    Must shine upon our grave.
Yet know, proud Vice, had I not given
To thee the robe I stole from heaven,
Thy shape of ugliness and fear
Had never gained admission here.

VICE

And know, that had I disdained to toil,
But sate in my loathsome cave the while,
And ne'er to these hateful sons of heaven,
GOLD, MONARCHY, and MURDER, given;
Hadst thou with all thine art essayed
One of thy games then to have played,
With all thine overweening boast,
Falshood! I tell thee thou hadst lost!—
Yet wherefore this dispute?—we tend,
Fraternal, to one common end;
In this cold grave beneath my feet,
Will our hopes, our fears, and our labours, meet.

FALSHOOD

I brought my daughter, RELIGION, on earth:
She smothered Reason's babes in their birth;
But dreaded their mother's eye severe,—
So the crocodile slunk off slily in fear,

And loosed her bloodhounds from the den . . .
They started from dreams of slaughtered men,
And, by the light of her poison eye,
Did her work o'er the wide earth frightfully:
The dreadful stench of her torches' flare,
Fed with human fat, polluted the air:
The curses, the shrieks, the ceaseless cries
Of the many-mingling miseries,
As on she trod, ascended high
And trumpeted my victory!—
Brother, tell what thou hast done.

VICE

I have extinguished the noon-day sun,
In the carnage-smoke of battles won:
Famine, murder, hell and power
Were glutted in that glorious hour
Which searchless fate had stamped for me
With the seal of her security . . .
For the bloated wretch on yonder throne
Commanded the bloody fray to rise.
Like me he joyed at the stifled moan
Wrung from a nation's miseries;
While the snakes, whose slime even him *defiled*,
In ecstacies of malice smiled:
They thought 'twas theirs,—but mine the deed!
Theirs is the toil, but mine the meed—
Ten thousand victims madly bleed.
They dream that tyrants goad them there
With poisonous war to taint the air:
These tyrants, on their beds of thorn,
Swell with the thoughts of murderous fame,
And with their gains to lift my name.
Restless they plan from night to morn:
I—I do all; without my aid
Thy daughter, that relentless maid,
Could never o'er a death-bed urge
The fury of her venomed scourge.

FALSHOOD

Brother, well:—the world is ours;
And whether thou or I have won,
The pestilence expectant lowers

On all beneath yon blasted sun.
Our joys, our toils, our honors meet
In the milk-white and wormy winding-sheet:
A short-lived hope, unceasing care,
Some heartless scraps of godly prayer,
A moody curse, and a frenzied sleep
Ere gapes the grave's unclosing deep,
A tyrant's dream, a coward's start,
The ice that clings to a priestly heart,
A judge's frown, a courtier's smile,
Make the great whole for which we toil;
And, brother, whether thou or I
Have done the work of misery,
It little boots: thy toil and pain,
Without my aid, were more than vain;
And but for thee I ne'er had sate
The guardian of heaven's palace gate.

[4] V.1–2

Thus do the generations of the earth
Go to the grave, and issue from the womb.

One generation passeth away and another generation cometh, but the earth abideth for ever. The sun also ariseth and the sun goeth down, and hasteth to his place where he arose. The wind goeth toward the south and turneth about unto the north, it whirleth about continually, and the wind returneth again according to his circuits. All the rivers run into the sea, yet the sea is not full; unto the place whence the rivers come, thither shall they return again.

Ecclesiastes, chap. i.

[5] V.4–6

Even as the leaves
Which the keen frost-wind of the waning year
Has scattered on the forest soil.

[*Shelley's note quotes in Greek Homer's* Iliad *VI.146–9.*]

[6] V.58

The mob of peasants, nobles, priests, and kings.

[*Shelley's note quotes in Latin Lucretius,* De Rerum Natura *II.1–14.*]

[7] V. 93–4

And statesmen boast
Of wealth!

[*Shelley's note, which begins, 'There is no real wealth but the labour of man', draws largely on the work of William Godwin to deplore the inequality in contemporary England and the legal system and social customs that perpetuate it, arguing that the taste for luxury and display and the unequal distribution of labour deny to rich and poor alike the benefits of that 'cultivated leisure' which promotes 'moral improvement'.*]

[8] V.112–13

or religion
Drives his wife raving mad.

I am acquainted with a lady of considerable accomplishments, and the mother of a numerous family, whom the Christian religion has goaded to incurable insanity. A parallel case is, I believe, within the experience of every physician.

Nam iam saepe homines patriam, carosque parentes
Prodiderunt, vitare Acherusia templa petentes.
Lucretius.

[9] V.189

Even love is sold.

Not even the intercourse of the sexes is exempt from the despotism of positive institution. Law pretends even to govern the indisciplinable wanderings of passion, to put fetters on the clearest deductions of reason, and, by appeals to the will, to subdue the involuntary affections of our nature. Love is inevitably consequent upon the perception of loveliness. Love withers under constraint: its very essence is liberty: it is compatible neither with obedience, jealousy, nor fear: it is there most pure, perfect, and unlimited, where its votaries live in confidence, equality, and unreserve.

How long then ought the sexual connection to last? what law ought to specify the extent of the grievances which should limit its duration? A husband and wife ought to continue so long united as they love each other: any law which should bind them to cohabitation for one moment after the decay of their affection, would be a most intolerable tyranny, and the most unworthy of toleration. How odious an usurpation of the right of private judgment should that law be considered, which should make the ties of friendship indissoluble, in spite of the caprices, the inconstancy, the fallibility, and capacity for improvement of the human mind. And by so much would the fetters of love be heavier and more unendurable than those of friendship, as love is more vehement and capricious, more dependent on those delicate peculiarities of imagination, and less capable of reduction to the ostensible merits of the object.

The state of society in which we exist is a mixture of feudal savageness and imperfect civilization. The narrow and unenlightened morality of the Christian religion is an aggravation of these evils. It is not even until lately that mankind have admitted that happiness is the sole end of the science of ethics, as of all other sciences; and that the fanatical idea of mortifying the flesh for the love of God has been discarded. I have heard, indeed, an ignorant collegian adduce, in favour of Christianity, its hostility to every worldly feeling!*

But if happiness be the object of morality, of all human unions and disunions; if the worthiness of every action is to be estimated by the quantity of pleasurable sensation it is calculated to produce, then the connection of the sexes is so long sacred as it contributes to the comfort of the parties, and is naturally dissolved when its evils are greater than its benefits. There is nothing immoral in this separation. Constancy has nothing virtuous in itself, independently of the pleasure it confers, and partakes of the temporizing spirit of vice in proportion as it endures tamely moral defects of magnitude in the object of its indiscreet choice. Love is free: to promise for ever to love the same woman, is not less absurd than to promise to believe the

* The first Christian emperor made a law by which seduction was punished with death: if the female pleaded her own consent, she also was punished with death; if the parents endeavoured to screen the criminals, they were banished and their estates were confiscated; the slaves who might be accessary were burned alive, or forced to swallow melted lead. The very offspring of an illegal love were involved in the consequences of the sentence.—*Gibbon's Decline and Fall, &c.* vol. ii. page 210. See also, for the hatred of the primitive Christians to love and even marriage, page 269 [Edward Gibbon, *The History of the Decline and Fall of the Roman Empire*, 6 vols (London: 1776–88)]. [Shelley's note]

same creed: such a vow, in both cases, excludes us from all enquiry. The language of the votarist is this: The woman I now love may be infinitely inferior to many others; the creed I now profess may be a mass of errors and absurdities; but I exclude myself from all future information as to the amiability of the one and the truth of the other, resolving blindly, and in spite of conviction, to adhere to them. Is this the language of delicacy and reason? Is the love of such a frigid heart of more worth than its belief?

The present system of constraint does no more, in the majority of instances, than make hypocrites or open enemies. Persons of delicacy and virtue, unhappily united to one whom they find it impossible to love, spend the loveliest season of their life in unproductive efforts to appear otherwise than they are, for the sake of the feelings of their partner or the welfare of their mutual offspring: those of less generosity and refinement openly avow their disappointment, and linger out the remnant of that union, which only death can dissolve, in a state of incurable bickering and hostility. The early education of their children takes its colour from the squabbles of the parents; they are nursed in a systematic school of ill humour, violence, and falshood. Had they been suffered to part at the moment when indifference rendered their union irksome, they would have been spared many years of misery: they would have connected themselves more suitably, and would have found that happiness in the society of more congenial partners which is for ever denied them by the despotism of marriage. They would have been separately useful and happy members of society, who, whilst united, were miserable, and rendered misanthropical by misery. The conviction that wedlock is indissoluble holds out the strongest of all temptations to the perverse: they indulge without restraint in acrimony, and all the little tyrannies of domestic life, when they know that their victim is without appeal. If this connection were put on a rational basis, each would be assured that habitual ill temper would terminate in separation, and would check this vicious and dangerous propensity.

Prostitution is the legitimate offspring of marriage and its accompanying errors. Women, for no other crime than having followed the dictates of a natural appetite, are driven with fury from the comforts and sympathies of society. It is less venial than murder; and the punishment which is inflicted on her who destroys her child to escape reproach, is lighter than the life of agony and disease to which the prostitute is irrecoverably doomed. Has a woman obeyed the impulse of unerring nature;—society declares war against her, pityless and eternal war: she must be the tame slave, she must make no reprisals;

theirs is the right of persecution, hers the duty of endurance. She lives a life of infamy: the loud and bitter laugh of scorn scares her from all return. She dies of long and lingering disease: yet *she* is in fault, *she* is the criminal, *she* the froward and untameable child,—and society, forsooth, the pure and virtuous matron, who casts her as an abortion from her undefiled bosom! Society avenges herself on the criminals of her own creation; she is employed in anathematizing the vice to-day, which yesterday she was the most zealous to teach. Thus is formed one tenth of the population of London: meanwhile the evil is twofold. Young men, excluded by the fanatical idea of chastity from the society of modest and accomplished women, associate with these vicious and miserable beings, destroying thereby all those exquisite and delicate sensibilities whose existence cold-hearted worldlings have denied; annihilating all genuine passion, and debasing that to a selfish feeling which is the excess of generosity and devotedness. Their body and mind alike crumble into a hideous wreck of humanity; idiotcy and disease become perpetuated in their miserable offspring, and distant generations suffer for the bigotted morality of their forefathers. Chastity is a monkish and evangelical superstition, a greater foe to natural temperance even than unintellectual sensuality; it strikes at the root of all domestic happiness, and consigns more than half of the human race to misery, that some few may monopolize according to law. A system could not well have been devised more studiously hostile to human happiness than marriage.

I conceive that, from the abolition of marriage, the fit and natural arrangement of sexual connection would result. I by no means assert that the intercourse would be promiscuous: on the contrary; it appears, from the relation of parent to child, that this union is generally of long duration, and marked above all others with generosity and self-devotion. But this is a subject which it is perhaps premature to discuss. That which will result from the abolition of marriage, will be natural and right, because choice and change will be exempted from restraint.

In fact, religion and morality, as they now stand, compose a practical code of misery and servitude: the genius of human happiness must tear every leaf from the accursed book of God, ere man can read the inscription on his heart. How would morality, dressed up in stiff stays and finery, start from her own disgusting image, should she look in the mirror of nature!

[10] VI.45–6

To the red and baleful sun
That faintly twinkles there.

[*Shelley's note proposes, citing contemporary scientific authorities, that the earth's axis in the planet's orbit round the sun is steadily becoming perpendicular to the equator; and that this phenomenon should gradually result in a mild and temperate climate over the entire globe conducive to 'true and comprehensive' health and to the development of human wisdom.*]

[11] VI.171–3

No atom of this turbulence fulfils
A vague and unnecessitated task,
Or acts but as it must and ought to act.

[*Shelley's note quotes in French from the Baron d'Holbach's* Système de la Nature *(1770) a passage setting out the principle that in physical as well as mental life every action is determined by the operation of material causes on the agent.*]

[12] VI.198

Necessity! thou mother of the world!

[*Following on from the previous note, Shelley defines the idea of Necessity:*] He who asserts the doctrine of Necessity, means that, contemplating the events which compose the moral and material universe, he beholds only an immense and uninterrupted chain of causes and effects, no one of which could occupy any other place than it does occupy, or acts in any other place than it does act. The idea of necessity is obtained by our experience of the connection between objects, the uniformity of the operations of nature, the constant conjunction of similar events, and the consequent inference of one from the other. Mankind are therefore agreed in the admission of necessity, if they admit that these two circumstances take place in voluntary action. Motive is, to voluntary action in the human mind, what cause is to effect in the material universe. The word liberty, as applied to mind, is analogous to the word chance, as applied to matter: they spring from an ignorance of the certainty of the conjunction of antecedents and consequents. [*The note goes on to deploy Necessity as a critical tool for impugning established doctrines of religion and canons of morality, borrowing arguments from Hume, Holbach and Godwin.*]

[13] VII.13

There is no God!

This negation must be understood solely to affect a creative Deity. The hypothesis of a pervading Spirit coeternal with the universe, remains unshaken.

A close examination of the validity of the proofs adduced to support any proposition, is the only secure way of attaining truth, on the advantages of which it is unnecessary to descant: our knowledge of the existence of a Deity is a subject of such importance, that it cannot be too minutely investigated; in consequence of this conviction we proceed briefly and impartially to examine the proofs which have been adduced. It is necessary first to consider the nature of belief.

When a proposition is offered to the mind, it perceives the agreement or disagreement of the ideas of which it is composed. A perception of their agreement is termed *belief*. Many obstacles frequently prevent this perception from being immediate; these the mind attempts to remove, in order that the perception may be distinct. The mind is active in the investigation, in order to perfect the state of perception of the relation which the component ideas of the proposition bear to each, which is passive: the investigation being confused with the perception, has induced many falsely to imagine that the mind is active in belief,—that belief is an act of volition,—in consequence of which it may be regulated by the mind. Pursuing, continuing this mistake, they have attached a degree of criminality to disbelief; of which, in its nature, it is incapable: it is equally incapable of merit.

Belief, then, is a passion, the strength of which, like every other passion, is in precise proportion to the degrees of excitement.

The degrees of excitement are three.

The senses are the sources of all knowledge to the mind; consequently their evidence claims the strongest assent.

The decision of the mind, founded upon our own experience, derived from these sources, claims the next degree.

The experience of others, which addresses itself to the former one, occupies the lowest degree.

(A graduated scale, on which should be marked the capabilities of propositions to approach to the test of the senses, would be a just barometer of the belief which ought to be attached to them.)

Consequently no testimony can be admitted which is contrary to reason; reason is founded on the evidence of our senses.

Every proof may be referred to one of these three divisions: it is to be considered what arguments we receive from each of them, which should convince us of the existence of a Deity.

1st. The evidence of the senses. If the Deity should appear to us, if he should convince our senses of his existence, this revelation would necessarily command belief. Those to whom the Deity has thus appeared have the strongest possible conviction of his existence. But the God of Theologians is incapable of local visibility.

2d. Reason. It is urged that man knows that whatever is, must either have had a beginning, or have existed from all eternity: he also knows, that whatever is not eternal must have had a cause. When this reasoning is applied to the universe, it is necessary to prove that it was created: until that is clearly demonstrated, we may reasonably suppose that it has endured from all eternity. We must prove design before we can infer a designer. The only idea which we can form of causation is derivable from the constant conjunction of objects, and the consequent inference of one from the other. In a case where two propositions are diametrically opposite, the mind believes that which is least incomprehensible;—it is easier to suppose that the universe has existed from all eternity, than to conceive a being beyond its limits capable of creating it: if the mind sinks beneath the weight of one, is it an alleviation to increase the intolerability of the burthen?

The other argument, which is founded on a man's knowledge of his own existence, stands thus. A man knows not only that he now is, but that once he was not; consequently there must have been a cause. But our idea of causation is alone derivable from the constant conjunction of objects and the consequent inference of one from the other; and, reasoning experimentally, we can only infer from effects, causes exactly adequate to those effects. But there certainly is a generative power which is effected by certain instruments: we cannot prove that it is inherent in these instruments; nor is the contrary hypothesis capable of demonstration: we admit that the generative power is incomprehensible; but to suppose that the same effect is produced by an eternal, omniscient, omnipotent being, leaves the cause in the same obscurity, but renders it more incomprehensible.

3d. Testimony. It is required that testimony should not be contrary to reason. The testimony that the Deity convinces the senses of men of his existence can only be admitted by us, if our mind considers it less probable that these men should have been deceived, than that the Deity should have appeared to them. Our reason can never admit the testimony of men, who not only declare that they were eye-witnesses of miracles, but that the Deity was irrational; for he commanded that he should be believed, he proposed the highest rewards for faith, eternal punishments for disbelief. We can only command voluntary actions; belief is not an act of volition; the mind is even passive, or involuntarily active: from this it is evident that we have no sufficient testimony, or rather that testimony is insufficient to prove the being of a God. It has been before shewn that it cannot be deduced from reason. They alone, then, who have been convinced by the evidence of the senses, can believe it.

Hence it is evident that, having no proofs from either of the three sources of conviction, the mind *cannot* believe the existence of a creative God: it is also evident, that, as belief is a passion of the mind, no degree of criminality is attachable to disbelief; and that they only are reprehensible who neglect to remove the false medium through which their mind views any subject of discussion. Every reflecting mind must acknowledge that there is no proof of the existence of a Deity.

[*The note continues, citing texts from Isaac Newton, Francis Bacon, Holbach, Pliny, Sir William Drummond (whom Shelley challenges) and Spinoza, in support of the contention that belief in the existence of a creative deity is an indemonstrable hypothesis.*]

[14] VII.67

Ahasuerus, rise!

[*The note narrates in prose the tormented existence of the Wandering Jew Ahasuerus, cursed by God to roam the earth until the Day of Judgement – based upon a translation from the German of C. F. D. Schubart's* Der ewige Jude: Eine lyrische Rhapsodie *(1783). Shelley claims, dubiously, that*] This fragment is the translation of part of some German work, whose title I have vainly endeavoured to discover. I picked it up, dirty and torn, some years ago, in Lincoln's-Inn Fields.

[15] VII.135–6

I will beget a Son, and he shall bear
The sins of all the world

[*The note sketches a sympathetic portrait of Jesus who lost his life 'in the cause of suffering humanity' while it mounts a critical assault on the distortions of Christian doctrine, the belief in miracles, prophecies and divine inspiration, and the coercions of institutional Christianity.*]

[16] VIII.203–7

Him, still from hope to hope the bliss pursuing,
Which from the exhaustless lore of human weal
Draws on the virtuous mind, the thoughts that rise
In time-destroying infiniteness, gift
With self-enshrined eternity, &c.

Time is our consciousness of the succession of ideas in our mind. Vivid sensation, of either pain or pleasure, makes the time seem long, as the common phrase is, because it renders us more acutely conscious of our ideas. If a mind be conscious of an hundred ideas during one minute, by the clock, and of two hundred during another, the latter of these spaces would actually occupy so much greater extent in the mind as two exceed one in quantity. If, therefore, the human mind, by any future improvement of its sensibility, should become conscious of an infinite number of ideas in a minute, that minute would be eternity. I do not hence infer that the actual space between the birth and death of a man will ever be prolonged; but that his sensibility is perfectible, and that the number of ideas which his mind is capable of receiving is indefinite. One man is stretched on the rack during twelve hours; another sleeps soundly in his bed: the difference of time perceived by these two persons is immense; one hardly will believe that half an hour has elapsed, the other could credit that centuries had flown during his agony. Thus, the life of a man of virtue and talent, who should die in his thirtieth year, is, with regard to his own feelings, longer than that of a miserable priest-ridden slave, who dreams out a century of dulness. The one has perpetually cultivated his mental faculties, has rendered himself master of his thoughts, can abstract and generalize amid the lethargy of every-day business;—the other can slumber over the brightest moments of his being, and is unable to remember the happiest hour of his life. Perhaps the perishing ephemeron enjoys a longer life than the tortoise.

Dark flood of time!
Roll as it listeth thee—I measure not
By months or moments thy ambiguous course.
Another may stand by me on the brink
And watch the bubble whirled beyond his ken
That pauses at my feet. The sense of love,
The thirst for action, and the impassioned thought
Prolong my being: if I wake no more,
My life more actual living will contain

Than some grey veteran's of the world's cold school,
Whose listless hours unprofitably roll,
By one enthusiast feeling unredeemed.

See Godwin's Pol. Jus. vol. i. p. 411;—and Condorcet, Esquisse d'un Tableau Historique des Progrès de l'Esprit Humain, Epoque ix.

[17] VIII.211–12

No longer now
He slays the lamb that looks him in the face.

I hold that the depravity of the physical and moral nature of man originated in his unnatural habits of life. The origin of man, like that of the universe of which he is a part, is enveloped in impenetrable mystery. His generations either had a beginning, or they had not. The weight of evidence in favour of each of these suppositions seems tolerably equal; and it is perfectly unimportant to the present argument which is assumed. The language spoken however by the mythology of nearly all religions seems to prove, that at some distant period man forsook the path of nature, and sacrificed the purity and happiness of his being to unnatural appetites. The date of this event seems to have also been that of some great change in the climates of the earth, with which it has an obvious correspondence. The allegory of Adam and Eve eating of the tree of evil, and entailing upon their posterity the wrath of God, and the loss of everlasting life, admits of no other explanation than the disease and crime that have flowed from unnatural diet. Milton was so well aware of this, that he makes Raphael thus exhibit to Adam the consequence of his disobedience.

Immediately a place
Before his eyes appeared: sad, noisome, dark:
A lazar-house it seem'd; wherein were laid
Numbers of all diseased: all maladies
Of ghastly spasm, or racking torture, qualms
Of heart-sick agony, all feverous kinds,
Convulsions, epilepsies, fierce catarrhs,
Intestine stone and ulcer, colic pangs,
Daemoniac frenzy, moping melancholy,
And moon-struck madness, pining atrophy,
Marasmus, and wide-wasting pestilence,
Dropsies, and asthmas, and joint-racking rheums.

And how many thousands more might not be added to this frightful catalogue!

The story of Prometheus is one likewise which, although universally admitted to be allegorical, has never been satisfactorily explained. Prometheus stole fire from heaven, and was chained for this crime to Mount Caucasus, where a vulture continually devoured his liver, that grew to meet its hunger. Hesiod says, that, before the time of Prometheus, mankind were exempt from suffering; that they enjoyed a vigorous youth, and that death, when at length it came, approached like sleep, and gently closed their eyes. Again, so general was this opinion, that Horace, a poet of the Augustan age, writes—

> Audax omnia perpeti,
> Gens humana ruit per vetitum nefas;
> Audax Iapeti genus
> Ignem fraude malâ gentibus intulit:
> Post ignem aetheriâ domo
> Subductum, macies et nova febrium
> Terris incubuit cohors,
> Semotique prius tarda necessitas
> Lethi corripuit gradum.

How plain a language is spoken by all this. Prometheus (who represents the human race) effected some great change in the condition of his nature, and applied fire to culinary purposes; thus inventing an expedient for screening from his disgust the horrors of the shambles. From this moment his vitals were devoured by the vulture of disease. It consumed his being in every shape of its loathsome and infinite variety, inducing the soul-quelling sinkings of premature and violent death. All vice arose from the ruin of healthful innocence. Tyranny, superstition, commerce, and inequality, were then first known, when reason vainly attempted to guide the wanderings of exacerbated passion. [...]

Man, and the animals whom he has infected with his society, or depraved by his dominion, are alone diseased. The wild hog, the mouflon, the bison, and the wolf, are perfectly exempt from malady, and invariably die either from external violence, or natural old age. But the domestic hog, the sheep, the cow, and the dog, are subject to an incredible variety of distempers; and, like the corrupters of their nature, have physicians who thrive upon their miseries. The supereminence of man is like Satan's, a supereminence of pain; and the majority of his species, doomed to penury, disease and crime, have reason to curse the untoward event, that by enabling him to communicate his sensations, raised him above the level of his fellow animals. But the steps that have been taken are irrevocable. The whole of human science is comprised in one question:—How can the advantages of intellect and civilization be reconciled with the liberty and pure pleasures of natural life? How can we take the benefits, and reject the evils of the system, which is now interwoven with all the fibres of our being?—I believe that abstinence from animal food and spirituous liquors would in a great measure capacitate us for the solution of this important question.

It is true, that mental and bodily derangement is attributable in part to other deviations from rectitude and nature than those which concern diet. The mistakes cherished by society respecting the connection of the sexes, whence the misery and diseases of unsatisfied celibacy, unenjoying prostitution, and the premature arrival of puberty necessarily spring; the putrid atmosphere of crowded cities; the exhalations of chemical processes; the muffling of our bodies in superfluous apparel; the absurd treatment of infants:—all these, and innumerable other causes, contribute their mite to the mass of human evil.

Comparative anatomy teaches us that man resembles frugivorous animals in everything, and carnivorous in nothing; he has neither claws wherewith to seize his prey, nor distinct and pointed teeth to tear the living fibre. A Mandarin of the first class, with nails two inches long, would probably find them alone inefficient to hold even a hare. After every subterfuge of gluttony, the bull must be degraded into the ox, and the ram into the wether, by an unnatural and inhuman operation, that the flaccid fibre may offer a fainter resistance to rebellious nature. It is only by softening and disguising dead flesh by culinary preparation, that it is rendered susceptible of mastication or digestion; and that the sight of its bloody juices and raw horror does not excite intolerable loathing and disgust. Let the advocate of animal food force himself to a decisive experiment on its fitness, and, as Plutarch recommends, tear a living lamb with his teeth, and plunging his head into its vitals, slake his thirst with the steaming blood; when fresh from the deed of horror, let him revert to the irresistible instincts of nature that would rise in judgment against it, and say, Nature formed me for such work as this. Then, and then only, would he be consistent. [. . .]

[*The passage omitted details the resemblances between human anatomy and that of herbivorous animals and remarks on the use of animal food and alcoholic beverages as acquired habits; when these are overcome, bodily and mental well-being naturally follow.*]

What is the cause of morbid action in the animal system? Not the air we breathe, for our fellow denizens of nature breathe the same uninjured; not the water we drink, (if remote from the pollutions of man and his inventions),* for the animals drink it too; not the earth we tread upon; not the unobscured sight of glorious nature, in the wood, the field, or the expanse of sky and ocean; nothing that we are or do in common with the undiseased inhabitants of the forest. Something then wherein we differ from them: our habit of altering our food by fire, so that our appetite is no longer a just criterion for the fitness of its gratification. Except in children, there remain no traces of that instinct which determines, in all other animals, what aliment is natural or otherwise; and so perfectly obliterated are they in the reasoning adults of our species, that it has become necessary to urge considerations drawn from comparative anatomy to prove that we are naturally frugivorous.

Crime is madness. Madness is disease. Whenever the cause of disease shall be discovered, the root, from which all vice and misery have so long overshadowed the globe, will lie bare to the axe. All the exertions of man, from that moment, may be considered as tending to the clear profit of his species. No sane mind in a sane body resolves upon a real crime. It is a man of violent passions, blood-shot eyes, and swollen veins, that alone can grasp the knife of murder. The system of a simple diet promises no Utopian advantages. It is no mere reform of legislation, whilst the furious passions and evil propensities of the human heart, in which it had its origin, are still unassuaged. It strikes at the root of all evil, and is an experiment which may be tried with success, not alone by nations, but by small societies, families, and even individuals. In no cases has a return to vegetable diet produced the slightest injury; in most it has been attended with changes undeniably beneficial. Should ever a physician be born with the genius of Locke, I am persuaded that he might trace all bodily and mental derangements to our unnatural habits, as clearly as that philosopher has traced all knowledge to sensation. What prolific sources of disease are not those mineral and vegetable poisons that have been introduced for its extirpation! How many thousands have become murderers and robbers, bigots and domestic tyrants, dissolute and abandoned adventurers, from the use of fermented liquors; who, had they slaked their thirst only with pure water, would have

* The necessity of resorting to some means of purifying water, and the disease which arises from its adulteration in civilized countries, is sufficiently apparent—see Dr. Lambe's Reports on Cancer. I do not assert that the use of water is in itself unnatural, but that the unperverted palate would swallow no liquid capable of occasioning disease. [Shelley's note]

lived but to diffuse the happiness of their own unperverted feelings. How many groundless opinions and absurd institutions have not received a general sanction from the sottishness and intemperance of individuals! Who will assert that, had the populace of Paris satisfied their hunger at the ever-furnished table of vegetable nature, they would have lent their brutal suffrage to the proscription-list of Robespierre? Could a set of men, whose passions were not perverted by unnatural stimuli, look with coolness on an auto da fé? Is it to be believed that a being of gentle feelings, rising from his meal of roots, would take delight in sports of blood? Was Nero a man of temperate life? could you read calm health in his cheek, flushed with ungovernable propensities of hatred for the human race? Did Muley Ismael's pulse beat evenly, was his skin transparent, did his eyes beam with healthfulness, and its invariable concomitants, cheerfulness and benignity? Though history has decided none of these questions, a child could not hesitate to answer in the negative. Surely the bile-suffused cheek of Buonaparte, his wrinkled brow, and yellow eye, the ceaseless inquietude of his nervous system, speak no less plainly the character of his unresting ambition than his murders and his victories. It is impossible, had Buonaparte descended from a race of vegetable feeders, that he could have had either the inclination or the power to ascend the throne of the Bourbons. The desire of tyranny could scarcely be excited in the individual, the power to tyrannize would certainly not be delegated by a society neither frenzied by inebriation nor rendered impotent and irrational by disease. Pregnant indeed with inexhaustible calamity is the renunciation of instinct, as it concerns our physical nature; arithmetic cannot enumerate, nor reason perhaps suspect, the multitudinous sources of disease in civilized life. Even common water, that apparently innoxious pabulum, when corrupted by the filth of populous cities, is a deadly and insidious destroyer.* Who can wonder that all the inducements held out by God Himself in the Bible to virtue should have been vainer than a nurse's tale; and that those dogmas, by which he has there excited and justified the most ferocious propensities, should have alone been deemed essential; whilst Christians are in the daily practice of all those habits, which have infected with disease and crime, not only the reprobate sons, but these favoured children of the common Father's love? Omnipotence itself could not save them from the consequences of this original and universal sin. [. . .]

The quantity of nutritious vegetable matter, consumed in fattening

* Lambe's Reports on Cancer. [Shelley's note]

the carcase of an ox, would afford ten times the sustenance, undepraving indeed, and incapable of generating disease, if gathered immediately from the bosom of the earth. The most fertile districts of the habitable globe are now actually cultivated by men for animals, at a delay and waste of aliment absolutely incapable of calculation. It is only the wealthy that can, to any great degree, even now, indulge the unnatural craving for dead flesh, and they pay for the greater license of the privilege by subjection to supernumerary diseases. Again, the spirit of the nation that should take the lead in this great reform, would insensibly become agricultural; commerce, with all its vice, selfishness and corruption, would gradually decline; more natural habits would produce gentler manners, and the excessive complication of political relations would be so far simplified, that every individual might feel and understand why he loved his country, and took a personal interest in its welfare. How would England, for example, depend on the caprices of foreign rulers, if she contained within herself all the necessaries, and despised whatever they possessed of the luxuries of life? How could they starve her into compliance with their views? Of what consequence would it be that they refused to take her woollen manufactures, when large and fertile tracts of the island ceased to be allotted to the waste of pasturage? On a natural system of diet, we should require no spices from India; no wines from Portugal, Spain, France, or Madeira; none of those multitudinous articles of luxury, for which every corner of the globe is rifled, and which are the causes of so much individual rivalship, such calamitous and sanguinary national disputes. In the history of modern times, the avarice of commercial monopoly, no less than the ambition of weak and wicked chiefs, seems to have fomented the universal discord, to have added stubbornness to the mistakes of cabinets, and indocility to the infatuation of the people. Let it ever be remembered, that it is the direct influence of commerce to make the interval between the richest and the poorest man wider and more unconquerable. Let it be remembered, that it is a foe to every thing of real worth and excellence in the human character. The odious and disgusting aristocracy of wealth is built upon the ruins of all that is good in chivalry or republicanism; and luxury is the forerunner of a barbarism scarce capable of cure. Is it impossible to realize a state of society, where all the energies of man shall be directed to the production of his solid happiness? Certainly, if this advantage (the object of all political speculation) be in any degree attainable, it is attainable only by a community, which holds out no factitious incentives to the avarice and ambition of the few, and which is internally organized for the liberty, security and comfort of the many. None must be entrusted with power (and money is the completest species of power) who do not stand pledged to use it exclusively for the general benefit. But the use of animal flesh and fermented liquors, directly militates with this equality of the rights of man. The peasant cannot gratify these fashionable cravings without leaving his family to starve. Without disease and war, those sweeping curtailers of population, pasturage would include a waste too great to be afforded. The labour requisite to support a family is far lighter* than is usually supposed. The peasantry work, not only for themselves, but for the aristocracy, the army, and the manufacturers. [. . .]

Let not too much however be expected from this system. The healthiest among us is not exempt from hereditary disease. The most symmetrical, athletic, and long-lived, is a being inexpressibly inferior to what he would have been, had not the unnatural habits of his ancestors accumulated for him a certain portion of malady and deformity. In the most perfect specimen of civilized man, something is still found wanting by the physiological critic. Can a return to nature, then, instantaneously eradicate predispositions that have been slowly taking root in the silence of innumerable ages?—Indubitably not. All that I contend for is, that from the moment of the relinquishing all unnatural habits, no new disease is generated; and that the predisposition to hereditary maladies gradually perishes, for want of its accustomed supply. In cases of consumption, cancer, gout, asthma, and scrofula, such is the invariable tendency of a diet of vegetables and pure water. [. . .]

I address myself not only to the young enthusiast, the ardent devotee of truth and virtue, the pure and passionate moralist, yet unvitiated by the contagion of the world. He will embrace a pure system, from its abstract truth, its beauty, its simplicity, and its promise of wide-extended benefit; unless custom has turned poison into food, he will hate the brutal pleasures of the chace by instinct; it will be a contemplation full of horror and disappointment to his mind, that beings capable of the gentlest and most admirable sympathies, should take delight in the death-pangs and last convulsions of

* It has come under the author's experience, that some of the workmen on an embankment in North Wales, who, in consequence of the inability of the proprietor to pay them, seldom received their wages, have supported large families by cultivating small spots of sterile ground by moonlight. In the notes to [Samuel] Pratt's Poem, 'Bread, or the Poor' [1802], is an account of an industrious labourer, who, by working in a small garden, before and after his day's task, attained to an enviable state of independence. [Shelley's note]

dying animals. The elderly man, whose youth has been poisoned by intemperance, or who has lived with apparent moderation, and is afflicted with a variety of painful maladies, would find his account in a beneficial change produced without the risk of poisonous medicines. The mother, to whom the perpetual restlessness of disease, and unaccountable deaths incident to her children, are the causes of incurable unhappiness, would on this diet experience the satisfaction of beholding their perpetual healths and natural playfulness.* The most valuable lives are daily destroyed by diseases, that it is dangerous to palliate and impossible to cure by medicine. How much longer will man continue to pimp for the gluttony of death, his most insidious, implacable, and eternal foe?

* See Mr. Newton's book. His children are the most beautiful and healthy creatures it is possible to conceive; the girls are perfect models for a sculptor; their dispositions are also the most gentle and conciliating; the judicious treatment, which they experience in other points, may be a correlative cause of this. In the first five years of their life, of 18,000 children that are born, 7,500 die of various diseases; and how many more of those that survive are not rendered miserable by maladies not immediately mortal? The quality and quantity of a woman's milk are materially injured by the use of dead flesh. In an island near Iceland, where no vegetables are to be got, the children invariably die of tetanus, before they are three weeks old, and the population is supplied from the main land.—Sir G. Mackenzie's Hist. of Iceland. See also Emile, chap. i. pages 53, 54, 56. [Shelley's note]

'Mine eyes were dim with tears unshed'

Mine eyes were dim with tears unshed;
Yes, I was firm—they did not flow.
My baffled looks did long yet dread
To meet your looks . . . I could not know
How anxiously they sought to shine
With soothing pity into mine.

To sit and curb the soul's mute rage
Which preys upon itself alone—
To curse that life which is the cage
Of fettered grief, that dares not groan,
Hiding from many a careless eye
The scorned load of agony,

Whilst you alone saw not regarded
The paleness you alone should see—
To spend years thus—and be rewarded
As you, sweet love, requited me
When none were nigh—oh, I did wake
From torture for that moment's sake.

Upon my heart your accents sweet
Of peace and pity fell like dew
On flowers half dead, thy lips did meet
Mine tremblingly, thy dark eyes threw
Their soft persuasion on my brain,
Charming away its dream of pain.

We are not happy, sweet, our state
Is strange, and full of doubt and fear;
More need for Truth, that ills and hate,
Reserve or censure come not near
Our sacred friendship, lest there be
No solace left for you and me.

Gentle and good and mild thou art,
  Nor can I live if thou appear
Aught but thyself—or turn thine heart
  Away from me or stoop to wear
The mask of scorn—although it be
To hide the love you feel for me.

'O! there are spirits of the air'

ΔΑΚΡΥΣΙ ΔΙΟΙΣΩ ΠΟΤΜΟΝ ΑΠΟΤΜΟΝ

O! there are spirits of the air,
  And genii of the evening breeze,
And gentle ghosts, with eyes as fair
  As star-beams among twilight trees:—
Such lovely ministers to meet
Oft hast thou turned from men thy lonely feet.

With mountain winds, and babbling springs,
  And moonlight seas, that are the voice
Of these inexplicable things
  Thou didst hold commune, and rejoice
When they did answer thee; but they
Cast, like a worthless boon, thy love away.

And thou hast sought in starry eyes
  Beams that were never meant for thine,
Another's wealth:—tame sacrifice
  To a fond faith! still dost thou pine?
Still dost thou hope that greeting hands,
Voice, looks, or lips, may answer thy demands?

Ah! wherefore didst thou build thine hope
  On the false earth's inconstancy?
Did thine own mind afford no scope
  Of love, or moving thoughts to thee?
That natural scenes or human smiles
Could steal the power to wind thee in their wiles?

Yes, all the faithless smiles are fled
Whose falsehood left thee broken-hearted;
The glory of the moon is dead;
Night's ghosts and dreams have now departed;
Thine own soul still is true to thee,
But changed to a foul fiend through misery.

This fiend, whose ghastly presence ever
Beside thee like thy shadow hangs,
Dream not to chase;—the mad endeavour
Would scourge thee to severer pangs.
Be as thou art. Thy settled fate,
Dark as it is, all change would aggravate.

A Summer-Evening Church-Yard, Lechlade, Gloucestershire

The wind has swept from the wide atmosphere
Each vapour that obscured the sunset's ray;
And pallid evening twines its beaming hair
In duskier braids around the languid eyes of day:
Silence and twilight, unbeloved of men,
Creep hand in hand from yon obscurest glen.

They breathe their spells towards the departing day,
Encompassing the earth, air, stars, and sea;
Light, sound, and motion own the potent sway,
Responding to the charm with its own mystery.
The winds are still, or the dry church-tower grass
Knows not their gentle motions as they pass.

Thou too, aerial Pile! whose pinnacles
Point from one shrine like pyramids of fire,
Obeyest in silence their sweet solemn spells,
Clothing in hues of heaven thy dim and distant spire,
Around whose lessening and invisible height
Gather among the stars the clouds of night.

The dead are sleeping in their sepulchres:
And, mouldering as they sleep, a thrilling sound
Half sense, half thought, among the darkness stirs,
Breathed from their wormy beds all living things around,
And mingling with the still night and mute sky
Its awful hush is felt inaudibly.

Thus solemnized and softened, death is mild
And terrorless as this serenest night:
Here could I hope, like some enquiring child
Sporting on graves, that death did hide from human sight
Sweet secrets, or beside its breathless sleep
That loveliest dreams perpetual watch did keep.

Sonnet. From the Italian of Dante
Dante Alighieri to Guido Cavalcanti

Guido, I would that Lappo, thou, and I,
Led by some strong enchantment, might ascend
A magic ship, whose charmed sails should fly
With winds at will where'er our thoughts might wend,
And that no change, nor any evil chance,
Should mar our joyous voyage; but it might be,
That even satiety should still enhance
Between our hearts their strict community:
And that the bounteous wizard then would place
Vanna and Bice and my gentle love,
Companions of our wandering, and would grace
With passionate talk wherever we might rove
Our time, and each were as content and free
As I believe that thou and I should be.

To Wordsworth

Poet of Nature, thou hast wept to know
That things depart which never may return:
Childhood and youth, friendship and love's first glow,
Have fled like sweet dreams, leaving thee to mourn.
These common woes I feel. One loss is mine
Which thou too feel'st, yet I alone deplore.

Thou wert as a lone star, whose light did shine
On some frail bark in winter's midnight roar:
Thou hast like to a rock-built refuge stood
Above the blind and battling multitude:
In honoured poverty thy voice did weave
Songs consecrate to truth and liberty,—
Deserting these, thou leavest me to grieve,
Thus having been, that thou shouldst cease to be.

Feelings of a Republican on the Fall of Bonaparte

I hated thee, fallen tyrant! I did groan
To think that a most unambitious slave,
Like thou, shouldst dance and revel on the grave
Of Liberty. Thou mightst have built thy throne
Where it had stood even now: thou didst prefer
A frail and bloody pomp which time has swept
In fragments towards oblivion. Massacre,
For this I prayed, would on thy sleep have crept,
Treason and Slavery, Rapine, Fear, and Lust,
And stifled thee, their minister. I know
Too late, since thou and France are in the dust,
That virtue owns a more eternal foe
Than force or fraud: old Custom, legal Crime,
And bloody Faith the foulest birth of time.

Mutability

We are as clouds that veil the midnight moon;
How restlessly they speed, and gleam, and quiver,
Streaking the darkness radiantly!—yet soon
Night closes round, and they are lost for ever:

Or like forgotten lyres, whose dissonant strings
Give various response to each varying blast,
To whose frail frame no second motion brings
One mood or modulation like the last.

We rest.—A dream has power to poison sleep;
  We rise.—One wandering thought pollutes the day;
We feel, conceive or reason, laugh or weep;
  Embrace fond woe, or cast our cares away:

It is the same!—For, be it joy or sorrow,
  The path of its departure still is free:
Man's yesterday may ne'er be like his morrow;
  Nought may endure but Mutability.

ALASTOR;

OR,

THE SPIRIT OF SOLITUDE

PREFACE

The poem entitled 'ALASTOR,' may be considered as allegorical of one of the most interesting situations of the human mind. It represents a youth of uncorrupted feelings and adventurous genius led forth by an imagination inflamed and purified through familiarity with all that is excellent and majestic, to the contemplation of the universe. He drinks deep of the fountains of knowledge, and is still insatiate. The magnificence and beauty of the external world sinks profoundly into the frame of his conceptions, and affords to their modifications a variety not to be exhausted. So long as it is possible for his desires to point towards objects thus infinite and unmeasured, he is joyous, and tranquil, and self-possessed. But the period arrives when these objects cease to suffice. His mind is at length suddenly awakened and thirsts for intercourse with an intelligence similar to itself. He images to himself the Being whom he loves. Conversant with speculations of the sublimest and most perfect natures, the vision in which he embodies his own imaginations unites all of wonderful, or wise, or beautiful, which the poet, the philosopher, or the lover could depicture. The intellectual faculties, the imagination, the functions of sense, have their respective requisitions on the sympathy of corresponding powers in other human beings. The Poet is represented as uniting these requisitions, and attaching them to a single image. He seeks in vain for a prototype of his conception. Blasted by his disappointment, he descends to an untimely grave.

The picture is not barren of instruction to actual men. The Poet's self-centred seclusion was avenged by the furies of an irresistible passion pursuing him to speedy ruin. But that Power which strikes the luminaries of the world with sudden darkness and extinction, by awakening them to too exquisite a perception of its influences, dooms to a slow and poisonous decay those meaner spirits that dare to abjure its dominion. Their destiny is more abject and inglorious as their delinquency is more contemptible and pernicious. They who, deluded by no generous error, instigated by no sacred thirst of doubtful knowledge, duped by no illustrious superstition, loving nothing on this earth, and cherishing no hopes beyond, yet keep aloof from sympathies with their kind, rejoicing neither in human joy nor mourning with human grief; these, and such as they, have their apportioned curse. They languish, because none feel with them their common nature. They are morally dead. They are neither friends, nor lovers, nor fathers, nor citizens of the world, nor benefactors of their country. Among those who attempt to exist without human sympathy, the pure and tender-hearted perish through the intensity and passion of their search after its communities, when the vacancy of their spirit suddenly makes itself felt. All else, selfish, blind, and torpid, are those unforeseeing multitudes who constitute, together with their own, the lasting misery and loneliness of the world. Those who love not their fellow-beings, live unfruitful lives, and prepare for their old age a miserable grave.

> 'The good die first,
> And those whose hearts are dry as summer dust,
> Burn to the socket!'

December 14, 1815.

Alastor; or, The Spirit of Solitude

> Nondum amabam, et amare amabam, quaerebam quid amarem, amans amare.
>
> *Confess. St. August.*

EARTH, ocean, air, beloved brotherhood!
If our great Mother has imbued my soul
With aught of natural piety to feel
Your love, and recompense the boon with mine;
If dewy morn, and odorous noon, and even,
With sunset and its gorgeous ministers,
And solemn midnight's tingling silentness;
If autumn's hollow sighs in the sere wood,
And winter robing with pure snow and crowns
Of starry ice the gray grass and bare boughs;

If spring's voluptuous pantings when she breathes
Her first sweet kisses, have been dear to me;
If no bright bird, insect, or gentle beast
I consciously have injured, but still loved
And cherished these my kindred; then forgive
This boast, beloved brethren, and withdraw
No portion of your wonted favour now!

Mother of this unfathomable world!
Favour my solemn song, for I have loved
Thee ever, and thee only; I have watched
Thy shadow, and the darkness of thy steps,
And my heart ever gazes on the depth
Of thy deep mysteries. I have made my bed
In charnels and on coffins, where black death
Keeps record of the trophies won from thee,
Hoping to still these obstinate questionings
Of thee and thine, by forcing some lone ghost
Thy messenger, to render up the tale
Of what we are. In lone and silent hours,
When night makes a weird sound of its own stillness,
Like an inspired and desperate alchymist
Staking his very life on some dark hope,
Have I mixed awful talk and asking looks
With my most innocent love, until strange tears
Uniting with those breathless kisses, made
Such magic as compels the charmed night
To render up thy charge: . . . and, though ne'er yet
Thou hast unveil'd thy inmost sanctuary,
Enough from incommunicable dream,
And twilight phantasms, and deep noonday thought,
Has shone within me, that serenely now
And moveless, as a long-forgotten lyre
Suspended in the solitary dome
Of some mysterious and deserted fane,
I wait thy breath, Great Parent, that my strain
May modulate with murmurs of the air,
And motions of the forests and the sea,
And voice of living beings, and woven hymns
Of night and day, and the deep heart of man.

There was a Poet whose untimely tomb
No human hands with pious reverence reared,
But the charmed eddies of autumnal winds
Built o'er his mouldering bones a pyramid
Of mouldering leaves in the waste wilderness:—
A lovely youth,—no mourning maiden decked
With weeping flowers, or votive cypress wreath,
The lone couch of his everlasting sleep:—
Gentle, and brave, and generous,—no lorn bard
Breathed o'er his dark fate one melodious sigh:
He lived, he died, he sung, in solitude.
Strangers have wept to hear his passionate notes,
And virgins, as unknown he past, have pined
And wasted for fond love of his wild eyes.
The fire of those soft orbs has ceased to burn,
And Silence, too enamoured of that voice,
Locks its mute music in her rugged cell.

By solemn vision, and bright silver dream,
His infancy was nurtured. Every sight
And sound from the vast earth and ambient air,
Sent to his heart its choicest impulses.
The fountains of divine philosophy
Fled not his thirsting lips, and all of great,
Or good, or lovely, which the sacred past
In truth or fable consecrates, he felt
And knew. When early youth had past, he left
His cold fireside and alienated home
To seek strange truths in undiscovered lands.
Many a wide waste and tangled wilderness
Has lured his fearless steps; and he has bought
With his sweet voice and eyes, from savage men,
His rest and food. Nature's most secret steps
He like her shadow has pursued, where'er
The red volcano overcanopies
Its fields of snow and pinnacles of ice
With burning smoke, or where bitumen lakes
On black bare pointed islets ever beat
With sluggish surge, or where the secret caves
Rugged and dark, winding among the springs
Of fire and poison, inaccessible
To avarice or pride, their starry domes

Of diamond and of gold expand above
Numberless and immeasurable halls,
Frequent with crystal column, and clear shrines
Of pearl, and thrones radiant with chrysolite.
Nor had that scene of ampler majesty
Than gems or gold, the varying roof of heaven
And the green earth lost in his heart its claims
To love and wonder; he would linger long
In lonesome vales, making the wild his home,
Until the doves and squirrels would partake
From his innocuous hand his bloodless food,
Lured by the gentle meaning of his looks,
And the wild antelope, that starts whene'er
The dry leaf rustles in the brake, suspend
Her timid steps to gaze upon a form
More graceful than her own.
                                        His wandering step
Obedient to high thoughts, has visited
The awful ruins of the days of old:
Athens, and Tyre, and Balbec, and the waste
Where stood Jerusalem, the fallen towers
Of Babylon, the eternal pyramids,
Memphis and Thebes, and whatsoe'er of strange
Sculptured on alabaster obelisk,
Or jasper tomb, or mutilated sphinx,
Dark Aethiopia in her desert hills
Conceals. Among the ruined temples there,
Stupendous columns, and wild images
Of more than man, where marble daemons watch
The Zodiac's brazen mystery, and dead men
Hang their mute thoughts on the mute walls around,
He lingered, poring on memorials
Of the world's youth, through the long burning day
Gazed on those speechless shapes, nor, when the moon
Filled the mysterious halls with floating shades
Suspended he that task, but ever gazed
And gazed, till meaning on his vacant mind
Flashed like strong inspiration, and he saw
The thrilling secrets of the birth of time.

Meanwhile an Arab maiden brought his food,
Her daily portion, from her father's tent,
And spread her matting for his couch, and stole
From duties and repose to tend his steps:—
Enamoured, yet not daring for deep awe
To speak her love:—and watched his nightly sleep,
Sleepless herself, to gaze upon his lips
Parted in slumber, whence the regular breath
Of innocent dreams arose: then, when red morn
Made paler the pale moon, to her cold home
Wildered, and wan, and panting, she returned.

The Poet wandering on, through Arabie
And Persia, and the wild Carmanian waste,
And o'er the aërial mountains which pour down
Indus and Oxus from their icy caves,
In joy and exultation held his way;
Till in the vale of Cashmire, far within
Its loneliest dell, where odorous plants entwine
Beneath the hollow rocks a natural bower,
Beside a sparkling rivulet he stretched
His languid limbs. A vision on his sleep
There came, a dream of hopes that never yet
Had flushed his cheek. He dreamed a veiled maid
Sate near him, talking in low solemn tones.
Her voice was like the voice of his own soul
Heard in the calm of thought; its music long,
Like woven sounds of streams and breezes, held
His inmost sense suspended in its web
Of many-coloured woof and shifting hues.
Knowledge and truth and virtue were her theme,
And lofty hopes of divine liberty,
Thoughts the most dear to him, and poesy,
Herself a poet. Soon the solemn mood
Of her pure mind kindled through all her frame
A permeating fire: wild numbers then
She raised, with voice stifled in tremulous sobs
Subdued by its own pathos: her fair hands
Were bare alone, sweeping from some strange harp
Strange symphony, and in their branching veins
The eloquent blood told an ineffable tale.
The beating of her heart was heard to fill
The pauses of her music, and her breath

Tumultuously accorded with those fits
Of intermitted song. Sudden she rose,
As if her heart impatiently endured
Its bursting burthen: at the sound he turned,
And saw by the warm light of their own life
Her glowing limbs beneath the sinuous veil
Of woven wind, her outspread arms now bare,
Her dark locks floating in the breath of night,
Her beamy bending eyes, her parted lips
Outstretched, and pale, and quivering eagerly.
His strong heart sunk and sickened with excess
Of love. He reared his shuddering limbs and quelled
His gasping breath, and spread his arms to meet
Her panting bosom: . . . she drew back a while,
Then, yielding to the irresistible joy,
With frantic gesture and short breathless cry
Folded his frame in her dissolving arms.
Now blackness veiled his dizzy eyes, and night
Involved and swallowed up the vision; sleep,
Like a dark flood suspended in its course,
Rolled back its impulse on his vacant brain.

Roused by the shock he started from his trance—
The cold white light of morning, the blue moon
Low in the west, the clear and garish hills,
The distinct valley and the vacant woods,
Spread round him where he stood. Whither have fled
The hues of heaven that canopied his bower
Of yesternight? The sounds that soothed his sleep,
The mystery and the majesty of Earth,
The joy, the exultation? His wan eyes
Gaze on the empty scene as vacantly
As ocean's moon looks on the moon in heaven.
The spirit of sweet human love has sent
A vision to the sleep of him who spurned
Her choicest gifts. He eagerly pursues
Beyond the realms of dream that fleeting shade;
He overleaps the bounds. Alas! alas!
Were limbs, and breath, and being intertwined
Thus treacherously? Lost, lost, for ever lost,
In the wide pathless desert of dim sleep,
That beautiful shape! Does the dark gate of death

Conduct to thy mysterious paradise,
O Sleep? Does the bright arch of rainbow clouds,
And pendent mountains seen in the calm lake,
Lead only to a black and watery depth,
While death's blue vault, with loathliest vapours hung,
Where every shade which the foul grave exhales
Hides its dead eye from the detested day,
Conduct, O Sleep, to thy delightful realms?
This doubt with sudden tide flowed on his heart,
The insatiate hope which it awakened, stung
His brain even like despair.
While day-light held
The sky, the Poet kept mute conference
With his still soul. At night the passion came,
Like the fierce fiend of a distempered dream,
And shook him from his rest, and led him forth
Into the darkness.—As an eagle grasped
In folds of the green serpent, feels her breast
Burn with the poison, and precipitates
Through night and day, tempest, and calm, and cloud,
Frantic with dizzying anguish, her blind flight
O'er the wide aëry wilderness: thus driven
By the bright shadow of that lovely dream,
Beneath the cold glare of the desolate night,
Through tangled swamps and deep precipitous dells,
Startling with careless step the moon-light snake,
He fled. Red morning dawned upon his flight,
Shedding the mockery of its vital hues
Upon his cheek of death. He wandered on
Till vast Aornos seen from Petra's steep
Hung o'er the low horizon like a cloud;
Through Balk, and where the desolated tombs
Of Parthian kings scatter to every wind
Their wasting dust, wildly he wandered on,
Day after day, a weary waste of hours,
Bearing within his life the brooding care
That ever fed on its decaying flame.
And now his limbs were lean; his scattered hair
Sered by the autumn of strange suffering
Sung dirges in the wind; his listless hand
Hung like dead bone within its withered skin;
Life, and the lustre that consumed it, shone

As in a furnace burning secretly
From his dark eyes alone. The cottagers,
Who ministered with human charity
His human wants, beheld with wondering awe
Their fleeting visitant. The mountaineer,
Encountering on some dizzy precipice
That spectral form, deemed that the Spirit of wind
With lightning eyes, and eager breath, and feet
Disturbing not the drifted snow, had paused
In its career: the infant would conceal
His troubled visage in his mother's robe
In terror at the glare of those wild eyes,
To remember their strange light in many a dream
Of after-times; but youthful maidens, taught
By nature, would interpret half the woe
That wasted him, would call him with false names
Brother, and friend, would press his pallid hand
At parting, and watch, dim through tears, the path
Of his departure from their father's door.

At length upon the lone Chorasmian shore
He paused, a wide and melancholy waste
Of putrid marshes. A strong impulse urged
His steps to the sea-shore. A swan was there,
Beside a sluggish stream among the reeds.
It rose as he approached, and with strong wings
Scaling the upward sky, bent its bright course
High over the immeasurable main.
His eyes pursued its flight.—'Thou hast a home,
Beautiful bird; thou voyagest to thine home,
Where thy sweet mate will twine her downy neck
With thine, and welcome thy return with eyes
Bright in the lustre of their own fond joy.
And what am I that I should linger here,
With voice far sweeter than thy dying notes,
Spirit more vast than thine, frame more attuned
To beauty, wasting these surpassing powers
In the deaf air, to the blind earth, and heaven
That echoes not my thoughts?' A gloomy smile
Of desperate hope wrinkled his quivering lips.

For sleep, he knew, kept most relentlessly
Its precious charge, and silent death exposed,
Faithless perhaps as sleep, a shadowy lure,
With doubtful smile mocking its own strange charms.

Startled by his own thoughts he looked around.
There was no fair fiend near him, not a sight
Or sound of awe but in his own deep mind.
A little shallop floating near the shore
Caught the impatient wandering of his gaze.
It had been long abandoned, for its sides
Gaped wide with many a rift, and its frail joints
Swayed with the undulations of the tide.
A restless impulse urged him to embark
And meet lone Death on the drear ocean's waste;
For well he knew that mighty Shadow loves
The slimy caverns of the populous deep.

The day was fair and sunny, sea and sky
Drank its inspiring radiance, and the wind
Swept strongly from the shore, blackening the waves.
Following his eager soul, the wanderer
Leaped in the boat, he spread his cloak aloft
On the bare mast, and took his lonely seat,
And felt the boat speed o'er the tranquil sea
Like a torn cloud before the hurricane.

As one that in a silver vision floats
Obedient to the sweep of odorous winds
Upon resplendent clouds, so rapidly
Along the dark and ruffled waters fled
The straining boat.—A whirlwind swept it on,
With fierce gusts and precipitating force,
Through the white ridges of the chafed sea.
The waves arose. Higher and higher still
Their fierce necks writhed beneath the tempest's scourge
Like serpents struggling in a vulture's grasp.
Calm and rejoicing in the fearful war
Of wave ruining on wave, and blast on blast
Descending, and black flood on whirlpool driven

With dark obliterating course, he sate:
As if their genii were the ministers
Appointed to conduct him to the light
Of those beloved eyes, the Poet sate
Holding the steady helm. Evening came on,
The beams of sunset hung their rainbow hues
High 'mid the shifting domes of sheeted spray
That canopied his path o'er the waste deep;
Twilight, ascending slowly from the east,
Entwin'd in duskier wreaths her braided locks
O'er the fair front and radiant eyes of day;
Night followed, clad with stars. On every side
More horribly the multitudinous streams
Of ocean's mountainous waste to mutual war
Rushed in dark tumult thundering, as to mock
The calm and spangled sky. The little boat
Still fled before the storm; still fled, like foam
Down the steep cataract of a wintry river;
Now pausing on the edge of the riven wave;
Now leaving far behind the bursting mass
That fell, convulsing ocean. Safely fled—
As if that frail and wasted human form,
Had been an elemental god.
At midnight
The moon arose: and lo! the etherial cliffs
Of Caucasus, whose icy summits shone
Among the stars like sunlight, and around
Whose cavern'd base the whirlpools and the waves
Bursting and eddying irresistibly
Rage and resound for ever.—Who shall save?—
The boat fled on,—the boiling torrent drove,—
The crags closed round with black and jagged arms,
The shattered mountain overhung the sea,
And faster still, beyond all human speed,
Suspended on the sweep of the smooth wave,
The little boat was driven. A cavern there
Yawned, and amid its slant and winding depths
Ingulphed the rushing sea. The boat fled on
With unrelaxing speed.—'Vision and Love!'
The Poet cried aloud, 'I have beheld
The path of thy departure. Sleep and death
Shall not divide us long!'

The boat pursued
The windings of the cavern. Day-light shone
At length upon that gloomy river's flow;
Now, where the fiercest war among the waves
Is calm, on the unfathomable stream
The boat moved slowly. Where the mountain, riven,
Exposed those black depths to the azure sky,
Ere yet the flood's enormous volume fell
Even to the base of Caucasus, with sound
That shook the everlasting rocks, the mass
Filled with one whirlpool all that ample chasm;
Stair above stair the eddying waters rose,
Circling immeasurably fast, and laved
With alternating dash the knarled roots
Of mighty trees, that stretched their giant arms
In darkness over it. I' the midst was left,
Reflecting, yet distorting every cloud,
A pool of treacherous and tremendous calm.
Seized by the sway of the ascending stream,
With dizzy swiftness, round, and round, and round,
Ridge after ridge the straining boat arose,
Till on the verge of the extremest curve,
Where, through an opening of the rocky bank,
The waters overflow, and a smooth spot
Of glassy quiet mid those battling tides
Is left, the boat paused shuddering.—Shall it sink
Down the abyss? Shall the reverting stress
Of that resistless gulph embosom it?
Now shall it fall?—A wandering stream of wind,
Breathed from the west, has caught the expanded sail,
And, lo! with gentle motion, between banks
Of mossy slope, and on a placid stream,
Beneath a woven grove it sails, and, hark!
The ghastly torrent mingles its far roar
With the breeze murmuring in the musical woods.
Where the embowering trees recede, and leave
A little space of green expanse, the cove
Is closed by meeting banks, whose yellow flowers
For ever gaze on their own drooping eyes,
Reflected in the crystal calm. The wave
Of the boat's motion marred their pensive task,
Which nought but vagrant bird, or wanton wind,

Or falling spear-grass, or their own decay
Had e'er disturbed before. The Poet longed
To deck with their bright hues his withered hair,
But on his heart its solitude returned,
And he forbore. Not the strong impulse hid
In those flushed cheeks, bent eyes, and shadowy frame,
Had yet performed its ministry: it hung
Upon his life, as lightning in a cloud
Gleams, hovering ere it vanish, ere the floods
Of night close over it.
The noonday sun
Now shone upon the forest, one vast mass
Of mingling shade, whose brown magnificence
A narrow vale embosoms. There, huge caves,
Scooped in the dark base of their aëry rocks
Mocking its moans, respond and roar for ever.
The meeting boughs and implicated leaves
Wove twilight o'er the Poet's path, as led
By love, or dream, or god, or mightier Death,
He sought in Nature's dearest haunt, some bank,
Her cradle, and his sepulchre. More dark
And dark the shades accumulate. The oak,
Expanding its immense and knotty arms,
Embraces the light beech. The pyramids
Of the tall cedar overarching, frame
Most solemn domes within, and far below,
Like clouds suspended in an emerald sky,
The ash and the acacia floating hang
Tremulous and pale. Like restless serpents, clothed
In rainbow and in fire, the parasites,
Starred with ten thousand blossoms, flow around
The gray trunks, and, as gamesome infants' eyes,
With gentle meanings, and most innocent wiles,
Fold their beams round the hearts of those that love,
These twine their tendrils with the wedded boughs
Uniting their close union; the woven leaves
Make net-work of the dark blue light of day,
And the night's noontide clearness, mutable
As shapes in the weird clouds. Soft mossy lawns
Beneath these canopies extend their swells,
Fragrant with perfumed herbs, and eyed with blooms
Minute yet beautiful. One darkest glen

Sends from its woods of musk-rose, twined with jasmine,
A soul-dissolving odour, to invite
To some more lovely mystery. Through the dell,
Silence and Twilight here, twin-sisters, keep
Their noonday watch, and sail among the shades,
Like vaporous shapes half seen; beyond, a well,
Dark, gleaming, and of most translucent wave,
Images all the woven boughs above,
And each depending leaf, and every speck
Of azure sky, darting between their chasms;
Nor aught else in the liquid mirror laves
Its portraiture, but some inconstant star
Between one foliaged lattice twinkling fair,
Or, painted bird, sleeping beneath the moon,
Or gorgeous insect floating motionless,
Unconscious of the day, ere yet his wings
Have spread their glories to the gaze of noon.

Hither the Poet came. His eyes beheld
Their own wan light through the reflected lines
Of his thin hair, distinct in the dark depth
Of that still fountain; as the human heart,
Gazing in dreams over the gloomy grave,
Sees its own treacherous likeness there. He heard
The motion of the leaves, the grass that sprung
Startled and glanced and trembled even to feel
An unaccustomed presence, and the sound
Of the sweet brook that from the secret springs
Of that dark fountain rose. A Spirit seemed
To stand beside him—clothed in no bright robes
Of shadowy silver or enshrining light,
Borrowed from aught the visible world affords
Of grace, or majesty, or mystery;—
But, undulating woods, and silent well,
And leaping rivulet, and evening gloom
Now deepening the dark shades, for speech assuming
Held commune with him, as if he and it
Were all that was,—only . . . when his regard
Was raised by intense pensiveness, . . . two eyes,
Two starry eyes, hung in the gloom of thought,
And seemed with their serene and azure smiles
To beckon him.

Obedient to the light
That shone within his soul, he went, pursuing
The windings of the dell.—The rivulet
Wanton and wild, through many a green ravine
Beneath the forest flowed. Sometimes it fell
Among the moss with hollow harmony
Dark and profound. Now on the polished stones
It danced; like childhood laughing as it went:
Then, through the plain in tranquil wanderings crept,
Reflecting every herb and drooping bud
That overhung its quietness.—'O stream!
Whose source is inaccessibly profound,
Whither do thy mysterious waters tend?
Thou imagest my life. Thy darksome stillness,
Thy dazzling waves, thy loud and hollow gulphs,
Thy searchless fountain, and invisible course
Have each their type in me: and the wide sky,
And measureless ocean may declare as soon
What oozy cavern or what wandering cloud
Contains thy waters, as the universe
Tell where these living thoughts reside, when stretched
Upon thy flowers my bloodless limbs shall waste
I' the passing wind!'
Beside the grassy shore
Of the small stream he went; he did impress
On the green moss his tremulous step, that caught
Strong shuddering from his burning limbs. As one
Roused by some joyous madness from the couch
Of fever, he did move; yet, not like him,
Forgetful of the grave, where, when the flame
Of his frail exultation shall be spent,
He must descend. With rapid steps he went
Beneath the shade of trees, beside the flow
Of the wild babbling rivulet, and now
The forest's solemn canopies were changed
For the uniform and lightsome evening sky.
Gray rocks did peep from the spare moss, and stemmed
The struggling brook: tall spires of windlestrae
Threw their thin shadows down the rugged slope,
And nought but knarled roots of ancient pines
Branchless and blasted, clenched with grasping roots

The unwilling soil. A gradual change was here,
Yet ghastly. For, as fast years flow away,
The smooth brow gathers, and the hair grows thin
And white, and where irradiate dewy eyes
Had shone, gleam stony orbs:—so from his steps
Bright flowers departed, and the beautiful shade
Of the green groves, with all their odorous winds
And musical motions. Calm, he still pursued
The stream, that with a larger volume now
Rolled through the labyrinthine dell; and there
Fretted a path through its descending curves
With its wintry speed. On every side now rose
Rocks, which, in unimaginable forms,
Lifted their black and barren pinnacles
In the light of evening, and its precipice
Obscuring the ravine, disclosed above,
Mid toppling stones, black gulphs and yawning caves,
Whose windings gave ten thousand various tongues
To the loud stream. Lo! where the pass expands
Its stony jaws, the abrupt mountain breaks,
And seems, with its accumulated crags,
To overhang the world: for wide expand
Beneath the wan stars and descending moon
Islanded seas, blue mountains, mighty streams,
Dim tracts and vast, robed in the lustrous gloom
Of leaden-coloured even, and fiery hills
Mingling their flames with twilight, on the verge
Of the remote horizon. The near scene,
In naked and severe simplicity,
Made contrast with the universe. A pine,
Rock-rooted, stretched athwart the vacancy
Its swinging boughs, to each inconstant blast
Yielding one only response, at each pause
In most familiar cadence, with the howl
The thunder and the hiss of homeless streams
Mingling its solemn song, whilst the broad river,
Foaming and hurrying o'er its rugged path,
Fell into that immeasurable void
Scattering its waters to the passing winds.

Yet the gray precipice and solemn pine
And torrent, were not all;—one silent nook
Was there. Even on the edge of that vast mountain,
Upheld by knotty roots and fallen rocks,
It overlooked in its serenity
The dark earth, and the bending vault of stars.
It was a tranquil spot, that seemed to smile
Even in the lap of horror. Ivy clasped
The fissured stones with its entwining arms,
And did embower with leaves for ever green,
And berries dark, the smooth and even space
Of its inviolated floor, and here
The children of the autumnal whirlwind bore,
In wanton sport, those bright leaves, whose decay,
Red, yellow, or etherially pale,
Rivals the pride of summer. 'Tis the haunt
Of every gentle wind, whose breath can teach
The wilds to love tranquillity. One step,
One human step alone, has ever broken
The stillness of its solitude:—one voice
Alone inspired its echoes;—even that voice
Which hither came, floating among the winds,
And led the loveliest among human forms
To make their wild haunts the depository
Of all the grace and beauty that endued
Its motions, render up its majesty,
Scatter its music on the unfeeling storm,
And to the damp leaves and blue cavern mould,
Nurses of rainbow flowers and branching moss,
Commit the colours of that varying cheek,
That snowy breast, those dark and drooping eyes.

The dim and horned moon hung low, and poured
A sea of lustre on the horizon's verge
That overflowed its mountains. Yellow mist
Filled the unbounded atmosphere, and drank
Wan moonlight even to fullness: not a star
Shone, not a sound was heard; the very winds,
Danger's grim playmates, on that precipice
Slept, clasped in his embrace.—O, storm of death!
Whose sightless speed divides this sullen night:
And thou, colossal Skeleton, that, still

Guiding its irresistible career
In thy devastating omnipotence,
Art king of this frail world, from the red field
Of slaughter, from the reeking hospital,
The patriot's sacred couch, the snowy bed
Of innocence, the scaffold and the throne,
A mighty voice invokes thee. Ruin calls
His brother Death. A rare and regal prey
He hath prepared, prowling around the world;
Glutted with which thou mayst repose, and men
Go to their graves like flowers or creeping worms,
Nor ever more offer at thy dark shrine
The unheeded tribute of a broken heart.

When on the threshold of the green recess
The wanderer's footsteps fell, he knew that death
Was on him. Yet a little, ere it fled,
Did he resign his high and holy soul
To images of the majestic past,
That paused within his passive being now,
Like winds that bear sweet music, when they breathe
Through some dim latticed chamber. He did place
His pale lean hand upon the rugged trunk
Of the old pine. Upon an ivied stone
Reclined his languid head, his limbs did rest,
Diffused and motionless, on the smooth brink
Of that obscurest chasm;—and thus he lay,
Surrendering to their final impulses
The hovering powers of life. Hope and despair,
The torturers, slept; no mortal pain or fear
Marred his repose, the influxes of sense,
And his own being unalloyed by pain,
Yet feebler and more feeble, calmly fed
The stream of thought, till he lay breathing there
At peace, and faintly smiling:—his last sight
Was the great moon, which o'er the western line
Of the wide world her mighty horn suspended,
With whose dun beams inwoven darkness seemed
To mingle. Now upon the jagged hills
It rests, and still as the divided frame
Of the vast meteor sunk, the Poet's blood,
That ever beat in mystic sympathy

With nature's ebb and flow, grew feebler still:
And when two lessening points of light alone
Gleamed through the darkness, the alternate gasp
Of his faint respiration scarce did stir
The stagnate night:—till the minutest ray
Was quenched, the pulse yet lingered in his heart.
It paused—it fluttered. But when heaven remained
Utterly black, the murky shades involved
An image, silent, cold, and motionless,
As their own voiceless earth and vacant air.
Even as a vapour fed with golden beams
That ministered on sunlight, ere the west
Eclipses it, was now that wonderous frame—
No sense, no motion, no divinity—
A fragile lute, on whose harmonious strings
The breath of heaven did wander—a bright stream
Once fed with many-voiced waves—a dream
Of youth, which night and time have quenched for ever,
Still, dark, and dry, and unremembered now.

O, for Medea's wondrous alchemy,
Which wheresoe'er it fell made the earth gleam
With bright flowers, and the wintry boughs exhale
From vernal blooms fresh fragrance! O, that God,
Profuse of poisons, would concede the chalice
Which but one living man has drained, who now,
Vessel of deathless wrath, a slave that feels
No proud exemption in the blighting curse
He bears, over the world wanders for ever,
Lone as incarnate death! O, that the dream
Of dark magician in his visioned cave,
Raking the cinders of a crucible
For life and power, even when his feeble hand
Shakes in its last decay, were the true law
Of this so lovely world! But thou art fled
Like some frail exhalation; which the dawn
Robes in its golden beams,—ah! thou hast fled!
The brave, the gentle, and the beautiful,
The child of grace and genius. Heartless things
Are done and said i' the world, and many worms
And beasts and men live on, and mighty Earth
From sea and mountain, city and wilderness,

In vesper low or joyous orison,
Lifts still its solemn voice:—but thou art fled—
Thou canst no longer know or love the shapes
Of this phantasmal scene, who have to thee
Been purest ministers, who are, alas!
Now thou art not. Upon those pallid lips
So sweet even in their silence, on those eyes
That image sleep in death, upon that form
Yet safe from the worm's outrage, let no tear
Be shed—not even in thought. Nor, when those hues
Are gone, and those divinest lineaments,
Worn by the senseless wind, shall live alone
In the frail pauses of this simple strain,
Let not high verse, mourning the memory
Of that which is no more, or painting's woe
Or sculpture, speak in feeble imagery
Their own cold powers. Art and eloquence,
And all the shews o' the world are frail and vain
To weep a loss that turns their lights to shade.
It is a woe too 'deep for tears,' when all
Is reft at once, when some surpassing Spirit,
Whose light adorned the world around it, leaves
Those who remain behind, not sobs or groans,
The passionate tumult of a clinging hope;
But pale despair and cold tranquillity,
Nature's vast frame, the web of human things,
Birth and the grave, that are not as they were.

Verses written on receiving a Celandine in a letter from England

I thought of thee, fair Celandine,
As of a flower aery blue
Yet small—thy leaves methought were wet
With the light of morning dew;
In the same glen thy star did shine
As the primrose and the violet,
And the wild briar bent over thee
And the woodland brook danced under thee.

Lovely thou wert in thine own glen
Ere thou didst dwell in song or story,
Ere the moonlight of a Poet's mind
Had arrayed thee with the glory
Whose fountains are the hearts of men—
Many a thing of vital kind
Had fed and sheltered under thee,
Had nourished their thoughts near to thee.

Yes, gentle flower, in thy recess
None might a sweeter aspect wear:
Thy young bud drooped so gracefully,
Thou wert so very fair—
Among the fairest ere the stress
Of exile, death and injury
Thus withering and deforming thee
Had made a mournful type of thee;

A type of that whence I and thou
Are thus familiar, Celandine—
A deathless Poet whose young prime
Was as serene as thine,
But he is changed and withered now,
Fallen on a cold and evil time;
His heart is gone—his fame is dim
And Infamy sits mocking him.

Celandine! Thou art pale and dead,
Changed from thy fresh and woodland state.
Oh! that thy bard were cold, but he

Has lived too long and late.
Would he were in an honoured grave,
But that, men say, now must not be
Since he for impious gold could sell
The love of those who loved him well.

That he, with all hope else of good,
Should be thus transitory
I marvel not—but that his lays
Have spared not their own glory,
That blood, even the foul god of blood,
With most inexpiable praise,
Freedom and truth left desolate,
He has been bought to celebrate!

They were his hopes which he doth scorn,
They were his foes the fight that won;
That sanction and that condemnation
Are now forever gone.
They need them not! Truth may not mourn
That with a liar's inspiration
Her majesty he did disown
Ere he could overlive his own.

They need them not, for Liberty,
Justice and philosophic truth
From his divine and simple song
Shall draw immortal youth
When he and thou shall cease to be,
Or be some other thing, so long
As men may breathe or flowers may blossom
O'er the wide Earth's maternal bosom.

The stem whence thou wert disunited
Since thy poor self was banished hither,
Now by that priest of Nature's care
Who sent thee forth to wither
His window with its blooms has lighted,
And I shall see thy brethren there,
And each like thee will aye betoken
Love sold, hope dead, and honour broken.

Hymn to Intellectual Beauty
[Version A]

1

The awful shadow of some unseen Power
Floats tho' unseen amongst us,—visiting
This various world with as inconstant wing
As summer winds that creep from flower to flower.—
Like moonbeams that behind some piny mountain shower,
It visits with inconstant glance
Each human heart and countenance;
Like hues and harmonies of evening,—
Like clouds in starlight widely spread,—
Like memory of music fled,—
Like aught that for its grace may be
Dear, and yet dearer for its mystery.

2

Spirit of BEAUTY, that doth consecrate
With thine own hues all thou dost shine upon
Of human thought or form,—where art thou gone?
Why dost thou pass away and leave our state,
This dim vast vale of tears, vacant and desolate?
Ask why the sunlight not forever
Weaves rainbows o'er yon mountain river,
Why aught should fail and fade that once is shewn,
Why fear and dream and death and birth
Cast on the daylight of this earth
Such gloom,—why man has such a scope
For love and hate, despondency and hope?

3

No voice from some sublimer world hath ever
To sage or poet these responses given—
Therefore the name of God and ghosts, and Heaven,
Remain the records of their vain endeavour,
Frail spells—whose uttered charm might not avail to sever,
From all we hear and all we see,
Doubt, chance, and mutability.
Thy light alone—like mist o'er mountains driven,
Or music by the night wind sent

Hymn to Intellectual Beauty
[Version B]

I

The Lovely shadow of some awful Power
   Walks though unseen amongst us, visiting
   This peopled world with as inconstant wing
As summer winds that creep from flower to flower,
Like moonbeams that behind some piny mountain shower
   It visits with a wavering glance
   Each human heart & countenance;—
Like hues and harmonies of evening—
   Like clouds in starlight widely spread
   Like memory of music fled
   Like aught that for its grace might be
Dear, & yet dearer for its mystery.

2

Shadow of Beauty!—that doth consecrate
   With thine own hues all thou dost fall upon
   Of human thought or form, Where art thou gone
Why dost thou pass away & leave our state
A dark deep vale of tears, vacant & desolate?
   Ask why the sun light not forever
   Weaves rainbows o'er yon mountain river
Ask why aught fades away that once is shewn
   Ask wherefore dream & death & birth
   Cast on the daylight of this earth
Such gloom,—why man has such a scope
For love & joy despondency & hope.

3

No voice from some sublimer world hath ever
   To wisest poets these responses given
   Therefore the name of God & Ghosts & Heaven
Remain yet records of their vain Endeavour—
Frail spells, whose uttered charm might not avail to sever
   From what we feel & what we see
   Doubt, Chance & mutability.
Thy shade alone like mists o'er mountains driven
   Or Music by the night-wind sent

[*Version A continued*]

Thro' strings of some still instrument,
Or moonlight on a midnight stream,
Gives grace and truth to life's unquiet dream.

4

Love, Hope, and Self-esteem, like clouds depart
And come, for some uncertain moments lent.
Man were immortal, and omnipotent,
Didst thou, unknown and awful as thou art,
Keep with thy glorious train firm state within his heart.
Thou messenger of sympathies,
That wax and wane in lovers' eyes—
Thou—that to human thought art nourishment,
Like darkness to a dying flame!
Depart not as thy shadow came,
Depart not—lest the grave should be,
Like life and fear, a dark reality.

5

While yet a boy I sought for ghosts, and sped
Thro' many a listening chamber, cave and ruin,
And starlight wood, with fearful steps pursuing
Hopes of high talk with the departed dead.
I called on poisonous names with which our youth is fed,
I was not heard—I saw them not—
When musing deeply on the lot
Of life, at that sweet time when winds are wooing
All vital things that wake to bring
News of buds and blossoming,—
Sudden, thy shadow fell on me;
I shrieked, and clasped my hands in extacy!

6

I vowed that I would dedicate my powers
To thee and thine—have I not kept the vow?
With beating heart and streaming eyes, even now
I call the phantoms of a thousand hours
Each from his voiceless grave: they have in visioned bowers
Of studious zeal or love's delight
Outwatched with me the envious night—

[*Version B continued*]

Thro' strings of some mute instrument
Or Moonlight on a forest stream
Gives truth & grace to life's tumultuous dream

4

Love, hope & self-esteem like clouds depart—
And come, for some uncertain moments lent.—
Man were immortal & omnipotent
Didst thou, unknown & awful as thou art
Keep with this glorious train firm state within his heart.
Thou messenger of sympathies
That wax & wane in lovers' eyes
Thou that to the poets thought art nourishment
As darkness to a dying flame
Depart not as thy shadow came!
Depart not!—lest the grave should be
Like life & fear a dark reality

5

While yet a boy I sought for Ghosts, & sped
Thro' many a lonely chamber, vault & ruin
And starlight wood, with fearful step pursuing
Hopes of strange converse with the storied dead
I called on that false name with which our youth is fed
He heard me not—I saw them not—
When musing deeply on the lot
Of Life, at that sweet time when winds are wooing
All vocal things that live to bring
News of buds & blossoming—
Sudden thy shadow fell on me
I shrieked & clasped my hands in extasy.

6

I vowed that I would dedicate my powers
To thee & thine—have I not kept the vow?
With streaming eyes & panting heart even now
I call the spectres of a thousand hours
Each from his voiceless grave, who have in visioned bowers
Of studious zeal or love's delight
Outwatched with me the waning night

[*Version A continued*]

They know that never joy illumed my brow
    Unlinked with hope that thou wouldst free
    This world from its dark slavery,
    That thou—O awful LOVELINESS,
Wouldst give whate'er these words cannot express.

7

The day becomes more solemn and serene
    When noon is past—there is a harmony
    In autumn, and a lustre in its sky,
Which thro' the summer is not heard or seen,
As if it could not be, as if it had not been!
    Thus let thy power, which like the truth
    Of nature on my passive youth
Descended, to my onward life supply
    Its calm—to one who worships thee,
    And every form containing thee,
    Whom, SPIRIT fair, thy spells did bind
To fear himself, and love all human kind.

[*Version B continued*]

To tell that never joy illumed my brow
Unlinked with hope that thou wouldst free
This world from its dark slavery
That thou, O, awful Loveliness!
Would give whate'er these words cannot express.

7

The day becomes more solemn & serene
When Noon is past—there is a harmony
In Autumn & a lustre in the sky
Which thro' the summer is not heard or seen
As if it could not be—as if it had not been—
Thus let thy shade—which like the truth
Of Nature on my passive youth
Descended, to my onward life supply
Its hues, to one that worships thee
And every form containing thee
Whom fleeting power! thy spells did bind
To fear himself & love all human Kind.

Mont Blanc

[Version A]

Lines Written in the Vale of Chamouni

I

The everlasting universe of things
Flows through the mind, and rolls its rapid waves,
Now dark—now glittering—now reflecting gloom—
Now lending splendour, where from secret springs
The source of human thought its tribute brings
Of waters,—with a sound but half its own,
Such as a feeble brook will oft assume
In the wild woods, among the mountains lone,
Where waterfalls around it leap for ever,
Where woods and winds contend, and a vast river
Over its rocks ceaselessly bursts and raves.

II

Thus thou, Ravine of Arve—dark, deep Ravine—
Thou many-coloured, many-voiced vale,
Over whose pines, and crags, and caverns sail
Fast cloud shadows and sunbeams: awful scene,
Where Power in likeness of the Arve comes down
From the ice gulphs that gird his secret throne,
Bursting through these dark mountains like the flame
Of lightning thro' the tempest;—thou dost lie,
Thy giant brood of pines around thee clinging,
Children of elder time, in whose devotion
The chainless winds still come and ever came
To drink their odours, and their mighty swinging
To hear—an old and solemn harmony;
Thine earthly rainbows stretched across the sweep
Of the ethereal waterfall, whose veil
Robes some unsculptured image; the strange sleep
Which when the voices of the desart fail
Wraps all in its own deep eternity;—
Thy caverns echoing to the Arve's commotion,
A loud, lone sound no other sound can tame;
Thou art pervaded with that ceaseless motion,
Thou art the path of that unresting sound—
Dizzy Ravine! and when I gaze on thee

Mont Blanc

[Version B]

Scene—Pont Pellisier in the vale of Servox

In day the eternal universe of things
Flows through the mind, & rolls its rapid waves
Now dark, now glittering; now reflecting gloom
Now lending splendour, where, from secret caves
The source of human thought its tribute brings
Of waters, with a sound not all it's own:
Such as a feeble brook will oft assume
In the wild woods among the mountains lone
Where waterfalls around it leap forever
Where winds & woods contend, & a vast river
Over its rocks ceaselessly bursts and raves

Thus thou Ravine of Arve, dark deep ravine,
Thou many coloured, many voiced vale!
Over whose rocks & pines & caverns sail
Fast cloud shadows & sunbeams—awful scene,
Where Power in likeness of the Arve comes down
From the ice gulphs that gird his secret throne
Bursting through these dark mountains like the flame
Of lightning thro the tempest—thou dost lie
Thy giant brood of pines around thee clinging
Children of elder time, in whose devotion
The charmed winds still come, & ever came
To drink thier odours, & thier mighty swinging
To hear, an old and solemn harmony;
Thine earthly rainbows stretched across the sweep
Of the aerial waterfall, whose veil
Robes some unsculptured image; even the sleep
The sudden pause that does inhabit thee
Which when the voices of the desart fail
And its hues wane, doth blend them all & steep
Thier periods in its own eternity;
Thy caverns echoing to the Arve's commotion
A loud lone sound no other sound can tame:
Thou art pervaded with such ceaseless motion
Thou art the path of that unresting sound
Ravine of Arve! & when I gaze on thee

[*Version A continued*]

I seem as in a trance sublime and strange
To muse on my own separate phantasy,
My own, my human mind, which passively
Now renders and receives fast influencings,
Holding an unremitting interchange
With the clear universe of things around;
One legion of wild thoughts, whose wandering wings
Now float above thy darkness, and now rest
Where that or thou art no unbidden guest,
In the still cave of the witch Poesy,
Seeking among the shadows that pass by,
Ghosts of all things that are, some shade of thee,
Some phantom, some faint image; till the breast
From which they fled recalls them, thou art there!

III

Some say that gleams of a remoter world
Visit the soul in sleep,—that death is slumber,
And that its shapes the busy thoughts outnumber
Of those who wake and live.—I look on high;
Has some unknown omnipotence unfurled
The veil of life and death? or do I lie
In dream, and does the mightier world of sleep
Spread far around and inaccessibly
Its circles? For the very spirit fails,
Driven like a homeless cloud from steep to steep
That vanishes among the viewless gales!
Far, far above, piercing the infinite sky,
Mont Blanc appears,—still, snowy, and serene—
Its subject mountains their unearthly forms
Pile around it, ice and rock; broad vales between
Of frozen floods, unfathomable deeps,
Blue as the overhanging heaven, that spread
And wind among the accumulated steeps;
A desart peopled by the storms alone,
Save when the eagle brings some hunter's bone,
And the wolf tracts her there—how hideously
Its shapes are heaped around! rude, bare, and high,
Ghastly, and scarred, and riven.—Is this the scene
Where the old Earthquake-daemon taught her young

[*Version B continued*]

I seem as in a vision deep & strange
To muse on my own various phantasy
My own, my human mind . . which passively
Now renders & recieves fast influencings
Holding an unforeseeing interchange
With the clear universe of things around:
A legion of swift thoughts, whose wandering wings
Now float above thy darkness, & now rest
Near the still cave of the witch Poesy
Seeking among the shadows that pass by,
Ghosts of the things that are, some form like thee,
Some spectre, some faint image; till the breast
From which they fled recalls them—thou art there

Some say that gleams of a remoter world
Visit the soul in sleep—that death is slumber
And that its shapes the busy thoughts outnumber
Of those who wake & live. I look on high
Has some unknown omnipotence unfurled
The vail of life & death? or do I lie
In dream, & does the mightier world of sleep
Spread far around, & inaccessibly
Its circles?—for the very spirit fails
Driven like a homeless cloud from steep to steep
That vanishes among the viewless gales.—
Far, far above, piercing the infinite sky
Mont Blanc appears, still, snowy & serene,
Its subject mountains thier unearthly forms
Pile round it—ice & rock—broad chasms between
Of frozen waves, unfathomable deeps
Blue as the overhanging Heaven, that spread
And wind among the accumulated steeps,
Vast desarts, peopled by the storms alone
Save when the eagle brings some hunter's bone
And the wolf watches her—how hideously
Its rocks are heaped around, rude bare & high
Ghastly & scarred & riven!—is this the scene
Where the old Earthquake demon taught her young

[*Version A continued*]

Ruin? Were these their toys? or did a sea
Of fire, envelope once this silent snow?
None can reply—all seems eternal now.
The wilderness has a mysterious tongue
Which teaches awful doubt, or faith so mild,
So solemn, so serene, that man may be
But for such faith with nature reconciled;
Thou hast a voice, great Mountain, to repeal
Large codes of fraud and woe; not understood
By all, but which the wise, and great, and good
Interpret, or make felt, or deeply feel.

IV

The fields, the lakes, the forests, and the streams,
Ocean, and all the living things that dwell
Within the daedal earth; lightning, and rain,
Earthquake, and fiery flood, and hurricane,
The torpor of the year when feeble dreams
Visit the hidden buds, or dreamless sleep
Holds every future leaf and flower;—the bound
With which from that detested trance they leap;
The works and ways of man, their death and birth,
And that of him and all that his may be;
All things that move and breathe with toil and sound
Are born and die; revolve, subside and swell.
Power dwells apart in its tranquillity
Remote, serene, and inaccessible:
And *this*, the naked countenance of earth,
On which I gaze, even these primaeval mountains
Teach the adverting mind. The glaciers creep
Like snakes that watch their prey, from their far fountains,
Slow rolling on; there, many a precipice,
Frost and the Sun in scorn of mortal power
Have piled: dome, pyramid, and pinnacle,
A city of death, distinct with many a tower
And wall impregnable of beaming ice.
Yet not a city, but a flood of ruin
Is there, that from the boundaries of the sky
Rolls its perpetual stream; vast pines are strewing
Its destined path, or in the mangled soil

[*Version B continued*]

Ruin? were these thier toys? or did a sea
Of fire envelope once this silent snow?
None can reply—all seems eternal now.
This wilderness has a mysterious tongue
Which teaches awful doubt, or faith so mild
So simple, so serene that man may be
In such a faith with Nature reconciled.
Ye have a doctrine Mountains to repeal
Large codes of fraud & woe—not understood
By all, but which the wise & great & good
Interpret, or make felt, or deeply feel.

The fields, the lakes, the forests & the streams
Ocean, & all the living things that dwell
Within the dædal Earth, lightning & rain,
Earthquake & lava flood & hurricane—
The torpor of the year, when feeble dreams
Visit the hidden buds, or dreamless sleep
Holds every future leaf & flower—the bound
With which from that detested trance they leap;
The works & ways of man, thier death & birth
And that of him, & all that his may be,
All things that move & breathe with toil & sound
Are born & die, revolve subside & swell—
Power dwells apart in deep tranquillity,
Remote, sublime, & inaccessible,
And this, the naked countenance of Earth
On which I gaze—even these primæval mountains
Teach the adverting mind.—the Glaciers creep
Like snakes that watch thier prey, from thier far fountains
Slow rolling on:—there, many a precipice
Frost & the Sun in scorn of human power
Have piled: dome, pyramid & pinnacle
A city of death, distinct with many a tower
And wall impregnable of shining ice . . . .
A city's phantom . . . but a flood of ruin
Is there, that from the boundaries of the sky
Rolls its eternal stream . . vast pines are strewing
Its destined path, or in the mangled soil

[*Version A continued*]

Branchless and shattered stand; the rocks, drawn down
From yon remotest waste, have overthrown
The limits of the dead and living world,
Never to be reclaimed. The dwelling-place
Of insects, beasts, and birds, becomes its spoil;
Their food and their retreat for ever gone,
So much of life and joy is lost. The race
Of man, flies far in dread; his work and dwelling
Vanish, like smoke before the tempest's stream,
And their place is not known. Below, vast caves
Shine in the rushing torrents' restless gleam,
Which from those secret chasms in tumult welling
Meet in the vale, and one majestic River,
The breath and blood of distant lands, for ever
Rolls its loud waters to the ocean waves,
Breathes its swift vapours to the circling air.

V

Mont Blanc yet gleams on high:—the power is there,
The still and solemn power of many sights,
And many sounds, and much of life and death.
In the calm darkness of the moonless nights,
In the lone glare of day, the snows descend
Upon that Mountain; none beholds them there,
Nor when the flakes burn in the sinking sun,
Or the star-beams dart through them:—Winds contend
Silently there, and heap the snow with breath
Rapid and strong, but silently! Its home
The voiceless lightning in these solitudes
Keeps innocently, and like vapour broods
Over the snow. The secret strength of things
Which governs thought, and to the infinite dome
Of heaven is as a law, inhabits thee!
And what were thou, and earth, and stars, and sea,
If to the human mind's imaginings
Silence and solitude were vacancy?

[*Version B continued*]

Branchless & shattered stand—the rocks drawn down
From yon remotest waste have overthrown
The limits of the dead & living world
Never to be reclaimed—the dwelling place
Of insects beasts & birds becomes its spoil,
Thier food & thier retreat for ever gone
So much of life & joy is lost—the race
Of man flies far in dread. his work & dwelling
Vanish like smoke before the tempests stream
And thier place is not known:—below, vast caves
Shine in the gushing torrents' restless gleam
Which from those secret chasms in tumult welling
Meet in the vale—& one majestic river
The breath & blood of distant lands, forever
Rolls its loud waters to the Ocean waves
Breathes its swift vapours to the circling air.

Mont Blanc yet gleams on high—the Power is there
The still & solemn Power of many sights
And many sounds, & much of life & death.
In the calm darkness of the moonless nights
Or the lone light of day the snows descend
Upon that mountain—none beholds them there—
Nor when the sunset wraps thier flakes in fire
Or the starbeams dart thro them—winds contend
Silently there, & heap the snows, with breath
Blasting & swift—but silently—its home
The voiceless lightning in these solitudes
Keeps innocently, & like vapour broods
Over the snow. the secret strength of things
Which governs thought, & to the infinite dome
Of Heaven is as a collumn, rests on thee,
And what were thou & Earth & Stars & Sea
If to the human minds imaginings
Silence and solitude were Vacancy

Dedication
before LAON AND CYTHNA

THERE IS NO DANGER TO A MAN, THAT KNOWS WHAT LIFE AND DEATH IS: THERE'S NOT ANY LAW EXCEEDS HIS KNOWLEDGE; NEITHER IS IT LAWFUL THAT HE SHOULD STOOP TO ANY OTHER LAW.

CHAPMAN.

TO MARY — —

1

So now my summer-task is ended, Mary,
And I return to thee, mine own heart's home;
As to his Queen some victor Knight of Faëry,
Earning bright spoils for her inchanted dome;
Nor thou disdain, that ere my fame become
A star among the stars of mortal night,
If it indeed may cleave its natal gloom,
Its doubtful promise thus I would unite
With thy beloved name, thou Child of love and light.

2

The toil which stole from thee so many an hour,
Is ended,—and the fruit is at thy feet!
No longer where the woods to frame a bower
With interlaced branches mix and meet,
Or where with sound like many voices sweet,
Water-falls leap among wild islands green,
Which framed for my lone boat a lone retreat
Of moss-grown trees and weeds, shall I be seen:
But beside thee, where still my heart has ever been.

3

Thoughts of great deeds were mine, dear Friend, when first
The clouds which wrap this world from youth did pass.
I do remember well the hour which burst
My spirit's sleep: a fresh May-dawn it was,
When I walked forth upon the glittering grass,
And wept, I knew not why; until there rose

From the near school-room, voices, that, alas!
Were but one echo from a world of woes—
The harsh and grating strife of tyrants and of foes.

4

And then I clasped my hands and looked around—
But none was near to mock my streaming eyes,
Which poured their warm drops on the sunny ground—
So without shame, I spake:—'I will be wise,
And just, and free, and mild, if in me lies
Such power, for I grow weary to behold
The selfish and the strong still tyrannise
Without reproach or check.' I then controuled
My tears, my heart grew calm, and I was meek and bold.

5

And from that hour did I with earnest thought
Heap knowledge from forbidden mines of lore,
Yet nothing that my tyrants knew or taught
I cared to learn, but from that secret store
Wrought linked armour for my soul, before
It might walk forth to war among mankind;
Thus power and hope were strengthened more and more
Within me, till there came upon my mind
A sense of loneliness, a thirst with which I pined.

6

Alas, that love should be a blight and snare
To those who seek all sympathies in one!—
Such once I sought in vain; then black despair,
The shadow of a starless night, was thrown
Over the world in which I moved alone:—
Yet never found I one not false to me,
Hard hearts, and cold, like weights of icy stone
Which crushed and withered mine, that could not be
Aught but a lifeless clog, until revived by thee.

7

Thou Friend, whose presence on my wintry heart
Fell, like bright Spring upon some herbless plain;
How beautiful and calm and free thou wert
In thy young wisdom, when the mortal chain

Of Custom thou didst burst and rend in twain,
And walked as free as light the clouds among,
Which many an envious slave then breathed in vain
From his dim dungeon, and my spirit sprung
To meet thee from the woes which had begirt it long.

8

No more alone through the world's wilderness,
Although I trod the paths of high intent,
I journeyed now: no more companionless,
Where solitude is like despair, I went.—
There is the wisdom of a stern content
When Poverty can blight the just and good,
When Infamy dares mock the innocent,
And cherished friends turn with the multitude
To trample: this was ours, and we unshaken stood!

9

Now has descended a serener hour,
And with inconstant fortune, friends return;
Tho' suffering leaves the knowledge and the power
Which says:—Let scorn be not repaid with scorn.
And from thy side two gentle babes are born
To fill our home with smiles, and thus are we
Most fortunate beneath life's beaming morn;
And these delights, and thou, have been to me
The parents of the Song I consecrate to thee.

10

Is it, that now my inexperienced fingers
But strike the prelude of a loftier strain?
Or, must the lyre on which my spirit lingers
Soon pause in silence, ne'er to sound again,
Tho' it might shake the Anarch Custom's reign,
And charm the minds of men to Truth's own sway
Holier than was Amphion's? I would fain
Reply in hope—but I am worn away,
And Death and Love are yet contending for their prey.

11

And what art thou? I know, but dare not speak:
Time may interpret to his silent years.
Yet in the paleness of thy thoughtful cheek,
And in the light thine ample forehead wears,
And in thy sweetest smiles, and in thy tears,
And in thy gentle speech, a prophecy
Is whispered, to subdue my fondest fears:
And thro' thine eyes, even in thy soul I see
A lamp of vestal fire burning internally.

12

They say that thou wert lovely from thy birth,
Of glorious parents, thou aspiring Child.
I wonder not—for One then left this earth
Whose life was like a setting planet mild,
Which clothed thee in the radiance undefiled
Of its departing glory; still her fame
Shines on thee, thro' the tempests dark and wild
Which shake these latter days; and thou canst claim
The shelter, from thy Sire, of an immortal name.

13

One voice came forth from many a mighty spirit,
Which was the echo of three thousand years;
And the tumultuous world stood mute to hear it,
As some lone man who in a desart hears
The music of his home:—unwonted fears
Fell on the pale oppressors of our race,
And Faith, and Custom, and low-thoughted cares,
Like thunder-stricken dragons, for a space
Left the torn human heart, their food and dwelling-place.

14

Truth's deathless voice pauses among mankind!
If there must be no response to my cry—
If men must rise and stamp with fury blind
On his pure name who loves them,—thou and I,
Sweet Friend! can look from our tranquillity
Like lamps into the world's tempestuous night,—
Two tranquil stars, while clouds are passing by
Which wrap them from the foundering seaman's sight,
That burn from year to year with unextinguished light.

To Constantia

Thy voice, slow rising like a spirit, lingers
O'er-shadowing me with soft and lulling wings;
The blood and life within thy snowy fingers
Teach witchcraft to the instrumental strings.
  My brain is wild, my breath comes quick,
  The blood is listening in my frame,
  And thronging shadows fast and thick
  Fall on my overflowing eyes,
  My heart is quivering like a flame;
As morning dew, that in the sunbeam dies,
I am dissolved in these consuming ecstasies.

I have no life, Constantia, but in thee;
Whilst, like the world-surrounding air, thy song
Flows on, and fills all things with melody:
Now is thy voice a tempest, swift and strong,
  On which, as one in trance upborne,
  Secure o'er woods and waves I sweep
  Rejoicing, like a cloud of morn:
  Now 'tis the breath of summer's night
  Which, where the starry waters sleep
Round western isles with incense blossoms bright,
Lingering, suspends my soul in its voluptuous flight.

A deep and breathless awe, like the swift change
Of dreams unseen, but felt in youthful slumbers;
Wild, sweet, yet incommunicably strange,
Thou breathest now, in fast ascending numbers:
  The cope of heaven seems rent and cloven
  By the enchantment of thy strain,
  And o'er my shoulders wings are woven
  To follow its sublime career,
  Beyond the mighty moons that wane
Upon the verge of nature's utmost sphere,
Till the world's shadowy walls are past, and disappear.

Cease, cease—for such wild lessons madmen learn:
Long thus to sink—thus to be lost and die
Perhaps is death indeed—Constantia turn!
Yes! in thine eyes a power like light doth lie,
  Even though the sounds its voice that were
  Between thy lips are laid to sleep—
  Within thy breath and on thy hair
  Like odour it is lingering yet—
  And from thy touch like fire doth leap:
Even while I write my burning cheeks are wet—
Such things the heart can feel and learn, but not forget!

Ozymandias

I met a traveller from an antique land,
Who said—'Two vast and trunkless legs of stone
Stand in the desart . . . Near them, on the sand,
Half sunk a shattered visage lies, whose frown,
And wrinkled lip, and sneer of cold command,
Tell that its sculptor well those passions read
Which yet survive, stamped on these lifeless things,
The hand that mocked them, and the heart that fed;
And on the pedestal, these words appear:
"My name is Ozymandias, King of Kings,
Look on my Works ye Mighty, and despair!"
No thing beside remains. Round the decay
Of that colossal Wreck, boundless and bare
The lone and level sands stretch far away.'—

Lines
Written among the Euganean Hills, October, 1818

Many a green isle needs must be
In the deep wide sea of misery,
Or the mariner, worn and wan,
Never thus could voyage on
Day and night, and night and day,
Drifting on his dreary way,
With the solid darkness black

Closing round his vessel's track;
Whilst above the sunless sky,
Big with clouds, hangs heavily,
And behind the tempest fleet
Hurries on with lightning feet,
Riving sail, and cord, and plank,
Till the ship has almost drank
Death from the o'er-brimming deep;
And sinks down, down, like that sleep
When the dreamer seems to be
Weltering through eternity;
And the dim low line before
Of a dark and distant shore
Still recedes, as ever still
Longing with divided will,
But no power to seek or shun,
He is ever drifted on
O'er the unreposing wave
To the haven of the grave.
What, if there no friends will greet;
What, if there no heart will meet
His with love's impatient beat;
Wander wheresoe'er he may,
Can he dream before that day
To find refuge from distress
In friendship's smile, in love's caress?
Then 'twill wreak him little woe
Whether such there be or no:
Senseless is the breast, and cold,
Which relenting love would fold;
Bloodless are the veins and chill
Which the pulse of pain did fill;
Every little living nerve
That from bitter words did swerve
Round the tortured lips and brow,
Are like sapless leaflets now
Frozen upon December's bough.
On the beach of a northern sea
Which tempests shake eternally,
As once the wretch there lay to sleep,
Lies a solitary heap,
One white skull and seven dry bones,

On the margin of the stones,
Where a few grey rushes stand,
Boundaries of the sea and land:
Nor is heard one voice of wail
But the sea-mews, as they sail
O'er the billows of the gale;
Or the whirlwind up and down
Howling, like a slaughtered town,
When a King in glory rides
Through the pomp of fratricides:
Those unburied bones around
There is many a mournful sound;
There is no lament for him,
Like a sunless vapour dim
Who once clothed with life and thought
What now moves nor murmurs not.

Aye, many flowering islands lie
In the waters of wide Agony:
To such a one this morn was led
My bark by soft winds piloted—
'Mid the mountains Euganean
I stood listening to the paean
With which the legioned rooks did hail
The sun's uprise majestical;
Gathering round with wings all hoar,
Thro' the dewy mist they soar
Like grey shades, till th' eastern heaven
Bursts, and then, as clouds of even
Flecked with fire and azure lie
In the unfathomable sky,
So their plumes of purple grain,
Starred with drops of golden rain,
Gleam above the sunlight woods,
As in silent multitudes
On the morning's fitful gale
Thro' the broken mist they sail,
And the vapours cloven and gleaming
Follow down the dark steep streaming,
Till all is bright, and clear, and still,
Round the solitary hill.

Beneath is spread like a green sea
The waveless plain of Lombardy,
Bounded by the vaporous air,
Islanded by cities fair;
Underneath day's azure eyes
Ocean's nursling, Venice lies,
A peopled labyrinth of walls,
Amphitrite's destined halls
Which her hoary sire now paves
With his blue and beaming waves.
Lo! the sun upsprings behind,
Broad, red, radiant, half reclined
On the level quivering line
Of the waters chrystalline;
And before that chasm of light,
As within a furnace bright,
Column, tower, and dome, and spire,
Shine like obelisks of fire,
Pointing with inconstant motion
From the altar of dark ocean
To the sapphire-tinted skies;
As the flames of sacrifice
From the marble shrines did rise,
As to pierce the dome of gold
Where Apollo spoke of old.

Sun-girt City, thou hast been
Ocean's child, and then his queen;
Now is come a darker day,
And thou soon must be his prey,
If the power that raised thee here
Hallow so thy watery bier.
A less drear ruin then than now,
With thy conquest-branded brow
Stooping to the slave of slaves
From thy throne, among the waves
Wilt thou be, when the sea-mew
Flies, as once before it flew,
O'er thine isles depopulate,
And all is in its antient state,
Save where many a palace gate
With green sea-flowers overgrown

Like a rock of ocean's own,
Topples o'er the abandoned sea
As the tides change sullenly.
The fisher on his watery way,
Wandering at the close of day,
Will spread his sail and seize his oar
Till he pass the gloomy shore,
Lest thy dead should, from their sleep
Bursting o'er the starlight deep,
Lead a rapid masque of death
O'er the waters of his path.

Those who alone thy towers behold
Quivering through aerial gold,
As I now behold them here,
Would imagine not they were
Sepulchres, where human forms,
Like pollution-nourished worms
To the corpse of greatness cling,
Murdered, and now mouldering:
But if Freedom should awake
In her omnipotence, and shake
From the Celtic Anarch's hold
All the keys of dungeons cold,
Where a hundred cities lie
Chained like thee, ingloriously,
Thou and all thy sister band
Might adorn this sunny land,
Twining memories of old time
With new virtues more sublime;
If not, perish thou and they!—
Clouds which stain truth's rising day
By her sun consumed away,
Earth can spare ye: while like flowers,
In the waste of years and hours,
From your dust new nations spring
With more kindly blossoming.

Perish—let there only be
Floating o'er thy hearthless sea
As the garment of the sky
Clothes the world immortally,

One remembrance, more sublime
Than the tattered pall of time
Which scarce hides thy visage wan;—
That a tempest-cleaving Swan
Of the songs of Albion,
Driven from his ancestral streams
By the might of evil dreams,
Found a nest in thee; and Ocean
Welcomed him with such emotion
That its joy grew his, and sprung
From his lips like music flung
O'er a mighty thunder-fit,
Chastening terror:—what though yet
Poesy's unfailing River,
Which thro' Albion winds forever
Lashing with melodious wave
Many a sacred Poet's grave,
Mourn its latest nursling fled?
What though thou with all thy dead
Scarce can for this fame repay
Aught thine own? oh, rather say
Though thy sins and slaveries foul
Overcloud a sunlike soul?
As the ghost of Homer clings
Round Scamander's wasting springs;
As divinest Shakespeare's might
Fills Avon and the world with light
Like Omniscient power which he
Imaged 'mid mortality;
As the love from Petrarch's urn
Yet amid yon hills doth burn,
A quenchless lamp by which the heart
Sees things unearthly;—so thou art,
Mighty Spirit—so shall be
The City that did refuge thee.

Lo, the sun floats up the sky
Like thought-winged Liberty,
Till the universal light
Seems to level plain and height;
From the sea a mist has spread,
And the beams of morn lie dead

On the towers of Venice now,
Like its glory long ago.
By the skirts of that grey cloud
Many-domed Padua proud
Stands, a peopled solitude,
'Mid the harvest-shining plain,
Where the peasant heaps his grain
In the garner of his foe,
And the milk-white oxen slow
With the purple vintage strain,
Heaped upon the creaking wain,
That the brutal Celt may swill
Drunken sleep with savage will;
And the sickle to the sword
Lies unchanged, though many a lord,
Like a weed whose shade is poison,
Overgrows this region's foizon,
Sheaves of whom are ripe to come
To destruction's harvest home:
Men must reap the things they sow,
Force from force must ever flow,
Or worse; but 'tis a bitter woe
That love or reason cannot change
The despot's rage, the slave's revenge.

Padua, thou within whose walls
Those mute guests at festivals,
Son and Mother, Death and Sin,
Played at dice for Ezzelin,
Till Death cried, 'I win, I win!'
And Sin cursed to lose the wager,
But Death promised, to assuage her,
That he would petition for
Her to be made Vice-Emperor,
When the destined years were o'er,
Over all between the Po
And the eastern Alpine snow,
Under the mighty Austrian.
Sin smiled so as Sin only can,
And since that time, aye, long before,
Both have ruled from shore to shore,
That incestuous pair, who follow

Tyrants as the sun the swallow,
As Repentance follows Crime,
And as changes follow Time.

In thine halls the lamp of learning,
Padua, now no more is burning;
Like a meteor, whose wild way
Is lost over the grave of day,
It gleams betrayed and to betray:
Once remotest nations came
To adore that sacred flame,
When it lit not many a hearth
On this cold and gloomy earth:
Now new fires from antique light
Spring beneath the wide world's might;
But their spark lies dead in thee,
Trampled out by tyranny.
As the Norway woodman quells,
In the depth of piny dells,
One light flame among the brakes,
While the boundless forest shakes,
And its mighty trunks are torn
By the fire thus lowly born:
The spark beneath his feet is dead,
He starts to see the flames it fed
Howling through the darkened sky
With a myriad tongues victoriously,
And sinks down in fear: so thou,
O tyranny, beholdest now
Light around thee, and thou hearest
The loud flames ascend, and fearest:
Grovel on the earth: aye, hide
In the dust thy purple pride!

Noon descends around me now:
'Tis the noon of autumn's glow,
When a soft and purple mist
Like a vaporous amethyst,
Or an air-dissolved star
Mingling light and fragrance, far
From the curved horizon's bound
To the point of heaven's profound,

Fills the overflowing sky;
And the plains that silent lie
Underneath, the leaves unsodden
Where the infant frost has trodden
With his morning-winged feet,
Whose bright print is gleaming yet;
And the red and golden vines,
Piercing with their trellised lines
The rough, dark-skirted wilderness;
The dun and bladed grass no less,
Pointing from this hoary tower
In the windless air; the flower
Glimmering at my feet; the line
Of the olive-sandalled Apennine
In the south dimly islanded;
And the Alps, whose snows are spread
High between the clouds and sun;
And of living things each one;
And my spirit which so long
Darkened this swift stream of song,
Interpenetrated lie
By the glory of the sky:
Be it love, light, harmony,
Odour, or the soul of all
Which from heaven like dew doth fall,
Or the mind which feeds this verse
Peopling the lone universe.

Noon descends, and after noon
Autumn's evening meets me soon,
Leading the infantine moon,
And that one star, which to her
Almost seems to minister
Half the crimson light she brings
From the sunset's radiant springs:
And the soft dreams of the morn
(Which like winged winds had borne
To that silent isle, which lies
'Mid remembered agonies,
The frail bark of this lone being)
Pass, to other sufferers fleeing,
And its antient pilot, Pain,
Sits beside the helm again.

Other flowering isles must be
In the sea of life and agony:
Other spirits float and flee
O'er that gulph: even now, perhaps,
On some rock the wild wave wraps,
With folded wings they waiting sit
For my bark, to pilot it
To some calm and blooming cove,
Where for me, and those I love,
May a windless bower be built,
Far from passion, pain, and guilt,
In a dell 'mid lawny hills,
Which the wild sea-murmur fills,
And soft sunshine, and the sound
Of old forests echoing round,
And the light and smell divine
Of all flowers that breathe and shine:
We may live so happy there,
That the spirits of the air,
Envying us, may even entice
To our healing paradise
The polluting multitude;
But their rage would be subdued
By that clime divine and calm,
And the winds whose wings rain balm
On the uplifted soul, and leaves
Under which the bright sea heaves;
While each breathless interval
In their whisperings musical
The inspired soul supplies
With its own deep melodies,
And the love which heals all strife
Circling, like the breath of life,
All things in that sweet abode
With its own mild brotherhood:
They, not it, would change; and soon
Every sprite beneath the moon
Would repent its envy vain,
And the earth grow young again.

JULIAN AND MADDALO
A CONVERSATION

The meadows with fresh streams, the bees with thyme,
The goats with the green leaves of budding spring,
Are saturated not—nor Love with tears.

Virgil's *Gallus.*

Count Maddalo is a Venetian nobleman of ancient family and of great fortune, who, without mixing much in the society of his countrymen, resides chiefly at his magnificent palace in that city. He is a person of the most consummate genius; and capable, if he would direct his energies to such an end, of becoming the redeemer of his degraded country. But it is his weakness to be proud: he derives, from a comparison of his own extraordinary mind with the dwarfish intellects that surround him, an intense apprehension of the nothingness of human life. His passions and his powers are incomparably greater than those of other men; and instead of the latter having been employed in curbing the former, they have mutually lent each other strength. His ambition preys upon itself, for want of objects which it can consider worthy of exertion. I say that Maddalo is proud, because I can find no other word to express the concentred and impatient feelings which consume him; but it is on his own hopes and affections only that he seems to trample, for in social life no human being can be more gentle, patient, and unassuming than Maddalo. He is cheerful, frank, and witty. His more serious conversation is a sort of intoxication; men are held by it as by a spell. He has travelled much; and there is an inexpressible charm in his relation of his adventures in different countries.

Julian is an Englishman of good family, passionately attached to those philosophical notions which assert the power of man over his own mind, and the immense improvements of which, by the extinction of certain moral superstitions, human society may be yet susceptible. Without concealing the evil in the world, he is for ever speculating how good may be made superior. He is a complete infidel, and a scoffer at all things reputed holy; and Maddalo takes a wicked pleasure in drawing out his taunts against religion. What Maddalo thinks on these matters is not exactly known. Julian, in spite of his heterodox opinions, is conjectured by his friends to possess some good qualities. How far this is possible, the pious reader will determine. Julian is rather serious.

Of the Maniac I can give no information. He seems by his own account to have been disappointed in love. He was evidently a very cultivated and amiable person when in his right senses. His story, told at length, might be like many other stories of the same kind: the unconnected exclamations of his agony will perhaps be found a sufficient comment for the text of every heart.

Julian and Maddalo
A Conversation

I rode one evening with Count Maddalo
Upon the bank of land which breaks the flow
Of Adria towards Venice:—a bare Strand
Of hillocks, heaped from ever-shifting sand,
Matted with thistles and amphibious weeds,
Such as from earth's embrace the salt ooze breeds
Is this;—an uninhabitable sea-side
Which the lone fisher, when his nets are dried,
Abandons; and no other object breaks
The waste, but one dwarf tree and some few stakes
Broken and unrepaired, and the tide makes
A narrow space of level sand thereon,
Where 'twas our wont to ride while day went down.
This ride was my delight.—I love all waste
And solitary places; where we taste
The pleasure of believing what we see
Is boundless, as we wish our souls to be:
And such was this wide ocean, and this shore
More barren than its billows;—and yet more
Than all, with a remembered friend I love
To ride as then I rode;—for the winds drove
The living spray along the sunny air
Into our faces; the blue heavens were bare,
Stripped to their depths by the awakening North,
And from the waves, sound like delight broke forth

Harmonizing with solitude, and sent
Into our hearts aërial merriment . . .
So, as we rode, we talked; and the swift thought,
Winging itself with laughter, lingered not
But flew from brain to brain,—such glee was ours—
Charged with light memories of remembered hours,
None slow enough for sadness; till we came
Homeward, which always makes the spirit tame.
This day had been cheerful but cold, and now
The sun was sinking, and the wind also.
Our talk grew somewhat serious, as may be
Talk interrupted with such raillery
As mocks itself, because it cannot scorn
The thoughts it would extinguish:—'twas forlorn
Yet pleasing, such as once, so poets tell,
The devils held within the dales of Hell
Concerning God, free will and destiny:
Of all that earth has been or yet may be,
All that vain men imagine or believe,
Or hope can paint or suffering may atchieve,
We descanted, and I (for ever still
Is it not wise to make the best of ill?)
Argued against despondency, but pride
Made my companion take the darker side.
The sense that he was greater than his kind
Had struck, methinks, his eagle spirit blind
By gazing on its own exceeding light.
—Meanwhile the sun paused ere it should alight,
Over the horizon of the mountains;—Oh
How beautiful is sunset, when the glow
Of Heaven descends upon a land like thee,
Thou Paradise of exiles, Italy!
Thy mountains, seas and vineyards and the towers
Of cities they encircle!—it was ours
To stand on thee, beholding it; and then
Just where we had dismounted the Count's men
Were waiting for us with the gondola.—
As those who pause on some delightful way
Tho' bent on pleasant pilgrimage, we stood
Looking upon the evening and the flood
Which lay between the city and the shore
Paved with the image of the sky . . . the hoar

And aery Alps towards the North appeared
Thro' mist, an heaven-sustaining bulwark reared
Between the East and West; and half the sky
Was roofed with clouds of rich emblazonry
Dark purple at the zenith, which still grew
Down the steep West into a wondrous hue
Brighter than burning gold, even to the rent
Where the swift sun yet paused in his descent
Among the many-folded hills: they were
Those famous Euganean hills, which bear
As seen from Lido thro' the harbour piles
The likeness of a clump of peaked isles—
And then—as if the Earth and Sea had been
Dissolved into one lake of fire, were seen
Those mountains towering as from waves of flame
Around the vaporous sun, from which there came
The inmost purple spirit of light, and made
Their very peaks transparent. 'Ere it fade,'
Said my Companion, 'I will shew you soon
A better station'—so, o'er the lagune
We glided, and from that funereal bark
I leaned, and saw the city, and could mark
How from their many isles in evening's gleam
Its temples and its palaces did seem
Like fabrics of enchantment piled to Heaven.
I was about to speak, when—'We are even
Now at the point I meant,' said Maddalo,
And bade the gondolieri cease to row.
'Look, Julian, on the West, and listen well
If you hear not a deep and heavy bell.'
I looked, and saw between us and the sun
A building on an island; such a one
As age to age might add, for uses vile;
A windowless, deformed and dreary pile
And on the top an open tower, where hung
A bell, which in the radiance swayed and swung.
We could just hear its hoarse and iron tongue.
The broad sun sunk behind it, and it tolled
In strong and black relief.—'What we behold
Shall be the madhouse and its belfry tower,'
Said Maddalo, 'and ever at this hour

Those who may cross the water hear that bell
Which calls the maniacs each one from his cell
To vespers.'—'As much skill as need to pray
In thanks or hope for their dark lot have they
To their stern maker,' I replied. 'O ho!
You talk as in years past,' said Maddalo.
''Tis strange men change not. You were ever still
Among Christ's flock a perilous infidel,
A wolf for the meek lambs—if you can't swim
Beware of Providence.' I looked on him,
But the gay smile had faded in his eye.
'And such,'—he cried, 'is our mortality
And this must be the emblem and the sign
Of what should be eternal and divine!—
And like that black and dreary bell, the soul
Hung in a heaven-illumined tower, must toll
Our thoughts and our desires to meet below
Round the rent heart and pray—as madmen do,
For what? they know not, till the night of death,
As sunset that strange vision, severeth
Our memory from itself, and us from all
We sought and yet were baffled!' I recall
The sense of what he said, altho' I mar
The force of his expressions. The broad star
Of day meanwhile had sunk behind the hill
And the black bell became invisible,
And the red tower looked grey, and all between
The churches, ships and palaces were seen
Huddled in gloom;—into the purple sea
The orange hues of heaven sunk silently.
We hardly spoke, and soon the gondola
Conveyed me to my lodgings by the way.

The following morn was rainy, cold and dim;
Ere Maddalo arose, I called on him,
And whilst I waited, with his child I played.
A lovelier toy sweet Nature never made,
A serious, subtle, wild, yet gentle being,
Graceful without design and unforeseeing,
With eyes—oh speak not of her eyes!—which seem
Twin mirrors of Italian Heaven, yet gleam

With such deep meaning, as we never see
But in the human countenance: with me
She was a special favourite: I had nursed
Her fine and feeble limbs when she came first
To this bleak world; and she yet seemed to know
On second sight her antient playfellow,
Less changed than she was by six months or so;
For after her first shyness was worn out
We sate there, rolling billiard balls about,
When the Count entered—salutations past—
'The words you spoke last night might well have cast
A darkness on my spirit—if man be
The passive thing you say, I should not see
Much harm in the religions and old saws
(Tho' I may never own such leaden laws)
Which break a teachless nature to the yoke:
Mine is another faith'—thus much I spoke
And noting he replied not, added: 'See
This lovely child, blithe, innocent and free;
She spends a happy time with little care
While we to such sick thoughts subjected are
As came on you last night—it is our will
That thus enchains us to permitted ill—
We might be otherwise—we might be all
We dream of happy, high, majestical.
Where is the love, beauty and truth we seek
But in our mind? and if we were not weak
Should we be less in deed than in desire?'
'Aye, if we were not weak—and we aspire
How vainly to be strong!' said Maddalo;
'You talk Utopia.' 'It remains to know,'
I then rejoined, 'and those who try may find
How strong the chains are which our spirits bind,
Brittle perchance as straw . . . We are assured
Much may be conquered, much may be endured
Of what degrades and crushes us. We know
That we have power over ourselves to do
And suffer—what, we know not till we try;
But something nobler than to live and die—
So taught those kings of old philosophy
Who reigned, before Religion made men blind;
And those who suffer with their suffering kind

Yet feel their faith, religion.' 'My dear friend,'
Said Maddalo, 'my judgement will not bend
To your opinion, tho' I think you might
Make such a system refutation-tight
As far as words go. I knew one like you
Who to this city came some months ago
With whom I argued in this sort, and he
Is now gone mad,—and so he answered me,—
Poor fellow! but if you would like to go
We'll visit him, and his wild talk will shew
How vain are such aspiring theories.'
'I hope to prove the induction otherwise,
And that a want of that true theory, still
Which seeks a "soul of goodness" in things ill,
Or in himself or others has thus bowed
His being—there are some by nature proud,
Who patient in all else demand but this:
To love and be beloved with gentleness;
And being scorned, what wonder if they die
Some living death? This is not destiny
But man's own wilful ill.' As thus I spoke
Servants announced the gondola, and we
Through the fast-falling rain and high-wrought sea
Sailed to the island where the madhouse stands.
We disembarked. The clap of tortured hands,
Fierce yells and howlings and lamentings keen,
And laughter where complaint had merrier been,
Moans, shrieks and curses and blaspheming prayers
Accosted us. We climbed the oozy stairs
Into an old court-yard. I heard on high
Then, fragments of most touching melody,
But looking up saw not the singer there—
Through the black bars in the tempestuous air
I saw, like weeds on a wrecked palace growing,
Long tangled locks flung wildly forth, and flowing,
Of those who on a sudden were beguiled
Into strange silence, and looked forth and smiled
Hearing sweet sounds.—Then I: 'Methinks there were
A cure of these with patience and kind care
If music can thus move . . . but what is he
Whom we seek here?' 'Of his sad history

I know but this,' said Maddalo, 'he came
To Venice a dejected man, and fame
Said he was wealthy, or he had been so;
Some thought the loss of fortune wrought him woe;
But he was ever talking in such sort
As you do—far more sadly—he seemed hurt,
Even as a man with his peculiar wrong,
To hear but of the oppression of the strong,
Or those absurd deceits (I think with you
In some respects, you know) which carry through
The excellent impostors of this Earth
When they outface detection—he had worth,
Poor fellow! but a humourist in his way.'—
'Alas, what drove him mad?' 'I cannot say;
A Lady came with him from France, and when
She left him and returned, he wandered then
About yon lonely isles of desart sand
Till he grew wild—he had no cash or land
Remaining,—the police had brought him here—
Some fancy took him and he would not bear
Removal; so I fitted up for him
Those rooms beside the sea, to please his whim,
And sent him busts and books and urns for flowers
Which had adorned his life in happier hours,
And instruments of music—you may guess
A stranger could do little more or less
For one so gentle and unfortunate,
And those are his sweet strains which charm the weight
From madmen's chains, and make this Hell appear
A heaven of sacred silence, hushed to hear.'—
'Nay, this was kind of you—he had no claim,
As the world says.'—'None—but the very same
Which I on all mankind were I as he
Fallen to such deep reverse;—his melody
Is interrupted now—we hear the din
Of madmen, shriek on shriek again begin;
Let us now visit him; after this strain
He ever communes with himself again,
And sees nor hears not any.' Having said
These words we called the keeper, and he led
To an apartment opening on the sea.—
There the poor wretch was sitting mournfully

Near a piano, his pale fingers twined
One with the other, and the ooze and wind
Rushed thro' an open casement, and did sway
His hair, and starred it with the brackish spray;
His head was leaning on a music book,
And he was muttering, and his lean limbs shook;
His lips were pressed against a folded leaf
In hue too beautiful for health, and grief
Smiled in their motions as they lay apart—
As one who wrought from his own fervid heart
The eloquence of passion, soon he raised
His sad meek face and eyes lustrous and glazed
And spoke—sometimes as one who wrote and thought
His words might move some heart that heeded not
If sent to distant lands; and then as one
Reproaching deeds never to be undone
With wondering self-compassion; then his speech
Was lost in grief, and then his words came each
Unmodulated, cold, expressionless;
But that from one jarred accent you might guess
It was despair made them so uniform:
And all the while the loud and gusty storm
Hissed thro' the window, and we stood behind
Stealing his accents from the envious wind
Unseen. I yet remember what he said
Distinctly: such impression his words made.

'Month after month,' he cried, 'to bear this load
And as a jade urged by the whip and goad
To drag life on, which like a heavy chain
Lengthens behind with many a link of pain!—
And not to speak my grief—O not to dare
To give a human voice to my despair,
But live and move, and wretched thing! smile on
As if I never went aside to groan
And wear this mask of falshood even to those
Who are most dear—not for my own repose—
Alas, no scorn or pain or hate could be
So heavy as that falshood is to me—
But that I cannot bear more altered faces
Than needs must be, more changed and cold embraces,

More misery, disappointment and mistrust
To own me for their father . . . Would the dust
Were covered in upon my body now!
That the life ceased to toil within my brow!
And then these thoughts would at the least be fled;
Let us not fear such pain can vex the dead.

'What Power delights to torture us? I know
That to myself I do not wholly owe
What now I suffer, tho' in part I may.
Alas, none strewed sweet flowers upon the way
Where wandering heedlessly, I met pale Pain
My shadow, which will leave me not again—
If I have erred, there was no joy in error,
But pain and insult and unrest and terror;
I have not as some do, bought penitence
With pleasure, and a dark yet sweet offence,
For then,—if love and tenderness and truth
Had overlived hope's momentary youth,
My creed should have redeemed me from repenting,
But loathed scorn and outrage unrelenting
Met love excited by far other seeming
Until the end was gained . . . as one from dreaming
Of sweetest peace, I woke, and found my state
Such as it is.—
'O Thou, my spirit's mate
Who, for thou art compassionate and wise,
Wouldst pity me from thy most gentle eyes
If this sad writing thou shouldst ever see—
My secret groans must be unheard by thee,
Thou wouldst weep tears bitter as blood to know
Thy lost friend's incommunicable woe.

'Ye few by whom my nature has been weighed
In friendship, let me not that name degrade
By placing on your hearts the secret load
Which crushes mine to dust. There is one road
To peace and that is truth, which follow ye!
Love sometimes leads astray to misery.
Yet think not tho' subdued—and I may well
Say that I am subdued—that the full Hell

Within me would infect the untainted breast
Of sacred nature with its own unrest;
As some perverted beings think to find
In scorn or hate a medicine for the mind
Which scorn or hate have wounded—O how vain!
The dagger heals not but may rend again . . .
Believe that I am ever still the same
In creed as in resolve, and what may tame
My heart, must leave the understanding free
Or all would sink in this keen agony—
Nor dream that I will join the vulgar cry,
Or with my silence sanction tyranny,
Or seek a moment's shelter from my pain
In any madness which the world calls gain,
Ambition or revenge or thoughts as stern
As those which make me what I am, or turn
To avarice or misanthropy or lust . . .
Heap on me soon, O grave, thy welcome dust!
Till then the dungeon may demand its prey,
And poverty and shame may meet and say—
Halting beside me on the public way—
"That love-devoted youth is ours—let's sit
Beside him—he may live some six months yet."
Or the red scaffold, as our country bends,
May ask some willing victim, or ye friends
May fall under some sorrow which this heart
Or hand may share or vanquish or avert;
I am prepared: in truth with no proud joy
To do or suffer aught, as when a boy
I did devote to justice and to love
My nature, worthless now! . . .
'I must remove
A veil from my pent mind. 'Tis torn aside!
O, pallid as death's dedicated bride,
Thou mockery which art sitting by my side,
Am I not wan like thee? at the grave's call
I haste, invited to thy wedding ball
To greet the ghastly paramour, for whom
Thou hast deserted me . . . and made the tomb
Thy bridal bed . . . but I beside your feet
Will lie and watch ye from my winding sheet—

Thus . . . wide awake tho' dead . . . yet stay, O stay!
Go not so soon—I know not what I say—
Hear but my reasons . . . I am mad, I fear,
My fancy is o'erwrought . . . thou art not here . . .
Pale art thou, 'tis most true . . . but thou art gone,
Thy work is finished . . . I am left alone!—

* * * * * * *

'Nay, was it I who wooed thee to this breast
Which, like a serpent, thou envenomest
As in repayment of the warmth it lent?
Didst thou not seek me for thine own content?
Did not thy love awaken mine? I thought
That thou wert she who said "You kiss me not
Ever, I fear you cease to love me now"—
In truth I loved even to my overthrow
Her, who would fain forget these words: but they
Cling to her mind, and cannot pass away.

* * * * * * *

'You say that I am proud—that when I speak
My lip is tortured with the wrongs which break
The spirit it expresses . . . Never one
Humbled himself before, as I have done!
Even the instinctive worm on which we tread
Turns, tho' it wound not—then with prostrate head
Sinks in the dust and writhes like me—and dies?
No: wears a living death of agonies!
As the slow shadows of the pointed grass
Mark the eternal periods, his pangs pass
Slow, ever-moving,—making moments be
As mine seem—each an immortality!

* * * * * * *

'That you had never seen me—never heard
My voice, and more than all had ne'er endured
The deep pollution of my loathed embrace—
That your eyes ne'er had lied love in my face—
That, like some maniac monk, I had torn out
The nerves of manhood by their bleeding root

With mine own quivering fingers, so that ne'er
Our hearts had for a moment mingled there
To disunite in horror—these were not
With thee, like some suppressed and hideous thought
Which flits athwart our musings, but can find
No rest within a pure and gentle mind . . .
Thou sealedst them with many a bare broad word
And cearedst my memory o'er them,—for I heard
And can forget not . . . they were ministered
One after one, those curses. Mix them up
Like self-destroying poisons in one cup,
And they will make one blessing, which thou ne'er
Didst imprecate for, on me,—death.

* * * * * * *

'It were
A cruel punishment for one most cruel,
If such can love, to make that love the fuel
Of the mind's hell—hate, scorn, remorse, despair:
But *me*—whose heart a stranger's tear might wear
As water-drops the sandy fountain-stone,
Who loved and pitied all things, and could moan
For woes which others hear not, and could see
The absent with the glance of phantasy,
And with the poor and trampled sit and weep,
Following the captive to his dungeon deep;
Me—who am as a nerve o'er which do creep
The else unfelt oppressions of this earth
And was to thee the flame upon thy hearth
When all beside was cold—that thou on me
Shouldst rain these plagues of blistering agony—
Such curses are from lips once eloquent
With love's too partial praise—let none relent
Who intend deeds too dreadful for a name
Henceforth, if an example for the same
They seek . . . for thou on me lookedst so, and so—
And didst speak thus . . . and thus . . . I live to shew
How much men bear and die not!

* * * * * * *

'Thou wilt tell
With the grimace of hate how horrible
It was to meet my love when thine grew less;
Thou wilt admire how I could e'er address
Such features to love's work . . . this taunt, tho' true,
(For indeed nature nor in form nor hue
Bestowed on me her choicest workmanship)
Shall not be thy defence . . . for since thy lip
Met mine first, years long past, since thine eye kindled
With soft fire under mine, I have not dwindled
Nor changed in mind or body, or in aught
But as love changes what it loveth not
After long years and many trials.
'How vain
Are words! I thought never to speak again
Not even in secret,—not to my own heart—
But from my lips the unwilling accents start
And from my pen the words flow as I write,
Dazzling my eyes with scalding tears . . . my sight
Is dim to see that charactered in vain
On this unfeeling leaf which burns the brain
And eats into it . . . blotting all things fair
And wise and good which time had written there.

'Those who inflict must suffer, for they see
The work of their own hearts and this must be
Our chastisement or recompense—O child!
I would that thine were like to be more mild
For both our wretched sakes . . . for thine the most
Who feelest already all that thou hast lost
Without the power to wish it thine again;
And as slow years pass, a funereal train
Each with the ghost of some lost hope or friend
Following it like its shadow, wilt thou bend
No thought on my dead memory?

* * * * * *

'Alas, love!
Fear me not . . . against thee I would not move
A finger in despite. Do I not live
That thou mayst have less bitter cause to grieve?

I give thee tears for scorn and love for hate
And that thy lot may be less desolate
Than his on whom thou tramplest, I refrain
From that sweet sleep which medicines all pain.
Then, when thou speakest of me, never say
He could forgive not. Here I cast away
All human passions, all revenge, all pride;
I think, speak, act no ill; I do but hide
Under these words like embers, every spark
Of that which has consumed me—quick and dark
The grave is yawning . . . as its roof shall cover
My limbs with dust and worms under and over
So let Oblivion hide this grief . . . the air
Closes upon my accents, as despair
Upon my heart—let death upon despair!'

He ceased, and overcome leant back awhile,
Then rising, with a melancholy smile
Went to a sofa, and lay down, and slept
A heavy sleep, and in his dreams he wept
And muttered some familiar name, and we
Wept without shame in his society.
I think I never was impressed so much;
The man who were not, must have lacked a touch
Of human nature . . . then we lingered not,
Although our argument was quite forgot,
But calling the attendants, went to dine
At Maddalo's; yet neither cheer nor wine
Could give us spirits, for we talked of him
And nothing else, till daylight made stars dim;
And we agreed his was some dreadful ill
Wrought on him boldly, yet unspeakable,
By a dear friend; some deadly change in love
Of one vowed deeply which he dreamed not of;
For whose sake he, it seemed, had fixed a blot
Of falshood on his mind which flourished not
But in the light of all-beholding truth,
And having stamped this canker on his youth
She had abandoned him . . . and how much more
Might be his woe, we guessed not—he had store
Of friends and fortune once, as we could guess
From his nice habits and his gentleness;

These were now lost . . . it were a grief indeed
If he had changed one unsustaining reed
For all that such a man might else adorn.
The colours of his mind seemed yet unworn;
For the wild language of his grief was high,
Such as in measure were called poetry,
And I remember one remark which then
Maddalo made. He said: 'Most wretched men
Are cradled into poetry by wrong;
They learn in suffering what they teach in song.'

If I had been an unconnected man
I, from this moment, should have formed some plan
Never to leave sweet Venice,—for to me
It was delight to ride by the lone sea;
And then, the town is silent—one may write
Or read in gondolas by day or night
Having the little brazen lamp alight,
Unseen, uninterrupted; books are there,
Pictures, and casts from all those statues fair
Which were twin-born with poetry, and all
We seek in towns, with little to recall
Regrets for the green country. I might sit
In Maddalo's great palace, and his wit
And subtle talk would cheer the winter night
And make me know myself, and the firelight
Would flash upon our faces, till the day
Might dawn and make me wonder at my stay.
But I had friends in London too: the chief
Attraction here, was that I sought relief
From the deep tenderness that maniac wrought
Within me—'twas perhaps an idle thought,
But I imagined that if day by day
I watched him, and but seldom went away,
And studied all the beatings of his heart
With zeal, as men study some stubborn art
For their own good, and could by patience find
An entrance to the caverns of his mind,
I might reclaim him from his dark estate:
In friendships I had been most fortunate—
Yet never saw I one whom I would call
More willingly my friend; and this was all

Accomplished not; such dreams of baseless good
Oft come and go in crowds and solitude
And leave no trace—but what I now designed
Made for long years impression on my mind.
The following morning urged by my affairs
I left bright Venice.
After many years
And many changes I returned; the name
Of Venice, and its aspect was the same;
But Maddalo was travelling far away
Among the mountains of Armenia.
His dog was dead. His child had now become
A woman; such as it has been my doom
To meet with few, a wonder of this earth
Where there is little of transcendent worth,
Like one of Shakespeare's women: kindly she
And with a manner beyond courtesy
Received her father's friend; and when I asked
Of the lorn maniac, she her memory tasked
And told as she had heard the mournful tale:
That the poor sufferer's health began to fail
Two years from my departure, but that then
The Lady who had left him, came again.
'Her mien had been imperious, but she now
Looked meek—perhaps remorse had brought her low.
Her coming made him better, and they stayed
Together at my father's—for I played
As I remember with the lady's shawl—
I might be six years old—but after all
She left him.' . . . 'Why, her heart must have been tough:
How did it end?' 'And was this not enough?
They met—they parted.'—'Child, is there no more?
Something within that interval which bore
The stamp of *why* they parted, *how* they met?'
'Yet if thine aged eyes disdain to wet
Those wrinkled cheeks with youth's remembered tears,
Ask me no more, but let the silent years
Be closed and ceared over their memory
As yon mute marble where their corpses lie.'
I urged and questioned still, she told me how
All happened—but the cold world shall not know.

Stanzas Written in Dejection—
December 1818, near Naples

The Sun is warm, the sky is clear,
The waves are dancing fast and bright,
Blue isles and snowy mountains wear
The purple noon's transparent might,
The breath of the moist earth is light
Around its unexpanded buds;
Like many a voice of one delight
The winds, the birds, the Ocean-floods;
The City's voice itself is soft, like Solitude's.

I see the Deep's untrampled floor
With green and purple seaweeds strown,
I see the waves upon the shore
Like light dissolved in star-showers, thrown;
I sit upon the sands alone;
The lightning of the noontide Ocean
Is flashing round me, and a tone
Arises from its measured motion,
How sweet! did any heart now share in my emotion.

Alas, I have nor hope nor health,
Nor peace within nor calm around,
Nor that content surpassing wealth
The sage in meditation found,
And walked with inward glory crowned;
Nor fame, nor power nor love nor leisure—
Others I see whom these surround,
Smiling they live and call life pleasure:
To me that cup has been dealt in another measure.

Yet now despair itself is mild
Even as the winds and waters are;
I could lie down like a tired child
And weep away the life of care
Which I have borne and yet must bear
Till Death like Sleep might steal on me,
And I might feel in the warm air
My cheek grow cold, and hear the sea
Breathe o'er my dying brain its last monotony.

Some might lament that I were cold,
As I, when this sweet day is gone,
Which my lost heart, too soon grown old,
Insults with this untimely moan—
They might lament,—for I am one
Whom men love not, and yet regret;
Unlike this Day, which, when the Sun
Shall on its stainless glory set,
Will linger though enjoyed, like joy in Memory yet.

The Two Spirits—An Allegory

First Spirit

O Thou who plumed with strong desire
Would float above the Earth—beware!
A shadow tracks thy flight of fire—
Night is coming.
Bright are the regions of the air
And when winds and beams [ ]
It were delight to wander there—
Night is coming!

Second Spirit

The deathless stars are bright above;
If I should cross the shade of night
Within my heart is the lamp of love
And that is day—
And the moon will smile with gentle light
On my golden plumes where'er they move;
The meteors will linger around my flight
And make night day.

First Spirit

But if the whirlwinds of darkness waken
Hail and Lightning and stormy rain—
See, the bounds of the air are shaken,
Night is coming.
The red swift clouds of the hurricane
Yon declining sun have overtaken,
The clash of the hail sweeps o'er the plain—
Night is coming.

Second Spirit

I see the glare and I hear the sound—
I'll sail on the flood of the tempest dark
With the calm within and light around
    Which make night day;
And thou when the gloom is deep and stark
Look from thy dull earth slumberbound—
My moonlike flight thou then mayst mark
    On high, far away.

Some say there is a precipice
Where one vast pine hangs frozen to ruin
O'er piles of snow and chasms of ice
    Mid Alpine mountains,
And that the leagued storm pursuing
That winged shape forever flies
Round those hoar branches, aye renewing
    Its aery fountains.

Some say when the nights are dry and clear
And the death dews sleep on the morass,
Sweet whispers are heard by the traveller
    Which make night day—
And a shape like his early love doth pass
Upborne by her wild and glittering hair,
And when he awakes on the fragrant grass
    He finds night day.

Sonnet ('Lift not the painted veil')

Lift not the painted veil which those who live
Call Life; though unreal shapes be pictured there,
And it but mimic all we would believe
With colours idly spread,—behind, lurk Fear
And Hope, twin Destinies, who ever weave
Their shadows o'er the chasm, sightless and drear.

I knew one who had lifted it—he sought,
For his lost heart was tender, things to love,
But found them not, alas! nor was there aught

The world contains, the which he could approve.
Through the unheeding many he did move,
A splendour among shadows, a bright blot
Upon this gloomy scene, a Spirit that strove
For truth, and like the Preacher found it not.

PROMETHEUS UNBOUND

A LYRICAL DRAMA IN FOUR ACTS

AUDISNE HAEC AMPHIARAE, SUB TERRAM ABDITE?

PREFACE

The Greek tragic writers, in selecting as their subject any portion of their national history or mythology, employed in their treatment of it a certain arbitrary discretion. They by no means conceived themselves bound to adhere to the common interpretation or to imitate in story as in title their rivals and predecessors. Such a system would have amounted to a resignation of those claims to preference over their competitors which incited the composition. The Agamemnonian story was exhibited on the Athenian theatre with as many variations as dramas.

I have presumed to employ a similar licence. The *Prometheus Unbound* of Aeschylus supposed the reconciliation of Jupiter with his victim as the price of the disclosure of the danger threatened to his empire by the consummation of his marriage with Thetis. Thetis, according to this view of the subject, was given in marriage to Peleus, and Prometheus, by the permission of Jupiter, delivered from his captivity by Hercules. Had I framed my story on this model, I should have done no more than have attempted to restore the lost drama of Aeschylus; an ambition, which, if my preference to this mode of treating the subject had incited me to cherish, the recollection of the high comparison such an attempt would challenge might well abate. But, in truth, I was averse from a catastrophe so feeble as that of reconciling the Champion with the Oppressor of mankind. The moral interest of the fable, which is so powerfully sustained by the sufferings and endurance of Prometheus, would be annihilated if we could conceive of him as unsaying his high language and quailing before his successful and perfidious adversary. The only imaginary being resembling in any degree Prometheus, is Satan; and Prometheus is, in my judgement, a more poetical character than Satan, because, in addition to courage, and majesty, and firm and patient opposition to omnipotent force, he is susceptible of being described as exempt from the taints of ambition, envy, revenge, and a desire for personal aggrandisement, which, in the Hero of *Paradise Lost*, interfere with the interest. The character of Satan engenders in the mind a pernicious casuistry which leads us to weigh his faults with his wrongs, and to excuse the former because the latter exceed all measure. In the minds of those who consider that magnificent fiction with a religious feeling, it engenders something worse. But Prometheus is, as it were, the type of the highest perfection of moral and intellectual nature, impelled by the purest and the truest motives to the best and noblest ends.

This Poem was chiefly written upon the mountainous ruins of the Baths of Caracalla, among the flowery glades, and thickets of odoriferous blossoming trees, which are extended in ever winding labyrinths upon its immense platforms and dizzy arches suspended in the air. The bright blue sky of Rome, and the effect of the vigorous awakening of spring in that divinest climate, and the new life with which it drenches the spirits even to intoxication, were the inspiration of this drama.

The imagery which I have employed will be found, in many instances, to have been drawn from the operations of the human mind, or from those external actions by which they are expressed. This is unusual in modern poetry, although Dante and Shakespeare are full of instances of the same kind: Dante indeed more than any other poet, and with greater success. But the Greek poets, as writers to whom no resource of awakening the sympathy of their contemporaries was unknown, were in the habitual use of this power; and it is the study of their works (since a higher merit would probably be denied to me) to which I am willing that my readers should impute this singularity.

One word is due in candour to the degree in which the study of contemporary writings may have tinged my composition, for such has been a topic of censure with regard to poems far more popular, and indeed more deservedly popular, than mine. It is impossible that any one who inhabits the same age with such writers as those who stand in the foremost ranks of our own, can conscientiously assure himself that his language and tone of thought may not have been modified by the study of the productions of those extraordinary intellects. It is true, that, not the spirit of their genius, but the forms in which it has manifested itself, are due less to the peculiarities of their own minds than to the peculiarity of the moral and intellectual condition of the minds among which they have been produced. Thus a number of writers possess the form, whilst they want the spirit of those whom, it is alleged, they imitate; because the former is the endowment of the age in which they live, and the latter must be the uncommunicated lightning of their own mind.

The peculiar style of intense and comprehensive imagery which distinguishes the modern literature of England, has not been, as a general power, the product of the imitation of any particular writer. The mass of capabilities remains at every period materially the same; the circumstances which awaken it to action perpetually change. If England were divided into forty republics, each equal in population and extent to Athens, there is no reason to suppose but that, under institutions not more perfect than those of Athens, each would produce philosophers and poets equal to those who (if we except Shakespeare) have never been surpassed. We owe the great writers of the golden age of our literature to that fervid awakening of the public mind which shook to dust the oldest and most oppressive form of the Christian religion. We owe Milton to the progress and development of the same spirit: the sacred Milton was, let it ever be remembered, a republican, and a bold inquirer into morals and religion. The great writers of our own age are, we have reason to suppose, the companions and forerunners of some unimagined change in our social condition or the opinions which cement it. The cloud of mind is discharging its collected lightning, and the equilibrium between institutions and opinions is now restoring, or is about to be restored.

As to imitation, poetry is a mimetic art. It creates, but it creates by combination and representation. Poetical abstractions are beautiful and new, not because the portions of which they are composed had no previous existence in the mind of man or in nature, but because the whole produced by their combination has some intelligible and beautiful analogy with those sources of emotion and thought, and with the contemporary condition of them: one great poet is a masterpiece of nature, which another not only ought to study but must study. He might as wisely and as easily determine that his mind should no longer be the mirror of all that is lovely in the visible universe, as exclude from his contemplation the beautiful which exists in the writings of a great contemporary. The pretence of doing it would be a presumption in any but the greatest; the effect, even in him, would be strained, unnatural, and ineffectual. A poet is the combined product of such internal powers as modify the nature of others; and of such external influences as excite and sustain these powers; he is not one, but both. Every man's mind is, in this respect, modified by all the objects of nature and art; by every word and every suggestion which he ever admitted to act upon his consciousness; it is the mirror upon which all forms are reflected, and in which they compose one form. Poets, not otherwise than philosophers, painters, sculptors, and musicians, are, in one sense, the creators, and, in another, the creations, of their age. From this subjection the loftiest do not escape. There is a similarity between Homer and Hesiod, between Aeschylus and Euripides, between Virgil and Horace, between Dante and Petrarch, between Shakespeare and Fletcher, between Dryden and Pope; each has a generic resemblance under which their specific distinctions are arranged. If this similarity be the result of imitation, I am willing to confess that I have imitated.

Let this opportunity be conceded to me of acknowledging that I have, what a Scotch philosopher characteristically terms, 'a passion for reforming the world': what passion incited him to write and publish his book, he omits to explain. For my part I had rather be damned with Plato and Lord Bacon, than go to Heaven with Paley and Malthus. But it is a mistake to suppose that I dedicate my poetical compositions solely to the direct enforcement of reform, or that I consider them in any degree as containing a reasoned system on the theory of human life. Didactic poetry is my abhorrence; nothing can be equally well expressed in prose that is not tedious and supererogatory in verse. My purpose has hitherto been simply to familiarize the highly refined imagination of the more select classes of poetical readers with beautiful idealisms of moral excellence; aware that until the mind can love, and admire, and trust, and hope, and endure, reasoned principles of moral conduct are seeds cast upon the highway of life which the unconscious passenger tramples into dust, although they would bear the harvest of his happiness. Should I live to accomplish what I purpose, that is, produce a systematical history of what appear to me to be the genuine elements of human society, let not the advocates of injustice and superstition flatter themselves that I should take Aeschylus rather than Plato as my model.

The having spoken of myself with unaffected freedom will need little apology with the candid; and let the uncandid consider that they injure me less than their own hearts and minds by misrepresentation. Whatever talents a person may possess to amuse and instruct others, be they ever so inconsiderable, he is yet bound to exert them: if his attempt be ineffectual, let the punishment of an unaccomplished purpose have been sufficient; let none trouble themselves to heap the dust of oblivion upon his efforts; the pile they raise will betray his grave which might otherwise have been unknown.

DRAMATIS PERSONAE

PROMETHEUS
DEMOGORGON
JUPITER
THE EARTH
OCEAN
APOLLO
MERCURY
HERCULES
ASIA, PANTHEA, IONE } OCEANIDES
THE PHANTASM OF JUPITER
THE SPIRIT OF THE EARTH
THE SPIRIT OF THE MOON
SPIRITS OF THE HOURS
SPIRITS, ECHOES, FAUNS, FURIES

ACT I

Scene, a Ravine of Icy Rocks in the Indian Caucasus. PROMETHEUS *is discovered bound to the precipice.* PANTHEA *and* IONE *are seated at his feet. Time, Night. During the Scene, Morning slowly breaks.*

Prometheus
Monarch of Gods and Daemons, and all Spirits
But One, who throng those bright and rolling worlds
Which Thou and I alone of living things
Behold with sleepless eyes! regard this Earth
Made multitudinous with thy slaves, whom thou
Requitest for knee-worship, prayer, and praise,
And toil, and hecatombs of broken hearts,
With fear and self-contempt and barren hope;
Whilst me, who am thy foe, eyeless in hate,
Hast thou made reign and triumph, to thy scorn,
O'er mine own misery and thy vain revenge.
Three thousand years of sleep-unsheltered hours
And moments aye divided by keen pangs
Till they seemed years, torture and solitude,

Scorn and despair,—these are mine empire.
More glorious far than that which thou surveyest
From thine unenvied throne, O Mighty God!
Almighty, had I deigned to share the shame
Of thine ill tyranny, and hung not here
Nailed to this wall of eagle-baffling mountain,
Black, wintry, dead, unmeasured; without herb,
Insect, or beast, or shape or sound of life.
Ah me! alas, pain, pain ever, for ever!

No change, no pause, no hope! Yet I endure.
I ask the Earth, have not the mountains felt?
I ask yon Heaven, the all-beholding Sun,
Has it not seen? The Sea, in storm or calm,
Heaven's ever-changing Shadow, spread below,
Have its deaf waves not heard my agony?
Ah me! alas, pain, pain ever, for ever!

The crawling glaciers pierce me with the spears
Of their moon-freezing crystals, the bright chains
Eat with their burning cold into my bones.
Heaven's winged hound, polluting from thy lips
His beak in poison not his own, tears up
My heart; and shapeless sights come wandering by,
The ghastly people of the realm of dream,
Mocking me: and the Earthquake-fiends are charged
To wrench the rivets from my quivering wounds
When the rocks split and close again behind;
While from their loud abysses howling throng
The genii of the storm, urging the rage
Of whirlwind, and afflict me with keen hail.
And yet to me welcome is day and night,
Whether one breaks the hoar frost of the morn,
Or starry, dim, and slow, the other climbs
The leaden-coloured east; for then they lead
Their wingless, crawling Hours, one among whom
—As some dark Priest hales the reluctant victim—
Shall drag thee, cruel King, to kiss the blood
From these pale feet, which then might trample thee
If they disdained not such a prostrate slave.
Disdain! Ah no! I pity thee. What ruin
Will hunt thee undefended through the wide Heaven!

How will thy soul, cloven to its depth with terror,
Gape like a Hell within! I speak in grief,
Not exultation, for I hate no more,
As then, ere misery made me wise. The curse
Once breathed on thee I would recall. Ye Mountains,
Whose many-voiced Echoes, through the mist
Of cataracts, flung the thunder of that spell!
Ye icy Springs, stagnant with wrinkling frost,
Which vibrated to hear me, and then crept
Shuddering through India! Thou serenest Air,
Through which the Sun walks burning without beams!
And ye swift Whirlwinds, who on poised wings
Hung mute and moveless o'er yon hushed abyss,
As thunder louder than your own made rock
The orbed world! if then my words had power,
Though I am changed so that aught evil wish
Is dead within; although no memory be
Of what is hate—let them not lose it now!
What was that curse? for ye all heard me speak.

First Voice: from the Mountains

Thrice three hundred thousand years
O'er the Earthquake's couch we stood:
Oft, as men convulsed with fears,
We trembled in our multitude.

Second Voice: from the Springs

Thunder-bolts had parched our water,
We had been stained with bitter blood,
And had run mute, 'mid shrieks of slaughter,
Through a city and a solitude.

Third Voice: from the Air

I had clothed, since Earth uprose,
Its wastes in colours not their own,
And oft had my serene repose
Been cloven by many a rending groan.

Fourth Voice: from the Whirlwinds

We had soared beneath these mountains
Unresting ages; nor had thunder,
Nor yon volcano's flaming fountains,
Nor any power above or under
Ever made us mute with wonder.

First Voice

But never bowed our snowy crest
As at the voice of thine unrest.

Second Voice

Never such a sound before
To the Indian waves we bore.
A pilot asleep on the howling sea
Leaped up from the deck in agony
And heard, and cried, 'Ah, woe is me!'
And died as mad as the wild waves be.

Third Voice

By such dread words from Earth to Heaven
My still realm was never riven:
When its wound was closed, there stood
Darkness o'er the day like blood.

Fourth Voice

And we shrank back: for dreams of ruin
To frozen caves our flight pursuing
Made us keep silence—thus—and thus—
Though silence is as hell to us.

The Earth

The tongueless Caverns of the craggy hills
Cried 'Misery!' then; the hollow Heaven replied,
'Misery!' And the Ocean's purple waves,
Climbing the land, howled to the lashing winds,
And the pale nations heard it,—'Misery!'

Prometheus

I hear a sound of voices: not the voice
Which I gave forth. Mother, thy sons and thou
Scorn him, without whose all-enduring will
Beneath the fierce omnipotence of Jove
Both they and thou had vanished like thin mist
Unrolled on the morning wind. Know ye not me,
The Titan? he who made his agony
The barrier to your else all-conquering foe?
Oh, rock-embosomed lawns, and snow-fed streams,
Now seen athwart frore vapours, deep below,
Through whose o'ershadowing woods I wandered once
With Asia, drinking life from her loved eyes,
Why scorns the spirit which informs ye, now
To commune with me? me alone, who checked—
As one who checks a fiend-drawn charioteer—
The falsehood and the force of Him who reigns
Supreme, and with the groans of pining slaves
Fills your dim glens and liquid wildernesses?
Why answer ye not, still? Brethren!

The Earth

They dare not.

Prometheus

Who dares? For I would hear that curse again . . .
Ha, what an awful whisper rises up!
'Tis scarce like sound: it tingles through the frame
As lightning tingles, hovering ere it strike.
Speak, Spirit! from thine inorganic voice
I only know that thou art moving near
And love. How cursed I him?

The Earth

How canst thou hear,
Who knowest not the language of the dead?

Prometheus

Thou art a living spirit; speak as they.

The Earth
I dare not speak like life, lest Heaven's fell King
Should hear, and link me to some wheel of pain
More torturing than the one whereon I roll.
Subtle thou art and good, and though the Gods
Hear not this voice, yet thou art more than God
Being wise and kind: earnestly hearken now.

Prometheus
Obscurely through my brain, like shadows dim,
Sweep awful thoughts, rapid and thick—I feel
Faint, like one mingled in entwining love.
Yet 'tis not pleasure.

The Earth
No, thou canst not hear:
Thou art immortal, and this tongue is known
Only to those who die . . .

Prometheus
And what art thou,
O melancholy Voice?

The Earth
I am the Earth,
Thy mother, she within whose stony veins,
To the last fibre of the loftiest tree
Whose thin leaves trembled in the frozen air,
Joy ran, as blood within a living frame,
When thou didst from her bosom, like a cloud
Of glory, arise, a spirit of keen joy!
And at thy voice her pining sons uplifted
Their prostrate brows from the polluting dust,
And our almighty Tyrant with fierce dread
Grew pale—until his thunder chained thee here.
Then—see those million worlds which burn and roll
Around us: their inhabitants beheld
My sphered light wane in wide Heaven; the sea
Was lifted by strange tempest, and new fire
From earthquake-rifted mountains of bright snow
Shook its portentous hair beneath Heaven's frown;
Lightning and Inundation vexed the plains;

Blue thistles bloomed in cities; foodless toads
Within voluptuous chambers panting crawled;
When Plague had fallen on man and beast and worm,
And Famine, and black blight on herb and tree;
And in the corn, and vines, and meadow-grass,
Teemed ineradicable poisonous weeds
Draining their growth, for my wan breast was dry
With grief; and the thin air, my breath, was stained
With the contagion of a mother's hate
Breathed on her child's destroyer—aye, I heard
Thy curse, the which, if thou rememberest not,
Yet my innumerable seas and streams,
Mountains, and caves, and winds, and yon wide air,
And the inarticulate people of the dead,
Preserve, a treasured spell. We meditate
In secret joy and hope those dreadful words,
But dare not speak them.

Prometheus

Venerable mother!
All else who live and suffer take from thee
Some comfort; flowers, and fruits, and happy sounds,
And love, though fleeting; these may not be mine.
But mine own words, I pray, deny me not.

The Earth
They shall be told. Ere Babylon was dust,
The Magus Zoroaster, my dead child,
Met his own image walking in the garden.
That apparition, sole of men, he saw.
For know there are two worlds of life and death:
One that which thou beholdest; but the other
Is underneath the grave, where do inhabit
The shadows of all forms that think and live
Till death unite them and they part no more;
Dreams and the light imaginings of men,
And all that faith creates or love desires,
Terrible, strange, sublime and beauteous shapes.
There thou art, and dost hang, a writhing shade
'Mid whirlwind-shaken mountains; all the Gods
Are there, and all the Powers of nameless worlds,
Vast, sceptred Phantoms; heroes, men, and beasts;

And Demogorgon, a tremendous Gloom;
And he, the Supreme Tyrant, throned
On burning Gold. Son, one of these shall utter
The curse which all remember. Call at will
Thine own ghost, or the ghost of Jupiter,
Hades or Typhon, or what mightier Gods
From all-prolific Evil, since thy ruin
Have sprung, and trampled on my prostrate sons.
Ask, and they must reply: so the revenge
Of the Supreme may sweep through vacant shades,
As rainy wind through the abandoned gate
Of a fallen palace.

Prometheus

Mother, let not aught
Of that which may be evil, pass again
My lips, or those of aught resembling me.
Phantasm of Jupiter, arise, appear!

Ione

My wings are folded o'er mine ears:
My wings are crossed over mine eyes:
Yet through their silver shade appears,
And through their lulling plumes arise,
A shape, a throng of sounds;
May it be no ill to thee
O thou of many wounds!
Near whom, for our sweet sister's sake,
Ever thus we watch and wake.

Panthea

The sound is of whirlwind underground,
Earthquake, and fire, and mountains cloven;
The Shape is awful like the sound,
Clothed in dark purple, star-inwoven.
A sceptre of pale gold
To stay steps proud, o'er the slow cloud
His veined hand doth hold.
Cruel he looks, but calm and strong,
Like one who does, not suffers wrong.

Phantasm of Jupiter
Why have the secret powers of this strange world
Driven me, a frail and empty phantom, hither
On direst storms? What unaccustomed sounds
Are hovering on my lips, unlike the voice
With which our pallid race hold ghastly talk
In darkness? And, proud Sufferer, who art thou?

Prometheus
Tremendous Image! as thou art must be
He whom thou shadowest forth. I am his foe,
The Titan. Speak the words which I would hear,
Although no thought inform thine empty voice.

The Earth
Listen! And though your echoes must be mute,
Grey mountains, and old woods, and haunted springs,
Prophetic caves, and isle-surrounding streams,
Rejoice to hear what yet ye cannot speak.

Phantasm
A spirit seizes me and speaks within:
It tears me as fire tears a thunder-cloud.

Panthea
See, how he lifts his mighty looks, the Heaven
Darkens above.

Ione
He speaks! O shelter me!

Prometheus
I see the curse on gestures proud and cold,
And looks of firm defiance, and calm hate,
And such despair as mocks itself with smiles,
Written as on a scroll . . . yet speak—O speak!

Phantasm

Fiend, I defy thee! with a calm, fixed mind,
All that thou canst inflict I bid to do;
Foul Tyrant both of Gods and Human-kind,
One only being shalt thou not subdue.

Rain then thy plagues upon me here,
Ghastly disease, and frenzying fear;
And let alternate frost and fire
Eat into me, and be thine ire
Lightning, and cutting hail, and legioned forms
Of furies, driving by upon the wounding storms.

Aye, do thy worst. Thou art omnipotent.
O'er all things but thyself I gave thee power,
And my own will. Be thy swift mischiefs sent
To blast mankind, from yon ethereal tower.
Let thy malignant spirit move
Its darkness over those I love:
On me and mine I imprecate
The utmost torture of thy hate;
And thus devote to sleepless agony
This undeclining head while thou must reign on high.

But thou who art the God and Lord—O thou
Who fillest with thy soul this world of woe,
To whom all things of Earth and Heaven do bow
In fear and worship—all-prevailing foe!
I curse thee! let a sufferer's curse
Clasp thee, his torturer, like remorse
Till thine Infinity shall be
A robe of envenomed agony;
And thine Omnipotence a crown of pain,
To cling like burning gold round thy dissolving brain.

Heap on thy soul, by virtue of this curse,
Ill deeds, then be thou damned, beholding good;
Both infinite as is the Universe,
And thou, and thy self-torturing solitude.
An awful image of calm power
Though now thou sittest, let the hour
Come, when thou must appear to be
That which thou art internally,
And after many a false and fruitless crime
Scorn track thy lagging fall through boundless space and time.

Prometheus

Were these my words, O Parent?

The Earth

They were thine.

Prometheus

It doth repent me: words are quick and vain;
Grief for a while is blind, and so was mine.
I wish no living thing to suffer pain.

The Earth

Misery, Oh misery to me
That Jove at length should vanquish thee.
Wail, howl aloud, Land and Sea,
The Earth's rent heart shall answer ye.
Howl, Spirits of the living and the dead,
Your refuge, your defence lies fallen and vanquished.

First Echo

Lies fallen and vanquished?

Second Echo

Fallen and vanquished?

Ione

Fear not: 'tis but some passing spasm,
The Titan is unvanquished still.
But see, where through the azure chasm
Of yon forked and snowy hill
Trampling the slant winds on high
With golden-sandalled feet, that glow
Under plumes of purple dye,
Like rose-ensanguined ivory,
A Shape comes now,
Stretching on high from his right hand
A serpent-cinctured wand.

Panthea

'Tis Jove's world-wandering herald, Mercury.

Ione

And who are those with hydra tresses
And iron wings that climb the wind,
Whom the frowning God represses
Like vapours steaming up behind,
Clanging loud, an endless crowd—

Panthea

These are Jove's tempest-walking hounds,
Whom he gluts with groans and blood,
When charioted on sulphurous cloud
He bursts Heaven's bounds.

Ione

Are they now led, from the thin dead
On new pangs to be fed?

Panthea

The Titan looks as ever, firm, not proud.

First Fury

Ha! I scent life!

Second Fury

Let me but look into his eyes!

Third Fury

The hope of torturing him smells like a heap
Of corpses, to a death-bird after battle.

First Fury

Darest thou delay, O Herald! take cheer, Hounds
Of Hell: what if the Son of Maia soon
Should make us food and sport? Who can please long
The Omnipotent?

Mercury

Back to your towers of iron,
And gnash, beside the streams of fire and wail,
Your foodless teeth . . . Geryon, arise! and Gorgon,

Chimaera, and thou Sphinx, subtlest of fiends,
Who ministered to Thebes Heaven's poisoned wine,
Unnatural love, and more unnatural hate:
These shall perform your task.

First Fury

Oh, mercy! mercy!
We die with our desire—drive us not back!

Mercury

Crouch then in silence.—
Awful Sufferer!
To thee unwilling, most unwillingly
I come, by the great Father's will driven down
To execute a doom of new revenge.
Alas! I pity thee, and hate myself
That I can do no more: aye from thy sight
Returning, for a season, Heaven seems Hell,
So thy worn form pursues me night and day,
Smiling reproach. Wise art thou, firm and good,
But vainly wouldst stand forth alone in strife
Against the Omnipotent; as yon clear lamps
That measure and divide the weary years
From which there is no refuge, long have taught
And long must teach. Even now thy Torturer arms
With the strange might of unimagined pains
The powers who scheme slow agonies in Hell,
And my commission is to lead them here,
Or what more subtle, foul, or savage fiends
People the abyss, and leave them to their task.
Be it not so! There is a secret known
To thee, and to none else of living things,
Which may transfer the sceptre of wide Heaven,
The fear of which perplexes the Supreme:
Clothe it in words, and bid it clasp his throne
In intercession; bend thy soul in prayer,
And like a suppliant in some gorgeous fane,
Let the will kneel within thy haughty heart:
For benefits and meek submission tame
The fiercest and the mightiest.

Prometheus

Evil minds
Change good to their own nature. I gave all
He has; and in return he chains me here
Years, ages, night and day: whether the Sun
Split my parched skin, or in the moony night
The crystal-winged snow cling round my hair—
Whilst my beloved race is trampled down
By his thought-executing ministers.
Such is the tyrant's recompense—'tis just:
He who is evil can receive no good;
And for a world bestowed, or a friend lost,
He can feel hate, fear, shame—not gratitude:
He but requites me for his own misdeed.
Kindness to such is keen reproach, which breaks
With bitter stings the light sleep of Revenge.
Submission, thou dost know I cannot try:
For what submission but that fatal word,
The death-seal of mankind's captivity,
Like the Sicilian's hair-suspended sword
Which trembles o'er his crown, would he accept,
Or could I yield? Which yet I will not yield.
Let others flatter Crime, where it sits throned
In brief Omnipotence; secure are they:
For Justice, when triumphant, will weep down
Pity, not punishment, on her own wrongs,
Too much avenged by those who err. I wait,
Enduring thus, the retributive hour
Which since we spake is even nearer now.
But hark, the hell-hounds clamour: fear delay!
Behold! Heaven lowers under thy Father's frown.

Mercury

Oh, that we might be spared: I to inflict,
And thou to suffer! Once more answer me:
Thou knowest not the period of Jove's power?

Prometheus

I know but this, that it must come.

Mercury

Alas!
Thou canst not count thy years to come of pain?

Prometheus

They last while Jove must reign; nor more, nor less
Do I desire or fear.

Mercury

Yet pause, and plunge
Into Eternity, where recorded time,
Even all that we imagine, age on age,
Seems but a point, and the reluctant mind
Flags wearily in its unending flight
Till it sink, dizzy, blind, lost, shelterless;
Perchance it has not numbered the slow years
Which thou must spend in torture, unreprieved?

Prometheus

Perchance no thought can count them—yet they pass.

Mercury

If thou might'st dwell among the Gods the while,
Lapped in voluptuous joy?

Prometheus

I would not quit
This bleak ravine, these unrepentant pains.

Mercury

Alas! I wonder at, yet pity thee.

Prometheus

Pity the self-despising slaves of Heaven,
Not me, within whose mind sits peace serene
As light in the sun, throned . . . How vain is talk!
Call up the fiends.

Ione

O, sister, look! White fire
Has cloven to the roots yon huge snow-loaded cedar;
How fearfully God's thunder howls behind!

Mercury
I must obey his words and thine—alas!
Most heavily remorse hangs at my heart!

Panthea
See where the child of Heaven, with winged feet,
Runs down the slanted sunlight of the dawn.

Ione
Dear sister, close thy plumes over thine eyes
Lest thou behold and die—they come, they come
Blackening the birth of day with countless wings,
And hollow underneath, like death.

First Fury
Prometheus!

Second Fury
Immortal Titan!

Third Fury
Champion of Heaven's slaves!

Prometheus
He whom some dreadful voice invokes is here,
Prometheus, the chained Titan. Horrible forms,
What and who are ye? Never yet there came
Phantasms so foul through monster-teeming Hell
From the all-miscreative brain of Jove;
Whilst I behold such execrable shapes,
Methinks I grow like what I contemplate,
And laugh and stare in loathsome sympathy.

First Fury
We are the ministers of pain and fear,
And disappointment, and mistrust, and hate,
And clinging crime; and as lean dogs pursue
Through wood and lake some struck and sobbing fawn,
We track all things that weep, and bleed, and live,
When the great King betrays them to our will.

Prometheus
O many fearful natures in one name,
I know ye, and these lakes and echoes know
The darkness and the clangour of your wings.
But why more hideous than your loathed selves
Gather ye up in legions from the deep?

Second Fury
We knew not that: Sisters, rejoice, rejoice!

Prometheus
Can aught exult in its deformity?

Second Fury
The beauty of delight makes lovers glad,
Gazing on one another: so are we.
As from the rose which the pale priestess kneels
To gather for her festal crown of flowers
The aerial crimson falls, flushing her cheek,
So from our victim's destined agony
The shade which is our form invests us round,
Else we are shapeless as our mother Night.

Prometheus
I laugh your power, and his who sent you here,
To lowest scorn.—Pour forth the cup of pain.

First Fury
Thou thinkest we will rend thee bone from bone,
And nerve from nerve, working like fire within?

Prometheus
Pain is my element, as hate is thine;
Ye rend me now: I care not.

Second Fury
Dost imagine
We will but laugh into thy lidless eyes?

Prometheus

I weigh not what ye do, but what ye suffer,
Being evil. Cruel was the Power which called
You, or aught else so wretched, into light.

Third Fury

Thou think'st we will live through thee, one by one,
Like animal life, and though we can obscure not
The soul which burns within, that we will dwell
Beside it, like a vain loud multitude
Vexing the self-content of wisest men:
That we will be dread thought beneath thy brain,
And foul desire round thine astonished heart,
And blood within thy labyrinthine veins
Crawling like agony.

Prometheus

Why, ye are thus now;
Yet am I king over myself, and rule
The torturing and conflicting throngs within,
As Jove rules you when Hell grows mutinous.

Chorus of Furies

From the ends of the Earth, from the ends of the Earth,
Where the night has its grave and the morning its birth,
Come, come, come!
O ye who shake hills with the scream of your mirth
When cities sink howling in ruin; and ye
Who with wingless footsteps trample the sea,
And close upon Shipwreck and Famine's track,
Sit chattering with joy on the foodless wreck;
Come, come, come!
Leave the bed, low, cold, and red,
Strewed beneath a nation dead;
Leave the hatred, as in ashes
Fire is left for future burning:
It will burst in bloodier flashes
When ye stir it, soon returning:
Leave the self-contempt implanted
In young spirits, sense-enchanted,
Misery's yet unkindled fuel:
Leave Hell's secrets half unchanted

To the maniac dreamer: cruel
More than ye can be with hate
Is he with fear.
Come, come, come!
We are steaming up from Hell's wide gate
And we burthen the blasts of the atmosphere,
But vainly we toil till ye come here.

Ione
Sister, I hear the thunder of new wings.

Panthea
These solid mountains quiver with the sound
Even as the tremulous air: their shadows make
The space within my plumes more black than night.

First Fury
Your call was as a winged car
Driven on whirlwinds fast and far;
It rapt us from red gulfs of war.

Second Fury
From wide cities, famine-wasted—

Third Fury
Groans half heard, and blood untasted—

Fourth Fury
Kingly conclaves stern and cold,
Where blood with gold is bought and sold—

Fifth Fury
From the furnace white and hot
In which—

A Fury
Speak not—whisper not;
I know all that ye would tell,
But to speak might break the spell
Which must bend the Invincible,
The stern of thought;
He yet defies the deepest power of Hell.

A Fury

Tear the veil!

Another Fury

It is torn.

Chorus

The pale stars of the morn
Shine on a misery dire to be borne.
Dost thou faint, mighty Titan? We laugh thee to scorn.
Dost thou boast the clear knowledge thou waken'dst for man?
Then was kindled within him a thirst which outran
Those perishing waters; a thirst of fierce fever,
Hope, love, doubt, desire—which consume him for ever.
One came forth of gentle worth
Smiling on the sanguine earth;
His words outlived him, like swift poison
Withering up truth, peace, and pity.
Look! where round the wide horizon
Many a million-peopled city
Vomits smoke in the bright air—
Hark that outcry of despair!
'Tis his mild and gentle ghost
Wailing for the faith he kindled:
Look again, the flames almost
To a glow-worm's lamp have dwindled:
The survivors round the embers
Gather in dread.
Joy, joy, joy!
Past ages crowd on thee, but each one remembers,
And the future is dark, and the present is spread
Like a pillow of thorns for thy slumberless head.

Semichorus I

Drops of bloody agony flow
From his white and quivering brow.
Grant a little respite now—
See! a disenchanted nation
Springs like day from desolation;
To Truth its state is dedicate,

And Freedom leads it forth, her mate;
A legioned band of linked brothers
Whom Love calls children—

Semichorus II

'Tis another's—
See how kindred murder kin!
'Tis the vintage-time for Death and Sin:
Blood, like new wine, bubbles within
Till Despair smothers
The struggling World—which slaves and tyrants win.
[*All the* FURIES *vanish, except one.*

Ione
Hark, sister! what a low yet dreadful groan
Quite unsuppressed is tearing up the heart
Of the good Titan, as storms tear the deep,
And beasts hear the sea moan in inland caves.
Darest thou observe how the fiends torture him?

Panthea
Alas, I looked forth twice, but will no more.

Ione
What didst thou see?

Panthea
A woeful sight: a youth
With patient looks nailed to a crucifix.

Ione
What next?

Panthea
The heaven around, the earth below
Was peopled with thick shapes of human death,
All horrible, and wrought by human hands,
And some appeared the work of human hearts,
For men were slowly killed by frowns and smiles:
And other sights too foul to speak and live
Were wandering by. Let us not tempt worse fear
By looking forth: those groans are grief enough.

Fury
Behold, an emblem: those who do endure
Deep wrongs for man, and scorn, and chains, but heap
Thousandfold torment on themselves and him.

Prometheus
Remit the anguish of that lighted stare;
Close those wan lips; let that thorn-wounded brow
Stream not with blood—it mingles with thy tears!
Fix, fix those tortured orbs in peace and death,
So thy sick throes shake not that crucifix,
So those pale fingers play not with thy gore.
O, horrible! Thy name I will not speak,
It hath become a curse. I see, I see
The wise, the mild, the lofty, and the just,
Whom thy slaves hate for being like to thee,
Some hunted by foul lies from their heart's home,
An early-chosen, late-lamented home,
As hooded ounces cling to the driven hind;
Some linked to corpses in unwholesome cells:
Some—hear I not the multitude laugh loud?—
Impaled in lingering fire: and mighty realms
Float by my feet, like sea-uprooted isles,
Whose sons are kneaded down in common blood
By the red light of their own burning homes.

Fury
Blood thou canst see, and fire; and canst hear groans;
Worse things, unheard, unseen, remain behind.

Prometheus
Worse?

Fury
                In each human heart terror survives
The ravin it has gorged: the loftiest fear
All that they would disdain to think were true:
Hypocrisy and custom make their minds
The fanes of many a worship, now outworn.
They dare not devise good for man's estate,
And yet they know not that they do not dare.
The good want power, but to weep barren tears.

The powerful goodness want: worse need for them.
The wise want love, and those who love want wisdom;
And all best things are thus confused to ill.
Many are strong and rich,—and would be just,—
But live among their suffering fellow-men
As if none felt: they know not what they do.

Prometheus
Thy words are like a cloud of winged snakes;
And yet, I pity those they torture not.

Fury
Thou pitiest them? I speak no more!
[*Vanishes.*

Prometheus
Ah woe!
Ah woe! Alas! pain, pain ever, forever!
I close my tearless eyes, but see more clear
Thy works within my woe-illumed mind,
Thou subtle tyrant . . . Peace is in the grave—
The grave hides all things beautiful and good:
I am a God and cannot find it there—
Nor would I seek it. For, though dread revenge,
This is defeat, fierce King, not victory!
The sights with which thou torturest gird my soul
With new endurance, till the hour arrives
When they shall be no types of things which are.

Panthea
Alas! what sawest thou?

Prometheus
There are two woes:
To speak and to behold; thou spare me one.
Names are there, Nature's sacred watch-words—they
Were borne aloft in bright emblazonry;
The nations thronged around, and cried aloud,
As with one voice, 'Truth, liberty, and love!'
Suddenly fierce confusion fell from Heaven
Among them—there was strife, deceit, and fear:
Tyrants rushed in, and did divide the spoil.
This was the shadow of the truth I saw.

The Earth
I felt thy torture, Son, with such mixed joy
As pain and Virtue give. To cheer thy state
I bid ascend those subtle and fair spirits
Whose homes are the dim caves of human thought,
And who inhabit, as birds wing the wind,
Its world-surrounding ether: they behold
Beyond that twilight realm, as in a glass,
The future: may they speak comfort to thee!

Panthea
Look, sister, where a troop of spirits gather,
Like flocks of clouds in spring's delightful weather,
Thronging in the blue air!

Ione
And see! more come,
Like fountain-vapours when the winds are dumb,
That climb up the ravine in scattered lines.
And hark! is it the music of the pines?
Is it the lake? Is it the waterfall?

Panthea
'Tis something sadder, sweeter far than all.

Chorus of Spirits
From unremembered ages we
Gentle guides and guardians be
Of Heaven-oppressed mortality;
And we breathe, and sicken not,
The atmosphere of human thought:
Be it dim and dank and grey
Like a storm-extinguished day,
Travelled o'er by dying gleams;
  Be it bright as all between
Cloudless skies and windless streams,
  Silent, liquid, and serene—
As the birds within the wind,
  As the fish within the wave,
As the thoughts of man's own mind
  Float through all above the grave,
We make there, our liquid lair,

Voyaging cloudlike and unpent
Through the boundless element—
Thence we bear the prophecy
Which begins and ends in thee!

Ione
More yet come, one by one: the air around them
Looks radiant as the air around a star.

First Spirit
On a battle-trumpet's blast
I fled hither, fast, fast, fast,
'Mid the darkness upward cast—
From the dust of creeds outworn,
From the tyrant's banner torn,
Gathering round me, onward borne,
There was mingled many a cry—
Freedom! Hope! Death! Victory!
Till they faded through the sky
And one sound above, around,
One sound beneath, around, above,
Was moving; 'twas the soul of love;
'Twas the hope, the prophecy
Which begins and ends in thee.

Second Spirit
A rainbow's arch stood on the sea
Which rock'd beneath, immoveably;
And the triumphant storm did flee,
Like a conqueror swift and proud,
Between, with many a captive cloud,
A shapeless, dark and rapid crowd,
Each by lightning riven in half:
I heard the thunder hoarsely laugh:
Mighty fleets were strewn like chaff
And spread beneath a hell of death
O'er the white waters. I alit
On a great ship lightning-split,
And speeded hither on the sigh
Of one who gave an enemy
His plank—then plunged aside to die.

Third Spirit

I sate beside a sage's bed,
And the lamp was burning red
Near the book where he had fed,
When a Dream with plumes of flame
To his pillow hovering came,
And I knew it was the same
Which had kindled long ago
Pity, eloquence, and woe;
And the world awhile below
Wore the shade its lustre made.
It has borne me here as fleet
As Desire's lightning feet:
I must ride it back ere morrow,
Or the sage will wake in sorrow.

Fourth Spirit

On a poet's lips I slept
Dreaming like a love-adept
In the sound his breathing kept;
Nor seeks nor finds he mortal blisses,
But feeds on the aërial kisses
Of shapes that haunt thought's wildernesses.
He will watch from dawn to gloom
The lake-reflected sun illume
The yellow bees i' the ivy-bloom,
Nor heed nor see, what things they be;
But from these create he can
Forms more real than living man,
Nurslings of immortality!—
One of these awakened me,
And I sped to succour thee.

Ione

Behold'st thou not two shapes from the east and west
Come, as two doves to one beloved nest,
Twin nurslings of the all-sustaining air
On swift still wings glide down the atmosphere?
And hark! their sweet, sad voices! 'tis despair
Mingled with love and then dissolved in sound.

Panthea
Canst thou speak, sister? all my words are drowned.

Ione
Their beauty gives me voice. See how they float
On their sustaining wings of skiey grain,
Orange and azure deepening into gold:
Their soft smiles light the air like a star's fire.

Chorus of Spirits
Hast thou beheld the form of Love?

Fifth Spirit
As over wide dominions
I sped, like some swift cloud that wings the wide air's wildernesses,
That planet-crested Shape swept by on lightning-braided pinions,
Scattering the liquid joy of life from his ambrosial tresses:
His footsteps paved the world with light—but as I past 'twas fading,
And hollow Ruin yawned behind: great sages bound in madness,
And headless patriots, and pale youths who perished, unupbraiding,
Gleamed in the night I wandered o'er—'till thou, O King of sadness,
Turned by thy smile the worst I saw to recollected gladness.

Sixth Spirit
Ah, sister! Desolation is a delicate thing:
It walks not on the Earth, it floats not on the air,
But treads with lulling footstep, and fans with silent wing
The tender hopes which in their hearts the best and gentlest bear,
Who, soothed to false repose by the fanning plumes above
And the music-stirring motion of its soft and busy feet,
Dream visions of aërial joy, and call the monster, Love,
And wake, and find the shadow Pain—as he whom now we greet.

Chorus

Though Ruin now Love's shadow be,
Following him destroyingly
  On Death's white and winged steed,
Which the fleetest cannot flee—
  Trampling down both flower and weed,
Man and beast, and foul and fair,
Like a tempest through the air;
Thou shalt quell this Horseman grim,
Woundless though in heart or limb.

Prometheus

Spirits! how know ye this shall be?

Chorus

In the atmosphere we breathe,
As buds grow red when the snow-storms flee
From spring gathering up beneath,
Whose mild winds shake the elder brake,
And the wandering herdsmen know
That the white-thorn soon will blow:
Wisdom, Justice, Love, and Peace,
When they struggle to increase,
Are to us as soft winds be
To shepherd boys—the prophecy
Which begins and ends in thee.

Ione

Where are the Spirits fled?

Panthea

Only a sense
Remains of them, like the omnipotence
Of music, when the inspired voice and lute
Languish, ere yet the responses are mute
Which through the deep and labyrinthine soul,
Like echoes through long caverns, wind and roll.

Prometheus

How fair these air-born shapes! and yet I feel
Most vain all hope but love; and thou art far,
Asia! who, when my being overflowed,

Wert like a golden chalice to bright wine
Which else had sunk into the thirsty dust.
All things are still: alas! how heavily
This quiet morning weighs upon my heart;
Though I should dream, I could even sleep with grief
If slumber were denied not . . . I would fain
Be what it is my destiny to be,
The saviour and the strength of suffering man,
Or sink into the original gulf of things . . .
There is no agony, and no solace left;
Earth can console, Heaven can torment no more.

Panthea
Hast thou forgotten one who watches thee
The cold dark night, and never sleeps but when
The shadow of thy spirit falls on her?

Prometheus
I said all hope was vain but love: thou lovest.

Panthea
Deeply in truth; but the Eastern star looks white,
And Asia waits in that far Indian vale
The scene of her sad exile—rugged once
And desolate and frozen like this ravine;
But now invested with fair flowers and herbs,
And haunted by sweet airs and sounds, which flow
Among the woods and waters, from the ether
Of her transforming presence—which would fade
If it were mingled not with thine. Farewell!

End of the First Act

ACT II

Scene i

Morning. A lovely Vale in the Indian Caucasus. ASIA, *alone.*

Asia

From all the blasts of Heaven thou hast descended:
Yes, like a spirit, like a thought, which makes
Unwonted tears throng to the horny eyes,
And beatings haunt the desolated heart,
Which should have learnt repose: thou hast descended
Cradled in tempests; thou dost wake, O Spring!
O child of many winds! As suddenly
Thou comest as the memory of a dream,
Which now is sad because it hath been sweet;
Like genius, or like joy which riseth up
As from the earth, clothing with golden clouds
The desert of our life . . .
This is the season, this the day, the hour;
At sunrise thou shouldst come, sweet sister mine . . .
Too long desired, too long delaying, come!
How like death-worms the wingless moments crawl!
The point of one white star is quivering still
Deep in the orange light of widening morn
Beyond the purple mountains; through a chasm
Of wind-divided mist the darker lake
Reflects it—now it wanes—it gleams again
As the waves fade, and as the burning threads
Of woven cloud unravel in pale air . . .
'Tis lost! and through yon peaks of cloudlike snow
The roseate sun-light quivers: hear I not
The Aeolian music of her sea-green plumes
Winnowing the crimson dawn?

[PANTHEA *enters*

I feel, I see
Those eyes which burn through smiles that fade in tears,
Like stars half quenched in mists of silver dew.
Beloved and most beautiful, who wearest

The shadow of that soul by which I live,
How late thou art! the sphered sun had climbed
The sea, my heart was sick with hope, before
The printless air felt thy belated plumes.

Panthea

Pardon, great Sister! but my wings were faint
With the delight of a remembered dream,
As are the noontide plumes of summer winds
Satiate with sweet flowers. I was wont to sleep
Peacefully, and awake refreshed and calm
Before the sacred Titan's fall, and thy
Unhappy love, had made, through use and pity,
Both love and woe familiar to my heart
As they had grown to thine: erewhile I slept
Under the glaucous caverns of old Ocean
Within dim bowers of green and purple moss,
Our young Ione's soft and milky arms
Locked then, as now, behind my dark, moist hair,
While my shut eyes and cheek were pressed within
The folded depth of her life-breathing bosom . . .
But not as now, since I am made the wind
Which fails beneath the music that I bear
Of thy most wordless converse; since dissolved
Into the sense with which love talks, my rest
Was troubled and yet sweet—my waking hours
Too full of care and pain.

Asia

Lift up thine eyes
And let me read thy dream.

Panthea

As I have said
With our sea-sister at his feet I slept.
The mountain mists, condensing at our voice
Under the moon, had spread their snowy flakes,
From the keen ice shielding our linked sleep . . .
Then two dreams came. One, I remember not.
But in the other his pale, wound-worn limbs
Fell from Prometheus, and the azure night

Grew radiant with the glory of that form
Which lives unchanged within, and his voice fell
Like music which makes giddy the dim brain,
Faint with intoxication of keen joy:
'Sister of her whose footsteps pave the world
With loveliness—more fair than aught but her
Whose shadow thou art—lift thine eyes on me!'
I lifted them: the overpowering light
Of that immortal shape was shadowed o'er
By love; which, from his soft and flowing limbs,
And passion-parted lips, and keen, faint eyes,
Steamed forth like vaporous fire; an atmosphere
Which wrapt me in its all-dissolving power,
As the warm ether of the morning sun
Wraps ere it drinks some cloud of wandering dew.
I saw not, heard not, moved not, only felt
His presence flow and mingle through my blood
Till it became his life, and his grew mine,
And I was thus absorbed—until it passed,
And like the vapours when the sun sinks down,
Gathering again in drops upon the pines,
And tremulous as they, in the deep night
My being was condensed; and as the rays
Of thought were slowly gathered, I could hear
His voice, whose accents lingered ere they died
Like footsteps of far melody: thy name
Among the many sounds alone I heard
Of what might be articulate; though still
I listened through the night when sound was none.
Ione wakened then, and said to me:
'Canst thou divine what troubles me to-night?
I always knew what I desired before,
Nor ever found delight to wish in vain.
But now I cannot tell thee what I seek;
I know not—something sweet, since it is sweet
Even to desire; it is thy sport, false sister!
Thou hast discovered some enchantment old,
Whose spells have stolen my spirit as I slept
And mingled it with thine;—for when just now
We kissed, I felt within thy parted lips
The sweet air that sustained me, and the warmth

Of the life-blood, for loss of which I faint,
Quivered between our intertwining arms.'
I answered not, for the Eastern star grew pale,
But fled to thee.

Asia
Thou speakest, but thy words
Are as the air: I feel them not . . . Oh, lift
Thine eyes, that I may read his written soul!

Panthea
I lift them, though they droop beneath the load
Of that they would express: what canst thou see
But thine own fairest shadow imaged there?

Asia
Thine eyes are like the deep, blue, boundless heaven
Contracted to two circles underneath
Their long, fine lashes; dark, far, measureless,—
Orb within orb, and line through line inwoven.

Panthea
Why lookest thou as if a spirit passed?

Asia
There is a change; beyond their inmost depth
I see a shade, a shape: 'tis He, arrayed
In the soft light of his own smiles, which spread
Like radiance from the cloud-surrounded moon.
Prometheus, it is thine! depart not yet!
Say not those smiles that we shall meet again
Within that bright pavilion which their beams
Shall build o'er the waste world? The dream is told.
What shape is that between us? Its rude hair
Roughens the wind that lifts it, its regard
Is wild and quick, yet 'tis a thing of air
For through its grey robe gleams the golden dew
Whose stars the noon has quenched not.

Dream
Follow! Follow!

Panthea
It is mine other dream.

Asia
It disappears.

Panthea
It passes now into my mind. Methought
As we sate here, the flower-infolding buds
Burst on yon lightning-blasted almond tree,
When swift from the white Scythian wilderness
A wind swept forth wrinkling the Earth with frost . . .
I looked, and all the blossoms were blown down;
But on each leaf was stamped, as the blue bells
Of Hyacinth tell Apollo's written grief—
O, follow, follow!

Asia
As you speak, your words
Fill, pause by pause, my own forgotten sleep
With shapes . . . methought among these lawns together
We wandered, underneath the young grey dawn,
And multitudes of dense white fleecy clouds
Were wandering in thick flocks along the mountains
Shepherded by the slow, unwilling wind;
And the white dew on the new-bladed grass,
Just piercing the dark earth, hung silently—
And there was more which I remember not;
But on the shadows of the moving clouds,
Athwart the purple mountain slope, was written
Follow, O follow! as they vanished by;
And on each herb, from which Heaven's dew had fallen,
The like was stamped as with a withering fire.
A wind arose among the pines; it shook
The clinging music from their boughs, and then
Low, sweet, faint sounds, like the farewell of ghosts,
Were heard: *O, follow, follow, follow me!*
And then I said: 'Panthea, look on me.'
But in the depth of those beloved eyes
Still I saw, *follow, follow!*

Echo

Follow, follow!

Panthea

The crags, this clear spring morning, mock our voices,
As they were spirit-tongued.

Asia

It is some being
Around the crags. What fine clear sounds! O, list!

Echoes (unseen)

Echoes we: listen!
We cannot stay:
As dew-stars glisten
Then fade away—
Child of Ocean!

Asia

Hark! Spirits speak. The liquid responses
Of their aërial tongues yet sound.

Panthea

I hear.

Echoes

O follow, follow,
As our voice recedeth
Through the caverns hollow,
Where the forest spreadeth;

(*More distant*)

O follow, follow!
Through the caverns hollow,
As the song floats thou pursue,
Where the wild bee never flew,
Through the noon-tide darkness deep,
By the odour-breathing sleep
Of faint night-flowers, and the waves
At the fountain-lighted caves,
While our music, wild and sweet,
Mocks thy gently falling feet,
Child of Ocean!

Asia
Shall we pursue the sound? It grows more faint
And distant.

Panthea
List! the strain floats nearer now.

Echoes
In the world unknown
Sleeps a voice unspoken;
By thy step alone
Can its rest be broken;
Child of Ocean!

Asia
How the notes sink upon the ebbing wind!

Echoes
O follow, follow!
Through the caverns hollow,
As the song floats thou pursue,
By the woodland noon-tide dew,
By the forests, lakes, and fountains,
Through the many-folded mountains,
To the rents, and gulfs, and chasms,
Where the Earth reposed from spasms,
On the day when He and thou
Parted, to commingle now,
Child of Ocean!

Asia
Come, sweet Panthea, link thy hand in mine,
And follow, ere the voices fade away.

Scene ii

A Forest, intermingled with Rocks and Caverns. ASIA *and* PANTHEA *pass into it. Two young Fauns are sitting on a Rock, listening.*

Semichorus I of Spirits

The path through which that lovely twain
  Have past, by cedar, pine, and yew,
  And each dark tree that ever grew,
  Is curtained out from Heaven's wide blue;
Nor sun, nor moon, nor wind, nor rain,
    Can pierce its interwoven bowers,
  Nor aught, save where some cloud of dew,
Drifted along the earth-creeping breeze
Between the trunks of the hoar trees,
    Hangs each a pearl in the pale flowers
  Of the green laurel, blown anew;
And bends, and then fades silently,
One frail and fair anemone:
Or when some star of many a one
That climbs and wanders through steep night,
Has found the cleft through which alone
Beams fall from high those depths upon,
Ere it is borne away, away,
By the swift Heavens that cannot stay—
It scatters drops of golden light,
Like lines of rain that ne'er unite:
And the gloom divine is all around;
And underneath is the mossy ground.

Semichorus II

There the voluptuous nightingales
  Are awake through all the broad noonday;
When one with bliss or sadness fails,
    And through the windless ivy-boughs,
  Sick with sweet love, droops dying away
On its mate's music-panting bosom;
Another from the swinging blossom,
    Watching to catch the languid close
  Of the last strain, then lifts on high
  The wings of the weak melody,
Till some new strain of feeling bear
  The song, and all the woods are mute;
When there is heard through the dim air
The rush of wings, and rising there
  Like many a lake-surrounded flute,
Sounds overflow the listener's brain
So sweet, that joy is almost pain.

Semichorus I

There those enchanted eddies play
Of echoes, music-tongued, which draw,
By Demogorgon's mighty law,
With melting rapture, or sweet awe,
All spirits on that secret way,
As inland boats are driven to Ocean
Down streams made strong with mountain-thaw;
And first there comes a gentle sound
To those in talk or slumber bound,
And wakes the destined: soft emotion
Attracts, impels them; those who saw
Say from the breathing Earth behind
There steams a plume-uplifting wind
Which drives them on their path, while they
Believe their own swift wings and feet
The sweet desires within obey:
And so they float upon their way,
Until, still sweet, but loud and strong,
The storm of sound is driven along,
Sucked up and hurrying: as they fleet
Behind, its gathering billows meet
And to the fatal mountain bear
Like clouds amid the yielding air.

First Faun

Canst thou imagine where those spirits live
Which make such delicate music in the woods?
We haunt within the least frequented caves
And closest coverts, and we know these wilds,
Yet never meet them, though we hear them oft:
Where may they hide themselves?

Second Faun

'Tis hard to tell:
I have heard those more skilled in spirits say,
The bubbles, which the enchantment of the sun
Sucks from the pale faint water-flowers that pave
The oozy bottom of clear lakes and pools,
Are the pavilions where such dwell and float
Under the green and golden atmosphere
Which noon-tide kindles through the woven leaves;

And when these burst, and the thin fiery air,
The which they breathed within those lucent domes,
Ascends to flow like meteors through the night,
They ride on them, and rein their headlong speed,
And bow their burning crests, and glide in fire
Under the waters of the earth again.

First Faun
If such live thus, have others other lives,
Under pink blossoms or within the bells
Of meadow flowers, or folded violets deep,
Or on their dying odours, when they die,
Or in the sunlight of the sphered dew?

Second Faun
Ay, many more which we may well divine.
But should we stay to speak, noontide would come,
And thwart Silenus find his goats undrawn,
And grudge to sing those wise and lovely songs
Of fate, and chance, and God, and Chaos old,
And Love, and the chained Titan's woful doom,
And how he shall be loosed, and make the Earth
One brotherhood: delightful strains which cheer
Our solitary twilights, and which charm
To silence the unenvying nightingales.

Scene iii

A Pinnacle of Rock among Mountains. ASIA *and* PANTHEA.

Panthea
Hither the sound has borne us—to the realm
Of Demogorgon, and the mighty portal,
Like a volcano's meteor-breathing chasm,
Whence the oracular vapour is hurled up
Which lonely men drink wandering in their youth,
And call truth, virtue, love, genius, or joy,
That maddening wine of life, whose dregs they drain
To deep intoxication; and uplift,
Like Maenads who cry loud, Evoe! Evoe!
The voice which is contagion to the world.

Asia
Fit throne for such a Power! Magnificent!
How glorious art thou, Earth! and if thou be
The shadow of some Spirit lovelier still,
Though evil stain its work, and it should be
Like its creation, weak yet beautiful,
I could fall down and worship that and thee—
Even now my heart adoreth—Wonderful!
Look, sister—ere the vapour dim thy brain:
Beneath is a wide plain of billowy mist,
As a lake, paving in the morning sky,
With azure waves which burst in silver light,
Some Indian vale . . . Behold it, rolling on
Under the curdling winds, and islanding
The peak whereon we stand—midway, around
Encinctured by the dark and blooming forests,
Dim twilight lawns, and stream-illumed caves,
And wind-enchanted shapes of wandering mist;
And far on high the keen sky-cleaving mountains
From icy spires of sun-like radiance fling
The dawn, as lifted Ocean's dazzling spray,
From some Atlantic islet scattered up,
Spangles the wind with lamp-like water-drops.
The vale is girdled with their walls—a howl
Of cataracts from their thaw-cloven ravines
Satiates the listening wind, continuous, vast,
Awful as silence—Hark! the rushing snow!
The sun-awakened avalanche! whose mass,
Thrice sifted by the storm, had gathered there
Flake after flake: in Heaven-defying minds
As thought by thought is piled, till some great truth
Is loosened, and the nations echo round,
Shaken to their roots, as do the mountains now.

Panthea
Look how the gusty sea of mist is breaking
In crimson foam, even at our feet!—it rises
As Ocean at the enchantment of the moon
Round foodless men wrecked on some oozy isle.

Asia
The fragments of the cloud are scattered up;
The wind that lifts them disentwines my hair;
Its billows now sweep o'er mine eyes—my brain
Grows dizzy—seest thou shapes within the mist?

Panthea
A countenance with beckoning smiles—there burns
An azure fire within its golden locks—
Another and another—hark! they speak!

Song of Spirits

To the Deep, to the Deep,
Down, down!
Through the shade of Sleep,
Through the cloudy strife
Of Death and of Life;
Through the veil and the bar
Of things which seem and are
Even to the steps of the remotest throne,
Down, down!

While the sound whirls around,
Down, down!
As the fawn draws the hound,
As the lightning the vapour,
As a weak moth the taper;
Death, Despair; Love, Sorrow;
Time both; to-day, to-morrow;
As steel obeys the spirit of the stone,
Down, down!

Through the grey, void Abysm,
Down, down!
Where the air is no prism,
And the moon and stars are not,
And the cavern-crags wear not
The radiance of Heaven,
Nor the gloom to Earth given;
Where there is One pervading, One alone,
Down, down!

In the depth of the Deep,
Down, down!
Like veiled lightning asleep,
Like the spark nursed in embers,
The last look Love remembers,
Like a diamond, which shines
On the dark wealth of mines,
A spell is treasured but for thee alone.
Down, down!

We have bound thee, we guide thee
Down, down!
With the bright form beside thee;
Resist not the weakness—
Such strength is in meekness
That the Eternal, the Immortal,
Must unloose through life's portal
The snake-like Doom coiled underneath his throne
By that alone!

Scene iv

The Cave of DEMOGORGON. ASIA *and* PANTHEA.

Panthea
What veiled form sits on that ebon throne?

Asia
The veil has fallen.

Panthea
I see a mighty Darkness
Filling the seat of power; and rays of gloom
Dart round, as light from the meridian sun,
Ungazed upon and shapeless—neither limb,
Nor form, nor outline; yet we feel it is
A living Spirit.

Demogorgon
Ask what thou wouldst know.

Asia
What canst thou tell?

Demogorgon
All things thou dar'st demand.

Asia
Who made the living world?

Demogorgon
God.

Asia
Who made all
That it contains—thought, passion, reason, will,
Imagination?

Demogorgon
God: Almighty God.

Asia
Who made that sense which, when the winds of spring
In rarest visitation, or the voice
Of one beloved heard in youth alone,
Fills the faint eyes with falling tears which dim
The radiant looks of unbewailing flowers,
And leaves this peopled earth a solitude
When it returns no more?

Demogorgon
Merciful God.

Asia
And who made terror, madness, crime, remorse,
Which from the links of the great chain of things
To every thought within the mind of man
Sway and drag heavily—and each one reels
Under the load towards the pit of death;
Abandoned hope, and love that turns to hate;
And self-contempt, bitterer to drink than blood;
Pain, whose unheeded and familiar speech
Is howling and keen shrieks, day after day;
And Hell, or the sharp fear of Hell?

Demogorgon
He reigns.

Asia
Utter his name: a world pining in pain
Asks but his name: curses shall drag him down.

Demogorgon
He reigns.

Asia
I feel, I know it: who?

Demogorgon
He reigns.

Asia
Who reigns? There was the Heaven and Earth at first,
And Light and Love; then Saturn, from whose throne
Time fell, an envious shadow; such the state
Of the earth's primal spirits beneath his sway,
As the calm joy of flowers and living leaves
Before the wind or sun has withered them
And semi-vital worms; but he refused
The birthrights of their being, knowledge, power,
The skill which wields the elements, the thought
Which pierces this dim universe like light,
Self-empire, and the majesty of love;
For thirst of which they fainted. Then Prometheus
Gave wisdom, which is strength, to Jupiter,
And with this law alone: 'Let man be free',
Clothed him with the dominion of wide Heaven.
To know nor faith, nor love, nor law; to be
Omnipotent but friendless, is to reign;
And Jove now reigned; for on the race of man
First famine, and then toil, and then disease,
Strife, wounds, and ghastly death unseen before,
Fell; and the unseasonable seasons drove,
With alternating shafts of frost and fire,
Their shelterless, pale tribes to mountain caves;
And in their desert hearts fierce wants he sent,
And mad disquietudes, and shadows idle

Of unreal good, which levied mutual war,
So ruining the lair wherein they raged.
Prometheus saw, and waked the legioned hopes
Which sleep within folded Elysian flowers,
Nepenthe, Moly, Amaranth, fadeless blooms,
That they might hide with thin and rainbow wings
The shape of Death; and Love he sent to bind
The disunited tendrils of that vine
Which bears the wine of life, the human heart;
And he tamed fire which, like some beast of prey,
Most terrible, but lovely, played beneath
The frown of man; and tortured to his will
Iron and gold, the slaves and signs of power,
And gems and poisons, and all subtlest forms
Hidden beneath the mountains and the waves.
He gave man speech, and speech created thought,
Which is the measure of the universe;
And Science struck the thrones of Earth and Heaven,
Which shook, but fell not; and the harmonious mind
Poured itself forth in all-prophetic song;
And music lifted up the listening spirit
Until it walked, exempt from mortal care,
Godlike, o'er the clear billows of sweet sound;
And human hands first mimicked and then mocked,
With moulded limbs more lovely than its own,
The human form, till marble grew divine,
And mothers, gazing, drank the love men see
Reflected in their race—behold, and perish.
He told the hidden power of herbs and springs,
And Disease drank and slept. Death grew like sleep.
He taught the implicated orbits woven
Of the wide-wandering stars, and how the sun
Changes his lair, and by what secret spell
The pale moon is transformed, when her broad eye
Gazes not on the interlunar sea;
He taught to rule, as life directs the limbs,
The tempest-wingèd chariots of the Ocean,
And the Celt knew the Indian. Cities then
Were built, and through their snow-like columns flowed
The warm winds, and the azure aether shone,
And the blue sea and shadowy hills were seen.

Such, the alleviations of his state,
Prometheus gave to man—for which he hangs
Withering in destined pain: but who rains down
Evil, the immedicable plague, which, while
Man looks on his creation like a God
And sees that it is glorious, drives him on
The wreck of his own will, the scorn of Earth,
The outcast, the abandoned, the alone?
Not Jove: while yet his frown shook Heaven, aye, when
His adversary from adamantine chains
Cursed him, he trembled like a slave. Declare
Who is his master? Is he too a slave?

Demogorgon
All spirits are enslaved which serve things evil:
Thou knowest if Jupiter be such or no.

Asia
Whom called'st thou God?

Demogorgon
I spoke but as ye speak,
For Jove is the supreme of living things.

Asia
Who is the master of the slave?

Demogorgon
If the Abysm
Could vomit forth its secrets:—but a voice
Is wanting, the deep truth is imageless;
For what would it avail to bid thee gaze
On the revolving world? what to bid speak
Fate, Time, Occasion, Chance and Change? To these
All things are subject but eternal Love.

Asia
So much I asked before, and my heart gave
The response thou hast given; and of such truths
Each to itself must be the oracle.
One more demand; and do thou answer me

As my own soul would answer, did it know
That which I ask. Prometheus shall arise
Henceforth the Sun of this rejoicing world:
When shall the destined hour arrive?

Demogorgon
Behold!

Asia
The rocks are cloven, and through the purple night
I see cars drawn by rainbow-winged steeds
Which trample the dim winds: in each there stands
A wild-eyed charioteer, urging their flight.
Some look behind, as fiends pursued them there,
And yet I see no shapes but the keen stars:
Others, with burning eyes, lean forth, and drink
With eager lips the wind of their own speed,
As if the thing they loved fled on before,
And now, even now, they clasped it. Their bright locks
Stream like a comet's flashing hair: they all
Sweep onward.

Demogorgon
These are the immortal Hours,
Of whom thou didst demand. One waits for thee.

Asia
A spirit with a dreadful countenance
Checks its dark chariot by the craggy gulf.
Unlike thy brethren, ghastly charioteer,
What art thou? Whither wouldst thou bear me? Speak!

Spirit
I am the shadow of a destiny
More dread than is my aspect: ere yon planet
Has set, the Darkness which ascends with me
Shall wrap in lasting night Heaven's kingless throne.

Asia
What meanest thou?

Panthea

That terrible shadow floats
Up from its throne, as may the lurid smoke
Of earthquake-ruined cities o'er the sea.
Lo! it ascends the Car . . . the coursers fly
Terrified: watch its path among the stars
Blackening the night!

Asia

Thus I am answered: strange!

Panthea

See, near the verge, another chariot stays;
An ivory shell inlaid with crimson fire,
Which comes and goes within its sculptured rim
Of delicate strange tracery; the young Spirit
That guides it has the dove-like eyes of hope;
How its soft smiles attracts the soul!—as light
Lures winged insects through the lampless air.

Spirit

My coursers are fed with the lightning,
They drink of the whirlwind's stream,
And when the red morning is bright'ning
They bathe in the fresh sunbeam;
They have strength for their swiftness, I deem:
Then ascend with me, Daughter of Ocean.

I desire—and their speed makes night kindle;
I fear—they outstrip the Typhoon;
Ere the cloud piled on Atlas can dwindle
We encircle the earth and the moon:
We shall rest from long labours at noon:
Then ascend with me, Daughter of Ocean.

Scene v

The Car pauses within a Cloud on the Top of a snowy Mountain.
ASIA, PANTHEA, *and the* SPIRIT OF THE HOUR.

Spirit
On the brink of the night and the morning
My coursers are wont to respire;
But the Earth has just whispered a warning
That their flight must be swifter than fire:
They shall drink the hot speed of desire!

Asia
Thou breathest on their nostrils, but my breath
Would give them swifter speed.

Spirit
Alas! it could not.

Panthea
Oh Spirit! pause, and tell whence is the light
Which fills this cloud—the sun is yet unrisen.

Spirit
The sun will rise not until noon. Apollo
Is held in Heaven by wonder; and the light
Which fills this vapour, as the aërial hue
Of fountain-gazing roses fills the water,
Flows from thy mighty sister.

Panthea
Yes, I feel . . .

Asia
What is it with thee, sister? Thou art pale.

Panthea
How thou art changed! I dare not look on thee;
I feel but see thee not. I scarce endure
The radiance of thy beauty. Some good change
Is working in the elements, which suffer
Thy presence thus unveiled. The Nereids tell
That on the day when the clear hyaline
Was cloven at thy uprise, and thou didst stand
Within a veined shell, which floated on
Over the calm floor of the crystal sea,
Among the Aegean isles, and by the shores

Which bear thy name, love, like the atmosphere
Of the sun's fire filling the living world,
Burst from thee, and illumined Earth and Heaven
And the deep ocean and the sunless caves
And all that dwells within them; till grief cast
Eclipse upon the soul from which it came:
Such art thou now; nor is it I alone,
Thy sister, thy companion, thine own chosen one,
But the whole world which seeks thy sympathy.
Hearest thou not sounds i' the air which speak the love
Of all articulate beings? Feelest thou not
The inanimate winds enamoured of thee? List!
[*Music*

Asia
Thy words are sweeter than aught else but his
Whose echoes they are: yet all love is sweet,
Given or returned. Common as light is love,
And its familiar voice wearies not ever.
Like the wide Heaven, the all-sustaining air,
It makes the reptile equal to the God:
They who inspire it most are fortunate,
As I am now; but those who feel it most
Are happier still, after long sufferings,
As I shall soon become.

Panthea
List! Spirits speak.

Voice (*in the air, singing*)
Life of Life! thy lips enkindle
With their love the breath between them;
And thy smiles before they dwindle
Make the cold air fire; then screen them
In those looks, where whoso gazes
Faints, entangled in their mazes.

Child of Light! thy limbs are burning
Through the vest which seems to hide them
As the radiant lines of morning
Through the clouds ere they divide them;
And this atmosphere divinest
Shrouds thee wheresoe'er thou shinest.

Fair are others;—none beholds thee,
  But thy voice sounds low and tender
Like the fairest—for it folds thee
  From the sight, that liquid splendour,
And all feel, yet see thee never,
As I feel now, lost for ever!

Lamp of Earth! where'er thou movest
  Its dim shapes are clad with brightness,
And the souls of whom thou lovest
  Walk upon the winds with lightness,
Till they fail, as I am failing,
Dizzy, lost . . . yet unbewailing!

Asia

  My soul is an enchanted boat
  Which, like a sleeping swan, doth float
Upon the silver waves of thy sweet singing;
  And thine doth like an angel sit
  Beside the helm conducting it,
Whilst all the winds with melody are ringing.
  It seems to float ever, for ever,
  Upon that many-winding river,
  Between mountains, woods, abysses,
  A paradise of wildernesses!
Till, like one in slumber bound,
Borne to the ocean, I float down, around,
Into a sea profound, of ever-spreading sound.

  Meanwhile thy spirit lifts its pinions
  In Music's most serene dominions,
Catching the winds that fan that happy Heaven.
  And we sail on, away, afar,
  Without a course, without a star,
But by the instinct of sweet music driven;
  Till through Elysian garden islets
  By thee, most beautiful of pilots,
  Where never mortal pinnace glided,
  The boat of my desire is guided:
Realms where the air we breathe is Love,
Which in the winds and on the waves doth move,
Harmonizing this Earth with what we feel above.

We have past Age's icy caves,
And Manhood's dark and tossing waves,
And Youth's smooth ocean, smiling to betray:
Beyond the glassy gulfs we flee
Of shadow-peopled Infancy,
Through Death and Birth, to a diviner day;
A paradise of vaulted bowers
Lit by downward-gazing flowers,
And watery paths that wind between
Wildernesses calm and green,
Peopled by shapes too bright to see,
And rest, having beheld; somewhat like thee;
Which walk upon the sea, and chant melodiously!

End of the Second Act

ACT III

Scene i

Heaven. JUPITER *on his Throne;* THETIS *and the other Deities assembled.*

Jupiter
Ye congregated Powers of Heaven, who share
The glory and the strength of him ye serve,
Rejoice! henceforth I am omnipotent.
All else had been subdued to me; alone
The soul of man, like unextinguished fire,
Yet burns towards Heaven with fierce reproach, and doubt,
And lamentation, and reluctant prayer,
Hurling up insurrection, which might make
Our antique empire insecure, though built
On eldest faith, and Hell's coeval, fear;
And though my curses through the pendulous air,
Like snow on herbless peaks, fall flake by flake,
And cling to it; though under my wrath's night
It climb the crags of life, step after step,
Which wound it, as ice wounds unsandalled feet,
It yet remains supreme o'er misery,
Aspiring, unrepressed; yet soon to fall:

Even now have I begotten a strange wonder,
That fatal child, the terror of the earth,
Who waits but till the destined Hour arrive,
Bearing from Demogorgon's vacant throne
The dreadful might of ever-living limbs
Which clothed that awful spirit unbeheld,
To redescend, and trample out the spark.

Pour forth Heaven's wine, Idaean Ganymede,
And let it fill the daedal cups like fire,
And from the flower-inwoven soil divine
Ye all-triumphant harmonies arise,
As dew from earth under the twilight stars:
Drink! be the nectar circling through your veins
The soul of joy, ye ever-living Gods,
Till exultation burst in one wide voice
Like music from Elysian winds.
And thou
Ascend beside me, veiled in the light
Of the desire which makes thee one with me,
Thetis, bright Image of Eternity!
When thou didst cry, 'Insufferable might!
God! Spare me! I sustain not the quick flames,
The penetrating presence; all my being,
Like him whom the Numidian seps did thaw
Into a dew with poison, is dissolved,
Sinking through its foundations'—even then
Two mighty spirits, mingling, made a third
Mightier than either, which, unbodied now
Between us, floats, felt although unbeheld,
Waiting the incarnation, which ascends
(Hear ye the thunder of the fiery wheels
Griding the winds?) from Demogorgon's throne.
Victory! victory! Feel'st thou not, O world,
The earthquake of his chariot thundering up
Olympus?

[*The Car of the* HOUR *arrives.* DEMOGORGON *descends and moves towards the Throne of* JUPITER

Awful shape, what art thou? Speak!

Demogorgon
Eternity. Demand no direr name.
Descend, and follow me down the abyss.
I am thy child, as thou wert Saturn's child;
Mightier than thee: and we must dwell together
Henceforth in darkness. Lift thy lightnings not.
The tyranny of Heaven none may retain,
Or reassume, or hold, succeeding thee:
Yet if thou wilt—as 'tis the destiny
Of trodden worms to writhe till they are dead—
Put forth thy might.

Jupiter
Detested prodigy!
Even thus beneath the deep Titanian prisons
I trample thee! thou lingerest?
Mercy! mercy!
No pity, no release, no respite! . . . Oh,
That thou wouldst make mine enemy my judge,
Even where he hangs, seared by my long revenge,
On Caucasus!—he would not doom me thus.
Gentle, and just, and dreadless, is he not
The monarch of the world? What then art thou?
No refuge! no appeal!
Sink with me then,
We two will sink on the wide waves of ruin,
Even as a vulture and a snake outspent
Drop, twisted in inextricable fight,
Into a shoreless sea. Let hell unlock
Its mounded oceans of tempestuous fire,
And whelm on them into the bottomless void
This desolated world, and thee, and me,
The conqueror and the conquered, and the wreck
Of that for which they combated.
Ai! Ai!
The elements obey me not . . . I sink . . .
Dizzily down—ever, for ever, down;
And, like a cloud, mine enemy above
Darkens my fall with victory! Ai! Ai!

Scene ii

The Mouth of a great River in the Island Atlantis. OCEAN *is discovered reclining near the Shore;* APOLLO *stands beside him.*

Ocean
He fell, thou sayest, beneath his conqueror's frown?

Apollo
Aye, when the strife was ended which made dim
The orb I rule, and shook the solid stars.
The terrors of his eye illumined Heaven
With sanguine light, through the thick ragged skirts
Of the victorious Darkness, as he fell:
Like the last glare of day's red agony,
Which, from a rent among the fiery clouds,
Burns far along the tempest-wrinkled Deep.

Ocean
He sunk to the abyss? to the dark void?

Apollo
An eagle so, caught in some bursting cloud
On Caucasus, his thunder-baffled wings
Entangled in the whirlwind, and his eyes
Which gazed on the undazzling sun, now blinded
By the white lightning, while the ponderous hail
Beats on his struggling form, which sinks at length
Prone, and the aërial ice clings over it.

Ocean
Henceforth the fields of Heaven-reflecting sea
Which are my realm, will heave, unstained with blood,
Beneath the uplifting winds, like plains of corn
Swayed by the summer air; my streams will flow
Round many-peopled continents, and round
Fortunate isles; and from their glassy thrones
Blue Proteus and his humid nymphs shall mark
The shadow of fair ships, as mortals see
The floating bark of the light-laden moon
With that white star, its sightless pilot's crest,

Borne down the rapid sunset's ebbing sea;
Tracking their path no more by blood and groans,
And desolation, and the mingled voice
Of slavery and command—but by the light
Of wave-reflected flowers, and floating odours,
And music soft, and mild, free, gentle voices,
That sweetest music, such as spirits love.

Apollo

And I shall gaze not on the deeds which make
My mind obscure with sorrow, as eclipse
Darkens the sphere I guide—but list, I hear
The small, clear, silver lute of the young Spirit
That sits i' the morning star.

Ocean

Thou must away?
Thy steeds will pause at even—till when, farewell.
The loud deep calls me home even now to feed it
With azure calm out of the emerald urns
Which stand forever full beside my throne.
Behold the Nereids under the green sea,
Their wavering limbs borne on the wind-like stream,
Their white arms lifted o'er their streaming hair
With garlands pied and starry sea-flower crowns,
Hastening to grace their mighty sister's joy.
[*A sound of waves is heard.*
It is the unpastured sea hungering for calm.
Peace, monster; I come now. Farewell.

Apollo

Farewell.

Scene iii

Caucasus. PROMETHEUS, HERCULES, IONE, *the* EARTH, SPIRITS; ASIA *and* PANTHEA *borne in the Car with the* SPIRIT OF THE HOUR.

[HERCULES *unbinds* PROMETHEUS, *who descends.*

Hercules
Most glorious among spirits, thus doth strength
To wisdom, courage, and long-suffering love,
And thee, who art the form they animate,
Minister like a slave.

Prometheus
Thy gentle words
Are sweeter even than freedom long desired
And long delayed.
Asia, thou light of life,
Shadow of beauty unbeheld; and ye,
Fair sister nymphs, who made long years of pain
Sweet to remember, through your love and care;
Henceforth we will not part. There is a Cave
All overgrown with trailing odorous plants,
Which curtain out the day with leaves and flowers,
And paved with veined emerald, and a fountain
Leaps in the midst with an awakening sound.
From its curved roof the mountain's frozen tears,
Like snow, or silver, or long diamond spires,
Hang downward, raining forth a doubtful light;
And there is heard the ever-moving air,
Whispering without from tree to tree, and birds,
And bees; and all around are mossy seats,
And the rough walls are clothed with long soft grass;
A simple dwelling, which shall be our own;
Where we will sit and talk of time and change,
As the world ebbs and flows, ourselves unchanged—
What can hide man from mutability?
And if ye sigh, then I will smile; and thou,
Ione, shalt chaunt fragments of sea-music,
Until I weep, when ye shall smile away
The tears she brought, which yet were sweet to shed.
We will entangle buds and flowers and beams
Which twinkle on the fountain's brim, and make
Strange combinations out of common things,
Like human babes in their brief innocence;
And we will search, with looks and words of love,
For hidden thoughts, each lovelier than the last,
Our unexhausted spirits, and like lutes
Touched by the skill of the enamoured wind,

Weave harmonies divine, yet ever new,
From difference sweet where discord cannot be;
And hither come, sped on the charmed winds
Which meet from all the points of heaven, as bees
From every flower aërial Enna feeds
At their known island-homes in Himera,
The echoes of the human world, which tell
Of the low voice of love, almost unheard,
And dove-eyed pity's murmured pain, and music,
Itself the echo of the heart, and all
That tempers or improves man's life, now free;
And lovely apparitions, dim at first,
Then radiant, as the mind, arising bright
From the embrace of beauty, whence the forms
Of which these are the phantoms, casts on them
The gathered rays which are reality,
Shall visit us, the progeny immortal
Of Painting, Sculpture, and rapt Poesy,
And arts, though unimagined, yet to be.
The wandering voices and the shadows these
Of all that man becomes, the mediators
Of that best worship, love, by him and us
Given and returned; swift shapes and sounds, which grow
More fair and soft as man grows wise and kind,
And veil by veil, evil and error fall . . .
Such virtue has the cave and place around.
[*Turning to the* SPIRIT OF THE HOUR.
For thee, fair Spirit, one toil remains. Ione,
Give her that curved shell, which Proteus old
Made Asia's nuptial boon, breathing within it
A voice to be accomplished, and which thou
Didst hide in grass under the hollow rock.

Ione

Thou most desired Hour, more loved and lovely
Than all thy sisters, this is the mystic shell;
See the pale azure fading into silver
Lining it with a soft yet glowing light:
Looks it not like lulled music sleeping there?

Spirit
It seems in truth the fairest shell of Ocean:
Its sound must be at once both sweet and strange.

Prometheus
Go, borne over the cities of mankind
On whirlwind-footed coursers: once again
Outspeed the sun around the orbed world;
And as thy chariot cleaves the kindling air,
Thou breathe into the many-folded shell,
Loosening its mighty music; it shall be
As thunder mingled with clear echoes: then
Return; and thou shalt dwell beside our cave.
[*Kissing the ground.*
And thou, O Mother Earth!—

The Earth
I hear, I feel;
Thy lips are on me, and thy touch runs down
Even to the adamantine central gloom
Along these marble nerves; 'tis life, 'tis joy,
And through my withered, old, and icy frame
The warmth of an immortal youth shoots down
Circling. Henceforth the many children fair
Folded in my sustaining arms—all plants,
And creeping forms, and insects rainbow-winged,
And birds, and beasts, and fish, and human shapes,
Which drew disease and pain from my wan bosom,
Draining the poison of despair—shall take
And interchange sweet nutriment; to me
Shall they become like sister-antelopes
By one fair dam, snow-white and swift as wind,
Nursed among lilies near a brimming stream.
The dew-mists of my sunless sleep shall float
Under the stars like balm; night-folded flowers
Shall suck unwithering hues in their repose:
And men and beasts in happy dreams shall gather
Strength for the coming day, and all its joy:
And death shall be the last embrace of her
Who takes the life she gave, even as a mother
Folding her child, says, 'Leave me not again!'

Asia
O mother! wherefore speak the name of death?
Cease they to love, and move, and breathe, and speak,
Who die?

The Earth
It would not avail to reply:
Thou art immortal, and this tongue is known
But to the uncommunicating dead.
Death is the veil which those who live call life:
They sleep, and it is lifted: and meanwhile
In mild variety the seasons mild—
With rainbow-skirted showers, and odorous winds,
And long blue meteors cleansing the dull night,
And the life-kindling shafts of the keen sun's
All-piercing bow, and the dew-mingled rain
Of the calm moonbeams, a soft influence mild—
Shall clothe the forests and the fields—aye, even
The crag-built deserts of the barren deep—
With ever-living leaves, and fruits, and flowers.
And Thou! There is a Cavern where my spirit
Was panted forth in anguish whilst thy pain
Made my heart mad, and those who did inhale it
Became mad too, and built a temple there,
And spoke, and were oracular, and lured
The erring nations round to mutual war,
And faithless faith, such as Jove kept with thee;
Which breath now rises, as amongst tall weeds
A violet's exhalation, and it fills
With a serener light and crimson air
Intense, yet soft, the rocks and woods around;
It feeds the quick growth of the serpent vine,
And the dark linked ivy tangling wild,
And budding, blown, or odour-faded blooms
Which star the winds with points of coloured light
As they rain through them, and bright golden globes
Of fruit, suspended in their own green heaven;
And, through their veined leaves and amber stems
The flowers whose purple and translucid bowls
Stand ever mantling with aërial dew,
The drink of spirits; and it circles round,

Like the soft waving wings of noonday dreams,
Inspiring calm and happy thoughts, like mine
Now thou art thus restored. This Cave is thine.
Arise! Appear!

[*A* SPIRIT *rises in the likeness of a winged child.*

This is my torch-bearer,
Who let his lamp out in old time with gazing
On eyes from which he kindled it anew
With love, which is as fire, sweet daughter mine,
For such is that within thine own. Run, wayward!
And guide this company beyond the peak
Of Bacchic Nysa, Maenad-haunted mountain,
And beyond Indus and its tribute rivers,
Trampling the torrent streams and glassy lakes
With feet unwet, unwearied, undelaying;
And up the green ravine, across the vale,
Beside the windless and crystalline pool
Where ever lies, on unerasing waves,
The image of a temple, built above,
Distinct with column, arch, and architrave,
And palm-like capital, and over-wrought,
And populous most with living imagery,
Praxitelean shapes, whose marble smiles
Fill the hushed air with everlasting love.
It is deserted now, but once it bore
Thy name, Prometheus; there the emulous youths
Bore to thy honour through the divine gloom
The lamp which was thine emblem . . . even as those
Who bear the untransmitted torch of hope
Into the grave, across the night of life,
As thou hast borne it most triumphantly
To this far goal of Time. Depart, farewell.
Beside that temple is the destined cave.

Scene iv

A Forest. In the Back-ground a Cave. PROMETHEUS, ASIA, PANTHEA, IONE, *and the* SPIRIT OF THE EARTH.

Ione
Sister, it is not earthly . . . how it glides
Under the leaves! how on its head there burns
A light like a green star, whose emerald beams
Are twined with its fair hair! how, as it moves,
The splendour drops in flakes upon the grass!
Knowest thou it?

Panthea
It is the delicate spirit
That guides the earth through heaven. From afar
The populous constellations call that light
The loveliest of the planets; and sometimes
It floats along the spray of the salt sea,
Or makes its chariot of a foggy cloud,
Or walks through fields or cities while men sleep,
Or o'er the mountain tops, or down the rivers,
Or through the green waste wilderness, as now,
Wondering at all it sees. Before Jove reigned
It loved our sister Asia, and it came
Each leisure hour to drink the liquid light
Out of her eyes, for which it said it thirsted
As one bit by a dipsas, and with her
It made its childish confidence, and told her
All it had known or seen, for it saw much,
Yet idly reasoned what it saw; and called her—
For whence it sprung it knew not, nor do I—
'Mother, dear Mother.'

Spirit of the Earth (*running to* ASIA)
Mother, dearest Mother!
May I then talk with thee as I was wont?
May I then hide my eyes in thy soft arms,
After thy looks have made them tired of joy?
May I then play beside thee the long noons,
When work is none in the bright silent air?

Asia
I love thee, gentlest being, and henceforth
Can cherish thee unenvied. Speak, I pray:
Thy simple talk once solaced, now delights.

Spirit of the Earth
Mother, I am grown wiser, though a child
Cannot be wise like thee, within this day;
And happier too; happier and wiser both.
Thou knowest that toads, and snakes, and loathly worms,
And venomous and malicious beasts, and boughs
That bore ill berries in the woods, were ever
An hindrance to my walks o'er the green world:
And that, among the haunts of humankind,
Hard-featured men, or with proud, angry looks,
Or cold, staid gait, or false and hollow smiles,
Or the dull sneer of self-loved ignorance,
Or other such foul masks, with which ill thoughts
Hide that fair being whom we spirits call man;
And women too, ugliest of all things evil,
(Though fair, even in a world where thou art fair,
When good and kind, free and sincere like thee),
When false or frowning made me sick at heart
To pass them, though they slept, and I unseen.
Well, my path lately lay through a great city
Into the woody hills surrounding it.
A sentinel was sleeping at the gate:
When there was heard a sound, so loud, it shook
The towers amid the moonlight, yet more sweet
Than any voice but thine, sweetest of all;
A long, long sound, as it would never end:
And all the inhabitants leapt suddenly
Out of their rest, and gathered in the streets,
Looking in wonder up to Heaven, while yet
The music pealed along. I hid myself
Within a fountain in the public square,
Where I lay like the reflex of the moon
Seen in a wave under green leaves; and soon
Those ugly human shapes and visages
Of which I spoke as having wrought me pain,
Past floating through the air, and fading still
Into the winds that scattered them; and those
From whom they past seemed mild and lovely forms
After some foul disguise had fallen, and all
Were somewhat changed; and after brief surprise
And greetings of delighted wonder, all
Went to their sleep again: and when the dawn

Came—wouldst thou think that toads, and snakes, and efts,
Could e'er be beautiful? yet so they were,
And that with little change of shape or hue:
All things had put their evil nature off.
I cannot tell my joy, when o'er a lake,
Upon a drooping bough with nightshade twined,
I saw two azure halcyons clinging downward
And thinning one bright bunch of amber berries
With quick long beaks, and in the deep there lay
Those lovely forms imaged as in a sky.
So with my thoughts full of these happy changes,
We meet again, the happiest change of all.

Asia
And never will we part, till thy chaste sister
Who guides the frozen and inconstant moon
Will look on thy more warm and equal light
Till her heart thaw like flakes of April snow,
And love thee.

Spirit of the Earth
What; as Asia loves Prometheus?

Asia
Peace, wanton, thou art yet not old enough.
Think ye, by gazing on each other's eyes
To multiply your lovely selves, and fill
With sphered fires the interlunar air?

Spirit of the Earth
Nay, Mother, while my sister trims her lamp
''Tis hard I should go darkling.

Asia
Listen! look!
[*The* SPIRIT OF THE HOUR *enters.*

Prometheus
We feel what thou hast heard and seen: yet speak.

Spirit of the Hour
Soon as the sound had ceased whose thunder filled
The abysses of the sky, and the wide earth,
There was a change . . . the impalpable thin air
And the all-circling sunlight were transformed,
As if the sense of love, dissolved in them,
Had folded itself round the sphered world.
My vision then grew clear, and I could see
Into the mysteries of the universe.
Dizzy as with delight I floated down,
Winnowing the lightsome air with languid plumes,
My coursers sought their birth-place in the sun,
Where they henceforth will live exempt from toil,
Pasturing flowers of vegetable fire;
And where my moonlike car will stand within
A temple, gazed upon by Phidian forms
Of thee, and Asia, and the Earth, and me,
And you fair nymphs, looking the love we feel,
In memory of the tidings it has borne;
Beneath a dome fretted with graven flowers,
Poised on twelve columns of resplendent stone,
And open to the bright and liquid sky.
Yoked to it by an amphisbaenic snake
The likeness of those winged steeds will mock
The flight from which they find repose. Alas,
Whither has wandered now my partial tongue
When all remains untold which ye would hear?
As I have said, I floated to the earth:
It was, as it is still, the pain of bliss
To move, to breathe, to be; I wandering went
Among the haunts and dwellings of mankind,
And first was disappointed not to see
Such mighty change as I had felt within
Expressed in outward things; but soon I looked,
And behold! thrones were kingless, and men walked
One with the other even as spirits do:
None fawned, none trampled; hate, disdain, or fear,
Self-love or self-contempt, on human brows
No more inscribed, as o'er the gate of hell,
'All hope abandon ye who enter here';
None frowned, none trembled, none with eager fear
Gazed on another's eye of cold command,

Until the subject of a tyrant's will
Became, worse fate, the abject of his own,
Which spurred him, like an outspent horse, to death.
None wrought his lips in truth-entangling lines
Which smiled the lie his tongue disdained to speak;
None, with firm sneer, trod out in his own heart
The sparks of love and hope till there remained
Those bitter ashes, a soul self-consumed,
And the wretch crept, a vampire among men,
Infecting all with his own hideous ill.
None talked that common, false, cold, hollow talk
Which makes the heart deny the *yes* it breathes,
Yet question that unmeant hypocrisy
With such a self-mistrust as has no name.
And women, too, frank, beautiful, and kind
As the free heaven which rains fresh light and dew
On the wide earth, past; gentle, radiant forms,
From custom's evil taint exempt and pure;
Speaking the wisdom once they could not think,
Looking emotions once they feared to feel,
And changed to all which once they dared not be,
Yet being now, made earth like Heaven; nor pride,
Nor jealousy, nor envy, nor ill shame,
The bitterest of those drops of treasured gall,
Spoilt the sweet taste of the nepenthe, love.

Thrones, altars, judgement-seats, and prisons—wherein,
And beside which, by wretched men were borne
Sceptres, tiaras, swords, and chains, and tomes
Of reasoned wrong, glozed on by ignorance,
Were like those monstrous and barbaric shapes,
The ghosts of a no more remembered fame,
Which from their unworn obelisks look forth
In triumph o'er the palaces and tombs
Of those who were their conquerors, mouldering round.
These imaged to the pride of Kings and Priests
A dark yet mighty faith, a power as wide
As is the world it wasted, and are now
But an astonishment; even so the tools
And emblems of its last captivity,
Amid the dwellings of the peopled earth,
Stand, not o'erthrown, but unregarded now.

And those foul shapes, abhorred by God and man,
Which under many a name and many a form
Strange, savage, ghastly, dark and execrable,
Were Jupiter, the tyrant of the world;
And which the nations, panic-stricken, served
With blood, and hearts broken by long hope, and love
Dragged to his altars soiled and garlandless,
And slain among men's unreclaiming tears,
Flattering the thing they feared, which fear was hate,
Frown, mouldering fast, o'er their abandoned shrines:
The painted veil, by those who were, called life,
Which mimick'd, as with colours idly spread,
All men believed and hoped, is torn aside;
The loathsome mask has fallen, the man remains
Sceptreless, free, uncircumscribed:—but man:
Equal, unclassed, tribeless, and nationless,
Exempt from awe, worship, degree,—the King
Over himself; just, gentle, wise:—but man:
Passionless? no—yet free from guilt or pain,
Which were, for his will made, or suffered them,
Nor yet exempt, though ruling them like slaves,
From chance, and death, and mutability,
The clogs of that which else might oversoar
The loftiest star of unascended Heaven,
Pinnacled dim in the intense inane.

End of the Third Act

ACT IV

Scene,—A part of the Forest near the Cave of PROMETHEUS. PANTHEA *and* IONE *are sleeping: they awaken gradually during the first Song.*

Voice of Unseen Spirits

The pale stars are gone!
For the Sun, their swift Shepherd,
To their folds them compelling
In the depths of the dawn,
Hastes, in meteor-eclipsing array, and they flee
Beyond his blue dwelling,
As fawns flee the leopard,
But where are ye?

A Train of dark Forms and Shadows passes by confusedly, singing.

Here, oh here!
We bear the bier
Of the Father of many a cancelled year!
Spectres we
Of the dead Hours be,
We bear Time to his tomb in eternity.

Strew, oh strew
Hair, not yew!
Wet the dusty pall with tears, not dew!
Be the faded flowers
Of Death's bare bowers
Spread on the corpse of the King of Hours!

Haste, oh haste!
As shades are chased,
Trembling, by day, from Heaven's blue waste,
We melt away,
Like dissolving spray,
From the children of a diviner day,
With the lullaby
Of winds that die
On the bosom of their own harmony!

Ione

What dark forms were they?

Panthea

The past Hours weak and grey,
With the spoil which their toil
Raked together
From the conquest but One could foil.

Ione

Have they past?

Panthea

They have past;
They outspeeded the blast;
While 'tis said, they are fled—

Ione
Whither, oh whither?

Panthea
To the dark, to the past, to the dead.

Voice of Unseen Spirits
Bright clouds float in heaven,
Dew-stars gleam on earth,
Waves assemble on ocean,
They are gathered and driven
By the storm of delight, by the panic of glee!
They shake with emotion,
They dance in their mirth—
But where are ye?

The pine boughs are singing
Old songs with new gladness,
The billows and fountains
Fresh music are flinging,
Like the notes of a spirit from land and from sea;
The storms mock the mountains
With thunder of gladness.
But where are ye?

Ione
What charioteers are these?

Panthea
Where are their chariots?

Semichorus of Hours I
The voice of the Spirits of Air and of Earth
Have drawn back the figured curtain of sleep
Which covered our being and darkened our birth
In the deep—

A Voice
In the deep?

Semichorus II
Oh, below the deep.

Semichorus I

An hundred ages we had been kept
Cradled in visions of hate and care,
And each one who waked as his brother slept,
Found the truth—

Semichorus II

Worse than his visions were!

Semichorus I

We have heard the lute of Hope in sleep;
We have known the voice of Love in dreams;
We have felt the wand of Power, and leap—

Semichorus II

As the billows leap in the morning beams.

Chorus

Weave the dance on the floor of the breeze,
Pierce with song Heaven's silent light,
Enchant the day that too swiftly flees,
To check its flight ere the cave of Night.

Once the hungry Hours were hounds
Which chased the Day like a bleeding deer,
And it limped and stumbled with many wounds
Through the nightly dells of the desert year.

But now—oh weave the mystic measure
Of music and dance and shapes of light,
Let the Hours, and the Spirits of might and pleasure,
Like the clouds and sunbeams, unite.

A Voice

Unite!

Panthea

See, where the Spirits of the human mind
Wrapt in sweet sounds, as in bright veils, approach.

Chorus of Spirits

We join the throng
Of the dance and the song,
By the whirlwind of gladness borne along;
As the flying-fish leap
From the Indian deep,
And mix with the sea-birds, half asleep.

Chorus of Hours

Whence come ye, so wild and so fleet,
For sandals of lightning are on your feet,
And your wings are soft and swift as thought,
And your eyes are as Love which is veiled not?

Chorus of Spirits

We come from the mind
Of human kind,
Which was late so dusk, and obscene, and blind;
Now 'tis an ocean
Of clear emotion,
A Heaven of serene and mighty motion.

From that deep abyss
Of wonder and bliss,
Whose caverns are crystal palaces;
From those skiey towers
Where Thought's crowned Powers
Sit watching your dance, ye happy Hours!

From the dim recesses
Of woven caresses,
Where lovers catch ye by your loose tresses;
From the azure isles
Where sweet Wisdom smiles,
Delaying your ships with her syren wiles.

From the temples high
Of Man's ear and eye,
Roofed over Sculpture and Poesy;
From the murmurings
Of the unsealed springs
Where Science bedews his Daedal wings.

Years after years,
Through blood and tears,
And a thick hell of hatreds, and hopes, and fears,
We waded and flew,
And the islets were few
Where the bud-blighted flowers of happiness grew.

Our feet now, every palm,
Are sandalled with calm,
And the dew of our wings is a rain of balm;
And, beyond our eyes,
The human love lies
Which makes all it gazes on Paradise.

Chorus of Spirits and Hours

Then weave the web of the mystic measure;
From the depths of the sky and the ends of the Earth,
Come, swift Spirits of might and of pleasure,
Fill the dance and the music of mirth,
As the waves of a thousand streams rush by
To an Ocean of splendour and harmony!

Chorus of Spirits

Our spoil is won,
Our task is done,
We are free to dive, or soar, or run;
Beyond and around,
Or within the bound
Which clips the world with darkness round.

We'll pass the eyes
Of the starry skies
Into the hoar deep to colonize:
Death, Chaos, and Night,
From the sound of our flight,
Shall flee, like mist from a tempest's might.

And Earth, Air, and Light,
And the Spirit of Might,
Which drives round the stars in their fiery flight;
And Love, Thought, and Breath,
The powers that quell Death,
Wherever we soar shall assemble beneath.

And our singing shall build
In the void's loose field
A world for the Spirit of Wisdom to wield;
We will take our plan
From the new world of man,
And our work shall be called the Promethean.

Chorus of Hours

Break the dance, and scatter the song;
Let some depart, and some remain.

Semichorus I

We, beyond heaven, are driven along—

Semichorus II

Us, the enchantments of earth retain—

Semichorus I

Ceaseless and rapid and fierce and free
With the Spirits which build a new earth and sea,
And a Heaven where yet Heaven could never be—

Semichorus II

Solemn, and slow, and serene, and bright,
Leading the Day, and outspeeding the Night,
With the Powers of a world of perfect light—

Semichorus I

We whirl, singing loud, round the gathering sphere,
Till the trees, and the beasts, and the clouds appear
From its chaos made calm by love, not fear—

Semichorus II

We encircle the Oceans and Mountains of Earth,
And the happy forms of its death and birth
Change to the music of our sweet mirth.

Chorus of Hours and Spirits

Break the dance, and scatter the song—
Let some depart, and some remain;
Wherever we fly we lead along
In leashes, like star-beams, soft and yet strong,
The clouds that are heavy with Love's sweet rain.

Panthea
Ha! They are gone!

Ione
Yet feel you no delight
From the past sweetness?

Panthea
As the bare green hill
When some soft cloud vanishes into rain,
Laughs with a thousand drops of sunny water
To the unpavilioned sky!

Ione
Even whilst we speak
New notes arise. What is that awful sound?

Panthea
'Tis the deep music of the rolling world,
Kindling within the strings of the waved air
Aeolian modulations.

Ione
Listen too,
How every pause is filled with under-notes,
Clear, silver, icy, keen awakening tones,
Which pierce the sense, and live within the soul,
As the sharp stars pierce winter's crystal air
And gaze upon themselves within the sea.

Panthea
But see where, through two openings in the forest
Which hanging branches overcanopy,
And where two runnels of a rivulet,
Between the close moss, violet-interwoven,
Have made their path of melody, like sisters
Who part with sighs that they may meet in smiles,
Turning their dear disunion to an isle
Of lovely grief, a wood of sweet sad thoughts;
Two visions of strange radiance float upon
The ocean-like enchantment of strong sound,
Which flows intenser, keener, deeper yet
Under the ground and through the windless air.

Ione
I see a chariot like that thinnest boat
In which the Mother of the Months is borne
By ebbing light into her western cave,
When she upsprings from interlunar dreams,
O'er which is curved an orblike canopy
Of gentle darkness, and the hills and woods,
Distinctly seen through that dusk airy veil,
Regard like shapes in an enchanter's glass;
Its wheels are solid clouds, azure and gold,
Such as the genii of the thunder-storm
Pile on the floor of the illumined sea
When the sun rushes under it; they roll
And move and grow as with an inward wind.
Within it sits a winged infant, white
Its countenance, like the whiteness of bright snow,
Its plumes are as feathers of sunny frost,
Its limbs gleam white, through the wind-flowing folds
Of its white robe, woof of aetherial pearl.
Its hair is white,—the brightness of white light
Scattered in strings; yet its two eyes are Heavens
Of liquid darkness, which the Deity
Within seems pouring, as a storm is poured
From jagged clouds, out of their arrowy lashes,
Tempering the cold and radiant air around
With fire that is not brightness; in its hand
It sways a quivering moon-beam, from whose point
A guiding power directs the chariot's prow
Over its wheeled clouds, which as they roll
Over the grass, and flowers, and waves, wake sounds
Sweet as a singing rain of silver dew.

Panthea
And from the other opening in the wood
Rushes, with loud and whirlwind harmony,
A sphere, which is as many thousand spheres,
Solid as crystal, yet through all its mass
Flow, as through empty space, music and light:
Ten thousand orbs involving and involved,
Purple and azure, white and green and golden,
Sphere within sphere; and every space between
Peopled with unimaginable shapes,

Such as ghosts dream dwell in the lampless deep,
Yet each inter-transpicuous; and they whirl
Over each other with a thousand motions,
Upon a thousand sightless axles spinning,
And with the force of self-destroying swiftness,
Intensely, slowly, solemnly roll on,
Kindling with mingled sounds, and many tones,
Intelligible words and music wild.
With mighty whirl the multitudinous Orb
Grinds the bright brook into an azure mist
Of elemental subtlety, like light;
And the wild odour of the forest flowers,
The music of the living grass and air,
The emerald light of leaf-entangled beams,
Round its intense yet self-conflicting speed,
Seem kneaded into one aerial mass
Which drowns the sense. Within the Orb itself,
Pillowed upon its alabaster arms,
Like to a child o'erwearied with sweet toil,
On its own folded wings, and wavy hair,
The Spirit of the Earth is laid asleep,
And you can see its little lips are moving
Amid the changing light of their own smiles,
Like one who talks of what he loves in dream.

Ione
'Tis only mocking the Orb's harmony . . .

Panthea
And from a star upon its forehead, shoot,
Like swords of azure fire, or golden spears
With tyrant-quelling myrtle overtwined,
Embleming Heaven and Earth united now,
Vast beams like spokes of some invisible wheel
Which whirl as the Orb whirls, swifter than thought,
Filling the abyss with sunlike lightnings,
And perpendicular now, and now transverse,
Pierce the dark soil, and as they pierce and pass,
Make bare the secrets of the Earth's deep heart;
Infinite mine of adamant and gold,
Valueless stones, and unimagined gems,
And caverns on crystalline columns poised

With vegetable silver overspread;
Wells of unfathomed fire, and water springs
Whence the great sea, even as a child is fed,
Whose vapours clothe Earth's monarch mountain-tops
With kingly, ermine snow. The beams flash on
And make appear the melancholy ruins
Of cancelled cycles; anchors, beaks of ships,
Planks turned to marble, quivers, helms, and spears,
And gorgon-headed targes, and the wheels
Of scythed chariots, and the emblazonry
Of trophies, standards, and armorial beasts,
Round which Death laughed, sepulchred emblems
Of dead destruction, ruin within ruin!
The wrecks beside of many a city vast,
Whose population which the Earth grew over
Was mortal, but not human; see, they lie,
Their monstrous works, and uncouth skeletons,
Their statues, homes and fanes; prodigious shapes
Huddled in grey annihilation, split,
Jammed in the hard, black deep; and over these
The anatomies of unknown winged things,
And fishes which were isles of living scale,
And serpents, bony chains, twisted around
The iron crags, or within heaps of dust
To which the tortuous strength of their last pangs
Had crushed the iron crags;—and over these
The jagged alligator, and the might
Of earth-convulsing behemoth, which once
Were monarch beasts, and on the slimy shores
And weed-overgrown continents of Earth
Increased and multiplied like summer worms
On an abandoned corpse, till the blue globe
Wrapt deluge round it like a cloke, and they
Yelled, gasped, and were abolished; or some God
Whose throne was in a comet, past, and cried
'Be not!'—and like my words they were no more.

The Earth

The joy, the triumph, the delight, the madness!
The boundless, overflowing, bursting gladness,
The vaporous exultation, not to be confined!

Ha! ha! The animation of delight
Which wraps me, like an atmosphere of light,
And bears me as a cloud is borne by its own wind!

The Moon

Brother mine, calm wanderer,
Happy globe of land and air,
Some Spirit is darted like a beam from thee,
Which penetrates my frozen frame,
And passes with the warmth of flame,
With love, and odour, and deep melody
Through me, through me!

The Earth

Ha! ha! The caverns of my hollow mountains,
My cloven fire-crags, sound exulting fountains,
Laugh with a vast and inextinguishable laughter.
The oceans, and the deserts, and the abysses
Of the deep air's unmeasured wildernesses
Answer from all their clouds and billows, echoing after.

They cry aloud as I do:—'Sceptred Curse,
Who all our green and azure universe
Threatenedst to muffle round with black destruction,
sending
A solid cloud to rain hot thunderstones,
And splinter and knead down my children's bones,
All I bring forth, to one void mass battering and blending.

'Until each crag-like tower, and storied column,
Palace, and obelisk, and temple solemn,
My imperial mountains crowned with cloud, and snow,
and fire;
My sea-like forests, every blade and blossom
Which finds a grave or cradle in my bosom,
Were stamped by thy strong hate into a lifeless mire.

'How art thou sunk, withdrawn, covered—drunk up
By thirsty nothing, as the brackish cup
Drain'd by a desert-troop, a little drop for all!
And from beneath, around, within, above,
Filling thy void annihilation, Love
Bursts in like light on caves cloven by the thunder-ball.'

The Moon

The snow upon my lifeless mountains
Is loosened into living fountains,
My solid oceans flow, and sing, and shine:
A spirit from my heart bursts forth,
It clothes with unexpected birth
My cold bare bosom: Oh! it must be thine
On mine, on mine!

Gazing on thee I feel, I know,
Green stalks burst forth, and bright flowers grow,
And living shapes upon my bosom move:
Music is in the sea and air,
Winged clouds soar here and there,
Dark with the rain new buds are dreaming of:
'Tis Love, all Love!

The Earth

It interpenetrates my granite mass,
Through tangled roots and trodden clay doth pass
Into the utmost leaves and delicatest flowers;
Upon the winds, among the clouds 'tis spread,
It wakes a life in the forgotten dead—
They breathe a spirit up from their obscurest bowers—

And like a storm, bursting its cloudy prison
With thunder, and with whirlwind, has arisen
Out of the lampless caves of unimagined being,
With earthquake shock and swiftness making shiver
Thought's stagnant chaos, unremoved for ever
Till Hate, and Fear, and Pain, light-vanquished shadows, fleeing,

Leave Man, who was a many sided mirror
Which could distort to many a shape of error
This true fair world of things—a sea reflecting Love;
Which over all his kind as the Sun's Heaven
Gliding o'er ocean, smooth, serene, and even,
Darting from starry depths radiance and life, doth move;

Leave Man, even as a leprous child is left
Who follows a sick beast to some warm cleft

Of rocks, through which the might of healing springs is poured;
  Then when it wanders home with rosy smile,
  Unconscious, and its mother fears awhile
It is a Spirit—then weeps on her child restored.

  Man, oh, not men! A chain of linked thought,
  Of love and might to be divided not,
Compelling the elements with adamantine stress;
  As the Sun rules, even with a tyrant's gaze,
  The unquiet Republic of the maze
Of Planets, struggling fierce towards Heaven's free wilderness:

  Man, one harmonious Soul of many a soul,
  Whose nature is its own divine control,
Where all things flow to all, as rivers to the sea;
  Familiar acts are beautiful through love;
  Labour and Pain and Grief in life's green grove
Sport like tame beasts—none knew how gentle they could be!

  His will, with all mean passions, bad delights,
  And selfish cares, its trembling satellites,
A spirit ill to guide, but mighty to obey,
  Is as a tempest-winged ship, whose helm
  Love rules, through waves which dare not overwhelm,
Forcing Life's wildest shores to own its sovereign sway.

  All things confess his strength. Through the cold mass
  Of marble and of colour his dreams pass—
Bright threads, whence mothers weave the robes their children wear;
  Language is a perpetual Orphic song,
  Which rules with Daedal harmony a throng
Of thoughts and forms, which else senseless and shapeless were.

  The Lightning is his slave; Heaven's utmost deep
  Gives up her stars, and like a flock of sheep
They pass before his eye, are numbered, and roll on!
  The Tempest is his steed,—he strides the air;
  And the abyss shouts from her depth laid bare,
'Heaven, hast thou secrets? Man unveils me; I have none.'

The Moon

The shadow of white Death has past
From my path in Heaven at last,
A clinging shroud of solid frost and sleep;
And through my newly-woven bowers,
Wander happy paramours,
Less mighty, but as mild as those who keep
Thy vales more deep.

The Earth

As the dissolving warmth of dawn may fold
A half-unfrozen dew-globe, green and gold
And crystalline, till it becomes a winged mist,
And wanders up the vault of the blue day,
Outlives the noon, and on the sun's last ray
Hangs o'er the sea, a fleece of fire and amethyst—

The Moon

Thou art folded, thou art lying
In the light which is undying
Of thine own joy, and Heaven's smile divine;
All suns and constellations shower
On thee a light, a life, a power
Which doth array thy sphere—thou pourest thine
On mine, on mine!

The Earth

I spin beneath my pyramid of night,
Which points into the heavens, dreaming delight,
Murmuring victorious joy in my enchanted sleep;
As a youth lulled in love-dreams, faintly sighing,
Under the shadow of his beauty lying,
Which round his rest a watch of light and warmth doth keep.

The Moon

As in the soft and sweet eclipse,
When soul meets soul on lovers' lips,
High hearts are calm, and brightest eyes are dull;
So, when thy shadow falls on me,
Then am I mute and still, by thee
Covered; of thy love, Orb most beautiful,
Full, oh, too full!

Thou art speeding round the sun,
Brightest world of many a one,
Green and azure sphere which shinest
With a light which is divinest
Among all the lamps of Heaven
To whom life and light is given;
I, thy crystal paramour,
Borne beside thee by a power
Like the polar Paradise,
Magnet-like, of lovers' eyes;
I, a most enamoured maiden
Whose weak brain is overladen
With the pleasure of her love,
Maniac-like around thee move,
Gazing, an insatiate bride,
On thy form from every side,
Like a Maenad, round the cup
Which Agave lifted up
In the weird Cadmaean forest.
Brother, whersoe'er thou soarest
I must hurry, whirl and follow
Through the heavens wide and hollow,
Sheltered by the warm embrace
Of thy soul from hungry space,
Drinking from thy sense and sight
Beauty, majesty, and might,
As a lover or cameleon
Grows like what it looks upon,
As a violet's gentle eye
Gazes on the azure sky
Until its hue grows like what it beholds,
As a grey and watery mist
Glows like solid amethyst
Athwart the western mountain it enfolds
When the sunset sleeps
Upon its snow—

The Earth

And the weak day weeps
That it should be so.
O gentle Moon, the voice of thy delight
Falls on me like thy clear and tender light

Soothing the seaman, borne the summer night
  Through isles for ever calm;
Oh gentle Moon, thy crystal accents pierce
The caverns of my pride's deep universe,
Charming the tiger Joy, whose tramplings fierce
  Made wounds which need thy balm.

Panthea
I rise as from a bath of sparkling water,
A bath of azure light, among dark rocks,
Out of the stream of sound.

Ione
Ah me! sweet sister,
The stream of sound has ebbed away from us,
And you pretend to rise out of its wave,
Because your words fall like the clear soft dew
Shaken from a bathing wood-nymph's limbs and hair.

Panthea
Peace! peace! A mighty Power, which is as darkness,
Is rising out of Earth, and from the sky
Is showered like night, and from within the air
Bursts, like eclipse which had been gathered up
Into the pores of sunlight—the bright Visions,
Wherein the singing spirits rode and shone,
Gleam like pale meteors through a watery night.

Ione
There is a sense of words upon mine ear—

Panthea
A universal sound like words: O, list!

Demogorgon
Thou Earth, calm empire of a happy soul,
  Sphere of divinest shapes and harmonies,
Beautiful orb! gathering as thou dost roll
  The Love which paves thy path along the skies:

The Earth
I hear: I am as a drop of dew that dies!

Demogorgon

Thou Moon, which gazest on the nightly Earth
With wonder, as it gazes upon thee,
Whilst each to men, and beasts, and the swift birth
Of birds, is beauty, love, calm, harmony:

The Moon

I hear: I am a leaf shaken by thee!

Demogorgon

Ye Kings of suns and stars, Daemons and Gods,
Etherial Dominations, who possess
Elysian, windless, fortunate abodes
Beyond Heaven's constellated wilderness:

A Voice from Above

Our great Republic hears: we are blest, and bless.

Demogorgon

Ye happy Dead, whom beams of brightest verse
Are clouds to hide, not colours to portray,
Whether your nature is that universe
Which once ye saw and suffered—

A Voice from Beneath

Or as they
Whom we have left, we change and pass away.

Demogorgon

Ye elemental Genii, who have homes
From man's high mind even to the central stone
Of sullen lead; from Heaven's star-fretted domes
To the dull weed some sea-worm battens on:

A Confused Voice

We hear: thy words waken Oblivion.

Demogorgon

Spirits whose homes are flesh: ye beasts and birds,
Ye worms and fish; ye living leaves and buds;
Lightning and wind; and ye untameable herds,
Meteors and mists, which throng air's solitudes:

A Voice

Thy voice to us is wind among still woods.

Demogorgon

Man, who wert once a despot and a slave;
A dupe and a deceiver; a decay;
A traveller from the cradle to the grave
Through the dim night of this immortal day:

All

Speak! thy strong words may never pass away.

Demogorgon

This is the day, which down the void abysm
At the Earth-born's spell yawns for Heaven's despotism,
And Conquest is dragged captive through the deep;
Love, from its awful throne of patient power
In the wise heart, from the last giddy hour
Of dread endurance, from the slippery, steep,
And narrow verge of crag-like agony, springs
And folds over the world its healing wings.

Gentleness, Virtue, Wisdom and Endurance:
These are the seals of that most firm assurance
Which bars the pit over Destruction's strength;
And if, with infirm hand, Eternity,
Mother of many acts and hours, should free
The serpent that would clasp her with his length,
These are the spells by which to re-assume
An empire o'er the disentangled Doom.

To suffer woes which Hope thinks infinite;
To forgive wrongs darker than Death or Night;
To defy Power, which seems omnipotent;
To love, and bear; to hope till Hope creates
From its own wreck the thing it contemplates;
Neither to change, nor falter, nor repent:
This, like thy glory, Titan! is to be
Good, great and joyous, beautiful and free;
This is alone Life, Joy, Empire, and Victory.

THE CENCI

A TRAGEDY, IN FIVE ACTS

DEDICATION

TO

LEIGH HUNT, Esq.

MY DEAR FRIEND,

I inscribe with your name, from a distant country, and after an absence whose months have seemed years, this the latest of my literary efforts.

Those writings which I have hitherto published, have been little else than visions which impersonate my own apprehensions of the beautiful and the just. I can also perceive in them the literary defects incidental to youth and impatience; they are dreams of what ought to be, or may be. The drama which I now present to you is a sad reality. I lay aside the presumptuous attitude of an instructor, and am content to paint, with such colours as my own heart furnishes, that which has been.

Had I known a person more highly endowed than yourself with all that it becomes a man to possess, I had solicited for this work the ornament of his name. One more gentle, honourable, innocent and brave; one of more exalted toleration for all who do and think evil, and yet himself more free from evil; one who knows better how to receive, and how to confer a benefit though he must ever confer far more than he can receive; one of simpler, and, in the highest sense of the word, of purer life and manners I never knew: and I had already been fortunate in friendships when your name was added to the list.

In that patient and irreconcilable enmity with domestic and political tyranny and imposture which the tenor of your life has illustrated, and which, had I health and talents should illustrate mine, let us, comforting each other in our task, live and die.

All happiness attend you!

Your affectionate friend,
PERCY B. SHELLEY.

Rome, May 29, 1819.

PREFACE

A Manuscript was communicated to me during my travels in Italy which was copied from the archives of the Cenci Palace at Rome, and contains a detailed account of the horrors which ended in the extinction of one of the noblest and richest families of that city during the Pontificate of Clement VIII, in the year 1599. The story is, that an old man having spent his life in debauchery and wickedness, conceived at length an implacable hatred towards his children; which shewed itself towards one daughter under the form of an incestuous passion, aggravated by every circumstance of cruelty and violence. This daughter, after long and vain attempts to escape from what she considered a perpetual contamination both of body and mind, at length plotted with her mother-in-law and brother to murder their common tyrant. The young maiden who was urged to this tremendous deed by an impulse which overpowered its horror, was evidently a most gentle and amiable being, a creature formed to adorn and be admired, and thus violently thwarted from her nature by the necessity of circumstance and opinion. The deed was quickly discovered and, in spite of the most earnest prayers made to the Pope by the highest persons in Rome, the criminals were put to death. The old man had during his life repeatedly bought his pardon from the Pope for capital crimes of the most enormous and unspeakable kind, at the price of a hundred thousand crowns; the death therefore of his victims can scarcely be accounted for by the love of justice. The Pope, among other motives for severity, probably felt that whoever killed the Count Cenci deprived his treasury of a certain and copious source of revenue.* Such a story, if told so as to present to the reader all the

* The Papal Government formerly took the most extraordinary precautions against the publicity of facts which offer so tragical a demonstration of its own wickedness and weakness; so that the communication of the MS. had become, until very lately, a matter of some difficulty. [Shelley's note]

feelings of those who once acted it, their hopes and fears, their confidences and misgivings, their various interests, passions and opinions acting upon and with each other, yet all conspiring to one tremendous end, would be as a light to make apparent some of the most dark and secret caverns of the human heart.

On my arrival at Rome I found that the story of the Cenci was a subject not to be mentioned in Italian society without awakening a deep and breathless interest; and that the feelings of the company never failed to incline to a romantic pity for the wrongs, and a passionate exculpation of the horrible deed to which they urged her, who has been mingled two centuries with the common dust. All ranks of people knew the outlines of this history, and participated in the overwhelming interest which it seems to have the magic of exciting in the human heart. I had a copy of Guido's picture of Beatrice which is preserved in the Colonna Palace, and my servant instantly recognized it as the portrait of *La Cenci*.

This national and universal interest which the story produces and has produced for two centuries and among all ranks of people in a great City, where the imagination is kept for ever active and awake, first suggested to me the conception of its fitness for a dramatic purpose. In fact it is a tragedy which has already received, from its capacity of awakening and sustaining the sympathy of men, approbation and success. Nothing remained as I imagined, but to clothe it to the apprehensions of my countrymen in such language and action as would bring it home to their hearts. The deepest and the sublimest tragic compositions, *King Lear* and the two plays in which the tale of Oedipus is told, were stories which already existed in tradition, as matters of popular belief and interest, before Shakespeare and Sophocles made them familiar to the sympathy of all succeeding generations of mankind.

This story of the Cenci is indeed eminently fearful and monstrous: any thing like a dry exhibition of it on the stage would be insupportable. The person who would treat such a subject must increase the ideal, and diminish the actual horror of the events, so that the pleasure which arises from the poetry which exists in these tempestuous sufferings and crimes may mitigate the pain of the contemplation of the moral deformity from which they spring. There must also be nothing attempted to make the exhibition subservient to what is vulgarly termed a moral purpose. The highest moral purpose aimed at in the highest species of the drama, is the teaching the human heart, through its sympathies and antipathies, the knowledge of itself; in proportion to the possession of which knowledge, every human being is wise, just, sincere, tolerant and kind. If dogmas can do more, it is well: but a drama is no fit place for the enforcement of them. Undoubtedly, no person can be truly dishonoured by the act of another; and the fit return to make to the most enormous injuries is kindness and forbearance, and a resolution to convert the injurer from his dark passions by peace and love. Revenge, retaliation, atonement, are pernicious mistakes. If Beatrice had thought in this manner she would have been wiser and better; but she would never have been a tragic character: the few whom such an exhibition would have interested, could never have been sufficiently interested for a dramatic purpose, from the want of finding sympathy in their interest among the mass who surround them. It is in the restless and anatomizing casuistry with which men seek the justification of Beatrice, yet feel that she has done what needs justification; it is in the superstitious horror with which they contemplate alike her wrongs and their revenge; that the dramatic character of what she did and suffered, consists.

I have endeavoured as nearly as possible to represent the characters as they probably were, and have sought to avoid the error of making them actuated by my own conceptions of right or wrong, false or true, thus under a thin veil converting names and actions of the sixteenth century into cold impersonations of my own mind. They are represented as Catholics, and as Catholics deeply tinged with religion. To a Protestant apprehension there will appear something unnatural in the earnest and perpetual sentiment of the relations between God and man which pervade the tragedy of the Cenci. It will especially be startled at the combination of an undoubting persuasion of the truth of the popular religion with a cool and determined perseverance in enormous guilt. But religion in Italy is not, as in Protestant countries, a cloak to be worn on particular days; or a passport which those who do not wish to be railed at carry with them to exhibit; or a gloomy passion for penetrating the impenetrable mysteries of our being, which terrifies its possessor at the darkness of the abyss to the brink of which it has conducted him. Religion coexists, as it were, in the mind of an Italian Catholic with a faith in that of which all men have the most certain knowledge. It is interwoven with the whole fabric of life. It is adoration, faith, submission, penitence, blind admiration; not a rule for moral conduct. It has no necessary connexion with any one virtue. The most atrocious villain may be rigidly devout, and without any shock to established faith, confess himself to be so. Religion pervades intensely the whole frame of society, and is according to the temper of the mind which it inhabits, a passion, a persuasion, an excuse, a refuge; never a check. Cenci himself built a chapel in the court of his Palace, and dedicated it to St. Thomas the Apostle, and established masses for the peace of his soul. Thus in the first scene of the fourth act Lucretia's design in exposing herself to the consequences of an expostulation with Cenci after having administered the opiate, was to induce him by a feigned tale to confess himself before death; this being esteemed by Catholics as essential to salvation; and she only relinquishes her purpose when she perceives that her perseverance would expose Beatrice to new outrages.

I have avoided with great care in writing this play the introduction of what is commonly called mere poetry, and I imagine there will scarcely be found a detached simile or a single isolated description, unless Beatrice's description of the chasm appointed for her father's murder should be judged to be of that nature.*

In a dramatic composition the imagery and the passion should interpenetrate one another, the former being reserved simply for the full development and illustration of the latter. Imagination is as the immortal God which should assume flesh for the redemption of mortal passion. It is thus that the most remote and the most familiar imagery may alike be fit for dramatic purposes when employed in the illustration of strong feeling, which raises what is low, and levels to the apprehension that which is lofty, casting over all the shadow of its own greatness. In other respects I have written more carelessly; that is, without an over-fastidious and learned choice of words. In this respect I entirely agree with those modern critics who assert that in order to move men to true sympathy we must use the familiar language of men. And that our great ancestors the antient English poets are the writers, a study of whom might incite us to do that for our own age which they have done for theirs. But it must be the real language of men in general and not that of any particular class to whose society the writer happens to belong. So much for what I have attempted; I need not be assured that success is a very different matter; particularly for one whose attention has but newly been awakened to the study of dramatic literature.

I endeavoured whilst at Rome to observe such monuments of this story as might be accessible to a stranger. The portrait of Beatrice at the Colonna Palace is admirable as a work of art: it was taken by

* An idea in this speech was suggested by a most sublime passage in *El Purgatorio de San Patricio* of Calderon: the only plagiarism which I have intentionally committed in the whole piece. [Shelley's note]

Guido during her confinement in prison. But it is most interesting as a just representation of one of the loveliest specimens of the workmanship of Nature. There is a fixed and pale composure upon the features: she seems sad and stricken down in spirit, yet the despair thus expressed is lightened by the patience of gentleness. Her head is bound with folds of white drapery from which the yellow strings of her golden hair escape, and fall about her neck. The moulding of her face is exquisitely delicate; the eye brows are distinct and arched: the lips have that permanent meaning of imagination and sensibility which suffering has not repressed and which it seems as if death scarcely could extinguish. Her forehead is large and clear; her eyes, which we are told were remarkable for their vivacity, are swollen with weeping and lustreless, but beautifully tender and serene. In the whole mien there is a simplicity and dignity which united with her exquisite loveliness and deep sorrow are inexpressibly pathetic. Beatrice Cenci appears to have been one of those rare persons in whom energy and gentleness dwell together without destroying one another: her nature was simple and profound. The crimes and miseries in which she was an actor and a sufferer are as the mask and the mantle in which circumstances clothed her for her impersonation on the scene of the world.

The Cenci Palace is of great extent; and though in part modernized, there yet remains a vast and gloomy pile of feudal architecture in the same state as during the dreadful scenes which are the subject of this tragedy. The Palace is situated in an obscure corner of Rome, near the quarter of the Jews, and from the upper windows you see the immense ruins of Mount Palatine half hidden under their profuse overgrowth of trees. There is a court in one part of the palace (perhaps that in which Cenci built the Chapel to St. Thomas), supported by granite columns and adorned with antique friezes of fine workmanship and built up, according to the antient Italian fashion, with balcony over balcony of open work. One of the gates of the palace formed of immense stones and leading through a passage, dark and lofty and opening into gloomy subterranean chambers, struck me particularly.

Of the Castle of Petrella, I could obtain no further information than that which is to be found in the manuscript.

DRAMATIS PERSONAE

COUNT FRANCESCO CENCI

GIACOMO } his sons
BERNARDO }

CARDINAL CAMILLO

ORSINO, a Prelate

SAVELLA, the Pope's Legate

OLIMPIO } Assassins
MARZIO }

ANDREA, servant to Cenci

Nobles—Judges—Guards—Servants

LUCRETIA, Wife of Cenci, and step-mother of his children

BEATRICE, his daughter

The scene lies principally in Rome, but changes during the Fourth Act to Petrella, a castle among the Apulian Apennines.

Time. During the Pontificate of Clement VIII.

ACT I

SCENE I.—*An apartment in the Cenci Palace. Enter* COUNT CENCI, *and* CARDINAL CAMILLO.

Camillo. That matter of the murder is hushed up
If you consent to yield his Holiness
Your fief that lies beyond the Pincian gate.—
It needed all my interest in the conclave
To bend him to this point: he said that you
Bought perilous impunity with your gold;
That crimes like yours if once or twice compounded
Enriched the Church, and respited from hell
An erring soul which might repent and live:—
But that the glory and the interest
Of the high throne he fills, little consist
With making it a daily mart of guilt
As manifold and hideous as the deeds
Which you scarce hide from men's revolted eyes.

Cenci. The third of my possessions—let it go!
Aye, I once heard the nephew of the Pope
Had sent his architect to view the ground,
Meaning to build a villa on my vines
The next time I compounded with his uncle:
I little thought he should outwit me so!
Henceforth no witness—not the lamp—shall see
That which the vassal threatened to divulge
Whose throat is choked with dust for his reward.
The deed he saw could not have rated higher
Than his most worthless life:—it angers me!
Respited me from Hell!—So may the Devil
Respite their souls from Heaven. No doubt Pope Clement,
And his most charitable nephews, pray
That the Apostle Peter and the saints
Will grant for their sake that I long enjoy
Strength, wealth, and pride, and lust, and length of days
Wherein to act the deeds which are the stewards
Of their revenue.—But much yet remains
To which they shew no title.

Camillo. Oh, Count Cenci!
So much that thou mightst honourably live
And reconcile thyself with thine own heart
And with thy God, and with the offended world.
How hideously look deeds of lust and blood
Thro' those snow white and venerable hairs!—
Your children should be sitting round you now,
But that you fear to read upon their looks
The shame and misery you have written there.
Where is your wife? Where is your gentle daughter?
Methinks her sweet looks, which make all things else
Beauteous and glad, might kill the fiend within you.
Why is she barred from all society
But her own strange and uncomplaining wrongs?
Talk with me, Count,—you know I mean you well.
I stood beside your dark and fiery youth
Watching its bold and bad career, as men
Watch meteors, but it vanished not—I marked
Your desperate and remorseless manhood; now
Do I behold you in dishonoured age

Charged with a thousand unrepented crimes.
Yet I have ever hoped you would amend,
And in that hope have saved your life three times.

Cenci. For which Aldobrandino owes you now
My fief beyond the Pincian.—Cardinal,
One thing, I pray you, recollect henceforth,
And so we shall converse with less restraint.
A man you knew spoke of my wife and daughter—
He was accustomed to frequent my house;
So the next day *his* wife and daughter came
And asked if I had seen him; and I smiled:
I think they never saw him any more.

Camillo. Thou execrable man, beware!—

Cenci. Of thee?
Nay this is idle:—We should know each other.
As to my character for what men call crime
Seeing I please my senses as I list,
And vindicate that right with force or guile,
It is a public matter, and I care not
If I discuss it with you. I may speak
Alike to you and my own conscious heart—
For you give out that you have half reformed me,
Therefore strong vanity will keep you silent
If fear should not; both will, I do not doubt.
All men delight in sensual luxury,
All men enjoy revenge; and most exult
Over the tortures they can never feel—
Flattering their secret peace with others' pain.
But I delight in nothing else. I love
The sight of agony, and the sense of joy,
When this shall be another's, and that mine.
And I have no remorse and little fear,
Which are, I think, the checks of other men.
This mood has grown upon me, until now
Any design my captious fancy makes
The picture of its wish, and it forms none
But such as men like you would start to know,

Is as my natural food and rest debarred
Until it be accomplished.

Camillo. Art thou not
Most miserable?

Cenci. Why, miserable?—
No.—I am what your theologians call
Hardened;—which they must be in impudence,
So to revile a man's peculiar taste.
True, I was happier than I am, while yet
Manhood remained to act the thing I thought;
While lust was sweeter than revenge; and now
Invention palls:—Aye, we must all grow old—
And but that there remains a deed to act
Whose horror might make sharp an appetite
Duller than mine—I'd do,—I know not what.
When I was young I thought of nothing else
But pleasure; and I fed on honey sweets:
Men, by St. Thomas! cannot live like bees
And I grew tired:—yet, till I killed a foe,
And heard his groans, and heard his children's groans,
Knew I not what delight was else on earth,
Which now delights me little. I the rather
Look on such pangs as terror ill conceals,
The dry fixed eyeball; the pale quivering lip,
Which tell me that the spirit weeps within
Tears bitterer than the bloody sweat of Christ.
I rarely kill the body which preserves,
Like a strong prison, the soul within my power,
Wherein I feed it with the breath of fear
For hourly pain.

Camillo. Hell's most abandoned fiend
Did never, in the drunkenness of guilt,
Speak to his heart as now you speak to me;
I thank my God that I believe you not.

[*Enter* ANDREA.

Andrea. My Lord, a gentleman from Salamanca
Would speak with you.

Cenci. Bid him attend me in
The grand saloon. [*Exit* ANDREA.

Camillo. Farewell; and I will pray
Almighty God that thy false, impious words
Tempt not his spirit to abandon thee. [*Exit* CAMILLO.

Cenci. The third of my possessions! I must use
Close husbandry, or gold, the old man's sword,
Falls from my withered hand. But yesterday
There came an order from the Pope to make
Fourfold provision for my cursed sons;
Whom I had sent from Rome to Salamanca,
Hoping some accident might cut them off;
And meaning if I could to starve them there.
I pray thee, God, send some quick death upon them!
Bernardo and my wife could not be worse
If dead and damned:—then, as to Beatrice—
[*looking around him suspiciously*
I think they cannot hear me at that door;
What if they should? And yet I need not speak
Though the heart triumphs with itself in words.
O, thou most silent air, that shalt not hear
What now I think! Thou, pavement, which I tread
Towards her chamber,—let your echoes talk
Of my imperious step scorning surprise,
But not of my intent!—Andrea!
[*Enter* ANDREA.

Andrea. My Lord?

Cenci. Bid Beatrice attend me in her chamber
This evening:—no, at midnight and alone. [*Exeunt.*

SCENE II.—*A garden of the Cenci Palace. Enter* BEATRICE *and* ORSINO, *as in conversation.*

Beatrice. Pervert not truth,
Orsino. You remember where we held
That conversation;—nay, we see the spot
Even from this cypress;—two long years are past

Since, on an April midnight, underneath
The moon-light ruins of mount Palatine,
I did confess to you my secret mind.

Orsino. You said you loved me then.

Beatrice. You are a Priest,
Speak to me not of love.

Orsino. I may obtain
The dispensation of the Pope to marry.
Because I am a Priest do you believe
Your image, as the hunter some struck deer,
Follows me not whether I wake or sleep?

Beatrice. As I have said, speak to me not of love;
Had you a dispensation, I have not;
Nor will I leave this home of misery
Whilst my poor Bernard, and that gentle lady
To whom I owe life, and these virtuous thoughts,
Must suffer what I still have strength to share.
Alas, Orsino! All the love that once
I felt for you, is turned to bitter pain.
Ours was a youthful contract, which you first
Broke, by assuming vows no Pope will loose.
And thus I love you still, but holily,
Even as a sister or a spirit might;
And so I swear a cold fidelity.
And it is well perhaps we shall not marry.
You have a sly, equivocating vein
That suits me not.—Ah, wretched that I am!
Where shall I turn? Even now you look on me
As you were not my friend, and as if you
Discovered that I thought so, with false smiles
Making my true suspicion seem your wrong.
Ah! No, forgive me; sorrow makes me seem
Sterner than else my nature might have been;
I have a weight of melancholy thoughts,
And they forbode,—but what can they forbode
Worse than I now endure?

Orsino. All will be well.
Is the petition yet prepared? You know
My zeal for all you wish, sweet Beatrice;
Doubt not but I will use my utmost skill
So that the Pope attend to your complaint.

Beatrice. Your zeal for all I wish;—Ah me, you are cold!
Your utmost skill . . . speak but one word . . . (*aside*) Alas!
Weak and deserted creature that I am,
Here I stand bickering with my only friend! [*To* ORSINO.
This night my father gives a sumptuous feast,
Orsino; he has heard some happy news
From Salamanca, from my brothers there,
And with this outward shew of love he mocks
His inward hate. 'Tis bold hypocrisy
For he would gladlier celebrate their deaths,
Which I have heard him pray for on his knees:
Great God! that such a father should be mine!
But there is mighty preparation made,
And all our kin, the Cenci, will be there,
And all the chief nobility of Rome.
And he has bidden me and my pale Mother
Attire ourselves in festival array.
Poor lady! She expects some happy change
In his dark spirit from this act; I none.
At supper I will give you the petition:
Till when—farewell.

Orsino. Farewell. (*Exit* BEATRICE.)
I know the Pope
Will ne'er absolve me from my priestly vow
But by absolving me from the revenue
Of many a wealthy see; and, Beatrice,
I think to win thee at an easier rate.
Nor shall he read her eloquent petition:
He might bestow her on some poor relation
Of his sixth cousin, as he did her sister,
And I should be debarred from all access.
Then as to what she suffers from her father,
In all this there is much exaggeration:—
Old men are testy and will have their way;

A man may stab his enemy, or his vassal,
And live a free life as to wine or women,
And with a peevish temper may return
To a dull home, and rate his wife and children;
Daughters and wives call this, foul tyranny.
I shall be well content if on my conscience
There rest no heavier sin than what they suffer
From the devices of my love—A net
From which she shall escape not. Yet I fear
Her subtle mind, her awe-inspiring gaze,
Whose beams anatomize me nerve by nerve
And lay me bare, and make me blush to see
My hidden thoughts.—Ah, no! A friendless girl
Who clings to me, as to her only hope:—
I were a fool, not less than if a panther
Were panic-stricken by the Antelope's eye,
If she escape me. [*Exit.*

SCENE III.—*A magnificent Hall in the Cenci Palace. A Banquet.*
Enter CENCI, LUCRETIA, BEATRICE, ORSINO, CAMILLO, NOBLES.

Cenci. Welcome, my friends and Kinsmen; welcome ye,
Princes and Cardinals, pillars of the church,
Whose presence honours our festivity.
I have too long lived like an Anchorite,
And in my absence from your merry meetings
An evil word is gone abroad of me;
But I do hope that you, my noble friends,
When you have shared the entertainment here,
And heard the pious cause for which 'tis given,
And we have pledged a health or two together,
Will think me flesh and blood as well as you;
Sinful indeed, for Adam made all so,
But tender-hearted, meek and pitiful.

First Guest. In truth, my Lord, you seem too light of heart,
Too sprightly and companionable a man,
To act the deeds that rumour pins on you.
(*To his companion*) I never saw such blythe and open cheer
In any eye!

Second Guest. Some most desired event,
In which we all demand a common joy,
Has brought us hither; let us hear it, Count.

Cenci. It is indeed a most desired event.
If when a parent from a parent's heart
Lifts from this earth to the great father of all
A prayer, both when he lays him down to sleep,
And when he rises up from dreaming it;
One supplication, one desire, one hope,
That he would grant a wish for his two sons
Even all that he demands in their regard—
And suddenly beyond his dearest hope,
It is accomplished, he should then rejoice,
And call his friends and kinsmen to a feast,
And task their love to grace his merriment,
Then honour me thus far—for I am he.

Beatrice (*to* LUCRETIA). Great God! How horrible!
Some dreadful ill
Must have befallen my brothers.

Lucretia. Fear not, Child,
He speaks too frankly.

Beatrice. Ah! My blood runs cold.
I fear that wicked laughter round his eye
Which wrinkles up the skin even to the hair.

Cenci. Here are the letters brought from Salamanca;
Beatrice, read them to your mother. God!
I thank thee! In one night didst thou perform,
By ways inscrutable, the thing I sought.
My disobedient and rebellious sons
Are dead!—Why, dead!—What means this change of cheer?
You hear me not, I tell you they are dead;
And they will need no food or raiment more:
The tapers that did light them the dark way
Are their last cost. The Pope, I think, will not
Expect I should maintain them in their coffins.
Rejoice with me—my heart is wondrous glad.
[LUCRETIA *sinks, half fainting;* BEATRICE *supports her.*

Beatrice. It is not true!—Dear lady, pray look up.
Had it been true, there is a God in Heaven,
He would not live to boast of such a boon.
Unnatural man, thou knowest that it is false.

Cenci. Aye, as the word of God; whom here I call
To witness that I speak the sober truth;—
And whose most favouring Providence was shewn
Even in the manner of their deaths. For Rocco
Was kneeling at the mass, with sixteen others,
When the church fell and crushed him to a mummy,
The rest escaped unhurt. Cristofano
Was stabbed in error by a jealous man,
Whilst she he loved was sleeping with his rival;
All in the self-same hour of the same night;
Which shews that Heaven has special care of me.
I beg those friends who love me, that they mark
The day a feast upon their calendars.
It was the twenty-seventh of December:
Aye, read the letters if you doubt my oath.
[*The assembly appears confused; several of the guests rise.*

First Guest. Oh, horrible! I will depart.—

Second Guest. And I.—

Third Guest. No, stay!
I do believe it is some jest; tho' faith!
'Tis mocking us somewhat too solemnly.
I think his son has married the Infanta,
Or found a mine of gold in El Dorado;
'Tis but to season some such news; stay, stay!
I see 'tis only raillery by his smile.

Cenci (*filling a bowl of wine, and lifting it up*).
Oh, thou bright wine whose purple splendour leaps
And bubbles gaily in this golden bowl
Under the lamp light, as my spirits do,
To hear the death of my accursed sons!
Could I believe thou wert their mingled blood,

Then would I taste thee like a sacrament,
And pledge with thee the mighty Devil in Hell,
Who, if a father's curses, as men say,
Climb with swift wings after their children's souls,
And drag them from the very throne of Heaven,
Now triumphs in my triumph!—But thou art
Superfluous; I have drunken deep of joy
And I will taste no other wine to night.
Here, Andrea! Bear the bowl around.

A Guest (*rising*). Thou wretch!
Will none among this noble company
Check the abandoned villain?

Camillo. For God's sake
Let me dismiss the guests! You are insane,
Some ill will come of this.

Second Guest. Seize, silence him!

First Guest. I will!

Third Guest. And I!

Cenci (*Addressing those who rise with a threatening gesture*).
Who moves? Who speaks?
(*Turning to the Company.*) 'tis nothing,
Enjoy yourselves.—Beware! For my revenge
Is as the sealed commission of a king
That kills, and none dare name the murderer.
[*The Banquet is broken up; several of the Guests are departing.*

Beatrice. I do entreat you, go not, noble guests;
What, although tyranny and impious hate
Stand sheltered by a father's hoary hair?
What, if 'tis he who clothed us in these limbs
Who tortures them, and triumphs? What, if we,
The desolate and the dead, were his own flesh,
His children and his wife, whom he is bound
To love and shelter? Shall we therefore find

No refuge in this merciless wide world?
Oh, think what deep wrongs must have blotted out
First love, then reverence in a child's prone mind
Till it thus vanquish shame and fear! O, think!
I have borne much, and kissed the sacred hand
Which crushed us to the earth, and thought its stroke
Was perhaps some paternal chastisement!
Have excused much, doubted; and when no doubt
Remained, have sought by patience, love and tears
To soften him, and when this could not be
I have knelt down through the long sleepless nights
And lifted up to God, the father of all,
Passionate prayers: and when these were not heard
I have still borne,—until I meet you here,
Princes and kinsmen, at this hideous feast
Given at my brothers' deaths. Two yet remain,
His wife remains and I, whom if ye save not,
Ye may soon share such merriment again
As fathers make over their children's graves.
Oh! Prince Colonna, thou art our near kinsman,
Cardinal, thou art the Pope's chamberlain,
Camillo, thou art chief justiciary,
Take us away!

Cenci. (*He has been conversing with* CAMILLO *during the first part of* BEATRICE*'s speech; he hears the conclusion, and now advances.*)
I hope my good friends here
Will think of their own daughters—or perhaps
Of their own throats—before they lend an ear
To this wild girl.

Beatrice (*not noticing the words of* CENCI).
Dare no one look on me?
None answer? Can one tyrant overbear
The sense of many best and wisest men?
Or is it that I sue not in some form
Of scrupulous law, that ye deny my suit?

Oh, God! That I were buried with my brothers!
And that the flowers of this departed spring
Were fading on my grave! And that my father
Were celebrating now one feast for all!

Camillo. A bitter wish for one so young and gentle;
Can we do nothing?—

Colonna. Nothing that I see.
Count Cenci were a dangerous enemy:
Yet I would second any one.

A Cardinal. And I.

Cenci. Retire to your chamber, insolent girl!

Beatrice. Retire thou, impious man! Aye hide thyself
Where never eye can look upon thee more!
Wouldst thou have honour and obedience
Who art a torturer? Father, never dream
Though thou mayst overbear this company,
But ill must come of ill.—Frown not on me!
Haste, hide thyself, lest with avenging looks
My brothers' ghosts should hunt thee from thy seat!
Cover thy face from every living eye,
And start if thou but hear a human step:
Seek out some dark and silent corner, there,
Bow thy white head before offended God,
And we will kneel around, and fervently
Pray that he pity both ourselves and thee.

Cenci. My friends, I do lament this insane girl
Has spoilt the mirth of our festivity.
Good night, farewell; I will not make you longer
Spectators of our dull domestic quarrels.
Another time.— [*Exeunt all but* CENCI *and* BEATRICE.
My brain is swimming round;
Give me a bowl of wine!
(*To* BEATRICE) Thou painted viper!

Beast that thou art! Fair and yet terrible!
I know a charm shall make thee meek and tame,
Now get thee from my sight! [*Exit* BEATRICE.
Here, Andrea,
Fill up this goblet with Greek wine. I said
I would not drink this evening; but I must;
For, strange to say, I feel my spirits fail
With thinking what I have decreed to do.—
[*Drinking the wine.*
Be thou the resolution of quick youth
Within my veins, and manhood's purpose stern,
And age's firm, cold, subtle villainy;
As if thou wert indeed my children's blood
Which I did thirst to drink! The charm works well;
It must be done; it shall be done, I swear! [*Exit.*

END OF THE FIRST ACT.

ACT II

SCENE I.—*An apartment in the Cenci Palace. Enter* LUCRETIA *and* BERNARDO.

Lucretia. Weep not, my gentle boy; he struck but me
Who have borne deeper wrongs. In truth, if he
Had killed me, he had done a kinder deed.
O, God Almighty, do thou look upon us,
We have no other friend but only thee!
Yet weep not; though I love you as my own
I am not your true mother.

Bernardo. Oh more, more,
Than ever mother was to any child,
That have you been to me! Had he not been
My father, do you think that I should weep?

Lucretia. Alas! Poor boy, what else couldst thou have done?
[*Enter* BEATRICE.

Beatrice (*in a hurried voice*).
Did he pass this way? Have you seen him, brother?
Ah! No, that is his step upon the stairs;
'Tis nearer now; his hand is on the door;
Mother, if I to thee have ever been
A duteous child, now save me! Thou, great God,
Whose image upon earth a father is,
Dost thou indeed abandon me! He comes;
The door is opening now; I see his face;
He frowns on others, but he smiles on me,
Even as he did after the feast last night.
[*Enter a Servant.*
Almighty God, how merciful thou art!
'Tis but Orsino's servant.—Well, what news?

Servant. My master bids me say, the Holy Father
Has sent back your petition thus unopened. [*Giving a paper.*
And he demands at what hour 'twere secure
To visit you again?

Lucretia. At the Ave Mary. [*Exit Servant.*
So, daughter, our last hope has failed; Ah me!
How pale you look; you tremble, and you stand
Wrapped in some fixed and fearful meditation,
As if one thought were over strong for you:
Your eyes have a chill glare; O, dearest child!
Are you gone mad? If not, pray speak to me.

Beatrice. You see I am not mad; I speak to you.

Lucretia. You talked of something that your father did
After that dreadful feast? Could it be worse
Than when he smiled, and cried, 'My sons are dead!'
And every one looked in his neighbour's face
To see if others were as white as he?
At the first word he spoke I felt the blood
Rush to my heart, and fell into a trance;
And when it past I sat all weak and wild;
Whilst you alone stood up, and with strong words
Checked his unnatural pride; and I could see
The devil was rebuked that lives in him.

Until this hour thus you have ever stood
Between us and your father's moody wrath
Like a protecting presence: your firm mind
Has been our only refuge and defence:
What can have thus subdued it? What can now
Have given you that cold melancholy look,
Succeeding to your unaccustomed fear?

Beatrice. What is it that you say? I was just thinking
'Twere better not to struggle any more.
Men, like my father, have been dark and bloody,
Yet never—O! Before worse comes of it
'Twere wise to die: it ends in that at last.

Lucretia. Oh, talk not so, dear child! Tell me at once
What did your father do or say to you?
He stayed not after that accursed feast
One moment in your chamber.—Speak to me.

Bernardo. Oh, sister, sister, prithee, speak to us!

Beatrice (*speaking very slowly with a forced calmness*).
It was one word, Mother, one little word;
One look, one smile. (*Wildly.*) Oh! He has trampled me
Under his feet, and made the blood stream down
My pallid cheeks. And he has given us all
Ditch water, and the fever-stricken flesh
Of buffaloes, and bade us eat or starve,
And we have eaten.—He has made me look
On my beloved Bernardo, when the rust
Of heavy chains has gangrened his sweet limbs,
And I have never yet despaired—but now!
What would I say? [*Recovering herself.*
Ah! No, 'tis nothing new.
The sufferings we all share have made me wild:
He only struck and cursed me as he passed;
He said, he looked, he did;—nothing at all
Beyond his wont, yet it disordered me.
Alas! I am forgetful of my duty,
I should preserve my senses for your sake.

Lucretia. Nay, Beatrice; have courage, my sweet girl.
If any one despairs it should be I
Who loved him once, and now must live with him
Till God in pity call for him or me.
For you may, like your sister, find some husband,
And smile, years hence, with children round your knees;
Whilst I, then dead, and all this hideous coil
Shall be remembered only as a dream.

Beatrice. Talk not to me, dear lady, of a husband.
Did you not nurse me when my mother died?
Did you not shield me and that dearest boy?
And had we any other friend but you
In infancy, with gentle words and looks,
To win our father not to murder us?
And shall I now desert you? May the ghost
Of my dead Mother plead against my soul
If I abandon her who filled the place
She left, with more, even, than a mother's love!

Bernardo. And I am of my sister's mind. Indeed
I would not leave you in this wretchedness,
Even though the Pope should make me free to live
In some blithe place, like others of my age,
With sports, and delicate food, and the fresh air.
Oh, never think that I will leave you, Mother!

Lucretia. My dear, dear children!
[*Enter* CENCI, *suddenly.*

Cenci. What, Beatrice here!
Come hither! [*She shrinks back, and covers her face.*
Nay, hide not your face, 'tis fair;
Look up! Why, yesternight you dared to look
With disobedient insolence upon me,
Bending a stern and an inquiring brow
On what I meant; whilst I then sought to hide
That which I came to tell you—but in vain.

Beatrice (*Wildly, staggering towards the door*).
Oh, that the earth would gape! Hide me, oh God!

Cenci. Then it was I whose inarticulate words
Fell from my lips, and who with tottering steps
Fled from your presence, as you now from mine.
Stay, I command you—from this day and hour
Never again, I think, with fearless eye,
And brow superior, and unaltered cheek,
And that lip made for tenderness or scorn,
Shalt thou strike dumb the meanest of mankind;
Me least of all. Now get thee to thy chamber!
Thou too, loathed image of thy cursed mother, [*To* BERNARDO.
Thy milky, meek face makes me sick with hate!
[*Exeunt* BEATRICE *and* BERNARDO.
(*Aside*.) So much has past between us as must make
Me bold, her fearful.—'Tis an awful thing
To touch such mischief as I now conceive:
So men sit shivering on the dewy bank,
And try the chill stream with their feet; once in . . .
How the delighted spirit pants for joy!

Lucretia (*advancing timidly towards him*).
Oh, husband! Pray forgive poor Beatrice,
She meant not any ill.

Cenci. Nor you perhaps?
Nor that young imp, whom you have taught by rote
Parricide with his alphabet? Nor Giacomo?
Nor those two most unnatural sons, who stirred
Enmity up against me with the Pope?
Whom in one night merciful God cut off:
Innocent lambs! They thought not any ill.
You were not here conspiring? You said nothing
Of how I might be dungeoned as a madman;
Or be condemned to death for some offence,
And you would be the witnesses?—This failing,
How just it were to hire assassins, or
Put sudden poison in my evening drink?
Or smother me when overcome by wine?
Seeing we had no other judge but God,
And he had sentenced me, and there were none
But you to be the executioners
Of his decree enregistered in heaven?
Oh, no! You said not this?

Lucretia. So help me God,
I never thought the things you charge me with!

Cenci. If you dare speak that wicked lie again
I'll kill you. What! It was not by your counsel
That Beatrice disturbed the feast last night?
You did not hope to stir some enemies
Against me, and escape, and laugh to scorn
What every nerve of you now trembles at?
You judged that men were bolder than they are;
Few dare to stand between their grave and me.

Lucretia. Look not so dreadfully! By my salvation
I knew not aught that Beatrice designed;
Nor do I think she designed any thing
Until she heard you talk of her dead brothers.

Cenci. Blaspheming liar! You are damned for this!
But I will take you where you may persuade
The stones you tread on to deliver you:
For men shall there be none but those who dare
All things—not question that which I command.
On Wednesday next I shall set out: you know
That savage rock, the Castle of Petrella,
'Tis safely walled, and moated round about:
Its dungeons underground, and its thick towers
Never told tales; though they have heard and seen
What might make dumb things speak.—Why do you linger?
Make speediest preparation for the journey! [*Exit* LUCRETIA.
The all-beholding sun yet shines; I hear
A busy stir of men about the streets;
I see the bright sky through the window panes:
It is a garish, broad, and peering day;
Loud, light, suspicious, full of eyes and ears,
And every little corner, nook and hole
Is penetrated with the insolent light.
Come darkness! Yet, what is the day to me?
And wherefore should I wish for night, who do
A deed which shall confound both night and day?
'Tis she shall grope through a bewildering mist
Of horror: if there be a sun in heaven
She shall not dare to look upon its beams;

Nor feel its warmth. Let her then wish for night;
The act I think shall soon extinguish all
For me: I bear a darker deadlier gloom
Than the earth's shade, or interlunar air,
Or constellations quenched in murkiest cloud,
In which I walk secure and unbeheld
Towards my purpose.—Would that it were done! [*Exit.*

SCENE II.—*A chamber in the Vatican. Enter* CAMILLO *and* GIACOMO, *in conversation.*

Camillo. There is an obsolete and doubtful law
By which you might obtain a bare provision
Of food and clothing—

Giacomo. Nothing more? Alas!
Bare must be the provision which strict law
Awards, and aged, sullen avarice pays.
Why did my father not apprentice me
To some mechanic trade? I should have then
Been trained in no highborn necessities
Which I could meet not by my daily toil.
The eldest son of a rich nobleman
Is heir to all his incapacities;
He has wide wants, and narrow powers. If you,
Cardinal Camillo, were reduced at once
From thrice-driven beds of down, and delicate food,
An hundred servants, and six palaces,
To that which nature doth indeed require?—

Camillo. Nay, there is reason in your plea; 'twere hard.

Giacomo. 'Tis hard for a firm man to bear: but I
Have a dear wife, a lady of high birth,
Whose dowry in ill hour I lent my father
Without a bond or witness to the deed:
And children, who inherit her fine senses,
The fairest creatures in this breathing world;
And she and they reproach me not. Cardinal,
Do you not think the Pope would interpose
And stretch authority beyond the law?

Camillo. Though your peculiar case is hard, I know
The Pope will not divert the course of law.
After that impious feast the other night
I spoke with him, and urged him then to check
Your father's cruel hand; he frowned and said,
'Children are disobedient, and they sting
Their fathers' hearts to madness and despair,
Requiting years of care with contumely.
I pity the Count Cenci from my heart;
His outraged love perhaps awakened hate,
And thus he is exasperated to ill.
In the great war between the old and young
I, who have white hairs and a tottering body,
Will keep at least blameless neutrality.'
[*Enter* ORSINO.
You, my good Lord Orsino, heard those words.

Orsino. What words?

Giacomo. Alas, repeat them not again!
There then is no redress for me, at least
None but that which I may atchieve myself,
Since I am driven to the brink.—But, say,
My innocent sister and my only brother
Are dying underneath my father's eye.
The memorable torturers of this land,
Galeaz Visconti, Borgia, Ezzelin,
Never inflicted on their meanest slave
What these endure; shall they have no protection?

Camillo. Why, if they would petition to the Pope
I see not how he could refuse it—yet
He holds it of most dangerous example
In aught to weaken the paternal power,
Being, as 'twere, the shadow of his own.
I pray you now excuse me. I have business
That will not bear delay. [*Exit* CAMILLO.

Giacomo. But you, Orsino,
Have the petition: wherefore not present it?

Orsino. I have presented it, and backed it with
My earnest prayers, and urgent interest;
It was returned unanswered. I doubt not
But that the strange and execrable deeds
Alledged in it—in truth they might well baffle
Any belief—have turned the Pope's displeasure
Upon the accusers from the criminal:
So I should guess from what Camillo said.

Giacomo. My friend, that palace-walking devil Gold
Has whispered silence to his Holiness:
And we are left, as scorpions ringed with fire,
What should we do but strike ourselves to death?
For he who is our murderous persecutor
Is shielded by a father's holy name,
Or I would— [*Stops abruptly*.

Orsino. What? Fear not to speak your thought.
Words are but holy as the deeds they cover:
A priest who has forsworn the God he serves;
A judge who makes Truth weep at his decree;
A friend who should weave counsel, as I now,
But as the mantle of some selfish guile;
A father who is all a tyrant seems,
Were the profaner for his sacred name.

Giacomo. Ask me not what I think; the unwilling brain
Feigns often what it would not; and we trust
Imagination with such phantasies
As the tongue dares not fashion into words,
Which have no words, their horror makes them dim
To the mind's eye.—My heart denies itself
To think what you demand.

Orsino. But a friend's bosom
Is as the inmost cave of our own mind
Where we sit shut from the wide gaze of day,
And from the all-communicating air.
You look what I suspected—

Giacomo. Spare me now!
I am as one lost in a midnight wood,
Who dares not ask some harmless passenger
The path across the wilderness, lest he,
As my thoughts are, should be—a murderer.
I know you are my friend, and all I dare
Speak to my soul that will I trust with thee.
But now my heart is heavy and would take
Lone counsel from a night of sleepless care.
Pardon me, that I say farewell—farewell!
I would that to my own suspected self
I could address a word so full of peace.

Orsino. Farewell!—Be your thoughts better or more bold.
[*Exit* GIACOMO.
I had disposed the Cardinal Camillo
To feed his hope with cold encouragement:
It fortunately serves my close designs
That 'tis a trick of this same family
To analyse their own and other minds.
Such self-anatomy shall teach the will
Dangerous secrets: for it tempts our powers,
Knowing what must be thought, and may be done,
Into the depth of darkest purposes:
So Cenci fell into the pit; even I,
Since Beatrice unveiled me to myself,
And made me shrink from what I cannot shun,
Shew a poor figure to my own esteem,
To which I grow half reconciled. I'll do
As little mischief as I can; that thought
Shall fee the accuser conscience.
(*After a pause*) Now what harm
If Cenci should be murdered?—Yet, if murdered,
Wherefore by me? And what if I could take
The profit, yet omit the sin and peril
In such an action? Of all earthly things
I fear a man whose blows outspeed his words;
And such is Cenci: and while Cenci lives
His daughter's dowry were a secret grave
If a priest wins her.—Oh, fair Beatrice!

Would that I loved thee not, or loving thee
Could but despise danger and gold and all
That frowns between my wish and its effect,
Or smiles beyond it! There is no escape . . .
Her bright form kneels beside me at the altar,
And follows me to the resort of men,
And fills my slumber with tumultuous dreams,
So when I wake my blood seems liquid fire;
And if I strike my damp and dizzy head
My hot palm scorches it: her very name,
But spoken by a stranger, makes my heart
Sicken and pant; and thus unprofitably
I clasp the phantom of unfelt delights
Till weak imagination half possesses
The self-created shadow. Yet much longer
Will I not nurse this life of feverous hours:
From the unravelled hopes of Giacomo
I must work out my own dear purposes.
I see, as from a tower, the end of all:
Her father dead; her brother bound to me
By a dark secret, surer than the grave;
Her mother scared and unexpostulating
From the dread manner of her wish atchieved:
And she!—Once more take courage, my faint heart;
What dares a friendless maiden matched with thee?
I have such foresight as assures success:
Some unbeheld divinity doth ever,
When dread events are near, stir up men's minds
To black suggestions; and he prospers best,
Not who becomes the instrument of ill,
But who can flatter the dark spirit, that makes
Its empire and its prey of other hearts
Till it become his slave . . . as I will do. [*Exit.*

END OF THE SECOND ACT.

ACT III

SCENE I.—*An apartment in the Cenci Palace.* LUCRETIA, *to her enter* BEATRICE.

Beatrice. (*She enters staggering, and speaks wildly.*)
Reach me that handkerchief!—My brain is hurt;
My eyes are full of blood; just wipe them for me . . .
I see but indistinctly . . .

Lucretia. My sweet child,
You have no wound; 'tis only a cold dew
That starts from your dear brow . . . Alas! Alas!
What has befallen?

Beatrice. How comes this hair undone?
Its wandering strings must be what blind me so,
And yet I tied it fast.—O, horrible!
The pavement sinks under my feet! The walls
Spin round! I see a woman weeping there,
And standing calm and motionless, whilst I
Slide giddily as the world reels . . . My God!
The beautiful blue heaven is flecked with blood!
The sunshine on the floor is black! The air
Is changed to vapours such as the dead breathe
In charnel pits! Pah! I am choked! There creeps
A clinging, black, contaminating mist
About me . . . 'tis substantial, heavy, thick,
I cannot pluck it from me, for it glues
My fingers and my limbs to one another,
And eats into my sinews, and dissolves
My flesh to a pollution, poisoning
The subtle, pure, and inmost spirit of life!
My God! I never knew what the mad felt
Before; for I am mad beyond all doubt!
(*More wildly.*) No, I am dead! These putrefying limbs
Shut round and sepulchre the panting soul
Which would burst forth into the wandering air! (*A pause.*)
What hideous thought was that I had even now?
'Tis gone; and yet its burthen remains here
O'er these dull eyes . . . upon this weary heart!
O, world! O, life! O, day! O, misery!

Lucretia. What ails thee, my poor child? She answers not:
Her spirit apprehends the sense of pain,
But not its cause; suffering has dried away
The source from which it sprung . . .

Beatrice (*franticly*). Like Parricide . . .
Misery has killed its father: yet its father
Never like mine . . . O, God! What thing am I?

Lucretia. My dearest child, what has your father done?

Beatrice (*doubtfully*). Who art thou, questioner? I have no father.
(*Aside*.) She is the madhouse nurse who tends on me,
It is a piteous office. [*To* LUCRETIA, *in a slow, subdued voice*.
Do you know
I thought I was that wretched Beatrice
Men speak of, whom her father sometimes hales
From hall to hall by the entangled hair;
At others, pens up naked in damp cells
Where scaly reptiles crawl, and starves her there,
Till she will eat strange flesh. This woful story
So did I overact in my sick dreams,
That I imagined . . . no, it cannot be!
Horrible things have been in this wild world,
Prodigious mixtures, and confusions strange
Of good and ill; and worse have been conceived
Than ever there was found a heart to do.
But never fancy imaged such a deed
As . . . [*Pauses, suddenly recollecting herself*.
Who art thou? Swear to me, ere I die
With fearful expectation, that indeed
Thou art not what thou seemest . . . Mother!

Lucretia. Oh!
My sweet child, know you . . .

Beatrice. Yet speak it not:
For then if this be truth, that other too
Must be a truth, a firm enduring truth,
Linked with each lasting circumstance of life,

Never to change, never to pass away.
Why so it is. This is the Cenci Palace;
Thou art Lucretia; I am Beatrice.
I have talked some wild words, but will no more.
Mother, come near me: from this point of time,
I am . . . [*Her voice dies away faintly.*

Lucretia. Alas! What has befallen thee, child?
What has thy father done?

Beatrice. What have I done?
Am I not innocent? Is it my crime
That one with white hair, and imperious brow,
Who tortured me from my forgotten years,
As parents only dare, should call himself
My father, yet should be!—Oh, what am I?
What name, what place, what memory shall be mine?
What retrospects, outliving even despair?

Lucretia. He is a violent tyrant, surely, child:
We know that death alone can make us free;
His death or ours. But what can he have done
Of deadlier outrage or worse injury?
Thou art unlike thyself; thine eyes shoot forth
A wandering and strange spirit. Speak to me,
Unlock those pallid hands whose fingers twine
With one another.

Beatrice. 'Tis the restless life
Tortured within them. If I try to speak
I shall go mad. Aye, something must be done;
What, yet I know not . . . something which shall make
The thing that I have suffered but a shadow
In the dread lightning which avenges it;
Brief, rapid, irreversible, destroying
The consequence of what it cannot cure.
Some such thing is to be endured or done:
When I know what, I shall be still and calm,
And never any thing will move me more.
But now!—Oh blood, which art my father's blood,
Circling thro' these contaminated veins,
If thou, poured forth on the polluted earth,

Could wash away the crime, and punishment
By which I suffer . . . no, that cannot be!
Many might doubt there were a God above
Who sees and permits evil, and so die:
That faith no agony shall obscure in me.

Lucretia. It must indeed have been some bitter wrong;
Yet what, I dare not guess. Oh, my lost child,
Hide not in proud impenetrable grief
Thy sufferings from my fear.

Beatrice. I hide them not.
What are the words which you would have me speak?
I, who can feign no image in my mind
Of that which has transformed me. I, whose thought
Is like a ghost shrouded and folded up
In its own formless horror. Of all words,
That minister to mortal intercourse,
Which wouldst thou hear? For there is none to tell
My misery: if another ever knew
Aught like to it, she died as I will die,
And left it, as I must, without a name.
Death! Death! Our law and our religion call thee
A punishment and a reward . . . Oh, which
Have I deserved?

Lucretia. The peace of innocence;
Till in your season you be called to heaven.
Whate'er you may have suffered, you have done
No evil. Death must be the punishment
Of crime, or the reward of trampling down
The thorns which God has strewed upon the path
Which leads to immortality.

Beatrice. Aye, death . . .
The punishment of crime. I pray thee, God,
Let me not be bewildered while I judge.
If I must live day after day, and keep
These limbs, the unworthy temple of thy spirit,
As a foul den from which what thou abhorrest
May mock thee, unavenged . . . it shall not be!
Self-murder . . . no, that might be no escape,

For thy decree yawns like a Hell between
Our will and it:—O! In this mortal world
There is no vindication and no law
Which can adjudge and execute the doom
Of that through which I suffer.

[*Enter* ORSINO.

(*She approaches him solemnly.*) Welcome, Friend!
I have to tell you that, since last we met,
I have endured a wrong so great and strange,
That neither life or death can give me rest.
Ask me not what it is, for there are deeds
Which have no form, sufferings which have no tongue.

Orsino. And what is he who has thus injured you?

Beatrice. The man they call my father: a dread name.

Orsino. It cannot be . . .

Beatrice. What it can be, or not,
Forbear to think. It is, and it has been;
Advise me how it shall not be again.
I thought to die; but a religious awe
Restrains me, and the dread lest death itself
Might be no refuge from the consciousness
Of what is yet unexpiated. Oh, speak!

Orsino. Accuse him of the deed, and let the law
Avenge thee.

Beatrice. Oh, ice-hearted counsellor!
If I could find a word that might make known
The crime of my destroyer; and that done,
My tongue should like a knife tear out the secret
Which cankers my heart's core; aye, lay all bare
So that my unpolluted fame should be
With vilest gossips a stale mouthed story;
A mock, a bye-word, an astonishment:—
If this were done, which never shall be done,
Think of the offender's gold, his dreaded hate,
And the strange horror of the accuser's tale,
Baffling belief, and overpowering speech;

Scarce whispered, unimaginable, wrapt
In hideous hints . . . Oh, most assured redress!

Orsino. You will endure it then?

Beatrice. Endure?—Orsino,
It seems your counsel is small profit.
[*Turns from him, and speaks half to herself.*
Aye,
All must be suddenly resolved and done.
What is this undistinguishable mist
Of thoughts, which rise, like shadow after shadow,
Darkening each other?

Orsino. Should the offender live?
Triumph in his misdeed? and make, by use,
His crime, whate'er it is, dreadful no doubt,
Thine element; until thou mayest become
Utterly lost; subdued even to the hue
Of that which thou permittest?

Beatrice (*to herself*). Mighty death!
Thou double-visaged shadow! Only judge!
Rightfullest arbiter! [*She retires absorbed in thought.*

Lucretia. If the lightning
Of God has e'er descended to avenge . . .

Orsino. Blaspheme not! His high Providence commits
Its glory on this earth, and their own wrongs
Into the hands of men; if they neglect
To punish crime . . .

Lucretia. But if one, like this wretch,
Should mock with gold, opinion, law and power?
If there be no appeal to that which makes
The guiltiest tremble? If because our wrongs,
For that they are unnatural, strange and monstrous,
Exceed all measure of belief? Oh, God!
If, for the very reasons which should make
Redress most swift and sure, our injurer triumphs?
And we the victims, bear worse punishment
Than that appointed for their torturer?

Orsino. Think not
But that there is redress where there is wrong,
So we be bold enough to seize it.

Lucretia. How?
If there were any way to make all sure,
I know not . . . but I think it might be good
To . . .

Orsino. Why, his late outrage to Beatrice;
For it is such, as I but faintly guess,
As makes remorse dishonour, and leaves her
Only one duty, how she may avenge:
You, but one refuge from ills ill endured;
Me, but one counsel . . .

Lucretia. For we cannot hope
That aid, or retribution, or resource
Will arise thence, where every other one
Might find them with less need. [BEATRICE *advances.*

Orsino. Then . . .

Beatrice. Peace, Orsino!
And, honoured Lady, while I speak, I pray,
That you put off, as garments overworn,
Forbearance and respect, remorse and fear,
And all the fit restraints of daily life,
Which have been borne from childhood, but which now
Would be a mockery to my holier plea.
As I have said, I have endured a wrong,
Which, though it be expressionless, is such
As asks atonement; both for what is past,
And lest I be reserved, day after day,
To load with crimes an overburthened soul,
And be . . . what ye can dream not. I have prayed
To God, and I have talked with my own heart,
And have unravelled my entangled will,
And have at length determined what is right.
Art thou my friend, Orsino? False or true?
Pledge thy salvation ere I speak.

Orsino. I swear
To dedicate my cunning, and my strength,
My silence, and whatever else is mine,
To thy commands.

Lucretia. You think we should devise
His death?

Beatrice. And execute what is devised,
And suddenly. We must be brief and bold.

Orsino. And yet most cautious.

Lucretia. For the jealous laws
Would punish us with death and infamy
For that which it became themselves to do.

Beatrice. Be cautious as ye may, but prompt. Orsino,
What are the means?

Orsino. I know two dull, fierce outlaws,
Who think man's spirit as a worm's, and they
Would trample out, for any slight caprice,
The meanest or the noblest life. This mood
Is marketable here in Rome. They sell
What we now want.

Lucretia. To-morrow before dawn,
Cenci will take us to that lonely rock,
Petrella, in the Apulian Apennines.
If he arrive there . . .

Beatrice. He must not arrive.

Orsino. Will it be dark before you reach the tower?

Lucretia. The sun will scarce be set.

Beatrice. But I remember
Two miles on this side of the fort, the road
Crosses a deep ravine; 'tis rough and narrow,
And winds with short turns down the precipice;
And in its depth there is a mighty rock,

Which has, from unimaginable years,
Sustained itself with terror and with toil
Over a gulph, and with the agony
With which it clings seems slowly coming down;
Even as a wretched soul hour after hour,
Clings to the mass of life; yet clinging, leans;
And leaning, makes more dark the dread abyss
In which it fears to fall: beneath this crag
Huge as despair, as if in weariness,
The melancholy mountain yawns . . . below,
You hear but see not an impetuous torrent
Raging among the caverns, and a bridge
Crosses the chasm; and high above there grow,
With intersecting trunks, from crag to crag,
Cedars, and yews, and pines; whose tangled hair
Is matted in one solid roof of shade
By the dark ivy's twine. At noonday here
'Tis twilight, and at sunset blackest night.

Orsino. Before you reach that bridge make some excuse
For spurring on your mules, or loitering
Until . . .

Beatrice. What sound is that?

Lucretia. Hark! No, it cannot be a servant's step;
It must be Cenci, unexpectedly
Returned . . . Make some excuse for being here.

Beatrice (*to* ORSINO, *as she goes out*).
That step we hear approach must never pass
The bridge of which we spoke.
[*Exeunt* LUCRETIA *and* BEATRICE.

Orsino. What shall I do?
Cenci must find me here, and I must bear
The imperious inquisition of his looks
As to what brought me hither: let me mask
Mine own in some inane and vacant smile.
[*Enter* GIACOMO, *in a hurried manner.*
How! Have you ventured hither? Know you then
That Cenci is from home?

Giacomo. I sought him here;
And now must wait till he returns.

Orsino. Great God!
Weigh you the danger of this rashness?

Giacomo. Aye!
Does my destroyer know his danger? We
Are now no more, as once, parent and child,
But man to man; the oppressor to the oppressed;
The slanderer to the slandered; foe to foe:
He has cast Nature off, which was his shield,
And Nature casts him off, who is her shame;
And I spurn both. Is it a father's throat
Which I will shake, and say, I ask not gold;
I ask not happy years; nor memories
Of tranquil childhood; nor home-sheltered love;
Though all these hast thou torn from me, and more;
But only my fair fame; only one hoard
Of peace, which I thought hidden from thy hate,
Under the penury heaped on me by thee,
Or I will . . . God can understand and pardon,
Why should I speak with man?

Orsino. Be calm, dear friend.

Giacomo. Well, I will calmly tell you what he did.
This old Francesco Cenci, as you know,
Borrowed the dowry of my wife from me,
And then denied the loan; and left me so
In poverty, the which I sought to mend
By holding a poor office in the state.
It had been promised to me, and already
I bought new clothing for my ragged babes,
And my wife smiled; and my heart knew repose.
When Cenci's intercession, as I found,
Conferred this office on a wretch, whom thus
He paid for vilest service. I returned
With this ill news, and we sate sad together
Solacing our despondency with tears
Of such affection and unbroken faith
As temper life's worst bitterness; when he,

As he is wont, came to upbraid and curse,
Mocking our poverty, and telling us
Such was God's scourge for disobedient sons.
And then, that I might strike him dumb with shame,
I spoke of my wife's dowry; but he coined
A brief yet specious tale, how I had wasted
The sum in secret riot; and he saw
My wife was touched, and he went smiling forth.
And when I knew the impression he had made,
And felt my wife insult with silent scorn
My ardent truth, and look averse and cold,
I went forth too: but soon returned again;
Yet not so soon but that my wife had taught
My children her harsh thoughts, and they all cried,
'Give us clothes, father! Give us better food!
What you in one night squander were enough
For months!' I looked, and saw that home was hell.
And to that hell will I return no more
Until mine enemy has rendered up
Atonement, or, as he gave life to me
I will, reversing nature's law . . .

Orsino. Trust me,
The compensation which thou seekest here
Will be denied.

Giacomo. Then . . . Are you not my friend?
Did you not hint at the alternative,
Upon the brink of which you see I stand,
The other day when we conversed together?
My wrongs were then less. That word parricide,
Although I am resolved, haunts me like fear.

Orsino. It must be fear itself, for the bare word
Is hollow mockery. Mark, how wisest God
Draws to one point the threads of a just doom,
So sanctifying it: what you devise
Is, as it were, accomplished.

Giacomo. Is he dead?

Orsino. His grave is ready. Know that since we met
Cenci has done an outrage to his daughter.

Giacomo. What outrage?

Orsino. That she speaks not, but you may
Conceive such half conjectures as I do,
From her fixed paleness, and the lofty grief
Of her stern brow bent on the idle air,
And her severe unmodulated voice,
Drowning both tenderness and dread; and last
From this; that whilst her step-mother and I,
Bewildered in our horror, talked together
With obscure hints; both self-misunderstood
And darkly guessing, stumbling, in our talk,
Over the truth, and yet to its revenge,
She interrupted us, and with a look
Which told before she spoke it, he must die . . .

Giacomo. It is enough. My doubts are well appeased;
There is a higher reason for the act
Than mine; there is a holier judge than me,
A more unblamed avenger. Beatrice,
Who in the gentleness of thy sweet youth
Hast never trodden on a worm, or bruised
A living flower, but thou hast pitied it
With needless tears! Fair sister, thou in whom
Men wondered how such loveliness and wisdom
Did not destroy each other! Is there made
Ravage of thee? O, heart, I ask no more
Justification! Shall I wait, Orsino,
Till he return, and stab him at the door?

Orsino. Not so; some accident might interpose
To rescue him from what is now most sure;
And you are unprovided where to fly,
How to excuse or to conceal. Nay, listen:
All is contrived; success is so assured
That . . .

[*Enter* BEATRICE.

Beatrice. 'Tis my brother's voice! You know me not?

Giacomo. My sister, my lost sister!

Beatrice. Lost indeed!
I see Orsino has talked with you, and
That you conjecture things too horrible
To speak, yet far less than the truth. Now, stay not,
He might return: yet kiss me; I shall know
That then thou hast consented to his death.
Farewell, farewell! Let piety to God,
Brotherly love, justice and clemency,
And all things that make tender hardest hearts
Make thine hard, brother. Answer not . . . farewell.
[*Exeunt severally.*

SCENE II.—*A mean apartment in* GIACOMO*'s house.* GIACOMO *alone.*

Giacomo. 'Tis midnight, and Orsino comes not yet.
[*Thunder, and the sound of a storm.*
What! can the everlasting elements
Feel with a worm like man? If so the shaft
Of mercy-winged lightning would not fall
On stones and trees. My wife and children sleep:
They are now living in unmeaning dreams:
But I must wake, still doubting if that deed
Be just which was most necessary. O,
Thou unreplenished lamp! whose narrow fire
Is shaken by the wind, and on whose edge
Devouring darkness hovers! Thou small flame,
Which, as a dying pulse rises and falls,
Still flickerest up and down, how very soon,
Did I not feed thee, wouldst thou fail and be
As thou hadst never been! So wastes and sinks
Even now, perhaps, the life that kindled mine:
But that no power can fill with vital oil
That broken lamp of flesh. Ha! 'tis the blood
Which fed these veins that ebbs till all is cold:
It is the form that moulded mine that sinks
Into the white and yellow spasms of death:
It is the soul by which mine was arrayed
In God's immortal likeness which now stands
Naked before Heaven's judgement seat! [*A bell strikes.*
One! Two!

The hours crawl on; and when my hairs are white,
My son will then perhaps be waiting thus,
Tortured between just hate and vain remorse;
Chiding the tardy messenger of news
Like those which I expect. I almost wish
He be not dead, although my wrongs are great;
Yet . . . 'tis Orsino's step . . .

[*Enter* ORSINO.

Speak!

Orsino. I am come
To say he has escaped.

Giacomo. Escaped!

Orsino. And safe
Within Petrella. He past by the spot
Appointed for the deed an hour too soon.

Giacomo. Are we the fools of such contingencies?
And do we waste in blind misgivings thus
The hours when we should act? Then wind and thunder,
Which seemed to howl his knell, is the loud laughter
With which Heaven mocks our weakness! I henceforth
Will ne'er repent of aught designed or done
But my repentance.

Orsino. See, the lamp is out.

Giacomo. If no remorse is ours when the dim air
Has drank this innocent flame, why should we quail
When Cenci's life, that light by which ill spirits
See the worst deeds they prompt, shall sink for ever?
No, I am hardened.

Orsino. Why, what need of this?
Who feared the pale intrusion of remorse
In a just deed? Altho' our first plan failed,
Doubt not but he will soon be laid to rest.
But light the lamp; let us not talk i' the dark.

Giacomo (*lighting the lamp*).
And yet once quenched I cannot thus relume
My father's life: do you not think his ghost
Might plead that argument with God?

Orsino. Once gone
You cannot now recall your sister's peace;
Your own extinguished years of youth and hope;
Nor your wife's bitter words; nor all the taunts
Which, from the prosperous, weak misfortune takes;
Nor your dead mother; nor . . .

Giacomo. O, speak no more!
I am resolved, although this very hand
Must quench the life that animated it.

Orsino. There is no need of that. Listen: you know
Olimpio, the castellan of Petrella
In old Colonna's time; him whom your father
Degraded from his post? And Marzio,
That desperate wretch, whom he deprived last year
Of a reward of blood, well earned and due?

Giacomo. I knew Olimpio; and they say he hated
Old Cenci so, that in his silent rage
His lips grew white only to see him pass.
Of Marzio I know nothing.

Orsino. Marzio's hate
Matches Olimpio's. I have sent these men,
But in your name, and as at your request,
To talk with Beatrice and Lucretia.

Giacomo. Only to talk?

Orsino. The moments which even now
Pass onward to tomorrow's midnight hour
May memorize their flight with death: ere then
They must have talked, and may perhaps have done,
And made an end . . .

Giacomo. Listen! What sound is that?

Orsino. The housedog moans, and the beams crack: nought else.

Giacomo. It is my wife complaining in her sleep:
I doubt not she is saying bitter things
Of me; and all my children round her dreaming
That I deny them sustenance.

Orsino. Whilst he
Who truly took it from them, and who fills
Their hungry rest with bitterness, now sleeps
Lapped in bad pleasures, and triumphantly
Mocks thee in visions of successful hate
Too like the truth of day.

Giacomo. If e'er he wakes
Again, I will not trust to hireling hands . . .

Orsino. Why, that were well. I must be gone; good night!
When next we meet may all be done—

Giacomo. And all
Forgotten—Oh, that I had never been! [*Exeunt.*

END OF THE THIRD ACT.

ACT IV

SCENE I.—*An apartment in the Castle of Petrella. Enter* CENCI.

Cenci. She comes not; yet I left her even now
Vanquished and faint. She knows the penalty
Of her delay: yet what if threats are vain?
Am I now not within Petrella's moat?
Or fear I still the eyes and ears of Rome?
Might I not drag her by the golden hair?
Stamp on her? Keep her sleepless till her brain
Be overworn? Tame her with chains and famine?
Less would suffice. Yet so to leave undone
What I most seek! No, 'tis her stubborn will

Which by its own consent shall stoop as low
As that which drags it down.

[*Enter* LUCRETIA.

Thou loathed wretch!
Hide thee from my abhorrence; Fly, begone!
Yet stay! Bid Beatrice come hither.

Lucretia. Oh,
Husband! I pray for thine own wretched sake
Heed what thou dost. A man who walks like thee
Thro' crimes, and thro' the danger of his crimes,
Each hour may stumble o'er a sudden grave.
And thou art old; thy hairs are hoary gray;
As thou wouldst save thyself from death and hell,
Pity thy daughter; give her to some friend
In marriage: so that she may tempt thee not
To hatred, or worse thoughts, if worse there be.

Cenci. What! like her sister who has found a home
To mock my hate from with prosperity?
Strange ruin shall destroy both her and thee
And all that yet remain. My death may be
Rapid, her destiny outspeeds it. Go,
Bid her come hither, and before my mood
Be changed, lest I should drag her by the hair.

Lucretia. She sent me to thee, husband. At thy presence
She fell, as thou dost know, into a trance;
And in that trance she heard a voice which said,
'Cenci must die! Let him confess himself!
Even now the accusing Angel waits to hear
If God, to punish his enormous crimes,
Harden his dying heart!'

Cenci. Why—such things are . . .
No doubt divine revealings may be made.
'Tis plain I have been favoured from above,
For when I cursed my sons they died.—Aye . . . so . . .
As to the right or wrong, that's talk . . . repentance . . .
Repentance is an easy moment's work
And more depends on God than me. Well . . . well . . .

I must give up the greater point, which was
To poison and corrupt her soul.

[*A pause;* LUCRETIA *approaches anxiously, and then shrinks back as he speaks.*

One, two;
Aye . . . Rocco and Cristofano my curse
Strangled: and Giacomo, I think, will find
Life a worse Hell than that beyond the grave:
Beatrice shall, if there be skill in hate,
Die in despair, blaspheming: to Bernardo,
He is so innocent, I will bequeath
The memory of these deeds, and make his youth
The sepulchre of hope, where evil thoughts
Shall grow like weeds on a neglected tomb.
When all is done, out in the wide Campagna,
I will pile up my silver and my gold;
My costly robes, paintings and tapestries;
My parchments and all records of my wealth,
And make a bonfire in my joy, and leave
Of my possessions nothing but my name;
Which shall be an inheritance to strip
Its wearer bare as infamy. That done,
My soul, which is a scourge, will I resign
Into the hands of him who wielded it;
Be it for its own punishment or theirs,
He will not ask it of me till the lash
Be broken in its last and deepest wound;
Until its hate be all inflicted. Yet,
Lest death outspeed my purpose, let me make
Short work and sure . . . [*Going.*

Lucretia. (*Stops him.*) Oh, stay! It was a feint:
She had no vision, and she heard no voice.
I said it but to awe thee.

Cenci. That is well.
Vile palterer with the sacred truth of God,
Be thy soul choked with that blaspheming lie!
For Beatrice worse terrors are in store
To bend her to my will.

Lucretia. Oh! to what will?
What cruel sufferings more than she has known
Canst thou inflict?

Cenci. Andrea! Go call my daughter,
And if she comes not tell her that I come.
What sufferings? I will drag her, step by step,
Thro' infamies unheard of among men:
She shall stand shelterless in the broad noon
Of public scorn, for acts blazoned abroad,
One among which shall be . . . What? Canst thou guess?
She shall become (for what she most abhors
Shall have a fascination to entrap
Her loathing will) to her own conscious self
All she appears to others; and when dead,
As she shall die unshrived and unforgiven,
A rebel to her father and her God,
Her corpse shall be abandoned to the hounds;
Her name shall be the terror of the earth;
Her spirit shall approach the throne of God
Plague-spotted with my curses. I will make
Body and soul a monstrous lump of ruin.
[*Enter* ANDREA.

Andrea. The lady Beatrice . . .

Cenci. Speak, pale slave! What
Said she?

Andrea. My Lord, 'twas what she looked; she said:
'Go tell my father that I see the gulph
Of Hell between us two, which he may pass,
I will not.' [*Exit* ANDREA.

Cenci. Go thou quick, Lucretia,
Tell her to come; yet let her understand
Her coming is consent: and say, moreover,
That if she come not I will curse her. [*Exit* LUCRETIA.
Ha!
With what but with a father's curse doth God
Panic-strike armed victory, and make pale

Cities in their prosperity? The world's Father
Must grant a parent's prayer against his child
Be he who asks even what men call me.
Will not the deaths of her rebellious brothers
Awe her before I speak? For I on them
Did imprecate quick ruin, and it came.
[*Enter* LUCRETIA.
Well; what? Speak, wretch!

Lucretia. She said, 'I cannot come;
Go tell my father that I see a torrent
Of his own blood raging between us.'

Cenci (*kneeling*). God!
Hear me! If this most specious mass of flesh,
Which thou hast made my daughter; this my blood,
This particle of my divided being;
Or rather, this my bane and my disease,
Whose sight infects and poisons me; this devil
Which sprung from me as from a hell, was meant
To aught good use; if her bright loveliness
Was kindled to illumine this dark world;
If nursed by thy selectest dew of love
Such virtues blossom in her as should make
The peace of life, I pray thee for my sake,
As thou the common God and Father art
Of her, and me, and all; reverse that doom!
Earth, in the name of God, let her food be
Poison, until she be encrusted round
With leprous stains! Heaven, rain upon her head
The blistering drops of the Maremma's dew,
Till she be speckled like a toad; parch up
Those love-enkindled lips, warp those fine limbs
To loathed lameness! All beholding sun,
Strike in thine envy those life-darting eyes
With thine own blinding beams!

Lucretia. Peace! Peace!
For thine own sake unsay those dreadful words.
When high God grants he punishes such prayers.

Cenci (leaping up, and throwing his right hand towards Heaven).
He does his will, I mine! This in addition,
That if she have a child . . .

Lucretia. Horrible thought!

Cenci. That if she ever have a child; and thou,
Quick Nature! I adjure thee by thy God,
That thou be fruitful in her, and encrease
And multiply, fulfilling his command,
And my deep imprecation! May it be
A hideous likeness of herself, that as
From a distorting mirror, she may see
Her image mixed with what she most abhors,
Smiling upon her from her nursing breast.
And that the child may from its infancy
Grow, day by day, more wicked and deformed,
Turning her mother's love to misery:
And that both she and it may live until
It shall repay her care and pain with hate,
Or what may else be more unnatural.
So he may hunt her through the clamorous scoffs
Of the loud world to a dishonoured grave.
Shall I revoke this curse? Go, bid her come,
Before my words are chronicled in heaven. [*Exit* LUCRETIA.
I do not feel as if I were a man,
But like a fiend appointed to chastise
The offences of some unremembered world.
My blood is running up and down my veins;
A fearful pleasure makes it prick and tingle:
I feel a giddy sickness of strange awe;
My heart is beating with an expectation
Of horrid joy.

[*Enter* LUCRETIA.

What? Speak!

Lucretia. She bids thee curse;
And if thy curses, as they cannot do,
Could kill her soul . . .

Cenci. She would not come. 'Tis well,
I can do both: first take what I demand,
And then extort concession. To thy chamber!
Fly ere I spurn thee: and beware this night
That thou cross not my footsteps. It were safer
To come between the tiger and his prey. [*Exit* LUCRETIA.
It must be late; mine eyes grow weary dim
With unaccustomed heaviness of sleep.
Conscience! Oh, thou most insolent of lies!
They say that sleep, that healing dew of heaven,
Steeps not in balm the foldings of the brain
Which thinks thee an imposter. I will go
First to belie thee with an hour of rest,
Which will be deep and calm, I feel: and then . . .
O, multitudinous Hell, the fiends will shake
Thine arches with the laughter of their joy!
There shall be lamentation heard in Heaven
As o'er an angel fallen; and upon Earth
All good shall droop and sicken, and ill things
Shall with a spirit of unnatural life
Stir and be quickened . . . even as I am now. [*Exit.*

SCENE II.—*Before the Castle of Petrella. Enter* BEATRICE *and* LUCRETIA *above on the ramparts.*

Beatrice. They come not yet.

Lucretia. 'Tis scarce midnight.

Beatrice. How slow
Behind the course of thought, even sick with speed,
Lags leaden-footed time!

Lucretia. The minutes pass . . .
If he should wake before the deed is done?

Beatrice. O, Mother! He must never wake again.
What thou hast said persuades me that our act
Will but dislodge a spirit of deep hell
Out of a human form.

Lucretia. 'Tis true he spoke
Of death and judgement with strange confidence
For one so wicked; as a man believing
In God, yet recking not of good or ill.
And yet to die without confession! . . .

Beatrice. Oh!
Believe that heaven is merciful and just,
And will not add our dread necessity
To the amount of his offences.
[*Enter* OLIMPIO *and* MARZIO, *below.*

Lucretia. See,
They come.

Beatrice. All mortal things must hasten thus
To their dark end. Let us go down.
[*Exeunt* LUCRETIA *and* BEATRICE *from above.*

Olimpio. How feel you to this work?

Marzio. As one who thinks
A thousand crowns excellent market price
For an old murderer's life. Your cheeks are pale.

Olimpio. It is the white reflexion of your own,
Which you call pale.

Marzio. Is that their natural hue?

Olimpio. Or 'tis my hate and the deferred desire
To wreak it, which extinguishes their blood.

Marzio. You are inclined then to this business?

Olimpio. Aye.
If one should bribe me with a thousand crowns
To kill a serpent which had stung my child,
I could not be more willing.
[*Enter* BEATRICE *and* LUCRETIA, *below.*
Noble ladies!

Beatrice. Are ye resolved?

Olimpio. Is he asleep?

Marzio. Is all
Quiet?

Lucretia. I mixed an opiate with his drink:
He sleeps so soundly . . .

Beatrice. That his death will be
But as a change of sin-chastising dreams,
A dark continuance of the Hell within him,
Which God extinguish! But ye are resolved?
Ye know it is a high and holy deed?

Olimpio. We are resolved.

Marzio. As to the how this act
Be warranted, it rests with you.

Beatrice. Well, follow!

Olimpio. Hush! Hark! What noise is that?

Marzio. Ha! some one comes!

Beatrice. Ye conscience-stricken cravens, rock to rest
Your baby hearts. It is the iron gate,
Which ye left open, swinging to the wind,
That enters whistling as in scorn. Come, follow!
And be your steps like mine, light, quick and bold. [*Exeunt.*

SCENE III.—*An apartment in the Castle. Enter* BEATRICE *and* LUCRETIA.

Lucretia. They are about it now.

Beatrice. Nay, it is done.

Lucretia. I have not heard him groan.

Beatrice. He will not groan.

Lucretia. What sound is that?

Beatrice. List! 'tis the tread of feet
About his bed.

Lucretia. My God!
If he be now a cold stiff corpse . . .

Beatrice. O, fear not
What may be done, but what is left undone:
The act seals all.

[*Enter* OLIMPIO *and* MARZIO.

Is it accomplished?

Marzio. What?

Olimpio. Did you not call?

Beatrice. When?

Olimpio. Now.

Beatrice. I ask if all is over?

Olimpio. We dare not kill an old and sleeping man;
His thin grey hair, his stern and reverent brow,
His veined hands crossed on his heaving breast,
And the calm innocent sleep in which he lay,
Quelled me. Indeed, indeed, I cannot do it.

Marzio. But I was bolder; for I chid Olimpio,
And bade him bear his wrongs to his own grave
And leave me the reward. And now my knife
Touched the loose wrinkled throat, when the old man
Stirred in his sleep, and said, 'God! hear, O, hear,
A father's curse! What, art thou not our father?'
And then he laughed. I knew it was the ghost
Of my dead father speaking through his lips,
And could not kill him.

Beatrice. Miserable slaves!
Where, if ye dare not kill a sleeping man,
Found ye the boldness to return to me
With such a deed undone? Base palterers!
Cowards and traitors! Why, the very conscience
Which ye would sell for gold and for revenge
Is an equivocation: it sleeps over
A thousand daily acts disgracing men;
And when a deed where mercy insults heaven . . .
Why do I talk?
[*Snatching a dagger from one of them and raising it.*
Hadst thou a tongue to say,
'She murdered her own father,' I must do it!
But never dream ye shall outlive him long!

Olimpio. Stop, for God's sake!

Marzio. I will go back and kill him.

Olimpio. Give me the weapon, we must do thy will.

Beatrice. Take it! Depart! Return! [*Exeunt* OLIMPIO *and* MARZIO.
How pale thou art!
We do but that which 'twere a deadly crime
To leave undone.

Lucretia. Would it were done!

Beatrice. Even whilst
That doubt is passing through your mind, the world
Is conscious of a change. Darkness and hell
Have swallowed up the vapour they sent forth
To blacken the sweet light of life. My breath
Comes, methinks, lighter, and the jellied blood
Runs freely thro' my veins. Hark!
[*Enter* OLIMPIO *and* MARZIO.
He is . . .

Olimpio. Dead!

Marzio. We strangled him that there might be no blood;
And then we threw his heavy corpse i' the garden
Under the balcony; 'twill seem it fell.

Beatrice (*giving them a bag of coin*).
Here, take this gold, and hasten to your homes.
And, Marzio, because thou wast only awed
By that which made me tremble, wear thou this!
[*Clothes him in a rich mantle.*
It was the mantle which my grandfather
Wore in his high prosperity, and men
Envied his state: so may they envy thine.
Thou wert a weapon in the hand of God
To a just use. Live long and thrive! And, mark,
If thou hast crimes, repent: this deed is none.
[*A horn is sounded.*

Lucretia. Hark, 'tis the castle horn; my God! it sounds
Like the last trump.

Beatrice. Some tedious guest is coming.

Lucretia. The drawbridge is let down; there is a tramp
Of horses in the court; fly, hide yourselves!
[*Exeunt* OLIMPIO *and* MARZIO.

Beatrice. Let us retire to counterfeit deep rest;
I scarcely need to counterfeit it now:
The spirit which doth reign within these limbs
Seems strangely undisturbed. I could even sleep
Fearless and calm: all ill is surely past.
[*Exeunt.*

SCENE IV.—*Another apartment in the Castle. Enter on one side the Legate* SAVELLA, *introduced by a servant, and on the other* LUCRETIA *and* BERNARDO.

Savella. Lady, my duty to his Holiness
Be my excuse that thus unseasonably
I break upon your rest. I must speak with
Count Cenci; doth he sleep?

Lucretia (*in a hurried and confused manner*). I think he sleeps;
Yet wake him not, I pray, spare me awhile,
He is a wicked and a wrathful man;
Should he be roused out of his sleep to-night,
Which is, I know, a hell of angry dreams,
It were not well; indeed it were not well.
Wait till day break . . . (*Aside.*) O, I am deadly sick!

Savella. I grieve thus to distress you, but the Count
Must answer charges of the gravest import,
And suddenly; such my commission is.

Lucretia (*with increased agitation*).
I dare not rouse him: I know none who dare . . .
'Twere perilous; . . . you might as safely waken
A serpent; or a corpse in which some fiend
Were laid to sleep.

Savella. Lady, my moments here
Are counted. I must rouse him from his sleep,
Since none else dare.

Lucretia (*aside*). O, terror! O, despair!
(*To* BERNARDO) Bernardo, conduct you the Lord Legate to
Your father's chamber. [*Exeunt* SAVELLA *and* BERNARDO.
[*Enter* BEATRICE.

Beatrice. 'Tis a messenger
Come to arrest the culprit who now stands
Before the throne of unappealable God.
Both Earth and Heaven, consenting arbiters,
Acquit our deed.

Lucretia. Oh, agony of fear!
Would that he yet might live! Even now I heard
The Legate's followers whisper as they passed
They had a warrant for his instant death.
All was prepared by unforbidden means
Which we must pay so dearly, having done.
Even now they search the tower, and find the body;

Now they suspect the truth; now they consult
Before they come to tax us with the fact;
O, horrible, 'tis all discovered!

Beatrice. Mother,
What is done wisely, is done well. Be bold
As thou art just. 'Tis like a truant child
To fear that others know what thou hast done,
Even from thine own strong consciousness, and thus
Write on unsteady eyes and altered cheeks
All thou wouldst hide. Be faithful to thyself,
And fear no other witness but thy fear.
For if, as cannot be, some circumstance
Should rise in accusation, we can blind
Suspicion with such cheap astonishment,
Or overbear it with such guiltless pride,
As murderers cannot feign. The deed is done,
And what may follow now regards not me.
I am as universal as the light;
Free as the earth-surrounding air; as firm
As the world's centre. Consequence, to me,
Is as the wind which strikes the solid rock
But shakes it not. [*A cry within and tumult.*

Voices. Murder! Murder! Murder!
[*Enter* BERNARDO *and* SAVELLA.

Savella (*to his followers*).
Go, search the castle round; sound the alarm;
Look to the gates that none escape!

Beatrice. What now?

Bernardo. I know not what to say . . . my father's dead.

Beatrice. How; dead! he only sleeps; you mistake, brother.
His sleep is very calm, very like death;
'Tis wonderful how well a tyrant sleeps.
He is not dead?

Bernardo. Dead; murdered.

Lucretia (*with extreme agitation*).
Oh, no, no,
He is not murdered though he may be dead;
I have alone the keys of those apartments.

Savella. Ha! Is it so?

Beatrice. My Lord, I pray excuse us;
We will retire; my mother is not well:
She seems quite overcome with this strange horror.
[*Exeunt* LUCRETIA *and* BEATRICE.

Savella. Can you suspect who may have murdered him?

Bernardo. I know not what to think.

Savella. Can you name any
Who had an interest in his death?

Bernardo. Alas!
I can name none who had not, and those most
Who most lament that such a deed is done;
My mother, and my sister, and myself.

Savella. 'Tis strange! There were clear marks of violence.
I found the old man's body in the moonlight
Hanging beneath the window of his chamber
Among the branches of a pine: he could not
Have fallen there, for all his limbs lay heaped
And effortless; 'tis true there was no blood . . .
Favour me, Sir; it much imports your house
That all should be made clear; to tell the ladies
That I request their presence. [*Exit* BERNARDO.
[*Enter Guards bringing in* MARZIO.

Guard. We have one.

Officer. My Lord, we found this ruffian and another
Lurking among the rocks; there is no doubt
But that they are the murderers of Count Cenci:
Each had a bag of coin; this fellow wore

A gold-inwoven robe, which shining bright
Under the dark rocks to the glimmering moon
Betrayed them to our notice: the other fell
Desperately fighting.

Savella. What does he confess?

Officer. He keeps firm silence; but these lines found on him
May speak.

Savella. Their language is at least sincere. [*Reads.*

'TO THE LADY BEATRICE.

That the atonement of what my nature
Sickens to conjecture may soon arrive,
I send thee, at thy brother's desire, those
Who will speak and do more than I dare
Write . . .
Thy devoted servant, Orsino.'

[*Enter* LUCRETIA, BEATRICE, *and* BERNARDO.

Knowest thou this writing, Lady?

Beatrice. No.

Savella. Nor thou?

Lucretia. (*Her conduct throughout the scene is marked by extreme agitation.*)
Where was it found? What is it? It should be
Orsino's hand! It speaks of that strange horror
Which never yet found utterance, but which made
Between that hapless child and her dead father
A gulph of obscure hatred.

Savella. Is it so?
Is it true, Lady, that thy father did
Such outrages as to awaken in thee
Unfilial hate?

Beatrice. Not hate, 'twas more than hate:
This is most true, yet wherefore question me?

Savella. There is a deed demanding question done;
Thou hast a secret which will answer not.

Beatrice. What sayest? My Lord, your words are bold
and rash.

Savella. I do arrest all present in the name
Of the Pope's Holiness. You must to Rome.

Lucretia. O, not to Rome! Indeed we are not guilty.

Beatrice. Guilty! Who dares talk of guilt? My Lord,
I am more innocent of parricide
Than is a child born fatherless . . . Dear Mother,
Your gentleness and patience are no shield
For this keen-judging world, this two-edged lie,
Which seems, but is not. What! will human laws,
Rather will ye who are their ministers,
Bar all access to retribution first,
And then, when heaven doth interpose to do
What ye neglect, arming familiar things
To the redress of an unwonted crime,
Make ye the victims who demanded it
Culprits? 'Tis ye are culprits! That poor wretch
Who stands so pale, and trembling, and amazed,
If it be true he murdered Cenci, was
A sword in the right hand of justest God.
Wherefore should I have wielded it? Unless
The crimes which mortal tongue dare never name
God therefore scruples to avenge.

Savella. You own
That you desired his death?

Beatrice. It would have been
A crime no less than his, if for one moment
That fierce desire had faded in my heart.
'Tis true I did believe, and hope, and pray,
Aye, I even knew . . . for God is wise and just,
That some strange sudden death hung over him.

'Tis true that this did happen, and most true
There was no other rest for me on earth,
No other hope in Heaven . . . now what of this?

Savella. Strange thoughts beget strange deeds; and here are both:
I judge thee not.

Beatrice. And yet, if you arrest me,
You are the judge and executioner
Of that which is the life of life: the breath
Of accusation kills an innocent name,
And leaves for lame acquittal the poor life
Which is a mask without it. 'Tis most false
That I am guilty of foul parricide;
Although I must rejoice, for justest cause,
That other hands have sent my father's soul
To ask the mercy he denied to me.
Now leave us free: stain not a noble house
With vague surmises of rejected crime;
Add to our sufferings and your own neglect
No heavier sum: let them have been enough:
Leave us the wreck we have.

Savella. I dare not, Lady.
I pray that you prepare yourselves for Rome:
There the Pope's further pleasure will be known.

Lucretia. O, not to Rome! O, take us not to Rome!

Beatrice. Why not to Rome, dear mother? There as here
Our innocence is as an armed heel
To trample accusation. God is there
As here, and with his shadow ever clothes
The innocent, the injured and the weak;
And such are we. Cheer up, dear Lady, lean
On me; collect your wandering thoughts. My Lord,
As soon as you have taken some refreshment,
And had all such examinations made
Upon the spot, as may be necessary
To the full understanding of this matter,
We shall be ready. Mother; will you come?

Lucretia. Ha! they will bind us to the rack, and wrest
Self-accusation from our agony!
Will Giacomo be there? Orsino? Marzio?
All present; all confronted; all demanding
Each from the other's countenance the thing
Which is in every heart! O, misery!
[*She faints, and is borne out.*

Savella. She faints: an ill appearance this.

Beatrice. My Lord,
She knows not yet the uses of the world.
She fears that power is as a beast which grasps
And loosens not: a snake whose look transmutes
All things to guilt which is its nutriment.
She cannot know how well the supine slaves
Of blind authority read the truth of things
When written on a brow of guilelessness:
She sees not yet triumphant Innocence
Stand at the judgement-seat of mortal man,
A judge and an accuser of the wrong
Which drags it there. Prepare yourself, my Lord;
Our suite will join yours in the court below. [*Exeunt.*

END OF THE FOURTH ACT.

ACT V

SCENE I.—*An apartment in* ORSINO*'s Palace. Enter* ORSINO *and* GIACOMO.

Giacomo. Do evil deeds thus quickly come to end?
O, that the vain remorse which must chastise
Crimes done, had but as loud a voice to warn
As its keen sting is mortal to avenge!
O, that the hour when present had cast off
The mantle of its mystery, and shewn
The ghastly form with which it now returns
When its scared game is roused, cheering the hounds

Of conscience to their prey! Alas! Alas!
It was a wicked thought, a piteous deed,
To kill an old and hoary-headed father.

Orsino. It has turned out unluckily, in truth.

Giacomo. To violate the sacred doors of sleep;
To cheat kind nature of the placid death
Which she prepares for overwearied age;
To drag from Heaven an unrepentant soul
Which might have quenched in reconciling prayers
A life of burning crimes . . .

Orsino. You cannot say
I urged you to the deed.

Giacomo. O, had I never
Found in thy smooth and ready countenance
The mirror of my darkest thoughts; hadst thou
Never with hints and questions made me look
Upon the monster of my thought, until
It grew familiar to desire . . .

Orsino. 'Tis thus
Men cast the blame of their unprosperous acts
Upon the abettors of their own resolve;
Or any thing but their weak, guilty selves.
And yet, confess the truth, it is the peril
In which you stand that gives you this pale sickness
Of penitence; Confess 'tis fear disguised
From its own shame that takes the mantle now
Of thin remorse. What if we yet were safe?

Giacomo. How can that be? Already Beatrice,
Lucretia and the murderer are in prison.
I doubt not officers are, whilst we speak,
Sent to arrest us.

Orsino. I have all prepared
For instant flight. We can escape even now,
So we take fleet occasion by the hair.

Giacomo. Rather expire in tortures, as I may.
What! will you cast by self-accusing flight
Assured conviction upon Beatrice?
She, who alone in this unnatural work,
Stands like God's angel ministered upon
By fiends; avenging such a nameless wrong
As turns black parricide to piety;
Whilst we for basest ends . . . I fear, Orsino,
While I consider all your words and looks,
Comparing them with your proposal now,
That you must be a villain. For what end
Could you engage in such a perilous crime,
Training me on with hints, and signs, and smiles,
Even to this gulph? Thou art no liar? No,
Thou art a lie! Traitor and murderer!
Coward and slave! But, no, defend thyself; [*Drawing.*
Let the sword speak what the indignant tongue
Disdains to brand thee with.

Orsino. Put up your weapon.
Is it the desperation of your fear
Makes you thus rash and sudden with a friend,
Now ruined for your sake? If honest anger
Have moved you, know, that what I just proposed
Was but to try you. As for me, I think,
Thankless affection led me to this point,
From which, if my firm temper could repent,
I cannot now recede. Even whilst we speak
The ministers of justice wait below:
They grant me these brief moments. Now if you
Have any word of melancholy comfort
To speak to your pale wife, 'twere best to pass
Out at the postern, and avoid them so.

Giacomo. O, generous friend! How canst thou pardon me?
Would that my life could purchase thine!

Orsino. That wish
Now comes a day too late. Haste; fare thee well!
Hear'st thou not steps along the corridor? [*Exit* GIACOMO.

I'm sorry for it; but the guards are waiting
At his own gate, and such was my contrivance
That I might rid me both of him and them.
I thought to act a solemn comedy
Upon the painted scene of this new world,
And to attain my own peculiar ends
By some such plot of mingled good and ill
As others weave; but there arose a Power
Which graspt and snapped the threads of my device
And turned it to a net of ruin . . . Ha! [*A shout is heard.*
Is that my name I hear proclaimed abroad?
But I will pass, wrapt in a vile disguise;
Rags on my back, and a false innocence
Upon my face, thro' the misdeeming crowd
Which judges by what seems. 'Tis easy then
For a new name and for a country new,
And a new life, fashioned on old desires,
To change the honours of abandoned Rome.
And these must be the masks of that within,
Which must remain unaltered . . . Oh, I fear
That what is past will never let me rest!
Why, when none else is conscious, but myself,
Of my misdeeds, should my own heart's contempt
Trouble me? Have I not the power to fly
My own reproaches? Shall I be the slave
Of . . . what? A word? which those of this false world
Employ against each other, not themselves;
As men wear daggers not for self-offence.
But if I am mistaken, where shall I
Find the disguise to hide me from myself,
As now I skulk from every other eye? [*Exit.*

SCENE II.—*A Hall of Justice.* CAMILLO, *Judges, etc., are discovered seated;* MARZIO *is led in.*

First Judge. Accused, do you persist in your denial?
I ask you, are you innocent, or guilty?
I demand who were the participators
In your offence? Speak truth and the whole truth.

Marzio. My God! I did not kill him; I know nothing;
Olimpio sold the robe to me from which
You would infer my guilt.

Second Judge. Away with him!

First Judge. Dare you, with lips yet white from the rack's kiss
Speak false? Is it so soft a questioner,
That you would bandy lover's talk with it
Till it wind out your life and soul? Away!

Marzio. Spare me! O, spare! I will confess.

First Judge. Then speak.

Marzio. I strangled him in his sleep.

First Judge. Who urged you to it?

Marzio. His own son Giacomo, and the young prelate
Orsino sent me to Petrella; there
The ladies Beatrice and Lucretia
Tempted me with a thousand crowns, and I
And my companion forthwith murdered him.
Now let me die.

First Judge. This sounds as bad as truth. Guards, there,
Lead forth the prisoners!
[*Enter* LUCRETIA, BEATRICE, *and* GIACOMO, *guarded*.
Look upon this man;
When did you see him last?

Beatrice. We never saw him.

Marzio. You know me too well, Lady Beatrice.

Beatrice. I know thee! How? where? when?

Marzio. You know 'twas I
Whom you did urge with menaces and bribes
To kill your father. When the thing was done
You clothed me in a robe of woven gold

And bade me thrive: how I have thriven, you see.
You, my Lord Giacomo, Lady Lucretia,
You know that what I speak is true.

[BEATRICE *advances towards him; he covers his face, and shrinks back.*

O, dart
The terrible resentment of those eyes
On the dead earth! Turn them away from me!
They wound: 'twas torture forced the truth. My Lords,
Having said this let me be led to death.

Beatrice. Poor wretch, I pity thee: yet stay awhile.

Camillo. Guards, lead him not away.

Beatrice. Cardinal Camillo,
You have a good repute for gentleness
And wisdom: can it be that you sit here
To countenance a wicked farce like this?
When some obscure and trembling slave is dragged
From sufferings which might shake the sternest heart
And bade to answer, not as he believes,
But as those may suspect or do desire
Whose questions thence suggest their own reply:
And that in peril of such hideous torments
As merciful God spares even the damned. Speak now
The thing you surely know, which is that you,
If your fine frame were stretched upon that wheel,
And you were told: 'Confess that you did poison
Your little nephew; that fair blue-eyed child
Who was the loadstar of your life':—and though
All see, since his most swift and piteous death,
That day and night, and heaven and earth, and time,
And all the things hoped for or done therein
Are changed to you, through your exceeding grief,
Yet you would say, 'I confess any thing':
And beg from your tormentors, like that slave,
The refuge of dishonourable death.
I pray thee, Cardinal, that thou assert
My innocence.

Camillo (*much moved*). What shall we think, my Lords?
Shame on these tears! I thought the heart was frozen
Which is their fountain. I would pledge my soul
That she is guiltless.

Judge. Yet she must be tortured.

Camillo. I would as soon have tortured mine own nephew
(If he now lived he would be just her age;
His hair, too, was her colour, and his eyes
Like hers in shape, but blue and not so deep)
As that most perfect image of God's love
That ever came sorrowing upon the earth.
She is as pure as speechless infancy!

Judge. Well, be her purity on your head, my Lord,
If you forbid the rack. His Holiness
Enjoined us to pursue this monstrous crime
By the severest forms of law; nay even
To stretch a point against the criminals.
The prisoners stand accused of parricide
Upon such evidence as justifies
Torture.

Beatrice. What evidence? This man's?

Judge. Even so.

Beatrice (*to* MARZIO).
Come near. And who art thou thus chosen forth
Out of the multitude of living men
To kill the innocent?

Marzio. I am Marzio,
Thy father's vassal.

Beatrice. Fix thine eyes on mine;
Answer to what I ask. [*Turning to the Judges.*
I prithee mark
His countenance: unlike bold calumny
Which sometimes dares not speak the thing it looks,
He dares not look the thing he speaks, but bends

His gaze on the blind earth.
(*To* MARZIO) What! wilt thou say
That I did murder my own father?

Marzio. Oh!
Spare me! My brain swims round . . . I cannot speak . . .
It was that horrid torture forced the truth.
Take me away! Let her not look on me!
I am a guilty miserable wretch;
I have said all I know; now, let me die!

Beatrice. My Lords, if by my nature I had been
So stern, as to have planned the crime alledged,
Which your suspicions dictate to this slave,
And the rack makes him utter, do you think
I should have left this two edged instrument
Of my misdeed; this man, this bloody knife
With my own name engraven on the heft,
Lying unsheathed amid a world of foes,
For my own death? That with such horrible need
For deepest silence, I should have neglected
So trivial a precaution, as the making
His tomb the keeper of a secret written
On a thief's memory? What is his poor life?
What are a thousand lives? A parricide
Had trampled them like dust; and, see, he lives!
(*Turning to* MARZIO.) And thou . . .

Marzio. Oh, spare me!
Speak to me no more!
That stern yet piteous look, those solemn tones,
Wound worse than torture.

(*To the Judges.*) I have told it all;
For pity's sake lead me away to death.

Camillo. Guards, lead him nearer the Lady Beatrice,
He shrinks from her regard like autumn's leaf
From the keen breath of the serenest north.

Beatrice. Oh, thou who tremblest on the giddy verge
Of life and death, pause ere thou answerest me;
So mayst thou answer God with less dismay:
What evil have we done thee? I, alas!
Have lived but on this earth a few sad years
And so my lot was ordered, that a father
First turned the moments of awakening life
To drops, each poisoning youth's sweet hope; and then
Stabbed with one blow my everlasting soul;
And my untainted fame; and even that peace
Which sleeps within the core of the heart's heart;
But the wound was not mortal; so my hate
Became the only worship I could lift
To our great father, who in pity and love,
Armed thee, as thou dost say, to cut him off;
And thus his wrong becomes my accusation;
And art thou the accuser? If thou hopest
Mercy in heaven, shew justice upon earth:
Worse than a bloody hand is a hard heart.
If thou hast done murders, made thy life's path
Over the trampled laws of God and man,
Rush not before thy Judge, and say: 'My maker,
I have done this and more; for there was one
Who was most pure and innocent on earth;
And because she endured what never any
Guilty or innocent endured before:
Because her wrongs could not be told, not thought;
Because thy hand at length did rescue her;
I with my words killed her and all her kin.'
Think, I adjure you, what it is to slay
The reverence living in the minds of men
Towards our ancient house, and stainless fame!
Think what it is to strangle infant pity,
Cradled in the belief of guileless looks,
Till it become a crime to suffer. Think
What 'tis to blot with infamy and blood
All that which shews like innocence, and is,
Hear me, great God! I swear, most innocent,
So that the world lose all discrimination
Between the sly, fierce, wild regard of guilt,
And that which now compels thee to reply
To what I ask: Am I, or am I not
A parricide?

Marzio. Thou art not!

Judge. What is this?

Marzio. I here declare those whom I did accuse
Are innocent. 'Tis I alone am guilty.

Judge. Drag him away to torments; let them be
Subtle and long drawn out, to tear the folds
Of the heart's inmost cell. Unbind him not
Till he confess.

Marzio. Torture me as ye will:
A keener pain has wrung a higher truth
From my last breath. She is most innocent!
Bloodhounds, not men, glut yourselves well with me;
I will not give you that fine piece of nature
To rend and ruin. [*Exit* MARZIO, *guarded*.

Camillo. What say ye now, my Lords?

Judge. Let tortures strain the truth till it be white
As snow thrice sifted by the frozen wind.

Camillo. Yet stained with blood.

Judge (*to* BEATRICE). Know you this paper, Lady?

Beatrice. Entrap me not with questions. Who stands here
As my accuser? Ha! wilt thou be he,
Who art my judge? Accuser, witness, judge,
What, all in one? Here is Orsino's name;
Where is Orsino? Let his eye meet mine.
What means this scrawl? Alas! Ye know not what,
And therefore on the chance that it may be
Some evil, will ye kill us?

[*Enter an Officer*.

Officer. Marzio's dead.

Judge. What did he say?

Officer. Nothing. As soon as we
Had bound him on the wheel, he smiled on us,
As one who baffles a deep adversary;
And holding his breath, died.

Judge. There remains nothing
But to apply the question to those prisoners,
Who yet remain stubborn.

Camillo. I overrule
Further proceedings, and in the behalf
Of these most innocent and noble persons
Will use my interest with the Holy Father.

Judge. Let the Pope's pleasure then be done. Meanwhile
Conduct these culprits each to separate cells;
And be the engines ready: for this night
If the Pope's resolution be as grave,
Pious, and just as once, I'll wring the truth
Out of those nerves and sinews, groan by groan. [*Exeunt.*

SCENE III.—*The cell of a prison.* BEATRICE *is discovered asleep on a couch. Enter* BERNARDO.

Bernardo. How gently slumber rests upon her face,
Like the last thoughts of some day sweetly spent
Closing in night and dreams, and so prolonged.
After such torments as she bore last night,
How light and soft her breathing comes. Ay, me!
Methinks that I shall never sleep again.
But I must shake the heavenly dew of rest
From this sweet folded flower, thus . . . wake! awake!
What, sister, canst thou sleep?

Beatrice (*awaking*). I was just dreaming
That we were all in Paradise. Thou knowest
This cell seems like a kind of Paradise
After our father's presence.

Bernardo. Dear, dear sister,
Would that thy dream were not a dream! O, God!
How shall I tell?

Beatrice. What wouldst thou tell, sweet brother?

Bernardo. Look not so calm and happy, or even whilst
I stand considering what I have to say
My heart will break.

Beatrice. See now, thou mak'st me weep:
How very friendless thou wouldst be, dear child,
If I were dead. Say what thou hast to say.

Bernardo. They have confessed; they could endure no more
The tortures . . .

Beatrice. Ha! What was there to confess?
They must have told some weak and wicked lie
To flatter their tormentors. Have they said
That they were guilty? O, white innocence,
That thou shouldst wear the mask of guilt to hide
Thine awful and serenest countenance
From those who know thee not!

[*Enter Judge with* LUCRETIA *and* GIACOMO, *guarded.*

Ignoble hearts!
For some brief spasms of pain, which are at least
As mortal as the limbs thro' which they pass,
Are centuries of high splendour laid in dust?
And that eternal honour which should live
Sunlike, above the reek of mortal fame,
Changed to a mockery and a bye-word? What!
Will you give up these bodies to be dragged
At horses' heels, so that our hair should sweep
The footsteps of the vain and senseless crowd,
Who, that they may make our calamity
Their worship and their spectacle, will leave
The churches and the theatres as void
As their own hearts? Shall the light multitude
Fling, at their choice, curses or faded pity,
Sad funeral flowers to deck a living corpse,
Upon us as we pass to pass away,
And leave . . . what memory of our having been?
Infamy, blood, terror, despair? O thou,
Who wert a mother to the parentless,

Kill not thy child! Let not her wrongs kill thee!
Brother, lie down with me upon the rack,
And let us each be silent as a corpse;
It soon will be as soft as any grave.
'Tis but the falsehood it can wring from fear
Makes the rack cruel.

Giacomo. They will tear the truth
Even from thee at last, those cruel pains:
For pity's sake say thou art guilty now.

Lucretia. O, speak the truth! Let us all quickly die;
And after death, God is our judge, not they;
He will have mercy on us.

Bernardo. If indeed
It can be true, say so, dear sister mine;
And then the Pope will surely pardon you,
And all be well.

Judge. Confess, or I will warp
Your limbs with such keen tortures . . .

Beatrice. Tortures! Turn
The rack henceforth into a spinning wheel!
Torture your dog, that he may tell when last
He lapped the blood his master shed . . . not me!
My pangs are of the mind, and of the heart,
And of the soul; aye, of the inmost soul,
Which weeps within tears as of burning gall
To see, in this ill world where none are true,
My kindred false to their deserted selves.
And with considering all the wretched life
Which I have lived, and its now wretched end,
And the small justice shewn by Heaven and Earth
To me or mine; and what a tyrant thou art,
And what slaves these; and what a world we make,
The oppressor and the oppressed . . . such pangs compel
My answer. What is it thou wouldst with me?

Judge. Art thou not guilty of thy father's death?

Beatrice. Or wilt thou rather tax high judging God
That he permitted such an act as that
Which I have suffered, and which he beheld;
Made it unutterable, and took from it
All refuge, all revenge, all consequence,
But that which thou hast called my father's death?
Which is or is not what men call a crime,
Which either I have done, or have not done;
Say what ye will. I shall deny no more.
If ye desire it thus, thus let it be,
And so an end of all. Now do your will;
No other pains shall force another word.

Judge. She is convicted, but has not confessed.
Be it enough. Until their final sentence
Let none have converse with them. You, young Lord,
Linger not here!

Beatrice. O, tear him not away!

Judge. Guards, do your duty.

Bernardo (embracing BEATRICE). Oh! would ye divide
Body from soul?

Officer. That is the headsman's business.
[*Exeunt all but* LUCRETIA, BEATRICE, *and* GIACOMO.

Giacomo. Have I confessed? Is it all over now?
No hope! No refuge! O, weak, wicked tongue
Which hast destroyed me, would that thou hadst been
Cut out and thrown to dogs first! To have killed
My father first, and then betrayed my sister;
Aye, thee! the one thing innocent and pure
In this black guilty world, to that which I
So well deserve! My wife! my little ones!
Destitute, helpless, and I . . . Father! God!
Canst thou forgive even the unforgiving,
When their full hearts break thus, thus! . . .
[*Covers his face and weeps.*

Lucretia. O, my child!
To what a dreadful end are we all come!
Why did I yield? Why did I not sustain
Those torments? Oh, that I were all dissolved
Into these fast and unavailing tears,
Which flow and feel not!

Beatrice. What 'twas weak to do,
'Tis weaker to lament, once being done;
Take cheer! The God who knew my wrong, and made
Our speedy act the angel of his wrath,
Seems, and but seems to have abandoned us.
Let us not think that we shall die for this.
Brother, sit near me; give me your firm hand,
You had a manly heart. Bear up! Bear up!
O, dearest Lady, put your gentle head
Upon my lap, and try to sleep awhile:
Your eyes look pale, hollow and overworn,
With heaviness of watching and slow grief.
Come, I will sing you some low, sleepy tune,
Not cheerful, nor yet sad; some dull old thing,
Some outworn and unused monotony,
Such as our country gossips sing and spin,
Till they almost forget they live: lie down!
So, that will do. Have I forgot the words?
Faith! They are sadder than I thought they were.

SONG

False friend, wilt thou smile or weep
When my life is laid asleep?
Little cares for a smile or a tear,
The clay-cold corpse upon the bier?
Farewell! Heigho!
What is this whispers low?
There is a snake in thy smile, my dear;
And bitter poison within thy tear.

Sweet sleep, were death like to thee,
Or if thou couldst mortal be,
I would close these eyes of pain;
When to wake? Never again.

O, World! Farewell!
Listen to the passing bell!
It says, thou and I must part,
With a light and a heavy heart. [*The scene closes.*

SCENE IV.—*A Hall of the Prison. Enter* CAMILLO *and* BERNARDO.

Camillo. The Pope is stern; not to be moved or bent.
He looked as calm and keen as is the engine
Which tortures and which kills, exempt itself
From aught that it inflicts; a marble form,
A rite, a law, a custom: not a man.
He frowned, as if to frown had been the trick
Of his machinery, on the advocates
Presenting the defences, which he tore
And threw behind, muttering with hoarse, harsh voice:
'Which among ye defended their old father
Killed in his sleep?' Then to another: 'Thou
Dost this in virtue of thy place; 'tis well.'
He turned to me then, looking deprecation,
And said these three words, coldly: 'They must die.'

Bernardo. And yet you left him not?

Camillo. I urged him still;
Pleading, as I could guess, the devilish wrong
Which prompted your unnatural parent's death.
And he replied: 'Paolo Santa Croce
Murdered his mother yester evening,
And he is fled. Parricide grows so rife
That soon, for some just cause no doubt, the young
Will strangle us all, dozing in our chairs.
Authority, and power, and hoary hair
Are grown crimes capital. You are my nephew,
You come to ask their pardon; stay a moment;
Here is their sentence; never see me more
Till, to the letter, it be all fulfilled.'

Bernardo. O, God, not so! I did believe indeed
That all you said was but sad preparation
For happy news. O, there are words and looks
To bend the sternest purpose! Once I knew them,
Now I forget them at my dearest need.
What think you if I seek him out, and bathe
His feet and robe with hot and bitter tears?
Importune him with prayers, vexing his brain
With my perpetual cries, until in rage
He strike me with his pastoral cross, and trample
Upon my prostrate head, so that my blood
May stain the senseless dust on which he treads,
And remorse waken mercy? I will do it!
O, wait till I return! [*Rushes out.*

Camillo. Alas! poor boy!
A wreck-devoted seaman thus might pray
To the deaf sea.
[*Enter* LUCRETIA, BEATRICE, *and* GIACOMO, *guarded.*

Beatrice. I hardly dare to fear
That thou bring'st other news than a just pardon.

Camillo. May God in heaven be less inexorable
To the Pope's prayers, than he has been to mine.
Here is the sentence and the warrant.

Beatrice (*wildly*). Oh,
My God! Can it be possible I have
To die so suddenly? So young to go
Under the obscure, cold, rotting, wormy ground!
To be nailed down into a narrow place;
To see no more sweet sunshine; hear no more
Blithe voice of living thing; muse not again
Upon familiar thoughts, sad, yet thus lost—
How fearful! to be nothing! Or to be . . .
What? O, where am I? Let me not go mad!
Sweet Heaven, forgive weak thoughts! If there should be
No God, no Heaven, no Earth in the void world;
The wide, grey, lampless, deep, unpeopled world!
If all things then should be . . . my father's spirit,
His eye, his voice, his touch surrounding me;

The atmosphere and breath of my dead life!
If sometimes, as a shape more like himself,
Even the form which tortured me on earth,
Masked in grey hairs and wrinkles, he should come
And wind me in his hellish arms, and fix
His eyes on mine, and drag me down, down, down!
For was he not alone omnipotent
On Earth, and ever present? Even tho' dead,
Does not his spirit live in all that breathe,
And work for me and mine still the same ruin,
Scorn, pain, despair? Who ever yet returned
To teach the laws of death's untrodden realm?
Unjust perhaps as those which drive us now,
O, whither, whither?

Lucretia. Trust in God's sweet love,
The tender promises of Christ: ere night,
Think we shall be in Paradise.

Beatrice. 'Tis past!
Whatever comes my heart shall sink no more.
And yet, I know not why, your words strike chill:
How tedious, false and cold seem all things. I
Have met with much injustice in this world;
No difference has been made by God or man,
Or any power moulding my wretched lot,
'Twixt good or evil, as regarded me.
I am cut off from the only world I know,
From light, and life, and love, in youth's sweet prime.
You do well telling me to trust in God,
I hope I do trust in him. In whom else
Can any trust? And yet my heart is cold.

[*During the latter speeches* GIACOMO *has retired conversing with* CAMILLO, *who now goes out;* GIACOMO *advances.*

Giacomo. Know you not, Mother . . . Sister, know you not?
Bernardo even now is gone to implore
The Pope to grant our pardon.

Lucretia. Child, perhaps
It will be granted. We may all then live
To make these woes a tale for distant years:
O, what a thought! It gushes to my heart
Like the warm blood.

Beatrice. Yet both will soon be cold.
O, trample out that thought! Worse than despair,
Worse than the bitterness of death, is hope:
It is the only ill which can find place
Upon the giddy, sharp and narrow hour
Tottering beneath us. Plead with the swift frost
That it should spare the eldest flower of spring:
Plead with awakening Earthquake, o'er whose couch
Even now a city stands, strong, fair and free;
Now stench and blackness yawns, like death. O, plead
With famine, or wind-walking Pestilence,
Blind lightning, or the deaf sea, not with man!
Cruel, cold, formal man; righteous in words,
In deeds a Cain. No, Mother, we must die:
Since such is the reward of innocent lives;
Such the alleviation of worst wrongs.
And whilst our murderers live, and hard, cold men,
Smiling and slow, walk thro' a world of tears
To death as to life's sleep; 'twere just the grave
Were some strange joy for us. Come, obscure Death,
And wind me in thine all-embracing arms!
Like a fond mother hide me in thy bosom,
And rock me to the sleep from which none wake.
Live ye, who live, subject to one another
As we were once, who now . . .

[BERNARDO *rushes in.*

Bernardo. Oh, horrible!
That tears, that looks, that hope poured forth in prayer,
Even till the heart is vacant and despairs,
Should all be vain! The ministers of death
Are waiting round the doors. I thought I saw
Blood on the face of one . . . what if 'twere fancy?
Soon the heart's blood of all I love on earth
Will sprinkle him, and he will wipe it off

As if 'twere only rain. O, life! O, world!
Cover me! let me be no more! To see
That perfect mirror of pure innocence
Wherein I gazed, and grew happy and good,
Shivered to dust! To see thee, Beatrice,
Who made all lovely thou didst look upon . . .
Thee, light of life . . . dead, dark! while I say, sister,
To hear I have no sister; and thou, Mother,
Whose love was a bond to all our loves . . .
Dead! The sweet bond broken!

[*Enter* CAMILLO *and Guards.*

They come! Let me
Kiss those warm lips before their crimson leaves
Are blighted . . . white . . . cold. Say farewell, before
Death chokes that gentle voice! O, let me hear
You speak!

Beatrice. Farewell, my tender brother. Think
Of our sad fate with gentleness, as now:
And let mild, pitying thoughts lighten for thee
Thy sorrow's load. Err not in harsh despair,
But tears and patience. One thing more, my child,
For thine own sake be constant to the love
Thou bearest us; and to the faith that I,
Tho' wrapt in a strange cloud of crime and shame,
Lived ever holy and unstained. And though
Ill tongues shall wound me, and our common name
Be as a mark stamped on thine innocent brow
For men to point at as they pass, do thou
Forbear, and never think a thought unkind
Of those, who perhaps love thee in their graves.
So mayest thou die as I do; fear and pain
Being subdued. Farewell! Farewell! Farewell!

Bernardo. I cannot say, farewell!

Camillo. O, Lady Beatrice!

Beatrice. Give yourself no unnecessary pain,
My dear Lord Cardinal. Here, Mother, tie
My girdle for me, and bind up this hair

In any simple knot; aye, that does well.
And yours I see is coming down. How often
Have we done this for one another; now
We shall not do it any more. My Lord,
We are quite ready. Well, 'tis very well.

THE END.

THE MASK OF ANARCHY

WRITTEN ON THE OCCASION OF THE MASSACRE AT MANCHESTER

As I lay asleep in Italy
There came a voice from over the Sea,
And with great power it forth led me
To walk in the visions of Poesy.

I met Murder on the way—
He had a mask like Castlereagh—
Very smooth he looked, yet grim;
Seven bloodhounds followed him:

All were fat; and well they might
Be in admirable plight,
For one by one, and two by two,
He tossed them human hearts to chew
Which from his wide cloak he drew.

Next came Fraud, and he had on,
Like Eldon, an ermined gown;
His big tears, for he wept well,
Turned to mill-stones as they fell.

And the little children, who
Round his feet played to and fro,
Thinking every tear a gem,
Had their brains knocked out by them.

Clothed with the Bible, as with light,
And the shadows of the night,
Like Sidmouth, next, Hypocrisy
On a crocodile rode by.

And many more Destructions played
In this ghastly masquerade,
All disguised, even to the eyes,
Like Bishops, lawyers, peers or spies.

Last came Anarchy: he rode
On a white horse, splashed with blood;
He was pale even to the lips,
Like Death in the Apocalypse.

And he wore a kingly crown,
And in his grasp a sceptre shone;
On his brow this mark I saw—
'I AM GOD, AND KING, AND LAW.'

With a pace stately and fast,
Over English land he passed,
Trampling to a mire of blood
The adoring multitude.

And a mighty troop around,
With their trampling shook the ground,
Waving each a bloody sword,
For the service of their Lord.

And with glorious triumph, they
Rode through England proud and gay,
Drunk as with intoxication
Of the wine of desolation.

O'er fields and towns, from sea to sea,
Passed the Pageant swift and free,
Tearing up, and trampling down;
Till they came to London town.

And each dweller, panic-stricken,
Felt his heart with terror sicken
Hearing the tempestuous cry
Of the triumph of Anarchy.

For with pomp to meet him came,
Clothed in arms like blood and flame,
The hired murderers, who did sing
'Thou art God, and Law, and King.

'We have waited, weak and lone
For thy coming, Mighty One!
Our purses are empty, our swords are cold,
Give us glory, and blood, and gold.'

Lawyers and priests, a motley crowd,
To the earth their pale brows bowed;
Like a bad prayer, not over loud,
Whispering—'Thou art Law and God.'—

Then all cried with one accord,
'Thou art King, and God, and Lord;
Anarchy, to thee we bow,
Be thy name made holy now!'

And Anarchy, the Skeleton,
Bowed and grinned to every one,
As well as if his education
Had cost ten millions to the nation.

For he knew the Palaces
Of our Kings were rightly his;
His the sceptre, crown, and globe,
And the gold-inwoven robe.

So he sent his slaves before
To seize upon the Bank and Tower,
And was proceeding with intent
To meet his pensioned Parliament,

When one fled past, a Maniac maid,
And her name was Hope, she said:
But she looked more like Despair,
And she cried out in the air:

'My father Time is weak and grey
With waiting for a better day;
See how idiot-like he stands,
Fumbling with his palsied hands!

'He has had child after child
And the dust of death is piled
Over every one but me—
Misery, oh, Misery!'

Then she lay down in the street,
Right before the horses' feet,
Expecting, with a patient eye,
Murder, Fraud and Anarchy.

When between her and her foes
A mist, a light, an image rose,
Small at first, and weak, and frail,
Like the vapour of a vale:

Till as clouds grow on the blast,
Like tower-crowned giants striding fast,
And glare with lightnings as they fly,
And speak in thunder to the sky,

It grew—a Shape arrayed in mail
Brighter than the viper's scale,
And upborne on wings whose grain
Was as the light of sunny rain:

On its helm, seen far away,
A planet, like the Morning's, lay;
And those plumes its light rained through
Like a shower of crimson dew.

With step as soft as wind it passed
O'er the heads of men—so fast
That they knew the presence there,
And looked,—but all was empty air.

As flowers beneath May's footstep waken,
As stars from Night's loose hair are shaken,
As waves arise when loud winds call,
Thoughts sprung where'er that step did fall.

And the prostrate multitude
Looked—and ankle-deep in blood,
Hope, that maiden most serene,
Was walking with a quiet mien:

And Anarchy, the ghastly birth,
Lay dead earth upon the earth;
The Horse of Death tameless as wind
Fled, and with his hoofs did grind
To dust, the murderers thronged behind.

A rushing light of clouds and splendour,
A sense awakening and yet tender
Was heard and felt—and at its close
These words of joy and fear arose

As if their own indignant Earth
Which gave the sons of England birth
Had felt their blood upon her brow,
And shuddering with a Mother's throe

Had turned every drop of blood
By which her face had been bedewed
To an accent unwithstood,—
As if her heart had cried aloud:

'Men of England, heirs of Glory,
Heroes of unwritten story,
Nurslings of one mighty Mother,
Hopes of her, and one another;

'Rise like Lions after slumber
In unvanquishable number,
Shake your chains to Earth like dew
Which in sleep had fallen on you—
Ye are many—they are few.

'What is Freedom?—ye can tell
That which slavery is, too well—
For its very name has grown
To an echo of your own.

''Tis to work and have such pay
As just keeps life from day to day
In your limbs, as in a cell
For the tyrants' use to dwell,

'So that ye for them are made,
Loom, and plough, and sword, and spade,
With or without your own will, bent
To their defence and nourishment.

''Tis to see your children weak
With their mothers pine and peak,
When the winter winds are bleak,—
They are dying whilst I speak.

''Tis to hunger for such diet
As the rich man in his riot
Casts to the fat dogs that lie
Surfeiting beneath his eye;

''Tis to let the Ghost of Gold
Take from Toil a thousandfold
More than e'er its substance could
In the tyrannies of old.

'Paper coin—that forgery
Of the title deeds, which ye
Hold to something of the worth
Of the inheritance of Earth.

''Tis to be a slave in soul
And to hold no strong controul
Over your own wills, but be
All that others make of ye.

'And at length when ye complain
With a murmur weak and vain
'Tis to see the Tyrant's crew
Ride over your wives and you—
Blood is on the grass like dew.

'Then it is to feel revenge
Fiercely thirsting to exchange
Blood for blood—and wrong for wrong—
Do not thus when ye are strong.

'Birds find rest, in narrow nest
When weary of their winged quest;
Beasts find fare, in woody lair
When storm and snow are in the air.

'Horses, oxen have a home
When from daily toil they come;
Household dogs, when the wind roars,
Find a home within warm doors.

'Asses, swine, have litter spread
And with fitting food are fed;
All things have a home but one—
Thou, Oh, Englishman, hast none!

'This is slavery—savage men,
Or wild beasts within a den
Would endure not as ye do—
But such ills they never knew.

'What art thou Freedom? O! could slaves
Answer from their living graves
This demand—tyrants would flee
Like a dream's dim imagery:

'Thou art not, as impostors say,
A shadow soon to pass away,
A superstition, and a name
Echoing from the cave of Fame.

'For the labourer thou art bread
And a comely table spread,
From his daily labour come,
In a neat and happy home.

'Thou art clothes, and fire, and food
For the trampled multitude—
No—in countries that are free
Such starvation cannot be
As in England now we see.

'To the rich thou art a check;
When his foot is on the neck
Of his victim, thou dost make
That he treads upon a snake.

'Thou art Justice—ne'er for gold
May thy righteous laws be sold
As laws are in England—thou
Shield'st alike the high and low.

'Thou art Wisdom—Freemen never
Dream that God will damn for ever
All who think those things untrue
Of which Priests make such ado.

'Thou art Peace—never by thee
Would blood and treasure wasted be
As tyrants wasted them, when all
Leagued to quench thy flame in Gaul.

'What if English toil and blood
Was poured forth, even as a flood?
It availed, Oh, Liberty!
To dim, but not extinguish thee.

'Thou art Love—the rich have kist
Thy feet, and like him following Christ,
Give their substance to the free
And through the rough world follow thee,

'Or turn their wealth to arms, and make
War for thy beloved sake
On wealth, and war, and fraud—whence they
Drew the power which is their prey.

'Science, Poetry and Thought
Are thy lamps; they make the lot
Of the dwellers in a cot
Such, they curse their Maker not.

'Spirit, Patience, Gentleness,
All that can adorn and bless
Art thou—let deeds not words express
Thine exceeding loveliness.

'Let a great Assembly be
Of the fearless and the free
On some spot of English ground
Where the plains stretch wide around.

'Let the blue sky overhead,
The green earth on which ye tread,
All that must eternal be
Witness the solemnity.

'From the corners uttermost
Of the bounds of English coast,
From every hut, village and town
Where those who live and suffer, moan
For others' misery or their own,

'From the workhouse and the prison
Where pale as corpses newly risen,
Women, children, young and old
Groan for pain, and weep for cold—

'From the haunts of daily life
Where is waged the daily strife
With common wants and common cares
Which sows the human heart with tares—

'Lastly from the palaces
Where the murmur of distress
Echoes, like the distant sound
Of a wind alive around

'Those prison halls of wealth and fashion
Where some few feel such compassion
For those who groan, and toil, and wail
As must make their brethren pale—

'Ye who suffer woes untold,
Or to feel, or to behold
Your lost country bought and sold
With a price of blood and gold—

'Let a vast assembly be,
And with great solemnity
Declare with measured words that ye
Are, as God has made ye, free—

'Be your strong and simple words
Keen to wound as sharpened swords,
And wide as targes let them be,
With their shade to cover ye.

'Let the tyrants pour around
With a quick and startling sound,
Like the loosening of a sea,
Troops of armed emblazonry.

'Let the charged artillery drive
Till the dead air seems alive
With the clash of clanging wheels,
And the tramp of horses' heels.

'Let the fixed bayonet
Gleam with sharp desire to wet
Its bright point in English blood
Looking keen as one for food.

'Let the horsemen's scimitars
Wheel and flash, like sphereless stars
Thirsting to eclipse their burning
In a sea of death and mourning.

'Stand ye calm and resolute,
Like a forest close and mute,
With folded arms and looks which are
Weapons of an unvanquished war,

'And let Panic, who outspeeds
The career of armed steeds
Pass, a disregarded shade
Through your phalanx undismayed.

'Let the laws of your own land,
Good or ill, between ye stand
Hand to hand, and foot to foot,
Arbiters of the dispute,

'The old laws of England—they
Whose reverend heads with age are grey,
Children of a wiser day;
And whose solemn voice must be
Thine own echo—Liberty!

'On those who first should violate
Such sacred heralds in their state
Rest the blood that must ensue,
And it will not rest on you.

'And if then the tyrants dare
Let them ride among you there,
Slash, and stab, and maim, and hew;—
What they like, that let them do.

'With folded arms and steady eyes,
And little fear, and less surprise
Look upon them as they slay
Till their rage has died away.

'Then they will return with shame
To the place from which they came,
And the blood thus shed will speak
In hot blushes on their cheek.

'Every woman in the land
Will point at them as they stand—
They will hardly dare to greet
Their acquaintance in the Street.

'And the bold, true warriors
Who have hugged Danger in wars
Will turn to those who would be free
Ashamed of such base company.

'And that slaughter, to the Nation
Shall steam up like inspiration,
Eloquent, oracular;
A volcano heard afar.

'And these words shall then become
Like oppression's thundered doom
Ringing through each heart and brain,
Heard again—again—again—

'Rise like lions after slumber
In unvanquishable number—
Shake your chains to earth like dew
Which in sleep had fallen on you—
Ye are many—they are few.'

THE END

PETER BELL THE THIRD

by Miching Mallecho, Esq[r].

Is it a party in a parlour—
Crammed just as they on earth were crammed—
Some sipping punch—some sipping tea;
But, as you by their faces see,
All silent and all—damned!

Peter Bell, by W. Wordsworth.

Ophelia: What means this, my lord?
Hamlet: Marry, this is miching mallecho;
it means mischief.

CONTENTS

DEDICATION

To Thomas Brown Esq[r]., the younger, H. F. &c. &c.

Dear Tom,

Allow me to request you to introduce Mr. Peter Bell to the respectable family of the Fudges; although he may fall short of those very considerable personages in the more active properties which characterize the Rat and the Apostate, I suspect that even you their historian will be forced to confess that he surpasses them in the more peculiarly legitimate qualification of intolerable dullness.

You know Mr. Examiner Hunt. That murderous and smiling villain at the mere sound of whose voice our susceptible friend the Quarterly fell into a paroxysm of eleutherophobia and foamed so much acrid gall that it burned the carpet in Mr. Murray's upper room, and eating a hole in the floor fell like rain upon our poor friend's head, who was scampering from room to room like a bear with a swarm of bees on his nose:—it caused an incurable ulcer and our poor friend has worn a wig ever since. Well, this monkey suckled with tiger's milk, this odious thief, liar, scoundrel, coxcomb and monster presented me to two of the Mr. Bells. Seeing me in his presence they of course uttered very few words and those with much caution. I scarcely need observe that they only kept company with him—at least I can certainly answer for one of them—in order to observe whether they could not borrow colours from any particulars of his private life for the denunciation they mean to make of him, as the member of an 'infamous and black conspiracy for diminishing the authority of that venerable canon, which forbids any man to marry his grandmother'; the effect of which on this our moral and religious nation is likely to answer the purpose of the contrivers. My intimacy with the younger Mr. Bell naturally sprung from this introduction to his brothers. And in presenting him to you, I have the satisfaction of being able to assure you that he is considerably the dullest of the three.

There is this particular advantage in an acquaintance with any one of the Peter Bells; that if you know one Peter Bell, you know three Peter Bells; they are not one but three; not three but one. An awful mystery, after having caused torrents of blood, and having been hymned by groans enough to deafen the music of the spheres, is at length illustrated to the satisfaction of all parties in the theological world, by the nature of Mr. Peter Bell.

Peter is a polyhedric Peter, or a Peter with many sides. He changes colours like a chameleon, and his coat like a snake. He is a Proteus of a Peter. He was at first sublime, pathetic, impressive, profound; then droll; then prosy and dull; and now dull—o so dull!—it is an ultra-legitimate dullness.

You will perceive that it is not necessary to consider Hell and the Devil as supernatural machinery. The whole scene of my epic is in 'this world which is'—(so Peter informed us before his conversion to *White Obi*)—

—the world of all of us, and *where*
We find our happiness, or not at all.

Let me observe that I have spent six or seven days in composing this sublime piece;—the orb of my moonlike genius has made the fourth part of its revolution round the dull earth which you inhabit, driving you mad whilst it has retained its calmness and its splendour, and I have been fitting this its last phase to 'occupy a permanent station in the literature of my country'.

Your works indeed, dear Tom, Sell better; but mine are far superior; the public is no judge: posterity sets all to rights.

Allow me to observe that so much has been written of Peter Bell that the present history can be considered only, like the *Iliad*, as a continuation of that series of cyclic poems which have already been candidates for bestowing immortality upon, at the same time that they receive it from, his character and adventures. In this point of view, I have violated no rule of syntax in beginning my composition with a conjunction; the full stop which closes the poem continued by me, being, like the full stops at the end of the *Iliad* and the *Odyssey*, a full stop of a very qualified import.

Hoping that the immortality which you have given to the Fudges, you will receive from them; and in the firm expectation that when London shall be the habitation of bitterns, when St. Paul's and Westminster Abbey shall stand, shapeless and nameless ruins, in the midst of an unpeopled marsh; when the piers of Waterloo bridge shall become the nuclei of islets of reeds and osiers and cast the jagged shadows of their broken arches on the solitary stream,—some transatlantic commentator will be weighing in the scales of some new and now unimagined system of criticism, the respective merits of the Bells and the Fudges, and of their historians,

I remain, Dear Tom
Yours sincerely
Miching Mallecho

December 1, 1819

P. S. Pray excuse the date of place; so soon as the profits of this publication come in, I mean to hire lodgings in a more respectable street.

Prologue

Peter Bells, one, two and three,
O'er the wide world wandering be:—
First, the antenatal Peter,
Wrapt in weeds of the same metre,
The so long predestined raiment
Clothed in which to walk his way meant
The second Peter; whose ambition
Is to link the proposition
As the mean of two extremes—
(This was learnt from Aldric's themes)
Shielding from the guilt of schism
The orthodoxal syllogism:
The first Peter—he who was
Like the shadow in the glass
Of the second, yet unripe,
His substantial antitype:—
Then came Peter Bell the Second,
Who henceforward must be reckoned
The body of a double soul—
And that portion of the whole
Without which the rest would seem
Ends of a disjointed dream.—
And the third is he who has
O'er the grave been forced to pass
To the other side, which is,—
Go and try else,— just like this.

Peter Bell the First was Peter
Smugger, milder, softer, neater,
Like the soul before it is
Born from *that* world into *this*.
The next Peter Bell was he
Predevote like you and me
To good or evil as may come;
His was the severer doom,—
For he was an evil Cotter

And a polygamic Potter.*
And the last is Peter Bell
Damned since our first Parents fell,
Damned eternally to Hell—
Surely he deserves it well!

Part First

Death

And Peter Bell, when he had been
With fresh-imported Hell-fire warmed,
Grew serious—from his dress and mien
'Twas very plainly to be seen
Peter was quite reformed.

His eyes turned up, his mouth turned down;
His accent caught a nasal twang;
He oiled his hair;† there might be heard
The grace of God in every word
Which Peter said or sang.

But Peter now grew old, and had
An ill no doctor could unravel;
His torments almost drove him mad;—
Some said it was a fever bad—
Some swore it was the gravel.

His holy friends then came about
And with long preaching and persuasion,
Convinced the patient, that without
The smallest shadow of a doubt
He was predestined to damnation.

* The oldest scholiasts read—a *dodecagamic* Potter; this is at once more descriptive and more megalophonous,—but the alliteration of the text had captivated the vulgar ears of the herd of later commentators. [Shelley's note]

† To those who have not duly appreciated the distinction between whale and Russia oil this attribute might rather seem to belong to the Dandy than the Evangelic. The effect, when to the windward, is indeed so similar that it requires a subtle Naturalist to discriminate the animals. They belong however to distinct genera. [Shelley's note]

They said:—'Thy name is Peter Bell;
Thy skin is of a brimstone hue;
Alive or dead—aye, sick or well—
The one God made to rhyme with hell;
The other, I think, rhymes with you.'

Then Peter set up such a yell!—
The nurse, who with some water gruel
Was climbing up the stairs as well
As her old legs could climb them—fell,
And broke them both—the fall was cruel.

The Parson from the casement leapt
Into the lake of Windermere—
And many an eel—though no adept
In God's right reason for it—kept
Gnawing his kidneys half a year.

And all the rest rushed through the door
And tumbled over one another,
And broke their skulls.—Upon the floor
Meanwhile sate Peter Bell, and swore,
And cursed his father and his Mother,

And raved of God, and sin, and death,
Blaspheming like an infidel;
And said, that with his clenched teeth,
He'd seize the Earth from underneath,
And drag it with him down to Hell.

As he was speaking came a spasm,
And wrenched his gnashing teeth asunder,
—Like one who sees a strange phantasm
He lay,—there was a silent chasm
Between his upper jaw and under.

And yellow death lay on his face;
And a fixed smile that was not human
Told, as I understand the case,
That he was gone to the wrong place:—
I heard all this from the old woman.

Then there came down from Langdale Pike
  A cloud with lightning, wind and hail;
It swept over the mountains like
An Ocean,—and I heard it strike
  The woods and crags of Grasmere vale.

And I saw the black storm come
  Nearer, minute after minute,
Its thunder made the cataracts dumb,
With hiss, and clash, and hollow hum
  It neared as if the Devil was in it.

The Devil *was* in it:—he had bought
  Peter for half a crown; and when
The storm which bore him vanished, nought
That in the house that storm had caught
  Was ever seen again.

The gaping neighbours came next day—
  They found all vanished from the shore:
The Bible, whence he used to pray
Half scorched under a hen-coop lay;
  Smashed glass—and nothing more!

Part Second

The Devil

The Devil, I safely can aver,
  Has neither hoof, nor tail, nor sting;
Nor is he, as some sages swear,
A spirit, neither here nor there,
  In nothing—yet in every thing.

He is—what we are; for sometimes
  The Devil is a gentleman;
At others a bard bartering rhymes
For sack; a statesman spinning crimes,
  A swindler, living as he can;

A thief who cometh in the night,
 With whole boots and net pantaloons,
Like someone whom it were not right
To mention;—or the luckless wight
 From whom he steals nine silver spoons.

But in this case he did appear
 Like a slop-merchant from Wapping
And with smug face, and eye severe
On every side did perk and peer
 Till he saw Peter dead or napping.

He had on an upper Benjamin
 (For he was of the driving schism)
In the which he wrapped his skin
From the storm he travelled in,
 For fear of rheumatism.

He called the ghost out of the corse;—
 It was exceedingly like Peter,—
Only its voice was hollow and hoarse—
It had a queerish look of course—
 Its dress too was a little neater.

The Devil knew not, his name and lot;
 Peter knew not that he was Bell:
Each had an upper stream of thought
Which made all seem as it was not;
 Fitting itself to all things well.

Peter thought he had parents dear,
 Brothers, sisters, cousins, cronies,
In the fens of Lincolnshire;
He perhaps had found them there
 Had he gone and boldly shown his

Solemn phiz in his own village;
 Where he thought, oft when a boy
He'd clombe the orchard walls to pillage
The produce of his neighbours' tillage
 With marvellous pride and joy.

And the Devil thought he had,
  'Mid the misery and confusion
Of an unjust war, just made
A fortune by the gainful trade
Of giving soldiers rations bad—
  The world is full of strange delusion—

That he had a mansion planned
  In a square like Grosvenor square,
That he was aping fashion, and
That he now came to Westmorland
  To see what was romantic there.

And all this, though quite ideal,—
  Ready at a breath to vanish,—
Was a state not more unreal
Than the peace he could not feel
  Or the care he could not banish.

After a little conversation
  The Devil told Peter, if he chose
He'd bring him to the world of fashion
By giving him a situation
  In his own service—and new clothes.

And Peter bowed, quite pleased and proud,
  And after waiting some few days
For a new livery—dirty yellow
Turned up with black—the wretched fellow
  Was bowled to Hell on the Devil's chaise.

Part Third

Hell

Hell is a city much like London;—
  A populous and a smoky city;
There are all sorts of people undone
And there is little or no fun done;
  Small justice shown, and still less pity.

There is a Castles, and a Canning,
  A Cobbett, and a Castlereagh;
All sorts of caitiff corpses planning
All sorts of cozening for trepanning
  Corpses less corrupt than they.

There is a * * *, who has lost
  His wits, or sold them, none knows which:
He walks about a double ghost,
And though as thin as Fraud almost—
  Ever grows more grim and rich.

There is a Chancery Court; a King;
  A manufacturing mob; a set
Of thieves who by themselves are sent
Similar thieves to represent;
  An Army;—and a public debt.

Which last is a scheme of Paper money,
  And means—being interpreted—
'Bees keep your wax—give us the honey
And we will plant while skies are sunny
  Flowers, which in winter serve instead.'

There is great talk of Revolution—
  And a great chance of Despotism—
German soldiers—camps—confusion—
Tumults—lotteries—rage—delusion—
  Gin—suicide and Methodism;

Taxes too, on wine and bread,
  And meat, and beer, and tea, and cheese
From which those patriots pure are fed
Who gorge before they reel to bed
  The tenfold essence of all these.

There are mincing women, mewing,
  (Like cats, who *amant miserè*,)*
Of their own virtue, and pursuing
Their gentler sisters to that ruin,
  Without which—what were chastity?†

Lawyers—judges—old hobnobbers
  Are there—Bailiffs—Chancellors—
Bishops—great and little robbers—
Rhymesters—pamphleteers—stock jobbers—
  Men of glory in the wars,—

Things whose trade is, over ladies
  To lean, and flirt, and stare, and simper,
Till all that is divine in woman
Grows cruel, courteous, smooth, inhuman,
  Crucified 'twixt a smile and whimper.

Thrusting, toiling, wailing, moiling,
  Frowning, preaching—such a riot!
Each with never ceasing labour
Whilst he thinks he cheats his neighbour
  Cheating his own heart of quiet.

And all these, meet at levees;—
  Dinners convivial and political;—
Suppers of epic poets;—teas,
Where small talk dies in agonies;—
  Breakfasts professional and critical;—

* One of the attributes in Linnaeus's description of the Cat. To a similar cause the caterwauling of more than one species of this genus is to be referred;—except indeed that the poor quadruped is compelled to quarrel with its own pleasures, whilst the biped is supposed only to quarrel with those of others. [Shelley's note]

† What would this husk and excuse for a Virtue be without its kernel prostitution, or the kernel prostitution without this husk of a Virtue? I wonder the Women of the Town do not form an association, like the Society for the Suppression of Vice, for the support of what may be considered the 'King, church and Constitution' of their order. But this subject is almost too horrible for a joke. [Shelley's note]

Lunches and snacks so aldermanic
  That one would furnish forth ten dinners,
Where reigns a Cretan-tongued panic
Lest news Russ, Dutch or Alemannic
  Should make some losers, and some winners;—

At conversazioni—balls—
  Conventicles and drawing-rooms—
Courts of law—committees—calls
Of a morning—clubs—book stalls—
  Churches—masquerades and tombs.

And this is Hell—and in this smother
  All are damnable and damned;
Each one damning, damns the other;
They are damned by one another,
  By none other are they damned.

'Tis a lie to say, 'God damns!'*
  Where was Heaven's Attorney General
When they first gave out such flams?
Let there be an end of shams;
  They are mines of poisonous mineral.

Statesmen damn themselves to be
  Cursed; and lawyers damn their souls
To the auction of a fee:
Churchmen damn themselves to see
  God's sweet love in burning coals.

The rich are damned beyond all cure
  To taunt, and starve, and trample on
The weak, and wretched: and the poor
Damn their broken hearts to endure
  Stripe on stripe, with groan on groan.

* This libel on our national oath, and this accusation of all our countrymen of being in the daily practice of solemnly asseverating the most enormous falshood I fear deserves the notice of a more active Attorney General than that here alluded to. [Shelley's note]

Sometimes the poor are damned indeed
To take,—not means for being blest,—
But Cobbett's snuff, revenge; that weed
From which the worms that it doth feed
Squeeze less than they before possessed.

And some few, like we know who,
Damned—but God alone knows why—
To believe their minds are given
To make this ugly Hell a Heaven;
In which faith they live and die.

Thus, as in a Town plague-stricken,
Each man be he sound or no
Must indifferently sicken;
As when day begins to thicken
None knows a pigeon from a crow,—

So good and bad, sane and mad,
The oppressor and the oppressed;
Those who weep to see what others
Smile to inflict upon their brothers;
Lovers, haters, worst and best;

All are damned—they breathe an air
Thick, infected, joy-dispelling:
Each pursues what seems most fair,
Mining like moles, through mind, and there
Scoop palace-caverns vast, where Care
In throned state is ever dwelling.

Part Fourth

Sin

Lo! Peter in Hell's Grosvenor square
A footman in the Devil's service!
And the misjudging world would swear
That every man in service there
To virtue would prefer vice.

But, Peter, though now damned, was not
  What Peter was before damnation.
Men oftentimes prepare a lot
Which ere it finds them, is not what
  Suits with their genuine station.

All things that Peter saw and felt
  Had a peculiar aspect to him;
And when they came within the belt
Of his own nature, seemed to melt
  Like cloud to cloud, into him.

And so the outward world uniting
  To that within him, he became
Considerably uninviting
To those, who meditation slighting,
  Were moulded in a different frame.

And he scorned them, and they scorned him;
  And he scorned all they did; and they
Did all that men of their own trim
Are wont to do to please their whim,
  Drinking, lying, swearing, play.

Such were his fellow servants: thus
  His virtue, like our own, was built
Too much on that indignant fuss
Hypocrite Pride stirs up in us
  To bully out another's guilt.

He had a mind which was somehow
  At once circumference and centre
Of all he might or feel or know;
Nothing went ever out, although
  Something did ever enter.

He had as much imagination
  As a pint-pot:—he never could
Fancy another situation
From which to dart his contemplation,
  Than that wherein he stood.

Yet his was individual mind,
And new-created all he saw
In a new manner, and refined
Those new creations, and combined
Them by a master-spirit's law,

Thus—though unimaginative,
An apprehension clear, intense,
Of his mind's work, had made alive
The things it wrought on; I believe
Wakening a sort of thought in sense.

But from the first 'twas Peter's drift
To be a kind of moral eunuch;
He touched the hem of Nature's shift,
Felt faint—and never dared uplift
The closest, all-concealing tunic.

She laughed the while, with an arch smile,
And kissed him with a sister's kiss,
And said—'My best Diogenes,
I love you well—but, if you please,
Tempt not again my deepest bliss.

''Tis you are cold—for I, not coy,
Yield love for love, frank, warm and true:
And Burns, a Scottish Peasant boy,—
His errors prove it—knew my joy
More, learned friend, than you.

'*Bocca baciata non perde ventura*
Anzi rinnuova come fa la luna:—
So thought Boccaccio, whose sweet words might cure a
Male prude like you from what you now endure, a
Low-tide in soul, like a stagnant laguna.'

Then Peter rubbed his eyes severe,
And smoothed his spacious forehead down
With his broad palm:—'twixt love and fear,
He looked, as he no doubt felt, queer;
And in his dream sate down.

The Devil was no uncommon creature;
  A leaden-witted thief—just huddled
Out of the dross and scum of nature;
A toadlike lump of limb and feature,
  With mind, and heart, and fancy muddled.

He was that heavy, dull, cold thing
  The Spirit of Evil well may be:
A drone too base to have a sting;
Who gluts, and limes his lazy wing,
  And calls lust, luxury.

Now he was quite, the kind of wight
  Round whom collect, at a fixed aera,
Venison, turtle, hock and claret,—
Good cheer—and those who come to share it—
  And best East Indian Madeira!

It was his fancy to invite
  Men of science, wit and learning;
Who came to lend each other light:—
He proudly thought that his gold's might
  Had set those spirits burning.

And men of learning, science, wit,
  Considered him as you and I
Think of some rotten tree, and sit
Lounging and dining under it,
  Exposed to the wide sky.

And all the while, with loose fat smile
  The willing wretch sat winking there,
Believing 'twas his power that made
That jovial scene—and that all paid
  Homage to his unnoticed chair.

Though to be sure this place was Hell;
  He was the Devil—and all they—
What though the claret circled well,
And wit, like ocean, rose and fell—
  Were damned eternally.

Part Fifth

Grace

Among the guests who often staid
  Till the Devil's petit soupers,
A man there came, fair as a maid,
And Peter noted what he said,
  Standing behind his master's chair.

He was a mighty poet—and
  A subtle-souled Psychologist;
All things he seemed to understand
Of old or new—of sea or land—
  But his own mind—which was a mist.

This was a man who might have turned
  Hell into Heaven—and so in gladness
A Heaven unto himself have earned;
But he in shadows undiscerned
  Trusted,—and damned himself to madness.

He spoke of Poetry, and how
  'Divine it was—a light—a love—
A spirit which like wind doth blow
As it listeth, to and fro;
  A dew rained down from God above,

'A Power which comes and goes like dream,
  And which none can ever trace—
Heaven's light on Earth—Truth's brightest beam,'
And when he ceased there lay the gleam
  Of those words upon his face.

Now Peter when he heard such talk
  Would, heedless of a broken pate
Stand like a man asleep, or baulk
Some wishing guest of knife or fork,
  Or drop and break his master's plate.

At night he oft would start and wake
  Like a lover, and began
In a wild measure songs to make
On moor, and glen, and rocky lake,
  And on the heart of man;—

And on the universal sky;—
  And the wide earth's bosom green;—
And the sweet, strange mystery
Of what beyond these things may lie,
  And yet remain unseen.

For in his thought he visited
  The spots in which, ere dead and damned,
He his wayward life had led;
Yet knew not whence the thoughts were fed
  Which thus his fancy crammed.

And these obscure remembrances
  Stirred such harmony in Peter,
That whensoever he should please,
He could speak of rocks and trees
  In poetic metre.

For though it was without a sense
  Of memory, yet he remembered well
Many a ditch and quickset fence;
Of lakes he had intelligence,
  He knew something of heath and fell.

He had also dim recollections
  Of pedlars tramping on their rounds,
Milk pans and pails, and odd collections
Of saws, and proverbs; and reflections
  Old parsons make in burying-grounds.

But Peter's verse was clear, and came
  Announcing from the frozen hearth
Of a cold age, that none might tame
The soul of that diviner flame
  It augured to the Earth:

Like gentle rains, on the dry plains,
  Making that green which late was grey,
Or like the sudden moon, that stains
Some gloomy chamber's windowpanes
  With a broad light like day.

For language was in Peter's hand
  Like clay while he was yet a potter;
And he made songs for all the land
Sweet both to feel and understand
  As pipkins late to mountain Cotter.

And Mr. ——, the Bookseller,
  Gave twenty pounds for some:—then scorning
A footman's yellow coat to wear,
Peter, too proud of heart I fear,
  Instantly gave the Devil warning.

Whereat the Devil took offence,
  And swore in his soul a great oath then,
'That for his damned impertinence,
He'd bring him to a proper sense
  Of what was due to gentlemen!'—

Part Sixth

Damnation

'O, that mine enemy had written
  A book!'—cried Job:—A fearful curse!
If to the Arab, as the Briton,
'Twas galling to be critic-bitten:—
  The Devil to Peter wished no worse.

When Peter's next new book found vent,
  The Devil to all the first Reviews
A copy of it slyly sent
With five-pound note as compliment,
  And this short notice—'Pray abuse.'

Then *seriatim*, month and quarter,
  Appeared such mad tirades—One said—
'Peter seduced Mrs. Foy's daughter,
Then drowned the Mother in Ullswater,
  The last thing as he went to bed.'

Another—'Let him shave his head!
  Where's Dr. Willis?—Or is he joking?
What does the rascal mean or hope,
No longer imitating Pope,
  In that barbarian Shakespeare poking?'

One more,—'Is incest not enough,
  And must there be adultery too?
Grace after meat? Miscreant and liar!
Thief! Blackguard! Scoundrel! Fool! Hell-fire
  Is twenty times too good for you.

'By that last book of yours WE think
  You've double damned yourself to scorn:
We warned you whilst yet on the brink
You stood. From your black name will shrink
  The babe that is unborn.'

All these Reviews the Devil made
  Up in a parcel, which he had
Safely to Peter's house conveyed.
For carriage ten-pence Peter paid—
  Untied them—read them—went half mad.

'What!'—Cried he,—'this is my reward
  For nights of thought, and days of toil?
Do poets, but to be abhorred
By men of whom they never heard,
  Consume their spirits' oil?

'What have I done to them?—and Who
  Is Mrs. Foy?—'Tis very cruel
To speak of me and Betty so!
Adultery! God defend me! Oh!
  I've half a mind to fight a duel.

'Or,' cried he, a grave look collecting,
  'Is it my genius, like the moon,
Sets those who stand her face inspecting,
(That face within their brain reflecting)
  Like a crazed bell chime, out of tune?'

For Peter did not know the town,
  But thought, as country readers do,
For half a guinea or a crown,
He bought oblivion or renown
  From God's own voice* in a review.

All Peter did on this occasion
  Was, writing some sad stuff in prose.
It is a dangerous invasion
When Poets criticise: their station
  Is to delight, not pose.

The Devil then sent to Leipsic fair,
  For Born's translation of Kant's book;
A world of words, tail-foremost, where
Right—wrong—false—true—and foul and fair
  As in a lottery wheel are shook.

Five thousand crammed octavo pages
  Of German psychologics,—he
Who his *furor verborum* assuages
Thereon, deserves just seven months' wages
  More than will e'er be due to me.

I looked on them nine several days,
  And then I saw that they were bad;
A friend, too, spoke in their dispraise,—
He never read them;—with amaze
  I found Sir William Drummond had.

* Vox populi, vox dei [The voice of the people is the voice of God]. As Mr. Godwin truly observes of a more famous saying, of some merit as a popular maxim, but totally destitute of philosophical accuracy. [Shelley's note]

When the book came, the Devil sent
  It to 'P. Verbovale Esquire',*
With a brief note of compliment,
By that night's Carlisle mail. It went
  And set his soul on fire.

Fire, which *ex luce praebens fumum*,
  Made him beyond the bottom see
Of truth's clear well—when I and you, Ma'am,
Go, as we shall do, *subter humum*,
  We may know more than he.

Now Peter ran to seed in soul,
  Into a walking paradox;—
For he was neither part nor whole,
Nor good, nor bad—nor knave, nor fool,
  —Among the woods and rocks

Furious he rode, where late he ran,
  Lashing and spurring his lame hobby;
Turned to a formal Puritan,
A solemn and unsexual man,—
  He half believed *White Obi*!

This steed in vision he would ride,
  High trotting over nine-inch bridges,
With Flibbertigibbet, imp of pride,
Mocking and mowing by his side—
A mad-brained goblin for a guide—
  Over cornfields, gates and hedges.

After these ghastly rides, he came
  Home to his heart, and found from thence
Much stolen of its accustomed flame;
His thoughts grew weak, drowsy and lame
  Of their intelligence.

* Quasi, *Qui valet verba.*—i.e. all the words which have been, are, or may be expended by, for, against, with, or on him. A sufficient proof of the utility of this History. Peter's progenitor who selected this name seems to have possessed *a pure anticipated cognition* of the nature and modesty of this ornament of his posterity. [Shelley's note]

To Peter's view, all seemed one hue;
He was no Whig, he was no Tory:
No Deist and no Christian he,—
He got so subtle, that to be
Nothing, was all his glory.

One single point in his belief
From his organization sprung,
The heart-enrooted faith, the chief
Ear in his doctrines' blighted sheaf,
That 'happiness is wrong'.

So thought Calvin and Dominic;
So think their fierce successors, who
Even now would neither stint nor stick
Our flesh from off our bones to pick,
If they might 'do their do'.

His morals thus were undermined:—
The old Peter—the hard, old Potter—
Was born anew within his mind:
He grew dull, harsh, sly, unrefined,
As when he tramped beside the Otter.*

In the death hues of agony
Lambently flashing from a fish,
Now Peter felt amused to see
Shades, like a rainbow's, rise and flee,
Mixed with a certain hungry wish.†

* A famous river in the new Atlantis of the Dynastophilic Pantisocratists. [Shelley's note]

† See the description of the beautiful colours produced during the agonising death of a number of trout, in the 4th part of a long poem in blank verse, published within a few years. That Poem contains curious evidence of the gradual hardening of a strong but circumscribed sensibility, of the perversion of a penetrating but panic-stricken understanding. The Author might have derived a lesson which he had probably forgotten from these sweet and sublime verses.

This lesson, Shepherd, let us two divide,
Taught both by what she [Nature] shews and what conceals,
Never to blend our pleasure or our pride
With sorrow of the meanest thing that feels. [Shelley's note]

So in his Country's dying face
   He looked—and lovely as she lay,
Seeking in vain his last embrace,
Wailing her own abandoned case,
   With hardened sneer he turned away:

And coolly to his own Soul said:—
   'Do you not think that we might make
A poem on her when she's dead?—
Or, no—a thought is in my head—
   Her shroud for a new sheet I'll take—

'My wife wants one.—Let who will, bury
   This mangled corpse!—And I and you,
My dearest Soul, will then make merry,
As the Prince Regent did with Sherry'—
   'Aye—and at last desert me too.'

And so his Soul would not be gay,
   But moaned within him; like a fawn,
Moaning within a cave, it lay
Wounded and wasting, day by day,
   Till all its life of life was gone.

As troubled skies stain waters clear,
   The storm in Peter's heart and mind,
Now made his verses dark and queer;
They were the ghosts of what they were,
   Shaking dim grave-clothes in the wind.

For he now raved enormous folly
   Of Baptisms, Sunday-schools and Graves;
'Twould make George Colman melancholy
To have heard him, like a male Molly,
   Chaunting those stupid staves.

Yet the Reviews, who heaped abuse
   On Peter, while he wrote for freedom,
So soon as in his song they spy
The folly which soothes Tyranny,
   Praise him, for those who feed 'em.

'He was a man, too great to scan;—
A planet lost in truth's keen rays:—
His virtue, awful and prodigious;—
He was the most sublime, religious,
Pure-minded Poet of these days.'

As soon as he read that—cried Peter;—
'Eureka! I have found the way
To make a better thing of metre
Than e'er was made by living creature
Up to this blessed day.'

Then Peter wrote odes to the Devil;—
In one of which he meekly said:—
'May Carnage and Slaughter,
Thy niece and thy daughter,
May Rapine and Famine,
Thy gorge ever cramming,
Glut thee with living and dead!

'May Death and Damnation,
And Consternation,
Flit up from Hell, with pure intent!
Slash them at Manchester,
Glasgow, Leeds and Chester;
Drench all with blood from Avon to Trent!

'Let thy body-guard yeomen
Hew down babes and women,
And laugh with bold triumph till Heaven be rent!
When Moloch in Jewry,
Munched children with fury
It was thou, Devil, dining with pure intent!'*

* It is curious to observe how often extremes meet. Cobbett and Peter use the same language for a different purpose: Peter is indeed a sort of metrical Cobbett. Cobbett is however more mischievous than Peter because he pollutes a holy and now unconquerable cause with the principles of legitimate murder; whilst the other only makes a bad one ridiculous and odious. If either Peter or Cobbett should see this note, each will feel more indignation at being compared to the other than at any censure implied in the moral perversions laid to their charge. [Shelley's note]

Part Seventh

Double Damnation

The Devil now knew, his proper cue—
  Soon as he read the ode, he drove
To his friend Lord McMurderchouse's,
A man of interest in both houses,
  And said:—'For money or for love

'Pray find some cure or sinecure,
  To feed from the superfluous taxes
A friend of ours—a Poet—fewer
Have fluttered tamer to the lure
  Than he.'—His Lordship stands and racks his

Stupid brains, while one might count
  As many beads as he had boroughs,—
At length replies;—from his mean front,
Like one who rubs out an account,
  Smoothing away the unmeaning furrows:—

'It happens fortunately, dear Sir,
  I can. I hope I need require
No pledge from you, that he will stir
In our affairs;—like Oliver,
  That he'll be worthy of his hire.'

These words exchanged, the news sent off
  To Peter:—home the Devil hied;
Took to his bed; he had no cough,
No doctor,—meat and drink enough,—
  Yet that same night he died.

The Devil's corpse was leaded down.—
  His decent heirs enjoyed his pelf:
Mourning coaches, many a one,
Followed his hearse along the town:—
  Where was the Devil himself?

When Peter heard of his promotion
His eyes grew like two stars for bliss:
There was a bow of sleek devotion
Engendering in his back; each motion
Seemed a Lord's shoe to kiss.

He hired a house, bought plate, and made
A genteel drive up to his door,
With sifted gravel neatly laid,—
As if defying all who said
Peter was ever poor.

But a disease soon struck into
The very life and soul of Peter—
He walked about—slept—had the hue
Of health upon his cheeks—and few
Dug better—none a heartier eater.

And yet—a strange and horrid curse
Clung upon Peter, night and day—
Month after month the thing grew worse,
And deadlier than in this my verse
I can find strength to say.

Peter was dull—he was at first
Dull—O, so dull—so very dull!
Whether he talked—wrote—or rehearsed—
Still with this dullness was he cursed—
Dull—beyond all conception—dull.—

No one could read his books—no mortal,
But a few natural friends, would hear him:—
The parson came not near his portal;—
His state was like that of the immortal
Described by Swift—no man could bear him.

His sister, wife and children yawned,
With a long, slow and drear ennui,
All human patience far beyond;
Their hopes of Heaven each would have pawned
Anywhere else to be.

But in his verse, and in his prose,
The essence of his dullness was
Concentred and compressed so close,—
'Twould have made Guatimozin doze
On his red gridiron of brass.

A printer's boy, folding those pages,
Fell slumberously upon one side:
Like those famed seven who slept three ages.
To wakeful frenzy's vigil rages
As opiates were the same applied.

Even the Reviewers who were hired
To do the work of his reviewing,
With adamantine nerves, grew tired;—
Gaping and torpid they retired,
To dream of what they should be doing.

And worse and worse, the drowsy curse
Yawned in him—till it grew a pest—
A wide contagious atmosphere,
Creeping like cold through all things near;
A power to infect, and to infest.

His servant maids and dogs grew dull;
His kitten, late a sportive elf;
The woods and lakes, so beautiful,
Of dim stupidity were full;
All grew dull as Peter's self.

The earth under his feet—the springs,
Which lived within it a quick life—
The Air—the Winds of many wings—
That fan it with new murmurings,
Were dead to their harmonious strife.

The birds and beasts within the wood;
The insects—and each creeping thing,
Were now a silent multitude;
Love's work was left unwrought:—no brood
Near Peter's house took wing.

And every neighbouring Cottager
  Stupidly yawned upon the other;
No jackass brayed;—no little cur
Cocked up his ears;—no man would stir
  To save a dying mother.

Yet all from that charmed district went,
  But some, half idiot and half knave,
Who, rather than pay any rent,
Would live, with marvellous content,
  Over his father's grave.

No bailiff dared within that space,
  For fear of the dull charm, to enter:
A man would bear upon his face,
For fifteen months, in any case,
  The yawn of such a venture.

Seven miles above—below—around—
  This pest of dullness holds its sway:
A ghastly life without a sound;
To Peter's soul the spell is bound—
  How should it ever pass away?

Finis.

*Ode to the West Wind**

I

O wild West Wind, thou breath of Autumn's being,
Thou, from whose unseen presence the leaves dead
Are driven, like ghosts from an enchanter fleeing,

Yellow, and black, and pale, and hectic red,
Pestilence-stricken multitudes: O thou
Who chariotest to their dark wintry bed

The winged seeds, where they lie cold and low,
Each like a corpse within its grave, until
Thine azure sister of the Spring shall blow

Her clarion o'er the dreaming earth, and fill
(Driving sweet buds like flocks to feed in air)
With living hues and odours plain and hill:

Wild Spirit, which art moving every where;
Destroyer and Preserver; hear, O hear!

II

Thou on whose stream, 'mid the steep sky's commotion,
Loose clouds like Earth's decaying leaves are shed,
Shook from the tangled boughs of Heaven and Ocean,

Angels of rain and lightning: there are spread
On the blue surface of thine airy surge,
Like the bright hair uplifted from the head

* This poem was conceived and chiefly written in a wood that skirts the Arno, near Florence, and on a day when that tempestuous wind, whose temperature is at once mild and animating, was collecting the vapours which pour down the autumnal rains. They began, as I foresaw, at sunset with a violent tempest of hail and rain, attended by that magnificent thunder and lightning peculiar to the Cisalpine regions.

The phenomenon alluded to at the conclusion of the third stanza is well known to naturalists. The vegetation at the bottom of the sea, of rivers, and of lakes, sympathises with that of the land in the change of seasons, and is consequently influenced by the winds which announce it. [Shelley's note]

Of some fierce Maenad, even from the dim verge
Of the horizon to the Zenith's height,
The locks of the approaching storm. Thou Dirge

Of the dying year, to which this closing night
Will be the dome of a vast sepulchre,
Vaulted with all thy congregated might

Of vapours, from whose solid atmosphere
Black rain, and fire, and hail will burst: O hear!

III

Thou who didst waken from his summer dreams
The blue Mediterranean, where he lay,
Lulled by the coil of his crystalline streams,

Beside a pumice isle in Baiae's bay,
And saw in sleep old palaces and towers
Quivering within the wave's intenser day,

All overgrown with azure moss and flowers
So sweet, the sense faints picturing them! Thou
For whose path the Atlantic's level powers

Cleave themselves into chasms, while far below
The sea-blooms and the oozy woods which wear
The sapless foliage of the Ocean, know

Thy voice, and suddenly grow grey with fear,
And tremble and despoil themselves: O hear!

IV

If I were a dead leaf thou mightest bear;
If I were a swift cloud to fly with thee;
A wave to pant beneath thy power, and share

The impulse of thy strength, only less free
Than thou, O Uncontroulable! If even
I were as in my boyhood, and could be

The comrade of thy wanderings over Heaven,
As then, when to outstrip thy skiey speed
Scarce seemed a vision, I would ne'er have striven

As thus with thee in prayer in my sore need.
Oh! lift me as a wave, a leaf, a cloud!
I fall upon the thorns of life! I bleed!

A heavy weight of hours has chained and bowed
One too like thee: tameless, and swift, and proud.

V

Make me thy lyre, even as the forest is:
What if my leaves are falling like its own!
The tumult of thy mighty harmonies

Will take from both a deep, autumnal tone,
Sweet though in sadness. Be thou, Spirit fierce,
My spirit! Be thou me, impetuous one!

Drive my dead thoughts over the universe
Like withered leaves to quicken a new birth!
And, by the incantation of this verse,

Scatter, as from an unextinguished hearth
Ashes and sparks, my words among mankind!
Be through my lips to unawakened Earth

The trumpet of a prophecy! O Wind,
If Winter comes, can Spring be far behind?

To S[idmouth] and C[astlereagh]

As from their ancestral oak
  Two empty ravens wind their clarion,
Yell by yell, and croak for croak,
When they scent the noonday smoke
  Of fresh human carrion:—

As two gibbering night-birds flit
From their bower of deadly yew
Thro' the night to frighten it—
When the moon is in a fit,
And the stars are none or few:—

As a shark and dogfish wait
Under an Atlantic isle
For the Negro ship whose freight
Is the theme of their debate,
Wrinkling their red gills the while:—

Are ye—two vultures sick for battle,
Two scorpions under one wet stone,
Two bloodless wolves whose dry throats rattle,
Two crows perched on the murrained cattle,
Two vipers tangled into one.

Love's Philosophy

The Fountains mingle with the River
And the Rivers with the Ocean;
The winds of Heaven mix for ever
With a sweet emotion;
Nothing in the world is single;
All things by a law divine
In one spirit meet and mingle.
Why not I with thine?—

See the mountains kiss high Heaven
And the waves clasp one another;
No sister-flower would be forgiven
If it disdained its brother,
And the sunlight clasps the earth
And the moonbeams kiss the sea—
What is all this sweet work worth
If thou kiss not me?

Goodnight

Goodnight? no love, the night is ill
   Which severs those it should unite;
Let us remain together still,
   Then it will be—'*good* night'.

How were the night without thee, good
   Though thy sweet wishes wing its flight?
Be it not said, thought, understood—
   Then it will be—'*good* night'.

The hearts that on each other beat
   From evening close to morning light
Have nights as good as they are sweet
   But never say 'good night'.

Time Long Past

Like the ghost of a dear friend dead
      Is Time long past.
A tone which is now forever fled,
A hope, which is now forever past,
A love, so sweet it could not last
      Was Time long past.

There were sweet dreams in the night
      Of Time long past;
And, was it sadness or delight,
Each day a shadow onward cast
Which made us wish it yet might last—
      That Time long past.

There is regret, almost remorse
      For Time long past.
'Tis like a child's beloved corse
A father watches, till at last
Beauty is like remembrance, cast
      From Time long past.

On a Dead Violet
To —

The odour from the flower is gone
  Which like thy kisses breathed on me;
The colour from the flower is flown
  Which glowed of thee and only thee.

A shrivelled, lifeless, vacant form
  It lies on my abandoned breast,
And mocks the heart which yet is warm
  With its cold, silent rest.

I weep—my tears revive it not,
  I sigh—it breathes no more on me;
Its mute and uncomplaining lot
  Is such as mine should be.

On the Medusa of Leonardo da Vinci, In the Florentine Gallery

It lieth, gazing on the midnight sky,
  Upon the cloudy mountain peak supine;
Below, far lands are seen tremblingly;
  Its horror and its beauty are divine.
Upon its lips and eyelids seems to lie
  Loveliness like a shadow, from which shine,
Fiery and lurid, struggling underneath,
The agonies of anguish and of death.

Yet it is less the horror than the grace
  Which turns the gazer's spirit into stone
Whereon the lineaments of that dead face
  Are graven, till the characters be grown
Into itself, and thought no more can trace;
  'Tis the melodious hues of beauty thrown
Athwart the darkness and the glare of pain,
Which humanize and harmonize the strain.

And from its head as from one body grow,
  As [ ] grass out of a watery rock,
Hairs which are vipers, and they curl and flow,
  And their long tangles in each other lock,
And with unending involutions shew
  Their mailed radiance, as it were to mock
The torture and the death within, and saw
The solid air with many a ragged jaw.

And from a stone beside, a poisonous eft
  Peeps idly into these Gorgonian eyes;
Whilst in the air a ghastly bat, bereft
  Of sense, has flitted with a mad surprise
Out of the cave this hideous light hath cleft,
  And he comes hastening like a moth that hies
After a taper; and the midnight sky
Flares, a light more dread than obscurity.

'Tis the tempestuous loveliness of terror;
  For from the serpents gleams a brazen glare
Kindled by that inextricable error
  Which makes a thrilling vapour of the air
Become a [ ] and ever-shifting mirror
  Of all the beauty and the terror there—
A woman's countenance, with serpent locks,
Gazing in death on heaven from those wet rocks.

To Night

Swiftly walk o'er the western wave,
    Spirit of Night!
Out of the misty eastern cave
Where, all the long and lone daylight
Thou wovest dreams of joy and fear,
Which make thee terrible and dear,—
    Swift be thy flight!

Wrap thy form in a mantle grey,
    Star-inwrought!
Blind with thine hair the eyes of day,
Kiss her until she be wearied out,

Then wander o'er city and sea and land
Touching all with thine opiate wand—
Come, long-sought!

When I arose and saw the dawn
I sighed for thee;
When Light rode high, and the dew was gone
And noon lay heavy on flower and tree,
And the weary Day turned to his rest
Lingering like an unloved guest,
I sighed for thee.

Thy brother Death came, and cried,
Wouldst thou me?
Thy sweet child Sleep, the filmy-eyed,
Murmured like a noontide bee,
Shall I nestle near thy side?
Wouldst thou me? And I replied,
No, not thee!

Death will come when thou art dead,
Soon, too soon—
Sleep will come when thou art fled;
Of neither would I ask the boon
I ask of thee, beloved Night—
Swift be thine approaching flight,
Come soon, soon!

England in 1819

An old, mad, blind, despised and dying King;
Princes, the dregs of their dull race, who flow
Through public scorn,—mud from a muddy spring;
Rulers who neither see nor feel nor know,
But leechlike to their fainting country cling
Till they drop, blind in blood, without a blow;
A people starved and stabbed on th' untilled field;
An army which liberticide and prey
Makes as a two-edged sword to all who wield;
Golden and sanguine laws which tempt and slay;
Religion Christless, Godless, a book sealed;

A senate, Time's worst statute, unrepealed,
Are graves from which a glorious Phantom may
Burst, to illumine our tempestuous day.

Song
To the Men of England

Men of England, wherefore plough
For the lords who lay ye low?
Wherefore weave with toil and care
The rich robes your tyrants wear?

Wherefore feed and clothe and save
From the cradle to the grave
Those ungrateful drones who would
Drain your sweat—nay, drink your blood?

Wherefore, Bees of England, forge
Many a weapon, chain and scourge,
That these stingless drones may spoil
The forced produce of your toil?

Have ye leisure, comfort, calm,
Shelter, food, love's gentle balm?
Or what is it ye buy so dear
With your pain and with your fear?

The seed ye sow, another reaps;
The wealth ye find, another keeps;
The robes ye weave, another wears;
The arms ye forge, another bears.

Sow seed—but let no tyrant reap:
Find wealth—let no impostor heap:
Weave robes—let not the idle wear:
Forge arms—in your defence to bear.

Shrink to your cellars, holes, and cells—
In halls ye deck another dwells.
Why shake the chains ye wrought? Ye see
The steel ye tempered glance on ye.

With plough and spade and hoe and loom
Trace your grave and build your tomb,
And weave your winding-sheet—till fair
England be your Sepulchre.

To — ('Corpses are cold in the tomb')

Corpses are cold in the tomb—
Stones on the pavement are dumb—
Abortions are dead in the womb
And their mothers look pale, like the death-white shore
Of Albion, free no more.

Her sons are as stones in the way—
They are masses of senseless clay—
They are trodden and move not away—
The abortion with which *she* travaileth
Is Liberty, smitten to death.

Then trample and dance, thou Oppressor!
For thy Victim is no redressor;
Thou art sole lord and possessor
Of her corpses and clods and abortions—they pave
Thy path to the grave.

Hearest thou the festival din
Of Death and Destruction and Sin,
And Wealth crying 'havoc!' within?
'Tis the Bacchanal triumph that makes truth dumb—
Thine Epithalamium—

Aye, marry thy ghastly wife!
Let Fear and Disquiet and Strife
Spread thy couch in the chamber of Life:
Marry *Ruin*, thou Tyrant, and Hell be thy guide
To the bed of the bride.

The Sensitive-Plant

PART FIRST

A Sensitive-plant in a garden grew,
And the young winds fed it with silver dew,
And it opened its fan-like leaves to the light
And closed them beneath the kisses of night.

And the Spring arose on the garden fair
Like the Spirit of love felt everywhere;
And each flower and herb on Earth's dark breast
Rose from the dreams of its wintry rest.

But none ever trembled and panted with bliss
In the garden, the field or the wilderness,
Like a doe in the noon-tide with love's sweet want
As the companionless Sensitive-plant.

The snow-drop and then the violet
Arose from the ground with warm rain wet,
And their breath was mixed with fresh odour, sent
From the turf, like the voice and the instrument.

Then the pied wind-flowers and the tulip tall,
And narcissi, the fairest among them all,
Who gaze on their eyes in the stream's recess
Till they die of their own dear loveliness;

And the Naiad-like lily of the vale
Whom youth makes so fair and passion so pale,
That the light of its tremulous bells is seen
Through their pavilions of tender green;

And the hyacinth purple, and white, and blue
Which flung from its bells a sweet peal anew
Of music so delicate, soft and intense,
It was felt like an odour within the sense;

And the rose like a nymph to the bath addrest,
Which unveiled the depth of her glowing breast,
Till, fold after fold, to the fainting air
The soul of her beauty and love lay bare;

And the wand-like lily which lifted up,
As a Maenad, its moonlight-coloured cup
Till the fiery star, which is its eye,
Gazed through clear dew on the tender sky;

And the jessamine faint, and the sweet tuberose,
The sweetest flower for scent that blows;
And all rare blossoms from every clime
Grew in that garden in perfect prime.

And on the stream whose inconstant bosom
Was prankt under boughs of embowering blossom
With golden and green light, slanting through
Their Heaven of many a tangled hue,

Broad water lilies lay tremulously,
And starry river-buds glimmered by,
And around them the soft stream did glide and dance
With a motion of sweet sound and radiance.

And the sinuous paths of lawn and of moss
Which led through the garden along and across,
Some open at once to the sun and the breeze,
Some lost among bowers of blossoming trees,

Were all paved with daisies and delicate bells
As fair as the fabulous asphodels,
And flow'rets which drooping as day drooped too
Fell into pavilions, white, purple, and blue,
To roof the glow-worm from the evening dew.

And from this undefiled Paradise
The flowers (as an infant's awakening eyes
Smile on its mother, whose singing sweet
Can first lull, and at last must awaken it),

When Heaven's blithe winds had unfolded them,
As mine-lamps enkindle a hidden gem,
Shone smiling to Heaven, and every one
Shared joy in the light of the gentle sun;

For each one was interpenetrated
With the light and the odour its neighbour shed,
Like young lovers whom youth and love make dear
Wrapped and filled by their mutual atmosphere.

But the Sensitive-plant which could give small fruit
Of the love which it felt from the leaf to the root,
Received more than all—it loved more than ever,
Where none wanted but it, could belong to the giver.

For the Sensitive-plant has no bright flower;
Radiance and odour are not its dower;
It loves, even like Love, its deep heart is full,
It desires what it has not—the beautiful!

The light winds which from unsustaining wings
Shed the music of many murmurings;
The beams which dart from many a star
Of the flowers whose hues they bear afar;

The plumed insects swift and free,
Like golden boats on a sunny sea,
Laden with light and odour, which pass
Over the gleam of the living grass;

The unseen clouds of the dew, which lie
Like fire in the flowers till the Sun rides high,
Then wander like spirits among the spheres,
Each cloud faint with the fragrance it bears;

The quivering vapours of dim noontide,
Which like a sea o'er the warm earth glide,
In which every sound, and odour, and beam
Move, as reeds in a single stream;

Each, and all, like ministering angels were
For the Sensitive-plant sweet joy to bear
Whilst the lagging hours of the day went by
Like windless clouds o'er a tender sky.

And when evening descended from Heaven above,
And the Earth was all rest, and the air was all love,
And delight, tho' less bright, was far more deep,
And the day's veil fell from the world of sleep,

And the beasts, and the birds, and the insects were drowned
In an ocean of dreams without a sound
Whose waves never mark, tho' they ever impress
The light sand which paves it—Consciousness;

(Only over head the sweet nightingale
Ever sang more sweet as the day might fail,
And snatches of its Elysian chant
Were mixed with the dreams of the Sensitive-plant).

The Sensitive-plant was the earliest
Up-gathered into the bosom of rest;
A sweet child weary of its delight,
The feeblest and yet the favourite—
Cradled within the embrace of night.

PART SECOND

There was a Power in this sweet place,
An Eve in this Eden; a ruling grace
Which to the flowers did they waken or dream,
Was as God is to the starry scheme.

A Lady, the wonder of her kind,
Whose form was upborne by a lovely mind
Which, dilating, had moulded her mien and motion
Like a sea-flower unfolded beneath the ocean,

Tended the garden from morn to even:
And the meteors of that sublunar Heaven,
Like the lamps of the air when night walks forth,
Laughed round her footsteps up from the Earth!

She had no companion of mortal race,
But her tremulous breath and her flushing face
Told, whilst the morn kissed the sleep from her eyes
That her dreams were less slumber than Paradise:

As if some bright Spirit for her sweet sake
Had deserted heaven while the stars were awake,
As if yet around her he lingering were,
Tho' the veil of daylight concealed him from her.

Her step seemed to pity the grass it prest;
You might hear by the heaving of her breast,
That the coming and going of the wind
Brought pleasure there and left passion behind.

And wherever her airy footstep trod,
Her trailing hair from the grassy sod
Erased its light vestige, with shadowy sweep,
Like a sunny storm o'er the dark green deep.

I doubt not the flowers of that garden sweet
Rejoiced in the sound of her gentle feet;
I doubt not they felt the spirit that came
From her glowing fingers thro' all their frame.

She sprinkled bright water from the stream
On those that were faint with the sunny beam;
And out of the cups of the heavy flowers
She emptied the rain of the thunder showers.

She lifted their heads with her tender hands
And sustained them with rods and ozier bands;
If the flowers had been her own infants she
Could never have nursed them more tenderly.

And all killing insects and gnawing worms
And things of obscene and unlovely forms
She bore, in a basket of Indian woof,
Into the rough woods far aloof,

In a basket of grasses and wild flowers full,
The freshest her gentle hands could pull
For the poor banished insects, whose intent,
Although they did ill, was innocent.

But the bee and the beam-like ephemeris
Whose path is the lightning's, and soft moths that kiss
The sweet lips of the flowers, and harm not, did she
Make her attendant angels be.

And many an antenatal tomb
Where butterflies dream of the life to come
She left, clinging round the smooth and dark
Edge of the odorous Cedar bark.

This fairest creature from earliest spring
Thus moved through the garden ministering
All the sweet season of summer tide,
And ere the first leaf looked brown—she died!

PART THIRD

Three days the flowers of the garden fair,
Like stars when the moon is awakened, were;
Or the waves of Baiae, ere luminous
She floats up through the smoke of Vesuvius.

And on the fourth, the Sensitive-plant
Felt the sound of the funeral chaunt
And the steps of the bearers heavy and slow,
And the sobs of the mourners deep and low;

The weary sound and the heavy breath
And the silent motions of passing death
And the smell, cold, oppressive and dank,
Sent through the pores of the coffin plank;

The dark grass, and the flowers among the grass,
Were bright with tears as the crowd did pass;
From their sighs the wind caught a mournful tone
And sate in the pines and gave groan for groan.

The garden once fair became cold and foul
Like the corpse of her who had been its soul,
Which at first was lovely as if in sleep,
Then slowly changed, till it grew a heap
To make men tremble who never weep.

Swift summer into the autumn flowed,
And frost in the mist of the morning rode
Though the noonday sun looked clear and bright,
Mocking the spoil of the secret night.

The rose leaves, like flakes of crimson snow,
Paved the turf and the moss below:
The lilies were drooping, and white, and wan,
Like the head and the skin of a dying man.

And Indian plants, of scent and hue
The sweetest that ever were fed on dew,
Leaf after leaf, day after day,
Were massed into the common clay.

And the leaves, brown, yellow, and grey, and red,
And white with the whiteness of what is dead,
Like troops of ghosts on the dry wind past;
Their whistling noise made the birds aghast.

And the gusty winds waked the winged seeds
Out of their birthplace of ugly weeds,
Till they clung round many a sweet flower's stem
Which rotted into the earth with them.

The water-blooms under the rivulet
Fell from the stalks on which they were set;
And the eddies drove them here and there
As the winds did those of the upper air.

Then the rain came down, and the broken stalks
Were bent and tangled across the walks;
And the leafless net-work of parasite bowers
Massed into ruin; and all sweet flowers.

Between the time of the wind and the snow
All loathliest weeds began to grow,
Whose coarse leaves were splashed with many a speck
Like the water-snake's belly and the toad's back.

And thistles, and nettles, and darnels rank,
And the dock, and henbane; and hemlock dank
Stretched out its long and hollow shank
And stifled the air, till the dead wind stank.

And plants at whose names the verse feels loath
Filled the place with a monstrous undergrowth,
Prickly, and pulpous, and blistering, and blue,
Livid, and starred with a lurid dew.

And agarics and fungi, with mildew and mould
Started like mist from the wet ground cold;
Pale, fleshy,—as if the decaying dead
With a spirit of growth had been animated!

Their mass rotted off them, flake by flake,
Till the thick stalk stuck like a murderer's stake,
Where rags of loose flesh yet tremble on high
Infecting the winds that wander by.

Spawn, weeds and filth, a leprous scum,
Made the running rivulet thick and dumb,
And at its outlet flags huge as stakes
Dammed it up with roots knotted like water-snakes.

And hour by hour, when the air was still,
The vapours arose which have strength to kill:
At morn they were seen, at noon they were felt,
At night they were darkness no star could melt.

And unctuous meteors from spray to spray
Crept and flitted in broad noon-day
Unseen; every branch on which they alit
By a venomous blight was burned and bit.

The Sensitive-plant like one forbid
Wept, and the tears, within each lid
Of its folded leaves which together grew,
Were changed to a blight of frozen glue.

For the leaves soon fell, and the branches soon
By the heavy axe of the blast were hewn;
The sap shrank to the root through every pore
As blood to a heart that will beat no more.

For Winter came—the wind was his whip—
One choppy finger was on his lip:
He had torn the cataracts from the hills
And they clanked at his girdle like manacles;

His breath was a chain which without a sound
The earth and the air and the water bound;
He came, fiercely driven in his Chariot-throne
By the tenfold blasts of the arctic zone.

Then the weeds which were forms of living death
Fled from the frost to the Earth beneath.
Their decay and sudden flight from frost
Was but like the vanishing of a ghost!

And under the roots of the Sensitive-plant
The moles and the dormice died for want.
The birds dropped stiff from the frozen air
And were caught in the branches naked and bare.

First there came down a thawing rain
And its dull drops froze on the boughs again;
Then there steamed up a freezing dew
Which to the drops of the thaw-rain grew;

And a northern whirlwind, wandering about
Like a wolf that had smelt a dead child out,
Shook the boughs thus laden and heavy and stiff
And snapped them off with his rigid griff.

When winter had gone and spring came back
The Sensitive-plant was a leafless wreck;
But the mandrakes and toadstools and docks and darnels
Rose like the dead from their ruined charnels.

CONCLUSION

Whether the Sensitive-plant, or that
Which within its boughs like a spirit sat
Ere its outward form had known decay,
Now felt this change,—I cannot say.

Whether that Lady's gentle mind,
No longer with the form combined
Which scattered love, as stars do light,
Found sadness, where it left delight,

I dare not guess; but in this life
Of error, ignorance and strife—
Where nothing is, but all things seem,
And we, the shadows of the dream,

It is a modest creed, and yet
Pleasant if one considers it,
To own that death itself must be,
Like all the rest,—a mockery.

That Garden sweet, that Lady fair,
And all sweet shapes and odours there,
In truth have never pass'd away—
'Tis we, 'tis ours, are changed—not they.

For love, and beauty, and delight
There is no death nor change: their might
Exceeds our organs—which endure
No light, being themselves obscure.

An Exhortation

Camelions feed on light and air:
  Poets' food is love and fame:
If in this wide world of care
  Poets could but find the same
With as little toil as they,
  Would they ever change their hue
  As the light camelions do,
Suiting it to every ray
Twenty times a-day?

Poets are on this cold earth
  As camelions might be,
Hidden from their early birth
  In a cave beneath the sea;
Where light is, camelions change:
  Where love is not, poets do:
  Fame is love disguised: if few
Find either, never think it strange
That poets range.

Yet dare not stain with wealth or power
  A poet's free and heavenly mind:
If bright camelions should devour
  Any food but beams and wind,
They would grow as earthly soon
  As their brother lizards are.
  Children of a sunnier star,
Spirits from beyond the moon,
O, refuse the boon!

Song of Apollo

The sleepless Hours who watch me as I lie
  Curtained with star-enwoven tapestries
From the broad moonlight of the open sky,
  Fanning the busy dreams from my dim eyes,
Waken me when their mother, the grey Dawn,
Tells them that Dreams and that the moon is gone.

Then I arise; and climbing Heaven's blue dome
 I walk over the mountains and the waves,
Leaving my robe upon the Ocean foam.
 My footsteps pave the clouds with fire; the caves
Are filled with my bright presence, and the air
Leaves the green Earth to my embraces bare.

The sunbeams are my shafts with which I kill
 Deceit, that loves the night and fears the day.
All men who do, or even imagine ill
 Fly me; and from the glory of my ray
Good minds, and open actions, take new might
Until diminished by the reign of night.

I feed the clouds, the rainbows and the flowers
 With their aetherial colours; the moon's globe
And the pure stars in their eternal bowers
 Are cinctured with my power as with a robe;
Whatever lamps on Earth or Heaven may shine
Are portions of one spirit; which is mine.

I stand at noon upon the peak of Heaven;
 Then with unwilling steps, I linger down
To the clouds of the Atlantic even.
 For grief that I depart they weep and frown—
What look is more delightful, than the smile
With which I soothe them from the Western isle?

I am the eye with which the Universe
 Beholds itself, and knows it is divine.
All harmony of instrument and verse,
 All prophecy and medicine are mine;
All light of art or nature—to my song
Victory and praise, in its own right, belong.

Song of Pan

From the forests and highlands
 We come, we come;
From the river-girt islands
 Where loud waves were dumb

Listening my sweet pipings.
The wind in the reeds and the rushes,
The bees in the bells of thyme,
The birds in the myrtle bushes,
The cicadae above in the lime,
And the lizards below in the grass,
Were silent as even old Tmolus was,
Listening my sweet pipings.

Liquid Peneus was flowing—
And all dark Tempe lay
In [?] shadow, outgrowing
The light of the dying day,
Speeded with my sweet pipings.
The sileni and sylvans and fauns
And the nymphs of the woods and the waves
To the edge of the moist river-lawns
And the brink of the dewy caves,
And all that did then attend and follow,
Were as silent for love, as you now, Apollo,
For envy of my sweet pipings.

I sang of the dancing stars,
I sang of the daedal Earth,
And of Heaven, and the giant wars,
And Love and Death and Birth;
And then I changed my pipings,
Singing how, down the vales of Maenalus
I pursued a maiden and clasped a reed:
Gods and men, we are all deluded thus!—
It breaks on our bosom and then we bleed;
They wept as I think both ye now would,
If envy or age had not frozen your blood,
At the sorrow of my sweet pipings.

The Cloud

I bring fresh showers for the thirsting flowers,
From the seas and the streams;
I bear light shade for the leaves when laid
In their noon-day dreams.

From my wings are shaken the dews that waken
  The sweet buds every one,
When rocked to rest on their mother's breast,
  As she dances about the sun.
I wield the flail of the lashing hail,
  And whiten the green plains under,
And then again I dissolve it in rain,
  And laugh as I pass in thunder.

I sift the snow on the mountains below,
  And their great pines groan aghast;
And all the night 'tis my pillow white,
  While I sleep in the arms of the blast.
Sublime on the towers of my skiey bowers,
  Lightning my pilot sits;
In a cavern under is fettered the thunder,
  It struggles and howls at fits;
Over earth and ocean, with gentle motion,
  This pilot is guiding me,
Lured by the love of the genii that move
  In the depths of the purple sea;
Over the rills, and the crags, and the hills,
  Over the lakes and the plains,
Wherever he dream, under mountain or stream
  The Spirit he loves remains;
And I all the while bask in heaven's blue smile,
  Whilst he is dissolving in rains.

The sanguine sunrise, with his meteor eyes,
  And his burning plumes outspread,
Leaps on the back of my sailing rack,
  When the morning star shines dead,
As on the jag of a mountain crag,
  Which an earthquake rocks and swings,
An eagle alit one moment may sit
  In the light of its golden wings.
And when Sunset may breathe, from the lit Sea beneath,
  Its ardours of rest and love,
And the crimson pall of eve may fall
  From the depth of Heaven above,
With wings folded I rest, on mine aëry nest,
  As still as a brooding dove.

That orbed maiden with white fire laden,
  Whom mortals call the moon,
Glides glimmering o'er my fleece-like floor,
  By the midnight breezes strewn;
And wherever the beat of her unseen feet,
  Which only the angels hear,
May have broken the woof of my tent's thin roof,
  The stars peep behind her, and peer;
And I laugh to see them whirl and flee,
  Like a swarm of golden bees,
When I widen the rent in my wind-built tent,
  Till the calm rivers, lakes, and seas,
Like strips of the sky fallen through me on high,
  Are each paved with the moon and these.

I bind the Sun's throne with a burning zone,
  And the moon's with a girdle of pearl;
The volcanoes are dim, and the stars reel and swim,
  When the whirlwinds my banner unfurl.
From cape to cape, with a bridge-like shape,
  Over a torrent sea,
Sunbeam-proof, I hang like a roof;
  The mountains its columns be!
The triumphal arch, through which I march
  With hurricane, fire, and snow,
When the Powers of the Air are chained to my chair,
  Is the million-coloured Bow;
The sphere-fire above its soft colours wove,
  While the moist earth was laughing below.

I am the daughter of Earth and Water,
  And the nursling of the sky;
I pass through the pores of the ocean and shores;
  I change, but I cannot die—
For after the rain, when with never a stain,
  The pavilion of Heaven is bare,
And the winds and sunbeams, with their convex gleams,
  Build up the blue Dome of Air,
I silently laugh at my own cenotaph,
  And out of the caverns of rain,
Like a child from the womb, like a ghost from the tomb,
  I arise, and unbuild it again.

'God save the Queen!'
[A New National Anthem]

God! prosper, speed and save,
God! raise from England's grave
  Her murdered Queen.
Pave with swift victory
The steps of Liberty
Whom Britons own to be
  Immortal Queen!

See, she comes throned on high,
On swift Eternity,
  God save the Queen!
Millions on millions wait
Firm, rapid, [ ], elate,
On her [?approaching] state,
  God save the Queen!

She is thine own pure soul
[?Moulding] the mighty whole,
  God save our Queen!
She is thine own deep love,
Rained down from Heaven above,
Wherever she rest or move,
  God save our Queen!

Wilder her enemies
In their own dark disguise,
  God save our Queen!
All earthly things that dare
Her sacred name to wear,
Strip them, as Kings [ ] bare;
  God save our Queen!

Be her eternal throne
Built in our hearts alone,
  God save our Queen!
Let the Oppressor hold
Canopied seats of gold,
She sits enthroned of old
  O'er our hearts, Queen.

Lips, touched by seraphim,
Breathe out the choral hymn,
God save the Queen!
Sweet as if Angels sang,
Loud as that [ ] clang
Wakening the world's dead gang,
God save the Queen!

Translation of Dante's Purgatorio, *Canto XXVIII, lines 1–51* *[Matilda Gathering Flowers]*

Earnest to explore within and all around
The divine wood, whose thick green living woof
Tempered the young day to the sight, I wound

Up the [green] slope, beneath the [forest's] roof,
With slow [soft] steps, leaving the abrupt shelf
And the [ ] aloof—

A gentle air which had within itself
No motion struck upon my forehead bare
Like the soft stroke of a continuous wind

In which the passive leaves tremblingly were
All bent towards that [part] where earliest
That sacred hill obscures the morning air,

Yet were they not so shaken from their rest
But that the birds, perched on the utmost spray
[Incessantly] renewing their blithe quest,

With perfect joy received the early day
Singing within the glancing leaves, whose sound
Kept one low burthen to their roundelay

Such as from bough to bough gathers around
The pine forest on bleak Chiassi's shore
When Aeolus Sirocco has unbound.

My slow steps had already borne me o'er
Such space within the antique wood, that I
Perceived not where I entered any more,

When lo, a stream whose little waves went by,
Bending towards the left the grass that grew
Upon its bank, impeded suddenly

My going on—waters of purest hue
On Earth, would appear turbid and impure
Compared with this, whose unconcealing dew,

Dark, dark, [yet] clear, moved under the obscure
Eternal shades, whose [?intense] [ ] [glooms]
No rays of moon or sunlight e'er endure.

I moved not with my feet, but amid the glooms
I pierced with my charmed sight, contemplating
The mighty multitude of fresh May blooms,

And then appeared to me—even like a thing
Which suddenly for blank astonishment
Dissolves all other thought, [ ]

A solitary woman, and she went
Singing and gathering flower after flower
With which her way was painted and besprent.

'Bright lady, who if looks had ever power
To bear firm witness of the heart within,
Dost bask under the beams of love, come lower

'[Towards] this bank; I prithee let me win
Thus much of thee that thou shouldst come anear
So I may hear thy song—like Proserpine

'Thou seemest to my fancy, singing here
And gathering flowers, at that [sweet] time when
She lost the spring and Ceres her . . . more dear.'

Evening. Ponte a Mare, Pisa

The sun is set, the swallows are asleep,
  The bats are flitting fast in the grey air;
The slow soft toads out of damp corners creep,
  And evening's breath, wandering here and there
Over the gleaming surface of the stream,
Wakes not one ripple from its summer dream.

There is no dew on the dry grass tonight,
  Nor damp within the shadow of the trees;
The wind is intermitting, dry and light,
  And in the inconstant motion of the breeze
The dust and straws are driven up and down
And whirled about the pavement of the Town.

Within the surface of the fleeting river
  The wrinkled image of the city lay
Immoveably unquiet—and forever
  It trembles but it never fades away;
Go to the Indies [ ]
You, being changed, will find it then as now.

The chasm in which the sun has sunk is shut
  By darkest barriers of cinereous cloud
Like mountain over mountain huddled but
  Growing and moving upwards in a crowd,
And over it a space of watery blue
Which the keen evening star is shining through.

And overhead hangs many a flaccid fold
  Of lurid thundersmoke most heavily,
A streak of dun and sulphureous gold

Ode to Liberty

Yet, Freedom, yet thy banner torn but flying,
Streams like a thunder-storm against the wind.
Byron

I

A glorious people vibrated again
The lightning of the nations: Liberty
From heart to heart, from tower to tower, o'er Spain,
Scattering contagious fire into the sky,
Gleamed. My soul spurned the chains of its dismay,
And, in the rapid plumes of song
Clothed itself, sublime and strong;
As a young eagle soars the morning clouds among,
Hovering in verse o'er its accustomed prey;
Till from its station in the heaven of fame
The Spirit's whirlwind rapt it, and the ray
Of the remotest sphere of living flame
Which paves the void was from behind it flung,
As foam from a ship's swiftness, when there came
A voice out of the deep: I will record the same.

II

The Sun and the serenest Moon sprang forth:
The burning stars of the abyss were hurled
Into the depths of heaven. The daedal earth,
That island in the ocean of the world,
Hung in its cloud of all-sustaining air:
But this divinest universe
Was yet a chaos and a curse,
For thou wert not: but power from worst producing worse,
The spirit of the beasts was kindled there,
And of the birds, and of the watery forms,
And there was war among them, and despair
Within them, raging without truce or terms:
The bosom of their violated nurse
Groan'd, for beasts warr'd on beasts, and worms on worms,
And men on men; each heart was as a hell of storms.

III

Man, the imperial shape, then multiplied
His generations under the pavilion
Of the Sun's throne: palace and pyramid,
Temple and prison, to many a swarming million,
Were, as to mountain-wolves their ragged caves.
This human living multitude
Was savage, cunning, blind, and rude,
For thou wert not; but o'er the populous solitude,
Like one fierce cloud over a waste of waves
Hung tyranny; beneath, sate deified
The sister-pest, congregator of slaves;
Into the shadow of her pinions wide,
Anarchs and priests who feed on gold and blood,
Till with the stain their inmost souls are dyed,
Drove the astonished herds of men from every side.

IV

The nodding promontories, and blue isles,
And cloud-like mountains, and dividuous waves
Of Greece, basked glorious in the open smiles
Of favouring heaven: from their enchanted caves
Prophetic echoes flung dim melody
On the unapprehensive wild.
The vine, the corn, the olive mild,
Grew savage yet, to human use unreconciled;
And, like unfolded flowers beneath the sea,
Like the man's thought dark in the infant's brain,
Like aught that is which wraps what is to be,
Art's deathless dreams lay veiled by many a vein
Of Parian stone; and yet a speechless child,
Verse murmured, and Philosophy did strain
Her lidless eyes for thee; when o'er the Aegean main

V

Athens arose: a city such as vision
Builds from the purple crags and silver towers
Of battlemented cloud, as in derision
Of kingliest masonry: the ocean-floors
Pave it; the evening sky pavilions it;
Its portals are inhabited
By thunder-zoned winds, each head

Within its cloudy wings with sunfire garlanded,
A divine work! Athens diviner yet
Gleamed with its crest of columns, on the will
Of man, as on a mount of diamond, set;
For thou wert, and thine all-creative skill
Peopled with forms that mock the eternal dead
In marble immortality, that hill
Which was thine earliest throne and latest oracle.

VI

Within the surface of Time's fleeting river
Its wrinkled image lies, as then it lay
Immoveably unquiet, and for ever
It trembles, but it cannot pass away!
The voices of its bards and sages thunder
With an earth-awakening blast
Through the caverns of the past;
Religion veils her eyes; Oppression shrinks aghast:
A winged sound of joy, and love, and wonder,
Which soars where Expectation never flew,
Rending the veil of space and time asunder!
One ocean feeds the clouds, and streams, and dew;
One sun illumines heaven; one spirit vast
With life and love makes chaos ever new,
As Athens doth the world with thy delight renew.

VII

Then Rome was, and from thy deep bosom fairest,
Like a wolf-cub from a Cadmaean Maenad,*
She drew the milk of greatness, though thy dearest
From that Elysian food was yet unweaned;
And many a deed of terrible uprightness
By thy sweet love was sanctified;
And in thy smile, and by thy side,
Saintly Camillus lived, and firm Atilius died.
But when tears stained thy robe of vestal whiteness,
And gold profaned thy Capitolian throne,
Thou didst desert, with spirit-winged lightness,
The senate of the tyrants: they sunk prone
Slaves of one tyrant: Palatinus sighed

* See the *Bacchae* of Euripides. [Shelley's note]

Faint echoes of Ionian song; that tone
Thou didst delay to hear, lamenting to disown.

VIII

From what Hyrcanian glen or frozen hill,
Or piny promontory of the Arctic main,
Or utmost islet inaccessible,
Didst thou lament the ruin of thy reign,
Teaching the woods and waves, and desart rocks,
And every Naiad's ice-cold urn,
To talk in echoes sad and stern,
Of that sublimest lore which man had dared unlearn?
For neither didst thou watch the wizard flocks
Of the Scald's dreams, nor haunt the Druid's sleep.
What if the tears rained through thy shattered locks
Were quickly dried? for thou didst groan, not weep,
When from its sea of death to kill and burn,
The Galilean serpent forth did creep,
And made thy world an undistinguishable heap.

IX

A thousand years the Earth cried, Where art thou?
And then the shadow of thy coming fell
On Saxon Alfred's olive-cinctured brow:
And many a warrior-peopled citadel,
Like rocks which fire lifts out of the flat deep,
Arose in sacred Italy,
Frowning o'er the tempestuous sea
Of kings, and priests, and slaves, in tower-crowned majesty;
That multitudinous anarchy did sweep
And burst around their walls, like idle foam,
Whilst from the human spirit's deepest deep
Strange melody with love and awe struck dumb
Dissonant arms; and Art, which cannot die,
With divine wand traced on our earthly home
Fit imagery to pave heaven's everlasting dome.

X

Thou huntress swifter than the Moon! thou terror
Of the world's wolves! thou bearer of the quiver
Whose sunlike shafts pierce tempest-winged Error,
As light may pierce the clouds when they dissever

In the calm regions of the orient day!
Luther caught thy wakening glance,
Like lightning, from his leaden lance
Reflected, it dissolved the visions of the trance
In which, as in a tomb, the nations lay;
And England's prophets hailed thee as their queen,
In songs whose music cannot pass away,
Though it must flow for ever: not unseen
Before the spirit-sighted countenance
Of Milton didst thou pass, from the sad scene
Beyond whose night he saw, with a dejected mien.

XI

The eager hours and unreluctant years
As on a dawn-illumined mountain stood,
Trampling to silence their loud hopes and fears,
Darkening each other with their multitude,
And cried aloud, Liberty! Indignation
Answered Pity from her cave;
Death grew pale within the grave,
And Desolation howled to the destroyer, Save!
When like heaven's sun girt by the exhalation
Of its own glorious light, thou didst arise,
Chasing thy foes from nation unto nation
Like shadows: as if day had cloven the skies
At dreaming midnight o'er the western wave,
Men started, staggering with a glad surprise,
Under the lightnings of thine unfamiliar eyes.

XII

Thou heaven of earth! what spells could pall thee then,
In ominous eclipse? a thousand years
Bred from the slime of deep oppression's den,
Dyed all thy liquid light with blood and tears,
Till thy sweet stars could weep the stain away;
How like Bacchanals of blood
Round France, the ghastly vintage, stood
Destruction's sceptred slaves, and Folly's mitred brood!
When one, like them, but mightier far than they,
The Anarch of thine own bewildered powers
Rose: armies mingled in obscure array,
Like clouds with clouds, darkening the sacred bowers

Of serene heaven. He, by the past pursued,
Rests with those dead, but unforgotten hours,
Whose ghosts scare victor kings in their ancestral towers.

XIII

England yet sleeps: was she not called of old?
Spain calls her now, as with its thrilling thunder
Vesuvius wakens Aetna, and the cold
Snow-crags by its reply are cloven in sunder:
O'er the lit waves every Aeolian isle
From Pithecusa to Pelorus
Howls, and leaps, and glares in chorus:
They cry, Be dim, ye lamps of heaven suspended o'er us.
Her chains are threads of gold, she need but smile
And they dissolve; but Spain's were links of steel,
Till bit to dust by virtue's keenest file.
Twins of a single destiny! appeal
To the eternal years enthroned before us,
In the dim West; impress as from a seal
All ye have thought and done! Time cannot dare conceal.

XIV

Tomb of Arminius! render up thy dead,
Till, like a standard from a watch-tower's staff,
His soul may stream over the tyrant's head;
Thy victory shall be his epitaph,
Wild Bacchanal of truth's mysterious wine,
King-deluded Germany,
His dead spirit lives in thee.
Why do we fear or hope? thou art already free!
And thou, lost Paradise of this divine
And glorious world! thou flowery wilderness!
Thou island of eternity! thou shrine
Where desolation clothed with loveliness
Worships the thing thou wert! O Italy,
Gather thy blood into thy heart; repress
The beasts who make their dens thy sacred palaces.

XV

O, that the free would stamp the impious name
Of KING into the dust! or write it there,
So that this blot upon the page of fame
Were as a serpent's path, which the light air

Erases, and the flat sands close behind!
    Ye the oracle have heard:
    Lift the victory-flashing sword,
And cut the snaky knots of this foul gordian word,
  Which weak itself as stubble, yet can bind
    Into a mass, irrefragably firm,
  The axes and the rods which awe mankind;
    The sound has poison in it, 'tis the sperm
Of what makes life foul, cankerous, and abhorred;
  Disdain not thou, at thine appointed term,
  To set thine armed heel on this reluctant worm.

XVI

O, that the wise from their bright minds would kindle
  Such lamps within the dome of this dim world,
That the pale name of PRIEST might shrink and dwindle
  Into the hell from which it first was hurled,
A scoff of impious pride from fiends impure;
    Till human thoughts might kneel alone
    Each before the judgement-throne
Of its own aweless soul, or of the power unknown!
  O, that the words which make the thoughts obscure
    From which they spring, as clouds of glimmering dew
  From a white lake blot heaven's blue portraiture,
    Were stript of their thin masks and various hue
And frowns and smiles and splendours not their own,
  Till in the nakedness of false and true
  They stand before their Lord, each to receive its due.

XVII

He who taught man to vanquish whatsoever
  Can be between the cradle and the grave
Crowned him the King of Life. O vain endeavour!
  If on his own high will a willing slave,
He has enthroned the oppression and the oppressor.
    What if earth can clothe and feed
    Amplest millions at their need,
And power in thought be as the tree within the seed?
  Or what if Art, an ardent intercessor,
    Diving on fiery wings to Nature's throne,
  Checks the great mother stooping to caress her,
    And cries: Give me, thy child, dominion
Over all height and depth? if Life can breed

New wants, and wealth from those who toil and groan
Rend of thy gifts and hers a thousandfold for one.

XVIII

Come Thou, but lead out of the inmost cave
Of man's deep spirit, as the morning-star
Beckons the Sun from the Eoan wave,
Wisdom. I hear the pennons of her car
Self-moving, like cloud charioted by flame;
Comes she not, and come ye not,
Rulers of eternal thought,
To judge, with solemn truth, life's ill-apportioned lot?
Blind Love, and equal Justice, and the Fame
Of what has been, the Hope of what will be?
O, Liberty! if such could be thy name
Wert thou disjoined from these, or they from thee:
If thine or theirs were treasures to be bought
By blood or tears, have not the wise and free
Wept tears, and blood like tears? The solemn harmony

XIX

Paused, and the spirit of that mighty singing
To its abyss was suddenly withdrawn;
Then, as a wild swan, when sublimely winging
Its path athwart the thunder-smoke of dawn,
Sinks headlong through the aerial golden light
On the heavy sounding plain,
When the bolt has pierced its brain;
As summer clouds dissolve, unburdened of their rain;
As a far taper fades with fading night,
As a brief insect dies with dying day,
My song, its pinions disarrayed of might,
Drooped; o'er it closed the echoes far away
Of the great voice which did its flight sustain,
As waves which lately paved his watery way
Hiss round a drowner's head in their tempestuous play.

To a Sky-Lark

Hail to thee, blithe Spirit!
Bird thou never wert,

That from Heaven, or near it,
  Pourest thy full heart
In profuse strains of unpremeditated art.

Higher still and higher
  From the earth thou springest
Like a cloud of fire;
  The blue deep thou wingest,
And singing still dost soar, and soaring ever singest.

In the golden lightning
  Of the sunken Sun,
O'er which clouds are brightning,
  Thou dost float and run;
Like an unbodied joy whose race is just begun.

The pale purple even
  Melts around thy flight;
Like a star of Heaven
  In the broad daylight
Thou art unseen, but yet I hear thy shrill delight,

Keen as are the arrows
  Of that silver sphere,
Whose intense lamp narrows
  In the white dawn clear,
Until we hardly see—we feel that it is there.

All the earth and air
  With thy voice is loud,
As when Night is bare
  From one lonely cloud
The moon rains out her beams—and Heaven is overflowed.

What thou art we know not;
  What is most like thee?
From rainbow clouds there flow not
  Drops so bright to see
As from thy presence showers a rain of melody.

Like a Poet hidden
  In the light of thought,

Singing hymns unbidden
Till the world is wrought
To sympathy with hopes and fears it heeded not:

Like a high-born maiden
In a palace-tower,
Soothing her love-laden
Soul in secret hour,
With music sweet as love—which overflows her bower:

Like a glow-worm golden
In a dell of dew,
Scattering unbeholden
Its aerial hue
Among the flowers and grass which screen it from the view:

Like a rose embowered
In its own green leaves,
By warm winds deflowered—
Till the scent it gives
Makes faint with too much sweet those heavy-wingèd thieves:

Sound of vernal showers
On the twinkling grass,
Rain-awakened flowers,
All that ever was
Joyous and clear and fresh, thy music doth surpass:

Teach us, Sprite or Bird,
What sweet thoughts are thine;
I have never heard
Praise of love or wine
That panted forth a flood of rapture so divine:

Chorus Hymeneal
Or triumphal chaunt
Matched with thine, would be all
But an empty vaunt,
A thing wherein we feel there is some hidden want.

What objects are the fountains
Of thy happy strain?

What fields or waves or mountains?
What shapes of sky or plain?
What love of thine own kind? what ignorance of pain?

With thy clear keen joyance
Languor cannot be:
Shadow of annoyance
Never came near thee:
Thou lovest; but ne'er knew love's sad satiety.

Waking or asleep,
Thou of death must deem
Things more true and deep
Than we mortals dream,
Or how could thy notes flow in such a crystal stream?

We look before and after
And pine for what is not:
Our sincerest laughter
With some pain is fraught;
Our sweetest songs are those that tell of saddest thought.

Yet if we could scorn
Hate and pride and fear;
If we were things born
Not to shed a tear,
I know not how thy joy we ever should come near.

Better than all measures
Of delightful sound,
Better than all treasures
That in books are found,
Thy skill to poet were, thou Scorner of the ground!

Teach me half the gladness
That thy brain must know,
Such harmonious madness
From my lips would flow,
The world should listen then—as I am listening now.

Letter to Maria Gisborne

The spider spreads her webs, whether she be
In poet's tower, cellar or barn or tree;
The silkworm in the dark green mulberry leaves
His winding sheet and cradle ever weaves;
So I, a thing whom moralists call worm,
Sit spinning still round this decaying form,
From the fine threads of verse and subtle thought—
No net of words in garish colours wrought
To catch the idle buzzers of the day—
But a soft cell, where when that fades away,
Memory may clothe in wings my living name
And feed it with the asphodels of fame,
Which in those hearts which most remember me
Grow, making love an immortality.

Whoever should behold me now, I wist,
Would think I were a mighty mechanist,
Bent with sublime Archimedean art
To breathe a soul into the iron heart
Of some machine portentous, or strange gin,
Which, by the force of figured spells might win
Its way over the sea, and sport therein;
For round the walls are hung dread engines, such
As Vulcan never wrought for Jove to clutch
Ixion or the Titans:—or the quick
Wit of that man of God, St. Dominic,
To convince Atheist, Turk, or Heretic,
Or those in philanthropic council met,
Who thought to pay some interest for the debt
They owed to Jesus Christ for their salvation,
By giving a faint foretaste of damnation
To Shakespeare, Sidney, Spenser and the rest
Who made our land an island of the blest,
When lamp-like Spain, who now relumes her fire
On Freedom's hearth, grew dim with Empire—
With thumbscrews, wheels, with tooth and spike and jag,
Which fishers found under the utmost crag
Of Cornwall and the storm-encompassed isles,
Where to the sky the rude sea rarely smiles

Unless in treacherous wrath, as on the morn
When the exulting elements in scorn
Satiated with destroyed destruction, lay
Sleeping in beauty on their mangled prey,
As panthers sleep;— and other strange and dread
Magical forms the brick floor overspread—
Proteus transformed to metal did not make
More figures, or more strange; nor did he take
Such shapes of unintelligible brass,
Or heap himself in such a horrid mass
Of tin and iron not to be understood;
And forms of unimaginable wood
To puzzle Tubal Cain and all his brood:
Great screws and cones, and wheels and grooved blocks,
The elements of what will stand the shocks
Of wave, and wind and time.—Upon the table
More knacks and quips there be than I am able
To catalogize in this verse of mine:—
A pretty bowl of wood—not full of wine,
But quicksilver, that dew which the gnomes drink
When at their subterranean toil they swink,
Pledging the daemons of the earthquake, who
Reply to them in lava—cry halloo!
And call out to the cities o'er their head,—
Roofs, towers, and shrines, the dying and the dead,
Crash through the chinks of earth—and then all quaff
Another rouse, and hold their sides and laugh.
This quicksilver no gnome has drunk—within
The walnut bowl it lies, veined and thin,
In colour like the wake of light that stains
The Tuscan deep, when from the moist moon rains
The inmost shower of its white fire—the breeze
Is still—blue heaven smiles over the pale seas.
And in this bowl of quicksilver—for I
Yield to the impulse of an infancy
Outlasting manhood—I have made to float
A rude idealism of a paper boat:
A hollow screw with cogs—Henry will know
The thing I mean and laugh at me—if so
He fears not I should do more mischief.—Next
Lie bills and calculations much perplexed,
With steamboats, frigates and machinery quaint

Traced over them in blue and yellow paint.
Then comes a range of mathematical
Instruments, for plans nautical and statical;
A heap of rosin, a queer broken glass
With ink in it, a china cup that was
What it will never be again, I think,
A thing from which sweet lips were wont to drink
The liquor doctors rail at—and which I
Will quaff in spite of them—and when we die
We'll toss up who died first of drinking tea,
And cry out heads or tails? where'er we be.
Near that a dusty paint box, some odd hooks,
A half-burnt match, an ivory block, three books
Where conic sections, spherics, logarithms,
To great Laplace, from Saunderson and Sims,
Lie heaped in their harmonious disarray
Of figures—disentangle them who may.
Baron de Tott's memoirs beside them lie,
And some odd volumes of old chemistry.
Near those a most inexplicable thing,
With lead in the middle—I'm conjecturing
How to make Henry understand—but no,
I'll leave, as Spenser says, with many mo,
This secret in the pregnant womb of time,
Too vast a matter for so weak a rhyme.

And here like some weird Archimage sit I,
Plotting dark spells and devilish enginery,
The self-impelling steam-wheels of the mind
Which pump up oaths from clergymen, and grind
The gentle spirit of our meek reviews
Into a powdery foam of salt abuse,
Ruffling the ocean of their self-content—
I sit, and smile or sigh as is my bent,
But not for them—Libeccio rushes round
With an inconstant and an idle sound,
I heed him more than them—the thunder-smoke
Is gathering on the mountains, like a cloak
Folded athwart their shoulders broad and bare;
The ripe corn under the undulating air
Undulates like an ocean—and the vines
Are trembling wide in all their trellised lines—

The murmur of the awakening sea doth fill
The empty pauses of the blast—the hill
Looks hoary through the white electric rain—
And from the glens beyond, in sullen strain
The interrupted thunder howls; above
One chasm of heaven smiles, like the eye of Love
On the unquiet world—while such things are,
How could one worth your friendship heed the war
Of worms? the shriek of the world's carrion jays,
Their censure, or their wonder, or their praise?

You are not here . . . the quaint witch Memory sees
In vacant chairs your absent images,
And points where once you sat, and now should be
But are not—I demand if ever we
Shall meet as then we met—and she replies,
Veiling in awe her second-sighted eyes;
'I know the past alone—but summon home
My sister Hope,— she speaks of all to come.'
But I, an old diviner, who know well
Every false verse of that sweet oracle,
Turned to the sad enchantress once again,
And sought a respite from my gentle pain,
In citing every passage o'er and o'er
Of our communion—how on the sea-shore
We watched the ocean and the sky together
Under the roof of blue Italian weather;
How I ran home through last year's thunderstorm
And felt the transverse lightning linger warm
Upon my cheek—and how we often made
Feasts for each other, where good will outweighed
The frugal luxury of our country cheer,
As well it might, were it less firm and clear
Than ours must ever be;—and how we spun
A shroud of talk to hide us from the sun
Of this familiar life, which seems to be
But is not,—or is but quaint mockery
Of all we would believe; or sadly blame
The jarring and inexplicable frame
Of this wrong world;—and then anatomize
The purposes and thoughts of men whose eyes
Were closed in distant years—or widely guess

The issue of the earth's great business,
When we shall be as we no longer are—
Like babbling gossips safe, who hear the war
Of winds, and sigh, but tremble not—or how
You listened to some interrupted flow
Of visionary rhyme, in joy and pain
Struck from the inmost fountains of my brain,
With little skill perhaps—or how we sought
Those deepest wells of passion and of thought
Wrought by wise poets in the waste of years,
Staining their sacred waters with our tears,
Quenching a thirst ever to be renewed!
Or how I, wisest lady! then indued
The language of a land which now is free,
And winged with thoughts of truth and majesty
Flits round the tyrant's sceptre like a cloud,
And bursts the peopled prisons, and cries aloud,
'My name is Legion!'—that majestic tongue
Which Calderon over the desert flung
Of ages and of nations; and which found
An echo in our hearts, and with the sound
Startled Oblivion—thou wert then to me
As is a nurse, when inarticulately
A child would talk as its grown parents do.
If living winds the rapid clouds pursue,
If hawks chase doves through the etherial way,
Huntsmen the innocent deer, and beasts their prey,
Why should not we rouse with the spirit's blast
Out of the forest of the pathless past
These recollected pleasures?
                                        You are now
In London, that great sea, whose ebb and flow
At once is deaf and loud, and on the shore
Vomits its wrecks, and still howls on for more.
Yet in its depth what treasures! You will see
That which was Godwin,—greater none than he
Though fallen—and fallen on evil times—to stand
Among the spirits of our age and land,
Before the dread tribunal of *to come*
The foremost—while Rebuke cowers pale and dumb.
You will see Coleridge—he who sits obscure
In the exceeding lustre, and the pure

Intense irradiation of a mind,
Which, with its own internal lightning blind,
Flags wearily through darkness and despair—
A cloud-encircled meteor of the air,
A hooded eagle among blinking owls.—
You will see Hunt—one of those happy souls
Who are the salt of the earth, and without whom
This world would smell like what it is—a tomb;
Who is, what others seem—his room no doubt
Is still adorned with many a cast from Shout,
With graceful flowers tastefully placed about,
And coronals of bay from ribbons hung,
And brighter wreaths in neat disorder flung,
The gifts of the most learn'd among some dozens
Of female friends, sisters-in-law, and cousins.
And there is he with his eternal puns,
Which beat the dullest brain for smiles, like duns
Thundering for money at a poet's door;
Alas! it is no use to say, 'I'm poor!'
Or oft in graver mood, when he will look
Things wiser than were ever read in book,
Except in Shakespeare's wisest tenderness.
You will see Hogg—and I cannot express
His virtues, though I know that they are great,
Because he locks, then barricades the gate
Within which they inhabit;—of his wit
And wisdom, you'll cry out when you are bit.
He is a pearl within an oyster shell,
One of the richest of the deep. And there
Is English Peacock with his mountain fair,
Turned into a Flamingo, that shy bird
That gleams i' the Indian air—have you not heard
When a man marries, dies, or turns Hindoo,
His best friends hear no more of him?—but you
Will see him, and will like him too, I hope,
With the milk-white Snowdonian antelope
Matched with this cameleopard.—His fine wit
Makes such a wound, the knife is lost in it;
A strain too learned for a shallow age,
Too wise for selfish bigots;—let his page
Which charms the chosen spirits of the time,
Fold itself up for the serener clime

Of years to come, and find its recompense
In that just expectation.—Wit and sense,
Virtue and human knowledge, all that might
Make this dull world a business of delight,
Are all combined in Horace Smith—and these,
With some exceptions which I need not tease
Your patience by descanting on,—are all
You and I know in London.
I recall
My thoughts, and bid you look upon the night.
As water does a sponge, so the moonlight
Fills the void, hollow, universal air—
What see you?—unpavilioned heaven is fair
Whether the moon, into her chamber gone,
Leaves midnight to the golden stars, or wan
Climbs with diminished beams the azure steep,
Or whether clouds sail o'er the inverse deep,
Piloted by the many-wandering blast,
And the rare stars rush through them dim and fast:—
All this is beautiful in every land.—
But what see you beside?—a shabby stand
Of hackney-coaches—a brick house or wall
Fencing some lordly court, white with the scrawl
Of our unhappy politics; or worse—
A wretched woman reeling by, whose curse
Mixed with the watchman's, partner of her trade,
You must accept in place of serenade—
Or yellow-haired Pollonia murmuring
To Henry some unutterable thing.
I see a chaos of green leaves and fruit
Built round dark caverns, even to the root
Of the living stems that feed them—in whose bowers
There sleep in their dark dew the folded flowers;
Beyond, the surface of the unsickled corn
Trembles not in the slumbering air, and borne
In circles quaint, and ever-changing dance,
Like winged stars the fire-flies flash and glance
Pale in the open moonshine, but each one
Under the dark trees seems a little sun,
A meteor tamed, a fixed star gone astray
From the silver regions of the Milky Way;—
Afar the contadino's song is heard,

Rude, but made sweet by distance—and a bird
Which cannot be the nightingale, and yet
I know none else that sings so sweet as it
At this late hour—and then all is still—
Now Italy or London, which you will!

Next winter you must pass with me; I'll have
My house by that time turned into a grave
Of dead despondence and low-thoughted care,
And all the dreams which our tormentors are.
Oh! that Hunt, Hogg, Peacock and Smith were there,
With everything belonging to them fair!—
We will have books, Spanish, Italian, Greek;
And ask one week to make another week
As like his father as I'm unlike mine,
Which is not his fault, as you may divine.
Though we eat little flesh and drink no wine,
Yet let's be merry: we'll have tea and toast,
Custards for supper, and an endless host
Of syllabubs and jellies and mince pies,
And other such lady-like luxuries—
Feasting on which we will philosophize!
And we'll have fires out of the Grand Duke's wood
To thaw the six weeks' winter in our blood.
And then we'll talk—what shall we talk about?
Oh! there are themes enough for many a bout
Of thought-entangled descant;—as to nerves,
With cones and parallelograms and curves
I've sworn to strangle them if once they dare
To bother me—when you are with me there,
And they shall never more sip laudanum
From Helicon or Himeros;*—well, come,
And in despite of God and of the devil,
We'll make our friendly philosophic revel
Outlast the leafless time—till buds and flowers
Warn the obscure inevitable hours
Sweet meeting by sad parting to renew—
'Tomorrow to fresh woods and pastures new.'

* Ἵμερος from which the river Himera was named, is, with some slight shade of difference, a synonym of Love. [Shelley's note]

To —— [the Lord Chancellor]

Thy country's curse is on thee, darkest Crest
  Of that foul, knotted, many-headed worm
Which rends our mother's bosom!—Priestly Pest!
  Masked Resurrection of a buried form!

Thy country's curse is on thee—Justice sold,
  Truth trampled, Nature's landmarks overthrown,
And heaps of fraud-accumulated gold
  Plead, loud as thunder, at destruction's throne.

And whilst that sure, slow Fate which ever stands
  Watching the beck of Mutability
Delays to execute her high commands
  And, though a nation weeps, spares thine and thee—

O let a father's curse be on thy soul
  And let a daughter's hope be on thy tomb;
Be both, on thy grey head, a leaden cowl
  To weigh thee down to thine approaching doom.

I curse thee! By a parent's outraged love,—
  By hopes long cherished and too lately lost,—
By gentle feelings thou couldst never prove,
  By griefs which thy stern nature never crossed;

By those infantine smiles of happy light
  Which were a fire within a stranger's hearth
Quenched even when kindled, in untimely night
  Hiding the promise of a lovely birth—

By those unpractised accents of young speech
  Which he who is a father thought to frame
To gentlest lore, such as the wisest teach—
  Thou strike the lyre of mind!—oh grief and shame!

By all the happy see in children's growth,
  That undeveloped flower of budding years—
Sweetness and sadness interwoven both,
  Source of the sweetest hopes, the saddest fears—

By all the days under a hireling's care
  Of dull constraint and bitter heaviness—
Oh wretched ye, if any ever were—
  Sadder than orphans—why not fatherless?

By the false cant which on their innocent lips
  Must hang like poison on an opening bloom,
By the dark creeds which cover with eclipse
  Their pathway from the cradle to the tomb—

By thy complicity with lust and hate:
  Thy thirst for tears—thy hunger after gold—
The ready frauds which ever on thee wait—
  The servile arts in which thou hast grown old.—

By thy most killing sneer, and by thy smile—
  By all the snares and nets of thy black den;
And—(for thou canst outweep the crocodile)—
  By thy false tears—those millstones braining men—

By all the hate which checks a father's love,
  By all the scorn which kills a father's care,
By those most impious hands which dared remove
  Nature's high bounds—by thee—and by despair—

Yes—the despair which bids a father groan
  And cry—'My children are no longer mine—
The blood within their veins may be mine own
  But, Tyrant, their polluted souls are thine';—

I curse thee, though I hate thee not.— O, slave!
  If thou couldst quench that earth-consuming Hell
Of which thou art a daemon, on thy grave
  This curse should be a blessing—Fare thee well!

THE WITCH OF ATLAS

To Mary
(on her objecting to the following poem, upon the score of its containing no human interest)

1

How, my dear Mary, are you critic-bitten
  (For vipers kill, though dead) by some review,
That you condemn these verses I have written
  Because they tell no story, false or true?
What, though no mice are caught by a young kitten,
  May it not leap and play as grown cats do,
Till its claws come? Prithee, for this one time,
Content thee with a visionary rhyme.

2

What hand would crush the silken-winged fly,
  The youngest of inconstant April's minions,
Because it cannot climb the purest sky
  Where the swan sings amid the sun's dominions?
Not thine. Thou knowest 'tis its doom to die
  When day shall hide within her twilight pinions,
The lucent eyes, and the eternal smile,
Serene as thine, which lent it life awhile.

3

To thy fair feet a winged Vision came
  Whose date should have been longer than a day,
And o'er thy head did beat its wings for fame,
  And in thy sight its fading plumes display;
The watery bow burned in the evening flame,
  But the shower fell, the swift sun went his way—
And that is dead.—O, let me not believe
That any thing of mine is fit to live!

4

Wordsworth informs us he was nineteen years
  Considering and retouching Peter Bell;
Watering his laurels with the killing tears
  Of slow, dull care, so that their roots to hell
Might pierce, and their wide branches blot the spheres
  Of heaven, with dewy leaves and flowers; this well
May be, for Heaven and Earth conspire to foil
The over-busy gardener's blundering toil.

5

My Witch indeed is not so sweet a creature
  As Ruth or Lucy, whom his graceful praise
Clothes for our grandsons—but she matches Peter,
  Though he took nineteen years, and she three days
In dressing. Light the vest of flowing metre
  She wears; he, proud as dandy with his stays,
Has hung upon his wiry limbs a dress
Like King Lear's 'looped and windowed raggedness'.

6

If you strip Peter, you will see a fellow
  Scorched by Hell's hyperequatorial climate
Into a kind of a sulphureous yellow,
  A lean mark, hardly fit to fling a rhyme at;
In shape a Scaramouch, in hue Othello.
  If you unveil my Witch, no Priest or Primate
Can shrive you of that sin,—if sin there be
In love, when it becomes idolatry.

The Witch of Atlas

1

Before those cruel Twins, whom at one birth
  Incestuous Change bore to her father Time,
Error and Truth, had hunted from the earth
  All those bright natures which adorned its prime,
And left us nothing to believe in, worth
  The pains of putting into learned rhyme,
A lady-witch there lived on Atlas' mountain
Within a cavern by a secret fountain.

2

Her mother was one of the Atlantides:
  The all-beholding Sun had ne'er beholden
In his wide voyage o'er continents and seas
  So fair a creature, as she lay enfolden
In the warm shadow of her loveliness;—
  He kissed her with his beams, and made all golden
The chamber of grey rock in which she lay—
She, in that dream of joy, dissolved away.

3

'Tis said, she first was changed into a vapour,
  And then into a cloud, such clouds as flit,
Like splendour-winged moths about a taper,
  Round the red west when the sun dies in it:
And then into a meteor, such as caper
  On hill-tops when the moon is in a fit:
Then into one of those mysterious stars
Which hide themselves between the Earth and Mars.

4

Ten times the Mother of the Months had bent
  Her bow beside the folding-star, and bidden
With that bright sign the billows to indent
  The sea-deserted sand—like children chidden,
At her command they ever came and went—
  Since in that cave a dewy splendour hidden
Took shape and motion: with the living form
Of this embodied Power, the cave grew warm.

5

A lovely lady garmented in light
  From her own beauty—deep her eyes, as are
Two openings of unfathomable night
  Seen through a temple's cloven roof—her hair
Dark—the dim brain whirls dizzy with delight
  Picturing her form; her soft smiles shone afar,
And her low voice was heard like love, and drew
All living things towards this wonder new.

6

And first the spotted cameleopard came,
  And then the wise and fearless elephant;
Then the sly serpent, in the golden flame
  Of his own volumes intervolved;—all gaunt
And sanguine beasts her gentle looks made tame.
  They drank before her at her sacred fount;
And every beast of beating heart grew bold,
Such gentleness and power even to behold.

7

The brinded lioness led forth her young,
  That she might teach them how they should forego
Their inborn thirst of death; the pard unstrung
  His sinews at her feet, and sought to know
With looks whose motions spoke without a tongue
  How he might be as gentle as the doe.
The magic circle of her voice and eyes
All savage natures did imparadise.

8

And old Silenus, shaking a green stick
  Of lilies, and the wood-gods in a crew
Came, blithe, as in the olive copses thick
  Cicadae are, drunk with the noonday dew:
And Dryope and Faunus followed quick,
  Teazing the God to sing them something new
Till in this cave they found the lady lone,
Sitting upon a seat of emerald stone.

9

And Universal Pan, 'tis said, was there,
  And though none saw him,—through the adamant
Of the deep mountains, through the trackless air,
  And through those living spirits, like a want
He past out of his everlasting lair
  Where the quick heart of the great world doth pant,
And felt that wondrous lady all alone,—
And she felt him upon her emerald throne.

10

And every nymph of stream and spreading tree
And every shepherdess of Ocean's flocks
Who drives her white waves over the green sea;
And Ocean with the brine on his grey locks,
And quaint Priapus with his company
All came, much wondering how the enwombed rocks
Could have brought forth so beautiful a birth;—
Her love subdued their wonder and their mirth.

11

The herdsmen and the mountain maidens came
And the rude kings of pastoral Garamant—
Their spirits shook within them, as a flame
Stirred by the air under a cavern gaunt:
Pigmies, and Polyphemes, by many a name,
Centaurs and Satyrs, and such shapes as haunt
Wet clefts,—and lumps neither alive nor dead,
Dog-headed, bosom-eyed and bird-footed.

12

For she was beautiful—her beauty made
The bright world dim, and every thing beside
Seemed like the fleeting image of a shade:
No thought of living spirit could abide—
Which to her looks had ever been betrayed—
On any object in the world so wide,
On any hope within the circling skies,
But on her form, and in her inmost eyes.

13

Which when the lady knew, she took her spindle
And twined three threads of fleecy mist, and three
Long lines of light such as the dawn may kindle
The clouds and waves and mountains with, and she
As many star-beams, ere their lamps could dwindle
In the belated moon, wound skilfully;
And with these threads a subtle veil she wove—
A shadow for the splendour of her love.

14

The deep recesses of her odorous dwelling
Were stored with magic treasures—sounds of air,
Which had the power all spirits of compelling,
Folded in cells of chrystal silence there;
Such as we hear in youth, and think the feeling
Will never die—yet ere we are aware,
The feeling and the sound are fled and gone,
And the regret they leave remains alone.

15

And there lay Visions swift, and sweet, and quaint,
Each in its thin sheath like a chrysalis;
Some eager to burst forth, some weak and faint
With the soft burthen of intensest bliss
It was its work to bear to many a saint
Whose heart adores that shrine which holiest is,
Even Love's—and others white, green, grey and black,
And of all shapes—and each was at her beck.

16

And odours in a kind of aviary
Of ever-blooming Eden-trees she kept,
Clipt in a floating net a love-sick Fairy
Had woven from dew-beams while the moon yet slept—
As bats at the wired window of a dairy,
They beat their vans; and each was an adept,
When loosed and missioned, making wings of winds,
To stir sweet thoughts or sad in destined minds.

17

And liquors clear and sweet, whose healthful might
Could medicine the sick soul to happy sleep,
And change eternal death into a night
Of glorious dreams—or if eyes needs must weep,
Could make their tears all wonder and delight,
She in her chrystal vials did closely keep:
If men could drink of those clear vials, 'tis said
The living were not envied of the dead.

18

Her cave was stored with scrolls of strange device,
The works of some Saturnian Archimage,
Which taught the expiations at whose price
Men from the Gods might win that happy age
Too lightly lost, redeeming native vice;
And which might quench the earth-consuming rage
Of gold and blood—till men should live and move
Harmonious as the sacred stars above.

19

And how all things that seem untameable,
Not to be checked and not to be confined,
Obey the spells of wisdom's wizard skill;
Time, Earth and Fire—the Ocean and the Wind
And all their shapes—and man's imperial will;
And other scrolls whose writings did unbind
The inmost lore of Love—let the prophane
Tremble to ask what secrets they contain.

20

And wondrous works of substances unknown,
To which the enchantment of her father's power
Had changed those ragged blocks of savage stone,
Were heaped in the recesses of her bower;
Carved lamps and chalices and phials which shone
In their own golden beams—each like a flower
Out of whose depth a fire-fly shakes his light
Under a cypress in a starless night.

21

At first she lived alone in this wild home,
And her own thoughts were each a minister,
Clothing themselves or with the ocean-foam,
Or with the wind, or with the speed of fire,
To work whatever purposes might come
Into her mind; such power her mighty Sire
Had girt them with, whether to fly or run,
Through all the regions which he shines upon.

22

The Ocean-nymphs and Hamadryades,
  Oreads and Naiads with long weedy locks,
Offered to do her bidding through the seas,
  Under the earth, and in the hollow rocks,
And far beneath the matted roots of trees
  And in the gnarled heart of stubborn oaks,
So they might live forever in the light
Of her sweet presence—each a satellite.

23

'This may not be,' the wizard maid replied;
  'The fountains where the Naiades bedew
Their shining hair at length are drained and dried;
  The solid oaks forget their strength, and strew
Their latest leaf upon the mountains wide;
  The boundless ocean, like a drop of dew
Will be consumed—the stubborn centre must
Be scattered, like a cloud of summer dust—

24

'And ye with them will perish one by one:
  If I must sigh to think that this shall be,
If I must weep when the surviving Sun
  Shall smile on your decay—Oh, ask not me
To love you till your little race is run;
  I cannot die as ye must—over me
Your leaves shall glance—the streams in which ye dwell
Shall be my paths henceforth, and so, farewell!'

25

She spoke and wept—the dark and azure well
  Sparkled beneath the shower of her bright tears,
And every little circlet where they fell
  Flung to the cavern-roof inconstant spheres
And intertangled lines of light—a knell
  Of sobbing voices came upon her ears
From those departing Forms, o'er the serene
Of the white streams and of the forest green.

26

All day the wizard lady sate aloof
  Spelling out scrolls of dread antiquity
Under the cavern's fountain-lighted roof;
  Or broidering the pictured poesy
Of some high tale upon her growing woof,
  Which the sweet splendour of her smiles could dye
In hues outshining heaven—and ever she
Added some grace to the wrought poesy.

27

While on her hearth lay blazing many a piece
  Of sandal wood, rare gums and cinnamon;
Men scarcely know how beautiful fire is—
  Each flame of it is as a precious stone
Dissolved in ever moving light, and this
  Belongs to each and all who gaze upon.
The Witch beheld it not, for in her hand
She held a woof that dimmed the burning brand.

28

This lady never slept, but lay in trance
  All night within the fountain—as in sleep.
Its emerald crags glowed in her beauty's glance:
  Through the green splendour of the water deep
She saw the constellations reel and dance
  Like fire-flies—and withal did ever keep
The tenour of her contemplations calm,
With open eyes, closed feet and folded palm.

29

And when the whirlwinds and the clouds descended
  From the white pinnacles of that cold hill,
She passed at dewfall to a space extended,
  Where in a lawn of flowering asphodel
Amid a wood of pines and cedars blended
  There yawned an inextinguishable well
Of crimson fire, full even to the brim
And overflowing all the margin trim.

30

Within the which she lay when the fierce war
   Of wintry winds shook that innocuous liquor
In many a mimic moon and bearded star,
   O'er woods and lawns—the serpent heard it flicker
In sleep, and dreaming still, he crept afar—
   And when the windless snow descended thicker
Than autumn leaves, she watched it as it came
Melt on the surface of the level flame.

31

She had a Boat which some say Vulcan wrought
   For Venus, as the chariot of her star;
But it was found too feeble to be fraught
   With all the ardours in that sphere which are,
And so she sold it, and Apollo bought
   And gave it to this daughter: from a car
Changed to the fairest and the lightest boat
Which ever upon mortal stream did float.

32

And others say, that when but three hours old
   The first-born Love out of his cradle leapt
And clove dun Chaos with his wings of gold,
   And like an horticultural adept,
Stole a strange seed, and wrapt it up in mould
   And sowed it in his mother's star, and kept
Watering it all the summer with sweet dew,
And with his wings fanning it as it grew.

33

The plant grew strong and green—the snowy flower
   Fell, and the long and gourd-like fruit began
To turn the light and dew by inward power
   To its own substance; woven tracery ran
Of light firm texture, ribbed and branching, o'er
   The solid rind, like a leaf's veined fan—
Of which Love scooped this boat—and with soft motion
Piloted it round the circumfluous ocean.

34

This boat she moored upon her fount, and lit
  A living spirit within all its frame,
Breathing the soul of swiftness into it.
  Couched on the fountain like a panther tame,
One of the twain at Evan's feet that sit—
  Or as on Vesta's sceptre a swift flame—
Or on blind Homer's heart a winged thought—
In joyous expectation lay the boat.

35

Then by strange art she kneaded fire and snow
  Together, tempering the repugnant mass
With liquid love—all things together grow
  Through which the harmony of love can pass;
And a fair Shape out of her hands did flow—
  A living Image, which did far surpass
In beauty that bright shape of vital stone
Which drew the heart out of Pygmalion.

36

A sexless thing it was, and in its growth
  It seemed to have developed no defect
Of either sex, yet all the grace of both—
  In gentleness and strength its limbs were decked;
The bosom swelled lightly with its full youth,
  The countenance was such as might select
Some artist that his skill should never die,
Imaging forth such perfect purity.

37

From its smooth shoulders hung two rapid wings,
  Fit to have borne it to the seventh sphere,
Tipt with the speed of liquid lightenings—
  Dyed in the ardours of the atmosphere.
She led her creature to the boiling springs
  Where the light boat was moored, and said: 'Sit here!'
And pointed to the prow, and took her seat
Beside the rudder with opposing feet.

38

And down the streams which clove those mountains vast,
  Around their inland islets, and amid
The panther-peopled forests, whose shade cast
  Darkness and odours, and a pleasure hid
In melancholy gloom, the pinnace past;
  By many a star-surrounded pyramid
Of icy crag cleaving the purple sky,
And caverns yawning round unfathomably.

39

The silver noon into that winding dell
  With slanted gleam athwart the forest-tops
Tempered like golden evening, feebly fell;
  A green and glowing light, like that which drops
From folded lilies in which glow-worms dwell
  When earth over her face night's mantle wraps;
Between the severed mountains lay on high
Over the stream, a narrow rift of sky.

40

And ever as she went, the Image lay
  With folded wings and unawakened eyes;
And o'er its gentle countenance did play
  The busy dreams, as thick as summer flies,
Chasing the rapid smiles that would not stay,
  And drinking the warm tears, and the sweet sighs
Inhaling, which, with busy murmur vain,
They had aroused from that full heart and brain.

41

And ever down the prone vale, like a cloud
  Upon a stream of wind, the pinnace went:
Now lingering on the pools, in which abode
  The calm and darkness of the deep content
In which they paused; now o'er the shallow road
  Of white and dancing waters all besprent
With sand and polished pebbles—mortal boat
In such a shallow rapid could not float.

42

And down the earthquaking cataracts which shiver
Their snow-like waters into golden air,
Or under chasms unfathomable ever
Sepulchre them, till in their rage they tear
A subterranean portal for the river,
It fled—the circling sunbows did upbear
Its fall down the hoar precipice of spray,
Lighting it far upon its lampless way.

43

And when the wizard lady would ascend
The labyrinths of some many winding vale
Which to the inmost mountain upward tend—
She called 'Hermaphroditus!' and the pale
And heavy hue which slumber could extend
Over its lips and eyes, as on the gale
A rapid shadow from a slope of grass,
Into the darkness of the stream did pass.

44

And it unfurled its heaven-coloured pinions,
With stars of fire spotting the stream below;
And from above into the Sun's dominions
Flinging a glory, like the golden glow
In which Spring clothes her emerald-winged minions,
All interwoven with fine feathery snow
And moonlight splendour of intensest rime
With which frost paints the pines in winter-time.

45

And then it winnowed the Elysian air
Which ever hung about that lady bright,
With its aetherial vans—and speeding there
Like a star up the torrent of the night
Or a swift eagle in the morning glare
Breasting the whirlwind with impetuous flight,
The pinnace, oared by those enchanted wings,
Clove the fierce streams towards their upper springs.

46

The water flashed like sunlight by the prow
  Of a noon-wandering meteor flung to Heaven;
The still air seemed as if its waves did flow
  In tempest down the mountains—loosely driven
The lady's radiant hair streamed to and fro:
  Beneath, the billows having vainly striven
Indignant and impetuous, roared to feel
The swift and steady motion of the keel.

47

Or, when the weary moon was in the wane
  Or in the noon of interlunar night,
The lady-witch in visions could not chain
  Her spirit; but sailed forth under the light
Of shooting stars, and bade extend amain
  Its storm-outspeeding wings, th' Hermaphrodite;
She to the Austral waters took her way
Beyond the fabulous Thamondocana,—

48

Where like a meadow which no scythe has shaven,
  Which rain could never bend, or whirl-blast shake,
With the Antarctic constellations paven,
  Canopus and his crew, lay th' Austral lake—
There she would build herself a windless haven
  Out of the clouds whose moving turrets make
The bastions of the storm, when through the sky
The spirits of the tempest thundered by.

49

A haven beneath whose translucent floor
  The tremulous stars sparkled unfathomably,
And around which, the solid vapours hoar,
  Based on the level waters, to the sky
Lifted their dreadful crags; and like a shore
  Of wintry mountains, inaccessibly
Hemmed in with rifts and precipices grey
And hanging crags, many a cove and bay.

50

And whilst the outer lake beneath the lash
  Of the wind's scourge, foamed like a wounded thing,
And the incessant hail with stony clash
  Ploughed up the waters, and the flagging wing
Of the roused cormorant in the lightning-flash
  Looked like the wreck of some wind-wandering
Fragment of inky thunder-smoke—this haven
Was as a gem to copy Heaven engraven,—

51

On which that lady played her many pranks,
  Circling the image of a shooting star,
Even as a tyger on Hydaspes' banks
  Outspeeds the antelopes which speediest are,
In her light boat; and many quips and cranks
  She played upon the water, till the car
Of the late moon, like a sick matron wan,
To journey from the misty east began.

52

And then she called out of the hollow turrets
  Of those high clouds, white, golden and vermilion,
The armies of her ministering Spirits—
  In mighty legions million after million
They came, each troop emblazoning its merits
  On meteor flags; and many a proud pavilion
Of the intertexture of the atmosphere
They pitched upon the plain of the calm mere.

53

They framed the imperial tent of their great Queen
  Of woven exhalations, underlaid
With lambent lightning-fire, as may be seen
  A dome of thin and open ivory inlaid
With crimson silk—cressets from the serene
  Hung there, and on the water for her tread
A tapestry of fleece-like mist was strewn,
Dyed in the beams of the ascending moon.

54

And on a throne o'erlaid with starlight, caught
  Upon those wandering isles of aëry dew,
Which highest shoals of mountain shipwreck not,
  She sate, and heard all that had happened new
Between the earth and moon since they had brought
  The last intelligence—and now she grew
Pale as that moon lost in the watery night—
And now she wept and now she laughed outright.

55

These were tame pleasures.—She would often climb
  The steepest ladder of the crudded rack
Up to some beaked cape of cloud sublime,
  And like Arion on the dolphin's back
Ride singing through the shoreless air. Oft time
  Following the serpent lightning's winding track,
She ran upon the platforms of the wind
And laughed to hear the fire-balls roar behind.

56

And sometimes to those streams of upper air
  Which whirl the earth in its diurnal round
She would ascend, and win the spirits there
  To let her join their chorus. Mortals found
That on those days the sky was calm and fair,
  And mystic snatches of harmonious sound
Wandered upon the earth where'er she past,
And happy thoughts of hope, too sweet to last.

57

But her choice sport was, in the hours of sleep
  To glide adown old Nilus, where he threads
Egypt and Aethiopia, from the steep
  Of utmost Axumè, until he spreads,
Like a calm flock of silver-fleeced sheep,
  His waters on the plain: and crested heads
Of cities and proud temples gleam amid,
And many a vapour-belted pyramid.

58

By Moeris and the Mareotid lakes,
   Strewn with faint blooms like bridal chamber floors,
Where naked boys bridling tame water-snakes
   Or charioteering ghastly alligators
Had left on the sweet waters mighty wakes
   Of those huge forms—within the brazen doors
Of the great Labyrinth slept both boy and beast,
Tired with the pomp of their Osirian feast.

59

And where within the surface of the river
   The shadows of the massy temples lie
And never are erased—but tremble ever
   Like things which every cloud can doom to die,
Through lotus-pav'n canals, and wheresoever
   The works of man pierced that serenest sky
With tombs, and towers, and fanes, 'twas her delight
To wander in the shadow of the night.

60

With motion like the spirit of that wind
   Whose soft step deepens slumber, her light feet
Past through the peopled haunts of human kind,
   Scattering sweet visions from her presence sweet,
Through fane and palace-court and labyrinth mined
   With many a dark and subterranean street
Under the Nile, through chambers high and deep
She past, observing mortals in their sleep.

61

A pleasure sweet doubtless it was to see
   Mortals subdued in all the shapes of sleep.
Here lay two sister-twins in infancy;
   There, a lone youth who in his dreams did weep;
Within, two lovers linked innocently
   In their loose locks which over both did creep
Like ivy from one stem;—and there lay calm
Old age with snow-bright hair and folded palm.

62

But other troubled forms of sleep she saw,
  Not to be mirrored in a holy song—
Distortions foul of supernatural awe,
  And pale imaginings of visioned wrong,
And all the code of custom's lawless law
  Written upon the brows of old and young:
'This,' said the wizard maiden, 'is the strife
Which stirs the liquid surface of man's life.'

63

And little did the sight disturb her soul—
  We, the weak mariners of that wide lake
Where'er its shores extend or billows roll,
  Our course unpiloted and starless make
O'er its wild surface to an unknown goal—
  But she in the calm depths her way could take
Where in bright bowers immortal forms abide
Beneath the weltering of the restless tide.

64

And she saw princes couched under the glow
  Of sunlike gems; and round each temple-court
In dormitories ranged, row after row,
  She saw the priests asleep—all of one sort,
For all were educated to be so.—
  The peasants in their huts, and in the port
The sailors she saw cradled on the waves,
And the dead lulled within their dreamless graves.

65

And all the forms in which those spirits lay
  Were to her sight like the diaphanous
Veils, in which those sweet ladies oft array
  Their delicate limbs, who would conceal from us
Only their scorn of all concealment: they
  Move in the light of their own beauty thus.
But these and all now lay with sleep upon them
And little thought a Witch was looking on them.

66

She all those human figures breathing there
   Beheld as living spirits—to her eyes
The naked beauty of the soul lay bare,
   And often through a rude and worn disguise
She saw the inner form most bright and fair—
   And then, she had a charm of strange device,
Which, murmured on mute lips with tender tone,
Could make that spirit mingle with her own.

67

Alas, Aurora! what wouldst thou have given
   For such a charm, when Tithon became grey?
Or how much, Venus, of thy silver Heaven
   Wouldst thou have yielded, ere Proserpina
Had half (oh! why not all?) the debt forgiven
   Which dear Adonis had been doomed to pay,
To any witch who would have taught you it?
The Heliad doth not know its value yet.

68

'Tis said in after times her spirit free
   Knew what love was, and felt itself alone—
But holy Dian could not chaster be
   Before she stooped to kiss Endymion
Than now this lady—like a sexless bee
   Tasting all blossoms and confined to none—
Among those mortal forms the wizard-maiden
Passed with an eye serene and heart unladen.

69

To those she saw most beautiful, she gave
   Strange panacea in a chrystal bowl.
They drank in their deep sleep of that sweet wave,
   And lived thenceforward as if some controul
Mightier than life, were in them; and the grave
   Of such, when death oppressed the weary soul,
Was as a green and overarching bower
Lit by the gems of many a starry flower.

70

For on the night that they were buried, she
  Restored the embalmer's ruining, and shook
The light out of the funeral lamps, to be
  A mimic day within that deathy nook;
And she unwound the woven imagery
  Of second childhood's swaddling bands and took
The coffin, its last cradle, from its niche
And threw it with contempt into a ditch.

71

And there the body lay, age after age,
  Mute, breathing, beating, warm and undecaying
Like one asleep in a green hermitage
  With gentle smiles about its eyelids playing
And living in its dreams beyond the rage
  Of death or life; while they were still arraying
In liveries ever new, the rapid, blind
And fleeting generations of mankind.

72

And she would write strange dreams upon the brain
  Of those who were less beautiful, and make
All harsh and crooked purposes more vain
  Than in the desart is the serpent's wake
Which the sand covers—all his evil gain
  The miser in such dreams would rise and shake
Into a beggar's lap;—the lying scribe
Would his own lies betray without a bribe.

73

The priests would write an explanation full,
  Translating hieroglyphics into Greek,
How the god Apis really was a bull
  And nothing more; and bid the herald stick
The same against the temple doors, and pull
  The old cant down; they licensed all to speak
Whate'er they thought of hawks, and cats, and geese,
By pastoral letters to each diocese.

74

The king would dress an ape up in his crown
  And robes, and seat him on his glorious seat,
And on the right hand of the sunlike throne
  Would place a gaudy mock-bird to repeat
The chatterings of the monkey.—Every one
  Of the prone courtiers crawled to kiss the feet
Of their great Emperor when the morning came,
And kissed—alas, how many kiss the same!

75

The soldiers dreamed that they were blacksmiths, and
  Walked out of quarters in somnambulism;
Round the red anvils you might see them stand
  Like Cyclopses in Vulcan's sooty abysm,
Beating their swords to ploughshares;—in a band
  The jailors sent those of the liberal schism
Free through the streets of Memphis, much, I wis,
To the annoyance of king Amasis.

76

And timid lovers who had been so coy
  They hardly knew whether they loved or not,
Would rise out of their rest, and take sweet joy
  To the fulfilment of their inmost thought;
And when next day the maiden and the boy
  Met one another, both, like sinners caught,
Blushed at the thing which each believed was done
Only in fancy—till the tenth moon shone;

77

And then the Witch would let them take no ill:
  Of many thousand schemes which lovers find,
The Witch found one,—and so they took their fill
  Of happiness in marriage warm and kind.
Friends who by practice of some envious skill,
  Were torn apart, a wide wound, mind from mind!
She did unite again with visions clear
Of deep affection and of truth sincere.

78

These were the pranks she played among the cities
  Of mortal men, and what she did to sprites
And Gods, entangling them in her sweet ditties
  To do her will, and shew their subtle slights,
I will declare another time; for it is
  A tale more fit for the weird winter nights
Than for these garish summer days, when we
Scarcely believe much more than we can see.

Sonnet: Political Greatness

Nor happiness, nor majesty nor fame,
Nor peace nor strength, nor skill in arms or arts
Shepherd those herds whom Tyranny makes tame:
Verse echoes not one beating of their hearts;
History is but the shadow of their shame;
Art veils her glass, or from the pageant starts
As to oblivion their blind millions fleet
Staining that Heaven with obscene imagery
Of their own likeness. What are numbers, knit
By force or custom? Man, who man would be,
Must rule the empire of himself; in it
Must be supreme, establishing his throne
On vanquished will; quelling the anarchy
Of hopes and fears; being himself alone.

Sonnet ('Ye hasten to the grave!')

Ye hasten to the grave! What seek ye there,
Ye restless thoughts, and busy purposes
Of the idle brain, which the world's livery wear?
O thou quick Heart which pantest to possess
All that pale Expectation feigneth fair!
Thou vainly curious mind which wouldest guess
Whence thou didst come, and whither thou must go,
And all, that never yet was known, wouldst know;
O whither hasten ye, that thus ye press
With such swift feet life's green and pleasant path
Seeking alike from happiness and woe
A refuge in the cavern of grey death?
O Heart and Mind and Thoughts, what thing do you
Hope to inherit in the grave below?

The Fugitives

1

The waters are flashing—
The white hail is dashing—
The lightnings are glancing—
The hoar spray is dancing—
Away!—
The whirlwind is rolling—
The thunder is tolling—
The forest is swinging—
The minster bells ringing—
Come away!
The Earth is like Ocean
Wreck-strewn and in motion:
Bird, beast, man and worm
Have crept out of the storm—
Come away!

2

'Our boat has one sail—
And the helmsman is pale—
A bold pilot I trow
Who should follow us now,'—
Shouted he.—
And she cried 'Ply the oar!
Put off gaily from shore'—
As she spoke, bolts of death
Mixed with hail, specked their path
O'er the sea.
And from isle, tower and rock
The blue beacon-cloud broke
And though dumb in the blast,
The red cannon flashed fast
From the lee.

3

And, fear'st thou, and fear'st thou?
And, see'st thou, and hear'st thou?
And, drive we not free

O'er the terrible Sea,
I and thou?
One boat-cloak doth cover
The loved and the lover—
Their blood beats one measure,
They murmur proud pleasure
Soft and low;
While around, the lashed Ocean,
Like mountains in motion,
Is withdrawn and uplifted,
Sunk, shattered and shifted
To and fro.

4

In the court of the fortress
Beside the pale portress,
Like a bloodhound well beaten,
The bridegroom stands, eaten
By shame.
On the topmost watch-turret,
As a death-boding spirit,
Stands the grey tyrant Father—
To his voice the mad weather
Seems tame;
And with Curses as wild
As e're clung to a child
He devotes to the blast
The best, loveliest and last
Of his name.

Memory ('Rose leaves, when the rose is dead')

Rose leaves, when the rose is dead,
Are heaped for the beloved's bed—
And so thy thoughts, when thou art gone,
Love itself shall slumber on . . .

Music, when soft voices die,
Vibrates in the memory.—
Odours, when sweet violets sicken,
Live within the sense they quicken.

Dirge for the Year

Orphan hours, the year is dead,
  Come and sigh, come and weep!
Merry hours smile instead,
  For the year is but asleep;
See it smiles as it is sleeping,
Mocking your untimely weeping.

As an Earthquake rocks a corse
  In its coffin in the clay,
So white Winter, that rough Nurse,
  Rocks the death-cold year today!
Solemn hours, wail aloud
For your mother in her shroud.

As the wild air stirs and sways
  The tree-swung cradle of a child,
So the breath of these rude days
  Rocks the year—be calm and mild,
Trembling hours, she will arise
With new love within her eyes . . .

January grey is here
  Like a sexton by her grave—
February bears the bier—
  March with grief doth howl and rave—
And April weeps—

EPIPSYCHIDION

Verses Addressed to the Noble and Unfortunate Lady Emilia V——, Now Imprisoned in the Convent of ——

> L'anima amante si slancia fuori del creato, e si crea nel infinito un Mondo tutto per essa, diverso assai da questo oscuro e pauroso baratro.
>
> HER OWN WORDS.

ADVERTISEMENT

The Writer of the following Lines died at Florence, as he was preparing for a voyage to one of the wildest of the Sporades, which he had bought, and where he had fitted up the ruins of an old building, and where it was his hope to have realised a scheme of life, suited perhaps to that happier and better world of which he is now an inhabitant, but hardly practicable in this. His life was singular; less on account of the romantic vicissitudes which diversified it, than the ideal tinge which it received from his own character and feelings. The present Poem, like the *Vita Nuova* of Dante, is sufficiently intelligible to a certain class of readers without a matter-of-fact history of the circumstances to which it relates; and to a certain other class it must ever remain incomprehensible, from a defect of a common organ of perception for the ideas of which it treats. Not but that, *gran vergogna sarebbe a colui, che rimasse cosa sotto veste di figura, o di colore rettorico: e domandato non sapesse denudare le sue parole da cotal veste, in guisa che avessero verace intendimento.*

The present poem appears to have been intended by the Writer as the dedication to some longer one. The stanza on the opposite page is almost a literal translation from Dante's famous Canzone

Voi, ch'intendendo, il terzo ciel movete, &c.

The presumptuous application of the concluding lines to his own composition will raise a smile at the expense of my unfortunate friend: be it a smile not of contempt, but pity.

S.

My Song, I fear that thou wilt find but few
Who fitly shall conceive thy reasoning,
Of such hard matter dost thou entertain;
Whence, if by misadventure, chance should bring
Thee to base company, (as chance may do),
Quite unaware of what thou dost contain,
I prithee, comfort thy sweet self again,
My last delight! tell them that they are dull,
And bid them own that thou art beautiful.

Epipsychidion

Sweet Spirit! Sister of that orphan one,
Whose empire is the name thou weepest on,
In my heart's temple I suspend to thee
These votive wreaths of withered memory.

Poor captive bird! who, from thy narrow cage,
Pourest such music, that it might assuage
The rugged hearts of those who prisoned thee,
Were they not deaf to all sweet melody;
This song shall be thy rose: its petals pale
Are dead, indeed, my adored Nightingale!
But soft and fragrant is the faded blossom,
And it has no thorn left to wound thy bosom.

High, spirit-wingèd Heart! who dost for ever
Beat thine unfeeling bars with vain endeavour,
'Till those bright plumes of thought, in which arrayed
It over-soared this low and worldly shade,
Lie shattered; and thy panting, wounded breast
Stains with dear blood its unmaternal nest!
I weep vain tears: blood would less bitter be,
Yet poured forth gladlier, could it profit thee.

Seraph of Heaven! too gentle to be human,
Veiling beneath that radiant form of Woman
All that is insupportable in thee
Of light, and love, and immortality!
Sweet Benediction in the eternal Curse!
Veiled Glory of this lampless Universe!
Thou Moon beyond the clouds! Thou living Form
Among the Dead! Thou Star above the Storm!
Thou Wonder, and thou Beauty, and thou Terror!
Thou Harmony of Nature's art! Thou Mirror
In whom, as in the splendour of the Sun,
All shapes look glorious which thou gazest on!
Aye, even the dim words which obscure thee now
Flash, lightning-like, with unaccustomed glow;
I pray thee that thou blot from this sad song
All of its much mortality and wrong,
With those clear drops, which start like sacred dew
From the twin lights thy sweet soul darkens through,
Weeping, till sorrow becomes ecstasy:
Then smile on it, so that it may not die.

I never thought before my death to see
Youth's vision thus made perfect. Emily,
I love thee; though the world by no thin name
Will hide that love, from its unvalued shame.
Would we two had been twins of the same mother!
Or, that the name my heart lent to another
Could be a sister's bond for her and thee,
Blending two beams of one eternity!
Yet were one lawful and the other true,
These names, though dear, could paint not, as is due,
How beyond refuge I am thine. Ah me!
I am not thine: I am a part of *thee*.

Sweet Lamp! my moth-like Muse has burnt its wings;
Or, like a dying swan who soars and sings,
Young Love should teach Time, in his own grey style,
All that thou art. Art thou not void of guile,
A lovely soul formed to be blest and bless?
A well of sealed and secret happiness,
Whose waters like blithe light and music are,
Vanquishing dissonance and gloom? A Star

Which moves not in the moving Heavens, alone?
A smile amid dark frowns? a gentle tone
Amid rude voices? a beloved light?
A Solitude, a Refuge, a Delight?
A lute, which those whom love has taught to play
Make music on, to soothe the roughest day
And lull fond grief asleep? a buried treasure?
A cradle of young thoughts of wingless pleasure?
A violet-shrouded grave of Woe?—I measure
The world of fancies, seeking one like thee,
And find—alas! mine own infirmity.

She met me, Stranger, upon life's rough way,
And lured me towards sweet Death; as Night by Day,
Winter by Spring, or Sorrow by swift Hope,
Led into light, life, peace. An antelope,
In the suspended impulse of its lightness,
Were less ethereally light: the brightness
Of her divinest presence trembles through
Her limbs, as underneath a cloud of dew
Embodied in the windless Heaven of June
Amid the splendour-winged stars, the Moon
Burns, inextinguishably beautiful:
And from her lips, as from a hyacinth full
Of honey-dew, a liquid murmur drops,
Killing the sense with passion; sweet as stops
Of planetary music heard in trance.
In her mild lights the starry spirits dance,
The sun-beams of those wells which ever leap
Under the lightnings of the soul—too deep
For the brief fathom-line of thought or sense.
The glory of her being, issuing thence,
Stains the dead, blank, cold air with a warm shade
Of unentangled intermixture, made
By Love, of light and motion: one intense
Diffusion, one serene Omnipresence,
Whose flowing outlines mingle in their flowing,
Around her cheeks and utmost fingers glowing
With the unintermitted blood, which there
Quivers, (as in a fleece of snow-like air
The crimson pulse of living morning quiver),
Continuously prolonged, and ending never,

Till they are lost, and in that Beauty furled
Which penetrates and clasps and fills the world;
Scarce visible from extreme loveliness.
Warm fragrance seems to fall from her light dress,
And her loose hair; and where some heavy tress
The air of her own speed has disentwined,
The sweetness seems to satiate the faint wind;
And in the soul a wild odour is felt,
Beyond the sense, like fiery dews that melt
Into the bosom of a frozen bud.—
See where she stands! a mortal shape indued
With love and life and light and deity,
And motion which may change but cannot die;
An image of some bright Eternity;
A shadow of some golden dream; a Splendour
Leaving the third sphere pilotless; a tender
Reflection of the eternal Moon of Love
Under whose motions life's dull billows move;
A Metaphor of Spring and Youth and Morning;
A Vision like incarnate April, warning,
With smiles and tears, Frost the Anatomy
Into his summer grave.
Ah, woe is me!
What have I dared? where am I lifted? how
Shall I descend, and perish not? I know
That Love makes all things equal: I have heard
By mine own heart this joyous truth averred:
The spirit of the worm beneath the sod
In love and worship, blends itself with God.

Spouse! Sister! Angel! Pilot of the Fate
Whose course has been so starless! O too late
Beloved! O too soon adored, by me!
For in the fields of immortality
My spirit should at first have worshipped thine,
A divine presence in a place divine;
Or should have moved beside it on this earth,
A shadow of that substance, from its birth;
But not as now:—I love thee; yes, I feel
That on the fountain of my heart a seal
Is set, to keep its waters pure and bright
For thee, since in those *tears* thou hast delight.

We—are we not formed, as notes of music are,
For one another, though dissimilar;
Such difference without discord, as can make
Those sweetest sounds, in which all spirits shake
As trembling leaves in a continuous air?

Thy wisdom speaks in me, and bids me dare
Beacon the rocks on which high hearts are wreckt.
I never was attached to that great sect,
Whose doctrine is, that each one should select
Out of the crowd a mistress or a friend,
And all the rest, though fair and wise, commend
To cold oblivion, though it is in the code
Of modern morals, and the beaten road
Which those poor slaves with weary footsteps tread,
Who travel to their home among the dead
By the broad highway of the world, and so
With one chained friend, perhaps a jealous foe,
The dreariest and the longest journey go.

True Love in this differs from gold and clay,
That to divide is not to take away.
Love is like understanding, that grows bright,
Gazing on many truths; 'tis like thy light,
Imagination! which from earth and sky,
And from the depths of human phantasy,
As from a thousand prisms and mirrors, fills
The Universe with glorious beams, and kills
Error, the worm, with many a sun-like arrow
Of its reverberated lightning. Narrow
The heart that loves, the brain that contemplates,
The life that wears, the spirit that creates
One object, and one form, and builds thereby
A sepulchre for its eternity.

Mind from its object differs most in this:
Evil from good; misery from happiness;
The baser from the nobler; the impure
And frail, from what is clear and must endure.
If you divide suffering and dross, you may
Diminish till it is consumed away;
If you divide pleasure and love and thought,

Each part exceeds the whole; and we know not
How much, while any yet remains unshared,
Of pleasure may be gained, of sorrow spared:
This truth is that deep well, whence sages draw
The unenvied light of hope; the eternal law
By which those live, to whom this world of life
Is as a garden ravaged, and whose strife
Tills for the promise of a later birth
The wilderness of this Elysian earth.

There was a Being whom my spirit oft
Met on its visioned wanderings, far aloft,
In the clear golden prime of my youth's dawn,
Upon the fairy isles of sunny lawn,
Amid the enchanted mountains, and the caves
Of divine sleep, and on the air-like waves
Of wonder-level dream, whose tremulous floor
Paved her light steps;—on an imagined shore,
Under the grey beak of some promontory
She met me, robed in such exceeding glory,
That I beheld her not. In solitudes
Her voice came to me through the whispering woods,
And from the fountains, and the odours deep
Of flowers, which, like lips murmuring in their sleep
Of the sweet kisses which had lulled them there,
Breathed but of *her* to the enamoured air;
And from the breezes whether low or loud,
And from the rain of every passing cloud,
And from the singing of the summer-birds,
And from all sounds, all silence. In the words
Of antique verse and high romance,—in form,
Sound, colour—in whatever checks that Storm
Which with the shattered present chokes the past;
And in that best philosophy, whose taste
Makes this cold common hell, our life, a doom
As glorious as a fiery martyrdom;
Her Spirit was the harmony of truth.—

Then, from the caverns of my dreamy youth
I sprang, as one sandalled with plumes of fire,
And towards the loadstar of my one desire,

I flitted, like a dizzy moth, whose flight
Is as a dead leaf's in the owlet light,
When it would seek in Hesper's setting sphere
A radiant death, a fiery sepulchre,
As if it were a lamp of earthly flame.—
But She, whom prayers or tears then could not tame,
Past, like a God throned on a winged planet,
Whose burning plumes to tenfold swiftness fan it,
Into the dreary cone of our life's shade;
And as a man with mighty loss dismayed,
I would have followed, though the grave between
Yawned like a gulf whose spectres are unseen:
When a voice said:—'O Thou of hearts the weakest,
The phantom is beside thee whom thou seekest.'
Then I—'where?'—the world's echo answered 'where!'
And in that silence, and in my despair,
I questioned every tongueless wind that flew
Over my tower of mourning, if it knew
Whither 'twas fled, this soul out of my soul;
And murmured names and spells which have controul
Over the sightless tyrants of our fate;
But neither prayer nor verse could dissipate
The night which closed on her; nor uncreate
That world within this Chaos, mine and me,
Of which she was the veiled Divinity,
The world I say of thoughts that worshipped her:
And therefore I went forth, with hope and fear
And every gentle passion sick to death,
Feeding my course with expectation's breath,
Into the wintry forest of our life;
And struggling through its error with vain strife,
And stumbling in my weakness and my haste,
And half bewildered by new forms, I past,
Seeking among those untaught foresters
If I could find one form resembling hers,
In which she might have masked herself from me.
There,—One, whose voice was venomed melody
Sate by a well, under blue night-shade bowers;
The breath of her false mouth was like faint flowers,
Her touch was as electric poison,—flame
Out of her looks into my vitals came,

And from her living cheeks and bosom flew
A killing air, which pierced like honey-dew
Into the core of my green heart, and lay
Upon its leaves; until, as hair grown grey
O'er a young brow, they hid its unblown prime
With ruins of unseasonable time.

In many mortal forms I rashly sought
The shadow of that idol of my thought.
And some were fair—but beauty dies away:
Others were wise—but honeyed words betray:
And One was true—oh! why not true to me?
Then, as a hunted deer that could not flee,
I turned upon my thoughts, and stood at bay,
Wounded and weak and panting; the cold day
Trembled, for pity of my strife and pain.
When, like a noon-day dawn, there shone again
Deliverance. One stood on my path who seemed
As like the glorious shape which I had dreamed,
As is the Moon, whose changes ever run
Into themselves, to the eternal Sun;
The cold chaste Moon, the Queen of Heaven's bright isles,
Who makes all beautiful on which she smiles,
That wandering shrine of soft yet icy flame
Which ever is transformed, yet still the same,
And warms not but illumines. Young and fair
As the descended Spirit of that sphere,
She hid me, as the Moon may hide the night
From its own darkness, until all was bright
Between the Heaven and Earth of my calm mind,
And, as a cloud charioted by the wind,
She led me to a cave in that wild place,
And sate beside me, with her downward face
Illumining my slumbers, like the Moon
Waxing and waning o'er Endymion.
And I was laid asleep, spirit and limb,
And all my being became bright or dim
As the Moon's image in a summer sea,
According as she smiled or frowned on me;
And there I lay, within a chaste cold bed:
Alas, I then was nor alive nor dead:—
For at her silver voice came Death and Life,

Unmindful each of their accustomed strife,
Masked like twin babes, a sister and a brother,
The wandering hopes of one abandoned mother,
And through the cavern without wings they flew,
And cried, 'Away, he is not of our crew.'
I wept, and though it be a dream, I weep.

What storms then shook the ocean of my sleep,
Blotting that Moon, whose pale and waning lips
Then shrank as in the sickness of eclipse;—
And how my soul was as a lampless sea,
And who was then its Tempest; and when She,
The Planet of that hour, was quenched, what frost
Crept o'er those waters, 'till from coast to coast
The moving billows of my being fell
Into a death of ice, immoveable;—
And then—what earthquakes made it gape and split,
The white Moon smiling all the while on it,
These words conceal:— If not, each word would be
The key of staunchless tears. Weep not for me!

At length, into the obscure Forest came
The Vision I had sought through grief and shame.
Athwart that wintry wilderness of thorns
Flashed from her motion splendour like the Morn's,
And from her presence life was radiated
Through the grey earth and branches bare and dead;
So that her way was paved, and roofed above
With flowers as soft as thoughts of budding love;
And music from her respiration spread
Like light,—all other sounds were penetrated
By the small, still, sweet spirit of that sound,
So that the savage winds hung mute around;
And odours warm and fresh fell from her hair
Dissolving the dull cold in the frore air:
Soft as an Incarnation of the Sun,
When light is changed to love, this glorious One
Floated into the cavern where I lay,
And called my Spirit, and the dreaming clay
Was lifted by the thing that dreamed below
As smoke by fire, and in her beauty's glow

I stood, and felt the dawn of my long night
Was penetrating me with living light:
I knew it was the Vision veiled from me
So many years—that it was Emily.

Twin Spheres of light who rule this passive Earth,
This world of love, this *me*; and into birth
Awaken all its fruits and flowers, and dart
Magnetic might into its central heart;
And lift its billows and its mists, and guide
By everlasting laws, each wind and tide
To its fit cloud, and its appointed cave;
And lull its storms, each in the craggy grave
Which was its cradle, luring to faint bowers
The armies of the rainbow-winged showers;
And, as those married lights, which from the towers
Of Heaven look forth and fold the wandering globe
In liquid sleep and splendour, as a robe;
And all their many-mingled influence blend,
If equal, yet unlike, to one sweet end;—
So ye, bright regents, with alternate sway
Govern my sphere of being, night and day!
Thou, not disdaining even a borrowed might;
Thou, not eclipsing a remoter light;
And, through the shadow of the seasons three,
From Spring to Autumn's sere maturity,
Light it into the Winter of the tomb,
Where it may ripen to a brighter bloom.
Thou too, O Comet beautiful and fierce,
Who drew the heart of this frail Universe
Towards thine own; till, wreckt in that convulsion,
Alternating attraction and repulsion,
Thine went astray and that was rent in twain;
Oh, float into our azure heaven again!
Be there love's folding-star at thy return;
The living Sun will feed thee from its urn
Of golden fire; the Moon will veil her horn
In thy last smiles; adoring Even and Morn
Will worship thee with incense of calm breath
And lights and shadows; as the star of Death
And Birth is worshipped by those sisters wild
Called Hope and Fear—upon the heart are piled

Their offerings,—of this sacrifice divine
A World shall be the altar.
Lady mine,
Scorn not these flowers of thought, the fading birth
Which from its heart of hearts that plant puts forth
Whose fruit, made perfect by thy sunny eyes,
Will be as of the trees of Paradise.

The day is come, and thou wilt fly with me.
To whatsoe'er of dull mortality
Is mine, remain a vestal sister still;
To the intense, the deep, the imperishable,
Not mine but me, henceforth be thou united
Even as a bride, delighting and delighted.
The hour is come:—the destined Star has risen
Which shall descend upon a vacant prison.
The walls are high, the gates are strong, thick set
The sentinels—but true love never yet
Was thus constrained: it overleaps all fence:
Like lightning, with invisible violence
Piercing its continents; like Heaven's free breath,
Which he who grasps can hold not; liker Death,
Who rides upon a thought, and makes his way
Through temple, tower, and palace, and the array
Of arms: more strength has Love than he or they;
For it can burst his charnel, and make free
The limbs in chains, the heart in agony,
The soul in dust and chaos.
Emily,
A ship is floating in the harbour now,
A wind is hovering o'er the mountain's brow;
There is a path on the sea's azure floor,
No keel has ever ploughed that path before;
The halcyons brood around the foamless isles;
The treacherous Ocean has forsworn its wiles;
The merry mariners are bold and free:
Say, my heart's sister, wilt thou sail with me?
Our bark is as an albatross, whose nest
Is a far Eden of the purple East;
And we between her wings will sit, while Night
And Day, and Storm, and Calm, pursue their flight,
Our ministers, along the boundless Sea,

Treading each other's heels, unheededly.
It is an isle under Ionian skies,
Beautiful as a wreck of Paradise,
And, for the harbours are not safe and good,
This land would have remained a solitude
But for some pastoral people native there,
Who from the Elysian, clear, and golden air
Draw the last spirit of the age of gold,
Simple and spirited; innocent and bold.
The blue Aegean girds this chosen home,
With ever-changing sound and light and foam,
Kissing the sifted sands, and caverns hoar;
And all the winds wandering along the shore
Undulate with the undulating tide:
There are thick woods where sylvan forms abide;
And many a fountain, rivulet, and pond,
As clear as elemental diamond,
Or serene morning air; and far beyond,
The mossy tracks made by the goats and deer
(Which the rough shepherd treads but once a year),
Pierce into glades, caverns, and bowers, and halls
Built round with ivy, which the waterfalls
Illumining, with sound that never fails
Accompany the noon-day nightingales;
And all the place is peopled with sweet airs;
The light clear element which the isle wears
Is heavy with the scent of lemon-flowers,
Which floats like mist laden with unseen showers,
And falls upon the eye-lids like faint sleep;
And from the moss violets and jonquils peep,
And dart their arrowy odour through the brain
'Till you might faint with that delicious pain.
And every motion, odour, beam, and tone,
With that deep music is in unison:
Which is a soul within the soul—they seem
Like echoes of an antenatal dream.—
It is an isle 'twixt Heaven, Air, Earth, and Sea,
Cradled, and hung in clear tranquillity;
Bright as that wandering Eden Lucifer,
Washed by the soft blue Oceans of young air.
It is a favoured place. Famine or Blight,
Pestilence, War and Earthquake, never light

Upon its mountain-peaks; blind vultures, they
Sail onward far upon their fatal way:
The winged storms, chaunting their thunder-psalm
To other lands, leave azure chasms of calm
Over this isle, or weep themselves in dew,
From which its fields and woods ever renew
Their green and golden immortality.
And from the sea there rise, and from the sky
There fall, clear exhalations, soft and bright,
Veil after veil, each hiding some delight,
Which Sun or Moon or zephyr draw aside,
Till the isle's beauty, like a naked bride
Glowing at once with love and loveliness,
Blushes and trembles at its own excess:
Yet, like a buried lamp, a Soul no less
Burns in the heart of this delicious isle,
An atom of th' Eternal, whose own smile
Unfolds itself, and may be felt not seen
O'er the grey rocks, blue waves, and forests green,
Filling their bare and void interstices.—
But the chief marvel of the wilderness
Is a lone dwelling, built by whom or how
None of the rustic island-people know:
'Tis not a tower of strength, though with its height
It overtops the woods; but, for delight,
Some wise and tender Ocean-King, ere crime
Had been invented, in the world's young prime,
Reared it, a wonder of that simple time,
An envy of the isles, a pleasure-house
Made sacred to his sister and his spouse.
It scarce seems now a wreck of human art,
But, as it were Titanic; in the heart
Of Earth having assumed its form, then grown
Out of the mountains, from the living stone,
Lifting itself in caverns light and high:
For all the antique and learned imagery
Has been erased, and in the place of it
The ivy and the wild-vine interknit
The volumes of their many twining stems;
Parasite flowers illume with dewy gems
The lampless halls, and when they fade, the sky
Peeps through their winter-woof of tracery

With Moon-light patches, or star atoms keen,
Or fragments of the day's intense serene;—
Working mosaic on their Parian floors.
And, day and night, aloof, from the high towers
And terraces, the Earth and Ocean seem
To sleep in one another's arms, and dream
Of waves, flowers, clouds, woods, rocks, and all that we
Read in their smiles, and call reality.

This isle and house are mine, and I have vowed
Thee to be lady of the solitude.—
And I have fitted up some chambers there
Looking towards the golden Eastern air,
And level with the living winds, which flow
Like waves above the living waves below.—
I have sent books and music there, and all
Those instruments with which high spirits call
The future from its cradle, and the past
Out of its grave, and make the present last
In thoughts and joys which sleep, but cannot die,
Folded within their own eternity.
Our simple life wants little, and true taste
Hires not the pale drudge Luxury, to waste
The scene it would adorn, and therefore still,
Nature, with all her children, haunts the hill.
The ring-dove, in the embowering ivy, yet
Keeps up her love-lament, and the owls flit
Round the evening tower, and the young stars glance
Between the quick bats in their twilight dance;
The spotted deer bask in the fresh moon-light
Before our gate, and the slow, silent night
Is measured by the pants of their calm sleep.
Be this our home in life, and when years heap
Their withered hours, like leaves, on our decay,
Let us become the over-hanging day,
The living soul of this Elysian isle,
Conscious, inseparable, one. Meanwhile
We two will rise, and sit, and walk together,
Under the roof of blue Ionian weather,
And wander in the meadows, or ascend
The mossy mountains, where the blue heavens bend
With lightest winds, to touch their paramour;

Or linger, where the pebble-paven shore,
Under the quick, faint kisses of the sea
Trembles and sparkles as with ecstacy,—
Possessing and possest by all that is
Within that calm circumference of bliss,
And by each other, till to love and live
Be one:—or, at the noontide hour, arrive
Where some old cavern hoar seems yet to keep
The moonlight of the expired night asleep,
Through which the awakened day can never peep;
A veil for our seclusion, close as Night's,
Where secure sleep may kill thine innocent lights;
Sleep, the fresh dew of languid love, the rain
Whose drops quench kisses till they burn again.
And we will talk, until thought's melody
Become too sweet for utterance, and it die
In words, to live again in looks, which dart
With thrilling tone into the voiceless heart,
Harmonizing silence without a sound.
Our breath shall intermix, our bosoms bound,
And our veins beat together; and our lips
With other eloquence than words, eclipse
The soul that burns between them, and the wells
Which boil under our being's inmost cells,
The fountains of our deepest life, shall be
Confused in passion's golden purity,
As mountain-springs under the morning Sun.
We shall become the same, we shall be one
Spirit within two frames, oh! wherefore two?
One passion in twin-hearts, which grows and grew,
'Till, like two meteors of expanding flame,
Those spheres instinct with it become the same,
Touch, mingle, are transfigured; ever still
Burning, yet ever inconsumable:
In one another's substance finding food,
Like flames too pure and light and unimbued
To nourish their bright lives with baser prey,
Which point to Heaven and cannot pass away:
One hope within two wills, one will beneath
Two overshadowing minds, one life, one death,
One Heaven, one Hell, one immortality,
And one annihilation. Woe is me!

The winged words on which my soul would pierce
Into the height of love's rare Universe,
Are chains of lead around its flight of fire.—
I pant, I sink, I tremble, I expire!

Weak Verses, go, kneel at your Sovereign's feet,
And say:—'We are the masters of thy slave;
What wouldest thou with us and ours and thine?'
Then call your sisters from Oblivion's cave,
All singing loud: 'Love's very pain is sweet,
But its reward is in the world divine
Which, if not here, it builds beyond the grave.'
So shall ye live when I am there. Then haste
Over the hearts of men, until ye meet
Marina, Vanna, Primus, and the rest,
And bid them love each other and be blest:
And leave the troop which errs, and which reproves,
And come and be my guest,—for I am Love's.

ADONAIS

An Elegy on the Death of John Keats, Author of Endymion, Hyperion Etc.

Ἀστὴρ πρὶν μὲν ἔλαμπες ἐνὶ ζωοῖσιν Ἑῷος·
νῦν δὲ θανὼν λάμπεις Ἕσπερος ἐν φθιμενοις.

PLATO

PREFACE

Φάρμακον ἦλθε, Βίων, ποτὶ σὸν στόμα, φάρμακον εἶδες.
Πῶς τευ τοῖς χείλεσσι ποτέδραμε, κοὐκ ἐγλυκάνθη;
Τίς δὲ βροτὸς τοσσοῦτον ἀνάμερος, ἢ κεράσαι τοι,
Ἒ δοῦναι λαλέοντι τὸ φάρμακον; ἔκφυγεν ᾠδάν.

MOSCHUS, EPITAPH. BION.

It is my intention to subjoin to the London edition of this poem, a criticism upon the claims of its lamented object to be classed among the writers of the highest genius who have adorned our age. My known repugnance to the narrow principles of taste on which several of his earlier compositions were modelled, prove, at least that I am an impartial judge. I consider the fragment of *Hyperion*, as second to nothing that was ever produced by a writer of the same years.

John Keats died at Rome of a consumption, in his twenty-fourth year, on the — of — 1821; and was buried in the romantic and lonely cemetery of the protestants in that city, under the pyramid which is the tomb of Cestius, and the massy walls and towers, now mouldering and desolate, which formed the circuit of ancient Rome. The cemetery is an open space among the ruins, covered in winter with violets and daisies. It might make one in love with death, to think that one should be buried in so sweet a place.

The genius of the lamented person to whose memory I have dedicated these unworthy verses, was not less delicate and fragile than it was beautiful; and where cankerworms abound, what wonder, if its young flower was blighted in the bud? The savage criticism on his *Endymion*, which appeared in the *Quarterly Review*, produced the most violent effect on his susceptible mind; the agitation thus originated ended in the rupture of a blood-vessel in the lungs; a rapid consumption ensued, and the succeeding acknowledgements from more candid critics, of the true greatness of his powers, were ineffectual to heal the wound thus wantonly inflicted.

It may be well said, that these wretched men know not what they do. They scatter their insults and their slanders without heed as to whether the poisoned shaft lights on a heart made callous by many blows, or one, like Keats's composed of more penetrable stuff. One of their associates, is, to my knowledge, a most base and unprincipled calumniator. As to *Endymion*; was it a poem, whatever might be its defects, to be treated contemptuously by those who had celebrated with various degrees of complacency and panegyric, *Paris*, and *Woman*, and a *Syrian Tale*, and Mrs. Lefanu, and Mr. Barrett, and Mr. Howard Payne, and a long list of the illustrious obscure? Are these the men, who in their venal good nature, presumed to draw a parallel between the Rev. Mr. Milman and Lord Byron? What gnat did they strain at here, after having swallowed all those camels? Against what woman taken in adultery, dares the foremost of these literary prostitutes to cast his opprobrious stone? Miserable man! you, one of the meanest, have wantonly defaced one of the noblest specimens of the workmanship of God. Nor shall it be your excuse, that, murderer as you are, you have spoken daggers, but used none.

The circumstances of the closing scene of poor Keats's life were not made known to me until the Elegy was ready for the press. I am given to understand that the wound which his sensitive spirit had received from the criticism of *Endymion*, was exasperated by the bitter sense of unrequited benefits; the poor fellow seems to have been hooted from the stage of life, no less by those on whom he had wasted the promise of his genius, than those on whom he had lavished his fortune and his care. He was accompanied to Rome, and attended in his last illness by Mr. Severn, a young artist of the highest promise, who, I have been informed 'almost risked his own life, and sacrificed every prospect to unwearied attendance upon his dying friend'. Had

I known these circumstances before the completion of my poem, I should have been tempted to add my feeble tribute of applause to the more solid recompense which the virtuous man finds in the recollection of his own motives. Mr. Severn can dispense with a reward from 'such stuff as dreams are made of'. His conduct is a golden augury of the success of his future career—may the unextinguished Spirit of his illustrious friend animate the creations of his pencil, and plead against Oblivion for his name!

Adonais

I

I weep for Adonais—he is dead!
O, weep for Adonais! though our tears
Thaw not the frost which binds so dear a head!
And thou, sad Hour, selected from all years
To mourn our loss, rouse thy obscure compeers,
And teach them thine own sorrow, say: with me
Died Adonais; till the Future dares
Forget the Past, his fate and fame shall be
An echo and a light unto eternity!

II

Where wert thou mighty Mother, when he lay,
When thy Son lay, pierced by the shaft which flies
In darkness? where was lorn Urania
When Adonais died? With veiled eyes,
'Mid listening Echoes, in her Paradise
She sate, while one, with soft enamoured breath,
Rekindled all the fading melodies,
With which, like flowers that mock the corse beneath,
He had adorned and hid the coming bulk of death.

III

O, weep for Adonais—he is dead!
Wake, melancholy Mother, wake and weep!
Yet wherefore? Quench within their burning bed
Thy fiery tears, and let thy loud heart keep
Like his, a mute and uncomplaining sleep;
For he is gone, where all things wise and fair

Descend;—oh, dream not that the amorous Deep
Will yet restore him to the vital air;
Death feeds on his mute voice, and laughs at our despair.

IV

Most musical of mourners, weep again!
Lament anew, Urania!—He died,
Who was the Sire of an immortal strain,
Blind, old, and lonely, when his country's pride,
The priest, the slave, and the liberticide,
Trampled and mocked with many a loathed rite
Of lust and blood; he went, unterrified,
Into the gulf of death; but his clear Sprite
Yet reigns o'er earth; the third among the sons of light.

V

Most musical of mourners, weep anew!
Not all to that bright station dared to climb;
And happier they their happiness who knew,
Whose tapers yet burn through that night of time
In which suns perished; others more sublime,
Struck by the envious wrath of man or God,
Have sunk, extinct in their refulgent prime;
And some yet live, treading the thorny road,
Which leads, through toil and hate, to Fame's serene abode.

VI

But now, thy youngest, dearest one, has perished,
The nursling of thy widowhood, who grew,
Like a pale flower by some sad maiden cherished,
And fed with true love tears, instead of dew;
Most musical of mourners, weep anew!
Thy extreme hope, the loveliest and the last,
The bloom, whose petals nipt before they blew
Died on the promise of the fruit, is waste;
The broken lily lies—the storm is overpast.

VII

To that high Capital, where kingly Death
Keeps his pale court in beauty and decay,
He came; and bought, with price of purest breath,
A grave among the eternal.—Come away!

Haste, while the vault of blue Italian day
Is yet his fitting charnel-roof! while still
He lies, as if in dewy sleep he lay;
Awake him not! surely he takes his fill
Of deep and liquid rest, forgetful of all ill.

VIII

He will awake no more, oh, never more!—
Within the twilight chamber spreads apace
The shadow of white Death, and at the door
Invisible Corruption waits to trace
His extreme way to her dim dwelling-place;
The eternal Hunger sits, but pity and awe
Soothe her pale rage, nor dares she to deface
So fair a prey, till darkness, and the law
Of change, shall o'er his sleep the mortal curtain draw.

IX

O, weep for Adonais!—The quick Dreams,
The passion-wingèd Ministers of thought,
Who were his flocks, whom near the living streams
Of his young spirit he fed, and whom he taught
The love which was its music, wander not,—
Wander no more, from kindling brain to brain,
But droop there, whence they sprung; and mourn their lot
Round the cold heart, where, after their sweet pain,
They ne'er will gather strength, or find a home again.

X

And one with trembling hands clasps his cold head,
And fans him with her moonlight wings, and cries;
'Our love, our hope, our sorrow, is not dead;
See, on the silken fringe of his faint eyes,
Like dew upon a sleeping flower, there lies
A tear some Dream has loosened from his brain.'
Lost Angel of a ruined Paradise!
She knew not 'twas her own; as with no stain
She faded, like a cloud which had outwept its rain.

XI

One from a lucid urn of starry dew
Washed his light limbs as if embalming them;
Another clipt her profuse locks, and threw
The wreath upon him, like an anadem,
Which frozen tears instead of pearls begem;
Another in her wilful grief would break
Her bow and winged reeds, as if to stem
A greater loss with one which was more weak;
And dull the barbed fire against his frozen cheek.

XII

Another Splendour on his mouth alit,
That mouth, whence it was wont to draw the breath
Which gave it strength to pierce the guarded wit,
And pass into the panting heart beneath
With lightning and with music: the damp death
Quenched its caress upon his icy lips;
And, as a dying meteor stains a wreath
Of moonlight vapour, which the cold night clips,
It flushed through his pale limbs, and past to its eclipse.

XIII

And others came . . . Desires and Adorations,
Winged Persuasions and veiled Destinies,
Splendours, and Glooms, and glimmering Incarnations
Of hopes and fears, and twilight Phantasies;
And Sorrow, with her family of Sighs,
And Pleasure, blind with tears, led by the gleam
Of her own dying smile instead of eyes,
Came in slow pomp;—the moving pomp might seem
Like pageantry of mist on an autumnal stream.

XIV

All he had loved, and moulded into thought,
From shape, and hue, and odour, and sweet sound,
Lamented Adonais. Morning sought
Her eastern watchtower, and her hair unbound,
Wet with the tears which should adorn the ground,
Dimmed the aerial eyes that kindle day;
Afar the melancholy thunder moaned,
Pale Ocean in unquiet slumber lay,
And the wild winds flew round, sobbing in their dismay.

XV

Lost Echo sits amid the voiceless mountains,
And feeds her grief with his remembered lay,
And will no more reply to winds or fountains,
Or amorous birds perched on the young green spray,
Or herdsman's horn, or bell at closing day;
Since she can mimic not his lips, more dear
Than those for whose disdain she pined away
Into a shadow of all sounds:—a drear
Murmur, between their songs, is all the woodmen hear.

XVI

Grief made the young Spring wild, and she threw down
Her kindling buds, as if she Autumn were,
Or they dead leaves; since her delight is flown,
For whom should she have waked the sullen year?
To Phoebus was not Hyacinth so dear
Nor to himself Narcissus, as to both
Thou Adonais: wan they stand and sere
Amid the faint companions of their youth,
With dew all turned to tears; odour, to sighing ruth.

XVII

Thy spirit's sister, the lorn nightingale
Mourns not her mate with such melodious pain;
Not so the eagle, who like thee could scale
Heaven, and could nourish in the sun's domain
Her mighty youth with morning, doth complain,
Soaring and screaming round her empty nest,
As Albion wails for thee: the curse of Cain
Light on his head who pierced thy innocent breast,
And scared the angel soul that was its earthly guest!

XVIII

Ah woe is me! Winter is come and gone,
But grief returns with the revolving year;
The airs and streams renew their joyous tone;
The ants, the bees, the swallows reappear;
Fresh leaves and flowers deck the dead Seasons' bier;
The amorous birds now pair in every brake,
And build their mossy homes in field and brere;
And the green lizard, and the golden snake,
Like unimprisoned flames, out of their trance awake.

XIX

Through wood and stream and field and hill and Ocean
A quickening life from the Earth's heart has burst
As it has ever done, with change and motion,
From the great morning of the world when first
God dawned on Chaos; in its steam immersed
The lamps of Heaven flash with a softer light;
All baser things pant with life's sacred thirst;
Diffuse themselves; and spend in love's delight,
The beauty and the joy of their renewed might.

XX

The leprous corpse touched by this spirit tender
Exhales itself in flowers of gentle breath;
Like incarnations of the stars, when splendour
Is changed to fragrance, they illumine death
And mock the merry worm that wakes beneath;
Nought we know, dies. Shall that alone which knows
Be as a sword consumed before the sheath
By sightless lightning?—th' intense atom glows
A moment, then is quenched in a most cold repose.

XXI

Alas! that all we loved of him should be,
But for our grief, as if it had not been,
And grief itself be mortal! Woe is me!
Whence are we, and why are we? of what scene
The actors or spectators? Great and mean
Meet massed in death, who lends what life must borrow.
As long as skies are blue, and fields are green,
Evening must usher night, night urge the morrow,
Month follow month with woe, and year wake year to sorrow.

XXII

He will awake no more, oh, never more!
'Wake thou,' cried Misery, 'childless Mother, rise
Out of thy sleep, and slake, in thy heart's core,
A wound more fierce than his with tears and sighs.'
And all the Dreams that watched Urania's eyes,
And all the Echoes whom their sister's song
Had held in holy silence, cried: 'Arise!'
Swift as a Thought by the snake Memory stung,
From her ambrosial rest the fading Splendour sprung.

XXIII

She rose like an autumnal Night, that springs
Out of the East, and follows wild and drear
The golden Day, which, on eternal wings,
Even as a ghost abandoning a bier,
Had left the Earth a corpse. Sorrow and fear
So struck, so roused, so rapt Urania;
So saddened round her like an atmosphere
Of stormy mist; so swept her on her way
Even to the mournful place where Adonais lay.

XXIV

Out of her secret Paradise she sped,
Through camps and cities rough with stone, and steel,
And human hearts, which to her aery tread
Yielding not, wounded the invisible
Palms of her tender feet where'er they fell:
And barbed tongues, and thoughts more sharp than they
Rent the soft Form they never could repel,
Whose sacred blood, like the young tears of May,
Paved with eternal flowers that undeserving way.

XXV

In the death chamber for a moment Death,
Shamed by the presence of that living Might,
Blushed to annihilation, and the breath
Revisited those lips, and life's pale light
Flashed through those limbs, so late her dear delight.
'Leave me not wild and drear and comfortless,
As silent lightning leaves the starless night!
Leave me not!' cried Urania: her distress
Roused Death: Death rose and smiled, and met her vain caress.

XXVI

'Stay yet awhile! speak to me once again;
Kiss me, so long but as a kiss may live;
And in my heartless breast and burning brain
That word, that kiss shall all thoughts else survive,
With food of saddest memory kept alive,
Now thou art dead, as if it were a part
Of thee, my Adonais! I would give
All that I am to be as thou now art!
But I am chained to Time, and cannot thence depart!

XXVII

'Oh gentle child, beautiful as thou wert,
Why didst thou leave the trodden paths of men
Too soon, and with weak hands though mighty heart
Dare the unpastured dragon in his den?
Defenceless as thou wert, oh where was then
Wisdom the mirrored shield, or scorn the spear?
Or hadst thou waited the full cycle, when
Thy spirit should have filled its crescent sphere,
The monsters of life's waste had fled from thee like deer.

XXVIII

'The herded wolves, bold only to pursue;
The obscene ravens, clamorous o'er the dead;
The vultures to the conqueror's banner true
Who feed where Desolation first has fed,
And whose wings rain contagion;—how they fled,
When like Apollo, from his golden bow,
The Pythian of the age one arrow sped
And smiled!—The spoilers tempt no second blow,
They fawn on the proud feet that spurn them lying low.

XXIX

'The sun comes forth, and many reptiles spawn;
He sets, and each ephemeral insect then
Is gathered into death without a dawn,
And the immortal stars awake again;
So is it in the world of living men:
A godlike mind soars forth, in its delight
Making earth bare and veiling heaven, and when
It sinks, the swarms that dimmed or shared its light
Leave to its kindred lamps the spirit's awful night.'

XXX

Thus ceased she: and the mountain shepherds came,
Their garlands sere, their magic mantles rent;
The Pilgrim of Eternity, whose fame
Over his living head like Heaven is bent,
An early but enduring monument,
Came, veiling all the lightnings of his song
In sorrow; from her wilds Ierne sent
The sweetest lyrist of her saddest wrong,
And love taught grief to fall like music from his tongue.

XXXI

Midst others of less note, came one frail Form,
A phantom among men; companionless
As the last cloud of an expiring storm
Whose thunder is its knell; he, as I guess,
Had gazed on Nature's naked loveliness,
Actaeon-like, and now he fled astray
With feeble steps o'er the world's wilderness,
And his own thoughts, along that rugged way,
Pursued, like raging hounds, their father and their prey.

XXXII

A pardlike Spirit beautiful and swift—
A Love in desolation masked;—a Power
Girt round with weakness;—it can scarce uplift
The weight of the superincumbent hour;
It is a dying lamp, a falling shower,
A breaking billow;—even whilst we speak
Is it not broken? On the withering flower
The killing sun smiles brightly: on a cheek
The life can burn in blood, even while the heart may break.

XXXIII

His head was bound with pansies overblown,
And faded violets, white, and pied, and blue;
And a light spear topped with a cypress cone,
Round whose rude shaft dark ivy tresses grew
Yet dripping with the forest's noonday dew,
Vibrated, as the ever-beating heart
Shook the weak hand that grasped it; of that crew
He came the last, neglected and apart;
A herd-abandoned deer struck by the hunter's dart.

XXXIV

All stood aloof, and at his partial moan
Smiled through their tears; well knew that gentle band
Who in another's fate now wept his own,
As in the accents of an unknown land
He sung new sorrow; sad Urania scanned
The Stranger's mien, and murmured: 'who art thou?'
He answered not, but with a sudden hand
Made bare his branded and ensanguined brow,
Which was like Cain's or Christ's—Oh! that it should be so!

XXXV

What softer voice is hushed over the dead?
Athwart what brow is that dark mantle thrown?
What form leans sadly o'er the white death-bed,
In mockery of monumental stone,
The heavy heart heaving without a moan?
If it be He, who, gentlest of the wise,
Taught, soothed, loved, honoured the departed one;
Let me not vex, with inharmonious sighs
The silence of that heart's accepted sacrifice.

XXXVI

Our Adonais has drunk poison—oh!
What deaf and viperous murderer could crown
Life's early cup with such a draught of woe?
The nameless worm would now itself disown:
It felt, yet could escape the magic tone
Whose prelude held all envy, hate, and wrong,
But what was howling in one breast alone,
Silent with expectation of the song,
Whose master's hand is cold, whose silver lyre unstrung.

XXXVII

Live thou, whose infamy is not thy fame!
Live! fear no heavier chastisement from me,
Thou noteless blot on a remembered name!
But be thyself, and know thyself to be!
And ever at thy season be thou free
To spill the venom when thy fangs o'erflow:
Remorse and Self-contempt shall cling to thee;
Hot Shame shall burn upon thy secret brow,
And like a beaten hound tremble thou shalt—as now.

XXXVIII

Nor let us weep that our delight is fled
Far from these carrion kites that scream below;
He wakes or sleeps with the enduring dead;
Thou canst not soar where he is sitting now.—
Dust to the dust! but the pure spirit shall flow
Back to the burning fountain whence it came,
A portion of the Eternal, which must glow
Through time and change, unquenchably the same,
Whilst thy cold embers choke the sordid hearth of shame.

XXXIX

Peace, peace! he is not dead, he doth not sleep—
He hath awakened from the dream of life—
'Tis we, who lost in stormy visions, keep
With phantoms an unprofitable strife,
And in mad trance, strike with our spirit's knife
Invulnerable nothings.—*We* decay
Like corpses in a charnel; fear and grief
Convulse us and consume us day by day,
And cold hopes swarm like worms within our living clay.

XL

He has outsoared the shadow of our night;
Envy and calumny and hate and pain,
And that unrest which men miscall delight,
Can touch him not and torture not again;
From the contagion of the world's slow stain
He is secure, and now can never mourn
A heart grown cold, a head grown grey in vain;
Nor, when the spirit's self has ceased to burn,
With sparkless ashes load an unlamented urn.

XLI

He lives, he wakes—'tis Death is dead, not he;
Mourn not for Adonais.—Thou young Dawn
Turn all thy dew to splendour, for from thee
The spirit thou lamentest is not gone;
Ye caverns and ye forests, cease to moan!
Cease ye faint flowers and fountains, and thou Air
Which like a mourning veil thy scarf hadst thrown
O'er the abandoned Earth, now leave it bare
Even to the joyous stars which smile on its despair!

XLII

He is made one with Nature: there is heard
His voice in all her music, from the moan
Of thunder, to the song of night's sweet bird;
He is a presence to be felt and known
In darkness and in light, from herb and stone,
Spreading itself where'er that Power may move
Which has withdrawn his being to its own;
Which wields the world with never wearied love,
Sustains it from beneath, and kindles it above.

XLIII

He is a portion of the loveliness
Which once he made more lovely: he doth bear
His part, while the one Spirit's plastic stress
Sweeps through the dull dense world, compelling there,
All new successions to the forms they wear;
Torturing th' unwilling dross that checks its flight
To its own likeness, as each mass may bear;
And bursting in its beauty and its might
From trees and beasts and men into the Heaven's light.

XLIV

The splendours of the firmament of time
May be eclipsed, but are extinguished not;
Like stars to their appointed height they climb
And death is a low mist which cannot blot
The brightness it may veil. When lofty thought
Lifts a young heart above its mortal lair,
And love and life contend in it, for what
Shall be its earthly doom, the dead live there
And move like winds of light on dark and stormy air.

XLV

The inheritors of unfulfilled renown
Rose from their thrones, built beyond mortal thought,
Far in the Unapparent. Chatterton
Rose pale, his solemn agony had not
Yet faded from him; Sidney, as he fought
And as he fell and as he lived and loved
Sublimely mild, a Spirit without spot,
Arose; and Lucan, by his death approved:
Oblivion as they rose shrank like a thing reproved.

XLVI

And many more, whose names on Earth are dark
But whose transmitted effluence cannot die
So long as fire outlives the parent spark,
Rose, robed in dazzling immortality.
'Thou art become as one of us,' they cry,
'It was for thee yon kingless sphere has long
Swung blind in unascended majesty,
Silent alone amid an Heaven of song.
Assume thy winged throne, thou Vesper of our throng!'

XLVII

Who mourns for Adonais? oh come forth
Fond wretch! and know thyself and him aright.
Clasp with thy panting soul the pendulous Earth;
As from a centre, dart thy spirit's light
Beyond all worlds, until its spacious might
Satiate the void circumference: then shrink
Even to a point within our day and night;
And keep thy heart light lest it make thee sink
When hope has kindled hope, and lured thee to the brink.

XLVIII

Or go to Rome, which is the sepulchre
O, not of him, but of our joy: 'tis nought
That ages, empires, and religions there
Lie buried in the ravage they have wrought;
For such as he can lend,—they borrow not
Glory from those who made the world their prey;
And he is gathered to the kings of thought
Who waged contention with their time's decay,
And of the past are all that cannot pass away.

XLIX

Go thou to Rome,—at once the Paradise,
The grave, the city, and the wilderness;
And where its wrecks like shattered mountains rise,
And flowering weeds, and fragrant copses dress
The bones of Desolation's nakedness
Pass, till the Spirit of the spot shall lead
Thy footsteps to a slope of green access
Where, like an infant's smile, over the dead,
A light of laughing flowers along the grass is spread.

L

And gray walls moulder round, on which dull Time
Feeds, like slow fire upon a hoary brand;
And one keen pyramid with wedge sublime,
Pavilioning the dust of him who planned
This refuge for his memory, doth stand
Like flame transformed to marble; and beneath,
A field is spread, on which a newer band
Have pitched in Heaven's smile their camp of death
Welcoming him we lose with scarce extinguished breath.

LI

Here pause: these graves are all too young as yet
To have outgrown the sorrow which consigned
Its charge to each; and if the seal is set,
Here, on one fountain of a mourning mind,
Break it not thou! too surely shalt thou find
Thine own well full, if thou returnest home,
Of tears and gall. From the world's bitter wind
Seek shelter in the shadow of the tomb.
What Adonais is, why fear we to become?

LII

The One remains, the many change and pass;
Heaven's light forever shines, Earth's shadows fly;
Life, like a dome of many-coloured glass,
Stains the white radiance of Eternity,
Until Death tramples it to fragments.—Die,
If thou wouldst be with that which thou dost seek!
Follow where all is fled!—Rome's azure sky,
Flowers, ruins, statues, music, words, are weak
The glory they transfuse with fitting truth to speak.

LIII

Why linger, why turn back, why shrink, my Heart?
Thy hopes are gone before: from all things here
They have departed; thou shouldst now depart!
A light is past from the revolving year,
And man, and woman; and what still is dear
Attracts to crush, repels to make thee wither.
The soft sky smiles,—the low wind whispers near:
'Tis Adonais calls! oh, hasten thither,
No more let Life divide what Death can join together.

LIV

That Light whose smile kindles the Universe,
That Beauty in which all things work and move,
That Benediction which the eclipsing Curse
Of birth can quench not, that sustaining Love
Which through the web of being blindly wove
By man and beast and earth and air and sea,
Burns bright or dim, as each are mirrors of
The fire for which all thirst, now beams on me,
Consuming the last clouds of cold mortality.

LV

The breath whose might I have invoked in song
Descends on me; my spirit's bark is driven,
Far from the shore, far from the trembling throng
Whose sails were never to the tempest given;
The massy earth and sphered skies are riven!
I am borne darkly, fearfully, afar;
Whilst burning through the inmost veil of Heaven,
The soul of Adonais, like a star,
Beacons from the abode where the Eternal are.

'When passion's trance is overpast'

When passion's trance is overpast,
If tenderness and truth could last
Or live, whilst all wild feelings keep
Some mortal slumber, dark and deep,
I should not weep, I should not weep!

It were enough to feel, to see
Thy soft eyes gazing tenderly,
And dream the rest—and burn and be
The secret food of fires unseen,
Could thou but be what thou hast been.

After the slumber of the year
The woodland violets reappear;
All things revive in field or grove
And sky and sea, but two, which move
And form all others—life and love.

Written on hearing the news of the death of Napoleon

1

What! alive and so bold, oh Earth?
  Art thou not overbold?
  What! leapest thou forth as of old
In the light of thy morning mirth,
The last of the flock of the starry fold?
Ha! leapest thou forth as of old?
Are not the limbs still when the ghost is fled,
And canst thou move, Napoleon being dead?

2

How! is not thy quick heart cold?
  What spark is alive on thy hearth?
  How! is not *his* death-knell knolled?
And livest *thou* still, Mother Earth?
Thou wert warming thy fingers old
O'er the embers covered and cold
Of that most fiery spirit, when it fled—
What, Mother, do you laugh now he is dead?

3

'Who has known me of old,' replied Earth,
'Or who has my story told?
It is thou who art overbold.'
And the lightning of scorn laughed forth
As she sung, 'To my bosom I fold
All my sons when their knell is knolled,
And so with living motion all are fed,
And the quick spring like weeds out of the dead.

4

'Still alive and still bold,' shouted Earth,
'I grow bolder and still more bold.
The dead fill me ten thousand fold
Fuller of speed and splendour and mirth.
I was cloudy, and sullen, and cold,
Like a frozen chaos uprolled
Till by the spirit of the mighty dead
My heart grew warm. I feed on whom I fed.

5

'Aye, alive and still bold,' muttered Earth,
'Napoleon's fierce spirit rolled
In terror, and blood, and gold,
A torrent of ruin to death from his birth.
Leave the millions who follow, to mould
The metal before it be cold,
And weave into his shame, which like the dead
Shrouds me, the hopes that from his glory fled.'

Epithalamium

Boys

Night! With all thine eyes look down!
Darkness weep thy holiest dew!
Never smiled the inconstant Moon
On a pair so true—
Haste coy Hour and quench all light,
Lest eyes see their own delight—
Haste swift Hour, and thy loved flight
Oft renew.

Girls

Fairies, sprites and angels keep her!
 Holy Stars! permit no wrong!
And return to wake the sleeper
 Dawn! ere it be long.
Oh joy! oh fear! there is not one
Of us can guess what may be done
In the absence of the Sun—
 Come along.

Boys

O linger long thou envious eastern lamp
 In the damp
 Caves of the deep.

Girls

Nay, return Vesper! urge thy lazy car!
 Swift unbar
 The gates of sleep.

Both

The golden gate of sleep unbar
 Where strength and beauty, met together,
Kindle their image—like a Star
 In a sea of glassy weather—
May the purple mist of love
Round them rise and with them move;
Nourishing each tender gem
Which like flowers will burst from them—
As the fruit is to the tree
May their children ever be.

The Aziola

'Do you not hear the Aziola cry?
Methinks she must be nigh'—
 Said Mary as we sate
In dusk, ere stars were lit or candles brought—
 And I who thought
This Aziola was some tedious woman
Asked, 'Who is Aziola?' How elate

I felt to know that it was nothing human,
No mockery of myself to fear or hate!—
And Mary saw my soul,
And laughed and said:—'Disquiet yourself not,
'Tis nothing but a little downy owl.'

Sad Aziola, many an eventide
Thy music I had heard
By wood and stream, meadow and mountain side,
And fields and marshes wide,—
Such as nor voice, nor lute, nor wind, nor bird
The soul ever stirred—
Unlike, and far sweeter than them all.—
Sad Aziola, from that moment I
Loved thee and thy sad cry.

HELLAS

A Lyrical Drama

ΜΑΝΤΙΣ ΕΙΜ' ΕΣΘΛΩΝ ἈΓΩΝΩΝ
Oedip. Colon.

TO
HIS EXCELLENCY
PRINCE ALEXANDER MAVROCORDATO
LATE SECRETARY FOR FOREIGN AFFAIRS
TO THE HOSPODAR OF WALLACHIA,
THE DRAMA OF HELLAS
IS INSCRIBED
AS AN IMPERFECT TOKEN
OF THE ADMIRATION, SYMPATHY, AND FRIENDSHIP
OF
THE AUTHOR.

Pisa,
November 1st, 1821.

PREFACE

The Poem of *Hellas*, written at the suggestion of the events of the moment, is a mere improvise, and derives its interest (should it be found to possess any) solely from the intense sympathy which the Author feels with the cause he would celebrate.

The subject in its present state, is insusceptible of being treated otherwise than lyrically, and if I have called this poem a drama from the circumstance of its being composed in dialogue, the licence is not greater than that which has been assumed by other poets who have called their productions epics, only because they have been divided into twelve or twenty-four books.

The *Persae* of Aeschylus afforded me the first model of my conception, although the decision of the glorious contest now waging in Greece being yet suspended forbids a catastrophe parallel to the return of Xerxes and the desolation of the Persians. I have, therefore, contented myself with exhibiting a series of lyric pictures, and with having wrought upon the curtain of futurity which falls upon the unfinished scene such figures of indistinct and visionary delineation as suggest the final triumph of the Greek cause as a portion of the cause of civilization and social improvement.

The drama (if drama it must be called) is, however, so inartificial that I doubt whether, if recited on the Thespian waggon to an Athenian village at the Dionysiaca, it would have obtained the prize of the goat. I shall bear with equanimity any punishment greater than the loss of such a reward which the Aristarchi of the hour may think fit to inflict.

The only *goat-song* which I have yet attempted has, I confess, in spite of the unfavourable nature of the subject, received a greater and a more valuable portion of applause than I expected or than it deserved.

Common fame is the only authority which I can alledge for the details which form the basis of the poem, and I must trespass upon the forgiveness of my readers for the display of newspaper erudition to which I have been reduced. Undoubtedly, until the conclusion of the war, it will be impossible to obtain an account of it sufficiently authentic for historical materials; but poets have their privilege, and it is unquestionable that actions of the most exalted courage have been performed by the Greeks, that they have gained more than one naval victory, and that their defeat in Wallachia was signalized by circumstances of heroism, more glorious even than victory.

The apathy of the rulers of the civilized world to the astonishing circumstance of the descendants of that nation to which they owe their civilization rising as it were from the ashes of their ruin is something perfectly inexplicable to a mere spectator of the shews of this mortal scene. We are all Greeks—our laws, our literature, our religion, our arts have their root in Greece. But for Greece, Rome, the instructor, the conqueror, or the metropolis of our ancestors would have spread no illumination with her arms, and we might still have been savages, and idolaters; or, what is worse, might have arrived at such a stagnant and miserable state of social institution as China and Japan possess.

The human form and the human mind attained to a perfection in Greece which has impressed its image on those faultless productions whose very fragments are the despair of modern art, and has propagated impulses which cannot cease, through a thousand channels of manifest or imperceptible operation to ennoble and delight mankind until the extinction of the race.

The modern Greek is the descendant of those glorious beings whom the imagination almost refuses to figure to itself as belonging to our kind, and he inherits much of their sensibility, their rapidity of conception, their enthusiasm and their courage. If in many instances he is degraded, by moral and political slavery to the practise of the basest vices it engenders, and that below the level of ordinary degradation; let us reflect that the corruption of the best produces the worst; and that habits which subsist only in relation to a peculiar state of social institution may be expected to cease so soon as that relation is dissolved. In fact, the Greeks, since the admirable novel of *Anastasius* could have been a faithful picture of their manners, have undergone most important changes; the flower of their Youth returning to their Country from the Universities of Italy, Germany and France have communicated to their fellow citizens the latest results of that social perfection of which their ancestors were the original source. The university of Chios contained before the breaking out of the Revolution eight hundred students, and among them several Germans and Americans. The munificence and energy of many of the Greek princes and merchants, directed to the renovation of their country with a spirit and a wisdom which has few examples, is above all praise.

The English permit their own oppressors to act according to their natural sympathy with the Turkish tyrant, and to brand upon their name the indelible blot of an alliance with the enemies of domestic happiness, of Christianity and civilization.

Russia desires to possess not to liberate Greece, and is contented to see the Turks, its natural enemies, and the Greeks, its intended slaves, enfeeble each other until one or both fall into its net. The wise and generous policy of England would have consisted in establishing the independence of Greece, and in maintaining it both against Russia and the Turk;—but when was the oppressor generous or just?

Should the English people ever become free they will reflect upon the part which those who presume to represent their will, have played in the great drama of the revival of liberty, with feelings which it would become them to anticipate. This is the age of the war of the oppressed against the oppressors, and every one of those ringleaders of the privileged gangs of murderers and swindlers called Sovereigns, look to each other for aid against the common enemy, and suspend their mutual jealousies in the presence of a mightier fear. Of this holy alliance all the despots of the earth are virtual members. But a new race has arisen throughout Europe, nursed in the abhorrence of the opinions which are its chains, and she will continue to produce fresh generations to accomplish that destiny which tyrants foresee and dread.

The Spanish peninsula is already free. France is tranquil in the enjoyment of a partial exemption from the abuses which its unnatural and feeble government are vainly attempting to revive. The seed of blood and misery has been sown in Italy and a more vigorous race is arising to go forth to the harvest. The world waits only the news of a revolution of Germany to see the Tyrants who have pinnacled themselves on its supineness precipitated into the ruin from which they shall never arise. Well do these destroyers of mankind know their enemy when they impute the insurrection in Greece to the same spirit before which they tremble throughout the rest of Europe, and that enemy well knows the power and the cunning of its opponents, and watches the moment of their approaching weakness and inevitable division to wrest the bloody sceptre from their grasp.—

DRAMATIS PERSONAE

MAHMUD
HASSAN
DAOOD
AHASUERUS, *a Jew*
Chorus of Greek Captive Women
Messengers, Slaves, and Attendants

Scene, *Constantinople.*
Time, *Sunset.*

SCENE. A Terrace on the Seraglio. MAHMUD *sleeping. An Indian Slave sitting beside his couch.*

Chorus of Greek Captive Women

We strew these opiate flowers
On thy restless pillow,—
They were stript from Orient bowers,
By the Indian billow.
Be thy sleep
Calm and deep,
Like theirs who fell, not ours who weep!

Indian

Away, unlovely dreams!
Away, false shapes of sleep!
Be his, as Heaven seems,
Clear and bright and deep!
Soft as love, and calm as death,
Sweet as a summer night without a breath.

Chorus

Sleep, sleep! our song is laden
With the soul of slumber;
It was sung by a Samian maiden
Whose lover was of the number
Who now keep
That calm sleep
Whence none may wake, where none shall weep.

Indian

I touch thy temples pale!
I breathe my soul on thee!
And could my prayers avail,
All my joy should be
Dead, and I would live to weep,
So thou might'st win one hour of quiet sleep.

Chorus

Breathe low, low!
The spell of the mighty mistress now
When Conscience lulls her sated snake
And Tyrants sleep, let Freedom wake.
Breathe! low—low
The words which like secret fire shall flow
Through the veins of the frozen earth—low, low!

Semichorus I

Life may change, but it may fly not;
Hope may vanish, but can die not;
Truth be veiled but still it burneth;
Love repulsed,—but it returneth!

Semichorus II

Yet were Life a charnel where
Hope lay coffined with despair;
Yet were Truth a sacred lie;
Love were Lust—

Semichorus I

If Liberty
Lent not Life its soul of light,
Hope its iris of delight,
Truth its prophet's robe to wear,
Love its power to give and bear.

Chorus

In the great Morning of the world
The spirit of God with might unfurled
The flag of Freedom over chaos,
  And all its banded Anarchs fled
Like Vultures frighted from Imaus
  Before an Earthquake's tread.—
So from Time's tempestuous dawn
Freedom's splendour burst and shone.—
Thermopylae and Marathon
Caught, like mountains beacon-lighted,
  The springing Fire.—The winged Glory
On Philippi half-alighted,
  Like an Eagle on a promontory.
Its unwearied wings could fan
The quenchless ashes of Milan.
From age to age, from man to man,
  It lived; and lit from land to land
  Florence, Albion, Switzerland.

Then Night fell—and as from night
Re-assuming fiery flight
From the West swift Freedom came
  Against the course of Heaven and doom,
A second sun arrayed in flame
  To burn, to kindle, to illume.
From far Atlantis its young beams
Chased the shadows and the dreams;
France with all her sanguine streams
  Hid but quenched it not; again
  Through clouds its shafts of glory rain
  From utmost Germany to Spain.

As an eagle fed with morning
Scorns the embattled tempest's warning
When she seeks her aiëry hanging
  In the mountain-cedar's hair
And her brood expect the clanging
  Of her wings through the wild air,
Sick with famine—Freedom so
To what of Greece remaineth now
Returns; her hoary ruins glow
Like orient mountains lost in day.
  Beneath the safety of her wings
Her renovated nurslings prey,
  And in the naked lightnings
Of truth they purge their dazzled eyes.
Let Freedom leave, where'er she flies,
A Desart, or a Paradise;
  Let the beautiful and the brave
  Share her glory, or a grave.

Semichorus I

With the gifts of gladness
  Greece did thy cradle strew—

Semichorus II

With the tears of sadness
  Greece did thy shroud bedew!

Semichorus I

With an orphan's affection
  She followed thy bier through Time;

Semichorus II

And at thy resurrection
Reappeareth, like thou, sublime!

Semichorus I

If Heaven should resume thee,
To Heaven shall her spirits ascend;

Semichorus II

If Hell should entomb thee,
To Hell shall her high hearts bend.

Semichorus I

If annihilation——

Semichorus II

Dust let her glories be!
And a name and a nation
Be forgotten, Freedom, with thee!

Indian

His brow grows darker—breathe not—move not.
He starts—he shudders—ye that love not,
With your panting loud and fast,
Have awakened him at last.

Mahmud [*starting from his sleep.*

Man the Seraglio-guard!—make fast the gate.
What! from a cannonade of three short hours?
'Tis false! that breach towards the Bosphorus
Cannot be practicable yet—who stirs?
Stand to the match! that when the foe prevails
One spark may mix in reconciling ruin
The conqueror and the conquered! Heave the tower
Into the gap—wrench off the roof!

[*Enter* HASSAN.

Ha! what!
The truth of day lightens upon my dream
And I am Mahmud, still,—

Hassan

Your sublime highness
Is strangely moved.

Mahmud

The times do cast strange shadows
On those who watch and who must rule their course,
Lest they being first in peril as in glory
Be whelmed in the fierce ebb—and these are of them.
Thrice has a gloomy vision hunted me
As thus from sleep into the troubled day;
It shakes me as the tempest shakes the sea,
Leaving no figure upon memory's glass.
Would that—no matter—thou didst say thou knewest
A Jew, whose spirit is a chronicle
Of strange and secret and forgotten things.
I bade thee summon him—'tis said his tribe
Dream, and are wise interpreters of dreams.

Hassan

The Jew of whom I spake is old—so old
He seems to have outlived a world's decay;
The hoary mountains and the wrinkled ocean
Seem younger still than he—his hair and beard
Are whiter than the tempest-sifted snow.
His cold pale limbs and pulseless arteries
Are like the fibres of a cloud instinct
With light, and to the soul that quickens them
Are as the atoms of the mountain-drift
To the winter wind—but from his eye looks forth
A life of unconsumed thought which pierces
The present, and the past, and the to-come.
Some say that this is he whom the great prophet
Jesus, the Son of Joseph, for his mockery
Mocked with the curse of immortality.—
Some feign that he is Enoch—others dream
He was preadamite and has survived
Cycles of generation and of ruin.
The Sage, in truth, by dreadful abstinence
And conquering penance of the mutinous flesh,
Deep contemplation and unwearied study
In years outstretched beyond the date of man,

May have attained to sovereignty and science
Over those strong and secret things and thoughts
Which others fear and know not.

Mahmud

I would talk
With this old Jew.

Hassan

Thy will is even now
Made known to him, where he dwells in a sea cavern
'Mid the Demonesi, less accessible
Than thou or God! He who would question him
Must sail alone at sunset where the stream
Of ocean sleeps around those foamless isles,
When the young moon is westering as now
And evening airs wander upon the wave;
And when the pines of that bee-pasturing isle,
Green Erebinthus, quench the fiery shadow
Of his gilt prow within the sapphire water,
Then must the lonely helmsman cry aloud,
Ahasuerus! and the caverns round
Will answer Ahasuerus! If his prayer
Be granted, a faint meteor will arise
Lighting him over Marmora, and a wind
Will rush out of the sighing pine forest
And with the wind a storm of harmony
Unutterably sweet, and pilot him
Through the soft twilight to the Bosphorus:
Thence at the hour and place and circumstance
Fit for the matter of their conference
The Jew appears. Few dare and few who dare
Win the desired communion—but that shout

[*a shout within*

Bodes——

Mahmud

Evil doubtless like all human sounds.
Let me converse with spirits.

Hassan

That shout again.

Mahmud
This Jew whom thou hast summoned—

Hassan
Will be here—

Mahmud
When the omnipotent hour to which are yoked
He, I, and all things shall compel—Enough.
Silence those mutineers—that drunken crew,
That crowd about the pilot in the storm.
Aye! strike the foremost shorter by a head.—
They weary me and I have need of rest.
Kings are like stars—they rise and set, they have
The worship of the world but no repose.
[*Exeunt severally.*

Chorus
Worlds on worlds are rolling ever
From creation to decay,
Like the bubbles on a river
Sparkling, bursting, borne away.
But they are still immortal
Who through Birth's orient portal
And Death's dark chasm hurrying to and fro,
Clothe their unceasing flight
In the brief dust and light
Gathered around their chariots as they go;
New shapes they still may weave,
New Gods, new Laws receive,
Bright or dim are they as the robes they last
On Death's bare ribs had cast.

A Power from the unknown God,
A Promethean Conqueror came;
Like a triumphal path he trod
The thorns of death and shame.
A mortal shape to him
Was like the vapour dim
Which the orient planet animates with light;
Hell, Sin and Slavery came
Like bloodhounds mild and tame,

Nor preyed, until their Lord had taken flight;
The moon of Mahomet
Arose, and it shall set,
While blazoned as on Heaven's immortal noon
The cross leads generations on.

Swift as the radiant shapes of sleep
From one whose dreams are Paradise
Fly, when the fond wretch wakes to weep,
And Day peers forth with her blank eyes;
So fleet, so faint, so fair,
The Powers of earth and air
Fled from the folding star of Bethlehem;
Apollo, Pan, and Love—
And even Olympian Jove—
Grew weak, for killing Truth had glared on them;
Our hills and seas and streams
Dispeopled of their dreams—
Their waters turned to blood, their dew to tears—
Wailed for the golden years.
[*Enter* MAHMUD, HASSAN, DAOOD, *and others.*

Mahmud
More gold? our ancestors bought gold with victory,
And shall I sell it for defeat?

Daood
The Janizars
Clamour for pay—

Mahmud
Go! bid them pay themselves
With Christian blood! Are there no Grecian virgins
Whose shrieks and spasms and tears they may enjoy?
No infidel children to impale on spears?
No hoary priests after that Patriarch
Who bent the curse against his country's heart,
Which clove his own at last? Go! bid them kill—
Blood is the seed of gold.

Daood

It has been sown,
And yet the harvest to the sicklemen
Is as a grain to each.

Mahmud

Then, take this signet.
Unlock the seventh chamber in which lie
The treasures of victorious Solyman,
An Empire's spoil stored for a day of ruin.
O spirit of my sires, is it not come?
The prey-birds and the wolves are gorged and sleep,
But these, who spread their feast on the red earth,
Hunger for gold, which fills not—see them fed;
Then, lead them to the rivers of fresh death.

[*Exit* DAOOD.

O, miserable dawn after a night
More glorious than the day which it usurped!
O, faith in God! O power on earth! O word
Of the great prophet, whose o'ershadowing wings
Darkened the thrones and idols of the West:
Now bright!—for thy sake cursed be the hour,
Even as a father by an evil child,
When th' orient moon of Islam roll'd in triumph
From Caucasus to white Ceraunia!
Ruin above, and anarchy below;
Terror without, and treachery within;
The chalice of destruction full, and all
Thirsting to drink, and who among us dares
To dash it from his lips? and where is hope?

Hassan

The lamp of our dominion still rides high,
One God is God—Mahomet is his prophet.
Four hundred thousand Moslems, from the limits
Of utmost Asia, irresistibly
Throng, like full clouds at the Sirocco's cry,
But not like them to weep their strength in tears:
They bear destroying lightning and their step
Wakes earthquake to consume and overwhelm
And reign in ruin. Phrygian Olympus,
Tmolus and Latmos and Mycale roughen

With horrent arms; and lofty ships even now
Like vapours anchored to a mountain's edge,
Freighted with fire and whirlwind, wait at Scala
The convoy of the ever-veering wind.
Samos is drunk with blood;—the Greek has paid
Brief victory with swift loss and long despair.
The false Moldavian serfs fled fast and far
When the fierce shout of Allah-illah-Allah!
Rose like the war-cry of the northern wind
Which kills the sluggish clouds, and leaves a flock
Of wild swans struggling with the naked storm.
So were the lost Greeks on the Danube's day!
If night is mute, yet the returning sun
Kindles the voices of the morning birds;
Nor at thy bidding less exultingly
Than birds rejoicing in the golden day,
The Anarchies of Africa unleash
Their tempest-winged cities of the sea
To speak in thunder to the rebel world.
Like sulphurous clouds half shattered by the storm
They sweep the pale Aegean, while the Queen
Of Ocean, bound upon her island-throne
Far in the West sits mourning that her sons
Who frown on Freedom spare a smile for thee.
Russia still hovers as an Eagle might
Within a cloud, near which a kite and crane
Hang tangled in inextricable fight,
To stoop upon the victor—for she fears
The name of Freedom even as she hates thine.
But recreant Austria loves thee as the Grave
Loves Pestilence, and her slow dogs of war
Fleshed with the chase come up from Italy
And howl upon their limits, for they see
The panther Freedom fled to her old cover
'Mid seas and mountains and a mightier brood
Crouch round. What Anarch wears a crown or mitre,
Or bears the sword, or grasps the key of gold,
Whose friends are not thy friends, whose foes thy foes?
Our arsenals and our armouries are full;
Our forts defy assault—ten thousand cannon
Lie ranged upon the beach, and hour by hour
Their earth-convulsing wheels affright the city;

The galloping of fiery steeds makes pale
The Christian merchant; and the yellow Jew
Hides his hoard deeper in the faithless earth.
Like clouds and like the shadows of the clouds
Over the hills of Anatolia
Swift in wide troops the Tartar chivalry
Sweep—the far flashing of their starry lances
Reverberates the dying light of day.
We have one God, one King, one hope, one law;
But many-headed Insurrection stands
Divided in itself, and soon must fall.

Mahmud
Proud words when deeds come short are seasonable.
Look, Hassan, on yon crescent moon emblazoned
Upon that shattered flag of fiery cloud
Which leads the rear of the departing day,
Wan emblem of an empire fading now.
See! how it trembles in the blood-red air
And like a mighty lamp whose oil is spent
Shrinks on the horizon's edge while from above
One star with insolent and victorious light
Hovers above its fall, and with keen beams
Like arrows through a fainting antelope
Strikes its weak form to death.

Hassan
Even as that moon
Renews itself——

Mahmud
Shall we be not renewed!
Far other bark than ours were needed now
To stem the torrent of descending time;
The spirit that lifts the slave before his lord
Stalks through the capitals of armed kings
And spreads his ensign in the wilderness,
Exults in chains, and when the rebel falls
Cries like the blood of Abel from the dust;
And the inheritors of the earth, like beasts
When earthquake is unleashed, with idiot fear
Cower in their kingly dens—as I do now.

What were Defeat when Victory must appal?
Or Danger when Security looks pale?
How said the messenger who from the fort
Islanded in the Danube, saw the battle
Of Bucharest?—that—

Hassan

Ibrahim's scymitar
Drew with its gleam swift victory from heaven,
To burn before him in the night of battle,
A light and a destruction——

Mahmud

Aye! the day
Was ours—but how?——

Hassan

The light Wallachians,
The Arnaut, Servian, and Albanian allies
Fled from the glance of our artillery
Almost before the thunderstone alit.
One half the Grecian army made a bridge
Of safe and slow retreat with Moslem dead;
The other—

Mahmud

Speak—tremble not.—

Hassan

Islanded
By victor myriads formed in hollow square
With rough and steadfast front, and thrice flung back
The deluge of our foaming cavalry;
Thrice their keen wedge of battle pierced our lines.
Our baffled army trembled like one man
Before a host, and gave them space, but soon
From the surrounding hills the batteries blazed,
Kneading them down with fire and iron rain:
Yet none approached till like a field of corn
Under the hook of the swart sickleman
The band, intrenched in mounds of Turkish dead,
Grew weak and few—then said the Pacha, 'Slaves,

Render yourselves—they have abandoned you—
What hope of refuge, or retreat or aid?
We grant your lives—' 'Grant that which is thine own!'
Cried one, and fell upon his sword and died!
Another—'God, and man, and hope abandon me
But I to them and to myself remain
Constant'—he bowed his head and his heart burst.
A third exclaimed, 'There is a refuge, tyrant,
Where thou darest not pursue and canst not harm
Should'st thou pursue; there we shall meet again.'
Then held his breath, and after a brief spasm
The indignant spirit cast its mortal garment
Among the slain;—dead earth upon the earth!
So these survivors, each by different ways,
Some strange, all sudden, none dishonourable,
Met in triumphant death; and when our army
Closed in, while yet wonder and awe and shame
Held back the base hyenas of the battle
That feed upon the dead and fly the living,
One rose out of the chaos of the slain:
And if it were a corpse which some dread spirit
Of the old saviours of the land we rule
Had lifted in its anger wandering by;—
Or if there burned within the dying man
Unquenchable disdain of death, and faith
Creating what it feigned;—I cannot tell—
But he cried—'Phantoms of the free, we come!
Armies of the Eternal, ye who strike
To dust the citadels of sanguine kings,
And shake the souls throned on their stony hearts,
And thaw their frostwork diadems like dew,—
O ye who float around this clime, and weave
The garment of the glory which it wears,
Whose fame though earth betray the dust it clasped,
Lies sepulchred in monumental thought;—
Progenitors of all that yet is great,
Ascribe to your bright senate, O accept
In your high ministrations, us, your Sons.
Us first, and the more glorious yet to come!
And ye, weak conquerors! giants who look pale
When the crushed worm rebels beneath your tread,
The vultures and the dogs, your pensioners tame,

Are overgorged, but like oppressors still
They crave the relic of destruction's feast;
The exhalations and the thirsty winds
Are sick with blood; the dew is foul with death;
Heaven's light is quenched in slaughter; thus, where'er
Upon your camps, cities, or towers, or fleets
The obscene birds the reeking remnants cast
Of these dead limbs,—upon your streams and mountains,
Upon your fields, your gardens, and your housetops,
Where'er the winds shall creep or the clouds fly
Or the dews fall or the angry sun look down
With poisoned light—Famine and Pestilence
And Panic shall wage war upon our side;
Nature from all her boundaries is moved
Against ye;—Time has found ye light as foam;
The Earth rebels; and Good and Evil stake
Their empire o'er the unborn world of men
On this one cast;—but ere the die be thrown
The renovated Genius of our race,
Proud umpire of the impious game, descends,
A seraph-winged Victory, bestriding
The tempest of the Omnipotence of God
Which sweeps all things to their appointed doom
And you to oblivion!'—more he would have said
But—

Mahmud

Died—as thou shouldst ere thy lips had painted
Their ruin in the hues of our success—
A rebel's crime gilt with a rebel's tongue!
Your heart is Greek, Hassan.

Hassan

It may be so:
A spirit not my own wrenched me within
And I have spoken words I fear and hate,
Yet would I die for—

Mahmud

Live! O live! outlive
Me and this sinking Empire.—But the fleet?—

Hassan
Alas!——

Mahmud
The fleet which like a flock of clouds
Chased by the wind flies the insurgent banner.
Our winged castles from their merchant ships!
Our myriads before their weak pirate bands!
Our arms before their chains! our years of Empire
Before their centuries of servile fear!
Death is awake, Repulse is on the waters!
They own no more the thunder-bearing banner
Of Mahmud, but like hounds of a base breed,
Gorge from a stranger's hand and rend their master.

Hassan
Latmos, and Ampelos and Phanae saw
The wreck——

Mahmud
The caves of the Icarian isles
Told each to the other in loud mockery,
And with the tongue as of a thousand echoes
First of the sea-convulsing fight—and, then,—
Thou darest to speak—senseless are the mountains;
Interpret thou their voice!

Hassan
My presence bore
A part in that day's shame. The Grecian fleet
Bore down at day-break from the North, and hung
As multitudinous on the ocean line
As cranes upon the cloudless Thracian wind.
Our squadron convoying ten thousand men
Was stretching towards Nauplia when the battle
Was kindled.—
First through the hail of our artillery
The agile Hydriote barks with press of sail
Dashed—ship to ship, cannon to cannon, man
To man were grappled in the embrace of war,
Inextricable but by death or victory—
The tempest of the raging fight convulsed

To its chrystalline depths that stainless sea
And shook Heaven's roof of golden morning clouds
Poised on a hundred azure mountain-isles.
In the brief trances of the artillery
One cry from the destroyed and the destroyer
Rose, and a cloud of desolation wrapt
The unforeseen event till the north wind
Sprung from the sea, lifting the heavy veil
Of battle-smoke—then Victory—Victory!
For as we thought three frigates from Algiers
Bore down from Naxos to our aid, but soon
The abhorred cross glimmered behind, before,
Among, around us; and that fatal sign
Dried with its beams the strength in Moslem hearts,
As the sun drinks the dew—what more? We fled!—
Our noonday path over the sanguine foam
Was beaconed,—and the glare struck the sun pale
By our consuming transports; the fierce light
Made all the shadows of our sails blood red
And every countenance blank. Some ships lay feeding
The ravening fire even to the water's level;
Some were blown up—some settling heavily
Sunk; and the shrieks of our companions died
Upon the wind that bore us fast and far
Even after they were dead—Nine thousand perished!
We met the vultures legioned in the air
Stemming the torrent of the tainted wind;
They, screaming from their cloudy mountain peaks,
Stooped through the sulphurous battle-smoke and perched
Each on the weltering carcase that we loved
Like its ill angel or its damned soul,
Riding upon the bosom of the sea.
We saw the dog-fish hastening to their feast,
Joy waked the voiceless people of the sea,
And ravening Famine left his ocean cave
To dwell with war, with us and with despair.
We met Night three hours to the west of Patmos
And with Night, tempest——

Mahmud

Cease!—

[*Enter a* MESSENGER.

Messenger

Your sublime Highness,
That Christian hound, the Muscovite Ambassador,
Has left the city—if the rebel fleet
Had anchored in the port, had Victory
Crowned the Greek legions in the hippodrome,
Panic were tamer—Obedience and Mutiny
Like Giants in contention, planet-struck,
Stand gazing on each other—there is peace
In Stamboul—

Mahmud

Is the grave not calmer still?
Its ruins shall be mine.

Hassan

Fear not the Russian:
The tiger leagues not with the stag at bay
Against the hunter—cunning, base, and cruel,
He crouches watching till the spoil be won
And must be paid for his reserve in blood.
After the war is fought yield the sleek Russian
That which thou can't not keep, his deserved portion
Of blood, which shall not flow through streets and fields,
Rivers and seas, like that which we may win,
But stagnate in the veins of Christian slaves!

[*Enter* SECOND MESSENGER.

Second Messenger

Nauplia, Tripolizza, Mothon, Athens,
Navarin, Artas, Monembasia,
Corinth and Thebes are carried by assault
And every Islamite who made his dogs
Fat with the flesh of Galilean slaves
Passed at the edge of the sword; the lust of blood
Which made our warriors drunk, is quenched in death,
But like a fiery plague breaks out anew
In deeds which make the Christian cause look pale
In its own light. The garrison of Patras
Has store but for ten days, nor is there hope
But from the Briton; at once slave and tyrant
His wishes still are weaker than his fears

Or he would sell what faith may yet remain
From the oaths broke in Genoa and in Norway;
And if you buy him not, your treasury
Is empty even of promises—his own coin.—
The freedman of a western poet chief
Holds Attica with seven thousand rebels
And has beat back the Pacha of Negropont—
The aged Ali sits in Yanina
A crownless metaphor of empire:
His name, that shadow of his withered might,
Holds our besieging army like a spell
In prey to Famine, Pest, and Mutiny;
He, bastioned in his citadel, looks forth
Joyless upon the sapphire lake that mirrors
The ruins of the city where he reigned
Childless and sceptreless. The Greek has reaped
The costly harvest his own blood matured,
Not the sower, Ali—who has bought a truce
From Ypsilanti with ten camel loads
Of Indian gold—

[*Enter a* THIRD MESSENGER.

Mahmud

What more?

Third Messenger

The Christian tribes
Of Lebanon and the Syrian wilderness
Are in revolt—Damascus, Hems, Aleppo
Tremble—the Arab menaces Medina,
The Ethiop has intrenched himself in Senaar
And keeps the Egyptian rebel well employed
Who denies homage, claims investiture
As price of tardy aid—Persia demands
The cities on the Tigris, and the Georgians
Refuse their living tribute. Crete and Cyprus
Like mountain-twins that from each other's veins
Catch the volcano-fire and earthquake spasm,
Shake in the general fever. Through the city
Like birds before a storm the Santons shriek
And prophesyings horrible and new
Are heard among the crowd—that sea of men

Sleeps on the wrecks it made, breathless and still.
A Dervise learned in the Koran preaches
That it is written how the sins of Islam
Must raise up a destroyer even now.
The Greeks expect a Saviour from the West
Who shall not come, men say, in clouds and glory:
But in the omnipresence of that spirit
In which all live and are. Ominous signs
Are blazoned broadly on the noonday sky.
One saw a red cross stamped upon the sun;
It has rained blood, and monstrous births declare
The secret wrath of Nature and her Lord.
The army encamped upon the Cydaris
Was roused last night by the alarm of battle
And saw two hosts conflicting in the air,
The shadows doubtless of the unborn time
Cast on the mirror of the night;—while yet
The fight hung balanced, there arose a storm
Which swept the phantoms from among the stars.
At the third watch the spirit of the plague
Was heard abroad flapping among the tents;
Those who relieved watch found the sentinels dead.
The last news from the camp is that a thousand
Have sickened, and——

[*Enter a* FOURTH MESSENGER.

Mahmud

And, thou, pale ghost, dim shadow
Of some untimely rumour—speak!

Fourth Messenger

One comes
Fainting with toil, covered with foam and blood:
He stood, he says, on Chelonite's
Promontory, which o'erlooks the isles that groan
Under the Briton's frown, and all their waters
Then trembling in the splendour of the moon—
When as the wandering clouds unveiled or hid
Her boundless light, he saw two adverse fleets
Stalk through the night in the horizon's glimmer,
Mingling fierce thunders and sulphurious gleams,
And smoke which strangled every infant wind

That soothed the silver clouds through the deep air.
At length the battle slept, but the Sirocco
Awoke and drove his flock of thunder clouds
Over the sea-horizon, blotting out
All objects—save that in the faint moon-glimpse
He saw, or dreamed he saw, the Turkish admiral
And two the loftiest of our ships of war
With the bright image of that Queen of Heaven
Who hid, perhaps, her face for grief, reversed;
And the abhorred cross—

[*Enter an* ATTENDANT.

Attendant

Your sublime highness,
The Jew, who—

Mahmud

Could not come more seasonably:
Bid him attend— I'll hear no more! too long
We gaze on danger through the mist of fear,
And multiply upon our shattered hopes
The images of ruin—come what will!
Tomorrow and tomorrow are as lamps
Set in our path to light us to the edge
Through rough and smooth, nor can we suffer aught
Which he inflicts not in whose hand we are.

[*exeunt.*

Semichorus I

Would I were the winged cloud
Of a tempest swift and loud,
I would scorn
The smile of morn
And the wave where the moon rise is born!
I would leave
The spirits of eve
A shroud for the corpse of the day to weave
From other threads than mine!
Bask in the deep blue noon divine
Who would,—not I.

Semichorus II

Whither to fly?

Semichorus I

Where the rocks that gird th' Aegean
Echo to the battle paean
Of the free—
I would flee,
A tempestuous herald of Victory,
My golden rain
For the Grecian slain
Should mingle in tears with the bloody main
And my solemn thunder knell
Should ring to the world the passing bell
Of Tyranny!

Semichorus II

Ha king! wilt thou chain
The rack and the rain,
Wilt thou fetter the lightning and hurricane?
The storms are free
But we?

Chorus

O Slavery! thou frost of the world's prime,
Killing its flowers and leaving its thorns bare!
Thy touch has stamped these limbs with crime,
These brows thy branding garland bear,
But the free heart, the impassive soul
Scorn thy controul!

Semichorus I

Let there be light! said Liberty,
And like sunrise from the sea,
Athens arose!—around her born,
Shone like mountains in the morn
Glorious States,—and are they now
Ashes, wrecks, oblivion?

Semichorus II

Go,
Where Thermae and Asopus swallowed
Persia, as the sand does foam.
Deluge upon deluge followed,—
Discord, Macedon and Rome:
And lastly Thou!

Semichorus I

Temples and towers,
Citadels and marts and they
Who live and die there, have been ours
And may be thine, and must decay,
But Greece and her foundations are
Built below the tide of war,
Based on the chrystalline sea
Of thought and its eternity;
Her citizens, imperial spirits,
Rule the present from the past,
On all this world of men inherits
Their seal is set—

Semichorus II

Hear ye the blast
Whose Orphic thunder thrilling calls
From ruin her Titanian walls?
Whose spirit shakes the sapless bones
Of Slavery? Argos, Corinth, Crete
Hear, and from their mountain thrones
The daemons and the nymphs repeat
The harmony.

Semichorus I

I hear! I hear!

Semichorus II

The world's eyeless charioteer,
Destiny, is hurrying by!
What faith is crushed, what empire bleeds
Beneath her earthquake-footed steeds?
What eagle-winged victory sits
At her right hand? what shadow flits

Before? what splendour rolls behind?
Ruin and Renovation cry
'Who but we?'

Semichorus I

I hear! I hear.
The hiss as of a rushing wind,
The roar as of an ocean foaming,
The thunder as of earthquake coming.
I hear! I hear!
The crash as of an empire falling,
The shrieks as of a people calling
'Mercy? Mercy!' how they thrill!
Then a shout of 'Kill! Kill! Kill!'
And then a small still voice, thus—

Semichorus II

For
Revenge and wrong bring forth their kind,
The foul cubs like their parents are,
Their den is in the guilty mind
And Conscience feeds them with despair.—

Semichorus I

In sacred Athens, near the fane
Of Wisdom, Pity's altar stood.—
Serve not the unknown God in vain,
But pay that broken shrine again,
Love for hate and tears for blood!
[*Enter* MAHMUD *and* AHASUERUS.

Mahmud

Thou art a man, thou sayest, even as we.

Ahasuerus

No more!

Mahmud

But raised above thy fellow men
By thought, as I by power.

Ahasuerus

Thou sayest so.

Mahmud

Thou art an adept in the difficult lore
Of Greek and Frank philosophy; thou numberest
The flowers, and thou measurest the stars;
Thou severest element from element;
Thy spirit is present in the past, and sees
The birth of this old world through all its cycles
Of desolation and of loveliness,
And when man was not, and how man became
The monarch and the slave of this low sphere,
And all its narrow circles—it is much—
I honour thee, and would be what thou art
Were I not what I am—but the unborn hour,
Cradled in fear and hope, conflicting storms,
Who shall unveil? Nor thou, nor I, nor any
Mighty or wise. I apprehended not
What thou hast taught me, but I now perceive
That thou art no interpreter of dreams;
Thou dost not own that art, device, or God,
Can make the future present—let it come!
Moreover thou disdainest us and ours;
Thou art as God whom thou contemplatest.

Ahasuerus

Disdain thee? not the worm beneath thy feet!
The Fathomless has care for meaner things
Than thou canst dream, and has made Pride for those
Who would be what they may not, or would seem
That which they are not—Sultan! talk no more
Of thee and me, the future and the past;
But look on that which cannot change—the One,
The unborn and the undying. Earth and ocean,
Space and the isles of life or light that gem
The sapphire floods of interstellar air,
This firmament pavilioned upon chaos,
With all its cressets of immortal fire
Whose outwall bastioned impregnably
Against the escape of boldest thoughts, repels them
As Calpe the Atlantic clouds—this Whole

Of suns, and worlds, and men, and beasts, and flowers,
With all the silent or tempestuous workings
By which they have been, are, or cease to be,
Is but a vision—all that it inherits
Are motes of a sick eye, bubbles and dreams;
Thought is its cradle and its grave, nor less
The future and the past are idle shadows
Of thought's eternal flight—they have no being.
Nought is but that which feels itself to be.

Mahmud

What meanest thou? thy words stream like a tempest
Of dazzling mist within my brain—they shake
The earth on which I stand, and hang like night
On Heaven above me. What can they avail?
They cast on all things surest, brightest, best,
Doubt, insecurity, astonishment.

Ahasuerus

Mistake me not! All is contained in each.
Dodona's forest to an acorn's cup
Is that which has been, or will be, to that
Which is—the absent to the present. Thought
Alone, and its quick elements, Will, Passion,
Reason, Imagination, cannot die;
They are, what that which they regard, appears,
The stuff whence mutability can weave
All that it hath dominion o'er, worlds, worms,
Empires and superstitions—what has thought
To do with time or place or circumstance?
Would'st thou behold the future?—ask and have!
Knock and it shall be opened—look and, lo!
The coming age is shadowed on the past
As on a glass.

Mahmud

Wild—wilder thoughts convulse
My spirit—did not Mahomet the Second
Win Stamboul?

Ahasuerus

Thou would'st ask that giant spirit
The written fortunes of thy house and faith—
Thou would'st cite one out of the grave to tell
How what was born in blood must die—

Mahmud

Thy words
Have power on me!—I see——

Ahasuerus

What hearest thou?

Mahmud

A far whisper——
Terrible silence—

Ahasuerus

What succeeds?

Mahmud

The sound
As of the assault of an imperial city——
The hiss of inextinguishable fire,—
The roar of giant cannon;—the earthquaking
Fall of vast bastions and precipitous towers,
The shock of crags shot from strange engin'ry,
The clash of wheels, and clang of armed hoofs
And crash of brazen mail as of the wreck
Of adamantine mountains—the mad blast
Of trumpets, and the neigh of raging steeds,
And shrieks of women whose thrill jars the blood
And one sweet laugh most horrible to hear
As of a joyous infant waked and playing
With its dead mother's breast, and now more loud
The mingled battle cry,—ha! hear I not
''Εν τούτῳ νίκη'—'Allah-Illah-Allah!'

Ahasuerus

The sulphurous mist is raised—thou see'st—

Mahmud

A chasm
As of two mountains in the wall of Stamboul
And in that ghastly breach the Islamites
Like giants on the ruins of a world
Stand in the light of sunrise. In the dust
Glimmers a kingless diadem, and one
Of regal port has cast himself beneath
The stream of war: another proudly clad
In golden arms spurs a Tartarian barb
Into the gap and with his iron mace
Directs the torrent of that tide of men
And seems—he is, Mahomet!

Ahasuerus

What thou see'st
Is but the ghost of thy forgotten dream.
A dream itself, yet, less, perhaps, than that
Thou callest reality. Thou mayest behold
How cities, on which empire sleeps enthroned,
Bow their tower'd crests to Mutability.
Poised by the flood, e'en on the height thou holdest,
Thou may'st now learn how the full tide of power
Ebbs to its depths.—Inheritor of glory
Conceived in darkness, born in blood, and nourished
With tears and toil, thou see'st the mortal throes
Of that whose birth was but the same. The Past
Now stands before thee like an Incarnation
Of the To-come; yet would'st thou commune with
That portion of thyself which was ere thou
Didst start for this brief race whose crown is death,
Dissolve with that strong faith and fervent passion
Which called it from the uncreated deep
Yon cloud of war with its tempestuous phantoms
Of raging death; and draw with mighty will
The imperial shade hither—

[*Exit* AHASUERUS.

Mahmud

Approach!

Phantom

I come
Thence whither thou must go! the grave is fitter
To take the living than give up the dead;
Yet has thy faith prevailed and I am here.
The heavy fragments of the power which fell
When I arose like shapeless crags and clouds
Hang round my throne on the abyss, and voices
Of strange lament soothe my supreme repose,
Wailing for glory never to return.——
A later Empire nods in its decay:
The autumn of a greener faith is come,
And wolfish Change, like winter, howls to strip
The foliage in which Fame, the eagle, built
Her aiëry, while Dominion whelped below.
The storm is in its branches, and the frost
Is on its leaves, and the blank deep expects
Oblivion on oblivion, spoil on spoil,
Ruin on ruin—thou art slow my son;
The Anarchs of the world of darkness keep
A throne for thee round which thine empire lies
Boundless and mute, and for thy subjects thou,
Like us, shalt rule the ghosts of murdered life,
The phantoms of the powers who rule thee now—
Mutinous passions, and conflicting fears
And hopes that sate themselves on dust and die,
Stript of their mortal strength, as thou of thine.
Islam must fall, but we will reign together
Over its ruins in the world of death—
And if the trunk be dry, yet shall the seed
Unfold itself even in the shape of that
Which gathers birth in its decay—Woe! woe!
To the weak people tangled in the grasp
Of its last spasms.

Mahmud

Spirit, woe to all!—
Woe to the wronged and the avenger! woe
To the destroyer; woe to the destroyed!
Woe to the dupe; and woe to the deceiver!
Woe to the oppressed; and woe to the oppressor!
Woe both to those that suffer and inflict,

Those who are born and those who die! but say,
Imperial shadow of the thing I am,
When, how, by whom, Destruction must accomplish
Her consummation?

Phantom

Ask the cold pale Hour
Rich in reversion of impending death
When he shall fall upon whose ripe grey hairs
Sit Care and Sorrow and Infirmity,
The weight which Crime whose wings are plumed with years
Leaves in his flight from ravaged heart to heart
Over the heads of men, under which burthen
They bow themselves unto the grave: fond wretch!
He leans upon his crutch and talks of years
To come, and how in hours of youth renewed
He will renew lost joys, and——

Voice without

Victory! Victory!
[*The* PHANTOM *vanishes.*

Mahmud
What sound of the importunate earth has broken
My mighty trance?

Voice without

Victory! Victory!

Mahmud
Weak lightning before darkness! poor faint smile
Of dying Islam! Voice which art the response
Of hollow weakness! Do I wake and live?
Were there such things or may the unquiet brain,
Vexed by the wise mad talk of the old Jew,
Have shaped itself these shadows of its fear?
It matters not!—for nought we see or dream,
Possess or lose or grasp at can be worth
More than it gives or teaches. Come what may,
The future must become the Past, and I
As they were to whom once this present hour,
This gloomy crag of Time to which I cling,

Seemed an Elysian isle of peace and joy
Never to be attained.——I must rebuke
This drunkenness of triumph ere it die,
And dying, bring despair. Victory? poor slaves!
[*Exit* MAHMUD.

Voice without
Shout in the jubilee of death! the Greeks
Are as a brood of lions in the net
Round which the kingly hunters of the earth
Stand smiling. Anarchs, ye whose daily food
Are curses, groans and gold, the fruit of death
From Thule to the Girdle of the World,
Come, feast! the board groans with the flesh of men;
The cup is foaming with a nation's blood,
Famine and Thirst await! eat, drink and die!

Semichorus I
Victorious Wrong with vulture scream
Salutes the risen sun, pursues the flying day!
I saw her, ghastly as a tyrant's dream,
Perch on the trembling pyramid of night,
Beneath which earth and all her realms pavilioned lay
In Visions of the dawning undelight.—
Who shall impede her flight?
Who rob her of her prey?

Voice without
Victory! Victory! Russia's famished Eagles
Dare not to prey beneath the crescent's light.
Impale the remnants of the Greeks? despoil?
Violate! make their flesh cheaper than dust!

Semichorus II
Thou Voice which art
The herald of the ill in splendour hid!
Thou echo of the hollow heart
Of monarchy, bear me to thine abode
When Desolation flashes o'er a world destroyed.
O bear me to those isles of jagged cloud
Which float like mountains on the earthquake, mid
The momentary oceans of the lightning,

Or to some toppling promontory proud
Of solid tempest whose black pyramid,
Riven, overhangs the founts intensely brightening
Of those dawn-tinted deluges of fire
Before their waves expire
When Heaven and Earth are light, and only light
In the thunder night!

Voice without
Victory! Victory! Austria, Russia, England
And that tame Serpent, that poor shadow, France,
Cry Peace, and that means Death when monarchs speak.
Ho, there! bring torches,—sharpen those red stakes,
These chains are light, fitter for slaves and poisoners
Than Greeks. Kill, plunder, burn! let none remain.

Semichorus I

Alas! for Liberty!
If numbers, wealth or unfulfilling years
Or fate can quell the free!
Alas! for Virtue when
Torments or contumely or the sneers
Of erring judging men
Can break the heart where it abides.
Alas! if Love whose smile makes this obscure world splendid
Can change with its false times and tides,
Like hope and terror—
Alas for Love!
And Truth, who wanderest lone and unbefriended,
If thou can'st veil thy lie-consuming mirror
Before the dazzled eyes of Error,
Alas for thee! Image of the Above.

Semichorus II

Repulse, with plumes from Conquest torn,
Led the Ten Thousand from the limits of the morn
Through many an hostile Anarchy!
At length they wept aloud and cried, 'The Sea! The Sea!'
Through exile, persecution and despair,
Rome was, and young Atlantis shall become
The wonder, or the terror or the tomb
Of all whose step wakes Power lulled in her savage lair.
But Greece was as a hermit child,

Whose fairest thoughts and limbs were built
To woman's growth, by dreams so mild,
She knew not pain or guilt;
And now—O Victory, blush! and Empire tremble
When ye desert the free—
If Greece must be
A wreck, yet shall its fragments reassemble
And build themselves again impregnably
In a diviner clime
To Amphionic music on some cape sublime,
Which frowns above the idle foam of Time.

Semichorus I

Let the tyrants rule the desart they have made—
Let the free possess the paradise they claim,
Be the fortune of our fierce oppressors weighed
With our ruin, our resistance and our name!

Semichorus II

Our dead shall be the seed of their decay,
Our survivors be the shadow of their pride,
Our adversity a dream to pass away—
Their dishonour a remembrance to abide!

Voice without

Victory! Victory! The bought Briton sends
The Keys of Ocean to the Islamite—
Now shall the blazon of the cross be veiled
And British skill directing Othman might,
Thunderstrike rebel Victory. O keep holy
This jubilee of unrevenged blood—
Kill, crush, despoil! Let not a Greek escape!

Semichorus I

Darkness has dawned in the East
On the noon of Time:
The death-birds descend to their feast,
From the hungry clime.—
Let Freedom and Peace flee far
To a sunnier strand,
And follow Love's folding star
To the Evening-land!

Semichorus II

The young moon has fed
Her exhausted horn
With the sunset's fire.
The weak day is dead,
But the night is not born,
And like Loveliness panting with wild desire
While it trembles with fear and delight,
Hesperus flies from awakening night
And pants in its beauty and speed with light
Fast flashing, soft and bright.
Thou beacon of love, thou lamp of the free!
Guide us far, far away,
To climes where now veiled by the ardour of day
Thou art hidden
From waves on which weary noon
Faints in her summer swoon
Between Kingless continents sinless as Eden,
Around mountains and islands inviolably
Prankt on the sapphire sea.

Semichorus I

Through the sunset of Hope
Like the shapes of a dream
What Paradise islands of glory gleam!
Beneath Heaven's cope,
Their shadows more clear float by—
The sound of their oceans, the light of their sky,
The music and fragrance their solitudes breathe
Burst, like morning on dream or like Heaven on death,
Through the walls of our prison;
And Greece which was dead is arisen!

Chorus

The world's great age begins anew,
The golden years return,
The earth doth like a snake renew
Her winter weeds outworn;
Heaven smiles, and faiths and empires gleam
Like wrecks of a dissolving dream.

A brighter Hellas rears its mountains
  From waves serener far,
A new Peneus rolls his fountains
  Against the morning-star,
Where fairer Tempes bloom, there sleep
Young Cyclads on a sunnier deep.

A loftier Argo cleaves the main,
  Fraught with a later prize;
Another Orpheus sings again,
  And loves, and weeps, and dies;
A new Ulysses leaves once more
Calypso for his native shore.

O, write no more the tale of Troy
  If earth Death's scroll must be!
Nor mix with Laian rage the joy
  Which dawns upon the free;
Although a subtler Sphinx renew
Riddles of death Thebes never knew.

Another Athens shall arise,
  And to remoter time
Bequeath, like sunset to the skies,
  The splendour of its prime.
And leave, if nought so bright may live,
All earth can take or Heaven can give.

Saturn and Love their long repose
  Shall burst, more bright and good
Than all who fell, than One who rose,
  Than many unsubdued;
Not gold, not blood their altar dowers
But votive tears and symbol flowers.

O cease! must hate and death return?
  Cease! must men kill and die?
Cease! drain not to its dregs the urn
  Of bitter prophecy.
The world is weary of the past,
O might it die or rest at last!

[SHELLEY'S] NOTES

Note 1 [l. 60]

The quenchless ashes of Milan

Milan was the centre of the resistance of the Lombard league against the Austrian tyrant. Frederic Barbarossa burnt the city to the ground, but Liberty lived in its ashes and it rose like an exhalation from its ruin. See Sismondi's *Histoire des Républiques Italiennes*, a book which has done much towards awakening the Italians to an imitation of their great ancestors.

Note 2 [l. 197]

The Chorus

The popular notions of Christianity are represented in this chorus as true in their relation to the worship they superseded, and that which in all probability they will supersede, without considering their merits in a relation more universal. The first stanza contrasts the immortality of the living and thinking beings which inhabit the planets, and to use a common and inadequate phrase, *clothe themselves in matter*, with the transience of the noblest manifestations of the external world.

The concluding verses indicate a progressive state of more or less exalted existence according to the degree of perfection which every distinct intelligence may have attained. Let it not be supposed that I mean to dogmatize upon a subject concerning which all men are equally ignorant, or that I think the Gordian knot of the origin of Evil can be disentangled by that or any similar assertions. The received hypothesis of a Being resembling men in the moral attributes of his nature having called us out of non-existence, and after inflicting on us the misery of the commission of error, should superadd that of the punishment and the privations consequent upon it, still would remain inexplicable and incredible. That there is a true solution of the riddle and that in our present state that solution is unattainable by us, are propositions which may be regarded as equally certain; meanwhile as it is the province of the poet to attach himself to those ideas which exalt and ennoble humanity, let him be permitted to have conjectured the condition of that futurity towards which we are all impelled by an inextinguishable thirst for immortality. Until better arguments can be produced than sophisms which disgrace the cause, this desire itself must remain the strongest and the only presumption that eternity is the inheritance of every thinking being.

Note 3 [l. 245]

No hoary priests after that Patriarch

The Greek Patriarch after having been compelled to fulminate an anathema against the insurgents was put to death by the Turks.

Fortunately the Greeks have been taught that they cannot buy security by degradation, and the Turks, though equally cruel, are less cunning than the smooth-faced Tyrants of Europe. As to the anathema, his Holiness might as well have thrown his mitre at Mount Athos for any effect that it produced. The Chiefs of the Greeks are almost all men of comprehension and enlightened views on religion and politics.

Note 4 [l. 563]

The freedman of a western poet chief

A Greek who had been Lord Byron's servant commands the insurgents in Attica. This Greek, Lord Byron informs me, though a poet and an enthusiastic patriot, gave him rather the idea of a timid and unenterprising person. It appears that circumstances make men what they are, and that we all contain the germ of a degree of degradation or of greatness whose connexion with our character is determined by events.

Note 5 [l. 598]

The Greeks expect a Saviour from the West

It is reported that this Messiah had arrived at a sea-port near Lacedaemon in an American brig. The association of names and ideas is irresistibly ludicrous, but the prevalence of such a rumour strongly marks the state of popular enthusiasm in Greece.

Note 6 [ll. 814–15]

The sound as of the assault of an imperial city

For the vision of Mahmud of the taking of Constantinople in 1453, see Gibbon's *Decline and Fall of the Roman Empire*, vol. 12, p. 223.

The manner of the invocation of the spirit of Mahomet the Second will be censured as over subtle. I could easily have made the Jew a regular conjuror and the phantom an ordinary ghost. I have preferred to represent the Jew as disclaiming all pretension or even belief in supernatural agency and as tempting Mahmud to that state of mind in which ideas may be supposed to assume the force of sensations through the confusion of thought with the objects of thought, and the excess of passion animating the creations of imagination.

It is a sort of natural magic, susceptible of being exercised in a degree by any one who should have made himself master of the secret associations of another's thoughts.

Note 7 [l. 1060]

The Chorus

The final chorus is indistinct and obscure as the event of the living drama whose arrival it foretells. Prophesies of wars, and rumours of wars &c., may safely be made by poet or prophet in any age, but to anticipate, however darkly, a period of regeneration and happiness is a more hazardous exercise of the faculty which bards possess or feign. It will remind the reader 'magno *nec* proximus intervallo' of Isaiah and Virgil, whose ardent spirits overleaping the actual reign of evil which we endure and bewail, already saw the possible and perhaps approaching state of society in which the *'lion shall lie down with the lamb'* and 'omnis feret omnia tellus'. Let these great names be my authority and my excuse.

Note 8 [ll. 1090–91]

Saturn and Love their long repose shall burst

Saturn and Love were among the deities of a real or imaginary state of innocence and happiness. *All* those *who fell*, or the gods of Greece, Asia, and Egypt; *the One who rose* or Jesus Christ, at whose appearance the idols of the Pagan world were amerced of their worship; and *the many unsubdued* or, the monstrous objects of the idolatry of China, India, the Antarctic islands, and the native tribes of America, certainly have reigned over the understandings of men in conjunction or in succession, during periods in which all we know of evil has been in a state of portentous, and until the revival of learning and the arts, perpetually increasing activity. The Grecian gods seem indeed to have been personally more innocent, although it cannot be said that as far as temperance and chastity are concerned they gave so edifying an example as their successor. The sublime human character of Jesus Christ was deformed by an imputed identification of it with a Demon, who tempted, betrayed and punished the innocent beings who were called into existence by his sole will; and for the period of a thousand years the spirit of this the most just, wise and benevolent of men has been propitiated with myriads of hecatombs of those who approached the nearest to his innocence and his wisdom, sacrificed under every aggravation of atrocity and variety of torture. The horrors of the Mexican, the Peruvian, and the Indian superstitions are well known.

'The flower that smiles today'

The flower that smiles today
   Tomorrow dies;
All that we wish to stay
   Tempts and then flies;
What is this world's delight?
Lightning, that mocks the night,
   Brief even as bright.—

Virtue, how frail it is!—
   Friendship, how rare!—
Love, how it sells poor bliss
   For proud despair!
But these though soon they fall,
Survive their joy, and all
   Which ours we call.—

Whilst skies are blue and bright,
   Whilst flowers are gay,
Whilst eyes that change ere night
   Make glad the day;
Whilst yet the calm hours creep
Dream thou—and from thy sleep
   Then wake to weep.

The Indian Girl's Song

I arise from dreams of thee
In the first sleep of night—
The winds are breathing low
And the stars are burning bright.
I arise from dreams of thee—
And a spirit in my feet
Has borne me—Who knows how?
To thy chamber window, sweet!—

The wandering airs they faint
On the dark silent stream—
The champak odours fail
Like sweet thoughts in a dream;
The nightingale's complaint—
It dies upon her heart—
As I must die on thine
O beloved as thou art!

O lift me from the grass!
I die, I faint, I fail!
Let thy love in kisses rain
On my lips and eyelids pale.
My cheek is cold and white, alas!
My heart beats loud and fast.
Oh press it close to thine again
Where it will break at last.

'Rough wind that moanest loud'

Rough wind that moanest loud,
  Grief too sad for song;
Wild wind when sullen cloud
  Knells all the night long;
Sad storm whose tears are vain,
Bare woods whose branches stain,
Deep caves and dreary main,
  Wail for the world's wrong.

Ah me, my heart is bare
  Like a winter bough;
The same blast of frozen air
  Bared it then that breaks it now;
Green leaves and crimson flowers
Clothed in the azure hours;
Death

To the Moon

Art thou pale for weariness
Of climbing Heaven, and gazing on the earth,
Wandering companionless
Among the stars that have a different birth,
And ever changing, like a joyless eye
That finds no object worth its constancy?

Remembrance

Swifter far than summer's flight,
Swifter far than happy night,
Swifter far than youth's delight
Art thou come and gone—
As the earth when leaves are dead—
As the Night when sleep is sped—
As the heart when joy is fled
I am left alone,—alone—

The swallow Summer comes again—
The owlet Night resumes her reign—
But the wild-swan Youth is fain
To fly with thee, false as thou—
My heart today desires tomorrow—
Sleep itself is turned to sorrow—
Vainly would my Winter borrow
Sunny leaves from any bough.

Lilies for a bridal bed,
Roses for a matron's head,
Violets for a maiden dead,—
Sadder flowers find for me.
On the living grave I bear
Scatter them without a tear;—
Let no friend, however dear,
Waste a hope, a fear, for me.

Lines to —— [Sonnet to Byron]

If I esteemed you less, Envy would kill
 Pleasure, and leave to Wonder and Despair
The ministration of the thoughts that fill
 My mind, which, like a worm whose life may share
A portion of the Unapproachable,
 Marks your creations rise as fast and fair
As perfect worlds at the creator's will,
 And bows itself before the godhead there.

But such is my regard, that, nor your fame
 Cast on the present by the coming hour,
Nor your well-won prosperity and power
 Move one regret for his unhonoured name
Who dares these words.—The worm beneath the sod
 May lift itself in worship to the God.

To —— ('The serpent is shut out from Paradise')

1

The serpent is shut out from Paradise—
The wounded deer must seek the herb no more
In which its heart's cure lies—
The widowed dove must cease to haunt a bower
Like that from which its mate with feigned sighs
Fled in the April hour—
I too, must seldom seek again
Near happy friends a mitigated pain.

2

Of hatred I am proud,—with scorn content;
Indifference, which once hurt me, is now grown
Itself indifferent.
But not to speak of love, Pity alone
Can break a spirit already more than bent.
The miserable one
Turns the mind's poison into food:
Its medicine is tears, its evil, good.

3

Therefore, if now I see you seldomer,
Dear friends, dear *friend*, know that I only fly
Your looks, because they stir
Griefs that should sleep, and hopes that cannot die.
The very comfort which they minister
I scarce can bear; yet I
(So deeply is the arrow gone)
Should quickly perish if it were withdrawn.

4

When I return to my cold home, you ask
Why I am not as I have lately been?
You spoil me for the task
Of acting a forced part in life's dull scene.
Of wearing on my brow the idle mask
Of author, great or mean,
In the world's carnival. I sought
Peace thus, and but in you I found it not.

5

Full half an hour today I tried my lot
With various flowers, and every one still said
'She loves me, loves me, not.'
And if this meant a Vision long since fled—
If it meant Fortune, Fame, or Peace of thought,
If it meant—(but I dread
To speak what you may know too well)
Still there was truth in the sad oracle.

6

The crane o'er seas and forests seeks her home.
No bird so wild, but has its quiet nest
When it no more would roam.
The sleepless billows on the Ocean's breast
Break like a bursting heart, and die in foam
And thus, at length, find rest.
Doubtless there is a place of peace
Where *my* weak heart and all its throbs will cease.

7

I asked her yesterday if she believed
That I had resolution. One who *had*
Would ne'er have thus relieved
His heart with words, but what his judgment bade
Would do, and leave the scorner unrelieved.—
These verses were too sad
To send to you, but that I know,
Happy yourself, you feel another's woe.

To Jane. The Invitation

Best and brightest, come away—
Fairer far than this fair day
Which like thee to those in sorrow
Comes to bid a sweet good-morrow
To the rough year just awake
In its cradle on the brake.—
The brightest hour of unborn spring
Through the winter wandering
Found it seems this halcyon morn
To hoar February born;
Bending from Heaven in azure mirth
It kissed the forehead of the earth
And smiled upon the silent sea,
And bade the frozen streams be free
And waked to music all their fountains
And breathed upon the frozen mountains,
And like a prophetess of May
Strewed flowers upon the barren way,
Making the wintry world appear
Like one on whom thou smilest, dear.

Away, away from men and towns
To the wild wood and the downs,
To the silent wilderness
Where the soul need not repress
Its music lest it should not find
An echo in another's mind,
While the touch of Nature's art
Harmonizes heart to heart.—

I leave this notice on my door
For each accustomed visitor—
'I am gone into the fields
To take what this sweet hour yields.
Reflexion, you may come tomorrow,
Sit by the fireside with Sorrow—
You, with the unpaid bill, Despair,
You, tiresome verse-reciter Care,
I will pay you in the grave,
Death will listen to your stave—
Expectation too, be off!
To-day is for itself enough—
Hope, in pity mock not woe
With smiles, nor follow where I go;
Long having lived on thy sweet food,
At length I find one moment's good
After long pain—with all your love
This you never told me of.'

Radiant Sister of the day,
Awake, arise and come away
To the wild woods and the plains
And the pools where winter-rains
Image all their roof of leaves,
Where the pine its garland weaves
Of sapless green and ivy dun
Round stems that never kiss the Sun—
Where the lawns and pastures be
And the sand hills of the sea—
Where the melting hoar-frost wets
The daisy-star that never sets,
And wind-flowers, and violets
Which yet join not scent to hue
Crown the pale year weak and new
When the night is left behind
In the deep east dun and blind
And the blue noon is over us,
And the multitudinous
Billows murmur at our feet
Where the earth and ocean meet,
And all things seem only one
In the universal Sun.—

To Jane—The Recollection

Now the last day of many days,
All beautiful and bright as thou,
The loveliest and the last, is dead.
Rise Memory, and write its praise!
Up to thy wonted work! come, trace
The epitaph of glory fled;
For now the Earth has changed its face,
A frown is on the Heaven's brow.

1

We wandered to the pine forest
  That skirts the Ocean foam;
The lightest wind was in its nest,
  The Tempest in its home;
The whispering waves were half asleep,
  The clouds were gone to play,
And on the bosom of the deep
  The smile of Heaven lay;
It seemed as if the hour were one
  Sent from beyond the skies,
Which scattered from above the sun
  A light of Paradise.

2

We paused amid the pines that stood
  The giants of the waste,
Tortured by storms to shapes as rude
  As serpents interlaced,
And soothed by every azure breath
  That under Heaven is blown
To harmonies and hues beneath,
  As tender as its own;
Now all the tree-tops lay asleep
  Like green waves on the sea,
As still as in the silent deep
  The Ocean woods may be.

3

How calm it was! the silence there
By such a chain was bound
That even the busy woodpecker
Made stiller with her sound
The inviolable quietness;
The breath of peace we drew
With its soft motion made not less
The calm that round us grew.—
There seemed from the remotest seat
Of the white mountain-waste,
To the soft flower beneath our feet
A magic circle traced,
A spirit interfused around
A thrilling silent life.
To momentary peace it bound
Our mortal nature's strife;—
And still I felt the centre of
The magic circle there
Was *one* fair form that filled with love
The lifeless atmosphere.

4

We paused beside the pools that lie
Under the forest bough—
Each seemed as 'twere, a little sky
Gulfed in a world below;
A firmament of purple light
Which in the dark earth lay
More boundless than the depth of night
And purer than the day,
In which the lovely forests grew
As in the upper air
More perfect, both in shape and hue,
Than any spreading there;
There lay the glade, the neighbouring lawn,
And through the dark green wood
The white sun twinkling like the dawn
Out of a speckled cloud.
Sweet views, which in our world above
Can never well be seen
Were imaged in the water's love

Of that fair forest green;
And all was interfused beneath
With an Elysian glow,
An atmosphere without a breath,
A softer day below—
Like one beloved, the scene had lent
To the dark water's breast
Its every leaf and lineament
With more than truth exprest;
Until an envious wind crept by,
Like an unwelcome thought
Which from the mind's too faithful eye
Blots one dear image out.—
Though thou art ever fair and kind
And forests ever green,
Less oft is peace in ——'s mind
Than calm in water seen.

'When the lamp is shattered'

When the lamp is shattered
The light in the dust lies dead—
When the cloud is scattered
The rainbow's glory is shed—
When the lute is broken
Sweet tones are remembered not—
When the lips have spoken
Loved accents are soon forgot.

As music and splendour
Survive not the lamp and the lute,
The heart's echoes render
No song when the spirit is mute—
No song—but sad dirges
Like the wind through a ruined cell
Or the mournful surges
That ring the dead seaman's knell.

When hearts have once mingled
Love first leaves the well-built nest—
The weak one is singled
To endure what it once possest.
O Love! who bewailest
The frailty of all things here,
Why choose you the frailest
For your cradle, your home and your bier?

Its passions will rock thee
As the storms rock the ravens on high—
Bright Reason will mock thee
Like the Sun from a wintry sky—
From thy nest every rafter
Will rot, and thine eagle home
Leave thee naked to laughter
When leaves fall and cold winds come.

'One word is too often prophaned'

One word is too often prophaned
For me to prophane it,
One feeling too falsely disdained
For thee to disdain it.
One hope is too like despair
For prudence to smother,
And Pity from thee more dear
Than that from another.

I can give not what men call love,—
But wilt thou accept not
The worship the heart lifts above
And the Heavens reject not—
The desire of the moth for the star,
Of the night for the morrow,
The devotion to something afar
From the sphere of our sorrow?

The Magnetic lady to her patient

'Sleep, sleep on, forget thy pain—
My hand is on thy brow,
My spirit on thy brain,
My pity on thy heart, poor friend;
And from my fingers flow
The powers of life, and like a sign
Seal thee from thine hour of woe,
And brood on thee, but may not blend
With thine.

'Sleep, sleep, sleep on—I love thee not—
Yet when I think that *he*
Who made and makes my lot
As full of flowers, as thine of weeds,
Might have been lost like thee,—
And that a hand which was not mine
Might then have charmed his agony
As I another's—my heart bleeds
For thine.

'Sleep, sleep, and with the slumber of
The dead and the unborn . . .
Forget thy life and love;
Forget that thou must wake—forever
Forget the world's dull scorn.—
Forget lost health, and the divine
Feelings which died in youth's brief morn;
And forget me, for I can never
Be thine.—

'Like a cloud big with a May shower
My soul weeps healing rain
On thee, thou withered flower.—
It breathes mute music on thy sleep—
Its odour calms thy brain—
Its light within thy gloomy breast
Spreads, like a second youth again—
By mine thy being is to its deep
Possest.—

'The spell is done—how feel you now?'
'Better, quite well,' replied
The sleeper—'What would do
You good when suffering and awake,
What cure your head and side?'
'What would cure that would kill me, Jane,
And as I must on earth abide
Awhile yet, tempt me not to break
My chain.'

With a Guitar. To Jane

Ariel to *Miranda*;—Take
This slave of music for the sake
Of him who is the slave of thee;
And teach it all the harmony,
In which thou can'st, and only thou,
Make the delighted spirit glow,
'Till joy denies itself again
And too intense is turned to pain;
For by permission and command
Of thine own *prince Ferdinand*
Poor Ariel sends this silent token
Of more than ever can be spoken;
Your guardian spirit Ariel, who
From life to life must still pursue
Your happiness, for thus alone
Can Ariel ever find his own;
From Prospero's enchanted cell,
As the mighty verses tell,
To the throne of Naples he
Lit you o'er the trackless sea,
Flitting on, your prow before,
Like a living meteor.
When you die, the silent Moon
In her interlunar swoon
Is not sadder in her cell
Than deserted Ariel;
When you live again on Earth
Like an unseen Star of birth
Ariel guides you o'er the sea

Of life from your nativity;
Many changes have been run
Since Ferdinand and you begun
Your course of love, and Ariel still
Has tracked your steps and served your will.
Now, in humbler, happier lot
This is all remembered not;
And now, alas! the poor sprite is
Imprisoned for some fault of his
In a body like a grave.—
From you, he only dares to crave
For his service and his sorrow
A smile today, a song tomorrow.

The artist who this idol wrought
To echo all harmonious thought
Felled a tree, while on the steep
The woods were in their winter sleep
Rocked in that repose divine
On the wind-swept Apennine;
And dreaming, some of autumn past
And some of spring approaching fast,
And some of April buds and showers
And some of songs in July bowers
And all of love,—and so this tree—
O that such our death may be—
Died in sleep and felt no pain
To live in happier form again,
From which, beneath Heaven's fairest star,
The artist wrought this loved guitar,
And taught it justly to reply
To all who question skilfully
In language gentle as thine own;
Whispering in enamoured tone
Sweet oracles of woods and dells
And summer winds in sylvan cells;
For it had learnt all harmonies
Of the plains and of the skies,
Of the forests and the mountains,
And the many-voiced fountains,
The clearest echoes of the hills,
The softest notes of falling rills,

The melodies of birds and bees,
The murmuring of summer seas,
And pattering rain and breathing dew
And airs of evening;—and it knew
That seldom heard mysterious sound,
Which, driven on its diurnal round
As it floats through boundless day
Our world enkindles on its way—
All this it knows, but will not tell
To those who cannot question well
The spirit that inhabits it:
It talks according to the wit
Of its companions, and no more
Is heard than has been felt before
By those who tempt it to betray
These secrets of an elder day.—
But, sweetly as its answers will
Flatter hands of perfect skill,
It keeps its highest holiest tone
For our beloved Jane alone.—

'Far, far away, O ye / Halcyons of Memory'

Far, far away, O ye
Halcyons of Memory,
Seek some far calmer nest
Than this abandoned breast—
No news of your false spring
To my heart's winter bring;
Once having gone, in vain
Ye come again.—

Vultures who build your bowers
High in the Future's towers,
Wake, for the spirit's blast
Over my peace has past;
Wrecked hopes on hopes are spread,
Dying joys choked by dead
Will serve your beaks for prey
Many a day.

'Tell me star, whose wings of light'

Tell me star, whose wings of light
Speed thee on thy fiery flight,
In what cavern of the night
  Will thy pinions close now?

Tell me Moon, thou pale and grey
Pilgrim of Heaven's homeless way,
In what depth of night or day
  Seekest thou repose now?

Weary wind who wanderest
Like the world's rejected guest,
Hast thou still some secret nest
  On some hill or billow?

THE TRIUMPH OF LIFE

Swift as a spirit hastening to his task
  Of glory and of good, the Sun sprang forth
Rejoicing in his splendour, and the mask

  Of darkness fell from the awakened Earth.
The smokeless altars of the mountain snows
  Flamed above crimson clouds, and at the birth

Of light, the Ocean's orison arose
  To which the birds tempered their matin lay.
All flowers in field or forest which unclose

  Their trembling eyelids to the kiss of day,
Swinging their censers in the element,
  With orient incense lit by the new ray

Burned slow and inconsumably, and sent
  Their odorous sighs up to the smiling air,
And in succession due, did Continent,

  Isle, Ocean, and all things that in them wear
The form and character of mortal mould
  Rise as the Sun their father rose, to bear

Their portion of the toil which he of old
  Took as his own and then imposed on them;
But I, whom thoughts which must remain untold

  Had kept as wakeful as the stars that gem
The cone of night, now they were laid asleep,
  Stretched my faint limbs beneath the hoary stem

Which an old chestnut flung athwart the steep
  Of a green Apennine: before me fled
The night; behind me rose the day; the Deep

  Was at my feet, and Heaven above my head
When a strange trance over my fancy grew
  Which was not slumber, for the shade it spread

Was so transparent that the scene came through
  As clear as when a veil of light is drawn
O'er evening hills they glimmer; and I knew

  That I had felt the freshness of that dawn,
Bathed in the same cold dew my brow and hair
  And sate as thus upon that slope of lawn

Under the self-same bough, and heard as there
  The birds, the fountains and the Ocean hold
Sweet talk in music through the enamoured air.
  And then a Vision on my brain was rolled . . .

As in that trance of wondrous thought I lay
  This was the tenour of my waking dream:
Methought I sate beside a public way

  Thick strewn with summer dust, and a great stream
Of people there was hurrying to and fro
  Numerous as gnats upon the evening gleam,

All hastening onward, yet none seemed to know
  Whither he went, or whence he came, or why
He made one of the multitude, yet so

  Was borne amid the crowd as through the sky
One of the million leaves of summer's bier.—
  Old age and youth, manhood and infancy,

Mixed in one mighty torrent did appear,
  Some flying from the thing they feared and some
Seeking the object of another's fear,

And others as with steps towards the tomb
Pored on the trodden worms that crawled beneath,
And others mournfully within the gloom

Of their own shadow walked, and called it death . . .
And some fled from it as it were a ghost,
Half fainting in the affliction of vain breath.

But more with motions which each other crost
Pursued or shunned the shadows the clouds threw
Or birds within the noonday ether lost,

Upon that path where flowers never grew;
And weary with vain toil and faint for thirst
Heard not the fountains whose melodious dew

Out of their mossy cells forever burst,
Nor felt the breeze which from the forest told
Of grassy paths, and wood lawns interspersed

With overarching elms and caverns cold
And violet banks where sweet dreams brood, but they
Pursued their serious folly as of old . . .

And as I gazed methought that in the way
The throng grew wilder, as the woods of June
When the South wind shakes the extinguished day,

And a cold glare, intenser than the noon
But icy cold, obscured with [ ] light
The Sun as he the stars. Like the young moon

When on the sunlit limits of the night
Her white shell trembles amid crimson air
And whilst the sleeping tempest gathers might

Doth, as a herald of its coming, bear
The ghost of her dead mother, whose dim form
Bends in dark ether from her infant's chair,

So came a chariot on the silent storm
Of its own rushing splendour, and a Shape
So sate within as one whom years deform

Beneath a dusky hood and double cape
Crouching within the shadow of a tomb,
And o'er what seemed the head a cloud like crape

Was bent, a dun and faint aetherial gloom
Tempering the light; upon the chariot's beam
A Janus-visaged Shadow did assume

The guidance of that wonder-winged team.
The Shapes which drew it in thick lightnings
Were lost: I heard alone on the air's soft stream

The music of their ever moving wings.
All the four faces of that charioteer
Had their eyes banded . . . little profit brings

Speed in the van and blindness in the rear,
Nor then avail the beams that quench the Sun
Or that their banded eyes could pierce the sphere

Of all that is, has been, or will be done—
So ill was the car guided, but it past
With solemn speed majestically on . . .

The crowd gave way, and I arose aghast,
Or seemed to rise, so mighty was the trance,
And saw like clouds upon the thunder-blast

The million with fierce song and maniac dance
Raging around; such seemed the jubilee
As when to greet some conqueror's advance

Imperial Rome poured forth her living sea
From senate-house and prison and theatre
When Freedom left those who upon the free

Had bound a yoke which soon they stooped to bear.
Nor wanted here the true similitude
Of a triumphal pageant, for where'er

The chariot rolled a captive multitude
Was driven; all those who had grown old in power
Or misery,—all who have their age subdued,

By action or by suffering, and whose hour
Was drained to its last sand in weal or woe,
So that the trunk survived both fruit and flower;

All those whose fame or infamy must grow
Till the great winter lay the form and name
Of their green earth with them forever low;

All but the sacred few who could not tame
Their spirits to the Conqueror, but as soon
As they had touched the world with living flame

Fled back like eagles to their native noon,
Or those who put aside the diadem
Of earthly thrones or gems, till the last one

Were there; for they of Athens and Jerusalem
Were neither mid the mighty captives seen
Nor mid the ribald crowd that followed them

Or fled before . . . Swift, fierce and obscene
The wild dance maddens in the van, and those
Who lead it, fleet as shadows on the green,

Outspeed the chariot and without repose
Mix with each other in tempestuous measure
To savage music . . . Wilder as it grows,

They, tortured by the agonizing pleasure,
Convulsed and on the rapid whirlwinds spun
Of that fierce spirit, whose unholy leisure

Was soothed by mischief since the world begun,
Throw back their heads and loose their streaming hair,
And in their dance round her who dims the Sun

Maidens and youths fling their wild arms in air
As their feet twinkle; now recede, and now
Bending within each other's atmosphere

Kindle invisibly; and as they glow
Like moths by light attracted and repelled,
Oft to new bright destruction come and go,

Till like two clouds into one vale impelled
That shake the mountains when their lightnings mingle
And die in rain—the fiery band which held

Their natures, snaps . . . the shock still may tingle—
One falls and then another in the path
Senseless, nor is the desolation single,

Yet ere I can say *where* the chariot hath
Past over them; nor other trace I find
But as of foam after the Ocean's wrath

Is spent upon the desert shore.—Behind,
Old men and women foully disarrayed
Shake their grey hair in the insulting wind,

Grasp in the dance and strain with limbs decayed
To reach the car of light which leaves them still
Farther behind and deeper in the shade.

But not the less with impotence of will
They wheel, though ghastly shadows interpose
Round them and round each other, and fulfil

Their work and to the dust whence they arose
Sink, and corruption veils them as they lie
And frost in these performs what fire in those.

Struck to the heart by this sad pageantry,
Half to myself I said, 'And what is this?
Whose shape is that within the car? and why'—

I would have added—'is all here amiss?'
But a voice answered . . . 'Life' . . . I turned and knew
(O Heaven have mercy on such wretchedness!)

That what I thought was an old root which grew
To strange distortion out of the hill side
Was indeed one of that deluded crew,

And that the grass which methought hung so wide
And white, was but his thin discoloured hair,
And that the holes it vainly sought to hide

Were or had been eyes.—'If thou canst forbear
To join the dance, which I had well forborne,'
Said the grim Feature, of my thought aware,

'I will now tell that which to this deep scorn
Led me and my companions, and relate
The progress of the pageant since the morn.

'If thirst of knowledge doth not thus abate,
Follow it thou even to the night, but I
Am weary' . . . Then like one who with the weight

Of his own words is staggered, wearily
He paused, and ere he could resume, I cried,
'First who art thou?' . . . 'Before thy memory

'I feared, loved, hated, suffered, did, and died,
And if the spark with which Heaven lit my spirit
Earth had with purer nutriment supplied

'Corruption would not now thus much inherit
Of what was once Rousseau—nor this disguise
Stained that within which still disdains to wear it.—

'If I have been extinguished, yet there rise
A thousand beacons from the spark I bore.'—
'And who are those chained to the car?' 'The Wise,

'The great, the unforgotten, they who wore
Mitres and helms and crowns, or wreathes of light,
Signs of thought's empire over thought; their lore

'Taught them not this—to know themselves; their might
Could not repress the mutiny within,
And for the morn of truth they feigned, deep night

'Caught them ere evening.' 'Who is he with chin
Upon his breast and hands crost on his chain?'
'The Child of a fierce hour; He sought to win

'The world, and lost all it did contain
Of greatness, in its hope destroyed; and more
Of fame and peace than Virtue's self can gain

'Without the opportunity which bore
Him on its eagle's pinion to the peak
From which a thousand climbers have before

'Fall'n as Napoleon fell.'—I felt my cheek
Alter to see the great form pass away
Whose grasp had left the giant world so weak

That every pigmy kicked it as it lay—
And much I grieved to think how power and will
In opposition rule our mortal day—

And why God made irreconcilable
Good and the means of good; and for despair
I half disdained mine eye's desire to fill

With the spent vision of the times that were
And scarce have ceased to be . . . 'Dost thou behold,'
Said then my guide, 'those spoilers spoiled, Voltaire,

'Frederic and Kant, Catharine, and Leopold,
Chained hoary anarch, demagogue and sage
Whose name the fresh world thinks already old—

'For in the battle Life and they did wage
She remained conqueror—I was overcome
By my own heart alone; which neither age

'Nor tears nor infamy nor now the tomb
Could temper to its object.' 'Let them pass'—
I cried—'the world and its mysterious doom

'Is not so much more glorious than it was
That I desire to worship those who drew
New figures on its false and fragile glass

'As the old faded.'—'Figures ever new
Rise on the bubble, paint them how you may;
We have but thrown, as those before us threw,

'Our shadows on it as it past away.
But mark how chained to the triumphal chair
The mighty phantoms of an elder day—

'All that is mortal of great Plato there
Expiates the joy and woe his master knew not;
That star that ruled his doom was far too fair—

'And Life, where long that flower of Heaven grew not,
Conquered the heart by love which gold or pain
Or age or sloth or slavery could subdue not.—

'And near walk the [ ] twain,
The tutor and his pupil, whom Dominion
Followed as tame as vulture in a chain.—

'The world was darkened beneath either pinion
Of him whom from the flock of conquerors
Fame singled as her thunder-bearing minion;

'The other long outlived both woes and wars
Throned in new thoughts of men, and still had kept
The jealous keys of truth's eternal doors

'If Bacon's spirit [ ] had not leapt
Like lightning out of darkness; he compelled
The Proteus shape of Nature's as it slept

'To wake and to unbar the caves that held
The treasure of the secrets of its reign.—
See the great bards of old who inly quelled

'The passions which they sung, as by their strain
May well be known: their living melody
Tempers its own contagion to the vein

'Of those who are infected with it—I
Have suffered what I wrote, or viler pain!—

'And so my words were seeds of misery—
Even as the deeds of others.'—'Not as theirs,'
I said—he pointed to a company

In which I recognized amid the heirs
Of Caesar's crime, from him to Constantine
The Anarchs old whose force and murderous snares

Had founded many a sceptre-bearing line
And spread the plague of blood and gold abroad,
And Gregory and John and men divine

Who rose like shadows between Man and god
Till that eclipse, still hanging under Heaven,
Was worshipped by the world o'er which they strode

For the true Sun it quenched.—'Their power was given
But to destroy,' replied the leader—'I
Am one of those who have created, even

'If it be but a world of agony.'—
'Whence camest thou and whither goest thou?
How did thy course begin,' I said, 'and why?

'Mine eyes are sick of this perpetual flow
Of people, and my heart of one sad thought.—
Speak.'— 'Whence I came, partly I seem to know,

'And how and by what paths I have been brought
To this dread pass, methinks even thou mayst guess;
Why this should be my mind can compass not—

'Whither the conqueror hurries me still less.
But follow thou, and from spectator turn
Actor or victim in this wretchedness

'And what thou wouldst be taught I then may learn
From thee.—Now listen . . . In the April prime
When all the forest tops began to burn

'With kindling green, touched by the azure clime
Of the young year, I found myself asleep
Under a mountain which from unknown time

'Had yawned into a cavern high and deep,
And from it came a gentle rivulet
Whose water like clear air in its calm sweep

'Bent the soft grass and kept for ever wet
The stems of the sweet flowers, and filled the grove
With sound which all who hear must needs forget

'All pleasure and all pain, all hate and love,
Which they had known before that hour of rest:
A sleeping mother then would dream not of

'The only child who died upon her breast
At eventide, a king would mourn no more
The crown of which his brow was dispossest

'When the sun lingered o'er the Ocean floor
To gild his rival's new prosperity.—
Thou wouldst forget thus vainly to deplore

'Ills, which if ills, can find no cure from thee,
The thought of which no other sleep will quell
Nor other music blot from memory—

'So sweet and deep is the oblivious spell.—
Whether my life had been before that sleep
The Heaven which I imagine, or a Hell

'Like this harsh world in which I wake to weep,
I know not. I arose and for a space
The scene of woods and waters seemed to keep,

'Though it was now broad day, a gentle trace
Of light diviner than the common Sun
Sheds on the common Earth, but all the place

'Was filled with many sounds woven into one
Oblivious melody, confusing sense
Amid the gliding waves and shadows dun;

'And as I looked the bright omnipresence
Of morning through the orient cavern flowed,
And the Sun's image radiantly intense

'Burned on the waters of the well that glowed
Like gold, and threaded all the forest maze
With winding paths of emerald fire—there stood

'Amid the sun, as he amid the blaze
Of his own glory, on the vibrating
Floor of the fountain, paved with flashing rays,

'A shape all light, which with one hand did fling
Dew on the earth, as if she were the Dawn
Whose invisible rain forever seemed to sing

'A silver music on the mossy lawn,
And still before her on the dusky grass
Iris her many-coloured scarf had drawn.—

'In her right hand she bore a chrystal glass
Mantling with bright Nepenthe;—the fierce splendour
Fell from her as she moved under the mass

'Of the deep cavern, and with palms so tender
Their tread broke not the mirror of its billow,
Glided along the river, and did bend her

'Head under the dark boughs, till like a willow
Her fair hair swept the bosom of the stream
That whispered with delight to be their pillow.—

'As one enamoured is upborne in dream
O'er lily-paven lakes mid silver mist
To wondrous music, so this shape might seem

'Partly to tread the waves with feet which kist
The dancing foam, partly to glide along
The airs that roughened the moist amethyst,

'Or the slant morning beams that fell among
The trees, or the soft shadows of the trees;
And her feet ever to the ceaseless song

'Of leaves and winds and waves and birds and bees
And falling drops moved in a measure new
Yet sweet, as on the summer evening breeze

'Up from the lake a shape of golden dew
Between two rocks, athwart the rising moon,
Dances i' the wind where eagle never flew.—

'And still her feet, no less than the sweet tune
To which they moved, seemed as they moved, to blot
The thoughts of him who gazed on them, and soon

'All that was seemed as if it had been not—
As if the gazer's mind was strewn beneath
Her feet like embers, and she, thought by thought,

'Trampled its fires into the dust of death,
As Day upon the threshold of the east
Treads out the lamps of night, until the breath

'Of darkness reillumine even the least
Of Heaven's living eyes—like day she came,
Making the night a dream; and ere she ceased

'To move, as one between desire and shame
Suspended, I said—"If, as it doth seem,
Thou comest from the realm without a name,

'"Into this valley of perpetual dream,
Shew whence I came, and where I am, and why—
Pass not away upon the passing stream."

'"Arise and quench thy thirst", was her reply.
And as a shut lily, stricken by the wand
Of dewy morning's vital alchemy,

'I rose; and, bending at her sweet command,
Touched with faint lips the cup she raised,
And suddenly my brain became as sand

'Where the first wave had more than half erased
The track of deer on desert Labrador,
Whilst the empty wolf from which they fled amazed

'Leaves his stamp visibly upon the shore
Until the second bursts—so on my sight
Burst a new Vision never seen before.—

'And the fair shape waned in the coming light
As veil by veil the silent splendour drops
From Lucifer, amid the chrysolite

'Of sunrise ere it strike the mountain tops—
And as the presence of that fairest planet,
Although unseen, is felt by one who hopes

'That his day's path may end as he began it
In that star's smile, whose light is like the scent
Of a jonquil when evening breezes fan it,

'Or the soft note in which his dear lament
The Brescian shepherd breathes, or the caress
That turned his weary slumber to content—

'So knew I in that light's severe excess
The presence of that shape which on the stream
Moved, as I moved along the wilderness,

'More dimly than a day-appearing dream,
The ghost of a forgotten form of sleep,
A light from Heaven whose half-extinguished beam

'Through the sick day in which we wake to weep
Glimmers, forever sought, forever lost.—
So did that shape its obscure tenour keep

'Beside my path as silent as a ghost;
But the new Vision, and its cold bright car,
With savage music, stunning music, crost

'The forest, and as if from some dread war
Triumphantly returning, the loud million
Fiercely extolled the fortune of her star.—

'A moving arch of victory, the vermilion
And green and azure plumes of Iris had
Built high over her wind-winged pavilion,

'And underneath aetherial glory clad
The wilderness, and far before her flew
The tempest of the splendour which forbade

'Shadow to fall from leaf or stone;—the crew
Seemed in that light like atomies that dance
Within a sunbeam;—some upon the new

'Embroidery of flowers that did enhance
The grassy vesture of the desert, played,
Forgetful of the chariot's swift advance;

'Others stood gazing till within the shade
Of the great mountain its light left them dim.—
Others outspeeded it, and others made

'Circles around it like the clouds that swim
Round the high moon in a bright sea of air,
And more did follow, with exulting hymn,

'The chariot and the captives fettered there,
But all like bubbles on an eddying flood
Fell into the same track at last and were

'Borne onward.—I among the multitude
Was swept; me sweetest flowers delayed not long,
Me not the shadow nor the solitude,

'Me not the falling stream's Lethean song,
Me, not the phantom of that early form
Which moved upon its motion,—but among

'The thickest billows of the living storm
I plunged, and bared my bosom to the clime
Of that cold light, whose airs too soon deform.—

'Before the chariot had begun to climb
The opposing steep of that mysterious dell,
Behold a wonder worthy of the rhyme

'Of him who from the lowest depths of Hell
Through every Paradise and through all glory
Love led serene, and who returned to tell

'In words of hate and awe the wondrous story
How all things are transfigured, except Love;
For deaf as is a sea which wrath makes hoary

'The world can hear not the sweet notes that move
The sphere whose light is melody to lovers—
A wonder worthy of his rhyme—the grove

'Grew dense with shadows to its inmost covers,
The earth was grey with phantoms, and the air
Was peopled with dim forms, as when there hovers

'A flock of vampire-bats before the glare
Of the tropic sun, bringing ere evening
Strange night upon some Indian isle,—thus were

'Phantoms diffused around, and some did fling
Shadows of shadows, yet unlike themselves,
Behind them, some like eaglets on the wing

'Were lost in the white blaze, others like elves
Danced in a thousand unimagined shapes
Upon the sunny streams and grassy shelves;

'And others sate chattering like restless apes
On vulgar hands, and over shoulders leapt.
Some made a cradle of the ermined capes

'Of kingly mantles, some upon the tiar
Of pontiffs sate like vultures, others played
Within the crown which girt with empire

'A baby's or an idiot's brow, and made
Their nests in it; the old anatomies
Sate hatching their base brood under the shade

'Of demon wings, and laughed from their dead eyes
To reassume the delegated power
Arrayed in which these worms did monarchize

'Who make this earth their charnel.—Others more
Humble, like falcons sate upon the fist
Of common men, and round their heads did soar,

'Or like small gnats and flies as thick as mist
On evening marshes, thronged about the brow
Of lawyer, statesman, priest and theorist,

'And others like discoloured flakes of snow
On fairest bosoms, and the sunniest hair
Fell, and were melted by the youthful glow

'Which they extinguished; for like tears, they were
A veil to those from whose faint lids they rained
In drops of sorrow.—I became aware

'Of whence those forms proceeded which thus stained
The track in which we moved; after brief space
From every form the beauty slowly waned,

'From every firmest limb and fairest face
The strength and freshness fell like dust, and left
The action and the shape without the grace

'Of life; the marble brow of youth was cleft
With care, and in the eyes where once hope shone
Desire like a lioness bereft

'Of its last cub, glared ere it died; each one
Of that great crowd sent forth incessantly
These shadows, numerous as the dead leaves blown

'In Autumn evenings from a poplar tree—
Each, like himself and like each other were,
At first, but soon distorted, seemed to be

'Obscure clouds moulded by the casual air;
And of this stuff the car's creative ray
Wrought all the busy phantoms that were there

'As the sun shapes the clouds—thus, on the way
Mask after mask fell from the countenance
And form of all, and long before the day

'Was old, the joy which waked like Heaven's glance
The sleepers in the oblivious valley, died,
And some grew weary of the ghastly dance

'And fell, as I have fallen by the way side,
Those soonest, from whose forms most shadows past
And least of strength and beauty did abide.'—

'Then, what is Life?' I said . . . the cripple cast
His eye upon the car which now had rolled
Onward, as if that look must be the last,

And answered . . . 'Happy those for whom the fold
Of

To Jane ('The keen stars were twinkling')

The keen stars were twinkling
And the fair moon was rising among them,
Dear Jane.
The guitar was tinkling
But the notes were not sweet 'till you sung them
Again.—
As the moon's soft splendour
O'er the faint cold starlight of Heaven
Is thrown—
So your voice most tender
To the strings without soul had then given
Its own.

The stars will awaken,
Though the moon sleep a full hour later,
Tonight;
No leaf will be shaken
While the dews of your melody scatter
Delight.
Though the sound overpowers
Sing again, with your dear voice revealing
A tone
Of some world far from ours,
Where music and moonlight and feeling
Are one.

Lines Written in the Bay of Lerici

Bright wanderer, fair coquette of Heaven,
To whom alone it has been given
To change and be adored for ever . . .
Envy not this dim world, for never
But once within its shadow grew
One fair as you, but far more true—
She left me at the silent time
When the moon had ceased to climb
The azure dome of Heaven's steep,
And like an albatross asleep,

Balanced on her wings of light,
Hovered in the purple night,
Ere she sought her Ocean nest
In the chambers of the west.—
She left me, and I staid alone
Thinking over every tone,
Which though now silent to the ear
The enchanted heart could hear
Like notes which die when born, but still
Haunt the echoes of the hill:
And feeling ever—O too much—
The soft vibrations of her touch
As if her gentle hand even now
Lightly trembles on my brow;
And thus although she absent were
Memory gave me all of her
That even fancy dares to claim.—
Her presence had made weak and tame
All passions, and I lived alone
In the time which is our own;
The past and future were forgot
As they had been, and would be, not.—
But soon, the guardian angel gone,
The demon reassumed his throne
In my faint heart . . . I dare not speak
My thoughts; but thus disturbed and weak
I sate and watched the vessels glide
Along the ocean bright and wide,
Like spirit-winged chariots sent
O'er some serenest element
To ministrations strange and far;
As if to some Elysian star
They sailed for drink to medicine
Such sweet and bitter pain as mine.—
And the wind that winged their flight
From the land came fresh and light,
And the scent of sleeping flowers
And the coolness of the hours
Of dew, and the sweet warmth of day
Was scattered o'er the twinkling bay;
And the fisher with his lamp
And spear, about the low rocks damp

Crept, and struck the fish who came
To worship the delusive flame:
Too happy, they whose pleasure sought
Extinguishes all sense and thought
Of the regret that pleasure [ ]
Seeking life alone, not peace.

THE PROSE

From *History of a Six Weeks' Tour*

Hôtel de Londres, Chamouni,
July 22d, 1816.

Near Maglans, within a league of each other, we saw two waterfalls. They were no more than mountain rivulets, but the height from which they fell, at least of *twelve* hundred feet, made them assume a character inconsistent with the smallness of their stream. The first fell from the overhanging brow of a black precipice on an enormous rock, precisely resembling some colossal Egyptian statue of a female deity. It struck the head of the visionary image, and gracefully dividing there, fell from it in folds of foam more like to cloud than water, imitating a veil of the most exquisite woof.[1] It then united, concealing the lower part of the statue, and hiding itself in a winding of its channel, burst into a deeper fall, and crossed our route in its path towards the Arve.

The other waterfall was more continuous and larger. The violence with which it fell made it look more like some shape which an exhalation[2] had assumed, than like water, for it streamed beyond the mountain, which appeared dark behind it, as it might have appeared behind an evanescent cloud.

The character of the scenery continued the same until we arrived at St. Martin (called in the maps Sallanches) the mountains perpetually becoming more elevated, exhibiting at every turn of the road more craggy summits, loftier and wider extent of forests, darker and more deep recesses.

The following morning we proceeded from St. Martin on mules to Chamouni, accompanied by two guides. We proceeded, as we had done the preceding day, along the valley of the Arve, a valley surrounded on all sides by immense mountains, whose rugged precipices are intermixed on high with dazzling snow. Their bases were still covered with the eternal forests, which perpetually grew darker and more profound as we approached the inner regions of the mountains.

On arriving at a small village, at the distance of a league from St. Martin, we dismounted from our mules, and were conducted by our guides to view a cascade. We beheld an immense body of water fall two hundred and fifty feet, dashing from rock to rock, and casting a spray which formed a mist around it, in the midst of which hung a multitude of sunbows, which faded or became unspeakably vivid, as the inconstant sun shone through the clouds. When we approached near to it, the rain of the spray reached us, and our clothes were wetted by the quick-falling but minute particles of water. The cataract fell from above into a deep craggy chasm at our feet, where, changing its character to that of a mountain stream, it pursued its course towards the Arve, roaring over the rocks that impeded its progress.

As we proceeded, our route still lay through the valley, or rather, as it had now become, the vast ravine, which is at once the couch and the creation of the terrible Arve. We ascended, winding between mountains whose immensity staggers the imagination. We crossed the path of a torrent, which three days since had descended from the thawing snow, and torn the road away.

We dined at Servoz, a little village, where there are lead and copper mines, and where we saw a cabinet of natural curiosities, like those of Keswick and Bethgelert.[3] We saw in this cabinet some chamois' horns, and the horns of an exceedingly rare animal called the bouquetin, which inhabits the desarts of snow to the south of Mont Blanc: it is an animal of the stag kind; its horns weigh at least twenty-seven English pounds. It is inconceivable how so small an animal could support so inordinate a weight. The horns are of a very peculiar conformation, being broad, massy, and pointed at the ends, and surrounded with a number of rings, which are supposed to afford an indication of its age: there were seventeen rings on the largest of these horns.

From Servoz three leagues remain to Chamouni.—Mont Blanc was before us—the Alps, with their innumerable glaciers on high all around, closing in the complicated windings of the single vale—forests inexpressibly beautiful, but majestic in their beauty—intermingled beech and pine, and oak, overshadowed our road, or receded, whilst lawns of such verdure as I have never seen before occupied these openings, and gradually became darker in their recesses. Mont Blanc was before us, but it was covered with cloud; its base, furrowed with dreadful gaps, was seen above. Pinnacles of snow intolerably bright, part of the chain connected with Mont Blanc, shone through the clouds at intervals on high. I never knew—I never imagined what mountains were before. The immensity of these aerial summits excited, when they suddenly burst upon the sight, a sentiment of extatic wonder, not unallied to madness. And remember this was all one scene, it all pressed home to our regard and our imagination. Though it embraced a vast extent of space, the snowy pyramids which shot into the bright blue sky seemed to overhang our path; the ravine, clothed with gigantic pines, and black with its depth below, so deep that the very roaring of the untameable Arve, which rolled through it, could not be heard above—all was as much our own, as if we had been the creators of such impressions in the minds of others as now occupied our own. Nature was the poet, whose harmony held our spirits more breathless than that of the divinest.

As we entered the valley of Chamouni (which in fact may be considered as a continuation of those which we have followed from Bonneville and Cluses) clouds hung upon the mountains at the distance perhaps of 6000 feet from the earth, but so as effectually to conceal not only Mont Blanc, but the other *aiguilles*,[4] as they call them here, attached and subordinate to it. We were travelling along the valley, when suddenly we heard a sound as of the burst of smothered thunder rolling above; yet there was something earthly in the sound, that told us it could not be thunder. Our guide hastily pointed out to us a part of the mountain opposite, from whence the sound came. It was an avalanche. We saw the smoke of its path among the rocks, and continued to hear at intervals the bursting of its fall. It fell on the bed of a torrent, which it displaced, and presently we saw its tawny-coloured waters also spread themselves over the ravine, which was their couch.

We did not, as we intended, visit the *Glacier de Boisson* to-day, although it descends within a few minutes' walk of the road, wishing to survey it at least when unfatigued. We saw this glacier which comes close to the fertile plain, as we passed, its surface was broken into a thousand unaccountable figures: conical and pyramidical crystalizations, more than fifty feet in height, rise from its surface, and precipices of ice, of dazzling splendour, overhang the woods and meadows of the vale. This glacier winds upwards from the valley, until it joins the masses of frost from which it was produced above, winding through its own ravine like a bright belt flung over the black region of pines. There is more in all these scenes than mere magnitude of proportion: there is a majesty of outline; there is an awful[5] grace in the very colours which invest these wonderful shapes—a charm which is peculiar to them, quite distinct even from the reality of their unutterable greatness.

July 24.

Yesterday morning we went to the source of the Arveiron. It is about a league from this village; the river rolls forth impetuously from an arch of ice, and spreads itself in many streams over a vast space of the valley, ravaged and laid bare by its inundations. The glacier by which its waters are nourished, overhangs this cavern and the plain, and the forests of pine which surround it, with terrible precipices of solid ice. On the other side rises the immense glacier of Montanvert, fifty miles in extent, occupying a chasm among mountains of inconceivable height, and of forms so pointed and abrupt, that they seem to pierce the sky. From this glacier we saw as we sat on a rock, close to one of the streams of the Arveiron, masses of ice detach themselves from on high, and rush with a loud dull noise into the vale. The violence of their fall turned them into powder, which flowed over the rocks in imitation of waterfalls, whose ravines they usurped and filled.

In the evening I went with Ducrée, my guide, the only tolerable person I have seen in this country, to visit the glacier of Boisson. This glacier, like that of Montanvert, comes close to the vale, overhanging the green meadows and the dark woods with the dazzling whiteness of its precipices and pinnacles, which are like spires of radiant crystal, covered with a net-work of frosted silver. These glaciers flow perpetually into the valley, ravaging in their slow but irresistible progress the pastures and the forests which surround them, performing a work of desolation in ages, which a river of lava might accomplish in an hour, but far more irretrievably; for where the ice has once descended, the hardiest plant refuses to grow; if even, as in some extraordinary instances, it should recede after its progress has once commenced. The glaciers perpetually move onward, at the rate of a foot each day, with a motion that commences at the spot where, on the boundaries of perpetual congelation, they are produced by the freezing of the waters which arise from the partial melting of the eternal snows. They drag with them from the regions whence they derive their origin, all the ruins of the mountain, enormous rocks, and immense accumulations of sand and stones. These are driven onwards by the irresistible stream of solid ice; and when they arrive at a declivity of the mountain, sufficiently rapid, roll down, scattering ruin. I saw one of these rocks which had descended in the spring, (winter here is the season of silence and safety) which measured forty feet in every direction.

The verge of a glacier, like that of Boisson, presents the most vivid image of desolation that it is possible to conceive. No one dares to approach it; for the enormous pinnacles of ice which perpetually fall, are perpetually reproduced. The pines of the forest, which bound it at one extremity, are overthrown and shattered to a wide extent at its base. There is something inexpressibly dreadful in the aspect of the few branchless trunks, which, nearest to the ice rifts, still stand in the uprooted soil. The meadows perish, overwhelmed with sand and stones. Within this last year, these glaciers have advanced three hundred feet into the valley. Saussure, the naturalist, says, that they have their periods of increase and decay:[6] the people of the country hold an opinion entirely different; but as I judge, more probable. It is agreed by all, that the snow on the summit of Mont Blanc and the neighbouring mountains perpetually augments, and that ice, in the form of glaciers, subsists without melting in the valley of Chamouni during its transient and variable summer. If the snow which produces this glacier must augment, and the heat of the valley is no obstacle to the perpetual existence of such masses of ice as have already descended into it, the consequence is obvious; the glaciers must augment and will subsist, at least until they have overflowed this vale.

I will not pursue Buffon's sublime but gloomy theory—that this globe which we inhabit will at some future period be changed into a mass of frost by the encroachments of the polar ice, and of that produced on the most elevated points of the earth.[7] Do you, who assert the supremacy of Ahriman,[8] imagine him throned among these desolating snows, among these palaces of death and frost, so sculptured in this their terrible magnificence by the adamantine[9] hand of necessity, and that he casts around him, as the first essays of his final usurpation, avalanches, torrents, rocks, and thunders, and above all these deadly glaciers, at once the proof and symbols of his reign;—add to this, the degradation of the human species—who in these regions are half deformed or idiotic, and most of whom are deprived of any thing that can excite interest or admiration. This is a part of the subject more mournful and less sublime; but such as neither the poet nor the philosopher should disdain to regard.

This morning we departed, on the promise of a fine day, to visit the glacier of Montanvert. In that part where it fills a slanting valley, it is called the Sea of Ice. This valley is 950 toises,[10] or 7600 feet above the level of the sea. We had not proceeded far before the rain began to fall, but we persisted until we had accomplished more than half of our journey, when we returned, wet through.

Chamouni, July 25th.

We have returned from visiting the glacier of Montanvert, or as it is called, the Sea of Ice, a scene in truth of dizzying wonder. The path that winds to it along the side of a mountain, now clothed with pines, now intersected with snowy hollows, is wide and steep. The cabin of Montanvert is three leagues from Chamouni, half of which distance is performed on mules, not so sure footed, but that on the first day the one which I rode fell in what the guides called a *mauvais pas*,[11] so that I narrowly escaped being precipitated down the mountain. We passed over a hollow covered with snow, down which vast stones are accustomed to roll. One had fallen the preceding day, a little time after we had returned: our guides desired us to pass quickly, for it is said that sometimes the least sound will accelerate their descent. We arrived at Montanvert, however, safe.

On all sides precipitous mountains, the abodes of unrelenting frost, surround this vale: their sides are banked up with ice and snow, broken, heaped high, and exhibiting terrific chasms. The summits are sharp and naked pinnacles, whose overhanging steepness will not even permit snow to rest upon them. Lines of dazzling ice occupy here and there their perpendicular rifts, and shine through the driving vapours with inexpressible brilliance: they pierce the clouds like things not belonging to this earth. The vale itself is filled with a mass of undulating ice, and has an ascent sufficiently gradual even to the remotest abysses of these horrible desarts. It is only half a league (about two miles) in breadth, and seems much less. It exhibits an appearance as if frost had suddenly bound up the waves and whirlpools of a mighty torrent. We walked some distance upon its surface. The waves are elevated about 12 or 15 feet from the surface of the mass, which is intersected by long gaps of unfathomable depth, the ice of whose sides is more beautifully azure than the sky. In these regions every thing changes, and is in motion. This vast mass of ice has one general progress, which ceases neither day nor night; it breaks and bursts for ever: some undulations sink while others rise; it is never the same. The echo of rocks, or of the ice and snow which fall from their overhanging precipices, or roll from their aerial summits, scarcely ceases for one moment. One would think that Mont Blanc, like the god of the Stoics,[12] was a vast animal, and that the frozen blood for ever circulated through his stony veins.

We dined (M***, C***, and I) on the grass, in the open air, surrounded by this scene. The air is piercing and clear. We returned down the mountain, sometimes encompassed by the driving vapours, sometimes cheered by the sunbeams, and arrived at our inn by seven o'clock.

Montalegre, July 28th.

The next morning we returned through the rain to St. Martin. The scenery had lost something of its immensity, thick clouds hanging over the highest mountains; but visitings of sunset intervened between the showers, and the blue sky shone between the accumulated clouds of snowy whiteness which brought them; the dazzling mountains sometimes glittered through a chasm of the clouds above our heads, and all the charm of its grandeur remained. We repassed *Pont Pellisier*, a wooden bridge over the Arve, and the ravine of the Arve. We repassed the pine forests which overhang the defile, the chateau of St. Michel, a haunted ruin, built on the edge of a precipice, and shadowed over by the eternal forest. We repassed the vale of Servoz, a vale more beautiful, because more luxuriant, than that of Chamouni. Mont Blanc forms one of the sides of this vale also, and the other is inclosed by an irregular amphitheatre of enormous mountains, one of which is in ruins, and fell fifty years ago into the higher part of the valley: the smoke of its fall was seen in Piedmont, and people went from Turin to investigate whether a volcano had not burst forth among the Alps. It continued falling many days, spreading, with the shock and thunder of its ruin, consternation into the neighbouring vales. In the evening we arrived at St. Martin. The next day we wound through the valley, which I have described before, and arrived in the evening at our home.

We have bought some specimens of minerals and plants, and two or three crystal seals, at Mont Blanc, to preserve the remembrance of having approached it. There is a cabinet of *Histoire Naturelle* at Chamouni, just as at Keswick, Matlock, and Clifton; the proprietor of which is the very vilest specimen of that vile species of quack that, together with the whole army of aubergistes[13] and guides, and indeed the entire mass of the population, subsist on the weakness and credulity of travellers as leaches subsist on the sick. The most interesting of my purchases is a large collection of all the seeds of rare alpine plants, with their names written upon the outside of the papers than contain them. These I mean to colonize in my garden in England, and to permit you to make what choice you please from them. They are companions which the Celandine[14]—the classic Celandine, need not despise; they are as wild and more daring than he, and will tell him tales of things even as touching and sublime as the gaze of a vernal poet.

Did I tell you that there are troops of wolves among these mountains? In the winter they descend into the vallies, which the snow occupies six months of the year, and devour every thing that they can find out of doors. A wolf is more powerful than the fiercest and strongest dog. There are no bears in these regions. We heard, when we were at Lucerne, that they were occasionally found in the forests which surround that lake. Adieu.

S.

From *Preface to* LAON AND CYTHNA;

OR, THE REVOLUTION OF THE GOLDEN CITY: A VISION OF THE NINETEENTH CENTURY. IN THE STANZA OF SPENSER

The Poem which I now present to the world, is an attempt from which I scarcely dare to expect success, and in which a writer of established fame might fail without disgrace. It is an experiment on the temper of the public mind, as to how far a thirst for a happier condition of moral and political society survives, among the enlightened and refined, the tempests which have shaken the age in which we live.[1] I have sought to enlist the harmony of metrical language, the etherial combinations of the fancy, the rapid and subtle transitions of human passion, all those elements which essentially compose a Poem, in the cause of a liberal and comprehensive morality, and in the view of kindling within the bosoms of my readers, a virtuous enthusiasm for those doctrines of liberty and justice, that faith and hope in something good, which neither violence, nor misrepresentation, nor prejudice, can ever totally extinguish among mankind. [. . .]

The panic which, like an epidemic transport, seized upon all classes of men during the excesses consequent upon the French Revolution, is gradually giving place to sanity. It has ceased to be believed, that whole generations of mankind ought to consign themselves to a hopeless inheritance of ignorance and misery, because a nation of men who had been dupes and slaves for centuries, were incapable of conducting themselves with the wisdom and tranquillity of freemen so soon as some of their fetters were partially loosened. That their conduct could not have been marked by any other characters than ferocity and thoughtlessness, is the historical fact from which liberty derives all its recommendations, and falshood the worst features of its deformity. There is a reflux in the tide of human things which bears the shipwrecked hopes of men into a secure haven, after the storms are past. Methinks, those who now live have survived an age of despair. [. . .]

I do not presume to enter into competition with our greatest contemporary Poets. Yet I am unwilling to tread in the footsteps of any who have preceded me. I have sought to avoid the imitation of any style of language or versification peculiar to the original minds of which it is the character, designing that even if what I have produced be worthless, it should still be properly my own. Nor have I permitted any system relating to mere words, to divert the attention of the reader from whatever interest I may have succeeded in creating, to my own ingenuity in contriving to disgust them according to the rules of criticism. I have simply clothed my thoughts in what appeared to me the most obvious and appropriate language. A person familiar with nature, and with the most celebrated productions of the human mind,[2] can scarcely err in following the instinct, with respect to selection of language, produced by that familiarity.

There is an education peculiarly fitted for a Poet, without which, genius and sensibility can hardly fill the circle of their capacities. No education indeed can entitle to this appellation a dull and unobservant mind, or one, though neither dull nor unobservant, in which the channels of communication between thought and expression have been obstructed or closed. How far it is my fortune to belong to either of the latter classes, I cannot know. I aspire to be something better. The circumstances of my accidental education[3] have been favourable to this ambition. I have been familiar from boyhood with mountains and lakes, and the sea, and the solitude of forests: Danger which sports upon the brink of precipices, has been my playmate. I have trodden the glaciers of the Alps, and lived under the eye of Mont Blanc.[4] I have been a wanderer among distant fields. I have sailed down mighty rivers,[5] and seen the sun rise and set, and the stars come forth, whilst I have sailed night and day down a rapid stream among mountains. I have seen populous cities, and have watched the passions which rise and spread, and sink and change amongst assembled multitudes of men. I have seen the theatre of the more visible ravages of tyranny and war, cities and villages reduced to scattered groups of black and roofless houses, and the naked inhabitants sitting famished upon their desolated thresholds.[6] I have conversed with living men of genius.[7] The poetry of ancient Greece and Rome, and modern Italy, and our own country, has been to me like external nature, a passion and an enjoyment. Such are the sources from which the materials for the imagery of my Poem have been drawn. I have considered Poetry in its most comprehensive sense, and have read the Poets and the Historians and the Metaphysicians* whose writings have been accessible to me, and have looked upon the beautiful and majestic scenery of the earth as common sources of those elements

* In this sense there may be such a thing as perfectibility in works of fiction, notwithstanding the concession often made by the advocates of human improvement, that perfectibility is a term applicable only to science. [Shelley's note][8]

which it is the province of the Poet to embody and combine. Yet the experience and the feelings to which I refer, do not in themselves constitute men Poets, but only prepares them to be the auditors of those who are. How far I shall be found to possess that more essential attribute of Poetry, the power of awakening in others sensations like those which animate my own bosom, is that which, to speak sincerely, I know not; and which with an acquiescent and contented spirit, I expect to be taught by the effect which I shall produce upon those whom I now address.

I have avoided, as I have said before, the imitation of any contemporary style. But there must be a resemblance which does not depend upon their own will, between all the writers of any particular age.[9] They cannot escape from subjection to a common influence which arises out of an infinite combination of circumstances belonging to the times in which they live, though each is in a degree the author of the very influence by which his being is thus pervaded. Thus, the tragic Poets of the age of Pericles;[10] the Italian revivers of ancient learning; those mighty intellects of our own country that succeeded the Reformation, the translators of the Bible, Shakespeare, Spenser, the Dramatists of the reign of Elizabeth, and Lord Bacon;* the colder spirits of the interval that succeeded;—all resemble each other, and differ from every other in their several classes. In this view of things, Ford[12] can no more be called the imitator of Shakespeare, than Shakespeare the imitator of Ford. There were perhaps few other points of resemblance between these two men, than that which the universal and inevitable influence of their age produced. And this is an influence which neither the meanest scribbler, nor the sublimest genius of any aera can escape; and which I have not attempted to escape. [. . .]

The Poem now presented to the Public occupied little more than six months in the composition. That period has been devoted to the task with unremitting ardour and enthusiasm. I have exercised a watchful and earnest criticism on my work as it grew under my hands. I would willingly have sent it forth to the world with that perfection which long labour and revision is said to bestow. But I found that if I should gain something in exactness by this method, I might lose much of the newness and energy of imagery and language as it flowed fresh from my mind. And although the mere composition occupied no more than six months, the thoughts thus arranged were slowly gathered in as many years. [. . .]

* Milton stands alone in the age which he illumined. [Shelley's note][11]

An Address to the People on the Death of the Princess Charlotte

By The Hermit of Marlow[1]

'We Pity the Plumage, but Forget the Dying Bird'[2]

I. The Princess Charlotte is dead. She no longer moves, nor thinks, nor feels. She is as inanimate as the clay with which she is about to mingle. It is a dreadful thing to know that she is a putrid corpse, who but a few days since was full of life and hope; a woman young, innocent, and beautiful, snatched from the bosom of domestic peace, and leaving that single vacancy which none can die and leave not.

II. Thus much the death of the Princess Charlotte has in common with the death of thousands. How many women die in childbed and leave their families of motherless children and their husbands to live on, blighted by the remembrance of that heavy loss? How many women of active and energetic virtues; mild, affectionate, and wise, whose life is as a chain of happiness and union, which once being broken, leaves those whom it bound to perish, have died, and have been deplored with bitterness, which is too deep for words? Some have perished in penury or shame, and their orphan baby has survived, a prey to the scorn and neglect of strangers. Men have watched by the bedside of their expiring wives, and have gone mad when the hideous death-rattle was heard within the throat, regardless of the rosy child sleeping in the lap of the unobservant nurse. The countenance of the physician had been read by the stare of this distracted husband, till the legible despair sunk into his heart. All this has been and is. You walk with a merry heart through the streets of this great city, and think not that such are the scenes acting all around you. You do not number in your thought the mothers who die in childbed. It is the most horrible of ruins:—In sickness, in old age, in battle, death comes as to his own home; but in the season of joy and hope, when life should succeed to life, and the assembled family expects one more, the youngest and the best beloved, that the wife, the mother—she for whom each member of the family was so dear to one another, should die!—Yet thousands of the poorest poor, whose misery is aggravated by what cannot be spoken now, suffer this. And have they no affections? Do not their hearts beat in their bosoms, and the tears gush from their eyes? Are they not human flesh and blood? Yet none weep for them—none mourn for them—none when their coffins are carried to the grave (if indeed the parish furnishes a coffin for all) turn aside and moralize upon the sadness they have left behind.

III. The Athenians did well to celebrate, with public mourning, the death of those who had guided the republic with their valour and their understanding, or illustrated it with their genius.[3] Men do well to mourn for the dead: it proves that we love something beside ourselves; and he must have a hard heart who can see his friend depart to rottenness and dust, and speed him without emotion on his voyage to 'that bourne whence no traveller returns.'[4] To lament for those who have benefitted the state, is a habit of piety yet more favourable to the cultivation of our best affections. When Milton died it had been well that the universal English nation had been clothed in solemn black, and that the muffled bells had tolled from town to town. The French nation should have enjoined a public mourning at the deaths of Rousseau and Voltaire. We cannot truly grieve for every one who dies beyond the circle of those especially dear to us; yet in the extinction of the objects of public love and admiration, and gratitude, there is something, if we enjoy a liberal mind, which has departed from within that circle. It were well done also, that men should mourn for any public calamity which has befallen their country or the world, though it be not death. This helps to maintain that connexion between one man and another, and all men considered as a whole, which is the bond of social life. There should be public mourning when those events take place which make all good men mourn in their hearts,—the rule of foreign or domestic tyrants, the abuse of public faith, the wresting of old and venerable laws to the murder of the innocent, the established insecurity of all those, the flower of the nation, who cherish an unconquerable enthusiasm for public good. Thus, if Horne Tooke and Hardy had been convicted of high treason,[5] it had been good that there had been not only the sorrow and the indignation which would have filled all hearts, but the external symbols of grief. When the French Republic was extinguished, the world ought to have mourned.

IV. But this appeal to the feelings of men should not be made lightly, or in any manner that tends to waste, on inadequate objects, those fertilizing streams of sympathy, which a public mourning should be the occasion of pouring forth. This solemnity should be used only to express a wide and intelligible calamity, and one which is felt to be such by those who feel for their country and for mankind; its character ought to be universal, not particular.

V. The news of the death of the Princess Charlotte, and of the execution of Brandreth, Ludlam, and Turner, arrived nearly at the same time. If beauty, youth, innocence, amiable manners, and the exercise of the domestic virtues could alone justify public sorrow when they are extinguished for ever, this interesting Lady would well deserve that exhibition. She was the last and the best of her race. But there were thousands of others equally distinguished as she, for private excellencies, who have been cut off in youth and hope. The accident of her birth neither made her life more virtuous nor her death more worthy of grief. For the public she had done nothing either good or evil; her education had rendered her incapable of either in a large and comprehensive sense. She was born a Princess; and those who are destined to rule mankind are dispensed with acquiring that wisdom and that experience which is necessary even to rule themselves. She was not like Lady Jane Grey, or Queen Elizabeth, a woman of profound and various learning. She had accomplished nothing, and aspired to nothing, and could understand nothing respecting those great political questions which involve the happiness of those over whom she was destined to rule. Yet this should not be said in blame, but in compassion: let us speak no evil of the dead. Such is the misery, such the impotence of royalty.—Princes are prevented from the cradle from becoming any thing which may deserve that greatest of all rewards next to a good conscience, public admiration and regret.

VI. The execution of Brandreth, Ludlam, and Turner, is an event of quite a different character from the death of the Princess Charlotte. These men were shut up in a horrible dungeon, for many months, with the fear of a hideous death and of everlasting hell thrust before their eyes; and at last were brought to the scaffold and hung. They too had domestic affections, and were remarkable for the exercise of private virtues. Perhaps their low station permitted the growth of those affections in a degree not consistent with a more exalted rank. They had sons, and brothers, and sisters, and fathers, who loved them, it should seem, more than the Princess Charlotte could be loved by those whom the regulations of her rank had held in perpetual estrangement from her. Her husband was to her as father, mother, and brethren. Ludlam and Turner were men of mature years, and the affections were ripened and strengthened within them. What these sufferers felt shall not be said. But what must have been the long and various agony of their kindred may be inferred from Edward Turner, who, when he saw his brother dragged along upon the hurdle,[6] shrieked horribly and fell in a fit, and was carried away like a corpse by two men. How fearful must have been their agony, sitting in solitude on that day when the tempestuous voice of horror from the crowd, told them that the head so dear to them was severed from the body! Yes—they listened to the maddening shriek which burst from the multitude: they heard the rush of ten thousand terror-stricken feet, the groans and the hootings which told them that the mangled and distorted head was then lifted into the air. The sufferers were dead. What is death? Who dares to say that which will come after the grave?* Brandreth was calm, and evidently believed that the consequences of our errors were limited by that tremendous barrier. Ludlam and Turner were full of fears, lest God should plunge them in everlasting fire. Mr. Pickering, the clergyman, was evidently anxious that Brandreth should not by a false confidence lose the single opportunity of reconciling himself with the Ruler of the future world. None knew what death was, or could know. Yet these men were presumptuously thrust into that unfathomable gulf, by other men, who knew as little and who reckoned not the present or the future sufferings of their victims. Nothing is more horrible than that man should for any cause shed the life of man. For all other calamities there is a remedy or a consolation. When that Power through which we live ceases to maintain the life which it has conferred, then is grief and agony, and the burthen which must be borne: such sorrow improves the heart. But when man sheds the blood of man, revenge, and hatred, and a long train of executions, and assassinations, and proscriptions, is perpetuated to remotest time.

VII. Such are the particular, and some of the general considerations depending on[8] the death of these men. But however deplorable, if it were a mere private or customary grief, the public, as the public, should not mourn. But it is more than this. The events which led to the death of those unfortunate men are a public calamity. I will not impute blame to the jury who pronounced them guilty of high treason, perhaps the law requires that such should be the denomination of their offence. Some restraint ought indeed to be imposed on those thoughtless men who imagine they can find in violence a remedy for violence, even if their oppressors had tempted them to this occasion

* 'Your death has eyes in his head—mine is not painted so.'—*Cymbeline.* [Shelley's note][7]

of their ruin. They are instruments of evil, not so guilty as the hands that wielded them, but fit to inspire caution. But their death, by hanging and beheading, and the circumstances of which it is the characteristic and the consequence, constitute a calamity such as the English nation ought to mourn with an unassuageable grief.

VIII. Kings and their ministers have in every age been distinguished from other men by a thirst for expenditure and bloodshed. There existed in this country, until the American war, a check,[9] sufficiently feeble and pliant indeed, to this desolating propensity. Until America proclaimed itself a republic, England was perhaps the freest and most glorious nation subsisting on the surface of the earth. It was not what is to the full desirable that a nation should be, but all that it can be, when it does not govern itself. The consequences however of that fundamental defect[10] soon became evident. The government which the imperfect constitution of our representative assembly threw into the hands of a few aristocrats, improved the method of anticipating the taxes by loans, invented by the ministers of William III, until an enormous debt had been created. In the war against the republic of France, this policy was followed up, until now, the *mere interest* of the public debt amounts to more than twice as much as the lavish expenditure of the public treasure, for maintaining the standing army, and the royal family, and the pensioners, and the placemen.[11] The effect of this debt is to produce such an unequal distribution of the means of living, as saps the foundation of social union and civilized life.[12] It creates a double aristocracy,[13] instead of one which was sufficiently burthensome before, and gives twice as many people the liberty of living in luxury and idleness, on the produce of the industrious and the poor. And it does not give them this because they are more wise and meritorious than the rest, or because their leisure is spent in schemes of public good, or in those exercises of the intellect and the imagination, whose creations ennoble or adorn a country. They are not like the old aristocracy men of pride and honour, *sans peur et sans tache*,[14] but petty piddling slaves who have gained a right to the title of public creditors, either by gambling in the funds,[15] or by subserviency to government, or some other villainous trade. They are not the 'Corinthian capital of polished society,'[16] but the petty and creeping weeds which deface the rich tracery of its sculpture. The effect of this system is, that the day labourer gains no more now by working sixteen hours a day than he gained before by working eight. I put the thing in its simplest and most intelligible shape. The labourer, he that tills the ground and manufactures cloth, is the man who has to provide, out of what he would bring home to his wife and children, for the luxuries and comforts of those, whose claims are represented by an annuity of forty-four millions a year levied upon the English nation. Before, he supported the army and the pensioners, and the royal family, and the landholders; and this is a hard necessity to which it was well that he should submit. Many and various are the mischiefs flowing from oppression, but this is the representative of them all; namely, that one man is forced to labour for another in a degree not only not necessary to the support of the subsisting distinctions among mankind, but so as by the excess of the injustice to endanger the very foundations of all that is valuable in social order, and to provoke that anarchy which is at once the enemy of freedom, and the child and the chastiser of misrule. The nation, tottering on the brink of two chasms,[17] began to be weary of a continuance of such dangers and degradations, and the miseries which are the consequence of them; the public voice loudly demanded a free representation of the people. It began to be felt that no other constituted body of men could meet the difficulties which impend. Nothing but the nation itself dares to touch the question as to whether there is any remedy or no to the annual payment of forty-four millions a year, beyond the necessary expenses of state, for ever and for ever. A nobler spirit also went abroad, and the love of liberty, and patriotism, and the self-respect attendant on those glorious emotions, revived in the bosoms of men. The government had a desperate game to play.

IX. In the manufacturing districts of England discontent and disaffection had prevailed for many years; this was the consequence of that system of double aristocracy produced by the causes before mentioned. The manufacturers, the helots[18] of our luxury, are left by this system famished, without affections, without health, without leisure or opportunity for such instruction as might counteract those habits of turbulence and dissipation, produced by the precariousness and insecurity of poverty. Here was a ready field for any adventurer who should wish for whatever purpose to incite a few ignorant men to acts of illegal outrage. So soon as it was plainly seen that the demands of the people for a free representation must be conceded if some intimidation and prejudice were not conjured up, a conspiracy of the most horrible atrocity was laid in train. It is impossible to know how far the higher members of the government are involved in the guilt of their infernal agents. It is impossible to know how numerous or how active they have been, or by what false hopes they are yet inflaming the untutored multitude to put their necks under the axe and into the halter. But thus much is known, that so soon as the whole nation lifted up its voice for parliamentary reform, spies were sent forth.[19] These were selected from the most worthless and infamous of mankind, and dispersed among the multitude of famished and illiterate labourers. It was their business if they found no discontent to create it. It was their business to find victims, no matter whether right or wrong. It was their business to produce upon the public an impression, that if any attempt to attain national freedom, or to diminish the burthens of debt and taxation under which we groan, were successful, the starving multitude would rush in, and confound all orders and distinctions, and institutions and laws, in common ruin. The inference with which they were required to arm the ministers was, that despotic power ought to be eternal. To produce this salutary impression, they betrayed some innocent and unsuspecting rustics into a crime whose penalty is a hideous death. A few hungry and ignorant manufacturers seduced by the splendid promises of these remorseless blood-conspirators, collected together in what is called rebellion against the state. All was prepared, and the eighteen dragoons assembled in readiness, no doubt, conducted their astonished victims to that dungeon which they left only to be mangled by the executioner's hand. The cruel instigators of their ruin retired to enjoy the great revenues which they had earned by a life of villainy. The public voice was overpowered by the timid and the selfish, who threw the weight of fear into the scale of public opinion, and parliament confided anew to the executive government those extraordinary powers[20] which may never be laid down, or which may be laid down in blood, or which the regularly constituted assembly of the nation must wrest out of their hands. Our alternatives are a despotism, a revolution, or reform.

X. On the 7th of November, Brandreth, Turner, and Ludlam ascended the scaffold. We feel for Brandreth the less, because it seems he killed a man. But recollect who instigated him to the proceedings which led to murder. On the word of a dying man, Brandreth tells us, that 'OLIVER[21] *brought him to this*'—that, '*but for* OLIVER, *he would not have been there*.' See, too, Ludlam and Turner, with their sons and brothers, and sisters, how they kneel together in a dreadful agony of prayer. Hell is before their eyes, and they shudder and feel sick with fear, lest some unrepented or some wilful sin should seal their doom in everlasting fire. With that dreadful penalty before their eyes—with that tremendous sanction for the truth of all he spoke,

Turner exclaimed loudly and distinctly, *while the executioner was putting the rope round his neck*, 'THIS IS ALL OLIVER AND THE GOVERNMENT.' What more he might have said we know not, because the chaplain prevented any further observations.[22] Troops of horse, with keen and glittering swords, hemmed in the multitudes collected to witness this abominable exhibition. 'When the stroke of the axe was heard, there was a burst of horror from the crowd.* The instant the head was exhibited, there was a tremendous shriek set up, and the multitude ran violently in all directions, as if under the impulse of sudden frenzy. Those who resumed their stations, groaned and hooted.' It is a national calamity, that we endure men to rule over us, who sanction for whatever ends a conspiracy which is to arrive at its purpose through such a frightful pouring forth of human blood and agony. But when that purpose is to trample upon our rights and liberties forever, to present to us the alternatives of anarchy and oppression, and triumph when the astonished nation accepts the latter at their hands, to maintain a vast standing army, and add, year by year, to a public debt, which, already, they know, cannot be discharged; and which, when the delusion that supports it fails, will produce as much misery and confusion through all classes of society as it has continued to produce of famine and degradation to the undefended poor; to imprison and calumniate those who may offend them, at will; when this, if not the purpose, is the effect of that conspiracy, how ought we not to mourn?

XI. Mourn then People of England. Clothe yourselves in solemn black. Let the bells be tolled. Think of mortality and change. Shroud yourselves in solitude and the gloom of sacred sorrow. Spare no symbol of universal grief. Weep—mourn—lament. Fill the great City—fill the boundless fields, with lamentation and the echo of groans. A beautiful Princess is dead:—she who should have been the Queen of her beloved nation, and whose posterity should have ruled it for ever. She loved the domestic affections, and cherished arts which adorn, and valour which defends. She was amiable and would have become wise, but she was young, and in the flower of youth the despoiler came. LIBERTY is dead. Slave! I charge thee disturb not the depth and solemnity of our grief by any meaner sorrow. If One has died who was like her that should have ruled over this land, like Liberty, young, innocent, and lovely, know that the power through which that one perished was God, and that it was a private grief. But *man* has

* These expressions are taken from the *Examiner*, Sunday, Nov. 9. [Shelley's note][23]

murdered Liberty, and whilst the life was ebbing from its wound, there descended on the heads and on the hearts of every human thing, the sympathy of an universal blast and curse. Fetters heavier than iron weigh upon us, because they bind our souls. We move about in a dungeon more pestilential than damp and narrow walls, because the earth is its floor and the heavens are its roof. Let us follow the corpse of British Liberty slowly and reverentially to its tomb: and if some glorious Phantom[24] should appear, and make its throne of broken swords and sceptres and royal crowns trampled in the dust, let us say that the Spirit of Liberty has arisen from its grave and left all that was gross and mortal there, and kneel down and worship it as our Queen.

From *On Christianity*

The being who has influenced in the most memorable manner the opinions and the fortunes of the human species, is Jesus Christ. At this day his name is connected with the devotional feelings of two hundred millions of the race of man. The institutions of the most civilised portion of the globe derive their authority from the sanction of his doctrines and to a certain extent are [imbued by their Spirit].[1] He is the God of our popular religion. His extraordinary Genius, the wide and rapid effect of his unexampled doctrines, his invincible gentleness and benignity, the devoted love borne to him by his adherents suggested a persuasion to them that he was something divine. The supernatural events which the historians of this wonderful man subsequently asserted to have been connected with every gradation of his career established the opinion. His death is said to have been accompanied by an accumulation of tremendous prodigies. Utter darkness fell upon the earth blotting the noonday Sun, dead bodies arising from their graves walked thro' the public streets, and an earthquake shook the astonished city, rending the rocks of the surrounding mountains.[2] The philosopher may attribute the application of these events to the death of a reformer or the events themselves to a visitation of that Universal Pan[3] who[4]

God

[. . .] We can distinctly trace in the tissue of his [Christ's] doctrines the persuasion that God is some universal being, differing both from man and from the mind of man.—According to Jesus Christ God is neither the Jupiter who sends rain upon the earth, nor the Venus thro' whom all living things are produced, nor the Vulcan who presides over the terrestrial element of fire, nor the Vesta[5] that preserves the light which is inshrined in the sun and moon and stars. He is neither the Proteus[6] or the Pan of the material world. But the word God according to the acceptation of Jesus Christ unites all the attributes which these denominations contain, and is the interfused and overruling Spirit of all the energy and wisdom included within the circle of existing things. It is important to observe that the author of the Christian system had a conception widely differing from the gross imaginations of the vulgar relatively to the ruling Power of the Universe. He every where represents this power as something mysteriously and illimitably pervading the frame of things. Nor do his doctrines practically assume any proposition which they theoretically deny. They do not represent God as a limitless and inconceivable mystery affirming at the same time his existence as a being subject to passion and capable[7]

Blessed are the pure in heart, for they shall see God[8]—blessed are those who have preserved internal sanctity of soul, who are conscious of no secret deceit, who are the same in act as they are in desire, who conceal no thought, no tendencies of thought, from their own conscience, who are faithful and sincere witnesses before the tribunal of their own judgement of all that passes within their mind. Such as these shall see God. What! After death shall their awakened eyes behold the King of Heaven, shall they stand in awe before the golden throne on which he sits, and gaze upon the venerable countenance of the paternal Monarch. Is this the reward of the virtuous and the pure? These are the idle dreams of the visionary or the pernicious representations of impostors who have fabricated from the very materials of wisdom a cloak for their own dwarfish and imbecile conceptions. Jesus Christ has said no more than the most excellent philosophers have felt and expressed, that virtue is its own reward. It is true that such an expression as he has used was prompted by the energy of genius, it was the overflowing enthusiasm of a [ ] poet, but it is not the less literally true, clearly repugnant to the mistaken conceptions of the multitude.—God, it has been asserted, was contemplated by Jesus Christ as every poet and every philosopher must have contemplated that mysterious principle. He considered that venerable word to express the overruling Spirit of the collective energy of the moral and material world. He affirms therefore no more than that a simple and sincere mind is an indispensable requisite of true knowledge and true happiness. He affirms that a being of pure and gentle habits will not fail in every thought, in every object of every thought, to be aware of benignant visitings from the invisible energies by which he is surrounded. Whosoever is free from the contamination of luxury and licence may go forth to the fields and to the woods inhaling joyous renovation from the breath of Spring, or catching from the odours and the sounds of autumn, some diviner mood of sweetest sadness which improves the solitary heart. Whosoever is no deceiver or destroyer of his fellow men, no liar, no flatterer, no murderer may walk among his species, deriving from the communion with all which they contain of beautiful or of majestic, some intercourse with the Universal God. Whoever has maintained with his own heart the strictest correspondence of confidence, who dares to examine and to estimate every imagination which suggests itself to his mind, who is that which he designs to become, and only aspires to that which the divinity of his own nature shall consider and approve . . . he, has already seen God.

We live and move and think, but we are not the creators of our own origin and existence, we are not the arbiters of every motion of our own complicated nature, we are not the masters of our own imaginations and moods of mental being . . . There is a power by which we are surrounded, like the atmosphere in which some motionless lyre[9] is suspended, which visits with its breath our silent chords, at will. Our most imperial and stupendous qualities, those on which the majesty and power of humanity is erected, are, relatively to the inferiour portion of its mechanism, indeed active and imperial; but they are the passive slaves of some higher and more omnipresent Power. This power is God. And those who have seen God, have, in the periods of their purer and more perfect nature, been harmonized by their own will, to so exquisite a consentaneity[10] of powers, as to give forth divinest melody when the breath of universal being sweeps over their frame.[11]

That those who are pure in heart shall see God, and that virtue is its own reward, may be considered as equivalent assertions. The former of these propositions is a metaphorical repetition of the latter. The advocates of literal interpretation have been the most efficacious enemies of those doctrines whose institutor they profess to venerate. They would assert, it[12]

[Revenge]

[. . .] Jesus Christ instructed his disciples to be perfect as their father in Heaven is perfect, declaring at the same time his belief that human perfection required the refraining from revenge or retribution in any of its various shapes.[13] The perfection of the human and the divine character is thus asserted to be the same: man by resembling God fulfills most accurately the tendencies of his nature, and God comprehends within itself all that constitutes human perfection. Thus God is a model thro' which the excellence of man is to be measured, whilst the *abstract* perfection of the human character is the type of the actual *perfection* of the divine. It is not to be believed that a person of such comprehensive views as Jesus Christ could have fallen into so manifest a contradiction as to assert that men would be tortured after death by that being whose character is held up as a model to human kind because he is incapable of malevolence or revenge. All the arguments which have been brought forward to justify retribution, fail when retribution is destined neither to operate as an example to other agents, nor to the offender himself. How feeble such reasoning is to be considered has been already shewn. But it is the character of an evil daemon to consign the beings whom he has endowed with sensation to improfitable anguish. The peculiar circumstances attendant on the conception of God casting sinners to burn in Hell forever, combine to render that conception the most perfect specimen of the greatest imaginable crime. Jesus Christ represented God as the principle of all good, the source of all happiness, the wise and benevolent creator and preserver of all living things. But the interpreters of his doctrine have confounded the good and the evil principle. They observed the emanations of these universal natures to be inextricably intangled in the world and, trembling before the power of the cause of all things, addressed to it such flattery as is acceptable to the ministers of human tyranny, attributing love and wisdom to those energies which they felt to be exerted indifferently for the purposes of benefit and calamity. Jesus Christ expressly asserts the distinction between the good and evil principle which it has been the practise of all theologians to confound. How far his doctrine or their interpretation may be true, it would scarcely have been worthwhile to enquire if the one did not afford an example and an incentive to the attainment of true virtue, whilst the other holds out a sanction and apology for every species of mean and cruel vice. [. . .]

Equality of Mankind

[. . .] Your physical wants are few, whilst those of your mind and heart cannot be numbered or described from their multitude and complication. To secure the gratification of the former men have made themselves the bondslaves of each other. They have cultivated these meaner wants to so great an excess as to judge nothing valuable or desirable but what relates to their gratification. Hence has arisen a system of passions which loses sight of the end which they were originally awakened to attain: Fame, power and gold are loved for their own sakes, are worshipped with a blind and habitual idolatry. The pageantry of empire, and the fame of irresistible might is contemplated by its possessor with unmeaning complacency, without a retrospect to the properties which first made him consider them of value. It is from the cultivation of the most contemptible properties of human nature, that the discord and torpor and [ ] by which the moral universe is disordered essentially depend. So long as these are the ties by which human society is connected, let it not be admired that they are fragile. Before man can be free and equal and truly wise he must cast aside the chains of habit and superstition, he must strip sensuality of its pomp and selfishness of its excuses, and contemplate actions and objects as they really are: He will discover the wisdom of universal love. He will feel the meanness and the injustice of sacrifising the leisure and the liberty of his fellow men to the indulgence of his physical appetites and becoming a party to their degradation by the consummation of his own [. . .][14]

Such, with those differences only incidental to the age and the state of society <in which> they were promulgated, appear to have been the doctrines of Jesus Christ. It is not too much to assert that they have been the doctrines of every just and compassionate mind that ever speculated on the social nature of man. The dogma of the equality of mankind has been advocated with various success in different ages of the world. It was imperfectly understood, but thro' a kind of instinct in its favour influenced considerably on the practise of antient Greece or Rome. Attempts to establish usages founded on this dogma have been made in modern Europe, in several instances since the revival of literature and the arts. Rousseau has vindicated this opinion with all the eloquence of sincere and earnest faith, and is perhaps the philosopher among the moderns who in the structure of his feelings and understanding resembles most nearly the mysterious sage of Judaea. It is impossible to read those passionate words in which Jesus Christ upbraids the pusillanimity and sensuality of mankind without being strongly reminded of the more connected and systematic enthusiasm of Rousseau.[15] 'No man', says Jesus Christ, 'can serve two masters'[16]

On Love

What is Love?—Ask him who lives what is life; ask him who adores what is God.

I know not the internal constitution of other men, or even of thine whom I now address. I see that in some external attributes they resemble me, but when misled by that appearance I have thought to appeal to something in common and unburthen my inmost soul to them I have found my language misunderstood like one in a distant and savage land. The more opportunities they have afforded me for experience the wider has appeared the interval between us, and to a greater distance have the points of sympathy been withdrawn. With a spirit ill fitted to sustain such proof,[1] trembling and feeble thro' its tenderness, I have every where sought and have found only repulse and disappointment.

Thou demandest what is Love.[2] It is that powerful attraction, towards all that we conceive or fear or hope beyond ourselves when we find within our own thoughts the chasm of an insufficient void and seek to awaken in all things that are a community with what we experience within ourselves. If we reason we would be understood; if we imagine we would that the airy children of our brain were born anew within another's; if we feel, we would that another's nerves should vibrate to our own, that the beams of their eyes should kindle at once and mix and melt into our own, that lips of motionless ice should not reply to lips quivering and burning with the heart's best blood. This is Love.[3] This is the bond and the sanction which connects not only man with man, but with every thing which exists. We are born into the world and there is something within us which from the instant that we live and move thirsts after its likeness. It is probably in correspondence with this law that the infant drains milk from the bosom of its mother. This propensity developes itself with the developement of our nature. We dimly see within our intellectual nature* a miniature as it were of our entire self, yet deprived of all that we condemn or despise, the ideal prototype[4] of every thing excellent or lovely that we are capable of conceiving as belonging to the nature of man. Not only the portrait of our external being, but an assemblage of the minutest particulars of which our nature is

* These words inefficient & metaphorical—Most words so—No help— [Shelley's note]

composed: a mirror whose surface reflects only the forms of purity and brightness: a soul within our soul[5] that describes a circle around its proper Paradise which pain and sorrow or evil dare not overleap.[6] To this we eagerly refer all sensations, thirsting that they should resemble or correspond with it. The discovery of its antitype:[7] the meeting with an understanding capable of clearly estimating the deductions of our own, an imagination which should enter into and seize upon the subtle and delicate peculiarities, which we have delighted to cherish and unfold in secret, with a frame whose nerves, like the chords of two exquisite lyres strung to the accompaniment of one delightful voice, vibrate with the vibrations of our own; and of a combination of all these in such proportion as the type within demands: this is the invisible and unattainable point to which Love tends; and to attain which it urges forth the powers of man to arrest the faintest shadow of that without the possession of which there is no rest or respite to the heart over which it rules. Hence in solitude, or in that deserted state when we are surrounded by human beings and yet they sympathise not with us, we love the flowers, the grass and the waters and the sky. In the motion of the very leaves of spring in the blue air there is then found a secret correspondence with our heart. There is eloquence in the tongueless wind and a melody in the flowing of brooks and the rustling of the reeds beside them which by their inconceivable[8] relation to something within the soul awaken the spirits to a dance of breathless rapture, and bring tears of mysterious tenderness to the eyes like the enthusiasm of patriotic success or the voice of one beloved singing to you alone. Sterne says that if he were in a desart he would love some cypress[9] . . . So soon as this want or power is dead, man becomes the living sepulchre of himself, and what yet survives is the mere husk of what once he was.—

On Life

Life, and the world, or whatever we call that which we are and feel, is an astonishing thing. The mist of familiarity obscures from us the wonder of our being. We are struck with admiration at some of its transient modifications; but it is itself the great miracle. What are changes of empires, the wreck of dynasties with the opinions which supported them; what is the birth and the extinction of religions and of political systems to life? What are the revolutions of the globe which we inhabit, and the operations of the elements of which it is composed, compared with life? What is the universe of stars and suns of[1] which this inhabited earth is one and their motions and their destiny compared with life? Life, the great miracle, we admire not, because it is so miraculous. It is well that we are thus shielded by the familiarity of what is at once so certain and so unfathomable from an astonishment which would otherwise absorb and overawe the functions of that which is [its] object.

If any artist (I do not say had executed) but had merely conceived in his mind the system of the sun and stars and planets, they not existing, and had painted to us in words or upon canvas, the spectacle now afforded by the nightly cope of Heaven and illustrated it by the wisdom of astronomy, great would be our admiration. Or had he imagined the scenery of this earth, the mountains, the seas and the rivers, and the grass and the flowers and the variety of the forms and masses of the leaves of the woods and the colours which attend the setting and the rising sun, and the hues of the atmosphere, turbid or serene, these things not before existing, truly we should have been astonished and it would have been more than a vain boast to have said of such a man, 'Non merita nome di creatore, sennon Iddio ed il Poeta.'[2] But now these things are looked on with little wonder and to be conscious of them with intense delight is esteemed to be the distinguishing mark of character of a refined and extraordinary person. The multitude of those men care not for them. It is thus with Life—that which includes all.

What is life? Thoughts and feelings arise, with or without our will, and we employ words to express them. We are born, and our birth is unremembered and our infancy remembered but in fragments. We live on, and in living we lose the apprehension of life. How vain it is to think that words can penetrate the mystery of our being. Rightly used they may make evident our ignorance to ourselves, and this is much. For what are we? Whence do we come, and whither do we go? Is birth the commencement, is death the conclusion of our being? What is birth and death?

The most refined abstractions of logic conduct to a view of life which, though startling to the apprehension, is in fact that which the habitual sense of its repeated combinations has extinguished in us. It strips, as it were, the painted curtain from this scene of things. I confess that I am one of those who am unable to refuse my assent to the conclusions of those philosophers, who assert that nothing exists but as it is perceived.

It is a decision against which all our persuasions struggle, and we must be long convicted, before we can be convinced that the solid universe of external things is 'such stuff as dreams are made of'.[3]—The shocking absurdities of the popular philosophy of mind and matter, and its fatal consequences in morals, their violent dogmatism concerning the source of all things, had early conducted me to materialism. This materialism is a seducing system to young and superficial minds. It allows its disciples to talk and dispenses them from thinking. But I was discontented with such a view of things as it afforded; man is a being of high aspirations 'looking both before and after,'[4] whose 'thoughts that wander through eternity',[5] disclaim alliance with transience and decay, incapable of imagining to himself annihilation, existing but in the future and the past, being, not what he is, but what he has been, and shall be. Whatever may be his true and final destination, there is a spirit within him at enmity with change and extinction.[6] This is the character of all life and being.—Each is at once the centre and the circumference; the point to which all things are referred, and the line within which all things are contained.—Such contemplations as these materialism and the popular philosophy of mind and matter, alike forbid; they are consistent only with the intellectual system.

It is absurd to enter into a long recapitulation of arguments sufficiently familiar to those enquiring minds whom alone a writer on abstruse subjects can be conceived to address. Perhaps the most clear and vigorous statement of the intellectual system is to be found in Sir W. Drummond's *Academical Questions*. After such an exposition it would be idle to translate into other words what could only lose its energy and fitness by the change. Examined point by point and word by word, the most discriminating intellects have been able to discover no train of thoughts in the process of its reasoning, which does not conduct inevitably to the conclusion which has been stated.

What follows from the admission? It establishes no new truth, it gives us no additional insight into our hidden nature, neither its action, nor itself. Philosophy, impatient as it may be to build, has much work yet remaining as pioneer[7] for the overgrowth of ages. It makes one step towards this object, however; it destroys error, and the roots of error. It leaves, what is too often the duty of the reformer in political and ethical questions to leave, a vacancy. It reduces the mind to that freedom in which it would have acted, but for the misuse of words and signs, the instruments of its own creation.—By signs, I would be understood in a wide sense, including what is properly meant by that term, and what I peculiarly mean. In this latter sense almost all familiar objects are signs, standing not for themselves but for others, in their capacity of suggesting one thought which shall lead to a train of thoughts.—Our whole life is thus an education of error.

Let us recollect our sensations as children. What a distinct and intense apprehension had we of the world and of ourselves. Many of the circumstances of social life were then important to us, which are now no longer so. But that is not the point of comparison on which I mean to insist. We less habitually distinguished all that we saw and felt from ourselves. They seemed as it were to constitute one mass. There are some persons who in this respect are always children. Those who are subject to the state called reverie[8] feel as if their nature were dissolved into the surrounding universe, or as if the surrounding universe were absorbed into their being. They are conscious of no distinction. And these are states which precede or accompany or follow an unusually intense and vivid apprehension of life. As men grow up, this power commonly decays, and they become mechanical and habitual agents. Their feelings and their reasonings are the combined result of a multitude of entangled thoughts, of a series of what are called impressions, blunted[9] by reiteration.

The view of life presented by the most refined deductions of the intellectual philosophy, is that of unity. Nothing exists but as it is perceived. The difference is merely nominal between those two classes of thought which are vulgarly distinguished by the names of ideas and of external objects. Pursuing the same thread of reasoning, the existence of distinct individual minds similar to that which is employed in now questioning its own nature, is likewise found to be a delusion. The words, *I*, *you*, *they* are not signs of any actual difference subsisting between the assemblage of thoughts thus indicated, but are merely marks employed to denote the different modifications of the one mind. Let it not be supposed that this doctrine conducts to the monstrous presumption, that I, the person who now write and think, am that one mind. I am but a portion of it. The words *I*, and *you* and *they* are grammatical devices, invented simply for arrangement and totally devoid of the intense and exclusive sense usually attached to them. It is difficult to find terms adequately to express so subtle a conception as that to which the intellectual philosophy has conducted us. We are on that verge where words abandon us, and what wonder if we grow dizzy to look down the dark abyss of—how little we know.

The relations of *things* remain unchanged by whatever system. By the word *things* is to be understood any object of thought, that is, any thought upon which any other thought is employed, with an apprehension of distinction. The relations of these remain unchanged; and such is the material of our knowledge.

What is the cause of life?—that is, how was it preceded,[10] or what agencies distinct from life, have acted or act upon life? All recorded generations of mankind have wearily busied themselves in inventing answers to this question. And the result has been . . . Religion. Yet, that the basis of[11] all things cannot be, as the popular philosophy alledges, mind is sufficiently evident. Mind, as far as we have any experience of its properties, and beyond that experience how vain is argument, cannot create, it can only perceive. It is said also to be the Cause. But cause is only a word expressing a certain state of the human mind with regard to the manner in which two thoughts[12] are apprehended to be related to each other.—If any one desires to know how unsatisfactorily the popular philosophy employs itself upon this great question, they need only impartially reflect upon the manner in which thoughts develope themselves in their minds.—It is infinitely improbable that the cause of mind, that is, of existence, is similar to mind. It is said that mind produces motion and it might as well have been said that motion produces mind.

The Coliseum[1]

At the hour of noon on the feast of the passover, an old man accompanied by a girl apparently his daughter entered the Coliseum at Rome. They immediately past thro' the Arena, and seeking a solitary chasm among the arches of the southern part of the ruin, selected a fallen column for their seat, and, clasping each other's hands, sate as in silent contemplation of the scene. But the eyes of the girl were fixed upon her father's lips, and his countenance sublime and sweet, but motionless as some Praxitelean image of the greatest of poets,[2] filled the silent air with smiles not reflected from external forms.

It was the great feast of the resurrection, and the whole native population of Rome, together with all the foreigners who flock from all parts of the earth to contemplate its celebration, were assembled round the Vatican. The most awful[3] religion of the world went forth surrounded by the emblazonry of mortal greatness, and mankind had assembled to wonder at and to worship the creations of their own power. No straggler was to be met with in the streets and grassy lanes which led to the Coliseum—the father and daughter had sought this spot immediately on their arrival.

A figure only visible at Rome in night or solitude, and then only to be seen amid the desolated temples of the Forum,[4] or gliding among the weed-grown galleries of the Coliseum, crost their path—His form which, tho' emaciated, displayed the elementary outlines of exquisite grace, was enveloped in an antient clamys[5]—which half-concealed his face. His snow white feet were fitted with ivory sandals delicately sculptured in the likeness of two female figures whose wings met upon the heel and whose eager and half-divided lips seemed quivering to meet. It was a face once seen never to be forgotten—the mouth and the moulding of the chin resembled the eager and impassioned tenderness of the statues of Antinous[6]—but instead of the effeminate sullenness of the eye and the narrow smoothness of the forehead shone an expression of profound and piercing thought; the brow was clear and open and his eyes deep, like two wells of christalline water which reflect the all-beholding heavens. Over all was spread a timid expression of womanish tenderness and hesitation which contrasted yet intermingled strangely with the abstracted and fearless character that predominated in his form and gestures.[7]

He avoided in an extraordinary degree all communication with the Italians, whose language he seemed scarcely to understand, but was occasionally seen to converse with some accomplished foreigner whose gestures and appearance might attract him amid his solemn haunts. He spoke Latin and especially Greek with fluency and with a peculiar but sweet accent—he had apparently acquired a knowledge of the northern languages of Europe. There was no circumstance connected with him that gave the least intimation of his country, his origin or his occupations. His dress was strange but splendid and solemn. He was forever alone. The literati of Rome thought him a curiosity but there was something in his manner unintelligible but impressive which awed their obtrusions[8] into distance and silence. The countrymen whose path he rarely crost returning by starlight from their market at Campo Vaccino called him with that strange mixture of religious and historical ideas so common in Italy, *Il Diavolo di Bruto*.[9]

Such was the figure which interrupted the contemplations (if they were so engaged) of the strangers by addressing them in the clear and exact but unidiomatic phrases of their native language—

'Strangers, you are two—behold the third in this great city to whom alone the spectacle of these mighty ruins is more delightful than the mockeries of a superstition which destroyed them.'

'I see nothing,' said the old man.

'What do you here then?'

'I listen to the sweet singing of the birds, and the sound of my daughter's breathing composes me like the soft murmur of waters—and I feel the sun-warm wind, and this is pleasant to me.'

'Wretched old man, know you not that these are the ruins of the Coliseum?'

'Alas! stranger,' said the girl in a voice like mournful music, 'speak not so—he is blind.'

The stranger's eyes were suddenly filled with tears and the lines of his countenance became relaxed. 'Blind!' he exclaimed in a tone of suffering which was more than an apology and seated himself apart on a flight of shattered and mossy stairs which wound up among the labyrinths of the ruin.

'My sweet Helen,' said the old man, 'you did not tell me that this was the Coliseum.'

'How should I tell you, dearest father, what I knew not—I was on the point of enquiring the way to that building when we entered this circle of ruins—and until the stranger accosted us I remained silent, subdued by the greatness of what I see.'

'It is your custom, sweetest child, to describe to me the objects that give you delight—you array them in the soft radiance of your words, and whilst you speak I only feel the infirmity which holds me in such dear dependance as a blessing. Why have you been silent now?'

'I know not—first the wonder and pleasure of the sight—then the words of the stranger, and then thinking on what he had said and how he had looked—and now, beloved father, your own words.'

'Well, I speak no more. What do you see?'

'I see a great circle of arches built upon arches, and walls giddily hanging upon walls, and stones like shattered crags overhanging the solid wall. In the crevices and on the vaulted roofs grow a multitude of shrubs, the wild olive and the myrtle—and intricate brambles and entangled weeds and plants I never saw before. The stones are immensely massive and they jut out one from the other. There are terrible rifts in the wall, and broad windows through which you see the blue heaven—There seems to be more than a thousand arches—some ruined, some entire, and they are all immensely high and wide—Some are shattered and stand forth in great heaps and the underwood is tufted on their crumbling summits—Around us lie enormous columns shattered and shapeless—and fragments of capitals and cornice fretted with delicate sculptures.'

'It is open to the blue sky?' said the old man.

'Yes. We see the liquid depth of Heaven above through the rifts and the windows; and the flowers and the weeds and the grass and creeping moss are nourished by its unforbidden rain—The blue sky is above, the wide bright blue sky—it flows thro' the great rents on high—and through the bare boughs of the marble-rooted fig-tree, and through the leaves and flowers of the weeds even to the dark arcades beneath—I see—I feel its clear and piercing beams fill the universe[10] and impregnate the joy-inspiring wind with warmth and light and interpenetrate all things, even me. Yes, and through the highest rift the noonday waning moon is hanging as it were out of the solid sky and this shews that the atmosphere has all the clearness which it rejoices me that you feel.'

'What else see you?'

'Nothing.'

'Nothing?'

'Only the bright green mossy ground, speckled by tufts of dewy clover grass that run into the interstices of the shattered arches and round the isolated pinnacles of ruin.'

'Like the lawny dells of soft short grass which wind among the pine forests and precipices in the Alps of Savoy.'

'Indeed, father, your eye has a vision more serene than mine.'

'And the great wrecked arches—the shattered masses of precipitous ruin, overgrown with the younglings of the forest and more like chasms rent by an earthquake among the mountains than like the vestige of what was human workmanship—What are they?'

'Things awe-inspiring and wonderful.'

'Are they not caverns such as the untamed elephant might chuse amid the Indian wilderness wherein to hide her cubs—such as, were the sea to overflow the earth, the mightiest monsters of the deep would change into their spacious chambers?'[11]

'Father, your words image forth what I would have expressed, but alas could not.'

'I hear the rustling of leaves and the sound of waters, but it does not rain, like the fast drops of a fountain among woods.'

'It falls from among the heaps of ruin over our heads—it is, I suppose—the water collected in the rifts by the showers—'

'A nursling of Man's art abandoned by his care and transformed by the inchantment of Nature into a likeness of her own creations, and destined to partake their immortality. Changed into a mountain cloven with woody dells which overhang its labyrinthine glades, and shattered into toppling precipices—Even the clouds intercepted by its craggy summit[12] feed its eternal fountains with their rain. By the column on which I sit I should judge that it had once been crowned by a temple or a theatre, and that on sacred days the radiant multitude wound up its craggy path to the spectacle of the sacrifize. It was such itself! Helen, what sound of wings is that?'

'It is the wild pigeons returning to their young. Do you not hear the murmur of those that are brooding in their nests?'

'Aye, it is the language of their happiness. They are as happy as we are, child, but in a different manner. They know not the sensations which this ruin excites within us. Yet it is pleasure to them to inhabit it, and the succession of its forms as they pass is connected with associations in their minds sacred to them as these to us. The internal nature of each being is surrounded by a circle not to be surmounted by his fellows; and it is this repulsion which constitutes the misfortune of the condition of life.[13] But there is a circle which comprehends as well as one which mutually excludes all things which feel. And with respect to man, his public and private happiness consists in diminishing the circumference which includes those resembling himself until they become one with him and he with them. It is because we enter into the meditations, designs and destinies of something beyond ourselves that the contemplation of the ruins of human power excites an elevating sense of awfulness and beauty. It is therefore that the Ocean, the glacier, the cataract, the tempest, the Volcano, have each a Spirit which animates the extremities of our frame with tingling joy.[14] It is therefore that the singing of birds and the motion of leaves, the sensation of the odorous earth beneath and the freshness of the living wind around, is sweet. And this is Love. This is the religion of eternity whose votaries have been exiled from among the multitude of mankind. O Power,' cried the old man, lifting his sightless eyes towards the undazzling sun, 'thou which interpenetratest all things, and without whom this glorious world were a blind and formless Chaos; Love, Author of good, God, King, Father, Friend of these thy worshippers. Two solitary hearts invoke thee. May they be divided never. If the contentions of mankind have been their misery, if to give and seek that happiness which thou art has been their choice and destiny, if in the contemplation of these majestic records of the power of their kind they see the shadow and [?the] prophecy of that which thou mayst have decreed that he should become; if the justice, the liberty, the loveliness, the truth which are thy footsteps [?have been sought by them,][15] divide them not. It is thine to unite, to eternize, to make outlive the grave those who have left the living memorials of thee. When this frame shall be senseless dust, may the hopes and the desires and the delights which animate it now, never be extinguished in my child; even, as if she were borne into the tomb, my memory would be the written monument of all her nameless excellencies.'

The old man's countenance and gestures radiant with the inspiration of his words sunk as he ceased into more than their accustomed calmness, for he heard his daughter's sobs, and remembered that he had spoken of death.

'My father, how can I outlive you?' said Helen.

'Do not let us talk of death,' said the old man, suddenly changing his tone. 'Heraclitus indeed died at my age, and if I had so sour a disposition,[16] there might be some danger for me. But Democritus reached 120 by the mere dint of a joyous and unconquerable mind; he only died at last because he had no gentle and beloved ministering spirit like my Helen for whom it would have been his delight to live. You remember his gay old sister requested him to put off starving himself to death until he had returned from the festival of Ceres, alledging that it would spoil her holiday if he refused to comply, as it was not permitted to appear in the procession immediately after the death of a relation; and how good-temperedly the sage acceded to her request.'[17]

The old man could not see his daughter's grateful smile but he felt the pressure of her hand by which it was expressed. 'In truth,' he continued, 'that mystery, Death, is a change which neither for ourselves nor for others is a just object of hope or fear. We know not if it be good or evil, we only know, it is. The old, the young, may alike die; no time, no place, no age, no foresight exempts us from death and the chance of death. We have no knowledge if death be a state of sensation, of any precaution which can make those sensations fortunate, if the existing series of events shall not produce that effect. Think not of death, or think of it as something common to us all. It has happened,' said he with a deep and suffering voice, 'that men have buried their children.'

'Alas! then, dearest father, how I pity you.—Let us speak no more.'

They arose to depart from the Coliseum, but the figure which had first accosted them interposed itself.

'Lady,' he said, 'if grief be an expiation of error, I have grieved deeply for the words which I spoke to your father. The men who antiently inhabited this spot, and those from whom they learned their wisdom,[18] respected infirmity and age. If I have rashly violated that venerable form at once majestic and defenceless, may I be forgiven?'

'It gives me pain to see how much your mistake afflicts you. That is my father,' she said; 'if you can forget, doubt not that we forgive.'

'You thought me one of those who are blind in spirit,' said the old man, 'and who deserve, if any human being can deserve, contempt and blame. Assuredly, contemplating this monument as I do, tho' in the mirror of my daughter's mind, I am filled with astonishment and delight; the spirit of departed generations seems to animate my limbs[19] and the life of extinguished ages circulate thro' all the fibres of my frame. Stranger, if I have expressed what you have ever felt, let us know each other more.'

'The sound of your voice and the harmony of your thoughts is delightful to me,' said the youth, 'and it is pleasure to see any form which expresses so much beauty and goodness as your daughter's; if you reward me for my rudeness by allowing me to know you, my error is already expiated; and you remember my ill words no more. I live a solitary life, and it is rare that I encounter any stranger with whom it is pleasant to talk; besides, their meditations, even though they be learned, do not always agree with mine, and though I can pardon this difference, they cannot. Nor have I ever explained the cause of the dress I wear and the difference which I perceive between my language and manners and those with whom I have intercourse. Not but that it is painful to me to live without communion with intelligent and affectionate beings. You are such, I feel: and[20]

Related Passage

Nor does a recollection of the use to which it may have been destined interfere with these emotions. Time has thrown its purple shadow athwart this scene, and no more is visible than the broad and everlasting character of human strength and genius, that pledge of all that is to be admirable and lovely in ages yet to come. Solemn temples, [?palaces][1] where the senate of the world assembled, triumphal arches and cloud-surrounded columns loaded with the sculptured annals of conquest and domination—What actions and deliberations have they been destined to inclose and to commemorate? Superstitious rites, which in their mildest form outrage reason and obscure the moral sense of mankind; schemes for wide extended murder and devastation and misrule and servitude; and lastly these schemes brought to their tremendous consummations and a human being returning in the midst of festival and solemn joy[2] with thousands and thousands of his inslaved and desolated species chained behind his chariot exhibiting, as titles to renown, the labour of ages and the admired creations of genius overthrown by the brutal force which was placed as a sword within his hand; and, contemplation fearful and abhorred! he himself, a being capable of the gentlest and best emotions, inspired with the persuasion that he has done a virtuous deed—We forget not these things.

From *On the Devil, and Devils*

To determine the Nature and functions of the Devil is no contemptible province of the European mythology.[1] Who or what he is, his origin, his habitation, his destiny, and his power, are subjects which puzzle the most acute Theologians, and on which no orthodox person can be induced to give a decisive opinion. He is the weak place of the popular religion, the vulnerable belly of the Crocodile.

The Manichaean philosophy[2] respecting the origin and government of the world, if not true is at least an hypothesis conformable to the experience of actual facts. To suppose that the world was created, and is superintended by two Spirits of a balanced power and opposite dispositions is simply a personification of the struggle which we experience within ourselves, and which we perceive in the operations of external things as they affect us, between good and evil. The supposition that the good Spirit is, or hereafter will be superiour, is a personification of the principle of hope, and that thirst for improvement without which, present evil would be intolerable. The vulgar are all Manichaeans: all that remains of the popular superstition is mere machinery and accompaniment. To abstract in contemplation from our sensations of pleasure and pain, all circumstance and limit,—to add those active powers of whose existence we are conscious within ourselves—to give to [?those] which are most pleasing to us a perpetual or an ultimate superiority, with all epithets of honourable addition, and to brand that which is displeasing with epithets ludicrous or horrible, predicting its ultimate defeat, is to pursue the process by which the vulgar arrive at the familiar notions of God and the Devil.

The Devil was clearly a Chaldaean invention, for we first hear of him after the return of the Jews from their second Assyrian captivity[3] [. . .][4] Those among Greek philosophers whose poetical imagination suggested a personification of the cause of the Universe, seemed nevertheless to have dispensed with the agency of the Devil [. . .][5] They accounted for evil by supposing that what is called matter is eternal and that God, in making the world, made not the best that he, or even inferior intelligences could concieve; but that he moulded the reluctant and stubborn materials ready to his hand into the nearest arrangement possible to the perfect archetype existing in his contemplation—in the same manner as a skilful watchmaker, who if he had diamonds and steel and brass and gold, can construct a time piece of the most accurate workmanship, could produce nothing beyond a coarse and imperfect clock if he were restricted to wood as his material.

The Christian theologians, however, have invariably rejected this hypothesis, on the ground that the eternity of matter is incompatible with the omnipotence of God. Like panic-stricken slaves in the presence of a jealous and suspicious despot, they have tortured themselves ever to devise a flattering sophism by which they might appease him by the most contradictory praises—endeavouring to reconcile omnipotence and benevolence and equity in the Author of an Universe where evil and good are inextricably intangled, and where the most admirable tendencies to happiness and preservation are forever baffled by misery and decay. The Christians therefore invented or adopted the Devil to extricate them from this difficulty.

The account they give us of the origin of the Devil is curious. Heaven, according to the popular creed, is a certain airy region inhabited by the Supreme being and a multitude of inferior spirits. With respect to the situation of it, theologians are not agreed, but it is generally supposed to be placed beyond the remotest constellation of the visible stars. These spirits are supposed, like those which reside in the bodies of animals and men, to have been created by God with a foresight of the consequences which would result from the mechanism of their nature. He made them as good as possible, but the nature of the substance out of which they were formed, or the unconquerable laws according to which that substance when created was necessarily modified prevented them from being so perfect as he could wish. Some say that he gave them free will, that is, that he made them without any very distinct apprehension of the results of his workmanship, leaving them an active power which might determine themselves to this or that action independently of the motives afforded by the regular operation of those impressions which were produced by the general agencies of the rest of his creation. This he is supposed to have done, that he might excuse himself to his own conscience for tormenting and annoying these unfortunate spirits, when they provoked him, by turning out worse than he expected. This account of the origin of evil, to make the best of it, does not seem more complimentary to the Supreme Being, or less derogatory to his omnipotence and goodness, than the Platonic scheme.[6]—

They then proceed to relate, gravely, that one fine Morning, a chief of these spirits took it into his head to rebel against God, having gained over to his cause a third part of the eternal angels who attended upon the Creator and Preserver of Heaven and Earth. After a series of desperate conflicts between those who remained faithful to the antient dynasty, and the insurgents, the latter were beaten, and driven into a place called Hell, which was rather their empire than their prison, and where God reserved them to be first the tempters and then the jailors and tormentors of a new race of beings whom he created under the same conditions of imperfection, and with the same foresight of an unfortunate result. The motive of this insurrection is not assigned by any of the earliest mythological writers. Milton supposes that on a particular day God chose to adopt as his son and *heir* (the reversion of an estate with an immortal incumbent would be worth little[7]) a *being* unlike the other spirits, who seems to have been supposed to be a detached portion of himself, and afterwards figured upon the earth in the well known character of Jesus Christ. The Devil is represented as conceiving high indignation at this preference; and as disputing the affair with arms. I cannot discover Milton's authority for this circumstance; but all agree in the fact of the insurrection, and the defeat, and the casting out into Hell.

Nothing can exceed the grandeur and the energy of the character of the Devil as expressed in *Paradise Lost*. He is a Devil very different from the popular personification of evil; and it is a mistake to suppose that he was intended for a personification of evil, implacable hate, and cunning refinement of device to inflict the utmost anguish on an enemy; these, which are venial in a slave, are not to be forgiven in a tyrant; these, which are redeemed by much that ennobles in one subdued, are marked by all that dishonours his conquest in the victor.

Milton's devil as a moral being is as far superior to his God, as one who perseveres in some purpose which he has conceived to be excellent in spite of adversity and torture is to one who in the cold security of undoubted triumph inflicts the most horrible revenge upon his enemy,—not from any mistaken notion of bringing him to repent of a perseverance in enmity but with the open and alledged design[8] of exasperating him to deserve new torments.

Milton so far violated all that part of the popular creed which is susceptible of being preached and defended in argument, as to alledge no superiority in moral virtue to God over his Devil [. . .][9] The writer who would have attributed majesty and beauty to the <character> of victorious and vindictive omnipotence, must have been contented with the character of a good Christian—he never could have been a great epic poet [. . .][10]

As it is, the Divine *Paradise Lost* has conferred on the whole modern mythology a systematic form; and when the immeasurable and unceasing mutability of time shall have added one more superstition[11] to those which have already arisen and decayed upon the earth, commentators and critics will be learnedly employed on elucidating the religion of ancestral Europe, only not utterly forgotten because it will have participated in the eternity of genius.

The Devil owes everything to Milton. Dante and Tasso[12] present us with a very gross idea of him. Milton divested him of a sting and hoofs and horns; [and] clothed him with the sublime grandeur of a graceful but tremendous Spirit.

I am afraid there is much laxity among the orthodox of the present day respecting a belief in the Devil. I recommend the Bishops to make a serious charge to their diocesans[13] on this dangerous latitude. The Devil is the outwork of the Christian faith; he is the weakest point—you may observe that infidels in their noviciate always begin by tremulously doubting the existence of the Devil. Depend on it that when a person once begins to think that perhaps there is no Devil, he is in a dangerous way. There may be observed in polite society a great deal of coquetting[14] about the Devil, especially among divines, which is singularly ominous. They qualify him as the evil Spirit—they consider him as synonymous with the flesh. They seem to wish to divest him of all personality; to reduce him from his abstract to his concrete; to reverse the means by which he was created in the mind; which they will by no means bear with respect to God. It is popular and well looked upon if you deny the Devil a 'local habitation and a name.'[15] Even the vulgar begin to scout[16] him. Hell is popularly considered as metaphorical, the torments of an evil conscience, and by no means capable of being topographically ascertained. No one likes to mention the torments of everlasting fire and the poisonous gnawing of the worm that liveth for ever and ever.[17] It is all explained away into the regrets and the reproaches of an evil conscience [. . .][18]

The Devil is Διάβολος,[19] an accuser [. . .][20] In this view, he is at once the informer—and the Attorney General [and] the jailor of the celestial tribunal. It is not good policy, or at least cannot be considered as a constitutional practise to unite these characters. The Devil must have a great interest to exert himself to procure a sentence of guilty from the judge; for I suppose there will be no jury at the resurrection—at least if there is, it will be so overawed by the bench and the counsel for *the Crown* as to ensure whatever verdict the court shall please to recommend. No doubt, that as an incentive to his exertions, half goes to the informer. What an army of spies and delators[21] all Hell must afford under the direction of that active magistrate the devil! [. . .][22] If the Devil takes but half the pleasure in tormenting a sinner which God does, who took the trouble to create them, and then to invent a system of casuistry by which he might excuse himself for devoting them to eternal torment, this reward must be considerable.

Conceive how the enjoyment of half the advantages to be derived from their ruin, whether in person or property, must irritate[23] the activity of a delator. Tiberius, or Bonaparte or Lord Castlereagh[24] never affixed any reward to the disclosure or the creation of conspiracies, equal to that which God's government has attached to the exertions of the Devil to tempt, betray and accuse unfortunate man. These two considerable personages are supposed to have entered into a sort of partnership in which the weaker has consented to bear all the odium of their common actions, and allow the stronger to talk of himself as a very honourable person, on condition of having a participation in what is the especial delight of both of them—burning men to all eternity. The dirty work is done by the Devil, in the same manner as some starving wretch will hire himself out to a king or a minister with a stipulation that he shall have some portion of the public spoil, as an instrument to betray a certain number of other starving wretches into circumstances of capital punishment, when they may think it convenient to edify the rest by hanging up a few of those whose murmurs are too loud.

It is far from inexplicable that earthly tyrants should employ these kind of agents, or that God should have done so with regard to the Devil and his angels, or that any depositary of power should take these measures with respect to those by whom he fears lest that power should be wrested from him. But to tempt mankind to incur everlasting damnation must on the part of God, and even on the part of the Devil, arise from that very disinterested love of tormenting and annoying which is seldom observed on earth except among old maids, eunuchs and priests. The thing that comes nearest to it is a troop of idle dirty boys baiting a cat. Cooks skinning eels and boiling lobsters alive and bleeding calves and whipping pigs to Death, naturalists anatomising dogs alive[25] (a dog has as good a right and a better excuse for anatomising a naturalist) are nothing compared to God and the Devil judging, damning, and then tormenting the soul of a miserable sinner. It is pretended that God dislikes it; but this is mere shamefacedness and coquetting, for he has everything his own way and he need not damn unless he likes. The Devil has a better excuse, for as he was entirely made by God he can have no tendency or disposition the seeds of which were not originally planted by his creator [. . .][26]

Christians in general will not admit the substance and presence of Devils upon the earth in modern times, or they suppose their agency to be more obscure and surreptitious in proportion as the histories of them approach to the present epoch, or indeed any epoch in which there has been a considerable progress in historical criticism and natural science. There were a number of Devils in Judaea in the time of Jesus Christ, and a great deal of reputation was gained both by him and others by what was called casting them out. A droll story is related amongst others of Jesus Christ having driven a legion of Devils into a herd of Pigs, who were so discomfited with these new inmates that they all threw themselves over the precipice into the lake and were drowned.[27] These were a set of hypocondriacal and high minded swine, very unlike any others of which we have authentic record; they disdained to live if they must live in so intimate a society with devils as that which was imposed on them; and the pig drivers were no doubt confounded at so heroical a resolution. What became of the Devils after the death of the pigs, whether they past into the fish, and thence by digestion thro' the stomach into the brain of Gadarean Ichthyophagists;[28] whether they returned to Hell, or remained in the water, the Historian has left as subjects of everlasting conjecture. I should be curious to know whether any half starved Jew picked up these pigs, and sold them at the market at Gadara, and what effect the bacon of a demoniac pig who had killed himself produced upon the consumers[29] [. . .][30]

The Devil and his angels are called the Powers of Air, and the Devil himself Lucifer [. . .][31] The Devil after having gradually assumed the horns, hoofs, tail and ears of the antient Gods of the Woods,[32] gradually lost them again; although wings had been added. It is inexplicable why men assigned them these additions as circumstances of terror and deformity. The Sylvans and Fauns with their leader the Great Pan were most poetical personages, and were connected in the imagination of Pagans with all that could enliven and delight. They were supposed to be innocent beings not greatly different in habits and manners from the shepherds and herdsmen of which they were the patron saints. But the Xtians contrived to turn the wrecks of the Greek mythology as well as the little they understood of their philosophy to purposes of deformity and falshood. I suppose the sting with which he was armed gave him a dragon like and viperous appearance very formidable.

I can sufficiently understand why the author of evil should have been typified under the image of a Serpent, that animal producing merely by its sight,[33] so strong an associated recollection of the malignity of many of its species. But this was eminently a practise confined to the Jews, whose earliest mythology suggested this animal as the cause of all evil. Among the Greeks the Serpent was considered as an auspicious and favourable being. He attended on Aesculapius and Apollo.[34] In Egypt the Serpent was an hieroglyph of eternity.[35] The Jewish account is, that the serpent, that is the animal, persuaded the original pair of human beings to eat of a fruit from which God had commanded them to abstain; and that in consequence God expelled them from the pleasant garden where he had before permitted them to reside. God on this occasion, it is said, assigned as a punishment to the serpent that its motion should be as it now is along the ground upon its belly; we are given to suppose that before this misconduct it hopped along upon its tail, a mode of progression which if I were a serpent I should think the severest punishment of the two. The Christians have turned this serpent into their Devil, and accommodated the whole story to their new scheme of sin and propitiation.[36]

From *A Philosophical View of Reform*

1st. Sentiment of the Necessity of change.
2nd. Practicability and Utility of such change.
3rd. State of Parties as regards it.
4th. Probable mode—Desirable mode.

Let us believe not only that is necessary because it is just and ought to be, but necessary because it is inevitable and must be.

Those who imagine that their personal interest is directly or indirectly concerned in maintaining the power in which they are clothed by the existing institutions of English Government do not acknowledge the necessity of a material change in those institutions. With this exception, there is no inhabitant of the British Empire of mature age and perfect understanding not fully persuaded of the necessity of Reform.

Introduction

From the dissolution of the Roman Empire, that vast and successful scheme for enslaving the most civilized portion of mankind, to the epoch of two recent wars,[1] have succeeded a series of schemes on a smaller scale, operating to the same effect. Sacred names borrowed from the life and opinions of Jesus Christ were employed as symbols of domination and imposture; and a system of liberty and equality, for such was the system preached by that great Reformer, was perverted to support oppression.—Not his doctrines, for they are too simple and direct to be susceptible of such perversion—but the mere names. Such was the origin of the Catholic Church, which, together with the several dynasties then beginning to consolidate themselves in Europe, means, being interpreted, a plan according to which the cunning and selfish few have employed the fears and hopes of the ignorant many to the Establishment of their own power and the destruction of the real interest of all.

The Republics and municipal governments of Italy opposed for some time a systematic and effectual resistance to the all-surrounding tyranny. The Lombard League defeated the armies of the despot in open field, and until Florence was betrayed to those flattered traitors <and> polished tyrants, the Medici, Freedom had one citadel wherein it could find refuge from a world which was its enemy.[2] Florence long balanced, divided, and weakened the strength of the Empire and the Popedom. To this cause, if to anything, was due the undisputed superiority of Italy in literature and the arts over all its contemporary nations, that union of energy and of beauty which distinguish from all other poets the writings of Dante, that restlessness of fervid power which expressed itself in painting and sculpture and in rude but daring architectural forms, and from which, conjointly from the creations of Athens, its predecessor and its image, Raphael and Michelangelo[3] drew the inspiration which created those forms and colours of what is now the astonishment of the world. The father of our own literature, Chaucer, wrought from the simple and powerful language of a nursling of this Republic[4] the basis of our own literature. And thus we owe, among other causes, the exact condition belonging to our own intellectual existence, to the generous disdain of submission which burned in the bosoms of men who filled a distant generation and inhabited another land.

When this resistance was overpowered, as what resistance to fraud and tyranny has not been overpowered, another was even then maturing. The progress of philosophy and civilization which ended in that imperfect emancipation of mankind from the yoke of priests and Kings called the Reformation, had already commenced. Exasperated by their long sufferings, inflamed by the sparks of that superstition from the flames of which they were emerging, the poor rose against their natural enemies, the rich, and repaid with bloody interest the tyranny of ages. One of the signs of the times was that the oppressed peasantry rose like the Negro slaves of a West Indian Plantation, and murdered their tyrants when they were unaware. For so dear is power that the tyrants themselves, neither then nor now nor ever, left or leave a path to freedom but thro their own blood. [. . .][5]

This new epoch was marked by the commencement of deeper enquiries into the forms of human nature than are compatible with an unreserved belief in any of those popular mistakes upon which popular systems of faith with respect to the agencies of the universe, with all their superstructure of political and religious tyranny, are built. Lord Bacon, Spinoza, Hobbes, Bayle, Montaigne,[6] regulated the reasoning powers, criticized the past history, exposed the errors, by illustrating their causes and their connexion, and anatomized the inmost nature of social man. Then, with a less interval of time than of genius, followed Locke[7] and the philosophers of his exact and intelligible but superficial school. Their illustrations of some of the minor consequences of the doctrines established by the sublime genius of their predecessors were correct, popular, simple, and energetic. Above all, they indicated inferences the most incompatible with the popular religions and the established governments of Europe.[8] Hartley, Berkeley and Hume,[9] following in a later age the traces of these inductions, have clearly established the certainty of our ignorance with respect to those obscure questions which under the name of religious truths have been the watchwords of con[tention] and the symbols of unjust power ever since they were distorted by the narrow passions of the immediate followers of Jesus from that meaning to which philosophers are even now restoring them.—A crowd of writers in France[10] seized upon the most popular topics of these doctrines, and developing those particular portions of the new philosophy which conducted to inferences at war with the dreadful oppressions under which that country groaned, made familiar to mankind the falshood of the pretences of their religious mediators and political oppressors. Considered as philosophers their error seems to have consisted chiefly [of] a limitedness of view; they told the truth, but not the whole truth. This might have arisen from the terrible sufferings of their countrymen inciting them rather to apply a portion of what had already been discovered to their immediate relief, than to pursue the abstractions of thought, as the great philosophers who preceded them had done, for the sake of a future and more universal advantage. Whilst that philosophy which, burying itself in the obscure parts of our nature, regards the truth and falsehood of dogmas relating to the cause of the universe, and the nature and manner of man's relation with it, was thus stripping Power of its darkest mask, Political philosophy, or that which considers the relations of Man as a social being, was assuming a precise form. This philosophy indeed sprang from and maintained a connexion with that other, as its parent. What would Swift and Bolingbroke and Sidney and Locke and Montesquieu, or even Rousseau, not to speak of political philosophers of our own age, Godwin and Bentham,[11] have been but for Lord Bacon, Montaigne, and Spinoza, and the other great luminaries of the preceding epoch? Something excellent and eminent, no doubt, the least of these would have been, but something different from and inferior to what they are. A series of these writers illustrated with more or less success the principles of human nature as applied to man in political society. A thirst for accommodating the existing forms according to which mankind are found divided to those rules of freedom and equality which were thus discovered as being the elementary principles according to which the happiness resulting from the social union ought to be produced and distributed, was kindled by these enquiries. Contemporary with this condition of the intell[ect,] all the powers of man seemed, though in most cases under forms highly inauspicious, to develop themselves with uncommon energy. The mechanical sciences attained to a degree of perfection which, though obscurely foreseen by Lord Bacon, it had been accounted madness to have prophesied in a preceding age. Commerce was pursued with a perpetually increasing vigour, and the same area of the Earth was perpetually compelled to furnish more and more subsistence. The means and sources of knowledge were thus increased together with knowledge itself, and the instruments of knowledge. The benefit of this increase of the powers of man became, in consequence of the inartificial[12] forms into which society continues to be distributed, an instrument of his additional evil. The capabilities of happiness were increased and applied to the augmentation of misery. Modern European society is thus an engine assumed to be <designed> for useful purposes, whose force is by a system of subtle mechanism augmented to the highest pitch, but which, instead of grinding corn or raising water, acts against itself and is perpetually wearing away and breaking to pieces the wheels of which it is composed.

The result of the labours of the political philosophers has been the establishment of the principle of Utility[13] as the substance, and liberty and equality as the forms, according to which the concerns of human life ought to be administered. By this test, the various institutions regulating political society have been tried and, as the undigested growth of the private passions, errors, and interests of barbarians and oppressors, have been condemned. And many new theories, more or less perfect, but all superior to the mass of evil which they would supplant, have been given to the world. [. . .][14]

The just and successful Revolt of America corresponded with a state of public opinion in Europe of which it was the first result. The French Revolution was the second. The oppressors of mankind had enjoyed (O that we could say suffered) a long and undisturbed reign in France, and to the pining famine, the shelterless destitution of the inhabitants of that country, had been added, and heaped up, insult harder to endure than misery. For the feudal system (the immediate causes and conditions of its institution having become obliterated) had degenerated into an instrument not only of oppression but of contumely; and both were unsparingly inflicted. Blind in the possession of strength, drunken as with the intoxication of ancestral greatness, the rulers perceived not that encrease of knowledge in their subjects which made its exercise insecure. They called soldiers to hew down the people when their power was already past. The tyrants were, as usual, the aggressors. Then the oppressed, having been rendered brutal, ignorant, servile, and bloody by long slavery, having had the intellectual thirst excited in them by the progress of civilization, satiated from fountains of literature poisoned by the spirit and the form of monarchy, arose and took a dreadful revenge on their oppressors. Their desire to wreak revenge to this extent, in itself a mistake, a crime, a calamity, arose from the same source as their other miseries and errors, and affords an additional proof of the necessity of that long-delayed change which it accompanied and disgraced. If a just and necessary revolution could have been accomplished with as little expense of happiness and order in a country governed by despotic as [in] one governed by free laws, equal liberty and justice would lose their chief recommendations, and tyranny be divested of its most revolting attributes. Tyranny entrenches itself within the existing interests of that great mass of the most refined citizens of a nation and says, 'If you dare trample upon these, be free.' [. . .][15]

Meanwhile England, the particular object for the sake of which these general considerations have been stated on the present occasion, has arrived, like the nations which surround it, at a crisis in its destiny.

The literature of England, an energetic development of which has ever followed or preceded a great and free development of the national will, has arisen, as it were, from a new birth.[16] In spite of that low-thoughted[17] envy which would undervalue, thro' a fear of comparison with its own insignificance, the eminence of contemporary merit, ours is in intellectual achievements a memorable age, and we live among such philosophers and poets as surpass beyond comparison any who have appeared in our nation since its last struggle for liberty. For the most unfailing herald, or companion, or follower, of an universal employment of the sentiments of a nation to the production of beneficial change is poetry, meaning by poetry an intense and impassioned power of communicating intense and impassioned impressions respecting man and nature. The persons in whom this power takes its abode may often, as far as regards many portions of their nature, have little correspondence with the spirit of good of which it is the minister. But although they may deny and abjure, they are yet compelled to serve, that which is seated on the throne of their own soul. And whatever systems they may professedly support, they actually advance the interests of Liberty. It is impossible to read the productions of our most celebrated writers, whatever may be their system relating to thought or expression, without being startled by the electric life which there is in their words. They measure the circumference or sound the depths of human nature with a comprehensive and all-penetrating spirit, at which they are themselves perhaps the most sincerely astonished, for it [is] less their own spirit than the spirit of their age. They are the priests of an unapprehended inspiration, the mirrors of gigantic forms which futurity casts upon the present, the words which express what they conceive not, the trumpet which sings to battle and feels not what it inspires, the influence which is moved not but moves. Poets and philosophers are the unacknowledged legislators of the world. [. . .][18]

On the Sentiment of the Necessity of Change

Two circumstances arrest the attention of those who turn their regard to the present political condition of the English nation; first, that there is an almost universal sentiment of the approach of some change to be wrought in the institutions of the government, and secondly, the necessity and desirableness of such a change. From the first of these propositions, it being matter of fact, no person addressing the public can dissent. The latter, from a general belief in which the former flows and on which it depends, is matter of opinion, but [one] which to the mind of all excepting those interested in maintaining the contrary is a doctrine so clearly established that even they, admitting that great abuses exist, are compelled to impugn it by insisting upon the specious topic that popular violence, by which they alone could be remedied, would be more injurious than the continuance of these abuses. But as those who argue thus derive for the most part great advantage and convenience from the continuance of these abuses, their estimation of the mischiefs of temporary popular violence, as compared with the mischiefs of permanent tyrannical and fraudulent forms of government, is likely, from the known principles of human nature, to be exaggerated. Such an estimate comes too with a worse grace from them who, if they would in opposition to their own unjust advantage, take the lead in reform, might spare the nation from the inconveniences of the temporary dominion of the poor, who by means of that very degraded condition which their insurrection would be designed to ameliorate are sufficiently incapable of discerning their own genuine and permanent advantage, tho' surely less incapable than those whose interests consist in proposing to themselves an object perfectly opposite and wholly incompatible with that advantage. These persons (I meant the government party) propose to us the dilemma of submitting to a despotism which is notoriously gathering like an avalanche year by year; or taking the risk of something which it must be confessed bears the aspect of a revolution. To this alternative we are reduced by the selfishness of those who taunt us with it. And the history of the world teaches us not to hesitate an instant in the decision, if indeed the power of decision be not already past. [. . .][19]

At the epoch adverted to,[20] the device of public credit was first systematically applied as an instrument of government. It was employed at the accession of William III less as a resource for meeting the financial exigencies of the state, than as a bond to connect those in the possession of property with those who had, by taking advantage of an accident of party, acceded to power. In the interval elapsed since that period it has accurately fulfilled the intention of its establishment, and has continued to add strength to the government, even until the present crisis. Now this device is one of those execrable contrivances of misrule which overbalance the material of common advantage produced by the progress of civilization, and increase the number of those who are idle in proportion to those who work, whilst it increases through the factitious wants of those indolent, priviledged persons, the quantity of work to be done. The rich, no longer being able to rule by force, have invented this scheme, that they may rule by fraud. [. . .][21]

The consequences of this transaction have been the establishment of a new aristocracy, which has its basis in fraud, as the old one has its basis in force. The hereditary landowners in England derived their title from royal grants—they are fiefs bestowed by conquerors, or church lands, or they have been bought by bankers and merchants from those persons [. . .] Let me be allowed to employ the word aristocracy in that ord[inary] sense which signifies that class of persons who possess a right to the produce of the labour of others, without dedicating to the common service any labour in return. This class of persons, whose existence is a prodigious anomaly in the social system, has ever constituted an inseparable portion of it, and there has never been an approach in practice towards any plan of political society modelled on equal justice, at least in the complicated mechanism of modern life.

Mankind seems to acquiesce, as in a necessary condition of the imbecility of their own will and reason, in the existence of an aristocracy. With reference to this imbecility, it has doubtless been the instrument of great social advantage, although the advantage would have been greater which might have been produced according to the forms of a just distribution of the goods and evils of life. The object therefore of all enlightened legislation and administration is to enclose within the narrowest practicable limits this order of drones. The effect of the financial impostures of the modern rulers of England has been to increase the numbers of the drones. Instead of one aristocracy the condition [to] which, in the present state of human affairs, the friends of justice and liberty are willing to subscribe as to an inevitable evil, they[22] have supplied us with two aristocracies. The one, consisting [of] the great land proprietors and merchants who receive and interchange the produce of this country with the produce of other countries; in this, because all other great communities have as yet acquiesced in it, we acquiesce. Connected with the members of [this aristocracy] is a certain generosity and refinement of manners and opinion which, although neither philosophy nor virtue has been that acknowledged substitute for them, at least is a religion which makes respected those venerable names. The [other] is an aristocracy of attorneys and excisemen,[23] and directors, and government pensioners, usurers, stock jobbers,[24] country bankers, with their dependents and descendants. These are a set of pelting[25] wretches in whose employment there is nothing to exercise, even to their distortion, the more majestic faculties of the soul. Though at bottom it is all trick, there is something magnificent in the chivalrous disdain of infamy connected with a gentleman. There is something to which—until you see through the base falshood upon which all inequality is founded—it is difficult for the imagination to refuse its respect, in the faithful and direct dealings of the substantial merchant.[26] But in the habits and lives of this new aristocracy created out of an increase [in] the public calamities, and whose existence must be determined by their termination, there is nothing to qualify our disapprobation. They eat and drink and sleep and, in the intervals of those <actions> being performed with most ridiculous ceremony and accompaniments, they cringe and lie. They poison the literature of the age in which they live, by requiring either the antitype[27] of their own mediocrity in books, or such stupid and distorted and inharmonious idealisms[28] as alone have the power to stir their torpid imaginations. [. . .][29]

The propositions which are the consequences or the corollaries to which the preceding reasoning seems to have conducted us are—

That the majority [of the] people of England are destitute and miserable, ill-clothed, ill-fed, ill-educated.

That they know this, and that they are impatient to procure a reform of the cause of their abject and wretched state.

That a cause of this peculiar misery is the unequal distribution which, under the form of the national debt, has been surreptitiously made of the products of their labour and the products of the labour of their ancestors; for all property is the produce of labour.

That the cause of that cause is a defect in the government.

That if they knew nothing of their condition, but believed that all they endured and all [they] were deprived of arose from the unavoidable condition of human life, this belief being an error, and the endurance of [which] enforces an injustice, every enlightened and honourable person, whatever may be the imagined interests of his peculiar class, ought to excite them to the discovery of the true state of the case and to the temperate but irresistible vindication of their rights.

A Reform in England is most just and necessary. What ought to be that reform?

A writer of the present day (a priest, of course, for his doctrines are those of a eunuch and of a tyrant) has stated that the evils of the poor arise from an excess of population,[30] and that after they have been stript naked by the tax gatherer and reduced to bread and tea and fourteen hours of hard labour by their masters, and after the frost has bitten their defenceless limbs, and the cramp has wrung like a disease within their bones, and hunger, and the suppressed revenge of hunger, has stamped the ferocity of want like the mark of Cain[31] upon their countenance, that the last tie by which Nature holds them to <the> benignant earth whose plenty is garnered up in the strongholds of their tyrants, is to be divided; that the single alleviation of their sufferings and their scorns, the one thing which made it impossible to degrade them below the beasts, which amid all their crimes and miseries yet separated a cynical and unmanly contamination, an anti-social cruelty, from all the soothing, elevating and harmonious gentlenesses of the sexual intercourse, and the humanizing charities of domestic life which are its appendages,—that this is to be obliterated. They are required to abstain from marrying under penalty of starvation. And it is threatened to deprive them of that property which is as strictly their birth right as a gentleman's land is his birth right, without giving them any compensation but the insulting advice to conquer, with minds undisciplined in the habits of higher gratification, a propensity which persons of the most consummate wisdom have been unable to resist, and which it is difficult to admire a person for having resisted. The doctrine of this writer is that the principle of population, when under no dominion of moral restraint, outstripping the sustenance produced by the labour of man, and that not in proportion to the number of inhabitants, but operating as equally in a thinly peopled community as in one where the population is enormous, [is][32] not a prevention but a check. So far a man might have been conducted by a train of reasoning which, though it may be shewn to be defective, would argue in the reasoner no selfish and slavish feelings. But he has the hardened insolence to propose as a remedy that the poor should be compelled (for what except compulsion is a threat of the confiscation of those funds which by the institutions of their country had been set apart for their sustenance in sickness or destitution?) to abstain from sexual intercourse, whilst the rich are to be permitted to add as many mouths to consume the products of the labour of the poor as they please.[33] If any new disadvantages are found to attach to the condition of social existence, those disadvantages ought not to be borne exclusively by one class of men, nor especially by that class whose ignorance leads them to exaggerate the advantages of sensual enjoyment, whose callous habits render domestic endearments more important to dispose them to resist the suggestions to violence and cruelty by which their situation ever exposes them to be tempted, and all whose other enjoyments are limited and few, whilst their sufferings are various and many. [. . .]

What is the Reform that We Desire?

Before we aspire after theoretical perfection in the amelioration of our political state, it is necessary that we possess those advantages which we have been cheated of, and [of] which the experience of modern times has proved that nations even under the present [conditions] are susceptible. 1st, we would regain these. 2d, we would establish some form of government which might secure us against such a series of events as have conducted us to a persuasion that the forms according to which it is now administered are inadequate to that purpose.

We would abolish the national debt.

We would disband the standing army.

We would, with every possible regard to the existing interests of the holders, abolish sinecures.[34]

We would, with every possible regard to the existing interests of the holders, abolish tithes.[35] And make all religions, all forms of opinion respecting the origin and government of the Universe, equal in the eye of the law.

We would make justice cheap, certain and speedy, and extend the institution of juries to every possible occasion of jurisprudence.

The national debt was chiefly contracted in two liberticide[36] wars, undertaken by the privileged classes of the country—the first, for the ineffectual purpose of tyrannizing over one portion of their subjects; the second, in order to extinguish the resolute spirit of obtaining these rights in another.

The labour which this money represents, and that which is represented by the money wrung for purposes of the same detestable character, out of the people since the commencement of the American war, would, if properly employed, have covered our land with monuments of architecture exceeding the sumptuousness and beauty of Aegypt and Athens; it might have made every peasant's cottage, surrounded with its garden, a little paradise of comfort, with every convenience desirable in civilized life; neat tables and chairs, and good beds, and a nice collection of useful books; and our ships manned by sailors well-paid and well-clothed might have kept watch round this glorious island against the less enlightened nations which assuredly would have envied, until they could have imitated, its prosperity. But the labour which is expressed by these sums has been diverted from these purposes of human happiness to the promotion of slavery, or the attempt at dominion, and a great portion of the sum in question is debt and must be paid.[37] Is it to remain unpaid forever, an eternal rent charge upon the land from which the inhabitants of these islands draw their subsistence? This were to pronounce the perpetual institution of two orders of aristocracy, and men are in a temper to endure one with some reluctance. Is it to be paid now? If so what are the funds, or when and how is it to be paid? The fact is that the national debt is a debt, not contracted by the whole nation towards a portion of it, but a debt contracted by the whole mass of the priviledged classes towards one particular portion of those classes. If the principal were paid, the whole property of those who possess property must be valued and the public creditor, whose property would have been included in this estimate, satisfied out of the proceeds. It has been said that all the land in the nation is mortgaged for the amount of the national debt. This is a partial statement. Not only all the land in the nation, but all the property of whatever denomination, all the houses and the furniture and the goods and every article of merchandise, and <the> property which is represented by the very money lent by the fund holder, who is bound to pay a certain portion as debtor, whilst he is to receive another certain portion as creditor. The property of the rich is mortgaged: to use the language of the law, let the mortgagee foreclose. [. . .][38]

There are two descriptions of property, which, without entering into the subtleties of a more refined moral theory as applicable to the existing forms of society, are entitled to two very different measures of forbearance and regard. And this forbearance and regard have by political institution usually been accorded in an inverse reason from what is just and natural. Labour, industry, economy, skill, genius, or any similar powers honourably and innocently exerted are the foundations of one description of property, and all true political institution ought to defend every man in the exercise of his discretion with respect to property so acquired. Of this kind is the principal part of the property enjoyed by those who are but one degree removed from the class which subsists by daily labour. [. . .] Property thus acquired men leave to their children. The absolute right becomes weakened by descent, first because it is only to avoid the greater evil of arbitrarily interfering with the discretion <of any man> in matters of property that the great evil of acknowledging any person to have an exclusive right to property who has not created it by his skill or labour is admitted; and secondly, because the mode of its having been originally acquired is forgotten, and it is confounded with the property acquired in a very different manner, and <the> principle upon which all property justly rests, after the great principle of the general advantage, becomes thus disregard[ed] and misunderstood. Yet the priviledge of disposing of property by will is one necessarily connected with the existing forms of domestic life, and exerted merely by those who have acquired property by industry or who have preserved it by economy, would never produce any great and invidious inequality of fortune. A thousand accidents would perpetually tend to level the accidental elevation, and the signs of property would perpetually recur to those whose deserving skill might attract, or whose labour might create it.

But there is another species of property, which has its foundation in usurpation or imposture or violence, without which, by the nature of things, immense aggregations of possessions of gold or land could never have been accumulated. Of this nature is the principal part of the property enjoyed by the aristocracy and by the great fund holders, the great majority of whose ancestors never either deserved it by their skill and talents or acquired and created it by their personal labour. It could not be that they deserved it, for if the honourable exertion of the most glorious imperial faculties of our nature had been the criterion of the possession of property, the posterity of Shakespeare, of Milton, of Hampden, of Lor[ ],[39] would be the wealthiest proprietors in England. It could not be that they acquired it by legitimate industry,—for besides that the real mode of acquisition is a matter of history, no honourable profession or honest trade, nor the hereditary exercise of it, ever in such numerous instances accumulated masses of property so vast as those enjoyed by the ruling orders in England. They were either grants from the feudal sovereigns whose right to what they granted was founded upon conquest or oppression, both a denial of all right; or they were the lands of the antient Catholic clergy which, according to the most acknowledged principles of public justice, reverted to the nation at their suppression, or they were the products of patents and monopolies, an exercise of sovereignty more pernicious than direct violence to the interests of a commercial nation; or in later times such property has been accumulated by dishonourable cunning and the taking advantage of a fictitious paper currency to obtain an unfair power over labour and the fruits of labour.

Property thus accumulated being transmitted from father to son acquires, as property of the more legitimate kind loses, force and sanction, but in a more limited manner. For not only on an examination and recurrence to first principles is it seen to have been founded on a violation of all that to which the latter owes its sacredness, but it is felt in its existence and perpetuation as a public burthen, and known as a rallying point to the ministers of tyranny, having the property of a snow ball, gathering as it rolls, and rolling until it bursts. [. . .]

What is meant by a Reform of parliament? If England were a Republic governed by one assembly; if there were no chamber of hereditary aristocracy which is at once an actual and a virtual representation of all who claim through rank or wealth superiority over their countrymen;

if there were no King who is as the rallying point <of all> those whose tendency is at once to <gather> and to confer that power which is consolidated at the expense of the nation, then[40]

The advocates of universal suffrage have reasoned correctly that no individual who is governed can be denied a direct share in the government of his country without supreme injustice. If we pursue the train of reasonings which have conducted to the conclusion, we discover that systems of social order still more incompatible than universal suffrage with any reasonable hope of instant accomplishment appear to be that which should result from a just combination of the elements of social life. I do not understand why those reasoners who propose at any price an immediate appeal to universal suffrage, because it is that which it is injustice to withhold, do not insist on the same ground on the immediate abolition, for instance, of monarchy and aristocracy, and the levelling of inordinate wealth, and an agrarian distribution, including the Parks and Chases of the rich, of the uncultivated districts of the country. No doubt the institution of universal suffrage would by necessary consequence tend to the abolition of these forms; because it is impossible that the people, having attained power, should fail to see what the demagogues now conceal from them [as] the legitimate consequence of the doctrines through which they had attained it. A Republic, however just in its principle, and glorious in its object, would, through <the> violence and sudden change which must attend it, incur a great risk of being as rapid in its decline as in its growth.

A civil war, which might be engendered by the passions attending on this mode of reform, would confirm in the mass of the nation those military habits which have been already introduced by our tyrants, and with which liberty is incompatible. From the moment that a man is a soldier, he becomes a slave. He is taught obedience; his will is no longer, which is the most sacred prerogative of man, guided by his own judgement. He is taught to despise human life and human suffering; this is the universal distinction of slaves. He is more degraded than a murderer; he is like the bloody knife, which has stabbed, and feels not; a murderer we may abhor and despise; a soldier is by profession beyond abhorrence and below contempt [. . .]

Probable Means

<That the House of> Commons should reform itself, uninfluenced by any fear that the people would, on their refusal, assume to itself that office, seems a contradiction. What need of Reform if it expresses the

will, and watches over the interests of the public? And if, as is sufficiently evident, it despises that will and neglects that interest, what motives would incite it to institute a reform which the aspect of the times renders indeed sufficiently perilous, but without which there will speedily be no longer anything in England to distinguish it from the basest and most abject community of slaves that ever existed.

The great principle of Reform consists in every individual of mature age and perfect understanding giving his consent to the institution and the continued existence of the social system which is instituted for his advantage and for the advantage of others in his situation. As in a great nation this is practically impossible, masses of individuals consent to qualify other individuals whom they delegate to superintend their concerns. These delegates have constitutional authority to exercise the functions of sovereignty; they unite in the highest degree the legislative and executive functions. A government that is founded on any other basis is a government of fraud or force, and aught on the first convenient occasion to be overthrown.

The grand principle of political reform is the natural equality of men; not with relation to their property, but to their rights. That equality in possessions which Jesus Christ so passionately taught is a moral rather than a political truth, and is such as social institutions cannot without mischief inflexibly secure. Morals and politics can only be considered as portions of the same science, with relation to a system of such absolute perfection as Plato and Rousseau and other reasoners have asserted, and as Godwin has, with irresistible eloquence, systematised and developed. Equality in possessions must be the last result of the utmost refinements of civilization; it is one of the conditions of that system of society, towards which with whatever hope of ultimate success, it is our duty to tend [. . .][41]

The last resort of resistance is undoubtedly insurrection.—The right of insurrection is derived from the employment of armed force to counteract the will of the nation. Let the government disband the standing army, and the purpose of resistance would be sufficiently fulfilled by the incessant agitation of the points of dispute before the courts of common law, and by an unwarlike display of the irresistible numbers and union of the people.

Before we enter into a consideration of the measures which might terminate in civil war, let us for a moment consider the nature and the consequences of war. This is the alternative which the unprincipled cunning of the tyrants <has> presented to us, and from which we must not [?shrink]. There is secret sympathy between Destruction and Power, between Monarchy and War; and the long experience of the history of all recorded time teaches us with what success they have played into each other's hands. War is a kind of superstition; the pageantry of arms and badges corrupts the imagination of men. How far more appropriate would be the symbols of an inconsolable grief—muffled drums, and melancholy music, and arms reversed, and the livery of sorrow rather than of blood. When men mourn at funerals, for what do they mourn in comparison with the calamities which they hasten with every circumstance of festivity to suffer and to inflict. Visit in imagination the scene of a field of battle, or a city taken by assault, collect into one group the groans and the distortions of the innumerable dying, the inconsolable grief and horror of their surviving friends, the hellish exultation, and unnatural drunkenness of destruction of the conquerors, the burning of the harvests and the obliteration of the traces of cultivation.—To this, in civil war is to be added the sudden disruption of the bonds of social life, and 'father against son'.

If there had never been war, there could never have been tyranny in the world; tyrants take advantage of the mechanical organization of armies to establish and defend their encroachments.—It is thus that the mighty advantages of the French Revolution have been almost compensated by a succession of tyrants (for demagogues, oligarchies, usurpers and legitimate Kings are merely varieties of the same class) from Robespierre to Louis 18.[42]

War, waged from whatever motive, extinguishes the sentiment of reason and justice in the mind. The motive is forgotten, or only adverted to in a mechanical and habitual manner. A sentiment of confidence in brute force and in a contempt of death and danger is considered as the highest virtue, when in truth, however indispensable, they are merely the means and the instruments, highly capable of being perverted to destroy the cause they were assumed to promote. [. . .][43]

A Defence of Poetry[1]

According to one mode of regarding those two classes of mental action which are called Reason and Imagination, the former may be considered as mind contemplating the relations borne by one thought to another, however produced; and the latter as mind acting upon those thoughts so as to colour them with its own light, and composing from them as from elements, other thoughts, each containing within itself the principle of its own integrity. The one is the τὸ ποιειν or the principle of synthesis, and has for its objects those forms which are common to universal nature and existence itself; the other is the τὸ λογιζειν[2] or principle of analysis, and its action regards the relations of things, simply as relations; considering thoughts, not in their integral unity, but as the algebraical representations which conduct to certain general results. Reason is the enumeration of quantities already known; Imagination the perception of the value of those quantities, both separately and as a whole. Reason respects the differences, and Imagination the similitudes of things. Reason is to Imagination as the instrument to the agent, as the body to the spirit, as the shadow to the substance.

Poetry, in a general sense, may be defined to be 'the expression of the Imagination': and poetry is connate[3] with the origin of man. Man is an instrument over which a series of external and internal impressions are driven, like the alternations of an ever-changing wind over an Aeolian lyre;[4] which move it, by their motion, to ever-changing melody. But there is a principle within the human being and perhaps within all sentient beings, which acts otherwise than in the lyre, and produces not melody alone, but harmony, by an internal adjustment of the sounds or motions thus excited to the impressions which excite them. It is as if the lyre could accommodate its chords to the motions of that which strikes them, in a determined proportion of sound; even as the musician can accommodate his voice to the sound of the lyre. A child at play by itself will express its delight by its voice and motions; and every inflexion of tone and every gesture will bear exact relation to a corresponding antitype[5] in the pleasurable impressions which awakened it; it will be the reflected image of that impression; and as the lyre trembles and sounds after the wind has died away, so the child seeks, by prolonging in its voice and motions the duration of the effect, to prolong also a consciousness of the cause. In relation to the objects which delight a child, these expressions are, what Poetry is to higher objects. The savage (for the savage is to ages what the child is to years) expresses the emotions produced in him by surrounding objects in a similar manner; and language and gesture together with plastic or pictorial imitation, become the image of the combined effect of those objects and of his apprehension of them. Man in society, with all his passions and his pleasures, next becomes the object of the passions and pleasures of man; an additional class of emotions produces an augmented treasure of expressions, and language, gesture, and the imitative arts become at once the representation and the medium, the pencil[6] and the picture, the chisel and the statue, the chord and the harmony. The social sympathies, or those laws from which as from its elements society results, begin to develope themselves from the moment that two human beings coexist; the future is contained within the present as the plant within the seed; and equality, diversity, unity, contrast, mutual dependence, become the principles alone capable of affording the motives according to which the will of a social being is determined to action, inasmuch as he is social; and constitute pleasure in sensation, virtue in sentiment, beauty in art, truth in reasoning, and love in the intercourse of kind. Hence men, even in the infancy of society, observe a certain order in their words and actions, distinct from that of the objects and the impressions represented by them, all expression being subject to the laws of that from which it proceeds. But let us dismiss those more general considerations which might involve an enquiry into the principles of society itself, and restrict our view to the manner in which the imagination is expressed upon its forms.

In the youth of the world, men dance and sing and imitate natural objects, observing in these actions, as in all others, a certain rhythm or order. And, although all men observe a similar, they observe not the same order, in the motions of the dance, in the melody of the song, in the combinations of language, in the series of their imitations of natural objects. For there is a certain order or rhythm belonging to each of these classes of mimetic[7] representation, from which the hearer and the spectator receive an intenser and a purer pleasure than from any other: the sense of an approximation to this order has been called taste, by modern writers. Every man, in the infancy of art, observes an order which approximates more or less closely to that from which this highest delight results: but the diversity is not sufficiently marked, as that its gradations should be sensible, except in those instances where the predominance of this faculty of approximation to the beautiful (for so we may be permitted to name the relation between this highest pleasure and its cause) is very great. Those in whom it exists in excess are poets, in the most universal sense of the word; and the pleasure resulting from the manner in which they express the influence of society or nature upon their own minds, communicates itself to others, and gathers a sort of reduplication from that community. Their language is vitally metaphorical; that is, it marks the before unapprehended relations of things, and perpetuates their apprehension, until the words which represent them become through time signs for portions or classes of thoughts, instead of pictures of integral thoughts; and then, if no new poets should arise to create afresh the associations which have been thus disorganized, language will be dead to all the nobler purposes of human intercourse. These similitudes or relations are finely said by Lord Bacon to be 'the same footsteps of nature impressed upon the various subjects of the world'[8]—and he considers the faculty which perceives them as the storehouse of axioms common to all knowledge. In the infancy of society every author is necessarily a poet, because language itself is poetry; and to be a poet is to apprehend the true and the beautiful, in a word the good which exists in the relation, subsisting, first between existence and perception, and secondly between perception and expression. Every original language near to its source is in itself the chaos of a cyclic poem:[9] the copiousness of lexicography[10] and the distinctions of grammar are the works of a later age, and are merely the catalogue and the form of the creations of Poetry.

But Poets, or those who imagine and express this indestructible order, are not only the authors of language and of music, of the dance and architecture and statuary and painting; they are the institutors of laws and the founders of civil society[11] and the inventors of the arts of life and the teachers, who draw into a certain propinquity with the beautiful and the true that partial apprehension of the agencies of the invisible world which is called religion. Hence all original religions are allegorical, or susceptible of allegory, and like Janus[12] have a double face of false and true. Poets, according to the circumstances of the age and nation in which they appeared, were called in the earlier epochs of the world legislators or prophets:[13] a poet essentially comprises and unites both these characters. For he not only beholds intensely the present as it is, and discovers those laws according to which present things ought to be ordered, but he beholds the future in the present, and his thoughts are the germs[14] of the flower and the fruit of latest time. Not that I assert poets to be prophets in the gross sense of the word, or that they can foretell the form as surely as they foreknow the spirit of events: such is the pretence of superstition which would make poetry an attribute of prophecy, rather than prophecy an attribute of poetry. A Poet participates in the eternal, the infinite and the one; as far as relates to his conceptions, time and place and number are not. The grammatical forms which express the moods of time, and the difference of persons and the distinction of place are convertible with respect to the highest poetry without injuring it as poetry, and the choruses of Aeschylus, and the Book of Job, and Dante's *Paradise* would afford more than any other writings examples of this fact, if the limits of this paper did not forbid citation. The creations of sculpture, painting and music are illustrations still more decisive.

Language, colour, form and religious and civil habits of action are all the instruments and the materials of poetry; they may all be called poetry by that figure of speech which considers the effect as a synonym of the cause. But poetry in a more restricted sense expresses those arrangements of language, and especially metrical language, which are created by that imperial faculty whose throne is curtained within the invisible nature of man. And this springs from the nature itself of language which is a more direct representation of the actions and passions of our internal being, and is susceptible of more various and delicate combinations than colour, form or motion, and is more plastic and obedient to the controul of that faculty of which it is the creation. For language is arbitrarily produced by the Imagination and has relation to thoughts alone; but all other materials, instruments and conditions of art have relations among each other, which limit and interpose between conception and expression. The former is as a mirror which reflects, the latter as a cloud which enfeebles, the light of which both are mediums of communication. Hence the fame of sculptors, painters and musicians, although the intrinsic powers of the great masters of these arts may yield in no degree to that of those who have employed language as the hieroglyphic of their thoughts, has never equalled that of poets in the restricted sense of the term; as two performers of equal skill will produce unequal effects from a guitar and a harp. The fame of legislators and founders of religions, so long as their institutions last, alone seems to exceed that of poets in the restricted sense: but it can scarcely be a question whether, if we deduct the celebrity which their flattery of the gross opinions of the vulgar usually conciliates, together with that which belonged to them in their higher character of poets, any excess will remain.

We have thus circumscribed the word Poetry within the limits of that art which is the most familiar and the most perfect expression of the faculty itself. It is necessary however to make the circle still narrower, and to determine the distinction between measured and unmeasured language; for the popular division into prose and verse is inadmissible in accurate philosophy.

Sounds as well as thoughts have relation both between each other and towards that which they represent, and a perception of the order of those relations has always been found connected with a perception of the order of the relations of thoughts. Hence the language of poets has ever affected a certain uniform and harmonious recurrence of sound without which it were not poetry, and which is scarcely less indispensable to the communication of its influence, than the words themselves without reference to that peculiar order. Hence the vanity of translation; it were as wise to cast a violet into a crucible that you might discover the formal principle of its colour and odour, as seek to transfuse from one language into another the creations of a poet. The plant must spring again from its seed or it will bear no flower—and this is the burthen of the curse of Babel.[15]

An observation of the regular mode of the recurrence of this harmony in the language of poëtical minds, together with its relation to music, produced metre, or a certain system of traditional forms of harmony and language. Yet it is by no means essential that a poet should accommodate his language to this traditional form, so that the harmony which is its spirit be observed. The practise is indeed convenient and popular and to be preferred, especially in such composition as includes much action: but every great poet must inevitably innovate upon the example of his predecessors in the exact structure of his peculiar versification. The distinction between poets and prose-writers is a vulgar error. The distinction between philosophers and poets has been anticipated. Plato was essentially a poet—the truth and splendour of his imagery and the melody of his language is the most intense that it is possible to conceive: he rejected the measure[16] of the epic, dramatic and lyrical forms, because he sought to kindle a harmony in thoughts divested of shape and action, and he forbore to invent any regular plan of rhythm which would include, under determinate forms, the varied pauses of his style. Cicero[17] sought to imitate the cadence of his periods[18] but with little success. Lord Bacon was a poet.[19] His language has a sweet and majestic rhythm which satisfies the sense no less than the almost superhuman wisdom of his philosophy satisfies the intellect; it is a strain which distends and then bursts the circumference of the reader's mind, and pours itself forth together with it into the universal element with which it has perpetual sympathy.—All the authors of revolutions in opinion are not only necessarily poets as they are inventors, nor even as their words unveil the permanent analogy of things by images which participate in the life of truth; but as their periods are harmonious and rhythmical and contain in themselves the elements of verse, being the echo of the eternal music.[20] Nor are those supreme poets, who have employed traditional forms of rhythm on account of the form and action of their subjects, less capable of perceiving and teaching the truth of things, than those who have omitted that form. Shakespeare, Dante and Milton (to confine ourselves to modern writers) are philosophers of the very loftiest power.

A Poem is the very image of life expressed in its eternal truth. There is this difference between a story and a poem, that a story is a catalogue of detached facts, which have no other bond of connexion than time, place, circumstance, cause and effect; the other is the creation of actions according to the unchangeable forms of human nature, as existing in the mind of the creator, which is itself the image of all other minds. The one is partial, and applies only to a definite period of time, and a certain combination of events which can never again recur; the other is universal, and contains within itself the germ of a relation to whatever motives or actions have place in the possible varieties of human nature. Time, which destroys the beauty and the use of the story of particular facts, stript of the poetry which should invest them, augments that of Poetry; and for ever developes new and wonderful applications of the eternal truth which it contains. Hence epitomes have been called the moths of just history;[21] they eat out the poetry of it. The story of particular facts is as a mirror which obscures and distorts that which should be beautiful: Poetry is a mirror which makes beautiful that which is distorted.

The parts of a composition may be poetical, without the composition as a whole being a poem. A single sentence may be considered as a whole though it may be found in the midst of a series of unassimilated portions; a single word even may be a spark of inextinguishable thought. And thus all the great historians, Herodotus, Plutarch, Livy,[22] were poets; and although the plan of these writers, especially that of Livy, constrained them from developing this faculty in its highest degree, they make copious and ample amends for their subjection, by filling all the interstices of their subjects with living images.

Having determined what is poetry, and who are poets, let us proceed to estimate its effects upon society.

Poetry is ever accompanied with pleasure: all spirits on which it falls, open themselves to receive the wisdom which is mingled with its delight. In the infancy of the world, neither poets themselves nor their auditors are fully aware of the excellency of poetry: for it acts in a divine and unapprehended manner, beyond and above consciousness: and it is reserved for future generations to contemplate and measure the mighty cause and effect in all the strength and splendour of their union. Even in modern times, no living poet ever arrived at the fulness of his fame; the jury which sits in judgement upon a poet, belonging as he does to all time, must be composed of his peers: it must be impanelled by Time from the selectest of the wise of many generations. A Poet is a nightingale who sits in darkness, and sings to cheer its own solitude with sweet sounds; his auditors are as men entranced by the melody of an unseen musician, who feel that they are moved and softened, yet know not whence or why. The poems of Homer and his contemporaries were the delight of infant Greece; they were the elements of that social system which is the column upon which all succeeding civilization has reposed. Homer embodied the ideal perfection of his age in human character; nor can we doubt that those who read his verses were awakened to an ambition of becoming like to Achilles, Hector and Ulysses:[23] the truth and beauty of friendship, patriotism and persevering devotion to an object, were unveiled to the depths in these immortal creations: the sentiments of the auditors must have been refined and enlarged by a sympathy with such great and lovely impersonations, until from admiring they imitated, and from imitation they identified themselves with the objects of their admiration. Nor let it be objected, that these characters are remote from moral perfection, and that they can by no means be considered as edifying patterns for general imitation. Every epoch under names more or less specious has deified its peculiar errors; Revenge is the naked Idol of the worship of a semi-barbarous age; and Self-deceit is the veiled Image of unknown evil before which luxury and satiety lie prostrate. But a poet considers the vices of his contemporaries as the temporary dress in which his creations must be arrayed, and which cover without concealing the eternal proportions of their beauty. An epic or dramatic personage is understood to wear them around his soul, as he may the antient armour or the modern uniform around his body; whilst it is easy to conceive a dress more graceful than either. The beauty of the internal nature cannot be so far concealed by its accidental vesture, but that the spirit of its form shall communicate itself to the very disguise, and indicate the shape it hides from the manner in which it is worn. A majestic form and graceful motions will express themselves through the most barbarous and tasteless costume. Few poets of the highest class have chosen to exhibit the beauty of their conceptions in its naked truth and splendour; and it is doubtful whether the alloy of costume, habit etc., be not necessary to temper this planetary music for mortal ears.[24]

The whole objection however of the immorality of poetry rests upon a misconception of the manner in which poetry acts to produce the moral improvement of man. Ethical science arranges the elements which poetry has created, and propounds schemes and proposes examples of civil and domestic life: nor is it for want of admirable doctrines that men hate, and despise, and censure, and deceive, and subjugate one another. But Poetry acts in another and a diviner manner. It awakens and enlarges the mind itself by rendering it the receptacle of a thousand unapprehended combinations of thought.

Poetry lifts the veil from the hidden beauty of the world; and makes familiar objects be as if they were not familiar; it reproduces all that it represents, and the impersonations clothed in its Elysian[25] light stand thenceforward in the minds of those who have once contemplated them, as memorials of that gentle and exalted content which extends itself over all thoughts and actions with which it coexists. The great secret of morals is Love; or a going out of our own nature, and an identification of ourselves with the beautiful which exists in thought, action or person, not our own.[26] A man to be greatly good, must imagine intensely and comprehensively; he must put himself in the place of another and of many others; the pains and pleasures of his species must become his own. The great instrument of moral good is the imagination: and poetry administers to the effect by acting upon the cause. Poetry enlarges the circumference of the imagination by replenishing it with thoughts of ever new delight, which have the power of attracting and assimilating to their own nature all other thoughts, and which form new intervals and interstices[27] whose void for ever craves fresh food. Poetry strengthens the faculty which is the organ of the moral nature of man in the same manner as exercise strengthens a limb. A Poet therefore would do ill to embody his own conceptions of right and wrong, which are usually those of his place and time, in his poetical creations, which participate in neither. By this assumption of the inferior office of interpreting the effect, in which perhaps after all he might acquit himself but imperfectly, he would resign a glory in a participation in the cause. There was little danger that Homer or any of the eternal poets, should have so far misunderstood themselves as to have abdicated this throne of their widest dominion. Those in whom the poetical faculty, though great, is less intense, as Euripides, Lucan, Tasso, Spenser, have frequently affected a moral aim; and the effect of their poetry is diminished in exact proportion to the degree in which they compel us to advert to this purpose.

Homer and the cyclic poets were followed at a certain interval by the dramatic and lyrical Poets of Athens, who flourished contemporaneously with all that is most perfect in the kindred expressions of the poetical faculty; architecture, painting, music, the dance, sculpture, philosophy, and we may add the forms of civil life. For although the scheme of Athenian society was deformed by many imperfections[28] which the poetry existing in Chivalry and Christianity has erased from the habits and institutions of modern Europe; yet never at any other period has so much energy, beauty and virtue been developed; never was blind strength and stubborn form so disciplined and rendered subject to the will of man, or that will less repugnant to the dictates of the beautiful and the true, as during the century which preceded the death of Socrates.[29] Of no other epoch in the history of our species have we records and fragments stamped so visibly with the image of the divinity in man. But it is Poetry alone, in form, in action or in language, which has rendered this epoch memorable above all others, and the storehouse of examples to everlasting time. For written poetry existed at that epoch simultaneously with the other arts, and it is an idle enquiry to demand which gave and which received the light, which all as from a common focus have scattered over the darkest periods of succeeding time. We know no more of cause and effect than a constant conjunction of events:[30] Poetry is ever found to coexist with whatever other arts contribute to the happiness and perfection of man. I appeal to what has already been established to distinguish between the cause and the effect.

It was at the period here adverted to, that the Drama had its birth; and however a succeeding writer may have equalled or surpassed those few great specimens of the Athenian drama which have been preserved to us, it is indisputable that the art itself never was understood or practised according to the true philosophy of it, as at Athens. For the Athenians employed language, action, music, painting, the dance, and religious institution to produce a common effect in the representation of the highest idealisms[31] of passion and of power; each division in the art was made perfect in its kind by artists of the most consummate skill, and was disciplined into a beautiful proportion and unity one towards the other. On the modern stage a few only of the elements capable of expressing the image of the poet's conception are employed at once. We have tragedy without music and dancing; and music and dancing without the highest impersonation of which they are the fit accompaniment, and both without religion and solemnity. Religious institution has indeed been usually banished from the stage. Our system of divesting the actor's face of a mask,[32] on which the many expressions appropriate to his dramatic character might be moulded into one permanent and unchanging expression, is favourable only to a partial and inharmonious effect; it is fit for nothing but a monologue, where all the attention may be directed to some great master of ideal mimicry. The modern practise of blending comedy with tragedy, though liable to great abuse in point of practise, is undoubtedly an extension of the dramatic circle; but the comedy should be as in *King Lear*, universal, ideal and sublime. It is perhaps the intervention of this principle which determines the balance in favour of *King Lear* against the *Oedipus Tyrannus* or the *Agamemnon*, or, if you will, the trilogies[33] with which they are connected; unless the intense power of the choral poetry, especially that of the latter, should be considered as restoring the equilibrium. *King Lear*, if it can sustain this comparison, may be judged to be the most perfect specimen of the dramatic art existing in the world; in spite of the narrow conditions to which the poet was subjected by the ignorance of the philosophy of the Drama which has prevailed in modern Europe. Calderón in his religious Autos[34] has attempted to fulfil some of the high conditions of dramatic representation neglected by Shakespeare; such as the establishing a relation between the drama and religion, and the accommodating them to music and dancing, but he omits the observation of conditions still more important, and more is lost than gained by a substitution of the rigidly-defined and ever-repeated idealisms of a distorted superstition[35] for the living impersonations of the truth of human passion.

But we digress.—The Author of the *Four Ages of Poetry* has prudently omitted to dispute on the effect of the Drama upon life and manners. For, if I know the knight by the device of his shield, I have only to inscribe *Philoctetes* or *Agamemnon* or *Othello* upon mine to put to flight the giant sophisms which have enchanted him, as the mirror of intolerable light, though on the arm of one of the weakest of the Paladins, could blind and scatter whole armies of necromancers and pagans.[36] The connexion of scenic exhibitions with the improvement or corruption of the manners of men, has been universally recognized: in other words, the presence or absence of poetry in its most perfect and universal form, has been found to be connected with good and evil in conduct or habit. The corruption which has been imputed to the drama as an effect begins, when the poetry employed in its constitution, ends: I appeal to the history of manners whether the gradations of the growth of the one and the decline of the other have not corresponded with an exactness equal to any other example of moral cause and effect.

The drama at Athens or wheresoever else it may have approached to its perfection, ever coexisted with the moral and intellectual greatness of the age. The tragedies of the Athenian poets are as mirrors in which the spectator beholds himself, under a thin disguise of circumstance, stript of all but that ideal perfection and energy which every one feels to be the internal type of all that he loves, admires and would become. The imagination is enlarged by a sympathy with pains and passions so mighty that they distend in their conception the capacity of that by which they are conceived; the good affections are strengthened by pity, indignation, terror and sorrow; and an exalted calm is prolonged from the satiety of this high exercise of them into the tumult of familiar life; even crime is disarmed of half its horror and all its contagion by being represented as the fatal consequence of the unfathomable agencies of nature; error is thus divested of its wilfulness; men can no longer cherish it as the creature of their choice. In a drama of the highest order there is little food for censure or hatred: it teaches rather self-knowledge and self-respect. Neither the eye or the mind can see itself unless reflected upon that which it resembles. The drama, so long as it continues to express poetry, is as a prismatic and many-sided mirror, which collects the brightest rays of human nature and divides and reproduces them from the simplicity of these elementary forms; and touches them with majesty and beauty, and multiplies all that it reflects, and endows it with the power of propagating its like wherever it may fall.

But in periods of the decay of social life, the drama sympathizes with that decay. Tragedy becomes a cold imitation of the form of the great masterpieces of antiquity, divested of all harmonious accompaniment of the kindred arts; and often the very form misunderstood: or a weak attempt to teach certain doctrines, which the writer considers as moral truths; and which are usually no more than specious flatteries of some gross vice or weakness with which the author in common with his auditors are infected. Hence what has been called the classical and the domestic drama. Addison's *Cato*[37] is a specimen of the one, and would it were not superfluous to cite examples of the other! To such purposes Poetry cannot be made subservient. Poetry is a sword of lightning ever unsheathed, which consumes the scabbard that would contain it. And thus we observe that all dramatic writings of this nature are unimaginative in a singular degree; they affect sentiment and passion: which divested of imagination are other names for caprice and appetite. The period in our own history of the grossest degradation of the drama is the reign of Charles II when all forms in which poetry had been accustomed to be expressed became hymns to the triumph of kingly power over liberty and virtue. Milton stood alone illuminating an age unworthy of him. At such periods the calculating principle pervades all the forms of dramatic exhibition, and poetry ceases to be expressed upon them. Comedy loses its ideal universality: wit succeeds to humour; we laugh from self-complacency and triumph instead of pleasure; malignity, sarcasm and contempt succeed to sympathetic merriment; we hardly laugh, but we smile. Obscenity, which is ever blasphemy against the divine beauty in life, becomes, from the very veil which it assumes, more active if less disgusting: it is a monster for which the corruption of society for ever brings forth new food, which it devours in secret.

The Drama being that form under which a greater number of modes of expression of poetry are susceptible of being combined than any other, the connexion of poetry and social good is more observable in the drama than in whatever other form. And it is indisputable that the highest perfection of human society has ever corresponded with the highest dramatic excellence: and that the corruption or the extinction of the drama in a nation where it has once flourished is a mark of a corruption of manners, and an extinction of the energies which sustain the soul of social life. But, as Machiavelli[38] says of political institutions, that life may be preserved and renewed, if men should arise capable of bringing back the drama to its principles. And this is true with respect to poetry in its most extended sense: all language, institution and form require not only to be produced but to be sustained: the office and character of a poet participates in the divine nature as regards providence no less than as regards creation.

Civil war, the spoils of Asia, and the fatal predominance first of the Macedonian, and then of the Roman arms, were so many symbols of the extinction or suspension of the creative faculty in Greece. The bucolic writers[39] who found patronage under the lettered tyrants of Sicily and Egypt were the latest representatives of its most glorious reign. Their poetry is intensely melodious; like the odour of the tuberose it overcomes and sickens the spirit with excess of sweetness; whilst the poetry of the preceding age was as a meadow-gale of June which mingles the fragrance of all the flowers of the field and adds a quickening and harmonizing spirit of its own which endows the sense with a power of sustaining its extreme delight. The bucolic and erotic delicacy in written poetry is correlative with that softness in statuary, music, and the kindred arts, and even in manners and institutions which distinguished the epoch to which we now refer. Nor is it the poetical faculty itself, or any misapplication of it, to which this want of harmony is to be imputed. An equal sensibility to the influence of the senses and the affections is to be found in the writings of Homer and Sophocles: the former especially has clothed sensual and pathetic images with irresistible attractions. Their superiority over these succeeding writers consists in the presence of those thoughts which belong to the inner faculties of our nature, not in the absence of those which are connected with the external: their incomparable perfection consists in a harmony of the union of all. It is not what the erotic poets have, but what they have not, in which their imperfection consists. It is not inasmuch as they were Poets, but inasmuch as they were not Poets, that they can be considered with any plausibility as connected with the corruption of their age. Had that corruption availed so as to extinguish in them the sensibility to pleasure, passion and natural scenery, which is imputed to them as an imperfection, the last triumph of evil would have been atchieved. For the end of social corruption is to destroy all sensibility to pleasure; and therefore it is corruption. It begins at the imagination and the intellect as at the core, and distributes itself thence as a paralyzing venom, through the affections into the very appetites, until all become a torpid mass in which sense hardly survives. At the approach of such a period, Poetry ever addresses itself to those faculties which are the last to be destroyed, and its voice is heard, like the footsteps of Astraea,[40] departing from the world. Poetry ever communicates all the pleasure which men are capable of receiving: it is ever still the light of life; the source of whatever of beautiful or generous or true can have place in an evil time. It will readily be confessed that those among the luxurious citizens of Syracuse and Alexandria who were delighted with the poems of Theocritus, were less cold, cruel and sensual than the remnant of their tribe. But corruption must utterly have destroyed the fabric of human society before Poetry can ever cease. The sacred links of that chain have never been entirely disjoined, which descending through the minds of many men is attached to those great minds whence as from a magnet the invisible effluence is sent forth which at once connects, animates and sustains the life of all.[41] It is the faculty which contains within itself the seeds at once of its own and of social renovation. And let us not circumscribe the effects of the bucolic and erotic poetry within the limits of the sensibility of those to whom it was addressed. They may have perceived the beauty of these immortal compositions, simply as fragments and isolated portions: those who are more finely organized, or born in a happier age, may recognize them as episodes of that great poem, which all poets, like the co-operating thoughts of one great mind, have built up since the beginning of the world.

The same revolutions within a narrower sphere had place in antient Rome: but the actions and forms of its social life never seem to have been perfectly saturated with the poetical element. The Romans appear to have considered the Greeks as the selectest treasuries of the selectest forms of manners and of nature and to have abstained from creating in measured language, sculpture, music or architecture, any thing which might bear a particular relation to their own condition whilst it should bear a general one to the universal constitution of the world. But we judge from partial evidence, and we judge perhaps partially. Ennius, Varro, Pacuvius and Accius,[42] all great poets, have been lost. Lucretius is in the highest, and Virgil in a very high sense, a creator. The chosen delicacy of the expressions of the latter are as a mist of light which conceal from us the intense and exceeding truth of his conceptions of nature. Livy is instinct with poetry. Yet Horace, Catullus, Ovid, and generally the other great writers of the Virgilian age, saw man and nature in the mirror of Greece. The institutions also and the religion of Rome were less poetical than those of Greece, as the shadow is less vivid than the substance. Hence Poetry in Rome seemed to follow rather than accompany the perfection of political and domestic society. The true Poetry of Rome lived in its institutions; for whatever of beautiful, true and majestic they contained could have sprung only from the faculty which creates the order in which they consist. The life of Camillus; the death of Regulus; the expectation of the senators in their godlike state of the victorious Gauls; the refusal of the Republic to make peace with Hannibal after the battle of Cannae,[43] were not the consequences of a refined calculation of the probable personal advantage to result from such a rhythm and order in the shews of life, to those who were at once the poets and the actors of these immortal dramas. The imagination beholding the beauty of this order, created it out of itself according to its own idea: the consequence was empire, and the reward everliving fame. These things are not the less poetry, *quia carent vate sacro*.[44] They are the episodes of that cyclic poem written by Time upon the memories of men. The Past, like an inspired rhapsodist,[45] fills the theatre of everlasting generations with their harmony.

At length the antient system of religion and manners had fulfilled the circle of its revolutions. And the world would have fallen into utter anarchy and darkness but that there were found poets among the authors of the Christian and Chivalric systems of manners and religion, who created forms of opinion and action never before conceived; which, copied into the imaginations of men, became as generals to the bewildered armies of their thoughts. It is foreign to the present purpose to touch upon the evil produced by these systems: except that we protest, on the ground of the principles already established, that no portion of it can be attributed to the poetry they contain.

It is probable that the poetry of Moses, Job, David, Solomon and Isaiah had produced a great effect upon the mind of Jesus and his disciples.[46] The scattered fragments preserved to us by the biographers of this extraordinary person, are all instinct with the most vivid poetry. But his doctrines seem to have been quickly distorted. At a certain period after the prevalence of a system of opinions founded upon those promulgated by him, the three forms into which Plato had distributed the faculties of mind[47] underwent a sort of apotheosis, and became the object of the worship of the civilised world. Here it is to be confessed that 'Light seems to thicken', and

> the crow makes wing to the rooky wood,
> Good things of day begin to droop and drowze
> And night's black agents to their preys do rouze.[48]

But mark how beautiful an order has sprung from the dust and blood of this fierce chaos! how the World, as from a resurrection, balancing itself on the golden wings of knowledge and of hope, has reassumed its yet unwearied flight into the Heaven of time! Listen to the music, unheard by outward ears, which is as a ceaseless and invisible wind nourishing its everlasting course with strength and swiftness.

The poetry in the doctrines of Jesus Christ, and the mythology and institutions of the Celtic[49] conquerors of the Roman Empire, outlived the darkness and the convulsions connected with their growth and victory, and blended themselves into a new fabric of manners and opinion. It is an error to impute the ignorance of the dark ages to the Christian doctrines or the predominance of the Celtic nations. Whatever of evil their agencies may have contained sprung from the extinction of the poetical principle, connected with the progress of despotism and superstition. Men, from causes too intricate to be here discussed, had become insensible and selfish: their own will had become feeble and yet they were its slaves, and thence the slaves of the will of others; lust, fear, avarice, cruelty and fraud characterised a race amongst whom no one was to be found capable of *creating* in form, language or institution. The moral anomalies of such a state of society are not justly to be charged upon any class of events immediately connected with them, and those events are most entitled to our approbation which could dissolve it most expeditiously. It is unfortunate for those who cannot distinguish words from thoughts that many of these anomalies have been incorporated into our popular religion.

It was not until the eleventh century that the effects of the poetry of the Christian and the Chivalric systems began to manifest themselves. The principle of equality had been discovered and applied by Plato in his *Republic*,[50] as the theoretical rule of the mode in which the materials of pleasure and of power produced by the common skill and labour of human beings ought to be distributed among them. The limitations of this rule were asserted by him to be determined only by the sensibility of each, or the utility to result to all. Plato, following the doctrines of Timaeus and Pythagoras,[51] taught also a moral and intellectual system of doctrine comprehending at once the past, the present and the future condition of man. Jesus Christ divulged the sacred and eternal truths contained in these views to mankind, and Christianity, in its abstract purity, became the exoteric expression of the esoteric[52] doctrines of the poetry and wisdom of antiquity. The incorporation of the Celtic nations with the exhausted population of the South, impressed upon it the figure of the poetry existing in their mythology and institutions. The result was a sum of the action and reaction of all the causes included in it; for it may be assumed as a maxim that no nation or religion can supersede any other without incorporating into itself a portion of that which it supersedes. The abolition of personal and domestic slavery, and the emancipation of women from a great part of the degrading restraints of antiquity were among the consequences of these events.

The abolition of personal slavery is the basis of the highest political hope that it can enter into the mind of man to conceive. The freedom of women produced the poetry of sexual love. Love became a religion, the idols of whose worship were ever present. It was as if the statues of Apollo and the Muses had been endowed with life and motion and had walked forth among their worshippers; so that earth became peopled by the inhabitants of a diviner world. The familiar appearances and proceedings of life became wonderful and heavenly; and a paradise was created as out of the wrecks of Eden. And as this creation itself is poetry, so its creators were poets; and language was the instrument of their art—'Galeotto fù il libro, e chi lo scrisse'.[53] The Provençal trouveurs, or inventors, preceded Petrarch,[54] whose verses are as spells which unseal the inmost enchanted fountains of the delight which is in the grief of Love. It is impossible to feel them without becoming a portion of that beauty which we contemplate: it were superfluous to explain how the gentleness and the elevation of mind connected with these sacred emotions can render men more amiable, and generous, and wise, and lift them out of the dull vapours of the little world of self. Dante understood the secret things of love even more than Petrarch. His *Vita Nuova*[55] is an inexhaustible fountain of purity of sentiment and language: it is the idealized history of that period, and those intervals of his life which were dedicated to love. His apotheosis of Beatrice in Paradise and the gradations of his own love and her loveliness, by which as by steps he feigns himself to have ascended to the throne of the Supreme Cause, is the most glorious imagination of modern poetry.[56] The acutest critics have justly reversed the judgement of the vulgar, and the order of the great acts of the 'Divine Drama',[57] in the measure of the admiration which they accord to the *Hell*, *Purgatory* and *Paradise*. The latter is a perpetual hymn to everlasting love. Love, which found a worthy poet in Plato[58] alone of all the antients, has been celebrated by a chorus of the greatest writers of the renovated world; and the music has penetrated the caverns of society, and its echoes still drown the dissonance of arms and superstition. At successive intervals Ariosto, Tasso, Shakespeare, Spenser, Calderón, Rousseau,[59] and the great writers of our own age, have celebrated the dominion of love, planting as it were trophies[60] in the human mind of that sublimest victory over sensuality and force. The true relation borne to each other by the sexes into which human kind is distributed has become less misunderstood; and if the error which confounded diversity with inequality of the powers of the two sexes has been partially recognized in the opinions and institutions of modern Europe, we owe this great benefit to the worship of which Chivalry was the law, and poets the prophets.

The poetry of Dante may be considered as the bridge thrown over the stream of time which unites the modern and antient world. The distorted notions of invisible things which Dante and his rival Milton have idealised are merely the mask and the mantle in which these great poets walk through eternity enveloped and disguised. It is a difficult question to determine how far they were conscious of the distinction which must have subsisted in their minds between their own creeds and that of the people. Dante at least appears to wish to mark the full extent of it by placing Riphaeus whom Virgil calls *justissimus unus*,[61] in Paradise, and observing a most heretical caprice in his distribution of rewards and punishments. And Milton's poem[62] contains within itself a philosophical refutation of that system of which, by a strange but natural antithesis, it has been a chief popular support. Nothing can exceed the energy and magnificence of the character of Satan as expressed in *Paradise Lost*. It is a mistake to suppose that he could ever have been intended for the popular personification of evil. Implacable hate, patient cunning, and a sleepless refinement of device to inflict the extremest anguish on an enemy, these things are evil; and although venial in a slave are not to be forgiven in a tyrant; although redeemed by much that ennobles his defeat in one subdued, are marked by all that dishonours his conquest in the victor. Milton's Devil as a moral being is as far superior to his God as one who perseveres in some purpose which he has conceived to be excellent in spite of adversity and torture, is to one who in the cold security of undoubted triumph inflicts the most horrible revenge upon his enemy—not from any mistaken notion of inducing him to repent of a perseverance in enmity, but with the alledged design[63] of exasperating him to deserve new torments. Milton has so far violated the popular creed (if this shall be judged to be a violation) as to have alledged no superiority of moral virtue to his God over his Devil. And this bold neglect of a direct moral purpose is the most decisive proof of the supremacy of Milton's genius. He mingled as it were the elements of human nature, as colours upon a single pallet, and arranged them into the composition of his great picture according to the laws of epic truth: that is, according to the laws of that principle by which a series of actions of the external universe and of intelligent and ethical beings is calculated to excite the sympathy of succeeding generations of mankind. The *Divina Commedia* and *Paradise Lost* have conferred upon modern mythology[64] a systematic form; and when change and time shall have added one more superstition to the mass of those which have arisen and decayed upon the earth, commentators will be learnedly employed in elucidating the religion of ancestral Europe, only not utterly forgotten because it will have been stamped with the eternity of genius.

Homer was the first, and Dante the second epic poet: that is, the second poet the series of whose creations bore a defined and intelligible relation to the knowledge, and sentiment, and religion, and political condition of the age in which he lived, and of the ages which followed it: developing itself in correspondence with their development. For Lucretius had limed the wings of his swift spirit in the dregs of the sensible world:[65] and Virgil, with a modesty that ill became his genius, had affected the fame of an imitator even whilst he created anew all that he copied; and none among the flock of mock-birds,[66] though their notes were sweet, Apollonius Rhodius, Quintus Calaber Smyrnaeus, Nonnus, Lucan, Statius or Claudian,[67] have sought even to fulfil a single condition of epic truth. Milton was the third Epic Poet: for if the title of epic in its highest sense be refused to the *Aeneid*, still less can it be conceded to the *Orlando Furioso*, the *Gerusalemme Liberata*, the *Lusiad* or the *Fairy Queen*.[68]

Dante and Milton were both deeply penetrated with the antient religion of the civilized world; and its spirit exists in their poetry probably in the same proportion as its forms survived in the unreformed worship of modern Europe. The one preceded and the other followed the Reformation at almost equal intervals. Dante was the first religious reformer, and Luther surpassed him rather in the rudeness and acrimony than in the boldness of his censures of papal usurpation. Dante was the first awakener of entranced Europe; he created a language in itself music and persuasion out of a chaos of inharmonious barbarisms.[69] He was the congregator of those great spirits who presided over the resurrection of learning; the Lucifer of that starry flock[70] which in the thirteenth century shone forth from republican Italy,[71] as from a heaven, into the darkness of the benighted world. His very words are instinct with[72] spirit; each is as a spark, a burning atom of inextinguishable thought; and many yet lie covered in the ashes of their birth, and pregnant with a lightning which has yet found no conductor. All high poetry is infinite; it is as the first acorn which contained all oaks potentially. Veil after veil may be undrawn and the inmost naked beauty of the meaning never exposed. A great poem is a fountain for ever overflowing with the waters of wisdom and delight; and after one person and one age has exhausted all its divine effluence which their peculiar relations enable them to share; another and yet another succeeds, and new relations are ever developed, the source of an unforeseen and an unconceived delight.

The age immediately succeeding to that of Dante, Petrarch and Boccaccio[73] was characterized by a revival of painting, sculpture, music and architecture. Chaucer caught the sacred inspiration, and the superstructure of English literature is based upon the materials of Italian invention.

But let us not be betrayed from a defence into a critical history of Poetry and its influence on society. Be it enough to have pointed out the effects of poets in the large and true sense of the word, upon their own and all succeeding times, and to revert to the partial instances cited as illustrations of an opinion the reverse of that attempted to be established in the *Four Ages of Poetry.*

But Poets have been challenged to resign the civic crown to reasoners and mechanists[74] on another plea. It is admitted that the exercise of the imagination is most delightful, but it is alledged that that of reason is more useful. Let us examine as the ground of this distinction what is here meant by Utility. Pleasure or good in a general sense, is that which the consciousness of a sensitive and intelligent being seeks, and in which when found it acquiesces. There are two kinds of pleasure, one durable, universal and permanent; the other transitory and particular. Utility may either express the means of producing the former or the latter. In the former sense, whatever strengthens and purifies the affections, enlarges the imagination, and adds a spirit to sense, is useful. But the meaning in which the Author of the *Four Ages of Poetry* seems to have employed the word utility is the narrower one of banishing the importunity of the wants of our animal nature, the surrounding men with security of life, the dispersing the grosser delusions of superstition, and the conciliating such a degree of mutual forbearance among men as may consist with the motives of personal advantage.

Undoubtedly the promoters of utility in this limited sense, have their appointed office in society. They follow the footsteps of poets, and copy the sketches of their creations into the book of common life. They make space and give time. Their exertions are of the highest value so long as they confine their administration of the concerns of the inferior powers of our nature within the limits of what is due to the superior ones. But whilst the sceptic destroys gross superstitions, let him spare to deface, as some of the French writers have defaced, the eternal truths charactered upon the imaginations of men. Whilst the mechanist[75] abridges, and the political economist combines, labour,[76] let them beware that their speculations, for want of a correspondence with those first principles which belong to the imagination, do not tend, as they have in modern England, to exasperate at once the extremes of luxury and want. They have exemplified the saying, 'To him that hath, more shall be given; and from him that hath not, the little that he hath shall be taken away.'[77] The rich have become richer, and the poor have become poorer; and the vessel of the state is driven between the Scylla and Charybdis[78] of anarchy and despotism. Such are the effects which must ever flow from an unmitigated exercise of the calculating faculty.

It is difficult to define pleasure in its highest sense; the definition involving a number of apparent paradoxes. For, from an inexplicable defect of harmony in the constitution of human nature, the pain of the inferior is frequently connected with the pleasures of the superior portions of our being. Sorrow, terror, anguish, despair itself are often the chosen expressions of an approximation to the highest good. Our sympathy in tragic fiction depends on this principle: tragedy delights by affording a shadow of the pleasure which exists in pain. This is the source also of the melancholy which is inseparable from the sweetest melody. The pleasure that is in sorrow, is sweeter than the pleasure of pleasure itself. And hence the saying, 'It is better to go to the house of mourning, than to the house of mirth.'[79] Not that this highest species of pleasure is necessarily linked with pain. The delight of love and friendship, the extacy of the admiration of nature, the joy of the perception and still more of the creation of poetry is often wholly unalloyed.

The production and assurance of pleasure in this highest sense is the true utility. Those who produce and preserve this pleasure are Poets or poetical philosophers.

The exertions of Locke, Hume, Gibbon, Voltaire, Rousseau,* and their disciples, in favour of oppressed and deluded humanity are entitled to the gratitude of mankind. Yet it is easy to calculate the degree of moral and intellectual improvement which the world would have exhibited, had they never lived. A little more nonsense would have been talked for a century or two; and perhaps a few more men, women and children burnt as heretics. We might not at this moment have been congratulating each other on the abolition of the Inquisition in Spain.[81] But it exceeds all imagination to conceive what would have been the moral condition of the world if neither Dante, Petrarch, Boccaccio, Chaucer, Shakespeare, Calderón, Lord Bacon, nor Milton had ever existed; if Raphael and Michael Angelo[82] had never been born; if the Hebrew poetry[83] had never been translated; if a revival of a study of Greek literature had never taken place; if no monuments of antient sculpture had been handed down to us; and if the poetry of the religion of the antient world had been extinguished together with its belief. The human mind could never, except by the intervention of these excitements, have been awakened to the invention of those grosser sciences, and that application of analytical reasoning to the aberrations of society, which it is now attempted to exalt over the direct expression of the inventive and creative faculty itself.

We have more moral, political and historical wisdom than we know how to reduce into practise: we have more scientific and economical knowledge than can be accommodated to the just distribution of the produce which it multiplies. The poetry in these systems of thought is concealed by the accumulation of facts and calculating processes. There is no want of knowledge respecting what is wisest and best in morals, government, and political economy, or at least what is wiser and better than what men now practise and endure. But we 'let *I dare not* wait upon *I would*, like the poor cat i' the adage'.[84] We want the creative faculty to imagine that which we know; we want the generous impulse to act that which we imagine; we want the poetry of life: our calculations have outrun conception; we have eaten more than we can digest. The cultivation of those sciences which have enlarged the limits of the empire of man over the external world, has,

* I follow the classification adopted by the author of the *Four Ages of Poetry*. But Rousseau was essentially a poet. The others, even Voltaire, were mere reasoners. [Shelley's note][80]

for want of the poetical faculty, proportionally circumscribed those of the internal world, and man, having enslaved the elements, remains himself a slave. To what but a cultivation of the mechanical arts in a degree disproportioned to the presence of the creative faculty which is the basis of all knowledge is to be attributed the abuse of all invention for abridging and combining labour, to the exasperation of the inequality of mankind?[85] From what other cause has it arisen that the discoveries which should have lightened, have added a weight to the curse imposed on Adam?[86] Poetry, and the principle of Self, of which money is the visible incarnation, are the God and Mammon[87] of the world.

The functions of the poetical faculty are twofold: by one it creates new materials of knowledge, and power, and pleasure; by the other it engenders in the mind a desire to reproduce and arrange them according to a certain rhythm and order, which may be called the beautiful and the good. The cultivation of poetry is never more to be desired than at periods when, from an excess of the selfish and calculating principle, the accumulation of the materials of external life exceed the quantity of the power of assimilating them to the internal laws of human nature. The body has then become too unwieldy for that which animates it.

Poetry is indeed something divine. It is at once the centre and circumference of knowledge;[88] it is that which comprehends all science, and that to which all science must be referred. It is at the same time the root and the blossom of all other systems of thought: it is that from which all spring, and that which adorns all; and that which if blighted denies the fruit and the seed, and withholds from the barren world the nourishment and the succession of the scions of the tree of life. It is the perfect and consummate surface and bloom of things; it is as the odour and the colour of the rose to the texture of the elements which compose it, as the form and splendour of unfaded beauty to the secrets of anatomy and corruption. What were Virtue, Love, Patriotism, Friendship—what were the scenery of this beautiful Universe which we inhabit, what were our consolations on this side of the grave, and what were our aspirations beyond it, if Poetry did not ascend to bring light and fire from those eternal regions where the owl-winged faculty of calculation dare not ever soar? Poetry is not like reasoning, a power to be exerted according to the determination of the will. A man cannot say, 'I will compose poetry'. The greatest poet even cannot say it: for the mind in creation is as a fading coal which some invisible influence, like an inconstant wind, awakens to transitory brightness: this power arises from within, like the colour of a flower which fades and changes as it is developed, and the conscious portions of our nature are unprophetic either of its approach or its departure. Could this influence be durable in its original purity and force, it is impossible to predict the greatness of the results: but when composition begins, inspiration is already on the decline, and the most glorious poetry that has ever been communicated to the world is probably a feeble shadow of the original conceptions of the poet. I appeal to the greatest Poets of the present day, whether it be not an error to assert that the finest passages of poetry are produced by labour and study. The toil and the delay recommended by critics can be justly interpreted to mean no more than a careful observation of the inspired moments, and an artificial connection of the spaces between their suggestions by the intertexture[89] of conventional expressions; a necessity only imposed by a limitedness of the poetical faculty itself. For Milton conceived the *Paradise Lost* as a whole before he executed it in portions. We have his own authority also for the Muse having 'dictated' to him 'the unpremeditated song'.[90] And let this be an answer to those who would alledge[91] the fifty-six various readings of the first line of the *Orlando Furioso*. Compositions so produced are to poetry what mosaic is to painting. This instinct and intuition of the poetical faculty is still more observable in the plastic and pictorial arts: a great statue or picture grows under the power of the artist as a child in the mother's womb, and the very mind which directs the hands in formation is incapable of accounting to itself for the origin, the gradations, or the media of the process.

Poetry is the record of the happiest and best moments of the happiest and best minds. We are aware of evanescent visitations of thought and feeling sometimes associated with place or person, sometimes regarding our own mind alone, and always arising unforeseen and departing unbidden, but elevating and delightful beyond all expression: so that even in the desire and the regret they leave there cannot but be pleasure, participating as it does in the nature of its object. It is as it were the interpenetration of a diviner nature through our own, but its footsteps are like those of a wind over the sea, which the coming calm erases, and whose traces remain only as on the wrinkled sand which paves it. These and corresponding conditions of being are experienced principally by those of the most delicate sensibility and the most enlarged imagination; and the state of mind produced by them is at war with every base desire. The enthusiasm of virtue, love, patriotism and friendship is essentially linked with such emotions; and whilst they last self appears as what it is, an atom to a

Universe. Poets are not only subject to these experiences as spirits of the most refined organization, but they can colour all that they combine with the evanescent hues of this etherial world; a word, a trait in the representation of a scene or a passion will touch the enchanted chord, and reanimate, in those who have ever experienced these emotions, the sleeping, the cold, the buried image of the past. Poetry thus makes immortal all that is best and most beautiful in the world; it arrests the vanishing apparitions which haunt the interlunations[92] of life, and veiling them or in language or in form sends them forth among mankind bearing sweet news of kindred joy to those with whom their sisters abide—abide, because there is no portal of expression from the caverns of the spirit which they inhabit into the universe of things. Poetry redeems from decay the visitations of the divinity in man.

Poetry turns all things to loveliness: it exalts the beauty of that which is most beautiful, and it adds beauty to that which is most deformed: it marries exultation and horror, grief and pleasure, eternity and change; it subdues to union under its light yoke all irreconcilable things. It transmutes all that it touches, and every form moving within the radiance of its presence is changed by wondrous sympathy to an incarnation of the spirit which it breathes: its secret alchemy turns to potable gold the poisonous waters which flow from death through life; it strips the veil of familiarity from the world, and lays bare the naked and sleeping beauty which is the spirit of its forms.

All things exist as they are perceived;[93] at least in relation to the percipient—'The mind is its own place, and of itself can make a Heaven of Hell, a Hell of Heaven'.[94] But Poetry defeats the curse which binds us to be subjected to the accident of surrounding impressions. And whether it spreads its own figured curtain or withdraws life's dark veil from before the scene of things, it equally creates for us a being within our being. It makes us the inhabitants of a world to which the familiar world is a chaos. It reproduces the common Universe of which we are portions and percipients, and it purges from our inward sight the film of familiarity[95] which obscures from us the wonder of our being. It compels us to feel that which we perceive, and to imagine that which we know. It creates anew the universe after it has been annihilated in our minds by the recurrence of impressions blunted by re-iteration. It justifies that bold and true word of Tasso: *Non merita nome di creatore se non Iddio ed il Poeta.*[96]

A Poet, as he is the author to others of the highest wisdom, pleasure, virtue and glory, so he ought personally to be the happiest, the best, the wisest and the most illustrious of men. As to his glory, let Time be challenged to declare whether the fame of any other institutor[97] of human life be comparable to that of a poet. That he is the wisest, the happiest and the best, inasmuch as he is a poet, is equally incontrovertible: the greatest Poets have been men of the most spotless virtue, of the most consummate prudence, and, if we would look into the interior of their lives, the most fortunate of men: and the exceptions, as they regard those who possessed the poetic faculty in a high yet inferior degree, will be found on consideration to confine rather than destroy the rule. Let us for a moment stoop to the arbitration of popular breath,[98] and usurping and uniting in our own persons the incompatible characters of accuser, witness, judge and executioner, let us decide without trial, testimony or form that certain motives of those who are 'there sitting where we dare not soar'[99] are reprehensible. Let us assume that Homer was a drunkard, that Virgil was a flatterer, that Horace was a coward, that Tasso was a madman, that Lord Bacon was a peculator, that Raphael was a libertine, that Spenser was a poet laureate.[100] It is inconsistent with this division of our subject to cite living poets, but Posterity has done ample justice to the great names now referred to. Their errors have been weighed and found to have been dust in the balance; if their sins 'were as scarlet, they are now white as snow': they have been washed in the blood of the mediator and the redeemer Time.[101] Observe in what a ludicrous chaos the imputations of real and of fictitious crime have been confused in the contemporary calumnies against poetry and poets;[102] consider how little is as it appears, or appears as it is; look to your own motives, and judge not, lest ye be judged.[103]

Poetry, as has been said, differs in this respect from logic, that it is not subject to the controul of the active powers of the mind, and that its birth and recurrence have no necessary connexion with consciousness or will. It is presumptuous to determine that these are the necessary conditions of all mental causation when mental effects are experienced insusceptible of being referred to them. The frequent recurrence of the poetical power, it is obvious to suppose, may produce in the mind an habit of order and harmony correlative with its own nature and with its effects upon other minds. But in the intervals of inspiration, and they may be frequent without being durable, a Poet becomes a man[104] and is abandoned to the sudden reflux of the influences under which others habitually live. But as he is more delicately organized than other men, and sensible to pain and pleasure both his own and that of others in a degree unknown to them, he will avoid the one and pursue the other with an ardour proportioned to this difference. And he renders himself obnoxious to[105] calumny, when he neglects to observe the circumstances under which these objects of universal pursuit and flight have disguised themselves in one another's garments.

But there is nothing necessarily evil in this error, and thus cruelty, envy, revenge, avarice, and the passions purely evil, have never formed any portion of the popular imputations on the lives of poets.

I have thought it most favourable to the cause of truth to set down these remarks according to the order in which they were suggested to my mind by a consideration of the subject itself, instead of following that of the treatise which excited me to make them public. Thus although devoid of the formality of a polemical reply, if the views which they contain be just, they will be found to involve a refutation of the *Four Ages of Poetry*, so far at least as regards the first division of the subject. I can readily conjecture what should have moved the gall of the learned and intelligent author of that paper; I confess myself like him unwilling to be stunned by the *Theseids* of the hoarse Codri of the day. Bavius and Maevius [106] undoubtedly are, as they ever were, insufferable persons. But it belongs to a philosophical critic to distinguish rather than confound.

The first of these remarks has related to Poetry in its elements and principles; and it has been shewn, as well as the narrow limits assigned them would permit, that what is called Poetry in a restricted sense has a common source with all other forms of order and of beauty according to which the materials of human life are susceptible of being arranged, and which is Poetry in an universal sense.

The second part will have for its object an application of these principles to the present state of the cultivation of Poetry, and a defence of the attempt to idealize the modern forms of manners and opinion, and compel them into a subordination to the imaginative and creative faculty. For the literature of England,[107] an energetic developement of which has ever preceded or accompanied a great and free developement of the national will, has arisen as it were from a new birth. In spite of the low-thoughted[108] envy which would undervalue contemporary merit, our own will be a memorable age in intellectual atchievements, and we live among such philosophers and poets as surpass beyond comparison any who have appeared since the last national struggle for civil and religious liberty. The most unfailing herald, companion and follower of the awakening of a great people to work a beneficial change in opinion or institution, is Poetry. At such periods there is an accumulation of the power of communicating and receiving intense and impassioned conceptions respecting man and nature. The persons in whom this power resides, may often as far as regards many portions of their nature, have little apparent correspondence with that spirit of good of which they are the ministers. But even whilst they deny and abjure, they are yet compelled to serve, the Power which is seated on the throne of their own soul. It is impossible to read the compositions of the most celebrated writers of the present day without being startled with the electric life which burns within their words. They measure the circumference and sound the depths of human nature with a comprehensive and all-penetrating spirit, and they are themselves perhaps the most sincerely astonished at its manifestations, for it is less their spirit than the spirit of the age.[109] Poets are the hierophants of an unapprehended inspiration,[110] the mirrors of the gigantic shadows which futurity casts upon the present, the words which express what they understand not, the trumpets which sing to battle and feel not what they inspire: the influence which is moved not, but moves. Poets are the unacknowledged legislators of the World.[111]

Notes

The notes give the primary manuscript (MS) or printed authority for each poem, as well as its dates of composition and of first publication. The commentaries aim to identify literary, historical and personal allusions and to furnish such additional information (e.g. prosodic, scientific) as clarifies or enhances the understanding of a text or passage. References are provided to works of criticism offering comment and interpretation of particular importance. Textual variants of substance only are recorded.

Unless otherwise attributed, translations from modern foreign languages are the editors'. Translations from Greek and Roman authors are taken from the Loeb Classical Library editions unless otherwise indicated; the Bible is cited from the Authorized King James Version (1611); Shakespeare's works from *William Shakespeare: The Complete Works*, edited by Stanley Wells and Gary Taylor (Oxford: Oxford University Press, 1988).

ABBREVIATIONS

Throughout, Percy Bysshe Shelley and Mary Wollstonecraft Shelley are abbreviated as PBS and MWS.

Shelley's Verse and Prose

A. Volumes published in PBS's lifetime (for a complete list with full bibliographical details, see Appendix: p. 881)

1810	*Original Poetry; by Victor and Cazire* (1810) [by PBS and his sister Elizabeth]
1810 (PFMN)	*Posthumous Fragments of Margaret Nicholson* (1810)
1813	*Queen Mab; A Philosophical Poem: With Notes* (1813)
1816	*Alastor; or, The Spirit of Solitude: and Other Poems* (1816)
1817	*History of a Six Weeks' Tour through a Part of France, Switzerland, Germany, and Holland: With Letters Descriptive of a Sail Round the Lake of Geneva, and of the Glaciers of Chamouni* (1817) [by PBS and MWS]

1817 (L&C) — *Laon and Cythna; or, The Revolution of the Golden City: A Vision of the Nineteenth Century. In the Stanza of Spenser* (1817) [withdrawn shortly after publication; see next entry]

1818 — *The Revolt of Islam; A Poem, in Twelve Cantos* (1818) [an expurgated version of *1817 (L&C)*]

1819 — *Rosalind and Helen, A Modern Eclogue; With Other Poems* (1819)

1820 — *Prometheus Unbound: A Lyrical Drama in Four Acts, With Other Poems* (1820)

1822 — *Hellas: A Lyrical Drama* (1822)

B. Later editions

1824 — *Posthumous Poems of Percy Bysshe* Shelley, ed. MWS (London: John and Henry Hunt, 1824)

1839 — *The Poetical Works of Percy Bysshe Shelley*, ed. MWS, 4 vols (London: Edward Moxon, 1839)

1840 — *The Poetical Works of Percy Bysshe Shelley*, ed. MWS (London: Edward Moxon, 1840) [a one-volume revised version with additions of *The Poetical Works* (1839) published in late 1839]

1840 (ELTF) — *Essays, Letters from Abroad, Translations and Fragments, by Percy Bysshe Shelley*, ed. MWS, 2 vols (London: Edward Moxon, 1840)

Chernaik — Judith Chernaik, *The Lyrics of Shelley* (Cleveland, Ohio, and London: Press of Case Western Reserve University, 1972)

Complete Poetry — *The Complete Poetry of Percy Bysshe Shelley*, 3 vols to date (Baltimore: Johns Hopkins University Press, 2000–2012): *Volume One*, ed. Donald H. Reiman and Neil Fraistat (2000); *Volume Two*, ed. Donald H. Reiman and Neil Fraistat (2004); *Volume Three*, ed. Donald H. Reiman, Neil Fraistat and Nora Crook (2012)

Esdaile — The Esdaile Notebook [a manuscript collection of PBS's early poems]

Esdaile 1964 — *The Esdaile Notebook*, ed. Kenneth Neill Cameron (New York: Alfred A. Knopf; London: Faber and Faber, 1964)

Forman 1876–7 — *The Poetical Works of Percy Bysshe Shelley*, ed. Harry Buxton Forman, 4 vols (London: Reeves and Turner, 1876–7)

Ingpen and Peck — *The Complete Works of Percy Bysshe Shelley*, ed. Roger Ingpen and Walter E. Peck, 10 vols (London: Ernst Benn, 1926–30)

Locock — *The Poems of Percy Bysshe Shelley*, ed. C. D. Locock, 2 vols (London: Methuen, 1911)

Major Works — *Percy Bysshe Shelley: The Major Works*, ed. Zachary Leader and Michael O'Neill (Oxford: Oxford University Press, 2003)

Norton 2002	*Shelley's Poetry and Prose*, ed. Donald H. Reiman and Neil Fraistat, 2nd edn (New York and London: W. W. Norton, 2002)
Notopoulos	*The Platonism of Shelley*, ed. James A. Notopoulos (Durham, NC: Duke University Press, 1949)
OSA	*Shelley: Poetical Works*, ed. Thomas Hutchinson (Oxford: Oxford University Press, 1905), corrected by G. M. Matthews, Oxford Standard Authors (Oxford: Oxford University Press, 1970)
Poems	*The Poems of Shelley*, 4 vols to date: *Volume One: 1804–1817*, ed. Geoffrey Matthews and Kelvin Everest (London: Longman, 1989); *Volume Two: 1817–1819*, ed. Kelvin Everest and Geoffrey Matthews (London: Pearson Education, 2000); *Volume Three: 1819–1820*, ed. Jack Donovan, Cian Duffy, Kelvin Everest and Michael Rossington (London: Pearson Education, 2011); *Volume Four: 1820–1821*, ed. Michael Rossington, Jack Donovan and Kelvin Everest (London: Routledge, 2013)
Prose	*Shelley's Prose; Or, The Trumpet of a Prophecy*, ed. David Lee Clark, corrected edition (London: Fourth Estate, 1988)
Prose Works	*The Prose Works of Percy Bysshe Shelley*, ed. E. B. Murray, vol. 1 (1811–18) (Oxford: Clarendon Press, 1993) [1 vol. to date]
Rossetti 1870	*The Poetical Works of Percy Bysshe Shelley*, ed. William Michael Rossetti, 2 vols (London: Edward Moxon, 1870)
Shelley Papers	*The Shelley Papers: Original Poems and Papers by Percy Bysshe Shelley*, ed. Thomas Medwin (London: Whittaker, Treacher and Co., 1833)
Webb 1995	*Percy Bysshe Shelley: Poems and Prose*, ed. Timothy Webb (London: J. M. Dent, 1995)

Manuscript Facsimiles

BSM	*The Bodleian Shelley Manuscripts*, general ed. Donald H. Reiman, 23 vols (New York and London: Garland, 1986–2002)
Massey	*Posthumous Poems of Shelley: Mary Shelley's Fair Copy Book*, ed. Irving Massey (Montreal: McGill-Queen's University Press, 1969)
MYR (Shelley)	*The Manuscripts of the Younger Romantics: Shelley*, general ed. Donald H. Reiman, 9 vols (New York and London: Garland, 1985–96)

Other Works Often Referenced

Bieri	James Bieri, *Percy Bysshe Shelley: A Biography*, 2 vols (Newark, Del.: University of Delaware Press, 2004, 2005)

Clairmont Journal	*The Journals of Claire Clairmont*, ed. Marion Kingston Stocking (Cambridge, Mass.: Harvard University Press, 1968)
Concordance	F. S. Ellis, *A Lexical Concordance to the Poetical Works of Percy Bysshe Shelley* (London: Bernard Quaritch, 1892)
Gisborne Journal	*Maria Gisborne & Edward E. Williams, Shelley's Friends: Their Journals and Letters*, ed. Frederick L. Jones (Norman, Okla.: University of Oklahoma Press, 1951)
Letters	*The Letters of Percy Bysshe Shelley*, ed. F. L. Jones, 2 vols (Oxford: Clarendon Press, 1964)
Life	*The Life of Percy Bysshe Shelley*, ed. Humbert Wolfe, 2 vols (London: Dent, 1933) [contains Thomas Jefferson Hogg's *Life of Shelley* (1858); Thomas Love Peacock's *Memoirs of Shelley* (1858–62); and Edward John Trelawny's *Recollections of the Last Days of Shelley and Byron* (1858)]
Medwin 1913	Thomas Medwin, *The Life of Percy Bysshe Shelley*, ed. H. Buxton Forman (Oxford: Oxford University Press, 1913) [a revised version of a work originally published in 2 vols, 1847]
MWS Journal	*The Journals of Mary Shelley*, ed. Paula R. Feldman and Diana Scott-Kilvert, 2 vols (Oxford: Oxford University Press, 1987)
MWS Letters	*The Letters of Mary Wollstonecraft Shelley*, ed. Betty T. Bennett, 3 vols (Baltimore and London: Johns Hopkins University Press, 1980–88)
OED	*The Oxford English Dictionary*
Peacock Works	*The Works of Thomas Love Peacock*, ed. H. F. B. Brett-Smith and C. E. Jones, 10 vols (London: Constable, 1924–34; reprinted New York: AMS Press, 1967)
SC	*Shelley and His Circle 1773–1822*, ed. Kenneth Neill Cameron, Donald H. Reiman and Doucet Devin Fisher, 10 vols to date (Cambridge, Mass.: Harvard University Press, 1961–2002)

Journals

ELH	*English Literary History*
KSJ	*Keats-Shelley Journal*
KSMB	*Keats-Shelley Memorial Bulletin*
KSR	*Keats-Shelley Review* [continuing *KSMB* from 1986]
MLR	*Modern Language Review*
PMLA	*Publications of the Modern Language Association of America*
RES	*Review of English Studies*
SiR	*Studies in Romanticism*

THE POEMS

The Irishman's Song

Text from *1810*, where it is dated October 1809. PBS's first poetic engagement with Irish politics, 'The Irishman's Song' was written before his initial visit to Ireland in 1812; it should be compared with other fruits of that expedition: the poems 'On Robert Emmet's Tomb' (p. 14) and 'The Tombs' (1812), as well as the pamphlets *An Address to the Irish People* (1812) and *Proposals for an Association of . . . Philanthropists* (1812). The overtly revolutionist sentiments of the 'Song' anticipate a comparable strain in PBS's later poetry on Ireland, a militant stance in marked contrast to the gradualist tenor of the *Address* and *Proposals*. The poem's ancestry reaches back to the plangent laments for departed Gaelic heroes in the poems that the Scot James Macpherson (1736–96) attributed to the ancient bard Ossian, of which the best known was the epic *Fingal* (1762). More recent verse on Celtic themes also left its mark on PBS's 'Song', in particular Walter Scott's *Lay of the Last Minstrel* (1805) from which *1810* borrows its epigraph: 'Call it not vain: – they do not err, / Who say, that when the Poet dies, / Mute Nature mourns her worshipper' (V.i.1–3). Scott goes on to imagine that, rather than Nature, it is those valiant and gentle souls whose memory has been given the second life of poetry who mourn the passing of the bard who bestowed it on them. The theme of forgotten heroism recovered in verse is shared by many of Thomas Moore's *Irish Melodies* (1808), from which PBS also drew inspiration, and where dormant Irish culture is celebrated and its harp called to reawaken. Both Scott and Moore assert an intimate link between the well-being of a people and the vigour of its poetry. The degree to which PBS adopts the idiom of national song from these two current contemporary best-sellers can be appreciated by comparing his final stanza with: 'Forget not our wounded companions, who stood / In the day of distress by our side; / While the moss of the valley grew red with their blood, / They stirr'd not, but conquer'd and died' ('War Song', ll. 17–20, in *Irish Melodies*); and with 'The phantom Knight, his glory fled, / Mourns o'er the field he heap'd with dead; / Mounts the wild blast that sweeps amain, / And shrieks along the battle-plain' (*Lay of the Last Minstrel* V.ii.13–16).

12 *Sloghan*: From the Gaelic *sluagh-ghairm* = battle-cry (literally 'host-shout'). In *The Lay of the Last Minstrel* the word is spelled 'slogan' and defined as 'the war-cry, or gathering word, of a Border clan' (I.vii).

15–16 The 'heroes' of l. 13 are either lying in the throes of death or their ghosts are already riding on the passing wind. *Poems* I emends *1810*'s 'Or' to 'As'.

Song ('Fierce roars the midnight storm')

Text from *1810*, where it is dated December 1809. The clear verbal and metrical debt to the 'wild and sad' air sung by the squire Fitz-Eustace in Walter Scott's *Marmion* (1808), III.x–xi, is noted by *Poems* I. PBS refashions his literary model, a complaint against a deceiving lover who abandons his true maiden, by transferring the guilt to Laura (a name established in lyric tradition as that of the beloved celebrated by the Italian humanist Petrarch (1304–74) in many of the poems of his *Canzoniere*) and having the song sung by her faithful and despairing lover.

'How eloquent are eyes!'

Text from *Esdaile*, where it is dated 1810. PBS spent much of the period 16 April to 5 May of that year in the company (chaperoned) of his fifteen-year-old cousin, Harriet Grove – an intense romantic attachment had developed between them – both at his home in Sussex and at her brother's house in London; the poem no doubt derives from these 'impassioned' days. Harriet's Diary for 1809 and 1810 (including entries for this period) is transcribed in *SC* II. Her relationship with PBS is recounted in detail in Desmond Hawkins, *Shelley's First Love* (London: Kyle Cathie, 1992). PBS follows established conventions of love poetry in deploying musical (ll. 6–7) and vernal (ll. 23–4) analogies while perhaps also alluding to actual conditions: Harriet Grove and the Shelley family shared a music teacher; PBS heard her play at a musical evening on 1 May; and the poem seems to want the completion of a musical setting. Physical love is de-emphasized throughout: in stanza 3 the lovers do not wish to prolong the moment of desire; instead they imagine it completing its course in the eternal spring of Heaven.

2 *rapt*: Enraptured.
5–8 More even than impassioned music, eyes summon rapture.
19–20 The sense seems to be: 'We burn for the eternity of "Heaven's unfading spring" (l. 23) when our love will be fulfilled.'

Fragment, or The Triumph of Conscience

Probably composed in summer 1810; published as the final poem in *1810*, from which the title is taken. A slightly different and untitled version, the text given here, appears in chapter 1 of PBS's Gothic romance *St. Irvyne* (1811), which he published anonymously while he was an undergraduate at Oxford. It is possible that PBS originally intended the 'Fragment' for the place it occupies in *St. Irvyne*, following the example of some Gothic novelists of the period, especially Anne Radcliffe (1764–1823), who embedded songs and poems at dramatically appropriate moments in their narratives. Certainly he provides a conventionally sublime setting for it: an evening among high Alpine peaks clad with dark pine forests where the noble Wolfstein, whose past includes an unspecified 'dreadful' event, has wandered to soothe the agitation of mind caused by his having joined a troop of bandits who are about to commit a savage robbery: 'At last he sank on a mossy bank, and, guided by the impulse of the moment, inscribed on a tablet the following lines; for the inaccuracy of which, the perturbation of him who wrote them, may account . . . Overcome by the wild retrospection of ideal [i.e. imaginary] horror, which these swiftly-written lines excited in his soul, Wolfstein tore the paper, on which he had written them, to pieces, and scattered them about him' (*Zastrozzi and St. Irvyne*, ed. Stephen C. Behrendt (Peterborough, Ont.: Broadview, 2002), pp. 165–6). By the early nineteenth century the fragment had acquired currency as a poetic form and could be presented (as it is here) as the product of an exceptionally heightened state of mind. Coleridge referred to 'Kubla Khan or, A Vision in a Dream' (written sometime between 1797 and 1800; published 1816) as both a 'fragment' and a 'psychological curiosity', while the final quarter of Byron's *The Giaour* (1813) is delivered by the despairing title-character in incomplete and disconnected recollections.

15 *upholding*: Raising up.

16 *Victoria*: The pedigree of the name in Gothic fiction is given in Kim Ian Michasiw's edition of Charlotte Dacre's *Zofloya, or The Moor* (Oxford: OUP World's Classics, 1997), p. 269. It is also the female form of 'Victor', the nom de plume adopted by PBS as joint author of *1810*, as well as the name later to be given by MWS to the creator of the monster in *Frankenstein* (1818).

17 *1810* reads: 'Her right hand a blood reeking dagger was bearing'.

Song ('Ah! faint are her limbs')

Written late summer/early autumn 1810, published in chapter 9 of PBS's Gothic romance *St. Irvyne*, which supplies our text. The orphaned Eloise de St. Irvyne has resisted the sinister but fascinating Nempere's attempts to seduce her (he will later succeed); playing her harp, she sings 'Ah! faint are her limbs' to him, explaining afterwards that ''tis a melancholy song; my poor brother wrote it, I remember, about ten days before he died. 'Tis a gloomy tale concerning him; he ill deserved the fate he met. Some future time I will tell it you; but now, 'tis very late.—Good-night' (*Zastrozzi and St. Irvyne*, ed. Behrendt (see headnote to previous poem), p. 232). The stanza and rhyme scheme are those of Sir Walter Scott's 'Helvellyn' (1805), which features a corpse exposed to the elements.

5 *whortle*: A low shrub bearing the bilberry.

6 *myrtle*: The common myrtle, traditionally sacred to Venus, is an evergreen shrub.

7 *kirtle*: A gown, skirt, or outer petticoat (*OED*).

The Monarch's funeral: An Anticipation

Dated 1810 in *Esdaile*, which provides our text, and probably composed in November or December of that year; published in *Esdaile 1964*. Lines 21–32, alluding to the Irish patriot Robert Emmet, might have been added following PBS's visit to Dublin (12 February–4 April 1812), as *Complete Poetry* II suggests. The poem was evidently prompted by the coincidence of two events: a recurrence of the illness and mental derangement from which George III had suffered intermittently since 1787 and the death of his daughter, the Princess Amelia, on 2 November. The king having been diagnosed as mentally incapable, a Regency Bill was introduced in Parliament on 20 December and passed on 5 February 1811, effectively ending George III's reign, although he survived until January 1820. As the title makes clear, the poem looks forward to the king's death and burial in Westminster Abbey (the 'Gothic . . . cathedral' of stanza 3). PBS's prose pamphlet *An Address to the People on the Death of the Princess Charlotte* (p. 605) similarly combines regret for a royal death and indignation at the injustices of the current social and political system.

21–32 Erin's 'uncoffined slain' is Robert Emmet, already the subject of 'lays' like Robert Southey's 'Written Immediately after Reading the Speech of Robert Emmet' (1803) and Thomas Moore's 'Oh! breathe not his name' (1807), as well as PBS's own 'On Robert Emmet's Tomb' (p. 14). Unclaimed after his execution by the British in September 1803, Emmet's body was buried in the paupers' graveyard in Dublin, whence it was later removed to an unknown location.

33 *Yet*: *Poems* I reads the word as 'Yes', which is possible.

34 *lay*: An alternative for 'lie', found in contemporary poets as a rhyme word.

38 Who will extort taxes from the poor in order to live in luxury?

57–8 The king's buried corpse fertilizes the earth. *Poems* I compares Erasmus Darwin's *Temple of Nature* (1803), IV.383–99: 'Hence when a monarch or a mushroom dies, / Awhile extinct the organic matter lies / . . . The wrecks of Death are but a change of forms; / Emerging matter from the grave returns.'

A Winter's Day

Undated in *Esdaile*, which supplies the text; probably written sometime before Christmas 1811 during PBS's stay at Keswick (November 1811–January 1812), though possibly while he was at Tremadoc in north Wales (November 1812–February 1813); published in *Esdaile 1964*. The poem takes a spring-like day in winter as the occasion for a meditation, conventional enough at first glance, on the 'transitory' (l. 29) – with a traditional closing emphasis on seizing the day. But PBS gives the poem a personal signature by linking the themes of Genius (in stanza 3, which has only six lines) and Passion (stanza 4). The struggle to realize high artistic aspirations and the troubles that beset early erotic attachment are topics much in evidence in his letters of the period from Keswick (*Letters* I, pp. 174–246), while in Wordsworth's *Poems, in Two Volumes* (1807) he had read of the trials that attend high creative gifts in both youth (e.g. 'Resolution and Independence') and age ('Ode: Intimations of Immortality'). These matters had immediate significance for one who had been expelled from Oxford for publishing critical views on religion, married against the wishes of his family, and seen his best friend (T. J. Hogg) make sexual advances to his new wife, while continuing to cherish ambitious plans for literary and political works to benefit his fellow beings.

1 *mockest*: The sense is of mimicry, deceptive imitation, in contrast to the sense of 'mockery' in l. 20.

7 *balm*: Balmy, i.e. soft and fragrant; the adjectival usage appears to be PBS's coinage.

26–7 In the inverted word order, 'springs' is the subject of the verb 'tell', i.e. 'declare' or 'reveal'.

To the Republicans of North America

Text from *Esdaile*, published in *Esdaile 1964*. Composed on or before 14 February 1812, when Shelley included it in a letter to Elizabeth Hitchener, untitled and without the fourth stanza, which, if then written, would have been out of keeping with the letter's vision of a 'society of peace and love' achieved through 'toleration and patience' (*Letters* I, pp. 251–5). Commentators have pointed out the poem's geographical vagaries. The MSS and PBS's letters (I, pp. 235, 272) indicate that the poem originally meant to celebrate liberation struggles in Spanish colonies in Central and South America, especially Mexico and perhaps Venezuela. In *Esdaile* PBS altered the 'New Spain' in the title to 'North America'. *Poems* I suggests that PBS may ultimately have wished his poem to address all republicans on both American continents.

15–16 The lines would be particularly appropriate to Dublin Castle, home of the British administration in Ireland, and to the squalor among Dublin's poor, which shocked PBS.

21 *Cotopaxi*: PBS's invocation of this active volcano in present-day Ecuador is an early instance of what would become his recurrent use of volcanic eruption as an emblem of revolution: e.g. *Prometheus Unbound* II.iii. 1–10 (p. 226); *The Mask of Anarchy*, ll. 364–7 (p. 368); and 'Ode to Liberty', ll. 181–7 (p. 432).

35–6 An allusion to Bertrand Barère de Vieuzac's celebrated speech to the French National Convention in 1792, advocating the death penalty for Louis XVI: 'L'arbre de la liberté ne croît qu'arrosé par le sang des tyrans' (The tree of liberty only grows when fed with the blood of tyrants).

40 A parody of Psalm 103:8: 'The Lord is merciful and gracious, slow to anger, and plenteous in mercy.'

45–50 The inversions in these lines can obscure the sense: 'When the patriot, whose immortal spirit will be forgiven for violence in the cause of liberty, dies, bereaved Earth may not speak his praise but can mourn him with a tear.'

On Robert Emmet's Tomb

In a letter of *c.*16 April 1812, PBS mentions having written 'some *verses* on Robert Emmet' (*Letters* I, p. 282); the lines, probably composed shortly before or just after the end, on 4 April 1812, of his first visit to Ireland, were later included in *Esdaile*, from which the present text is taken. Lines 21–8 were published in Edward Dowden, *The Life of Percy Bysshe Shelley*, 2 vols (London: Kegan Paul, Trench & Co., 1886), the entire poem in *Esdaile 1964*. Long admired by Shelley, Emmet was the leader of a short-lived insurrection in Dublin in July 1803 which aimed to establish a provisional government in hopes of galvanizing the country to a general uprising against British rule. He was executed on 20 September, having been arrested while lingering in the city for an answer to his declaration of love for Sarah Curran, the daughter of the prominent lawyer John Philpot Curran, whom PBS met in Dublin in March 1812. Curran had acted as defence counsel for some members of the Society of United Irishmen, the nationalist movement of which Emmet himself was an active member, and which had carried out the unsuccessful insurrection of 1798 with military aid from France.

The circumstances of Emmet's arrest, together with his youth (he was twenty-five) and the eloquence of his final speech from the dock, won him both popular and poetic acclaim as a Romantic exemplar of patriotic nationalism. Robert Southey's 'Written Immediately after Reading the Speech of Robert Emmet' (1803) and Thomas Moore's 'Oh! breathe not his name' (1807) and 'She is far from the land where her young hero sleeps' (1811) are only three of the many lyric responses to Emmet's fate. As well as the sentiments, PBS's poem shares the line of four anapaests (two unstressed syllables followed by a stressed one) of the first of Moore's poetic tributes mentioned above and the stanza rhyming *abab* of the second. Lines 21–4 allude to Emmet's celebrated last injunction, which tradition has preserved with variations: 'let no man write my epitaph . . . and my tomb remain uninscribed, until other times, and other men, can do justice to my character; – when my country takes her place among the nations of the earth, then and not till then – let my epitaph be written' (cited in Marianne Elliott, *Robert Emmet: The Making of a Legend* (London: Profile Books, 2003), p. 85). The location of Emmet's unmarked tomb ('distinguished in lowliness', l. 10) was, and remains, unknown; in the early nineteenth century it was presumed to be the only blank slab in St Michan's churchyard in Dublin, which PBS visited, but some now suggest that it is in Glasnevin cemetery. The poem expands upon the revolutionist sentiments in PBS's other poetic reactions to the condition of Ireland, including 'The Irishman's Song' (p. 5).

7 *shamrock*: The three-leaved national symbol of Ireland.

10 *relics*: Remains.

17–24 PBS suggests that the responses elicited by the lowliness and anonymity of Emmet's burial place are guarantors of Ireland's eventual freedom. Compare the similar view of the patriot's grave in ll. 21–5 of 'To Liberty' (p. 15).

18 Recalling Emmet's speech from the dock: 'I am going to my cold and silent grave . . . I have but one request to ask at my departure from this world, it is the charity of its silence!' (Elliott, *Robert Emmet*, p. 85).

23 *caressed*: Spelled 'carest' in *Esdaile.*

26–7 *its lifespring . . . their memory*: The 'lifespring' of Emmet's name, the 'memory' of his 'foes' (l. 23).

To Liberty

Text from *Esdaile*, published in Dowden, *Life* (see headnote to previous poem). The exact date of composition is unknown, but strong verbal and thematic similarities suggest a time shortly before PBS began work on *Queen Mab* in spring 1812. The 'Tyrant' of stanzas 1–3 may have been suggested by Napoleon, who in the period mid 1810–late 1811 reached the zenith of his power in Europe; but the stanzas have an evident general application as well. PBS's generation inherited a rich literary and pictorial tradition that attributed symbolic value to ruins. The tenor of stanzas 4 and 5 – which anticipate Canto IX of *Queen Mab* (p. 77) and parallel the sentiments and images of T. L.

Peacock's poem *Palmyra* (1806) – derives particularly from *Les Ruines, ou Méditation sur les révolutions des empires* (1791) by Constantin, Comte de Volney (1757–1820): the defining assertion, by a French revolutionary theorist, of the transience of monarchical authority as evidenced in its decayed monuments. Volney's book, translated as *Ruins of Empires* (1795), had considerable currency in England from the late 1790s and was a favourite of the young Shelley. Lines 21–5 can be compared with 'On Robert Emmet's Tomb' (p. 14) and 'The Tombs' (1812), poems which similarly invest the grave of the patriot with the power to inspire revolutionary revenge, a defiant note which somewhat abruptly heralds the dawn of 'Virtue, Truth and Peace' (l. 45) in the present poem. PBS developed such a moral evolution in detail in *Prometheus Unbound*: see especially I.218–305, III.iii (pp. 195, 243).

16 *pure*: *Complete Poetry* II and *Esdaile 1964* read the word, ambiguously formed in the MS, as 'free'.

28 *her Atlantic throne*: America.

36–9 Both Volney's *Ruines* and his *Voyage en Syrie et en Égypte* (1787) express indignation at the cost in human suffering of constructing the pyramids, as does Peacock's *Palmyra*.

38 *footstone*: The foundation stone of the pyramid; or – perhaps the meaning here – its base.

Written on a Beautiful Day in Spring

Probably composed in spring 1812 at Nant Gwyllt ('Wild Brook' in Welsh, pronounced *nant guithlt*) in central Wales, near PBS's cousin Thomas Grove's estate at Cwm Elan (the valley of the Elan river, pronounced *coom eelan*), where PBS had stayed for about four weeks the previous summer. The text is from *Esdaile*, first publication in *Esdaile 1964*. *Poems* I notes the resemblance between ll. 1–2 and the opening lines of Fragment VII in Sydney Owenson's *The Lay of an Irish Harp; or, Metrical Fragments* (1807) – 'There was a day when simply but to BE, / To live, to breathe, was purest ecstasy' – which develop a conventional opposition between carefree childhood and careworn age. The contrast in PBS's poem is rather between self-consciousness and that self-forgetfulness (the 'strange mental wandering' of l. 1) in which mind and feeling become as one under the influence of exquisitely pleasurable sensations offered by the natural world – a state which anticipates the pure bliss of Heaven. This Shelleyan theme modifies the evident debt to Wordsworth's early poems, such as 'Tintern Abbey', 'Lines Written in Early Spring' and 'Lines written at a small distance from my house'. David Duff, 'Shelley's "Foretaste of Heaven"', *Wordsworth Circle* 31 (2000), pp. 149–58, provides an informative consideration of the poem, its sources and its place in PBS's poetic development.

5 *unpercipient*: Not perceiving; the word appears to be PBS's coinage.

10 *it*: The 'mental wandering' of l. 1.

11 *it*: The antecedent is 'Sensation' (l. 8).

15 *the frame*: The body.

'Dark Spirit of the desart rude'

Text from *Esdaile*, published in *Esdaile 1964*. Date of composition uncertain but probably spring 1812. PBS and his wife Harriet spent the period from mid April to late June in Wales, at Nant Gwyllt and Cwm Elan (see headnote to previous poem), in the country of mountains and valleys through which the river Elan (named in l. 10) flows; ll. 30–33 set the poem in spring. In 'Dark Spirit' PBS imagines a natural scene near his current residence as expressing what eighteenth-century aesthetics had defined as the 'sublime' – a relation between an observer and a landscape in which the fear and awe inspired by such phenomena as the dark woods and jagged peaks of the present poem convey insights inaccessible to reason. See headnote to 'Mont Blanc' (p. 718). The poet's search for a natural equivalent of the *genius loci*, or presiding spirit of the place, settles at last on the oak (traditional symbol of royalty), which, blasted by lightning, represents all kings, who despoil their subjects, yet themselves waste away. Milton had compared the fallen Satan to a 'scathed' oak in *Paradise Lost* I.612–15; PBS is probably also remembering *Coombe-Ellen*, a poem written by the Reverend William Lisle Bowles in 1798 while a guest of PBS's cousin Thomas Grove at Cwm Elan. See note to l. 35 below.

Title 'desart' is the usual spelling in PBS's verse.

1–15 Grammatically the lines make a single sentence, addressing a question ('Art thou . . . ?', ll. 12–15) to the 'Dark Spirit' (l. 1) that 'Wavest . . . force' (l. 11).

6 *jetty*: Jet-black.

12 *sooty and fearful fowl*: A raven.

35 *desolate Oak*: Cp. Bowles's *Coombe-Ellen*, ll. 54–7: 'Upon the adverse bank, wither'd and stript / Of all its pleasant leaves, a scathed oak / Hangs desolate; once sov'reign of the scene, / Perhaps, proud of its beauty and its strength.' To Bowles the barren oak stands as a reminder of the inevitable coming of age and infirmity.

45 *that race*: The race of kings.

The Retrospect: Cwm Elan 1812

Composed between early May and mid June 1812 while PBS and his wife Harriet, just returned in disappointment from their first campaign for reform in Ireland, were staying in Wales at Nant Gwyllt, then at nearby Cwm Elan (see headnote to 'Written on a Beautiful Day in Spring': p. 689). The text is from *Esdaile*: lines 15–168 were first published in Edward Dowden's *Life of Percy Bysshe Shelley* (1886), the complete poem in *Esdaile 1964*. The previous year PBS had spent about four weeks (early July to early August) at Cwm Elan. Expelled from Oxford in March, at odds with his father, anxious about his health, and contemplating an elopement with Harriet, his mental state had been intensely agitated, even to entertaining suicidal thoughts (*Letters* I, pp. 117–31). 'The Retrospect' develops from a contrast between the two sojourns which produced in him, he wrote to William Godwin on 25 April 1812, a divided consciousness: 'the place where we now reside is in the neighbourhood of scenes marked deeply on my mind by the thoughts which possessed it when present among them. The ghosts of these old friends have a dim & strange appearance when resuscitated in a situation so altered as mine is, since I felt that they were alive' (*Letters* I, p. 287).

PBS took the occasion to give imaginative form in a condensed poetic narrative to what he regarded as the chief formative elements of his life to date. He would undertake such a self-examination in verse at later periods – in, for example, 'Hymn to Intellectual Beauty' (p. 134), the Dedication before *Laon and Cythna* (p. 148) and *Epipsychidion* (p. 474). His poem works a variation on a type practised by the earlier generation of Romantic poets, a meditative review of the author's personal life set in a particularized landscape. It shares the title and other features of Southey's 'The Retrospect' (1795) and shows the influence of Wordsworth's 'Tintern Abbey' (1798) and 'Ode: Intimations of Immortality' (1807). David Duff analyses the poem in '"The Casket of my Unknown Mind": The 1813 Volume of Minor Poems', in *The Unfamiliar Shelley*, ed. Alan M. Weinberg and Timothy Webb (Farnham: Ashgate, 2009), pp. 55–60.

5–7 In ancient Greek myth, the Titan Kronos, traditionally assimilated to Chronos (Time), devoured his children to prevent them from usurping his place in the heavens. PBS's reference to Time as feminine may appropriate the sex of the earth as in Shakespeare's Sonnet XIX.1–2: 'Devouring Time, blunt thou the lion's paws, / And make the earth devour her own sweet brood.'

15 *wildered*: Lost, gone astray.

24–8 The rushing of the 'wild brook', as internalized in the mind of the poet, drives out his baleful thoughts.

65–70 In 1810 an informal engagement between PBS and his cousin Harriet Grove (see headnote to 'How eloquent are eyes!': p. 684) was terminated against his wishes, Harriet's family regarding his opinions, writings and conduct as unsuitable for her. PBS considered that both she and they had betrayed him.

73 The biblical language recalls two passages from Psalms: 'As the hart panteth after the water brooks, so panteth my soul after thee, O God' (42:1); and 'If I take the wings of the morning, and dwell in the uttermost parts of the sea; Even there shall thy hand lead me, and thy right hand shall hold me' (139:9–10).

78–83 The allure of his family name attracted many but they neither perceived nor influenced his inner self.

84–91 The patriot willing to perish for freedom's sake could never find friends among those who benefit from tyranny.

95 *of unprofitable mould*: Of a kind that brought no worldly reward.

112–13 Adapting ll. 8–9 of 'Dark Spirit of the desart rude' (p. 17). Other adaptations of PBS's own verse up to l. 123 are noted in *Poems* I and *Complete Poetry* II.

120–21 In Classical myth, the nymph Echo, rejected by Narcissus, concealed herself in the woods to hide her grief.

136–43 PBS imagines his change from summer 1811 to summer 1812 as the metamorphosis of a grave-worm into a butterfly. Cp. 'Written on a Beautiful Day in Spring', l. 18 (p. 16).

QUEEN MAB

Originally conceived in December 1811 as a portrait of 'a perfect state of society; though still earthly' (*Letters* I, p. 201), and written mostly between spring 1812 and spring 1813, *Queen Mab* (*QM*) was not offered for sale but printed in a limited edition of 250 copies and distributed privately, to avoid the risk of prosecution for the poem's forthright anti-monarchical and anti-religious opinions. Our text is from this edition (1813). The Queen Mab of the title is the 'fairies' midwife' who is evoked in a celebrated passage of Shakespeare's *Romeo and Juliet* (I.iv.53–95) as the architect of sleepers' dreams, and who features in the title of popular eighteenth-century collections of fairy tales and stories for children. The visionary frame of the poem intends to recall these precedents as well as the scenes of instruction delivered by a supernatural being in ancient and modern epics such as Virgil's *Aeneid* VI and Milton's *Paradise Lost* XI–XII. The polemical conspectus of past, present and future that Mab unveils to the spirit of the sleeping Ianthe in *QM* II–IX draws upon a long tradition of critical thought. Its principal sources range from the Roman poet Lucretius (98–*c.*55 BC) through the French materialist Baron d'Holbach (1723–89) and the revolutionary theorist Constantin, Comte de Volney (1757–1820) to the sceptical empiricism of the Scottish philosopher David Hume (1711–76) and the English political radicals Thomas Paine (1737–1809), William Godwin (1756–1836) and Mary Wollstonecraft (1759–97) – and extends to contemporary writers on astronomy, diet and health. Ideas gathered from these form the chief intellectual underpinning of Mab's revelations as well as of the seventeen prose notes, which provide a further dimension of philosophical and scientific authority.

In furnishing his poem with notes, PBS was following the example of such didactic works as Erasmus Darwin's *The Botanic Garden . . . With Philosophical Notes* (1791), in which an imaginative survey in verse is supported with extensive references to botanical science and plant lore. The style mixes what PBS described as 'blank heroic verse' and 'blank lyrical measure': that is, unrhymed lines of ten syllables whose dominant pattern is an unstressed followed by a stressed syllable, varied by shorter unrhymed lines of different lengths and stress patterns (*Letters* I, p. 352); he cites as precedents the flexible verse of the choruses of Greek tragedies, of Milton's *Samson Agonistes* (1671) and of Robert Southey's narrative poem *Thalaba the Destroyer* (1801). For the many additional influences *Poems* I and *Complete Poetry* II may be consulted.

The 1813 edition of *QM* was a finely produced and relatively expensive volume which might, PBS claimed, be read by aristocratic youth (*Letters* I, p. 361). The appearance of cheaper pirated editions from 1821, of which PBS disapproved (*Letters* II, p. 298), attracted both fiercely vituperative attacks on him and prosecution for some of the poem's publishers. But, having thus illegitimately been introduced to a broad readership, *QM* gained remarkable currency among Chartists, socialists, Marxists and freethinkers right through the nineteenth century.

General introductions to *QM* may be found in Carlos Baker, *Shelley's Major Poetry: The Fabric of a Vision* (London: Oxford University Press, 1948), and in the works by Kenneth Neill Cameron, David Duff and Stuart Sperry listed under 'Critical Sources' in Further Reading (p. xxxix). PBS's vegetarianism is considered in Timothy Morton, *Shelley and the Revolution in Taste* (Cambridge: Cambridge University Press, 1994); Bouthaina Shaaban, 'Shelley and the Chartists', in *Shelley: Poet and Legislator of the World*, ed. Betty T. Bennett and Stuart Curran (Baltimore: Johns Hopkins University Press, 1996), pp. 114–25, investigates PBS's presence in the journals of that movement.

Epigraph 1 Voltaire frequently ended his letters with this injunction, which may be translated 'Crush the vile thing', where 'thing' = 'superstition and intolerance'.

Epigraph 2 The opening lines (1–7) of Lucretius' *De Rerum Natura* (On the Nature of Things), Book IV: 'I wander through a pathless region of poetry where no one has trod before me. I delight to approach virgin springs, to drink from them and to pluck unfamiliar flowers [PBS omits the phrase 'seeking an illustrious crown for my head'] with which the Muses have never yet wreathed anyone's brows. First, because I teach lofty matters, then because I go on to free the mind from the tight knots of superstition' (editors' translation).

Epigraph 3 'Give me a place to stand and I will move the earth.' This celebrated remark, attributed to the Greek mathematician, astronomer and physicist Archimedes (*c.*287–212 BC), had been adopted by radical writers as a slogan for the power of ideas to bring about change, and notably by Thomas Paine at the beginning of *Rights of Man*, Part II (1792).

*To Harriet ******

The dedicatory poem is addressed to Harriet Westbrook, PBS's wife since August 1811: 'flowers' (l. 11) and 'Each flowret' (l. 15) refer to the shorter poems in *Esdaile* which PBS at first planned to publish with *QM*. The Dedication before *Laon and Cythna* (p. 148), addressed to MWS, offers an interesting comparison.

11 *wilding*: Wild, uncultivated.
15 *flowret*: i.e. floweret, a small flower.

Queen Mab

I.2 In Classical mythology, Death and Sleep were the children of Night. Line 1 revises the opening line of Southey's *Thalaba the Destroyer* (1801): 'How beautiful is night!'

I.27 *Ianthe*: PBS's and Harriet's first child, born 23 June 1813, was named Eliza Ianthe. The name derives from the Greek, 'violet flower'. An ocean nymph in Greek mythology, Ianthe, in Ovid's *Metamorphoses*, is a beautiful girl of Crete loved by another girl, Iphis, who is transformed into a young man in order to marry her. Carlos Baker, *Shelley's Major Poetry*, p. 26, lists other possible sources.

I.43 *parasite*: Any climbing plant could be designated as such.

I.52 *that strange lyre*: An Aeolian or wind harp, conventional emblem of poetic inspiration. See *Alastor*, ll. 39–49 (p. 114).

I.53 *genii*: Spirits or minor deities associated with natural phenomena. See *Prometheus Unbound* I.42 (p. 189).

I.61 *pennons*: Wings.

I.82–3 Purely translucent, the fairy chariot does not bend light by refraction.

I.98 *fair star*: The planet Venus as the morning star.

I.102 *purpureal*: 'Purple', and possibly (a secondary Latin sense) 'bright', 'shining'.

I.108 *amaranth*: A mythical flower that never fades.

I.128 *day-stars*: Both the morning star and the sun are so called.

I.134 *Instinct with*: Quickened by, energized by, as in I.271.

I.188 *immurement*: Confinement, as if within walls. See II.61.

I.200 *disparted*: Dispersed.

I.242–3 See PBS's Note [1].

I.252–3 See PBS's Note [2].

I.259 *Hesperus*: The planet Venus as the evening star.

II.21 *fane*: Temple.

II.37 *circumambient*: Surrounding.

II.51–4 The meaning of these lines turns on the sense of 'for' in l. 52. *Locock*, taking 'for' as 'on account of', understands that Ianthe does not refrain from tasting the 'varied bliss'. *Poems* I takes 'for' as 'despite', so that Ianthe chooses not to enjoy the pleasures of the palace which are the reward of virtue and wisdom. *Complete Poetry* II, reading 'for' as 'in order to obtain', concludes that Ianthe refrains from raising virtuous scruples in order to enjoy the delights the palace affords.

II.59 *meed*: Reward.

II.98 *intellectual eye*: The mind's eye.

II.108 *chain of nature*: The totality of interconnected causes and effects operating in the universe.

II.110 *Palmyra*: An important ancient trading city on the east–west caravan route through the Syrian desert which reached the height of its affluence and power in the third century AD – when, having engaged in conflict with Rome, it was conquered and destroyed by the emperor Aurelian (reigned AD 270–75). The extensive remains of Palmyra furnished matter for reflections on the transience of human prosperity and grandeur in Volney's *Les Ruines* (1791), translated as *Ruins of Empires* (1795; see headnote to 'To Liberty': p. 688), and Peacock's *Palmyra* (1806).

II.132 *scite*: Site, an unusual contemporary spelling.

II.137–48 The building at Jerusalem (Salem) of a magnificent and lavishly appointed temple during King Solomon's reign in the tenth century BC was accomplished by imposing heavy taxation on the king's subjects and by large-scale forced labour. See 1 Kings 5–8 and 2 Chronicles 2–5.

II.148 *a dotard's*: Solomon's.

II.149–61 In order to enforce a similar judgement on the Israelites of the Old Testament in the pamphlet *A Refutation of Deism* (1814), PBS cites their savage treatment of the Midianites, in obedience to God's command to Moses in Numbers 31:1–18 (*Prose Works* I, p. 102).

II.153 *Promiscuous*: Indiscriminately.
II.155 *he*: Moses.
II.158–60 *tales . . . credits*: Which religion repeats to frighten its adherents into believing them.
II.176 *Where Socrates expired*: i.e. Athens.
a tyrant's slave: Local rulers in Greece were subject to the Sultan of the Ottoman Empire.
II.179–81 The Rome that once produced courageous, wise and benevolent figures is now home to the Pope, leader of a fraudulent religion. Marcus Tullius Cicero (106–43 BC) was a rational enquirer over a range of topics and a political orator. Antoninus may refer either to Antoninus Pius, emperor AD 138–61, admired for integrity and gentleness; or to Marcus Aurelius Antoninus, emperor AD 161–80, Stoic philosopher and author of *Meditations*.
II.182–210 As *Poems* I points out, some features of the 'stately city' (l. 187) appear to have been suggested by Tenochtitlán (built on the site of the present Mexico City), capital of the Aztec empire, which was described in D. F. S. Clavigero's *History of Mexico* (trans. 1787). Robert Southey's narrative poem *Madoc* (1805), which PBS had read, introduces the fictional city Aztlan as the capital of the Aztecs, citing authorities in footnotes.
II.182 *ten thousand*: A rhetorical exaggeration.
II.231 *viewless*: Invisible.
III.17 *imbecility*: Weakness, feebleness.
III.32 *nickname*: Here and in IV.212 (where it is a noun) the word signifies '(to conceal with) a deceptive verbal mask'.
III.46 *palled*: Diminished, dulled.
III.110 *mechanic*: Manual labourer.
hind: Agricultural worker.
III.111 *stubborn glebe*: Resistant soil – a phrase borrowed from Gray's 'Elegy Written in a Country Churchyard' (1751), l. 26.
III.124 *genders*: Engenders.
III.157 *impassive*: Both the senses 'invulnerable' and 'immovable' are possible.
III.182 *Lowered*: Scowled, frowned.
IV.10 *depend*: Hang down.
IV.14 *idly*: Motionless.
IV.24 *vesper*: Hesperus, the evening star.
IV.33–70 This scene of war has been taken as evoking the siege and occupation of Moscow by the French in August 1812, the setting fire to the city by the Russians and the debacle of the French retreat. But, as *Complete Poetry* II points out, although some details are consistent with those events, others are not – so that the passage is better understood as a general condemnation of the horrors of war bearing some analogy to recent events.
IV.66 *outsallying*: A 'sally' is 'a sudden rush (out) from a besieged place upon the enemy' (*OED*).
IV.82–3 PBS's prophecy combines two references common in contemporary radical writers: to John the Baptist's accusation of the Pharisees and

Sadducees in Matthew 3:7–10: 'O generation of vipers . . . the axe is laid unto the root of the trees: therefore every tree which bringeth not forth good fruit is hewn down, and cast into the fire'; and to the upas tree, supposed to poison the atmosphere and lay waste the country round it, according to legend. The latter is developed further in IV.262–5, V.44–52, VI.207–8.

IV.86 *the serpent's famine*: 'The Upas-tree's hunger for its victims' (*Poems* I).

IV.98 *Partial in*: Inclined/biased towards.

IV.102 *But*: Only, merely.

IV.122 *tenement*: Abode (in a human body).

IV.127–38 The newborn soul's oppression by customary power parallels the lot of the child factory-worker sequestered from fresh air and daylight.

IV.178–9 See PBS's Note [3].

IV.212 *nick-name*: See note to III.32.

IV.240 *thy master*: Jesus.

IV.255 *nerveless*: Listless, lacking vigour.

IV.262–5 See note to IV.82–3.

V.1–2 See PBS's Note [4].

V.4–6 See PBS's Note [5].

V.13 *lawn*: Glade, open space among trees.

V.34 *impassive by*: Not responsive to.

V.44 See note to IV.82–3.

V.58 See PBS's Note [6].

V.64–8 Referring principally, though not exclusively, to the production of sugar on West Indian estates worked by African slaves and the military conflicts between European powers in the region. See PBS's Note [17].

V.72 *slaves*: Exploited factory labourers are primarily intended, as ll. 76–7 indicate.

V.80 *wealth of nations*: Recalling the title of Adam Smith's landmark work of political economy *An Inquiry into the Nature and Causes of the Wealth of Nations* (1776), the classic analysis of the working of free and open markets and the role of capital in promoting them; but PBS's specific target here is the withering effect of commercial greed.

V.93–4 See PBS's Note [7].

V.98–101 See note to VII.33–6 and PBS's Note [15].

V.112–13 See PBS's Note [8].

V.116 *famished offsprings scream*: *Complete Poetry* II makes a good case for retaining the *1813* reading 'offsprings', 'scream' then being a verb and 'offsprings' an acceptable early nineteenth-century plural.

V.135 *plastic*: Capable of being moulded.

V.137–46 The lines recall a well-known passage in Gray's 'Elegy', ll. 45–76.

V.140 *vulgar*: Pertaining to ordinary or common people.

Cato: The Roman soldier, statesman and author Marcus Porcius Cato (234–149 BC), proverbially stern, upright and public-spirited, remained active into old age.

V.147–66 PBS's elementary statement of the doctrine of Perfectibility is chiefly indebted to Godwin's *Enquiry Concerning Political Justice* (1793), where it is formulated as 'the faculty of being continually made better and receiving perpetual improvement' – without ever attaining perfection (1798 edn), ed. Isaac Kramnick (Harmondsworth: Penguin Books, 1976), pp. 144–5.

V.166 *mean lust*: Petty cravings.

V.177 *light of heaven*: *Poems* I detects an allusion to an increased window tax reintroduced in 1797 to defray the cost of the war against France.

V.189–96 See PBS's Note [9].

V.194–5 *pestilence . . . sensualism*: Venereal disease.

V.196 *hydra-headed*: In Greek myth, the Lernaean Hydra was a monstrous serpent with many heads and poisonous breath and blood.

V.223–7 The virtuous man's actions for the general good require no other reward or recognition than those provided by his own feelings.

VI.4 *periods*: The rhetorical passages into which Mab's lessons are divided.

VI.36–8 PBS again deploys the legend of the scorpion's suicide when surrounded by fire in IX.43–5 and in *The Cenci* II.ii.70–71 (p. 300).

VI.41 The idea that the revolution of the seven planets in their orbits round the earth created harmonious music, emblem of cosmic concord, was a commonplace dating from antiquity. See VIII.17–30.

VI.45–6 See PBS's Note [10].

VI.54–238 In *1839* MWS omitted the remainder of this canto and all of Canto VII.

VI.72–102 A slightly modified version of these lines appeared as an independent poem in *1816* under the title 'Superstition'.

VI.74–9 That the uninformed and extravagant infant mind of humanity first attributed divinity to the great forms of nature, was a hypothesis maintained by contemporary critics of orthodox theology such as Holbach.

VI.111 Ironically recalling the words of Sin in *Paradise Lost* II.787–9: 'I fled, and cried out Death; / Hell trembled at the hideous name, and sighed / From all her caves, and back resounded Death.'

VI.132 *horrent*: Shuddering with horror.

VI.154 *sublunary*: Beneath the moon, and so (according to traditional astronomy) subject to change and decay, unlike the immutable planets and stars.

VI.167 *uprooted ocean-fords*: 'Ford' can designate a shallow tract of the ocean (*OED* n. 2a); *Complete Poetry* II suggests that the phrase designates a waterspout, i.e. a gyrating column of mist, water and spray created by the action of a whirlwind on the sea (*OED* n. 3).

VI.171–3 See PBS's Note [11].

VI.188 *virtue*: Strength, power.

VI.198 See PBS's Note [12].

VI.207 *poison-tree*: See note to IV.82–3.

VI.220–38 The sense appears to be: 'When inevitable change has destroyed the temples of sanguinary religion, a temple to the Spirit of Nature/Necessity (ll. 197–8) will subsist unalterably.' This 'fane' is simply the *sensitive extension of the world* (l. 231), an elusive phrase that may mean either the world as perceived by the senses or – more likely – the world of sentient beings.

VII.13 An ironic rejoinder to Psalm 14:1: 'The fool hath said in his heart, There is no God.' See PBS's Note [13].

VII.15–26 The passage affirms the view that the infinity of interlinked causes evident in nature denies the hypothesis that there is a first cause, God, which created the world.

VII.23 *exterminable*: The reasoning of the passage seems to demand a meaning opposite to the usual sense of the word, 'that may be exterminated'. *OED* remarks: 'used by Shelley for "illimitable"'.

VII.30 PBS's principal source for these names appears to have been Volney's *Ruins*, which identifies *Seeva* (Shiva), representing destruction (but also generation), as one of the trinity of Hindu gods together with Vishnu and Brahma. 'Buddh' is Buddha and 'Foh' the Chinese form of 'Buddha'. Jehovah or Yahweh is the Hebrew god of the Old Testament, sometimes addressed or referred to as 'Lord' (Hebrew 'Adonai').

VII.33–6 Recalling the Hindu procession of Juggernaut, from Jagannath, a title of the god Vishnu; an image of the god was pulled along on a huge wagon attended by Brahmins (members of the priestly cast) under the wheels of which devotees were said to throw themselves. See V.98–101.

VII.43 *iron age*: PBS adapts the ancient commonplace (as in Ovid, *Metamorphoses* I) of accounting for the imperfection of the world by imagining that it has declined from a golden through a silver and then a bronze age to the present age of iron.

VII.49–59 The knowledge that Ianthe has so far acquired has been called up from a complete and accurate record of time indistinctly present in all minds and which needs only to be awakened to be recognized as true.

VII.53 *Tablets*: Here the word signifies a notebook (as *Poems* I points out) – in which the lessons the pupil Ianthe has learned are permanently inscribed.

VII.65 *purblind*: Myopic; figuratively 'dull' or 'stupid'.

VII.67 *Ahasuerus*: See PBS's Note [14]. One of the names by which the Wandering Jew of legend was known. In the Preface to PBS's early poem *The Wandering Jew* (1810) the subject is described as 'an imaginary personage, noted for the various and contradictory traditions which have prevailed concerning him' (*Poems* I, p. 41). He appears again in *Hellas*, ll. 738 ff. (p. 538).

VII.99 *paeans*: Hymns.

VII.100 *A murderer*: Moses, who kills an Egyptian in Exodus 2:12 and in 32:26–8 directs the sons of Levi to slaughter in God's name 3,000 idolatrous Israelites.

VII.119 *woman's blood*: Probably alluding to the slaughter of captive Midian women by the Israelites in Numbers 31:14–18.

VII.135–6 See PBS's Note [15].

VII.149 *reprobation*: The condition of being condemned to, specifically predestined to, eternal damnation.

VII.156 Alluding to Matthew 22:14: 'For many are called, but few are chosen.'

VII.170–72 Ahasuerus' interpretation of Christ's words in Matthew 10:34: 'I came not to send peace, but a sword.'

VII.192 *ghastily*: Adverbial form of 'ghastly'.

VII.195–9 Appropriating Satan's defiant 'Better to reign in hell, than serve in heaven' and his determination 'To wage by force or guile eternal war / Irreconcilable, to our grand foe' (*Paradise Lost* I.263, 121–2).

VII.208 *So*: 'So did they' or perhaps 'Therefore'.

VII.218 Recalling the prophetic vision in Revelation 14:18–19: 'Thrust in thy sharp sickle, and gather the clusters of the vine of the earth; for her grapes are fully ripe. And the angel thrust in his sickle into the earth, and gathered the vine of the earth, and cast it into the great winepress of the wrath of God.'

VII.219 *the red cross*: Symbol of militant Christianity.

VII.221 *exterminated faith*: One of the Christian heresies eradicated by the bloody persecution of its adherents.

VII.232–3 Those fanatics who slaughtered in God's name believed they acted guiltlessly.

VII.241–53 The freedom that has begun to emerge following the progress of reason has mitigated the worst impulses of the zealous, frustrating divine malevolence.

VII.259–60 The fallen angels are described as 'forest oaks' scathed by 'heaven's fire' in *Paradise Lost* I.612–15.

VIII.3–5 Kronos the Titan, associated with Chronos ('Time'), devoured his children as soon as they were born, it having been foretold that one of them would dethrone him. Kronos' sister and wife, Rhea, tricked him by wrapping a stone in infant's clothes and giving it to him to swallow instead of her newborn son Zeus, whom she concealed. Once grown, Zeus made Kronos vomit up the children he had eaten; together they and Zeus defeated him and ruled in his stead.

VIII.17–30 See note to VI.41.

VIII.37 *Glow mantling*: Suffused with the 'glow of health'.

VIII.86 *basilisk*: Alluding to the prophecy of an age of peace in Isaiah 11:8: 'And the suckling child shall play on the hole of the asp, and the weaned child shall put his hand on the cockatrice' den.' The 'cockatrice', another name for the basilisk, was a legendary reptile (supposedly hatched by a serpent from a cock's egg, i.e. a hen's egg without a yolk) whose poisonous look and breath were deadly.

VIII.108 *consentaneous*: Mutual, concurring.

VIII.115 *mantles*: Spreads foaming over the surface.

VIII.120–21 There will be no more winter.

VIII.124–8 Recalling Isaiah 11:6–7: 'The wolf also shall dwell with the lamb, and the leopard shall lie down with the kid; and the calf and the young lion and the fatling together; and a little child shall lead them . . . and the lion shall eat straw like the ox' – examples of PBS's contention in Note [17] that abstaining from flesh in favour of a vegetable diet would result in moral improvement.

VIII.129–30 *nightshade's . . . Poisons no more*: The beautiful plant with poisonous berries ceases to be toxic. Cp. *Prometheus Unbound* III.iv.78–85 (p. 251).

VIII.132 *mantles*: Foams.

VIII.183–6 Referring to the British military campaigns of 1798–1807 against the French in Egypt, regarded as the birthplace of the fraudulent monopoly of power by a league of priests and kings.

VIII.194 *the train-bearer of slaves*: The menial servant of tyrants, who are themselves the true slaves. See III.32, IV.246, IX.94.

VIII.203–7 *Him, still . . . eternity*: A slightly altered version of these difficult lines in *1813* serves as the key to PBS's Note [16]:

> Him, (still from hope to hope the bliss pursuing,
> Which, from the exhaustless lore of human weal
> Dawns on the virtuous mind,) the thoughts that rise
> In time-destroying infiniteness, gift
> With self-enshrined eternity, &c.

The convoluted syntax in each version obscures both the order of subject, predicate, object – 'thoughts', 'gift', 'Him' – and the sense: 'Hope prompts him to seek the happiness that leads the virtuous mind to educate itself in the knowledge of human well-being; and the unbounded thoughts that arise from this pursuit endow him with an autonomous immortality.'

VIII.211–12 See PBS's Note [17].

VIII.222 *prune*: Preen.

VIII.226–7 *prerogative . . . equals*: Man ceases to kill animals, regarding them as his fellow-creatures.

IX.29–30 A theme amply developed in 'Ozymandias' (p. 153).

IX.48 MWS omitted this line from *1839* and did not restore it, as she did other censored passages, in *1840*.

IX.76 *sweet bondage*: Sexual love.

IX.86 *senselessness*: Absence of sensual feeling.

IX.130 *wreck*: The remains of something ruined.

IX.149–63 PBS here conceives of human destiny in its broadest terms by combining the idea of perfectibility with that of metempsychosis or the transmigration of souls through successive material existences.

IX.154 *Bicker*: Flash, gleam.

IX.175 *gulph-dream*: A dream of falling into a gulf.

[SHELLEY'S] NOTES

Editorial summaries of excised passages of significance are given in italics within square brackets.

[1] The astronomical information is taken from the source that PBS credits in Note [2], William Nicholson's *The British Encyclopedia, or Dictionary of Arts and Sciences* (1809).

[2] p. 83 *awful:* Awe-inspiring.
p. 84 *necessity . . . itself*: See VI.197 ff. and Note [12].
The works of his fingers: Ironically alluding to the praise of God in Psalm 8:3–9: 'When I consider thy heavens, the work of thy fingers . . . how excellent is thy name in all the earth!'

[3] The first three paragraphs are taken with minor variations from William Godwin's *The Enquirer: Reflections on Education, Manners, and Literature* (1797). The verse dialogue, one of the titles that PBS collected in *Esdaile* but did not publish, appears to have been composed before he began to work on *QM*. Commentators have found models for the poem in

the exchange between the witches in *Macbeth* I.iii.1–35 and in Coleridge's castigation of the war policy of William Pitt in 'Fire, Famine, and Slaughter' (1798).

p. 84 *trepanned*: Inveigled, tricked.

[4] Quoted with minor inaccuracies from Ecclesiastes 1:4–7.

[5] The Greek quotation from Homer's *Iliad* is translated by Robert Fagles (Harmondsworth: Penguin Books, 1991), p. 200, as follows: 'Like the generations of leaves, the lives of mortal men. / Now the wind scatters the old leaves across the earth, / now the living timber bursts with the new buds / and spring comes round again. And so with men: / as one generation comes to life, another dies away.'

[6] The Latin quotation from Lucretius, *De Rerum Natura* II.1–14, is translated by R. E. Latham in *On the Nature of the Universe* (Harmondsworth: Penguin Books, 1951), p. 60, as follows:

> What joy it is, when out at sea the stormwinds are lashing the waters, to gaze from the shore at the heavy stress some other man is enduring! Not that anyone's afflictions are in themselves a source of delight; but to realize from what troubles you yourself are free is joy indeed. What joy, again, to watch opposing hosts marshalled on the field of battle when you have yourself no part in their peril! But this is the greatest joy of all: to stand aloof in a quiet citadel, stoutly fortified by the teaching of the wise, and to gaze down from that elevation on others wandering aimlessly in a vain search for the way of life, pitting their wits one against another, disputing for precedence, struggling night and day with unstinted effort to scale the pinnacles of wealth and power. O joyless hearts of men! O minds without vision!

[8] The two Latin verses are from Lucretius, *De Rerum Natura* III.85–6: 'Many a time before now men have betrayed their country and their beloved parents in an effort to escape the halls of Hell' (trans. Latham, *On the Nature of the Universe*, p. 98).

[9] p. 92 *one tenth of the population of London*: An extreme, perhaps exaggerated, estimate of the number of prostitutes in the metropolis.

[13] This note reproduces, with some additions and modifications, *The Necessity of Atheism* (*NofA*), the pamphlet jointly authored by PBS and his friend and fellow-undergraduate Thomas Jefferson Hogg, which led to their expulsion from Oxford in March 1811. The most significant additions to the text of the pamphlet are: the first paragraph; 'of the relation . . . bear to each' (third paragraph); '(A graduated scale . . . attached to them)'; 'But the God of Theologians is incapable of local visibility' ('1st . . . the senses'); 'We must prove design before we can infer a designer' and 'beyond its limits' ('2d. Reason'); 'or involuntarily active' ('3d. Testimony'); 'creative' (final paragraph). Important excisions from and alterations to *NofA* are given in the notes below.

p. 95 *least incomprehensible*: 'less incomprehensible' (*NofA*).

there must have been a cause: After this phrase, *NofA* reads: 'But what does this prove?'

omnipotent being: 'Almighty Being' (*NofA*).

p. 96 *either of*: 'any of' (*NofA*).
neglect to remove: 'willingly neglect to remove' (*NofA*).
views any subject of discussion: 'views the subject' (*NofA*). At this point and before the final sentence *NofA* reads: 'It is almost unnecessary to observe, that the general knowledge of the deficiency of such proof, cannot be prejudicial to society: Truth has always been found to promote the best interests of mankind.—'
no proof of the existence of a Deity: As a concluding flourish *NofA* adds 'Q.E.D.' (abbreviating the Latin formula *Quod erat demonstrandum*, 'Which was to be demonstrated'; i.e. 'What was to be proved has been proven').

[16] See note to VIII.203–7. The verse 'Dark flood of time . . . unredeemed' quotes lines 58–69 of PBS's unpublished poem 'To Harriet' ('It is not blasphemy to hope'), written in 1812 and included in *Esdaile*. The citations at the end of the note identify PBS's principal sources, Godwin's *Political Justice* (1793) and Nicolas de Condorcet's *Esquisse d'un tableau historique* (1795).

[17] This note is substantially identical to PBS's pamphlet *A Vindication of Natural Diet* (1813), which appears to have been printed shortly before the notes to *QM*, as *Complete Poetry* II argues. PBS adopted a vegetarian diet at the beginning of 1812 and largely kept to it for the rest of his life. His principal sources for pamphlet and note were John Frank Newton's *The Return to Nature; or, A Defence of the Vegetable Regimen* (1811), Joseph Ritson's *An Essay on Abstinence from Animal Food as a Moral Duty* (1802) and Dr William Lambe's *Reports on the Effects of a Peculiar Regimen on Scirrhous Tumours and Cancerous Ulcers* (1809). Timothy Morton's *Shelley and the Revolution in Taste* (Cambridge: Cambridge University Press, 1994) considers PBS's vegetarianism in the context of contemporary debates on animal rights, diet and health.

The verse is from *Paradise Lost* XI.477–88, the words of the Archangel Michael (and not Raphael) to Adam prophesying the effects on humans of 'intemperance . . . / In meats and drinks'.

The Latin verse is from Horace, *Odes* I.iii.25–33: 'The human species, audacious enough to endure anything, plunges into forbidden sacrilege. The audacious son [Prometheus] of Iapetus by an act of criminal deception brought fire to the nations. After the theft of fire from its heavenly home, a wasting disease and an unprecedented troop of fevers fell upon the earth, and the doom of a distant death, which up to then was slow in coming, quickened its step.'

p. 99 *the shambles*: The slaughterhouse.
mouflon: Wild sheep.
p. 100 *It is true . . . mass of human evil*: This paragraph does not appear in *A Vindication*.
p. 102 *Muley Ismael*: Sultan of Morocco from 1672 to 1727, notorious for cruelty.

'Mine eyes were dim with tears unshed'

MWS printed this enigmatic lyric without date and with the title 'To—' in *1824* and placed it among the poems of 1821 in *1839*; earlier, in transcribing it from PBS's draft, she had entitled it 'To MWG' (Mary Wollstonecraft Godwin) and dated it June 1814 before cancelling the initials. Some commentators and editors have considered the earlier year as the more likely, MWS as indeed the addressee, and composition to have taken place between the mutual declaration of love that PBS and the sixteen-year-old Mary Godwin (MWS) made on 26 June and their elopement on 28 July. Many details of the poem are susceptible of being understood in that context. See *Poems* I, pp. 442–3. But evidence that the poem is more likely to have been composed in 1820–21 and addressed to Claire Clairmont has been adduced by Nora Crook in 'Mary Shelley's Concealing "To—": (Re)addressing Poems', *Wordsworth Circle* 43:1 (Winter 2012), pp. 12–20: see note to ll. 13–14. The present text, which differs in some respects from that in MWS's editions of PBS's poems and later ones, has been edited from Bodleian MS Shelley adds. e. 12, pp. 8–11, a rough draft, unfinished in places and not always confidently legible. Some punctuation has been supplied and some readings are conjectural.

6 *into*: 'upon' is an uncancelled alternative in the MS.

13–14 These lines are very difficult to decipher in the MS. The present text adopts the reading offered by Nora Crook after a detailed study of the MS ('Mary Shelley's Concealing "To —"', pp. 14–16), which gives the sense: 'Only you saw the paleness in my face that otherwise went unseen, it having been intended for you alone.' Other readings have been proposed, for example in *Poems* I: 'Whilst you alone then not regarded / The tie which you alone should be'; i.e. 'You alone, in loving me, disregarded the fact that I was married – you only, by virtue of our love, deserving to be my wife.' *1824* reads: 'Whilst thou alone, then not regarded, / The [ ] thou alone should be'.

15–18 Mary declared her love for PBS before he confessed his for her (*Letters* I, p. 403).

24 'Turning to bliss its wayward pain' is an uncancelled alternative in the MS.

'O! there are spirits of the air'

Published in *1816*, from which the present text is taken; probably composed in 1815. MWS noted in *1839* that the poem 'was addressed in idea to Coleridge, whom [PBS] never knew; and at whose character he could only guess imperfectly, through his writings, and accounts he heard of him from some who knew him well. He regarded his change of opinions as rather an act of will than conviction, and believed that in his inner heart he would be haunted by what Shelley considered the better and holier aspirations of his youth' (III, pp. 15–16). These remarks have influenced understanding of 'O! there are spirits' as addressed to a well-known writer who had adopted conservative views while remaining inwardly attached to his earlier progressive ones; as such it may be set against the more directly political confrontation of 'To Wordsworth'

(p. 109), also published in *1816*. PBS was well acquainted with Coleridge's 'France: An Ode' (1798), which combines an account of the author's solitary wanderings in nature with a statement of his altered political sympathies towards revolutionary France. But rather than treating politics explicitly, the moral portrait and condensed narrative of 'O! there are spirits' have largely to do with the complex, and hazardous, character of imaginative inspiration – its relation to nature, to love and to the self. Stanzas 3–6 might allude to the effects of the married Coleridge's infatuation for Wordsworth's sister-in-law Sara Hutchinson, which is implicit in 'Dejection: An Ode' (1802).

Title There is no title in *1816*, the text being preceded solely by the epigraph; in *1839* MWS adopted 'To * * * *' as the title.

Epigraph 'I shall endure in tears an unhappy lot' – from Euripides, *Hippolytus* 1142–4. In *1816* the Greek is incorrectly printed; the text here is that edited by W. S. Barrett (Oxford: Clarendon Press, 1964). Preceded by the phrase 'for your misfortune', the words are spoken by the Chorus to Hippolytus, who has been banished by his father Theseus following a false accusation of rape by his stepmother Phaedra, who has hanged herself in despair at her love for her stepson.

1–6 *Poems* I notes a number of echoes of Coleridge's poems in these lines.

9 *inexplicable things*: The 'lovely ministers' of the preceding stanza. Cp. *Alastor*, l. 6 (p. 113).

15–16 *tame sacrifice / To a fond faith*: The sense is obscure – perhaps either: (1) 'You naïvely thought you could elicit a response to your love from one who was meant for another'; or (2) 'Your orthodox religious convictions prevented you from finding outside marriage the love you might have enjoyed.'

25–6 The lines would be appropriate to the disappointments in love that PBS recounts as his own in 'The Retrospect: Cwm Elan 1812', ll. 65–70 (p. 20), and in the Dedication before *Laon and Cythna*, stanza 6 (p. 149).

A Summer-Evening Church-Yard, Lechlade, Gloucestershire

Text from *1816*, where the poem was first published. PBS, Mary Godwin (as MWS then was), T. L. Peacock and Claire Clairmont's brother Charles visited Lechlade in the first week of September 1815, during a boating expedition on the Thames. They had originally intended to visit the river's source, but shallow water prevented their going further than Lechlade, where they stayed for two nights before turning back. Years later, Peacock remembered that 'A Summer-Evening Church-Yard' was written during this stay. As well as the setting, the poem adopts the pensive and melancholy idiom of eighteenth-century 'graveyard poetry' – in comparing the onset of death to the fall of evening, for example – though such consolation as it offers involves no reference to religion, a conspicuous absence in view of the central position given to the church and surrounding graves.

5 *Silence and twilight*: The personifications are repeated in *Alastor*, l. 455 (p. 125).

9 *own*: Accept.

13–14 The church of St Lawrence, Lechlade, has a central spire surrounded by four smaller pinnacles.
pyramids of fire: The word 'pyramid' was thought to designate 'flame-shaped', its first syllable deriving from the Greek for 'fire'.

15 *their*: Refers to 'Silence and twilight' of l. 5.

24 *Its awful hush is felt inaudibly*: Cp. *Alastor*, l. 30: 'When night makes a weird sound of its own stillness' (p. 114).

25–30 PBS reworks the elements of this stanza in the fourth stanza of 'Stanzas Written in Dejection—December 1818, near Naples' (p. 180), an example, among many, of self-revision in his poetry.

Sonnet. From the Italian of Dante

The original of this translation is Dante's well-known sonnet 'Guido, i' vorrei che tu e Lapo ed io'; the Italian text can be found, with English version and commentary, in *Dante's Lyric Poetry*, ed. K. Foster and P. Boyde, 2 vols (Oxford: Clarendon Press, 1967), I, pp. 30–31, II, pp. 52–4. The text there given, the one accepted by modern scholarship, differs slightly from the one translated by Shelley: see note to l. 10. Guido Cavalcanti and Lapo (the usual spelling) Gianni De' Ricevuti were friends of Dante and fellow authors who shared his ideas on a modern vernacular style in lyric poetry. In thirteenth-century Florence, it was customary for poets to comment on each other's poems in verse; Guido Cavalcanti's reply to this sonnet is given in *Dante's Lyric Poetry* I, pp. 30–32, and PBS's translation of it in *Poems* I, pp. 453–4, and *Complete Poetry* III, pp. 325, 942–6. Timothy Webb examines Shelley's rendering of Dante's sonnet 'Guido, i' vorrei che' in relation to the original in *The Violet in the Crucible* (Oxford: Oxford University Press, 1976), p. 281. The date of the sonnet is uncertain, though PBS may have composed it, as *Poems* I suggests, in early September 1815 shortly after returning from an excursion up the Thames by boat in company with T. L. Peacock, Mary Godwin (as MWS then was) and Claire Clairmont's brother Charles (see headnote to previous poem). Dante's sonnet provided a set of themes that PBS would celebrate throughout his verse: the idealized journey by boat, the small community bound together by love and intellectual friendship, the high excitement of 'passionate talk' (l. 12) – and the intricate connections of all these to the practice of poetry. Our text is from *1816*.

8 *strict*: Close.

10 Editors have wondered whether 'my' might not be a mistake or misprint because it was Bice (the familiar form of 'Beatrice') who was Dante's love. 'Vanna' is familiar for 'Giovanna'. The two named women in standard modern texts are Vanna and Lagia, the beloved of Guido and Lapo respectively.

To Wordsworth

Published in *1816*, from which the text is taken; composed between September 1814 and October 1815, when the *Alastor* volume went to press. In addition to its engagement with Wordsworth's poetry generally, as indicated below, the poem may be regarded as PBS's reaction to Wordsworth's *The Excursion* (August 1814), in which the older poet dramatizes his disappointment with the outcome of the French Revolution while endorsing the post-war political and religious status quo in Britain. MWS's journal entry for 14 September 1814 records that 'Shelley . . . brings home Wordsworth's "Excursion", of which we read a part, much disappointed. He is a slave' (*MWS Journal* I, p. 25). PBS never met Wordsworth, though he had hoped to do so during a stay at Keswick between November 1811 and January 1812. This sonnet laments Wordsworth's apostasy, ironically applying a theme that Wordsworth had made his own – 'That things depart which never may return' (l. 2) – to an examination of Wordsworth's own departure from his earlier support for humanitarian and libertarian ideals. PBS's critical apostrophe may be regarded as an ironic revision of Wordsworth's evocation of Milton's austere and high-minded example in the sonnet 'London, 1802' (1807), l. 9 of which – 'Thy soul was like a Star and dwelt apart' – is echoed in l. 7 here. PBS's ambiguous response to Wordsworth ('That such a man should be such a poet!', *Letters* II, p. 26) would continue throughout his career, notably in 'Verses written on receiving a Celandine in a letter from England' (p. 132) and *Peter Bell the Third* (p. 369). PBS varies the pattern of the Shakespearean sonnet by placing the traditional final couplet in ll. 9–10.

1–4 Wordsworth's most celebrated treatment of this theme occurs in the first stanza of his 'Ode: Intimations of Immortality' (1807): 'It is not now as it hath been of yore;— / Turn whereso'er I may, / By night or day, / The things which I have seen I now can see no more.'

9–10 The lines adapt one of the cardinal sources of PBS's conception of the philosopher-poet, Lucretius' *De Rerum Natura* (On the Nature of Things) II.1–14, in which the Roman poet imagines the pleasures of contemplating with a serene mind the blind struggles of ambition and greed. See editorial note to PBS's Note [6] to *Queen Mab* V.58 (p. 701).

11 *honoured poverty*: In a letter of 15 December 1811, PBS wrote enthusiastically from Keswick that 'Wordsworth . . . yet retains the integrity of his independance [sic], but his poverty is such that he is frequently obliged to beg for a shirt to his back' (*Letters* I, pp. 208–9).

12 *liberty*: One of the sections in Wordsworth's *Poems, in Two Volumes* (1807) is entitled 'Sonnets Dedicated to Liberty'.

Feelings of a Republican on the Fall of Bonaparte

Published in *1816*, which furnishes our text; date of composition uncertain but probably written in late 1815 as ll. 10–14 would be more appropriate to the harsh and restrictive post-Waterloo settlement imposed by the Allies on France than to the more generous terms of the Treaty of Paris of May 1814, which followed Napoleon's first abdication the previous month. But Charles E. Robinson argues that an unnamed poem that PBS sent to Byron in June 1814 could be this one (*KSJ* 35 (1986), pp. 104–10). In a letter of late August 1815, PBS deplores 'the enormities of their [i.e. the Allies'] troops', adding: 'In considering the political events of the day I endeavour to divest my mind of temporary sensations, to consider them as already historical' (*Letters* I, p. 430) – a point of view consistent with the elevated and generalized idiom of this poem. Napoleon's final defeat and exile to St Helena prompt PBS to recall the complex and ambivalent attitude towards the emperor which he shared with many radical and liberal contemporaries. He made numerous assessments of Napoleon in his poetry and prose: e.g. *Letters* I, pp. 345–6; 'Ode to Liberty' XII (p. 431); 'Written on hearing the news of the death of Napoleon' (p. 508); *The Triumph of Life*, ll. 215–34 (p. 577); and *A Philosophical View of Reform* (p. 636). See also Cian Duffy, '"The Child of a Fierce Hour": Shelley and Napoleon Bonaparte', *SIR* 43 (2004), pp. 399–416.

2 *unambitious slave*: The ironic paradox taxes the former emperor with a lack of those truly noble aspirations which would have prevented his moral enslavement to the vices of monarchs through the ages – territorial greed and the exercise of arbitrary power.

3 *shouldst*: Agrees with 'thou' rather than 'slave' (l. 2).

12 *owns*: Recognizes.

13–14 *old Custom, legal Crime, / And bloody Faith*: Referring to the provisions of the treaties restoring the Bourbon dynasty in France but with particular reference ('bloody Faith') to the Treaty of the Holy Alliance of September 1815 by which the rulers of Russia, Austria and Prussia claimed divine sanction for their authority and pledged to govern their nations according to the principles of Christian fraternity as set out in Holy Scripture. Liberals considered the Holy Alliance a cover of pious hypocrisy for the restoration of 'legitimacy', i.e. dynastic sovereignty, in Europe.

Mutability

These polished verses with their dramatic closing paradox appeared in *1816*, from which the text is taken. They are likely to have been written sometime during the year preceding publication of the volume in February 1816. PBS was keenly interested in the nature and functioning of the mind, returning to the subject at intervals in succeeding years: see 'On Love' (p. 618) and 'On Life' (p. 619). The 'psychology' of stanzas 2 and 3 derives from the empiricists John Locke (1632–1704) and David Hume (1711–76), in whose thought the mind is primarily a theatre for a succession of fleeting sense-impressions and the ideas arising from them – which leads Hume in particular to question traditional conceptions of a stable personal identity. See Timothy Clark, *Embodying Revolution: The Figure of the Poet in Shelley* (Oxford: Clarendon Press, 1989), pp. 13–43, 66–70. In a larger sense, PBS's lyric takes up one of literature's venerable themes, the unceasing change to which the world and human things are subject. *Poems* I cites Ovid, *Metamorphoses* XV.178–355 and Spenser's 'Two Cantos of Mutabilitie' (*Faerie Queene* VII.vii.13–56) as relevant precedents; *Complete Poetry* III refers to one of PBS's favoured texts, Lucretius' *De Rerum Natura* (On the Nature of Things), which imagines the universe as a perpetual flow of atomic particles. To these may be added *The Philosophy of Melancholy* (1812) in which PBS's friend T. L. Peacock identifies the steady contemplation of universal mutability as promoting that 'philosophical melancholy' which is 'the most copious source of virtue, of courage, and of genius' (*Peacock Works* VI, p. 186). PBS returned often to the theme of ineluctable change – for example in 'The flower that smiles today' (p. 554), to which MWS gave the title 'Mutability' when she included it in *1824*.

14 *still is free*: Is always open.

ALASTOR; OR, THE SPIRIT OF SOLITUDE

Composed in autumn–winter 1815 (the Preface is dated 14 December) during PBS's residence at Bishopsgate, near Windsor; published the following February in a volume entitled *Alastor; or, The Spirit of Solitude: and Other Poems* (1816), together with eleven shorter poems, six of which are included here: 'O! there are spirits of the air', 'A Summer-Evening Church-Yard, Lechlade, Gloucestershire', 'Sonnet. From the Italian of Dante', 'To Wordsworth', 'Feelings of a Republican on the Fall of Bonaparte' and 'Mutability' (pp. 107–10). Our text is taken from *1816*.

PBS's friend T. L. Peacock remembered suggesting the unusual title: 'He was at a loss for a title, and I proposed that which he adopted . . . The Greek word 'Αλάστωρ is an evil genius [i.e. malevolent spirit] . . . The poem treated the spirit of solitude as a spirit of evil. I mention the true meaning of the word, because many have supposed *Alastor* to be name of the hero of the poem' (*Peacock Works* VIII, p. 100). The sense of 'an avenging spirit' also had some currency at the time (*OED*). In the poem, the 'Spirit of Solitude' designates not a supernatural being but rather a morbid state of mind in which sympathetic idealism collapses into solipsism. PBS evoked the mental impulses involved in a letter to T. J. Hogg shortly before he began to compose *Alastor*: 'It excites my wonder to consider the perverted energies of the human mind . . . who is there that will not pursue phantoms, spend his choicest hours in hunting after dreams, and wake only to perceive his error and regret that death is so near?' (*Letters* I, pp. 429–30). MWS's 'Note on *Alastor*' in *1839* claims that it 'contains an individual interest only' (as against the broad political concerns of *Queen Mab*: p. 23); and PBS introduced it to the Laureate Robert Southey as his 'first serious attempt to interest the best feelings of the human heart' (*Letters* I, p. 462). In *1839* MWS recalled that in spring 1815 PBS had been diagnosed as suffering from pulmonary consumption and identifies his apprehension of death, the sudden disappearance of his symptoms, and a chastened backward glance at his own early philosophic radicalism as conditions that shaped the major themes of *Alastor*.

Alastor is PBS's first sustained examination of what would become a central topic of his work: the scope, responsibility and potential dysfunction of the poetic imagination. These have an obvious autobiographical dimension, but his claim in the Preface that 'The picture is not barren of instruction to actual men' (p. 112) has prompted attempts to discover in the Poet-protagonist features belonging to Wordsworth and Coleridge, who also receive particular assessments in the *Alastor* volume: see 'To Wordsworth' (p. 109) and 'O! there are spirits of the air' (p. 107). In reading *Alastor* the different estimates of the Poet's destiny in the first and second paragraphs of the Preface should be noted; one should also bear in mind the differences between the narrative that is sketched in the Preface and the one that unfolds in the poem, as well as the different roles assigned to the narrator of the poem and its principal character – neither of whom is simply to be identified with PBS himself or any other.

The volume received only a few, largely hostile and uncomprehending, reviews when it appeared, but has since come to be regarded as one of the landmark collections of the second generation of British Romantic poets. The title-poem has attracted important critical commentary; a representative sample would include: G. Kim Blank, *Wordsworth's Influence on Shelley* (London: Palgrave Macmillan, 1988); Kenneth Neill Cameron, *Shelley: The Golden Years* (Cambridge, Mass.: Harvard University Press, 1974), pp. 219–33; Timothy Clark, *Embodying Revolution: The Figure of the Poet in Shelley* (Oxford: Clarendon Press, 1989), pp. 47–53; Cian Duffy, *Shelley and the Revolutionary Sublime* (Cambridge: Cambridge University Press, 2005), pp. 73–83; Donald Maddox, 'Shelley's *Alastor* and the Legacy of Rousseau', *SiR* 9 (1970), pp. 82–98; Paul Mueschke and Earl Griggs, 'Wordsworth as the Prototype of the Poet in Shelley's *Alastor*', *PMLA* 49 (1934), pp. 229–45; Joseph Raben, 'Coleridge as the Prototype of the Poet in Shelley's *Alastor*', *RES* 17 (1966), pp. 278–92; and Earl Wasserman, *Shelley: A Critical Reading* (Baltimore: Johns Hopkins University Press, 1971), pp. 15–46.

Preface Compare this early development with the 'education peculiarly fitted for a poet', an idealized account of PBS's own poetic vocation, in the Preface to *Laon and Cythna* (p. 603), written about a year later in autumn 1817.
p. 112 *requisitions*: Claims.
Blasted: Blighted.
Power: The idea of a 'Power' inherent in nature figures in 'Hymn to Intellectual Beauty', l. 1 (p. 134), and 'Mont Blanc', l. 16 (p. 140).
p. 113 *doubtful*: Apparently combining the obsolete sense 'to be dreaded' with the more usual 'uncertain'.
All else: Completely different.
'The good . . . socket': A slight misquotation of Wordsworth, *The Excursion* (1814) I.500–502. The lines describe the poor cottager Margaret; although she is kindly, loving and industrious, the harsh material conditions of her existence, the loss of her soldier husband in war and the death of her child have destroyed her will to live.
socket: The hollow part of a candlestick that holds the candle.

Epigraph 'I was not yet in love, and I was in love with love, I sought what I might love, loving to love.' The Latin quotation is composed from a longer passage in St Augustine's *Confessions* III.i, in which the saint declares that his impulse to love was unconscious longing for God. The sense that PBS attaches to words is set out in the Preface. In *Esdaile* (*SC* IV, p. 1005) he applied the quotation to his younger self, and later inscribed it in a notebook in 1814 (*Clairmont Journal*, p. 61).

2 *our great Mother*: The forces of nature personified as maternal. See note to ll. 18–19.

3 *natural piety*: Reverence for nature; echoing Wordsworth's 'My heart leaps up' (1807), ll. 7–9: 'The Child is Father of the man; / And I could wish my days to be / Bound each to each by natural piety', lines which were set as an epigraph to 'Ode: Intimations of Immortality' in Wordsworth's *Poems* (1815).

8 *sere*: Dried, withered.

14 *consciously*: Intentionally; PBS became a vegetarian in 1812, defending the 'vegetable regimen' himself in his Note [17] to *Queen Mab* VIII.211–12 (p. 98).

18–19 *Mother . . . song*: The appeal to nature for inspiration replaces the similar appeal to the Muse in ancient Greek and Roman poetry.
21 *Thy shadow*: The operations of nature cannot be perceived directly, but only through its manifestations in the material world. Cp. 'Hymn to Intellectual Beauty', ll. 1–2 (p. 134).
23–9 *I have made . . . what we are*: PBS's friend Hogg records (*Life* I, pp. 36–7) PBS's youthful watching for ghosts, and in a letter to him of January 1811 the nineteen-year-old PBS claims to 'have been most of the night pacing a church yard' (*Letters* I, p. 39). Cp. 'Hymn to Intellectual Beauty', ll. 49–54, which describe a similar quest for 'high talk with the departed dead' (p. 136).
26 *obstinate questionings*: Wordsworth, 'Ode: Intimations of Immortality', ll. 142–3: 'those obstinate questionings / Of sense and outward things'. In Wordsworth's poem, adults retain vestiges of the lively sense of their own divine origins they experienced in childhood.
29–37 *In lone . . . thy charge*: Just such a session is recorded by PBS in *MWS Journal* (7 October 1814): 'soon after' the 'witching time of night' he asked 'whether it is not horrible to feel the silence of night tingling in our ears'. He and Claire Clairmont then 'continued to sit by the fire at intervals engaging in awful conversation relative to the nature of these mysteries'.
42 *lyre*: The instrument here functions like the Aeolian harp (from Aeolus or Eolus, the god of the wind), a hollow box stringed across its opening which produced sounds when exposed to wind or breeze, and the subject of Coleridge's 'Effusion XXXV' (1796; later retitled 'The Eolian Harp').
44 *fane*: Temple.
49 *deep heart of man*: A Wordsworthian phrase; relevant passages would include: 'Ode: Intimations of Immortality', ll. 190–206; 'Tintern Abbey' (1798), ll. 94–112; 'Michael' (1800), ll. 29–33.
56 *votive cypress wreath*: In ancient Rome, boughs of cypress, sacred to Pluto, were carried at funerals as an offering to the gods.
67–8 Wordsworth's account of the Wanderer's development in *The Excursion* I.301–2 – 'In dreams, in study, and in ardent thought, / Thus was he reared' – is one among many parallels between his early life and that of the Poet in *Alastor*.
67 *silver*: As well as evoking glowing colour, the word suggests the sense 'gently melodious'.
71 *divine philosophy*: Recalling Milton, *Comus*, l. 475: 'How charming is divine philosophy!'
85 *bitumen lakes*: i.e. of naturally occurring pitch.
93 *Frequent with*: 'Crowded with' (a Latinism).
94 *chrysolite*: A green or yellowish-green gemstone.
101 *bloodless food*: Vegetable fare; see note to l. 14.
104 *brake*: Thicket.
suspend: i.e. 'would suspend'.
106–28 The Poet's journey is both geographical and historical, taking him through the countries of the eastern Mediterranean and up the Nile in search of the origins of European civilization in the great cities of

increasingly ancient cultures: Greek (Athens), Phoenician (Tyre, Balbec or Baalbek), Jewish (Jerusalem), Babylonian (Babylon), Egyptian (Memphis, Thebes), finally arriving in Ethiopia, which, according to some writers, was the seat of Paradise. Tyre and Baalbek were in what is now Lebanon; Babylon in Iraq, south of Baghdad.

109–10 *the waste . . . Jerusalem*: Jerusalem was sacked by the future Roman emperor Titus Flavius in AD 70.

118 *daemons*: Spirits that mediate between gods and men.

119–28 *The Zodiac's brazen mystery . . . birth of time*: A celebrated zodiac in the temple of the goddess Hathor at Dendera on the Nile was considered by some contemporary thinkers to be the earliest representation of natural forces as divine, evidence that religion originated in the worship of nature. It is now displayed in the Louvre.

120 *mute thoughts . . . mute walls*: Because the temples are now unfrequented and abandoned or, perhaps, as *Complete Poetry* III suggests, because hieroglyphics had not yet been deciphered.

126–7 *till meaning . . . inspiration*: Adapting Wordsworth, 'I wandered lonely as a Cloud' (1807), ll. 11–16: 'I gaz'd – and gaz'd [on a crowd of daffodils] . . . For oft when on my couch I lie / In vacant or in pensive mood, / They flash upon that inward eye / Which is the bliss of solitude.'

140–45 *The Poet . . . vale of Cashmire*: Continuing eastward, the Poet passes through Arabia, Iran (Persia), the Kerman desert ('the wild Carmanian waste') in south-eastern Iran, then over the Hindu Kush or Indian Caucasus (source of the Indus and Oxus rivers and setting of *Prometheus Unbound* I: p. 188) and on into the valley of Kashmir on the border between modern India and Pakistan. Contemporary speculation located the origin of the human race in Kashmir, in which the scene of *Prometheus Unbound* II.i (p. 217) is laid.

149–91 PBS describes the impulses that generate the Poet's vision in the Preface. The psychology developed in his prose essay 'On Love' (p. 618) also serves as a commentary on the present passage. The portrait of the 'veiled maid' draws upon his reading in contemporary 'Oriental' prose fiction and poetry, for which see the notes on *Alastor* in *Poems* I and *Complete Poetry* III. The gap between an idealized and an actual erotic object, a major preoccupation of PBS's life and poetry, is articulated in, for example, *Letters* I, pp. 95, 429–30.

163 *numbers*: Verse; here accompanied by a stringed instrument.

167 *symphony*: Harmony.

172 *intermitted*: Interrupted, ceasing at intervals.

189 *Involved*: Enveloped.

193 *blue*: Often associated with sickness and death in PBS's verse, e.g. in ll. 216 and 598 and 'The Plague's blue kisses' (*Laon and Cythna*, l. 2766).

196–200 *Whither have fled . . . exultation*: Echoing Wordsworth, 'Ode: Intimations of Immortality', ll. 56–7: 'Whither is fled the visionary gleam? / Where is it now, the glory and the dream?'

207 *He overleaps the bounds*: i.e. between the imagined and the real.

211–19 *Does . . . delightful realms*: The supposition in 'Mont Blanc', ll. 49–52, varies the tenor of the question: 'Some say that gleams of a remoter world /

Visit the soul in sleep,—that death is slumber, / And that its shapes the busy thoughts outnumber / Of those who wake and live' (p. 142).

228–32 A similar struggle between a serpent and an eagle has an important symbolic function in *Laon and Cythna* I.viii–xiv.

229–31 *precipitates . . . her blind flight*: Rushes headlong, recklessly.

239–44 The Poet reverses direction, now travelling north and west through modern Pakistan, Afghanistan, Tajikistan, Uzbekistan and Iran. Commentators have identified Aornos as modern Pir Sarai in Pakistan, Petra as the Rock of Soghdiana in Uzbekistan: each was the site of a victory won by the armies of Alexander the Great. The city of Balk or Balkh is in Afghanistan. The 'tombs / Of Parthian kings' in northern Iran were destroyed by the Roman emperor Caracalla in the third century AD.

249 *Sered*: See l. 8 and note.

272 *Chorasmian shore*: Probably the eastern shore of the Caspian Sea but possibly the western shore of the Aral Sea. Chorasmia (or Khwarezm) is an area lying between the two along the Oxus (or Amu Darya) river in modern Turkmenistan and Uzbekistan.

291 *wrinkled his quivering lips*: PBS substituted the reading 'convulsed his curling lips' in a copy of the *Alastor* volume presented to Leigh Hunt (M. Quinn, *KSJ* 35 (1986), pp. 17–20).

297 *fair fiend*: Apparently the 'veiled maid' the Poet sees in his dream in ll. 151–91, because the vision of her is both lovely and demonic.

299 *shallop*: A small boat.

330 *genii*: Spirits associated with natural phenomena.

352 *etherial*: Rising high into the air.

353 *Caucasus*: Mountain range in the Republic of Georgia, to the east of the Caspian Sea, which the Poet has just crossed.

382 *knarled*: Here and at l. 530 an obsolete (in England) form of 'gnarled'; perhaps (as *Forman 1876–7* suggests) the initial letter *k* is to be pronounced, as it then was in Scotland.

406 *yellow flowers*: Narcissi. In Ovid's *Metamorphoses* III.344–511, the beautiful youth Narcissus, as punishment for scorning his admirers, is made to fall in love with his own reflection in a pool; dying of grief at not being able to possess the image, he is transformed into a flower.

409 *pensive*: Frequent in Wordsworth, this is the only occurrence of the word in PBS's poetry, though 'pensiveness' appears in l. 489 in a related context. See note to ll. 126–7.

422 *brown*: Dark.

424 *aëry*: High in the air.

425 The caves echo the sound of the wind among the forest trees.

426 *implicated*: Intertwined.

439–45 The contemporary sense of 'parasite' suggested symbiosis rather than exploitation. PBS uses the term in this sense in *Queen Mab* I.43 (p. 25).

448 *lawns*: Grassy clearings.

455 PBS varies the image in 'A Summer-Evening Church-Yard, Lechlade, Gloucestershire', ll. 5–6: 'Silence and twilight, unbeloved of men, / Creep hand in hand from yon obscurest glen' (p. 108).

465 *painted*: Brightly and variously coloured.

476 *Startled*: Started, moved abruptly.
glanced: Sprang aside.

479–88 The Spirit has the appearances of the natural surroundings and communicates with the Poet through its sounds.

490 *Two starry eyes*: Recalling the 'beamy bending eyes' of the veiled maid in l. 179; the crescent-points of the setting moon in l. 654 look back to both images.

507 *searchless*: Undiscoverable; like the other adjectives in ll. 503–8, this one has a figurative as well as a physical sense.

517–22 The fever-patient, not the Poet, is 'Forgetful of the grave'.

528 *windlestrae*: A dry withered stalk of grass.

543–50 Taking 'it' as referring to 'ravine', the sense of the passage is that while the high rocks darken the depths of the ravine, 'gulphs and . . . caves' which echo the sound of the stream can be discerned higher up.

583 *children*: i.e. lesser breezes or gusts, the offspring of the 'autumnal whirlwind'.

588–90 *One step . . . one voice*: The 'step' is the Poet's, the 'voice' apparently that of the Spirit that in ll. 479–92 beckons him, assuming the sounds of the surrounding natural phenomena.

609–24 The shift of address in this passage is also a shift to a political idiom comparable to that of *Queen Mab* (p. 23). The sense is that Death, who rules the world – as witness the pernicious instances in ll. 614–17 – is called by his brother Ruin to feast on a 'rare and regal prey', apparently including both royal rulers and the Poet himself, who is at the point of death (cp. ll. 690–95). Thereafter, men will die naturally rather than as victims, no longer crushed by oppression and injustice.

610 *sightless*: Invisible, possibly also 'blind'.

651 *meteor*: The moon; in contemporary usage, 'meteor' could signify any luminous atmospheric appearance.

654 *two lessening points of light*: The moon is setting and only the tips of its crescent remain visible above the horizon. See note to l. 490.

657 *stagnate*: Stagnant.

660 *involved*: Enveloped.

672–5 The sorceress Medea restored her husband Jason's aged father to youth by means of a magic potion which she prepared in a cauldron. Leaves and fruit burst from the withered olive branch with which she stirred the mixture, some drops of which, falling to the ground, caused flowers and grass to spring up – according to the account in Ovid's *Metamorphoses* VII.275–81.

675–81 The narrator asks that God, who has inflicted so many ills on humanity, would grant it the gift of immortality. The 'one living man' is Ahasuerus, the Wandering Jew of legend, the subject of an early poem by PBS and a character in both *Queen Mab* (note to VII.67: p. 698) and *Hellas* (ll. 135–61, 738 ff.: pp. 520–21, 538). Ahasuerus was condemned to roam the earth eternally as a punishment for having refused help to Christ on the road to Calvary.

681–6 The 'dark magician' is an alchemist attempting to concoct the elixir of life, which confers immortality. See ll. 31–2, 672–5 and note.

694 *vesper*: Evening prayer.
705 *senseless*: That cannot feel or perceive.
713 The quotation is from the concluding line of Wordsworth's 'Ode: Intimations of Immortality': 'To me the meanest flower that blows can give / Thoughts that do often lie too deep for tears.'

Verses written on receiving a Celandine in a letter from England

PBS drafted this poem in Switzerland in summer 1816; MWS transcribed a fair copy at Marlow the following year; it was not published until 1925 in the *Boston Herald* for 21 December: see *BSM* XI and *MYR (Shelley)* V. The fair copy, on which the present text is based, is very lightly punctuated; a minimum of additional punctuation has been supplied. The celandine of the title (see notes on ll. 1–3 below) was apparently included in a letter sent from England by Shelley's friend T. L. Peacock. Years later Claire Clairmont recalled her and MWS's delight when PBS came from his study and handed them the 'Verses' (*MYR (Shelley)* V.17, 28). Wordsworth's *Poems, in Two Volumes* (London: Longman, 1807) contains three poems on the lesser celandine, which is identified (vol. I, p. 15) by its familiar name, common pilewort, and whose bright yellow blossoms can be seen in March and April opening to the sun and closing at evening or in cloudy weather. PBS's 'Verses' makes a critical address to Wordsworth with an eye on these poems – taking off from 'There's a flower that shall be mine, / 'Tis the little Celandine' in the first of them, while turning to sarcastic use the role Wordsworth assigns to the flower in the third poem as emblem of the human passage from prodigal youth to helpless age. PBS adapts further details from these and other of Wordsworth's poems (see M. Quinn, *KSJ* 36 (1987), pp. 88–109).

In 1813 Wordsworth had accepted a salaried government post as a Distributor of Stamps for his region, in effect a collector of revenue; PBS and Peacock regarded the appointment as a political reward for his increasing conservatism as well as the motive for his support for post-Waterloo conservatism in Britain. See 'To Wordsworth' (p. 109) and 'An Exhortation' (p. 418). Strategic echoes of Milton and Shakespeare (ll. 30, 62–3) introduce a comparison on the themes of artistic integrity and posthumous fame which is unflattering to Wordsworth – although PBS is careful to acknowledge the power of what he considered to be the older man's immortal early verse.

1–2 These frankly puzzling lines have occasioned much commentary. The blossom of both the lesser celandine (*Ranunculus ficaria*) and the greater celandine (*Chelidonium majus*) is yellow, as PBS well knew. Otherwise the two flowers are botanically distinct, the former a member of the buttercup family, the latter of the poppy family. PBS's 'blue' may allude, for the benefit of the Greek scholar Peacock, to the derivation of 'celandine' from the Greek *chelidon* = 'swallow', whose steel-blue upper feathers in flight might suggest the image of 'a flower aery blue'. *Complete Poetry* III, citing PBS's phrase 'the classic celandine' (see following note), points out that there is a celandine described as blue in Theocritus' *Idyll* XIII.41 and glosses the lines plausibly: 'When I received a withered specimen of a Celandine, I thought of an ideal Celandine – classically blue and unwithered.' One might also suggest a tongue-in-cheek reading: 'I thought that the Celandine, even the smaller variety, was blue' – which would allude to private coded meanings involving both varieties of celandine, and both colours, which PBS and Peacock entertained, perhaps preferring the 'classic' blue greater celandine as a playful jibe against Wordsworth's association with the smaller flower. See also ll. 65–72 and notes.

3 *Yet small*: The name *Chelidonium* was principally applied (as in Pliny, *Natural History* XXXV.89) to the greater celandine, popularly called 'swallowwort' because its blossoms appeared with the arrival of the swallow and disappeared when it departed. It may be the blossom of this plant that PBS was sent (see previous note) and that he writes of to Peacock on 27 July 1816 (*Letters* I, p. 501), in relation to the Alpine seeds he has purchased to cultivate in England: 'They are companions which the celandine, the classic celandine, need not despise.'

25–6 *A type of . . . thus familiar*: An emblem of that (i.e. the 'deathless Poet' of the next line) which now brings us intimately together.

30 Recalling Milton's reference (*Paradise Lost* VII.25–6) to the dangers surrounding him immediately after the Restoration because of his support for Parliament during the Civil Wars: 'though fallen on evil days, / On evil days though fallen, and evil tongues'.

45–8 Alluding to Wordsworth's celebration of the Allied victory at Waterloo in 'Ode. The Morning of the Day Appointed for a General Thanksgiving. January 18, 1816' (1816); liberal opinion was especially outraged by ll. 277–82: 'We bow our heads before Thee, and we laud / And magnify thy name, Almighty God! / But thy most dreaded instrument, / In working out a pure intent, / Is Man – arrayed for mutual slaughter,— / Yea, Carnage is thy daughter!'

49–56 The stanza is tortuously phrased. The sense appears to be: 'He scorns hopes that had been his own; the victors he now praises were once his foes. He no longer promotes hope or condemns tyranny. But neither hope nor opposition to tyranny needs his approval. Truth need not lament that he disowned her before his inspiration had waned.'

56 *overlive*: Outlive.

57–60 The praise of Wordsworth's early poetry in these lines ironically recalls the compensations he discovers in age for loss of youthful vision ('Ode: Intimations of Immortality' (1807), ll. 182–9): 'We will grieve not, rather find / Strength in what remains behind . . . In years that bring the philosophic mind.'

62–3 Echoing Shakespeare's claim in Sonnet XVIII.13–14: 'So long as men can breathe or eyes can see, / So long lives this, and this gives life to thee.'

65–72 In fact each stem of the lesser celandine bears only one flower. The greater celandine bears several blossoms on an umbel at the end of its stem.

67 *priest of Nature*: Apparently Peacock, who sent the celandine and who perhaps had written that he had placed the original stem in his window; PBS humorously refers to him as a priest about the time the poem was written (*Letters* I, p. 490) – though ll. 67–8 also glance at Wordsworth, who describes the visionary Youth in 'Ode: Intimations of Immortality' (l. 72) as 'Nature's Priest'.

Hymn to Intellectual Beauty

Before leaving Switzerland for England at the end of August 1816, MWS transcribed into a notebook three poems that PBS had written that summer: 'Hymn to Intellectual Beauty' and two otherwise unknown sonnets. PBS himself entered into the same notebook, which remained with Byron in Geneva, a copy of the poem then entitled 'Scene—Pont Pellisier in the vale of Servox', later to be retitled 'Mont Blanc' (p. 140). The following month the notebook would appear to have been entrusted by Byron to his friend Scrope Davies, who brought it to England but neglected to return it to PBS; when he left England in 1820, Davies deposited a trunk containing the notebook and other papers with his bankers. The trunk was only rediscovered in 1976 in a branch of Barclay's Bank in London. The texts of 'Hymn to Intellectual Beauty' and of 'Mont Blanc' in the Scrope Davies notebook differ significantly from their first appearance in print. On PBS's return to England, he sent a version of the 'Hymn' derived from his first draft for publication to the liberal weekly *The Examiner*, but the editor, Leigh Hunt, mislaid it. As the fair copy in the Scrope Davies notebook had not been delivered, PBS would seem to have returned to his draft and produced a finished version of the poem for the second time. This was eventually published in *The Examiner* on Sunday 19 January 1817. Probably 'Mont Blanc' was similarly recovered from the draft MS for publication at the end of 1817. Judith Chernaik and Timothy Burnett reconstruct the complex textual history of each poem in *RES* n.s. 29 (1978), pp. 36–49.

Although not prepared for the press, the texts of PBS's poems in the Scrope Davies notebook are clean, legible and complete in themselves. They are reproduced here, each headed 'Version B', facing the versions published in *The Examiner* and in *1817*, which are headed 'Version A' and which are the ones to which the annotations are keyed. The Version B texts are given as they appear in the MSS transcribed by MWS and PBS – with insufficient punctuation, inconsistent capitalization and indentation, unexpanded ampersands and peculiar spellings. As such, they offer not only a rare occasion to compare the published texts of two of PBS's major poems with an earlier variant derived from the same draft, but also display the features of a stage of composition immediately preceding final submission for print.

In *1839* MWS recalls how PBS's 'Hymn' 'was conceived during his voyage round the lake [of Geneva] with Lord Byron'. PBS describes this excursion by boat (22–30 June 1816) in *Letters* I, pp. 480–88, and in *1817*, pp. 107–39 (see the extract: p. 595). The Alpine scenes he then observed affected him intensely; he later recalled that the poem had been 'composed under the influence of feelings which agitated me even to tears' (*Letters* I, p. 517). The surviving draft (*BSM* XI), lacking stanza 4, was probably made during the tour of the lake or shortly afterwards and the poem finished by late August 1816.

The 'Hymn' of PBS's title announces the religious character of a poem which incorporates a number of the traditional elements of prayer: praise offered to a mysterious Power, petition for its aid, confession of childhood errors, and renewal of a vow – in this case following upon a visionary crisis in youth. The poem borrows eclectically from religious and ethical traditions: biblical language is adopted equally with that of secular humanism, while the political implications of ll. 68–70 may have put contemporary readers in mind of the hymns sung during the public ceremonies of the French Revolution to such abstractions as Liberty and Reason. The development of the seven stanzas is underpinned by a discreet structure of argument. Visitations of the Spirit of Beauty, which the poet apprehends through the transient appearances of nature, together with the intense mental and emotive experiences that he recalls in stanzas 5 and 6, support a tentative affirmation: that an immanent force which cannot be known directly, but only through its intermittent interventions in the natural sphere, is the cause of all that the senses, the mind and the affections recognize as beautiful. This power is the Intellectual Beauty that is addressed throughout as if it were a deity, although no such claim is made explicitly. The phrase 'Intellectual Beauty' occurs in a number of authors that PBS had read, notably in chapter 3 of Mary Wollstonecraft's *A Vindication of the Rights of Woman* (1792), where it signifies the mental excellence of a woman as opposed to her mere physical attractions; and in chapter 10 of William Godwin's *Memoirs of the Author of A Vindication of the Rights of Woman* (1798), where Mary Wollstonecraft herself is credited with possessing an intuitive perception of that Beauty which is proper to the things of the mind. But it should be stressed that PBS's poem aims to redefine Intellectual Beauty in his own language and to his own purposes, the text elaborating with notable particularity the special cluster of meanings that he attaches to the idea. Good investigations of the sources and contexts of the term can be found in: N. Brown, *KSR* 2 (1987), pp. 91–104; *Chernaik*, pp. 32–40; *Complete Poetry* III, pp. 476–82; and *Poems* I, pp. 522–5.

1 *awful*: Inspiring awe.

6 *glance*: A sudden movement producing a flash or gleam.

13 *doth*: 'Dost' would be the correct form for an address to the 'Spirit of Beauty' in the second-person singular, as in ll. 14 and 16; but 'doth' is confirmed by both draft and first version.

16 *state*: Condition, lot.

17 *vale of tears*: The phrase derives from the Vulgate version of Psalm 84:5–6 (H. W. White and N. Rogers, *KSMB* 24, pp. 16–18) and traditionally signified the temporary afflictions of this world in contrast to the eternal bliss of heaven.

23 *scope*: Capacity.

27 *name of God and ghosts, and Heaven*: the *Examiner* version reads: 'names of Demon, Ghost, and Heaven'. The reading adopted here was entered by PBS on a clipping of the *Examiner* text of the poem (*MYR (Shelley)* V). The draft reads: 'names of Ghosts & God & Heaven' (*BSM* XI); Version B gives: 'name of God & Ghosts & Heaven'. The removal of 'God' from the *Examiner* text may have been the result of Leigh Hunt's anxieties; prosecution for blasphemous libel was a real danger in 1817 (see headnote to the extract from the Preface to *Laon and Cythna*: p. 854).

34 *still instrument*: An Aeolian or wind harp, which gives out music as the wind blows upon it. Cp. *Alastor*, ll. 42–9 and note on l. 42 (pp. 114, 710).

36 Echoing John 1:14: 'And the Word was made flesh, and dwelt among us, (and we beheld his glory, the glory as of the only begotten of the Father,) full of grace and truth.'

37 *Self-esteem*: Here replaces Faith as the third of what were traditionally known as Theological Virtues: Faith, Hope, Charity (Love).

41 *firm state*: Unshakeable sway.

49–72 Cp. stanzas 3–5 of the Dedication before *Laon and Cythna* (p. 148).

49 MWS confirms in a sketch of PBS's early life that as a boy he sat up at night hoping to see ghosts. See *BSM* XXII, pp. 270–71, and cp. *Alastor*, ll. 23–9 (p. 114).

53–4 *poisonous names . . . I was not heard*: Both draft and Version B read: 'false name . . . He heard me not'. PBS's original 'He' probably intended God (cp. l. 27) and so was altered to avoid offence – as l. 27 seems to have been. But the context admits the possibility that it was the Devil's aid which was being invoked to raise the spirits of the dead. This would be consistent with the occult experiments of the young PBS as described by his sister (T. J. Hogg in *Life* I, pp. 22–6). The precise reference of the revision 'poisonous names' is still less clear; it may include other demons, magicians, perhaps saints, and even the 'God' of l. 27. Cp. *Queen Mab* IV.112–13: 'specious names, / Learnt in soft childhood's unsuspecting hour' (p. 47).

58 *buds*: Given as 'birds' in *The Examiner*. PBS corrected what was evidently a misprint on a clipping of the *Examiner* text (*MYR (Shelley)* V), so restoring the reading of both draft and first version.

84 *fear*: Wariness and self-suspicion, combined with the sense 'revere, show reverence, especially towards God' – as in 'The Lord taketh pleasure in them that fear him' (Psalm 147:11). PBS's line reformulates as fundamental principles of a secular ethics two biblical injunctions: one frequent in the Old Testament, e.g. 'Ye shall walk after the Lord your God, and fear him, and keep his commandments' (Deuteronomy 13:4); the other in the New Testament, e.g. 'Thou shalt love thy neighbour as thyself' (Mark 12:31). The worship of Intellectual Beauty as conceived in the poem inspires instead the Shelleyan virtue of self-respect (cp. the 'Self-esteem' which stands in place of Faith in l. 37) as well as generalizing the love of one's neighbour to include all of humanity.

Mont Blanc

Written between 22 July and 29 August 1816; published late the following year in *1817*, which provides our Version A text. The Preface to *1817* introduces the poem as having been 'composed under the immediate impression of the deep and powerful feelings excited by the objects which it attempts to describe; and as an undisciplined overflowing of the soul, rests its claim to approbation on an attempt to imitate the untameable wildness and inaccessible solemnity from which those feelings sprang'. *1817* also contains a journal-letter recounting the excursion to Mont Blanc from 21 to 27 July during which the poem was conceived and probably drafted at least in part. This letter (see the extract from *1817* (pp. 595–601) and *Letters* I, pp. 495–502) and the parallel account in *MWS Journal* I, pp. 112–21, provide a revealing commentary on 'Mont Blanc'. The Shelleys followed an established itinerary for tourists, and PBS's poem refashions a language of response to much-described sights which had become current coin.

For the existence of two finished versions of the poem, reproduced here as 'Version A' and 'Version B', see the headnote to the previous poem, 'Hymn to Intellectual Beauty'. Annotations are to the *1817* text, Version A.

In 1816 the valley of Chamonix presented an even more arresting spectacle than it does today. From the middle of the sixteenth century until 1820, its glaciers grew steadily – thereafter climatic changes slowly decreased their mass – so that the Shelleys saw them both rising higher and descending further towards the neighbouring forests and villages than at present, winding sinuously beneath the high peaks like rivers of ice. In some contemporary descriptions the valley appears as distinctly hostile and menacing, qualities which MWS turned to effect in *Frankenstein* (1818) by setting the first interview between Victor Frankenstein and the creature to which he has given life on the glacier known as the *Mer de Glace*.

Mont Blanc and its environs, the most dramatic mountainscape in western Europe, were fast becoming the site par excellence in which orthodox religious convictions could confront that species of the sublime which was held to affirm faith through wonder and awe at the transcendent power of the Deity as revealed in the most majestic of His works. Resisting the expected and conventional response, PBS made a characteristically provocative gesture when he described himself (in Greek) as an atheist (and also as a republican and lover of mankind) in various visitors' albums in and near Chamonix (G. de Beer, *KSMB* 9 (1958), pp. 1–15). Climbers had reached the summit of Mont Blanc itself in 1786 and the ascent had been accomplished several times since by naturalist-mountaineers. The perspectives opened up by contemporary geology and the study of comparative religion (see the extract from *1817*: p. 595) suggested new lines of enquiry and new modes of imagining the scene, while avoiding any recourse to final causes.

In the poem PBS also evidently intended a specific riposte to the psalmodic enthusiasm of Coleridge's 'Hymn before Sun-Rise, in the Vale of Chamouni' (1802). As against such ecstatic affirmations of immanent divinity as Coleridge's, Shelley's 'Mont Blanc' maintains a tone of sceptical uncertainty; its rhetorical modes are interrogation, speculation, hypothesis. The observer-poet's mixed horror and elation combine with the steady gaze of sceptical rationalism to prompt doubts as to the nature of knowledge itself. The result is a bleak and unsettling lyricism which yet carries a sense of exhilarated wonder.

Revealing commentary is provided in: *Chernaik*; Cian Duffy, *Shelley and the Revolutionary Sublime* (Cambridge: Cambridge University Press, 2005); William Keach, *Shelley's Style* (New York and London: Methuen, 1984); Nigel Leask, 'Mont Blanc's Mysterious Voice: Shelley and Huttonian Earth Science', in *The Third Culture: Literature and Science*, ed. Elinor Shaffer (Berlin and New York: De Gruyter, 1998); Angela Leighton, *Shelley and the Sublime* (Oxford: Oxford University Press, 1984); Michael O'Neill, *The Human Mind's Imaginings* (Oxford: Clarendon Press, 1989); and Earl Wasserman, *Shelley: A Critical Reading* (Baltimore and London: Johns Hopkins University Press, 1971).

Subtitle *Chamouni*: Both the draft title (*BSM* XI) and that of Version B indicate that PBS originally fixed the poem's viewpoint at a specific location, where 'he lingered on the Bridge of Arve' (MWS's 'Note on the Poems of 1816' in *1839*), i.e. Pont Pélissier between the village of Servoz and the entrance to the valley of Chamonix proper. See the extract from *1817* (p. 595). As the poem proceeds, it develops its perspective to include sights that he observed both before and after this overwhelming initial impression.

1–11 The natural scene is taken as an emblem of the human mind, which perceives the physical universe as a vast stream of sensations while mingling with them thoughts from its own concealed source.

15 *awful*: Dreadful; inspiring mingled fear and awe.

16 *Power*: The might of the rushing torrent suggests the presence of a divinity (*OED* Power 5.II.7), whose nature is absolute force and strength, enthroned on the summit of Mont Blanc, and which the poet cannot perceive directly. The analogy with the God who speaks from within a cloud on Mount Sinai to Moses (Exodus 24:15–18) is developed with radical revisions throughout the poem.

27–9 When read along with the draft and with the longer version of these lines in Version B, ll. 27–31, the sense appears to be that in the momentary stillness of wind, river and trees a peculiar impression is created of the primeval and permanent nature of the scene.

27 *unsculptured image*: Shaped by natural forces rather than by a human sculptor. The lines recall the effect of an actual waterfall on the rock below it which PBS observed on the route to Chamonix. See the extract from *1817* (p. 595).

34–40 The dimensions and dramatic perspectives of the place overwhelm the mind, inducing an imaginative vision ('phantasy') of itself as the very ravine that it perceives. See the extract from *1817* (p. 595).

41–8 These difficult lines represent the mind's efforts to make an adequate rational and imaginative grasp of the tremendous spectacle of the ravine, which continues to be addressed directly as 'thee' and 'thou', as it has been since l. 12. In ll. 45–6, 'shadows' and 'Ghosts' are in apposition.

44 *the witch Poesy*: Dragons, demons and witches (like the Witch of the Alps in Byron's *Manfred* (1817), II.ii) were among the fabulous beings long imagined as inhabiting these and other remote Alpine regions. A local legend accounted for the current condition of the once verdant valley of Chamonix as the result of a curse by a witch who, disguised as a poor old woman, had been refused bed and board by the inhabitants (F. Bidaut and J. Gendrault, *La Mer de Glace et le Montenvers: une légende, une histoire, un site* (Servoz: Edimontagne, 1997), pp. 11–12).

49 *remoter*: Imperceptible by the senses.

53 *unfurled*: Both the (opposing) senses 'drawn aside' and 'spread out' are possible.

59 *viewless*: Invisible.

63–6 Contemporary observers frequently noted that the glaciers of Chamonix resembled bodies of water agitated by the wind whose peaks and waves had suddenly been frozen. See the extract from *1817* (p. 595).

69 *tracts*: Traces, follows.

72 *Earthquake-daemon*: PBS imagines the work of gnome-like subterranean beings who cause earthquakes in 'Letter to Maria Gisborne', ll. 58–65 (p. 439).

76–9 This passage has occasioned much commentary, the meaning of l. 79 being particularly contested. PBS's draft and Version B (l. 89) read: 'In such a faith with Nature reconciled.' The alteration to 'But for such faith' (the phrase is heavily cancelled in the draft) in the *1817* text appears to carry the sense that the wild spectacle presented by Mont Blanc and its surroundings teaches two possible lessons: (1) doubt, adopted with appropriate dread and awe, regarding the doctrines of a divinely created and providentially directed nature; (2) religious conviction so calm and untroubled that it brings the believer as close as such faith can do to reconciliation with a natural order whose cause is evidently both remote from human concerns and inaccessible to thought – a reconciliation that might be complete were it not for such lingering faith.

81 *codes*: The word can denote both a system of secular law and a body of religious prescription.

84–95 The passage appears to be inspired by the opening lines of Lucretius, *De Rerum Natura* (On the Nature of Things; I.1–20), which include the phrase *daedala tellus* ('daedal earth', l. 86) = 'earth the intricate artificer', though the sense here has usually been understood passively to mean 'intricately fashioned earth'.

100 *adverting*: Observant, attentive.

105 *distinct with*: Adorned or decorated with.

120 *And their place is not known*: The exact phrase occurs in Nahum 3:17 apropos of the transience of earthly power, and closely resembles one in Psalm 103:15–16 (which served for morning prayer in the Anglican Psalter) on the brevity of human life.

120–23 Referring to the source of the river Arveiron, which flowed out of a cavern in a glacier – a favourite subject for contemporary prints. See the extract from *1817* (p. 595) for PBS's visit to it.

123 *one majestic River*: The Rhône, which flows out of Lake Geneva (into which the Arve flows) to the Mediterranean.

Dedication
before LAON AND CYTHNA

PBS finished composing the twelve cantos of his epic-romance *Laon and Cythna; or, The Revolution of the Golden City: A Vision of the Nineteenth Century. In the Stanza of Spenser* by 23 September 1817 (see headnote to the extract from the Preface to *Laon and Cythna*: p. 854). Between then and mid November he added the Preface as well as this lengthy Dedication to Mary (Wollstonecraft Shelley) – the complete name is cancelled in his fair-copy MS – whom he had married on 30 December of the previous year, two weeks after learning of the suicide of his first wife, Harriet. *Laon and Cythna* was on sale by early December; our text is from *1817 (L&C)*. In March 1817 the Court of Chancery had denied PBS the custody of his two children by Harriet. By late 1817 PBS and MWS had themselves had three children, of whom two were alive: William, born 24 January 1816, and Clara, born 2 September 1817. The Dedication incorporates two autobiographical strains, intellectual and affective, as well as announcing the formation of a literary alliance between PBS and

MWS. In stanza 9 the genesis of *Laon and Cythna* is attributed to love and domestic fulfilment. Compare 'To Harriet *****', PBS's dedication of *Queen Mab* to his then wife, Harriet Westbrook (p. 23). Like the twelve cantos of *Laon and Cythna*, the Dedication is written in the stanza of Spenser's *The Faerie Queene* (1590–96), which comprise eight lines of ten syllables and a concluding line of twelve syllables, rhyming *ababbcbcc*.

Epigraph From George Chapman's play *The Conspiracy of Charles Duke of Byron* (1608), by way of an extract in Charles Lamb's *Specimens of English Dramatic Poets, Who Lived About the Time of Shakespeare* (1808). Chapman's lines evidently epitomized for PBS the ambition and daring necessary to undertake a poem with the high aims of *Laon and Cythna*, as well as recalling the poet he regarded as best qualified for the task, Byron, in whose company he had spent a good part of the preceding summer.

3 *Knight of Faëry*: 'Elfin Knight' (as Redcrosse Knight is styled in Spenser's *Faerie Queene*) was one of Mary's pet-names for PBS and one he used in 1817 as a nom de plume. 'Faëry' is fairyland.

4 *dome*: A stately home, mansion.

9 *beloved name*: MWS was the daughter of the liberal authors William Godwin and Mary Wollstonecraft. See note to l. 38 below.

19–45 PBS's unhappy experiences with both his schoolmasters and fellow schoolboys, especially at Eton (1804–10), contributed to the epiphany and self-dedication to oppose tyranny that are here imagined. Although the precise details cannot be verified, such an experience formed an important element in PBS's conception of the course of his life. He recounts a comparable episode in 'Hymn to Intellectual Beauty', stanzas 5 and 6 (pp. 136–7), and attributes to the Maniac in *Julian and Maddalo*, ll. 380–82 (p. 173), a similar youthful decision to devote himself to 'justice' and 'love'.

38 *forbidden mines of lore*: The radical and progressive authors who challenged received religious and political ideas and who had formed the outlook of the young PBS – among them the Roman poet Lucretius, the French revolutionary theorist Volney, Thomas Paine, Mary Wollstonecraft and William Godwin. See headnote to *Queen Mab* (p. 692).

41 *armour for my soul*: Adapting the injunction to the Christian in Ephesians 6:11–17 to 'put on the whole armour of God', as had Spenser in the 'Letter of the Authors' (to Sir Walter Raleigh) explaining the allegory of the *Faerie Queene* (Longman edition, p. 738).

46–54 Looking back from his union with MWS, which he regards as fulfilling his destiny in love, PBS finds only despair and betrayal in his earlier attachments to women. The lines appear to encode his relations with his cousin Harriet Grove (see 'How eloquent are eyes!': p. 6) and his deceased wife, Harriet Westbrook (see PBS's dedicatory poem before *Queen Mab*, 'To Harriet *****': p. 23).

54 *clog*: A weight that hinders or obstructs.

58–9 *mortal chain / Of Custom*: The sixteen-year-old Mary Godwin declared her love for PBS, a married man, in June 1814 and, against her father's wishes, eloped with him the following month – in defiance of conventional social morality.

60–62 The meaning is clarified when 'breathed' is understood as 'breathed forth'. Those slaves imprisoned in their dungeons by Custom exhale dark clouds of disapproval which MWS's action penetrates like light.

86 *Anarch Custom's reign*: The Greek word *anarchos* signifies 'without a leader'. The sense here is that Custom is not a true ruler but rather a tyrant whose sway is misrule.

88 *Amphion*: In Greek mythology, Amphion, son of Zeus and Antiope, was both poet and the father of music, having been given the lyre by Hermes. He helped build Thebes, legend relating that the stones of the wall around the city moved into place by themselves, in response to the sweet melodies he played.

89–90 While composing *1817 (L&C)* PBS suffered from ill-health, which made him fear for his life and determined him to 'leave some record of myself' in a major poem (*Letters* I, p. 577).

91–2 PBS is hinting at some future literary fame for MWS, who was responsible for the bulk of *1817* and had written *Frankenstein*, which would be published early the following year. Both works were issued anonymously.

99 *vestal fire*: Vesta was the Roman goddess of the hearth in whose temple a perpetual fire, held to guarantee the well-being of the state, was tended by an order of women, the Vestal Virgins, dedicated from youth to the task.

102 *One*: MWS's mother, Mary Wollstonecraft, died on 10 September 1797, eleven days after giving birth to her.

108–9 *thy Sire . . . One voice*: Referring to MWS's father, William Godwin, whom PBS identifies in both the draft and fair-copy MSS as the author of *An Enquiry Concerning Political Justice* (1793), which proposed a theory of rational anarchism based on the principle of human perfectibility.

109–10 Defining Godwin's 'voice' as inspired by the best thinkers and writers of ancient and modern Europe.

115 *low-thoughted*: Petty, mean-spirited.

118–21 PBS is affirming his intention to speak to the present post-revolutionary period when Truth's voice has been temporarily silenced.

121–6 The images in these lines are adapted from Lucretius, *De Rerum Natura* (On the Nature of Things) II.1–5, which praise the retired sage who observes with philosophic calm the vain struggles of the unenlightened as if watching a man weltering on the raging sea (see *Queen Mab*, editorial note to PBS's note [6]: p. 701), and III.1–2 and V.11–12, which liken true wisdom to a light illuminating the darkness of error.

To Constantia

Written between mid 1817 and January 1818 while the Shelley household was living at Marlow; published in the *Oxford University and City Herald* (*OH*) on 31 January 1818, which supplies our text, over the signature 'Pleyel'. The name recalls the novel *Wieland; or, The Transformation* (1798), by the American Charles Brockden Brown (1771–1810), in which the character Henry Pleyel is the lover of Clara Wieland. But it may also have been suggested by the composer Ignaz Pleyel (1757–1831), the founder in 1807 of a piano-manufacturing company. It is generally agreed that 'To Constantia' was inspired by the singing of MWS's stepsister, Claire Clairmont, an accomplished musician, who at Marlow accompanied herself on the piano that PBS and Leigh Hunt acquired at the end of April 1817. The 'Constantia' of the title was PBS's familiar name for Claire (given name 'Clara') as well as alluding to Constantia Dudley, the owner of an exquisite singing voice in another of Brown's novels, *Ormond* (1799); Peacock records PBS's high admiration for her character (*Peacock Works* VIII, p. 77). Brown's fiction was a favourite with the Shelleys, and the exchange of playful nicknames was common in their circle at Marlow, as well as later. On 19 January 1818, Claire transcribed a copy of the poem, very likely the one to be sent to *OH* (*Clairmont Journal*, p. 79), which she and PBS kept secret from MWS. Judith Chernaik recovered the *OH* text and printed it in 1969. See *MYR (Shelley)* V and *Chernaik*, pp. 52–8, 195–7.

'To Constantia' explores the transformative effects on the listener of a woman singing, a theme that PBS also developed in Asia's lyric in *Prometheus Unbound* II.v.72–110 (pp. 238–9) and in 'To Jane' ('The keen stars were twinkling') (p. 589). The highly unusual stanza form of eleven lines of eight, ten or twelve syllables rhyming (*ababcdcedee*) lends a traditional motif of the personal lyric something of the formal breadth and intricacy of a Pindaric ode (see 'Ode to Liberty': p. 427) as well as its rhythmic variety and verbal music.

Neville Rogers, 'Music at Marlow', *KSMB* 5 (1953), pp. 20–25, gives the history of the piano in question. Jean de Palacio's 'Music and Musical Themes in Shelley's Poetry', *MLR* 59 (1964), pp. 345–59, includes a consideration of 'To Constantia'. *Chernaik*, pp. 52–8, offers an acute exegesis, while Paul A. Vatalaro, *Shelley's Music: Fantasy, Authority and the Object Voice* (Burlington, Vt.: Ashgate, 2009), examines PBS's poems on music from a psychoanalytic standpoint.

31–2 If 'moons' is understood as satellites of other planets than the earth and 'sphere' as 'domain', then the sense would be 'beyond the furthest limit of the universe where heavenly bodies wane'. Cp. *1817 (L&C)*, ll. 1344–5: 'Beyond the sun, beyond the stars that wane / On the verge of formless space'.

44 PBS's draft reads: 'Alas that the torn heart can bleed but not forget' (*BSM* III).

Ozymandias

Probably written in late December 1817, perhaps as PBS's contribution to a friendly sonnet-writing competition with the stockbroker and man of letters Horace Smith, who visited the Shelleys in Marlow on the twenty-sixth and twenty-seventh of the month (*MWS Journal* I, p. 188). Leigh Hunt published PBS's sonnet in *The Examiner* for 11 January 1818 over the signature 'Glirastes', which has been plausibly interpreted as a compound of the Latin word for 'dormouse' and the Greek for 'lover'; one of PBS's pet-names for MWS was 'the dormouse'. Horace Smith's poem, which appeared in *The Examiner* for 1 February 1818, reads as follows:

OZYMANDIAS

In Egypt's sandy silence, all alone,
  Stands a gigantic Leg, which far off throws
  The only shadow that the Desart knows:—
  "I am great OZYMANDIAS," saith the stone,
  "The King of Kings; this mighty City shows
  "The wonders of my hand."—The City's gone,—
  Nought but the Leg remaining to disclose
The site of this forgotten Babylon.

We wonder,—and some Hunter may express
Wonder like ours, when thro' the wilderness
  Where London stood, holding the Wolf in chace,
He meets some fragment huge, and stops to guess
  What powerful but unrecorded race
Once dwelt in that annihilated place.

'Ozymandias' is the Greek name for the Egyptian Pharaoh Ramses II (reigned 1279–1213 BC). Whether directly or indirectly, both PBS and Smith will have been acquainted with a description of the huge statue of Ozymandias in the temple he erected at Thebes, first given in the *Library of History* of Diodorus Siculus, a Sicilian-Greek historian of the first century BC. They might also have known that negotiations were in progress to bring to the British Museum the massive bust of Ramses II, part of a larger seated colossus, which had been removed from the temple. The bust, which did not arrive until spring 1818, was put on display in 1820 and is still exhibited in the British Museum. In his long reign Ramses II undertook a grandiose programme of monumental building, of which the temple at Thebes was a spectacular example. It is this vainglorious ostentation as symptom and emblem of monarchical power that provokes the irony of both PBS and Horace Smith.

Widely cited and anthologized, the sonnet is one of the best-known short poems in the English language. The sculpted figure of Ozymandias as PBS imagines it has been regularly invoked in political discourse – appearing, for example, on the front page of *The Times* (London) on 10 April 2003 beneath a photo of the toppling of the statue of Saddam Hussein in Baghdad – while the name 'Ozymandias' has been appropriated in fantasy and science fiction, graphic novels, the lyrics of popular songs and television series.

Our text is from the *Examiner* printing, though some punctuation and capitalization have been adopted from PBS's fair-copy MS (*BSM* III).

4–8 The displeasure and scorn on the sculpted face have outlived both the discerning sculptor who duplicated (and thereby derided) them, and the Pharaoh's heart that nourished them.

Lines Written among the Euganean Hills, October, 1818

Composed October 1818, with at least one later addition (see note to ll. 165–6); published in *1819*, from which the text is taken, apart from ll. 56–112 – which follow a fragment of MWS's transcription for the press (now in the Huntington Library: HM331: see *MYR (Shelley)* III) – and ll. 165–205, which follow a fragment of PBS's MS now in the Beinecke Library at Yale University (Tinker Collection 1897; see *MYR (Shelley)* VIII). In early October 1818, PBS was living at I Cappuccini, a villa at Este about twenty miles south-west of Padua which Byron had rented for the summer but had chosen not to occupy – preferring to remain in Venice, some thirty-five miles to the north-east. PBS's letter to T. L. Peacock of 8 October 1818 (*Letters* II, pp. 41–4) sketches a visual and moral portrait of Venice as well as describing the view from the villa at Este and the nearby Euganean Hills (pronounced with an accent on the third syllable: *Euganèan*), a view also described by MWS in her note on *Julian and Maddalo* in *1839* (*OSA*, pp. 203–4).

PBS's 'Advertisement' to *1819* (dated 20 December 1818) reveals that the poem

> was written after a day's excursion among those lovely mountains which surround what was once the retreat, and where is now the sepulchre, of Petrarch. If anyone is inclined to condemn the insertion of the introductory lines, which image forth the sudden relief of a state of deep despondency by the radiant visions disclosed by the sudden burst of an Italian sunrise in autumn on the highest peak of those delightful mountains, I can only offer as my excuse, that they were not erased at the request of a dear friend [MWS], with whom added years of intercourse only add to my apprehension of its value, and who would have had more right than any one to complain, that she has not been able to extinguish in me the very power of delineating sadness.

PBS's 'Lines' continue a tradition of English verse in which the poet's wide survey of his natural surroundings from a lofty vantage point prompts reflections on history, politics and poetry itself, as well as recommending the ideal of a tranquil and retired life. Sir John Denham's 'Cooper's Hill' (1642) and John Dyer's 'Grongar Hill' (1726) are among the better-known examples. This mode PBS combines with that of the extended lyric of personal crisis as practised by both Coleridge and Wordsworth; his title imitates the specificity of Wordsworth's 'Lines Written a Few Miles above Tintern Abbey, on Revisiting the Banks of the Wye During a Tour, July 13, 1798'. Byron's blending of loco-descriptive and confessional poetry in *Childe Harold's Pilgrimage* (especially Canto IV, 1818) is also a major influence. The image in the 'introductory lines' (1–65) of human existence as a dark and relentless voyage to death cheered only by the occurrence of fertile islands PBS developed from his own dejection, brought on by personal affliction – in particular the death of the one-year-old Clara Shelley on 24 September and the painful events of his life in the England he had left behind the previous March. These and other sources are identified by Donald H. Reiman in *PMLA* 77 (1962), pp. 404–13, in *Poems* II, pp. 428–9, and in *Chernaik*, pp. 80–81. The passage does not invite precise interpretation as autobiography, however; its symbolic idiom is designed both to conceal specific details and to open up a broader range of meaning.

1–2 In *Julian and Maddalo*, ll. 77–9, PBS evokes the view from Venice of 'Those famous Euganean hills, which bear / As seen from Lido through the harbour piles / The likeness of a clump of peaked isles' (p. 166).

10 *Big with*: Heavily pregnant with.

13 *Riving*: Ripping apart.

18 *Weltering*: Tumbling, as if tossed by waves.

27–8 *Poems* II compares the series of rhetorical questions in Pope's 'Elegy to the Memory of an Unfortunate Lady' (1717), ll. 55–62. See also note to l. 36 below.

34 *wreak*: Cause (harm or injury).

36 *Senseless*: Unable to perceive or feel. *Poems* II compares Pope, 'Elegy to the Memory of an Unfortunate Lady', l. 33: 'Cold is that breast which warm'd the world before.'

45–65 The passage has been interpreted both as allegorized autobiography and as generalized image of human woe. *Chernaik*, pp. 80–81, detects a debt to the celebrated choral ode on the calamities of existence in Sophocles' *Oedipus at Colonus* (ll. 1239–44), in which man is likened to a shore perpetually beaten by winter tempests from the north. See also references at the end of the headnote above.

54 *sea-mews*: Seagulls.

59 *pomp*: Ostentatious victory celebration.

71 *paean*: Song of praise, originally a hymn to Apollo the sun god, patron of medicine and prophecy.

90–91 On 8 October 1818, PBS wrote to Peacock from Este: 'We see just before [us] the wide flat plains of Lombardy, in which we see the sun & moon rise and set, & the evening star, & all the golden magnificence of autumnal clouds' (*Letters* II, p. 43). Lombardy is the region of northern Italy west of the Veneto.

97 *Amphitrite*: In Greek myth Amphitrite, queen of the sea, was the daughter of Oceanus (her 'sire', l. 98) and wife of Poseidon, god of the sea.

111–14 The spectacle of Venice at sunrise suggests a comparison with ancient sacrificial altars from which flames rose as they did at Delphi (and other shrines) where the prophecies of Apollo were delivered.

115–20 Venice, known as 'Queen of the Adriatic', will again be overwhelmed by the sea, the original source of her wealth and power.

121–8 Formerly a republic, Venice had been taken by Napoleon in 1797, ceded to Austria in 1798, retaken by France in 1806, and restored to Austria by the Congress of Vienna after Napoleon's final defeat at Waterloo in 1815. PBS maintains that when Venice has been reclaimed by the ocean it will be less devastated than it is at present under Austrian tyranny.

123 *the slave of slaves*: Both Austria and the powers that granted her dominion over Venice are morally enslaved by the exercise of tyranny.

139 *starlight*: Contemporary form of 'starlit'.

140 *masque of death*: A symbolic drama imagined as enacted by the dead, perhaps one resembling a kind of procession in which the participants dressed as resurrected corpses and paraded through the streets as reminders of mortality.

142–9 On 8 October 1818, PBS wrote to Peacock: 'I had no conception of the excess to which avarice, cowardice, superstition, ignorance, passionless lust, & all the inexpressible brutalities which degrade human nature could be carried, until I had lived a few days among the Venetians' (*Letters* II, p. 43).

152 *Celtic Anarch*: Austrian tyrant. 'Celtic' is here used in the Classical sense to indicate a barbarian northern people (see also l. 223); while 'Anarch', from the Greek 'without a leader', designates an oppressor who lacks any genuine title to rule.

165–6 PBS's MS of ll. 167–205 (see headnote) instructs the publisher to insert these lines after 'From thy dust shall nations spring / With more kindly blossoming'. The MS version alters the address as printed in *1819* from second-person plural (referring to the 'hundred cities' of l. 154, which are addressed as 'ye' in l. 163) to the second-person singular, indicating Venice. The plural 'your' seems to make better sense in the context, and in the MS PBS may be quoting from memory or from an earlier version of the poem than the one he sent to be printed. But it is also possible, though he does not say so specifically, that he wished to alter 'your' to 'thy' and 'new' to 'shall' – as Donald H. Reiman argues in *MYR (Shelley)* VIII, p. 188. *Norton 2002* cites in support of 'thy' and 'shall' PBS's corrections in a privately owned copy of *1819*.

174–7 *Swan . . . dreams*: Byron, then England's (Albion's) best-known poet, who had taken up residence in Venice following his departure from England in the wake of scandals surrounding his personal life.

178–83 *Ocean . . . terror*: PBS considered that the apostrophe to Ocean at the close of Byron's *Childe Harold's Pilgrimage*, Canto IV (1818), stanzas 179–84, proved his greatness as a poet despite the desperate pessimism of the rest of the poem (*Letters* II, pp. 57–8).

184 Alluding to the 'rich stream' of poetry flowing eternally from Mount Helicon in ancient Greece in Thomas Gray's 'The Progress of Poesy' (1757), stanza I.i.

194–5 The river Scamander (Karamenderes in modern Turkey) in the Trojan plain is the scene of many battles in Homer's *Iliad*.

197 *Avon*: The river from which the birthplace of Shakespeare, Stratford-upon-Avon, takes its name.

200–203 The Italian Renaissance poet and scholar Francesco Petrarca (1304–74) lived the final years of his life in the town of Arquà in the Euganean Hills and is buried there. For Petrarch as love poet, see *A Defence of Poetry* (p. 651).

218–19 The Italian farmer labours for the benefit of the Austrian occupier. See *Letters* II, p. 43.

228 *foizon*: (Usually spelled 'foison') abundant harvest.

238–48 PBS borrows from both *Paradise Lost* II.648–870, where Satan and Sin are figured as father and mother; and from Coleridge, *The Rime of the Ancient Mariner* (1798), ll. 191–4 in the 1805 version, where 'Death' and 'Life-in-Death' throw dice for the soul of the mariner. Ezzelin is Ezzelino da Romano (1194–1259), a brutal tyrant who ruled Padua and much of its environs, until he was deposed in a bloody revolt. The river Po flows across northern Italy from the Alps and into the Adriatic, near Venice.

256–7 The University of Padua, founded in 1222, is one of the oldest in Europe.

258 *meteor*: In PBS's day, the term was applied to a variety of luminous atmospheric phenomena, from will-o'-the-wisps to 'falling stars'.

269–79 *Poems* II compares Mary Wollstonecraft's account of a forest fire near Oslo in her *Letters Written . . . in Sweden, Norway, and Denmark* (1796), Letter 15: 'Fires of this kind are occasioned by the wind suddenly rising when the farmers are burning roots of trees, stalks of beans, &c. with which they manure the ground. The devastation must, indeed, be terrible, when this, literally speaking, wild fire, runs along the forest, flying from top to top, and crackling amongst the branches.'

271 *brakes*: Thickets, undergrowth.

289 *an air-dissolved star*: Whose light is dispersed in the atmosphere like 'fragrance' (l. 290).

306 *olive-sandalled Apennine*: The Apennine Mountains run down the centre of the Italian peninsula with olive groves at their feet.

323 *that one star*: The planet Venus appearing as evening star (Hesperus).

335–73 PBS imagines a similar island paradise in *Epipsychidion*, ll. 407–590 (pp. 485–90).

362–9 The meaning of these lines has been much discussed and the punctuation variously altered: see *Locock* I, p. 592; *Poems* II, p. 442; *Major Works*, p. 738. *1819*'s punctuation, retained here, requires the verb 'supplies' (l. 364) to be understood as repeated before 'All things' (l. 368).

JULIAN AND MADDALO

PBS drew many of the details for this poem (hereafter *JM*) from his visit to Byron in Venice on 23–4 August 1818; composition began in September–October and continued the following year. Our text of the poem is taken from the fair copy which PBS sent to Leigh Hunt on 15 August 1819, now in the Pierpont Morgan Library (MS MA 974: see *MYR (Shelley)* VIII). PBS notes that this 'was composed at Este last year' and asks Hunt to have it published anonymously (*Letters* II, p. 108). But Hunt did not do so and it remained unpublished until *1824*, which is the sole authority for the preface and epigraph. MWS dates this text 'Rome, May 1819' and says that it had 'received the author's ultimate corrections' (*1824*, p. vii) but she was uncertain about the composition date, amending it to 1820 in *1839* before deciding on 1818 in *1840*.

Using the Socratic device of dialogue, *JM* reflects on a number of philosophical, political and personal issues through 'a conversation' between the two interlocutors named in the title. When PBS sent the poem to Hunt in August 1819, he assured him that 'two of the characters you will recognise' (*Letters* II, p. 108) and most commentators accept that Julian and Maddalo are fictional versions of PBS and Byron; indeed, PBS's cousin Thomas Medwin records Byron saying of Maddalo that PBS 'does not make me cut a good figure' (*Medwin's Conversations of Lord Byron*, ed. Ernest J. Lovell, Jnr (Princeton, NJ: Princeton University Press, 1966), p. 119).

Two issues loomed large in PBS's relationship with Byron in August 1818. The first, and the main reason for PBS's visit to Byron in Venice, was the ongoing discussion about the custody of Allegra, Byron's illegitimate daughter with Claire Clairmont, and (presumably) the original of Maddalo's 'child', introduced in ll. 143–50. Second was PBS's disappointment with Byron's much-anticipated *Childe Harold's Pilgrimage: Canto the Fourth* (1818): the poem is pessimistic about the possibilities of human improvement and PBS felt that this would damage support for political reform. In a letter to T. L. Peacock of 17 or 18 December 1818, PBS says of *Childe Harold*, IV Canto, that the 'spirit in which it is written is, if insane, the most wicked & mischievous insanity that ever was given forth. It is a kind of obstinate & self-willed folly in which he [i.e. Byron] hardens himself. I remonstrated with him in vain on the tone of mind from which such a view of things alone arises' (*Letters* II, p. 58). To a certain extent, *JM* reprises this 'remonstrance', with the idealistic Julian attempting to convince the fatalistic Maddalo that human nature and society can be perfected. But the poem narrates – as its subtitle suggests – a conversation rather than an argument won, and PBS is careful to maintain critical distance from both Julian's and Maddalo's positions, each exposing the strengths and limitations of the other's arguments.

Of the Maniac whom Julian and Maddalo visit in the latter part of the poem PBS wrote to Hunt that he is 'also in some degree a painting from nature, but, with respect to time and place, ideal [i.e. imaginary]' (*Letters* II, p. 108). Commentators have variously interpreted the Maniac as a reflection of PBS's guilt over the collapse of his marriage to Harriet Westbrook, or of Byron's guilt over the failure of his marriage to Annabella Milbanke and his complex relationship with his half-sister Augusta. Comparisons have also been drawn with the fate of the sixteenth-century Italian poet Torquato Tasso, who was imprisoned and driven insane after attempting to pursue a relationship with Leonora d'Este, the daughter of his patron. Byron had written a 'Lament of Tasso' in 1817 and, in a letter of 20 April 1818, PBS told Peacock that he meant to devote 'this summer & indeed the next year' to 'the composition of a tragedy on the subject of Tasso's madness, which I find upon inspection is, if properly treated, admirably dramatic & poetical' (*Letters* II, p. 8; only one draft, 'Scene' and a 'Song', survive of this project). *JM* may be compared with PBS's other, broadly contemporary engagement with Venice and Byron in 'Lines Written among the Euganean Hills, October, 1818' (p. 153).

JM is in iambic pentameter couplets, and PBS observed to Hunt that he had employed 'a certain familiar style of language to express the actual way in which people talk with each other whom education and a certain refinement of sentiment have placed above the use of vulgar idioms' (*Letters* II, p. 108). Commentators have noted stylistic similarities with Leigh Hunt's *The Story of Rimini* (1816) and John Keats's *Endymion* (1818), both of which also employ iambic pentameter couplets as part of an urbane and cultured style.

Influential biographical readings of the poem include William Brewer, *The Shelley-Byron Conversation* (Gainesville: University Press of Florida, 1994), pp. 39–56, and Charles E. Robinson, *Shelley and Byron: The Snake and Eagle Wreathed in Fight* (Baltimore: Johns Hopkins University Press, 1976), pp. 73–106. For critical readings, see: Kelvin Everest, 'Shelley's Doubles: An

Approach to *Julian and Maddalo*', in Kelvin Everest (ed.), *Shelley Revalued* (Leicester: Leicester University Press, 1983), pp. 63–88; Nick Johnston, 'Shelley, Julian and the Narratives of *Julian and Maddalo*', *KSR* 14 (2000), pp. 34–41; Geoffrey Matthews, '*Julian and Maddalo*: The Draft and the Meaning', *Studia Neophilologica* 35 (1963), pp. 57–84; and Vincent Newey, 'The Shelleyan Psycho-Drama: *Julian and Maddalo*', in Miriam Allott (ed.), *Essays on Shelley* (Totawa, NJ: Barnes & Noble, 1982), pp. 71–104.

Epigraph Excerpted from PBS's own (partial) translation of Virgil, *Eclogues* X.29–30, made in June 1818. The words are spoken by Pan in an attempt to correct the excessive grief of Gallus, Virgil's friend and patron, at the loss of his would-be lover, Lycoris.

Preface *Count Maddalo*: The two seventeenth-century Italian biographies of Torquato Tasso (1544–95) which PBS read in spring 1818 in preparation for his drama on the life of the poet identify a Count Maddalo Fucci as responsible for betraying the secret of Tasso's love for Leonora d'Este, and a 'Count Maddalo' features in PBS's draft scene for the play (see *Poems* II, pp. 365–7).

p. 163 *capable, if he would direct*: In 1816, PBS had written to Byron to urge him to make his work 'a fountain from which the thoughts of other men shall draw strength and beauty' (*Letters* I, p. 507).

his degraded country: The reference is both to Italy, 'degraded' by Austrian occupation (see note to ll. 121–8 of 'Lines Written among the Euganean Hills': p. 727), and, implicitly, to contemporary England.

But it is . . . human life: Cp. PBS's description of Byron in his letter to Peacock of 17 or 18 December 1818, as 'heartily & deeply discontented with himself, & contemplating in the distorted mirror of his own thoughts, the nature & the destiny of man, what can he behold but objects of contempt & despair?' (*Letters* II, p. 58).

concentred: Self-focused.

1–3 *I rode . . . Venice*: Cp. PBS's letter to MWS of 23 August 1818 in which he describes the day's events: '[Byron] took me in his gondola . . . across the laguna to a long sandy island which defends Venise [*sic*] from the Adriatic. When we disembarked, we found his horses waiting for us, & we rode along the sands of the sea talking' (*Letters* II, p. 36).

2–3 *the bank of land . . .Venice*: The Lido di Venezia, which shields Venice from the Adriatic Sea.

36–9 *Our talk . . . extinguish*: Our conversation became more serious, as conversation often does when we try and fail to dismiss sobering thoughts with witty, self-ironic chatter.

40 *so poets tell*: As Milton did in *Paradise Lost* II.555–61; the phrase introduces ll. 41–5 here.

46 *descanted*: Discussed at length.

51 *struck . . . blind*: Cp. PBS's account of Coleridge in 'Letter to Maria Gisborne', ll. 202–8 (pp. 442–3), and Byron's 'Lament of Tasso' (1817), ll. 1–2.

67 *hoar*: Grey or white with age; here implying snow-capped.

74 *rent*: Torn gap.

77–9 PBS develops the island-mountain simile in more detail in his 'Lines Written among the Euganean Hills, October, 1818' (p. 153).

88 *that funereal bark*: Cp. PBS's description of gondolas in his letter to Peacock of 8 October 1818: 'the gondolas themselves are things of a most romantic & picturesque appearance; I can only compare them to moths of which a coffin might have been the chrysalis. They are hung with black, & painted black, & carpeted with grey' (*Letters* II, p. 42).

111 *vespers*: Evening prayers.

115–18 *You were ever . . . Providence*: Maddalo's quip might recall an incident in July 1816, when PBS and Byron ran into difficulties during a sailing trip on Lake Geneva and their boat appeared near sinking. PBS could not swim; Byron was an excellent swimmer (see *Letters* I, p. 483). The phrase 'A wolf for the meek lambs' alludes to John 10:11–12, in which Christ contrasts the good shepherd who gives his life for his sheep and the hireling who abandons them to the wolf.

143–55 Biographical readings usually associate Maddalo's child with Allegra, Byron's illegitimate daughter with Claire Clairmont. Claire had sent the fifteen-month-old Allegra to Byron in Venice in April 1818, believing that he could better provide for her. Hence PBS had not seen Allegra for four months when he arrived in Venice in August 1818. PBS describes Allegra's 'deep blue eyes', her 'seriousness' and 'vivacity' in a letter of 15 August 1821 (*Letters* II, p. 334).

144 *toy*: Plaything, companion in play.

162 *old saws*: Proverbial sayings.

163 *never own*: Never acknowledge.

164 *teachless*: Incapable of being taught; here meaning 'free'.

170–76 *it is our will . . . desire*: Cp. 'Ode to Liberty', ll. 241–5: 'He who taught man to vanquish whatsoever / Can be between the cradle and the grave / Crowned him the King of Life. O vain endeavour! / If on his own high will a willing slave, / He has enthroned the oppression and the oppressor' (p. 433); and MWS's 'Note on *Prometheus Unbound*': 'Shelley believed that mankind had only to will that there should be no evil, and there would be none' (*1839* II, p. 133).

175–6 *and . . . desire*: Cp. *Macbeth* I.vii.39–41: 'Art thou afeared / To be the same in thine own act and valour / As thou art in desire?'

188–9 PBS refers to the pre-Christian thought of Classical Greece and Rome.

190–91 *And those . . . religion*: Those whose religion leads them to sympathy with others, or those for whom such sympathy has the force of religion.

204 *"soul of goodness"*: Cp. Shakespeare, *Henry V* IV.i.3–4: 'There is some soul of goodness in things evil / Would men observingly distil it out.'

218 This line is not in *1824*.

238 *peculiar*: Specific, particular.

244 *humourist*: Two senses are possible: someone subject to the humours (i.e. of unstable feelings), or someone with a sense of humour.

252–8 *Poems* II compares a similar act of kindness by Glenarvon, Caroline Lamb's portrait of Byron in her eponymous novel of 1816.

301 *jade*: A worn-out horse.

302–3 PBS describes convicts chained in St Peter's Square in a letter of 6 April 1819 to Peacock from Rome (*Letters* II, p. 93).

320 *What . . . torture us*: Cp. *Prometheus Unbound* II.iv.100–101 (p. 233), in which Asia asks Demogorgon 'who rains down / Evil, the immedicable plague'.

354–7 Nora Crook and Derek Guiton, in *Shelley's Venomed Melody* (Cambridge: Cambridge University Press, 1986), p. 137, suggest that PBS 'refers here to the homeopathic principle [which seeks the cure for an illness or injury in its cause], but warns against a single-minded application of it'.

380–82 *as when . . . nature*: PBS recalls such a youthful crisis in 'Hymn to Intellectual Beauty', ll. 49–62 (p. 136), and in the Dedication before *Laon and Cythna*, ll. 19–36 (p. 148–9).

383 *pent*: Imprisoned.

384–5 In PBS's draft of these lines, the Maniac refers to a 'Laura' at this point, Petrarch (buried in the nearby Euganean Hills) and his unrequited love for Laura of Avignon. *Poems* II observes that John Black's *Life of Tasso*, 2 vols (London: John Murray, 1810), II, p. 242, records that the imprisoned and ailing poet confused 'illusions' of the mind with 'external impressions' and frequently conversed with an imagined 'familiar spirit'.

416–19 *As the slow . . . immortality:* Cp. *Prometheus Unbound* I.13–14: 'And moments aye divided by keen pangs / Till they seemed years' (p. 188).

433 *cearedst*: *1824* reads 'seard'st'. *OED* cites 'cear' as an obsolete form of 'sear' = 'to dry or burn'. *Poems* II, p. 686, emends to 'ceredst', suggesting that PBS's spelling is an alternative for both 'seared' (burned, dried) and 'sered' (embalmed). Cp. l. 614 and note.

438 *imprecate for, on me*: Wish upon me as a curse.

450 Echoing Ecclesiastes 4:1: 'So I returned, and considered all the oppressions that are done under the sun.'

504 *words like embers, every spark*: Cp. 'Ode to the West Wind', ll. 66–7 (p. 400), and *The Triumph of Life*, ll. 206–7, 386–8 (pp. 577, 582–3).

536 *nice*: Refined.

541–2 That is, language that would have been called poetry if it had been metrical. In his letter to Hunt of 15 August 1819, PBS says of the 'style of language' used in *JM* that 'passion exceeding a certain limit touches the boundaries of that which is ideal [i.e. imaginary]. Strong passion expresses itself in metaphor borrowed from objects alike remote or near, and casts over all the shadow of its own greatness' (*Letters* II, p. 108).

561 *make me know myself*: Echoing the famous advice, 'Know Thyself', of the oracle at Delphi. Cp. *Adonais*, ll. 415–16: 'come forth / Fond wretch! and know thyself and him aright' (p. 505); and *The Triumph of Life*, ll. 211–12: 'their lore / Taught them not this—to know themselves' (p. 577).

586–7 Byron studied the Armenian language at a monastery in Venice.

588 *His dog was dead*: Byron kept a sequence of Newfoundland dogs as favoured pets, and elegized the first – Boatswain – in a poem of November 1808.

588–9 *His child . . . woman*: Byron and Claire's daughter Allegra was to die, from malaria or pneumonia, on 20 April 1822, aged five.

595 *lorn*: Forlorn, i.e. 'miserable' or 'abandoned'.

597 The fair copy that PBS sent to Hunt begins direct speech at this point, but this seems incompatible with the reference to 'my departure' in l. 598. Editors have differed as to where direct speech should begin.

608–15 *Child . . . lie*: The distribution of the dialogue in these lines is uncertain. In PBS's fair copy the lines are compressed into the edge of the page, leaving it impossible to discern any intended punctuation. Editors tend to assign the question in l. 608 to Julian and ll. 609–15 to Maddalo's daughter. However, the division between the speakers given here is also possible: that Julian asks an extended question in ll. 608–10, to which Maddalo's daughter replies in ll. 611–15. In PBS's fair copy, 'Yet' in l. 611 replaces a cancelled 'But', which, as *Poems* II observes, 'might enforce a pause and help suggest a change of speaker'.

614 *ceared*: See note to l. 433 above.

Stanzas Written in Dejection—December 1818, near Naples

Composed, as the title indicates, in December 1818, and first published in *1824*. PBS's draft is in the Bodleian Library (*BSM* XV), and there are two autograph fair copies, one in the Pierpont Morgan Library (*MYR (Shelley)* V) and the other in the Bodleian (MS Shelley e. 5: see *BSM* XXI). Our text follows the Bodleian fair copy, evidently the later of the two. The poem was one of a number which PBS gathered together in November 1820 as his 'saddest verses' and planned to publish with *Julian and Maddalo* (*Letters* II, p. 246). The 'dejection' of the title resulted from several converging causes: PBS's poor health, a malicious reference to his personal life (though not by name) in the *Quarterly Review* for May 1818, the death of his daughter Clara that September and the depression of spirits it occasioned in MWS, and the complications surrounding Elena Adelaide, PBS's 'Neapolitan charge' (*Letters* II, p. 211): a child registered as his and MWS's in February 1819 and as having been born the previous December, but whose relationship to them remains unclear (*MWS Journal* I, pp. 249–50; *Bieri* II, pp. 103 ff.). The 'Stanzas' take the form of modified Spenserian stanzas, and commentators have noted the influence of Wordsworth's 'Ode: Intimations of Immortality' (1807) and Coleridge's 'Dejection: An Ode' (1802). *Chernaik*, pp. 74–80, offers a close and informative reading.

1–4 In a letter of 23–4 January 1819, PBS wrote to T. L. Peacock of the view from Pompeii, just south of Naples, which he and MWS had visited on 22 December: 'Above & between the multitudinous shafts of the [?sunshiny] columns, was seen the blue sea reflecting the purple heaven of noon above it, & supporting as it were on its line the dark lofty mountains of Sorrento, of a blue inexpressibly deep, & tinged towards their summits with streaks of new-fallen snow' (*Letters* II, p. 73).

10–11 In a letter of 17 or 18 December 1818, PBS described for Peacock an excursion by boat from Naples: 'there was not a cloud in the sky nor a wave upon the sea which was so translucent that you could see the hollow caverns clothed with the glaucous sea-moss, & the leaves & branches of those delicate weeds that pave the unequal bottom of the water' (*Letters* II, p. 61).

10 *untrampled*: Never having been trod upon, and so intact, undamaged.

21–3 Various candidates for this 'sage' have been proposed, including Socrates and Marcus Aurelius, but PBS may not have had a specific individual in mind.

23 *inward glory crowned*: The phrase recalls the characterization of regenerated man in *Prometheus Unbound* III.iv.196–7, who is 'King / Over himself' (p. 254), and 'Sonnet: Political Greatness', ll. 10–13: 'Man, who man would be, / Must rule the empire of himself; in it / Must be supreme, establishing his throne / On vanquished will' (p. 470).

The Two Spirits—An Allegory

First published in *1824*. Our copy-text is PBS's draft in the Bodleian Library (MS Shelley adds. e. 12: see *BSM* XVIII), the only authoritative source. It appears to date from late 1818, although in *1839* MWS grouped the poem with those written in 1820. The draft, which never reached finished form, is rough and not always resolved, so that more editorial intervention than usual has been necessary, including conjectural readings in some lines. At the head of the draft PBS has written 'The good die first', the first words of a reflection from Wordsworth's *The Excursion* (1814), I.500–502, which he had quoted in the Preface to *Alastor* (p. 113). Beneath it are the cancelled lines 'Two genii [i.e. spirits] stood before me in a dream / Seest thou not the shades of even'. The poem's title invites interpretation – without pre-empting it – of the spirits' dialogue on freedom and constraint, boldness and caution, and the transforming power of love.

15 *meteors*: The term could signify any luminous atmospheric body or appearance.

37 *leagued*: *BSM* XVIII reads PBS's difficult draft as 'languid', as do *1824*, *Chernaik* and most modern editors. The sense of 'leagued' would be, as *Poems* II suggests, that the 'storm' is composed of various destructive powers conjoined, as in ll. 17–24.

42 *death dews*: Noxious vapour (miasma) rising from swampy ground ('the morass') was regarded as carrying disease.

Sonnet ('Lift not the painted veil')

In *1839* MWS dated this sonnet 1818, but later editors have proposed a date of composition between the middle of that year and spring 1820. There is a draft in PBS's hand in the Bodleian Library (*BSM* XVIII) and an autograph fair copy in the Pierpont Morgan Library (MS MA 406: see *MYR (Shelley)* V). We follow *Poems* II in taking as copy-text the printing in *1839*, as this seems likely to embody PBS's latest revisions. Substantive verbal differences between *1839* and PBS's fair copy and *1824* (where the poem was first published) are recorded in the notes below. *Prometheus Unbound* III.iv.190–92 (p. 254) employs the imagery and language of lines 1–4 of this poem for a contrary purpose, to imagine the mind's liberation from deceptive illusion. The traditional order of the Petrarchan or Italian sonnet into octave followed by sestet is here reversed, and an unorthodox rhyme scheme adopted.

6 *1824* reads: 'The shadows, which the world calls substance, there.' *sightless*: 'Impenetrable by vision' (*OED*).
7–14 Cp. the fate of the 'one frail Form' in *Adonais*, ll. 271–306 (p. 501).
13 PBS's fair copy reads: 'Cast on this gloomy world—a thing which strove'.
14 *the Preacher*: The preacher of Ecclesiastes, who declares that 'all is vanity' but who 'sought to find out acceptable words: and that which was written was upright, even words of truth' (12:8–10).

PROMETHEUS UNBOUND

PBS would have been familiar from his school days with Aeschylus' drama *Prometheus Bound* and the outline of its lost sequel, the seminal retelling of the myth of the Titan Prometheus whom Zeus (PBS uses the Roman name, Jupiter) punished for bringing to earth fire stolen from heaven (out of pity for the lot of humanity) by chaining him to a rock in the Caucasus where each day an eagle devoured his liver which was continually renewed. On his release, Prometheus revealed to Jupiter that an oracle had foretold that, were he to marry the nymph Thetis, a son born of their union would be greater than his father and dethrone him. See also note to first stage direction and PBS's Note [17] to *Queen Mab* VIII.211–12 (p. 98) In a letter of 1823, MWS suggested that PBS had 'the idea' of writing his own version of the myth after passing through Les Échelles, in the French Alps, on their journey to Italy in March 1818 (*MWS Letters* II, p. 357); for an account by PBS of these mountains, see his entry in MWS's journal for 26 March 1818 (*MWS Journal* I, p. 200).

PBS probably began *Prometheus Unbound* (*PU*) in late summer or early autumn 1818 and composition continued, with varying intensity, until December 1819. *PU* was published in *1820*, in August of that year. After PBS received a copy, he wrote to Charles Ollier on 10 November that it was 'certainly most beautifully printed' but also 'regretted that the errors of the press are so numerous' (*Letters* II, p. 246). Our text is based on *1839*, which MWS edited using 'a list of errata prepared by Shelley himself' (II, p. 140). We have taken some readings and presentational features from *1820* and from PBS's fair copy in the Bodleian Library (see *BSM* XI) when these seemed preferable. For a detailed account of the compositional and textual history of *PU*, see *Poems* II, pp. 456–65, and the commentary in *BSM* XI, pp. lxii–lxxv.

PU is a work of extraordinary scope and ambition which embodies many of the fundamental concerns of PBS's thought (for assessments of its complexity by PBS himself and by MWS, see *Letters* II, p. 246, and *1839* II, p. 135). It is at once a narrative of political change, of geophysical transformation, and of the liberation of the human mind from various forms of intellectual and ideological enslavement, which PBS identifies as both cause and consequence of any successful reformation of the structures of power. Two characters whom PBS introduces to the story of Prometheus are central to these transitions. The first is Asia, Prometheus' beloved, one of the Oceanides, daughters of the Titan Oceanus/Ocean (the presiding divinity of the ocean and rivers) and his sister Tethys; her role in *PU* suggests that love is the central principle of the moral world and the only true agent of lasting personal and political reform. The second is Demogorgon, a shadowy figure whom MWS in her note on *PU* in *1839* describes as 'the Primal Power of the world' (II, p. 134). Often understood by commentators as a personification of the natural laws governing the universe, Demogorgon's presence in *PU* suggests that it is only through recognizing and abiding by those laws that humanity can find genuine and lasting freedom. As *Poems* II, p. 468, observes, Demogorgon is also 'the one figure in whom most levels of [*PU*] coincide': in the terms of the Classical myth, he represents the mysterious child destined to overthrow Jupiter; but he also stands for the physical energies of the earth, and the irresistible historical impetus towards political liberty. For further commentary, see note to II.iv.1–7.

PU also represents an impressive and innovative advance in PBS's poetic technique. Subtitled 'A Lyrical Drama' and described by PBS as having 'characters & mechanism of a kind yet unattempted' (*Letters* II, p. 94), *PU* blends blank-verse narrative with lyric and choral elements into a hybrid form which draws upon Classical Greek drama, established English and European genres, and other more contemporary, experimental forms, such as Byron's 'dramatic poem' *Manfred* (1817). For considerations of the ways in which PBS's stylistic innovations in *PU* relate to its thematic concerns, see, for example: Susan Hawk Brisman, '"Unsaying His High Language": The Problem of Voice in *Prometheus Unbound*', *SiR* 16 (1977), pp. 51–86; Kelvin Everest, '"Mechanism of a Kind Yet Unattempted": The Dramatic Action of *Prometheus Unbound*', in P. J. Kitson (ed.), *Coleridge, Keats, and Shelley* (London: Palgrave, 1996), pp. 186–201; Jennifer Wallace, *Shelley and Greece* (Basingstoke: Macmillan, 1997), pp. 147–8; and Timothy Webb, 'The Unascended Heaven: Shelley's Use of Negatives in *Prometheus Unbound*', in Kelvin Everest (ed.), *Shelley Revalued* (Leicester: Leicester University Press, 1983), pp. 37–62.

Critical discussion of *PU* has been extensive, and most monographs on PBS offer an extended analysis. Dedicated studies of note include: Stuart Curran, 'The Political Prometheus', *SiR* 25/3 (1986), pp. 429–55; Carl Grabo, *A Newton Among Poets: Shelley's Use of Science in Prometheus Unbound* (Chapel Hill, NC: University of North Carolina Press, 1968); Richard Isomaki, 'Love as Cause in *Prometheus Unbound*', *Studies in English Literature* 29/4 (1989), pp. 655–73; Geoffrey Matthews, 'A Volcano's Voice in Shelley', *ELH* 24/3 (1957), pp. 191–228; Tilottama Rajan, 'Deconstruction or Reconstruction: Reading Shelley's *Prometheus Unbound*', *SiR* 23/3 (1984), pp. 317–38; Stuart Sperry, 'Necessity and the Role of the Hero in *Prometheus Unbound*', *PMLA* 96/2 (1981), pp. 242–54; and Earl Wasserman, *Shelley's Prometheus Unbound: A Critical Reading* (Baltimore: Johns Hopkins University Press, 1966).

Epigraph 'Do you hear this, Amphiaraus, in your home beneath the earth?' Amphiaraus became an oracular god after Zeus saved his life by having the earth swallow him and hide him from his enemies. The quotation is from *Epigoni*, a lost play by Aeschylus, quoted in Cicero's *Tusculan Disputations*, where it is used to challenge the Stoic doctrine that suffering is of no consequence. In a notebook PBS addresses it to Aeschylus' ghost (*BSM* XV).

PREFACE

p. 184 *Agamemnonian story*: The subject of Aeschylus' *Oresteia* trilogy, which was produced in 458 BC and which dramatizes the myth in which King Agamemnon, his wife Clytemnestra and their son Orestes are trapped in a cycle of murder and vengeance until the intervention of Athena, who settles the matter by submitting it to the decision of public justice.

catastrophe: Denouement, resolution of the plot.

p. 185 *casuistry*: 'The part of Ethics which resolves cases of conscience . . . in which there appears to be a conflict of duties' (*OED*).

Baths of Caracalla: The extensive ruins of public baths, which were opened in AD 217 in the reign of the emperor Caracalla (Marcus Aurelius Antoninus), located south-east of the ancient centre of Rome.

pp. 185–7 *One word . . . unknown*: PBS added the last five paragraphs to the Preface after he read the *Quarterly Review* for April 1819 which attacked his character and poetry in a review of *Laon and Cythna/The Revolt of Islam* (1817–18); among its many criticisms, the periodical questioned the originality of PBS's work, claiming it was a debased imitation of Wordsworth.

p. 187 *Fletcher*: Shakespeare's younger contemporary John Fletcher (1579–1625) is best known for his dramatic collaborations with Sir Francis Beaumont (1584–1616) but wrote plays with several other authors as well as on his own account.

'a passion for reforming the world': In chapter 2 of T. L. Peacock's satire *Nightmare Abbey* (1818), Scythrop Glowry, a character based on PBS, suffers from 'the *passion for reforming the world*' (*Peacock Works*, p. 22). The 'Scotch philosopher' is Robert Forsyth, to whose *Principles of Moral Science* (1805) Peacock attributes the phrase.

For my part . . . Malthus: For Lord Bacon, see note 11 to the extract from the Preface to *Laon and Cythna* (p. 856). William Paley (1743–1805) was a conservative theologian and author of *Principles of Moral and Political Philosophy* (1785) and *Natural Theology* (1802), whose ideas PBS considers and rejects in his *A Refutation of Deism* (1814). Thomas Malthus (1766–1834) was the author of *An Essay on the Principle of Population* (1798); see note 30 to 'From *A Philosophical View of Reform*' (p. 870).

seeds . . . life: Alluding to the Parable of the Sower in Matthew 13:3–9.

ACT I

Stage direction *Indian Caucasus*: The Hindu Kush, a mountain range in central Asia (largely in modern Pakistan and Afghanistan) considered by some in PBS's day to be the birthplace of humanity and of civilization. PBS sets the action of the drama there rather than its traditional location in the Caucasus Mountains in Georgia.

1 *Daemons*: Plato's *Symposium*, which PBS translated, describes daemons as beings intermediate between gods and mortals.

2 *But One*: Prometheus, or perhaps Demogorgon.

7 *hecatombs*: Sacrifices of numerous victims; in ancient Greece, the sacrifice of a hundred oxen.

9–11 The phrase 'eyeless in hate' may refer either to 'me' or 'thou' – appropriately, as Prometheus and Jupiter have become reflections one of the other.

42 *genii*: Beings representing aspects and activities of the natural world.

53–9 Prometheus' mental shift from hatred to pity is the moral condition of the subsequent dramatic action.

59 *recall*: Here meaning both 'remember' and 'revoke'.

61 *spell*: Here and elsewhere in *PU* (e.g. IV.555) meaning 'words with transformative and/or binding effect'.

64–5 *Thou serenest . . . without beams*: In the note to *Queen Mab* I.242–3 (p. 83), PBS explains that beyond the earth's atmosphere sunlight has no rays.

82–3 Colour is produced by the interaction of sunlight with the earth's atmosphere (air); it is not a property of things in themselves.

95–8 Cp. Coleridge, *The Rime of the Ancient Mariner* (1798), ll. 554–63 (1805 version).

99–102 Echoing biblical accounts of the crucifixion of Jesus, e.g. Luke 23:44–6.

121 *frore*: Frozen.

135 *inorganic*: Inanimate; the Spirit of the Earth has no body. Cp. *OED* 2, citing this line: 'Not furnished with or acting by bodily or material organs'.

137 *And love*: And that you love (me).

141–2 *some wheel . . . roll*: In Greek myth, Zeus tortures Ixion, one of the Titans, by binding him to a burning and ever-spinning wheel. Wasserman, *Shelley: A Critical Reading*, pp. 262 ff., suggests that PBS is alluding here to the ecliptic (the apparent annual path of the sun around the earth), which determines the seasons.

150–51 *this tongue . . . die*: See ll. 243–5.

153 *stony veins*: Cp. PBS's letter of July 1816 to Peacock from Chamonix: 'One would think that Mont Blanc was a living being & that the frozen blood forever circulated slowly thro' his stony veins' (*Letters* I, p. 500).

170 *Blue thistles*: PBS and his contemporaries often associate the colour blue with disease and illness.

178 *contagion*: Here indicating transmission of disease, but cp. II.iii.10.

192 *Zoroaster*: Also known as Zarathustra. A Persian sage (Magus) and mystic known to PBS and his contemporaries as the author of a system of belief which viewed existence as a perpetual struggle between the opposed principles of good (Ormuzd) and evil (Ahriman). No source for Zoroaster's encounter with his double has been identified but the Zoroastrian belief in *fravashis*, or guardian spirits, is relevant. See Stuart Curran, *Shelley's Annus Mirabilis* (San Marino, Calif.: Huntington Library, 1975), pp. 68–74.

195–209 The notion of two parallel worlds, material and immaterial, is found in various ancient traditions, Platonic, Neoplatonic and others.

212 *Hades or Typhon*: In Classical myth, Hades was the lord of the underworld; Typhon, a dragon-like monster and one of Prometheus' fellow Titans, was imprisoned by Zeus beneath Mount Etna.

229 *our sweet sister*: Asia: the third Oceanid and Prometheus' beloved.

236 *To stay steps*: To steady [its] steps.

278 *imprecate*: To invoke, or call down upon.

289 In Classical myth, both Hercules and Creusa, the daughter of Creon, were killed by poisoned robes.

292–3 Echoing Milton, *Paradise Lost* I.215–18.

296 *awful*: Inspiring terror and awe.

324–5 *serpent-cinctured wand . . . Mercury*: The messenger of the gods in Classical myth, Mercury is often depicted carrying a caduceus, a short staff with two serpents wrapped around it.

326 *hydra tresses*: The Hydra was a monstrous many-headed serpent.

331 *Jove's tempest-walking hounds*: The Furies (Erinyes): female spirits whom the Greek gods send to punish those guilty of serious crimes. PBS's Furies threaten Prometheus with physical pain (ll. 475–91) and, when this fails, move on to mental torments, showing Prometheus visions of the perversion of the philanthropic teachings of Jesus by institutional Christianity (ll. 546–60), of the failure of the French Revolution (ll. 564–77), and of the corruption and injustice of the world (ll. 618–31).

342 *Son of Maia*: Maia was one of the Pleiades and mother of Hermes/Mercury by Zeus.

345 *the streams of fire and wail*: In Greek myth, Phlegethon (river of fire) and Cocytus (river of lamentation) were two of the traditional five rivers of the underworld. See *Paradise Lost* II.575–86.

346–9 *Geryon . . . hate*: Monsters from Classical myth. Geryon was a three-headed giant slain by Hercules; Medusa was a Gorgon slain by Perseus; the Chimaera, a mythical beast composed of goat, lion and snake, was slain by Bellerophon. Sophocles' Theban plays tell how Oedipus solves the riddle of the monstrous Sphinx before proceeding, unwittingly, to murder his father and marry his mother; his sons subsequently murder each other. So his story exemplifies both 'Unnatural love' and 'unnatural hate'.

387 *thought-executing ministers*: The phrase has been understood as meaning 'those who carry out Jove's thought' and/or 'those who destroy thought'.

398–9 *the Sicilian's . . . o'er his crown*: Dionysius I, tyrant of Syracuse, compelled the courtier Damocles to dine under a sword suspended by a single horse-hair so that he might appreciate the insecurity of rule.

409 *lowers*: i.e. 'lours', 'threatens', presumably by darkening.

450 *Notopoulos*, p. 227, suggests that this idea, which features in various forms in PBS's writings, derives from Thomas Paine's *Rights of Man* (1791): 'It is the faculty of the human mind to become what it contemplates, and to act in unison with its object' (ed. Eric Foner and Henry Collins (Harmondsworth: Penguin Books, 1984), p. 109). See III.iii.49–53 and *A Defence of Poetry* (p. 651).

479 *lidless*: Always open; unsleeping.

492–4 Cp. 'Sonnet: Political Greatness', ll. 10–14 (p. 470).

506–9 Cp. 'Ode to the West Wind', ll. 63–70 (p. 400).

530 *Kingly conclaves*: No doubt to be understood as referring in particular to the Congress of Vienna (1814–15), which was convened to decide the partition and governance of post-Napoleonic Europe, and which PBS and many of his contemporaries regarded as having legitimized reactionary royal authority.

546 *One came forth*: i.e. Jesus Christ.

563 *pillow of thorns*: Recalling the crown of thorns placed on Christ's head in e.g. Matthew 27:29.

567 *a disenchanted nation*: Coleridge, 'France: An Ode' (1798), l. 28, describes France, in the early phase of the Revolution, as a 'disenchanted nation', i.e. freed from the spell of tyranny.

573–7 The lines suggest parallels with recent historical events, such as the Reign of Terror (1793–4), the wars of revolutionary and imperial France (1792–1815), and the restoration of the European monarchies post-Waterloo (1815).

609 *ounces*: Leopards.

619 *ravin*: Prey.

622 *fanes*: Temples.

625–8 Cp. *The Triumph of Life*, ll. 228–31 (p. 577).

631 *they know not what they do*: Echoing the words of Jesus on the cross (e.g. Luke 23:34).

651 *'Truth, liberty, and love!'*: Cp. the French revolutionary slogan: *Liberty, Equality, Fraternity*; see also John 8:32: 'And ye shall know the truth, and the truth shall make you free.'

658 *subtle and fair spirits*: The first four of these immaterial ('subtle') beings represent qualities inherent in general and individual human thought which offer hope for the future of humanity as an antidote to the Furies' counsels of despair. The fifth and sixth spirits exemplify the intimate relation of hope and despair in even the enlightened mind.

765 *That planet-crested Shape*: Love, associated with the planet Venus.

769 *unupbraiding*: Without rebuking or criticizing; one of a number of unusual negative constructions in *PU*; see Webb, 'The Unascended Heaven', in Everest (ed.), *Shelley Revalued*, pp. 37–62.

772–9 PBS is adapting the imagery of Plato, *Symposium* 195.

782 Cp. Revelation 6:8: 'And I looked, and behold a pale horse: and his name that sat on him was Death.'

825 *the Eastern star*: The planet Venus, as the morning star.

830–31 *And haunted . . . waters*: Adapting Shakespeare, *The Tempest* III.ii. 138–40: 'The isle is full of noises, / Sounds, and sweet airs, that give Delight and hurt not.'

ACT II

Scene i

1–9 *Poems* II cites this passage, as well as ll. 27, 35–8, 92 and 107–8 of this scene, as evidence that the action of the poem is to be considered sequential rather than simultaneous.

3 *horny*: An unusual usage: 'semi-opaque like horn' (*OED*); hence (perhaps) 'dull', 'cloudy'.

26–7 The beating of Panthea's wings through the morning air makes music: see ll. 50–52. Aeolus was the mythical keeper of the winds.

43 *erewhile*: i.e. 'Before the sacred Titan's fall' (l. 40).

44 *glaucous*: 'Of dull or pale green colour passing into greyish blue' (*OED*).

62–7 Recalling the Gospel episode, e.g. Matthew 17:1–6, in which Christ is transfigured.

133–41 This complex sequence involves several elements: the almond-tree, which flowers early, heralds the spring. Its blossoms are killed by an icy wind from the north (for the ancient Greeks, Scythia indicated lands to the north of the Black Sea; this is the region in which the action of Aeschylus' *Prometheus Bound* is set). Each fallen almond leaf bears the message '*O, follow, follow!*', just as the hyacinth's petals were imagined as bearing the sorrowful cry 'ai' in memory of Apollo's love for Hyacinth, who had been transformed into the flower after his early death. Apollo was the Greek god of the sun, and patron of poetry, prophecy and medicine. The priestesses of some ancient oracles traditionally wrote their prophecies on leaves.

Scene ii

Stage direction As Geoffrey Matthews notes, in 'A Volcano's Voice in Shelley', the scenery of *PU* II.ii, through which Asia and Panthea journey on their way to the cave of Demogorgon, is based upon the lush volcanic landscapes of Lake Agnano and the Astroni crater near Naples, which PBS visited in the spring of 1819 (see *Letters* II, p. 77). The scene (like much of *PU* II) is also indebted to both ancient and contemporary speculation about volcanic activity, e.g. the account of 'the breathing earth' (ll. 50–56), which combines early nineteenth-century natural philosophy with Classical notions of the inspirational or intoxicating properties of volcanic gases. See also II.iii.1–10.

Fauns: A faun was a rural semi-divinity, half man and half goat.

10 Cp. Shakespeare, *A Midsummer Night's Dream* II.i.14–15: 'I must go seek some dewdrops here, / And hang a pearl in every cowslip's ear.'

70–82 These lines derive from the debate among some contemporary natural philosophers on the question whether flammable hydrogen gas, released from water plants by the sunlight, might be the cause of various luminous atmospheric phenomena ('meteors').

90 Silenus is a satyr (part man, part goat), repository of ancient myth and wisdom and tutor to Dionysus, the god of wine and ecstasy. Here he would be 'thwart' (cross, testy) to find his herd of goats 'undrawn' (unmilked).

Scene iii

Stage direction Asia and Panthea have reached the summit of a volcano, from which gas is being expelled (ll. 3–4); the cave of Demogorgon is located in the depths of the crater beneath them. Many of the details recall PBS's account of his ascent of Vesuvius on 16 December 1818 (*Letters* II, p. 62–3).

4 *the oracular vapour*: The priestess who delivered the responses of the Oracle at Delphi was reputed to draw her inspiration from vapours rising from a chasm.

9–10 In Greek myth, Maenads were the frenzied female followers of Dionysus; their ritual cry was 'Evoe!'. Equivocal figures, they express both transformative energies and the dangers of intoxication, hence the ambivalence of 'The voice' in l. 10, where 'contagion' can be construed in either a positive or a negative sense. Cp. I.178.

28–42 PBS's draft of these lines indicates that he intended them as a response to an attack, in the *Quarterly Review* for May 1818, on his atheism and on the absence of pious awe before mountain landscapes in *History of a Six Weeks' Tour* (1817) and 'Mont Blanc' (p. 140). See Timothy Webb, '"The Avalanche of Ages": Shelley's Defence of Atheism and *Prometheus Unbound*', *KSMB* 35 (1984), pp. 1–39.

70 *stone*: Lodestone; magnetic iron oxide.

79 *one*: Demogorgon is intended, here and in l. 95 ('the Eternal, the Immortal').

97 *snake-like Doom*: Fate, or destiny; 'snake-like' suggests an association with eternity (sometimes represented as a serpent devouring its own tail).

Scene iv

Stage direction Asia and Panthea have reached the cave of Demogorgon, at the bottom of the volcanic crater. As Geoffrey Matthews observes, in 'A Volcano's Voice in Shelley', one current theory held that volcanic eruptions were triggered by the interaction of sea water and molten magma in subterranean caverns. Hence, the entry of the Oceanides to Demogorgon's cave appropriately precipitates a symbolic eruption, and the various accounts of Jupiter's fall in ll. 129, 150 ff. and III.i–ii draw upon that scientific dimension.

1–7 Commentators have found sources for PBS's conception of Demogorgon in T. L. Peacock's *Rhododaphne* (1818), where Demogorgon is named as the supreme earthly power; in Boccaccio's *Genealogia Deorum Gentilium* (1472), which was Peacock's source; and in a range of Classical texts, including Lucan's *Pharsalia*. PBS's description of Demogorgon in these lines recalls Milton's portrait of Death in *Paradise Lost* II.666–70. Carl Grabo suggests that the 'rays of gloom' (l. 3) emitted by Demogorgon might allude to infra-red radiation, which the astronomer William Herschel had discovered in 1800; see also IV.225–30 (*A Newton Among Poets*, p. 47). Paul Foot finds in the name 'Demogorgon' the etymological sense 'people-monster', thereby suggesting that the character is linked in PBS's mind with the (revolutionary) political energies of the crowd (*Red Shelley* (London: Bookmarks, 1984), pp. 193–201 (p. 194)).

32–4 *There was . . . shadow*: Uranus (Heaven) and Gaia (Earth) were the parents of the Titans, including Saturn (Greek 'Kronos', associated with Chronos (Time)).

52 *unseasonable seasons*: Both Classical and Christian traditions regarded the seasons as the consequence of a fall from an original Golden or Edenic age of perpetual spring.

61 In Classical mythology, nepenthe was a drug which caused forgetfulness of sorrow. According to Homer, *Odyssey* X.302–6, moly was the flower which Hermes gave to Odysseus to protect him from the enchanted potion of Circe. Amaranth here is a mythical, unfading flower growing only in Paradise.

77–9 Recalling Christ's walking on the water, e.g. Matthew 14:25–6.

80–84 A difficult passage, of uncertain meaning. The general sense appears to be: 'Sculptors first copied the human body and then created idealized versions of it, inspiring love in the mothers who beheld such idealized forms and hoped that their own children would share such perfection.' Some commentators find a reference to the idea that a child in the womb is influenced by an intense impression on its mother during pregnancy. As *Poems* II, p. 562, observes, 'the subject of *behold, and perish* is presumably the *men* of line 83, but the grammar is dislocated and the sense unclear'.

91 *interlunar*: The period between the old and the new moon. Cp. 'With a Guitar. To Jane', l. 24 (p. 566).

94 *Celt*: Used loosely to indicate a northern European.

101 *immedicable*: Not capable of being healed.

102–3 *Man . . . glorious*: The prerogative of divinity, as in Genesis 1:31, 'And God saw every thing that he had made, and, behold, it was very good', and Satan's address to the Sun in *Paradise Lost* IV.32–4: 'O thou that with surpassing glory crowned, / Look'st from thy sole dominion like the God / Of this new world.'

107 *adamantine*: Unbreakable.

156–9 *See . . . tracery*: The chariot that attends Asia recalls Aphrodite, the goddess of love, one of whose emblems is the seashell. Cp. II.v.20–25, where Asia's emergence from the ocean on a seashell recalls the myth of the birth of Aphrodite.

171 *Atlas*: Traditionally the highest point on earth, Mount Atlas was thought in ancient times to stand in the far west of the known world; it was associated with the Titan Atlas, brother to Prometheus, who was condemned by Zeus to support the heavens on his shoulders for having joined the war against the Olympian gods.

Scene v

2 *respire*: Catch their breath.

7 *it could not*: The cosmic cataclysm that has begun must take its course, keeping even the sun from rising until noon (l. 10).

20 *Nereids*: Sea deities, daughters of Nereus, the sea god.

21 *the clear hyaline*: The glassy sea, as in l. 24.

98–110 Asia's lyric traces, according to a broadly Platonic scheme, a journey from age back to birth and through that portal to the eternal realm peopled by spirits – from which the soul enters the world. Commentators have suggested that PBS may be reversing the account of the soul's progress from eternity to manhood in Wordsworth's 'Ode: Intimations of Immortality' (1807), ll. 58–84. See III. iii.113–14 and note.

ACT III

Scene i

11 *the pendulous air*: Cp. Shakespeare, *King Lear* III.iv.64–5: 'Now, all the plagues that in the pendulous air / Hang fated o'er men's faults light on thy daughters!'

18–19 *Even now . . . fatal child*: Jupiter's child by Thetis who, he assumes, will secure his reign, but whom Prometheus knows will be his undoing. See also note to ll. 33–9 below. Jupiter's words echo *Paradise Lost* V.603–4: 'This day I have begot whom I declare / My only Son.'

25 *Idaean Ganymede*: Ganymede was a young Trojan prince who was abducted by Jupiter from Mount Ida (in what is now north-west Turkey) and became the cup-bearer of the gods.

26 *daedal*: Intricately crafted; from Daedalus, the Greek master craftsman and father of Icarus. Cp. 'Mont Blanc', l. 86 (p. 144).

33–9 *And thou . . . presence*: In Classical myth, Zeus/Jupiter ensures that Thetis, a sea goddess, is married to a mortal after Prometheus reveals that her son will become greater than his father; Thetis marries Peleus, and gives birth to Achilles. Thetis' account of her rape draws on the story of Semele – a mortal woman raped by Jupiter and destroyed by the intensity of his presence. See Ovid, *Metamorphoses* III.259 ff., XI.229–65.

40–41 *Like him . . . poison*: Lucan, *Pharsalia* IX.762–88, recounts how Sabellus was 'dissolved' after being bitten by a seps (a highly poisonous, mythical snake) in the Numidian desert.

48 *Griding*: Cutting or scraping with a grating sound.

51 **Stage direction** *The Car of the* HOUR: The chariot driven by the 'spirit with a dreadful countenance' from II.iv.142–4.

62 *Titanian*: The Titans were imprisoned underground in Tartarus, below Hades, after their defeat by Zeus and his divine allies.

72–3 *a vulture and a snake . . . fight*: PBS introduces similar images of archetypal combat in *Laon and Cythna* (1817), I.vi–xiv, and *Alastor*, ll. 227–32 (p. 119).

Scene ii

Stage direction *Atlantis*: A legendary island in the Atlantic west of Gibraltar in Plato's *Timaeus* and *Critias*; sometimes associated in PBS's work with America.

19 *unstained with blood*: Because naval warfare, piracy and the slave trade will all have ceased to be.

24 *Blue Proteus*: A shape-shifting god of the sea. Cp. III.iii.65.

26–8 P. H. Butter (ed.), *Shelley: Alastor and Other Poems, Prometheus Unbound with Other Poems, Adonais* (London and Glasgow: Collins, 1970), suggests that the complex image likens the moon with a star at its tip to a boat ('bark') guided by an invisible ('sightless') pilot with a star as his crest.

49 *unpastured*: Unfed (with the 'calm' it hungers for).

Scene iii

10 *a Cave*: It is not clear whether this cave is the same as the 'Cavern' which Earth describes and allots to Prometheus in ll. 124–47, although here Prometheus does not mention any adjacent 'temple' (l. 127). Both locations revise Plato's image of the cave as a theatre of deceptive illusion in *Republic* 514–19: instead these caves are privileged places from which Prometheus and Asia will observe the operations of a regenerated, post-revolutionary consciousness.

15 *the mountain's frozen tears*: Stalactites.

22–9 The passage borrows from *King Lear* V.iii.8–19.

42–3 Proserpina/Persephone was snatched away by Pluto/Hades as she gathered flowers in a mountain meadow near Enna in central Sicily (see Ovid, *Metamorphoses* V.385–96). Himera was a Greek town on the north coast of Sicily.

49–56 Adapting the Platonic notion that the intimate experience of beauty transforms the mind, finally rendering it capable of immortal creations. See note to I.450.

64–8 The association of Asia with a curved shell given by Proteus (see note to III.ii.24) links her with the mythical Aphrodite, born on a seashell.

96–9 *to me . . . brimming stream*: Echoing the Song of Solomon 4:5: 'Thy two breasts are like two young roes that are twins, which feed among the lilies.'

113–14 *Death . . . lifted*: Cp. III.iv.190–92, 'Sonnet' ('Lift not the painted veil') (p. 182) and 'Mont Blanc', ll. 53–4 (p. 142).

124 *Cavern*: See note to II.iii.4 and to the stage direction for II.iv.

136 *ivy*: Sacred to Dionysus.

154–5 *Bacchic Nysa . . . Indus*: Dionysus/Bacchus was born in the semi-legendary mountains of Nysa, which some Classical authors locate in India; hence 'beyond' Indus, a river which flows through Tibet, India and Pakistan.

165 Praxiteles (fourth century BC) was one of the foremost sculptors of ancient Athens.

168–70 *there the . . . emblem*: At the Athenian festival of Lampadephoria, young men competed in races while carrying torches in honour of Prometheus' gift of fire to humanity.

168 *emulous*: Both 'competing' and 'desiring to imitate'.

Scene iv

Stage direction In this scene, PBS associates the Spirit of the Earth with electricity and electrical phenomena: many contemporary scientists believed that electricity was the fundamental force animating the physical universe. The Spirit has also been likened to the god Eros, Aphrodite's son.

2–4 *on its . . . hair*: Carl Grabo relates this image to the Leyden jar, an early form of electrical battery, which emits a green light when charged (*A Newton Among Poets*, p. 126).

8 *populous*: 'Numerous', or perhaps 'full of life', i.e. 'populated'.

19 *dipsas*: A mythical snake, whose bite was supposed to induce severe thirst.

54 *a sound*: No doubt a blast from the 'curved shell' given by Prometheus to the Spirit of the Hour in III.iii.64–8.

65–7 *Those ugly human shapes . . . the air*: Lucretius, *De Rerum Natura* (On the Nature of Things) IV.30–37, describes the *simulacra* or filmy images which leave the surface of all material objects and float in the air.

74 *efts*: Small lizards.

79–82 *nightshade . . . long beaks*: Kingfishers ('halcyons'), vegetarians since the fall of Jupiter, eat nightshade, formerly poisonous, which is now innocuous.

111–24 PBS borrowed details for these lines from a sculpture, in the Vatican Museum, of the Chariot of the Moon whose horses are linked by a two-headed ('amphisbaenic') snake. Phidias was the pre-eminent sculptor of Athens in the fifth century BC. See Donald H. Reiman, *Romantic Texts and Contexts* (Columbia, Mo.: University of Missouri Press, 1987), pp. 278–83.

120 *will mock*: Will imitate, though in the stillness of marble, the motion of the steeds they represent.

136 *'All hope . . . here'*: The inscription over the gate of Hell in Dante's *Inferno* III.9.

140 *abject*: Here, a noun: 'outcast'.

167 *glozed on*: Given a specious and deceptive commentary.

187 *unreclaiming*: Unprotesting.

204 *inane*: Empty space.

ACT IV

11 *the Father*: Jupiter; he is called 'the King of Hours' (l. 20) by the 'dead Hours' (l. 13) which he has ruled; hence 'Time' has not ended (l. 14), only that period of time dominated by Jupiter.

34 *One*: Prometheus.

58 *the figured curtain*: Cp. III.iii.113–14 and note.

109–10 The consciousness of time may be slowed down by love ('siren wiles') and the experience of wisdom.

140 *clips*: Circumscribes, encloses.

169 *gathering sphere*: Perhaps alluding to the speculation of some contemporary scientists that new planets were formed from the particles and gases in nebulae.

184 *unpavilioned*: Uncovered, open.

207 *Mother of the Months*: A conventional poeticism for the moon.

209 *interlunar*: Between the disappearance of the old and the reappearance of the new moon.

213 *Regard like*: Resemble, look like; *OED* (v. 10) cites this instance as a rare and obsolete sense.

219 The 'winged infant' that directs the moon-chariot has details in common with the visionary figures in Daniel 7:9 and Revelation 1:14.

230 *fire that is not brightness*: Perhaps referring to infra-red radiation, a phenomenon investigated by the astronomer William Herschel (1738–1822)

and the chemist Humphry Davy (1778–1829). For Herschel, see also note to II.iv.1–7.

236–68 Panthea's vision recalls that of 'the likeness of the glory of the Lord' in Ezekiel 1:28 which influenced Milton's image of the chariot of divine power in *Paradise Lost* VI.749–852. It also draws upon contemporary scientific speculation on the atomic composition of matter. See Thomas Reisner, 'Some Scientific Models for Shelley's "Multitudinous Orb"', *KSJ* 23 (1974), pp. 52–9.

246 *inter-transpicuous*: 'Visible between or through each other' (*OED*, citing this instance).

261 *drowns the sense*: Is sublime; i.e. overwhelms the senses.

269 *mocking*: Imitating.

272 *tyrant-quelling myrtle*: 'Tyrant-quelling' is borrowed from Coleridge, 'France: An Ode', l. 37. In ancient Greece, myrtle was sacred to Aphrodite, goddess of love, and associated with the struggle for liberty, recollecting Harmodius and Aristogeiton, who slew the tyrant Hipparchus of Athens in 514 BC, having concealed their daggers in ceremonial myrtle branches.

275–318 In these lines, PBS condenses information from contemporary scientific thinking on a range of topics, including geology (ll. 280–83), the water cycle (ll. 284–7), archaeological studies on the evolution and destruction of civilizations and species, including proto-hominids (ll. 287–316), either gradually or by a catastrophe such as a flood (ll. 314–16). Lines 316–18 dramatize the suggestion, by Pierre-Simon Laplace, *Exposition du système du monde* (1796), that these extinctions might have been precipitated by the impact or near miss of a comet displacing the oceans.

281 *Valueless*: Punning on the two meanings of 'priceless' and 'worthless'.

283 *vegetable silver*: Of a substance combining mineral and vegetable; cp. 'vegetable fire' (III.iv.110).

291 *gorgon-headed targes*: Light shields decorated with the head of a monster (gorgon) which had snakes in place of hair. See headnote to 'On the Medusa of Leonardo da Vinci, In the Florentine Gallery' (p. 776).

303 *anatomies*: Skeletons.

319–502 PBS's playful equation of gravitational with erotic attraction in this dialogue reaffirms love as the governing principle of the universe.

388–93 King Bladud, the legendary founder of the city of Bath, having been exiled as a child because of his leprosy, became a swineherd. Noticing that those of his pigs that bathed in the warm mud of a marsh did not suffer from skin disease, he followed their example and was cured and returned to his father's court.

415 *Orphic*: In Greek myth, Orpheus was the first poet. His verse and music were credited with magical powers.

444 *my pyramid of night*: The conical shadow which the earth casts away from the sun into space.

455 *Covered*: The word has a sexual connotation.

473–5 In Euripides, *The Bacchae* 1051 ff., Agave, the daughter of Cadmus, unwittingly kills her son Pentheus while in the frenzy of a Dionysian ritual.

526 *birth*: Species, or race.

529–30 Cp. the orders of angels enumerated in *Paradise Lost* V.600–601: 'Hear, all ye Angels, Progeny of Light, / Thrones, Dominations, Princedoms, Virtues, Powers.'

539 *elemental Genii*: Spirits representing natural phenomena.

555 *Earth-born*: Prometheus, who, as a Titan, descended from Uranus (the Heavens) and Gaia (the Earth).

562–9 The stanza echoes and revises the defeat and imprisonment of the Devil in Revelation 20:1–3.

575 Cp. Satan's defiant words in *Paradise Lost* I.94–6: 'Yet not for those, / Nor what the potent victor in his rage / Can else inflict, do I repent or change.'

THE CENCI

According to MWS, PBS had the idea for *The Cenci* after seeing in the Palazzo Colonna at Rome on 22 April 1819 a portrait then believed to be of Beatrice Cenci, by Guido Reni (*1839* II, p. 274; the identity of both sitter and artist is now doubted). On 11 May, PBS, MWS and Claire Clairmont visited the Palazzo Cenci in Rome and three days later MWS records that PBS 'writes his tragedy' (*MWS Journal* I, p. 263). As he makes clear in his Preface, PBS drew on a historical account in Italian of the Cenci family. MWS had copied this in May 1818 from an MS in the possession of the Shelleys' friend John Gisborne, and began to translate it, perhaps with some help from PBS, in May 1819 (see *Poems* II, pp. 865–75); the translation was published in *1840* and is reproduced in *BSM* X. Notes on the Cenci family in PBS's hand also survive, in the Huntington Library (see *MYR (Shelley)* IV). Composition was interrupted by the death of William Shelley on 7 June and not resumed until PBS, MWS and Claire had moved to the Villa Valsovano, near Livorno, on 17 June, where Mary says 'the principal part' was written (*1839* II, p. 276). PBS and MWS made the press copy in August and an edition of 250 copies had been printed by Glauco Masi at Livorno by 21 September (*Letters* II, p. 119).

PBS hoped that *The Cenci* could be performed in London and, conscious of his scandalous reputation in England, sent a copy, no doubt with the title-page, Dedication and Preface removed, to T. L. Peacock on 10 September, asking him to 'procure for me its presentation at Covent Garden' (*Letters* II, p. 102). PBS had in mind two of the leading actors of the day, Edmund Kean and Eliza O'Neill, for the parts of Count Cenci and Beatrice. However, Thomas Harris, the manager of Covent Garden, found PBS's depiction of the subject of Cenci's rape of his daughter 'so objectionable, that he could not even submit the part to Miss O'Neil [sic] for perusal' (*1839* II, p. 279) and rejected the play outright for performance. *The Cenci* was first performed privately in 1886 and in public in 1922, each time in London.

Apart from a few brief fragments, the only recorded surviving manuscripts of *The Cenci* are those of the Dedication and the Preface (*MYR (Shelley)* IV). In autumn 1819, PBS had the 250 copies of the play that were printed in Italy sent to Charles Ollier in London, where *The Cenci* was published early the following year, dated 1819. In April 1820, PBS sent a list of errata in the 1819 text to Ollier, who published a second edition (the only one of PBS's works to reach an authorized second edition in his lifetime) in spring 1821. Our text is based on the 1819 Italian printing, though we have incorporated readings from the 1821 edition, from the list of errata, and from the alterations in PBS's and MWS's hand in a copy of the 1819 text that PBS inscribed to his friend John Taafe, which are given in *Poems* II.

The Cenci owes much to the English tragedies of the Renaissance period, especially Shakespeare's *Hamlet* and *Macbeth*, although commentators have also discerned the influence of a range of other dramatic forms, including Classical Greek tragedy. At the heart of the play is Beatrice's murderous response to the abuse which she and her family suffer at the hands of her father and the 'restless and anatomizing casuistry', as PBS puts it in his Preface, which this response prompts in the audience as they 'seek the justification of Beatrice, yet feel that she has done what needs justification' (p. 276). Comparable enquiry into the ethics of force and retribution is present in *Prometheus Unbound* (p. 184) and *Hellas* (p. 512), examples of PBS's sustained interrogation of the role of violence in the political process: can violence ever be a legitimate or even a necessary response to oppression, or is it only ever an instrument for breeding further violence? MWS records that PBS was 'writing the Cenci, when the news of the Manchester Massacre reached us' (*1839* II, p. 205) – which prompted *The Mask of Anarchy* (p. 357), an important poetic engagement with the issue of retribution for authorized carnage.

The Cenci is the third work in verse by PBS to treat explicitly the topic of incest, which he, in a letter of 16 November 1819, describes as a 'very poetical circumstance' which can consist in either 'the excess of love or of hate' (*Letters* II, p. 154). *Laon and Cythna* (1817) and 'Rosalind and Helen' (1818) offer a view of incest more in keeping with what PBS, in his letter, calls 'that defiance of every thing for the sake of another which clothes itself in the glory of the highest heroism' (*Letters* II, p. 154). Cenci's abuse of his daughter, conversely, typifies 'that cynical rage which confounding the good & bad in existing opinions breaks through them for the purpose of rioting in selfishness & antipathy' (*Letters* II, p. 154). Aware of the obstacle that the theme of incest posed to representation on the contemporary stage, PBS took pains to treat the subject with 'peculiar delicacy', as he wrote to Peacock (*Letters* II, p. 102). Apart from the 'Song' which closes Act V, Scene iii, *The Cenci* is in blank verse dialogue throughout, with little of what PBS, in his Preface, describes as 'mere poetry' (p. 277), i.e. imagery beyond what is strictly required for the development of dramatic plot and character. PBS goes on to state the principles on which he based his choice of language in the paragraph beginning 'In a dramatic composition' (p. 277).

Critical commentaries include: Jonathan Bate, *Shakespeare and the English Romantic Imagination* (Oxford: Clarendon Press, 1986), pp. 202–21; Paul A. Cantor, '"A Distorting Mirror": Shelley's *The Cenci* and Shakespearean Tragedy', in G. B. Evans (ed.), *Shakespeare: Aspects of Influence*, Harvard English Studies 7 (Cambridge, Mass.: Harvard University Press, 1976), pp. 91–108; Stuart Curran, *Shelley's Cenci: Scorpions Ringed with Fire* (Princeton, NJ: Princeton University Press, 1970); D. Harrington-Lueker,

'Imagination versus Introspection: *The Cenci* and *Macbeth*', *KSJ* 32 (1983), pp. 172–89; Jacqueline Mulhallen, *The Theatre of Shelley* (Cambridge: Open Book Publishers, 2010), pp. 85–113; and Earl Wasserman, *Shelley: A Critical Reading* (Baltimore, Md.: Johns Hopkins University Press, 1971), pp. 84–128.

Dedication Leigh Hunt (1784–1859); poet, essayist and editor of the liberal weekly *The Examiner*, Hunt had been a close friend and supporter of PBS since 1817. He had been imprisoned from 1813 to 1815 for criticizing in print the Prince Regent in an instance of the 'political tyranny' to which PBS alludes in the final paragraph (p. 273).

p. 273 *a sad reality*: On 15 December 1819, PBS wrote to Charles Ollier of his plans to write poems 'the subjects of which will all be drawn from dreadful or beautiful realities' (*Letters* II, p. 164).

PREFACE

p. 274 *Clement VIII* (1536–1605): Pope from 30 January 1592.

p. 275 *Guido's picture*: See headnote.

p. 276 *Revenge ... mistakes*: Cp. *Hellas*, ll. 729–30: 'Revenge and wrong bring forth their kind, / The foul cubs like their parents are' (p. 538).
anatomizing casuistry: Close moral analysis of a difficult case. In his Preface to *Prometheus Unbound*, PBS attributes to Milton's characterization of Satan in *Paradise Lost* a comparable 'pernicious casuistry' (p. 185).

p. 277 *those modern critics ... to belong*: The use of *familiar language* as proper to poetry had been variously argued by Wordsworth in the Preface to *Lyrical Ballads* (1800), Coleridge in *Biographia Literaria* (1817) and Leigh Hunt in the Preface to *The Story of Rimini* (1816).
[Shelley's note]: See note to III.i.243–65 for the 'speech' to which PBS refers in his footnote. Earlier in 1819, PBS was introduced by Maria Gisborne to the work of the Spanish Golden Age dramatist and poet Pedro Calderón de la Barça (1600–1681).

p. 278 *Mount Palatine*: The Palatine Hill in central Rome, traditional site of the first settlement of the city.
Castle of Petrella: See note to II.i.168.

ACT I

Scene i

1 *the murder*: Referred to by Cenci in ll. 21–3.

3 *fief*: Land.
Pincian gate: Part of the fortifications of ancient Rome; now at the northern end of the Via Vittorio Veneto.

4 *conclave*: Gathering of cardinals and the Pope; the Papal Court.

7 *compounded*: Settled by (punitive) payment.

16 *nephew*: Perhaps a euphemism for 'illegitimate son'; Cenci's reply implies nepotism and corruption in the papacy.

51 *meteors*: Any atmospheric phenomenon could be so denominated.
57 *Aldobrandino*: The nephew of the Pope. The family name of the historical Clement VIII was Aldobrandini.
69 *list*: Wish.
87 *captious*: Both 'entrapping' and 'capacious'.
94 *Hardened*: Obdurately closed to divine influence.
113 *the bloody sweat of Christ*: Cp. Luke 22:44 on Christ in the Garden of Gethsemane, on the eve of the crucifixion: 'his sweat was as it were great drops of blood falling down to the ground.'
114–15 The image of the body as a prison for the soul is Platonic, e.g. *Phaedo* 82d–e.
121 *Salamanca*: A city in north-western Spain.
127 *Close husbandry*: Care in expenditure.
141–4 Cp. *Macbeth* II.i.56–8: 'Thou sure and firm-set earth, / Hear not my steps which way they walk, for fear / Thy very stones prate of my whereabout.'

Scene ii

23 *loose*: Loosen, untie.
75 *vassal*: Changed on PBS's list of errata from 'slave' in the first edition.
85 *anatomize*: Literally, 'dissect'; figuratively, 'analyse in great detail'.

Scene iii

4 *Anchorite*: Hermit.
60 *a mummy*: 'A pulpy substance or mass', specifically of 'dead flesh' (see *OED* n. 1, b–c).
68 *the twenty-seventh of December*: Comparing Cenci with the biblical King Herod, who is said to have ordered the slaughter of all male children under two years of age (Matthew 2:16–18), a massacre remembered in the Christian calendar on 28 December, the Feast of the Holy Innocents. Cp. II.i.133–6.
73 *the Infanta*: The title of the daughter of the King of Spain (in l. 39, the news of the death of Cenci's sons is communicated in letters from Salamanca).
74 *El Dorado*: In Spanish, 'the golden one', a legendary city of fabulous wealth believed to be located in the Spanish Americas.
77–90 Cenci, raising the cup of wine, parodies the Christian rite ('sacrament', l. 82) of the Eucharist.
108–10 The sense of these difficult lines seems to be: 'Imagine the wrongs which must have been done not only to cause the devotion and respect for my father to be erased, but also to embolden me to speak out in public against him like this.'
109 *prone*: Impressionable.
126 *Prince Colonna*: Head of one of the oldest aristocratic households in Rome.
127 *chamberlain*: Responsible for managing the Pope's household.

151 *ill must come of ill*: A succinct statement of the ethical principle embodied in *The Cenci*. Cp. *Macbeth* V.i.68–9, 'Unnatural deeds / Do breed unnatural troubles', and *Hellas*, ll. 729–30 (p. 538). Cp. also IV.iv.139.

151–3 *Frown . . . seat*: Recalling the appearance of Banquo's ghost to Macbeth in *Macbeth* III.iv.

ACT II

Scene i

26 *secure*: Presumably combining the two senses: sure of finding her and sure of finding her alone.

27 *At the Ave Mary*: At the hour of the Angelus, the Catholic devotion performed morning, noon and evening, in which the Hail Mary (Ave Maria) features prominently. Since Act II, Scene i, evidently takes place the morning after the banquet in Act I, Scene iii (see II.i.106), Lucretia probably means either noon or 6 p.m.

71 *gangrened*: Made rotten.

86 *coil*: Turbulent existence; drawing on *Hamlet* III.i.68–70: 'For in that sleep of death what dreams may come / When we have shuffled off this mortal coil / Must give us pause.'

111 Commentators have identified a number of precedents for Beatrice's wish to be swallowed up in the earth, including: Aeschylus, *Persae* 915–17; Virgil, *Aeneid* X.675–6; and Marlowe, *Doctor Faustus* V.ii.88.

142 *sudden*: Fast-acting.

168 *Castle of Petrella*: Rocca Cenci, in the village of Petrella Salto, north-east of Rome. See note to III.i.240. For detailed discussion of the ambiguities in PBS's account of the castle and its location, see *Poems* II, pp. 737n and 767n.

174 *The all-beholding sun*: Cp. Shakespeare, *Romeo and Juliet* I.ii.94: 'the all-seeing sun'.

177 Cp. *Romeo and Juliet* III.ii.25, 'the garish sun', and Milton, *Il Penseroso*, l. 141, 'day's garish eye'.

181–3 Cp. *Macbeth* I.v.49–53: 'Come, thick night, / And pall thee in the dunnest smoke of hell, / That my keen knife see not the wound it makes, / Nor heaven peep through the blanket of the dark / To cry "Hold, hold!"'

190 *the earth's shade*: The shadow cast by the earth into space in the direction opposite the sun.

interlunar: The period of darkness between the old and the new moon. Cp. 'With a Guitar. To Jane', l. 24 (p. 566).

Scene ii

14 *thrice-driven beds of down*: Cp. Shakespeare, *Othello* I.iii.230: 'My thrice-driven bed of down'; 'thrice-driven' indicates beds made up of only the smallest, softest feathers separated from the larger, coarser ones.

49 Gian Galeazzo Visconti (1351–1402) became ruler of Milan after seizing control from his uncle; a patron of the arts, he also conducted a lengthy and bloody struggle to unite and rule northern Italy. Cesare Borgia

(?1475/6–1507), statesman, soldier and one-time cardinal, was ruler of a territory in northern Italy which he sought to extend by treachery and open conflict. The illegitimate son of Pope Alexander VI, his power depended upon the continued support of the papacy. Ezzelino III da Romano (1194–1259) was leader of the Ghibellines in Lombardy and the Veneto; ruler of Verona, Vicenza and Padua, he was notorious for his cruelty. PBS also refers to 'Ezzelin' in 'Lines Written among the Euganean Hills, October, 1818', l. 239 (p. 159), and would have read about all three 'memorable torturers' (l. 48) in J.-C.-L. Simonde de Sismondi, *Histoire des républiques italiennes du moyen âge* (2nd edn, 1818).

70–71 *scorpions . . . death*: Cp. similar imagery in Byron, *The Giaour* (1813), ll. 422–38. Cp. also PBS's *A Declaration of Rights* (1812) (*Prose Works* I, p. 57); *Queen Mab* VI.36–8 (p. 58); and *Laon and Cyntha* XI.viii.

89 *the inmost cave of our own mind*: The image (Platonic in origin) is not uncommon in PBS's work, e.g. 'Mont Blanc', ll. 34–48 (p. 140), and *Julian and Maddalo*, l. 573 (p. 178); cp. also the prose fragment in Bodleian MS Shelley adds. c. 4 ff. 184^{r}–184^{v}: 'thought can with difficulty visit the intricate & winding chambers which it *inhabits* . . . The caverns of the mind are obscure & shadowy, or pervaded with a lustre, beautifully bright indeed, but *shining* not beyond their portals' (see *BSM* XXI, pp. 192–5).

110 Cp. PBS's letter to MWS of 10 August 1821: 'What is passing in the heart of another rarely escapes the observation of one who is a strict anatomist of his own' (*Letters* II, p. 324).

120 *fee*: Buy off, bribe.

130–31 *and all . . . its effect*: *Poems* II compares this with *Macbeth* I.v.44–6: 'That no compunctious visitings of nature / Shake my fell purpose, nor keep peace between / The'effect and it.'

147 Cp. Shakespeare, *Richard III* II.iv.52–3: 'Welcome destruction, blood, and massacre! / I see, as in a map, the end of all.'

ACT III

Scene i

13 Cp. Marlowe, *Doctor Faustus* V.ii.78: 'See where Christ's blood streams in the firmament!'

16–17 *There creeps . . . mist*: Cp. *Paradise Lost* IX.180, describing Satan 'Like a black mist low creeping'.

26–8 Cp. Shakespeare, *Richard II* I.iii.187–9: 'By this time, had the King permitted us, / One of our souls had wandered in the air, / Banished this frail sepulchre of our flesh.'

34–7 An instance of what in post-Freudian terminology would be called post-traumatic repression: Beatrice's suffering effaces her memory of its cause, or 'father' (in a double sense).

44 *hales*: Hauls, drags.

48 *strange flesh*: Cp. Shakespeare, *Anthony and Cleopatra* I.iv.67: 'It is reported thou didst eat strange flesh'. In Jude 7 the cities of Sodom and Gomorrah are reproached with eating 'strange flesh'.

52 *Prodigious*: Combining the senses of 'extraordinary' and 'monstrous'.

86–7 *something ... know not*: Echoing the words of the old king in Shakespeare, *King Lear* II.ii.454–5: 'I will do such things – / What they are, yet I know not.' *Poems* II compares this with Leigh Hunt on the political situation in England in *The Examiner* for 3 January 1819, p. 1: 'all classes feel that something, as the phrase is, must be done.' PBS quotes Beatrice's speech in his letter to Charles Ollier of 6 September 1819, in which he deplores the Peterloo Massacre (see *The Mask of Anarchy* and headnote (pp. 357, 759), and *Letters* II, p. 117; see also *Letters* II, p. 120).

101 *and so die*: And die in that doubt.

129 *the unworthy ... spirit*: An echo of 1 Corinthians 6:19: 'know ye not that your body is the temple of the Holy Ghost.'

132–4 *Self-murder ... it*: Cp. *Hamlet* I.ii.129–32: 'O that this too too solid flesh would melt, / Thaw, and resolve itself into a dew, / Or that the Everlasting had not fixed / His canon 'gainst self-slaughter!'

157–60 *aye ... astonishment*: Cp. Deuteronomy 28:37: 'And thou shalt become an astonishment, a proverb, and a byword, among all nations'.

178 *double-visaged*: Two-faced; recalling representations of the Roman god Janus.

208–9 Echoing Satan in *Paradise Lost* IV.108–9: 'So farewell hope, and with hope farewell fear, / Farewell remorse.'

240 *Apulian Apennines*: PBS seems mistaken in his geography: the Appenine Mountains run the length of the Italian peninsula, but Apulia is the extreme south-eastern region of Italy whereas Petrella is located north-east of Rome.

243–65 This is the speech which PBS, in his Preface, identifies as the sole instance in *The Cenci* of 'mere poetry', although the images suggest both the dark intentions of the principal characters and their precarious moral state. The 'sublime passage' of *El Purgatorio de San Patricio* on which he says it is based has been identified as II.2019–26. See Curran, *Shelley's Cenci*, pp. 120–21. Beatrice's description also recalls Coleridge, 'Kubla Khan' (1816), ll. 16–25.

293 *fair*: Pure, untainted.

319 *specious*: Deceptively plausible. Cp. IV.i.115.

324 *ardent*: Passionate, fervent; in contrast to his wife's 'look averse and cold' and to Cenci's 'specious tale' in l. 319.

Scene ii

8–18 The imagery and sentiment are drawn from *Othello* V.ii.7–15.

51–2 *And yet ... life*: Echoing Othello, contemplating the murder of Desdemona: 'I know not where is that Promethean heat / That can thy light relume' (V.ii.12–13).

54 *recall*: Restore.

62 *castellan*: 'The governor of a castle' (*OED*).

66 *a reward of blood*: Presumably, payment for a murder.

ACT IV

Scene i

5 *the eyes and ears of Rome*: Cenci wonders whether he need be apprehensive of his deeds becoming known in Rome, even though, as *Poems* II points out, Petrella stood outside Roman jurisdiction.

8–12 Cenci wants Beatrice to 'consent' rather than be forced to accept his abuse, so that he may destroy her body and soul. See IV.i.44–5, 93–5.

55 *the wide Campagna*: Sparsely populated countryside around Rome.

83 *blazoned*: Proclaimed.

114–67 'As to Cenci's curse—', PBS wrote to his cousin, Thomas Medwin, on 20 July 1820: 'I know not whether I can defend it or no. I wish I may be able, since, as it often happens respecting the worst part of an author's work, it is a particular favourite with me' (*Letters* II, p. 219). The curse has a notable precedent in King Lear's cursing of his daughters (e.g. I.iv. 254–69, II.ii.335–41).

115 *specious*: Deceptively fair and attractive.

131 *Maremma*: A large area of wetland along the coast of Tuscany; associated, like the Campagna Romana, with disease and banditry.

140 *That if she have a child*: MWS comments in her 'Note' on *The Cenci*: 'In speaking of his mode of treating this main incident, Shelley said that it might be remarked that, in the course of the play, he had never mentioned expressly Cenci's worst crime. Every one knew what it must be, but it was never imaged in words—the nearest allusion to it being that portion of Cenci's curse, beginning, "That if she have a child", &c.' (*1840*, p. 159).

144 Cp. Genesis 1:22: 'Be fruitful, and multiply, and fill the waters in the seas, and let fowl multiply in the earth.'

145 *imprecation*: Curse.

162 *some unremembered world*: Recalling the Platonic idea of the pre-existence of the soul which the soul forgets at birth.

172 *spurn*: Kick.

173–4 *It were . . . prey*: Cp. *King Lear* I.i.122: 'Come not between the dragon and his wrath.'

187–9 *All good . . . quickened*: Cp. *Macbeth* III.ii.53–4: 'Good things of day begin to droop and drowse, / Whiles night's black agents to their preys do rouse.'

Scene ii

11 *recking*: Considering, caring for.

12 *to die without confession*: The fate of old Hamlet, murdered by his brother Claudius, as well as that which Prince Hamlet contemplates for Claudius. See *Hamlet* II.v.76–9, III.iii.74–95.

33 *the Hell within him*: Cp. *Paradise Lost* IV.18–21: 'Horror and doubt distract / His troubled thoughts, and from the bottom stir / The hell within him, for within him hell / He brings, and round about him.'

Scene iii

1–35 These lines draw on the conversation between Macbeth and Lady Macbeth following the murder of Duncan in *Macbeth* II.ii.1–18. *Poems* II observes that PBS also 'follows closely the language' of MWS's translation of the MS account of the Cenci family.

25 *palterers*: Prevaricators, tricksters.

28 *equivocation*: A falsehood expressed in a form of words that is true in itself. Beatrice accuses Marzio and Olimpio of showing mercy in a case justly demanding an unflinching conscience when they have been habitually indifferent in dishonourable matters. Cp. *Macbeth* II.iii.7–11: 'Faith, here's an equivocator that could swear in both the scales against either scale, who committed treason enough for God's sake, yet could not equivocate to heaven.'

42 *light of life*: Recalling Christ's words in John 8:12: 'I am the light of the world: he that followeth me shall not walk in darkness, but shall have the light of life.' Cp. also *Prometheus Unbound* III.iii.6 (p. 244).

43 *jellied*: Congealed, coagulated.

57–8 *Hark . . . trump*: Cp. *Macbeth* II.iii.80–82: 'What's the business, / That such a hideous trumpet calls to parley / The sleepers of the house?'

58 *tedious*: Perhaps combining the senses of 'irritating' and 'late-arriving'.

Scene iv

Stage direction *Legate*: 'An ecclesiastic deputed to represent the Pope and armed with his authority' (*OED*).

13 *suddenly*: Immediately.

28 PBS seems to have introduced this ironic twist to the story, although such devices are familiar practice in Classical and Renaissance tragedy.

44 *cheap*: Easily feigned.

49 *Free . . . air*: Cp. *Macbeth* III.iv.22: 'As broad and general as the casing air'.

76 *effortless*: 'Lifeless; with no sign of struggle' (*Major Works*).

79 *Poems* II observes that the historical Marzio was apprehended some four months after Cenci's murder. Olimpio was killed almost nine months after (cp. IV.iv.86–7).

127–9 *Unless . . . avenge*: Unless God will avenge crimes that people are unwilling to address. Cp. IV.iv.151.

151 *rejected*: Unacknowledged.

ACT V

Scene i

12 Cp. *Romeo and Juliet* III.iv.1: 'Things have fall'n out, sir, so unluckily.'

85 *vile*: Mean, wretched.

87 *misdeeming*: 'Misjudging, wrongly supposing' (*OED*).

Scene ii

50–55 MWS says that PBS recalls in these lines the grief that 'haunted' him after the death of their son William on 7 June (*1839* II, p. 275n).

59–61 *What shall . . . fountain*: *Poems* II compares this with Webster, *The Duchess of Malfi* IV.ii.364–6: 'where were / These penitent fountains while she was living? / O, they were frozen up!'

164 *pain*: Rendered 'pang' in the second edition, though the change is not on PBS's list of errata.

169 *strain*: Playing on the two senses of 'filter' ('sifted', l. 170) and 'place under stress'.

172–3 *Entrap . . . accuser*: Cp. Webster, *The White Devil* III.ii.225–6: 'If you be my accuser / Pray cease to be my judge.'

182 *deep*: Cunning, artful.

189 *pleasure*: i.e. 'will', but with a pun on 'enjoyment'.

191 *engines*: Instruments of torture.

Scene iii

89 Cp. Iago being led to torture in *Othello* V.ii.310: 'From this time forth I never will speak word.'

125 *monotony*: i.e. 'monotone', sound without variation.

Scene iv

13 *looking deprecation*: His look expressing disapproval.

18–20 According to MWS's translation of the Italian account of the Cenci family (see headnote, p. 749), the news that one Paolo Santa Croce had recently murdered his mother influenced the Pope to deny a pardon to Lucretia, Giacomo and Beatrice. See *BSM* X, pp. 214–17.

47–55 The lines draw on Claudio's speech in Shakespeare, *Measure for Measure* III.i.118–32.

56 *Let me not go mad*: Cp. *King Lear* I.v.45: 'O, let me not be mad, not mad, sweet heaven!'

76–7 Echoing the words of Jesus on the cross to the 'good thief' in Luke 23:43: 'Verily I say unto thee, To day shalt thou be with me in paradise.'

80–81 Cp. *Hamlet* I.ii.133–4: 'How weary, stale, flat, and unprofitable / Seem to me all the uses of this world!'

100 *narrow*: Brief.

101–7 *Plead . . . man*: *Poems* II compares this with Shakespeare, *The Merchant of Venice* IV.i.70–79.

106 *wind-walking Pestilence*: According to the miasmatic theory of disease, infectious vapours rising from rotting vegetable matter were carried on the wind.

136 This line lacks a tenth syllable. Some editors emend to 'was as a bond'.

THE MASK OF ANARCHY

The Mask of Anarchy (*MA*) is PBS's primary imaginative response to one of the defining events of English national life in the early nineteenth century. On 16 August 1819, tens of thousands of demonstrators gathered on St Peter's Field near the centre of Manchester for a mass protest against the hardship of the labouring poor and in support of electoral reform. They were to be addressed by well-known speakers from the reform movement. When constables, struggling to make their way through the dense crowd, were unable to carry out the orders of the magistrates to arrest the leaders of the meeting, the local mounted yeomanry was called to their aid. These inexperienced volunteers, acting both brutally and ineffectively, soon required the reinforcement of regular cavalry and infantry who were instructed to disperse the crowd. In the melee some dozen or more of the demonstrators were killed and hundreds wounded. There were women and children among the injured. That unarmed English civilians, legally and peacefully assembled, should be assaulted by mounted troops aroused widespread shock and consternation and inspired the ironic title of 'Peterloo' which was soon applied to the day's events as a sarcastic allusion to the military victory at Waterloo four years previously. Shortly after 16 August, the home secretary, Lord Sidmouth, wrote to the civil authorities in Manchester to convey the Prince Regent's congratulations to them and to the yeomanry for their decisive intervention to preserve the peace.

The news from Manchester reached PBS in Livorno on 5 September. The following day he wrote to his publisher, Charles Ollier, that 'the torrent of my indignation has not yet done boiling in my veins', and to T. L. Peacock three days later that in the bloody confrontation of 16 August he could hear 'the distant thunders of the terrible storm which is approaching' (*Letters* II, pp. 117, 119). In this mood of outrage and foreboding, he set to work on *MA*, completed it rapidly and posted it to Leigh Hunt on 23 September for immediate publication in *The Examiner* newspaper (*MWS Journal* I, p. 298, *Letters* II, p. 152). But Hunt dared not risk legal sanctions by publishing so inflammatory a poem at a time of increased government vigilance of the press. *MA* was not to appear until 1832, after the passage of the First Reform Bill, in a separate volume with a preface by Hunt, but omitting the subtitle, which was not printed until *Forman 1876–7*.

For information about Peterloo PBS relied on newspapers sent to him by Peacock, especially *The Examiner* for 22 and 29 August, which gave ample accounts of the events of the day and the opposing reactions they provoked. His sense of the matter, expressed in a letter to *The Examiner* of 3 November, which again Hunt did not publish, was fiercely indignant: 'We hear that a troop of the enraged master manufacturers are let loose with sharpened swords upon a multitude of their starving dependents & in spite of the remonstrances of the regular troops that they ride over them & massacre without distinction of sex or age, & cut off women's breasts and dash the heads of infants against the stones' (*Letters* II, p. 136). But in *MA* he chose not to incorporate any actual details of the skirmish or any direct reference to the local actors or to dramatize conflicting political opinions. Instead he opted for a formal hybrid: a dream vision (ll. 1–4) that draws largely on the New Testament (especially

Revelation), delivered as a symbolic narrative in a popular ballad stanza, and which borrows its title and fictional development from the mask (or masque), a dramatic pageant with courtly origins featuring allegorical personages and a plot that typically affirms the legitimacy of royal and aristocratic power. Leigh Hunt had given an example of the mask as vehicle for a progressive political viewpoint in his *The Descent of Liberty* (1815), which celebrates not the return of the conservative old order but the hopes of liberal opinion for increased freedom and solidarity in Europe after the first defeat of Napoleon in 1814. The 'Mask' of PBS's title also signifies the disguises that arbitrary authority and its supporters assume, whether trappings of office or religious devotion or tendentious language, to conceal the self-interest that lies behind what Leigh Hunt calls in his leading article in *The Examiner* for 22 August 1819 'the Brazen Masks of power'. Looking beneath these disguises, *MA* reveals that it is the established political order and not the movement for reform which is the source of anarchy in its usual sense of 'social confusion and disorder', while bringing to the fore another sense of the word, 'misrule', as underlying cause.

Our text is taken from MWS's fair copy with corrections by PBS which was sent to Leigh Hunt on 23 September 1819 and which is now in the Library of Congress (MMC 1399): there is a facsimile in *MYR (Shelley)* II.

The extensive commentary on *MA* includes: Stephen C. Behrendt, *Shelley and His Audiences* (Lincoln, Nebr.: University of Nebraska Press, 1989), pp. 196–204; Richard Cronin, *Shelley's Poetic Thoughts* (London: Macmillan, 1981), pp. 39–55, and *The Politics of Romantic Poetry* (Basingstoke: Macmillan, 2000), pp. 173–80; Stuart Curran, *Shelley's Annus Mirabilis* (San Marino, Calif.: Huntington Library, 1975), pp. 185–93; Steven E. Jones, *Shelley's Satire: Violence, Exhortation, and Authority* (DeKalb, Ill.: Northern Illinois University Press, 1994), pp. 94–123; Michael Henry Scrivener, *Radical Shelley* (Princeton, NJ: Princeton University Press, 1982), pp. 199–210; and Susan J. Wolfson, *Formal Charges: The Shaping of Poetry in British Romanticism* (Stanford, Calif.: Stanford University Press, 1997), pp. 195–204.

6 *Castlereagh*: See headnote to 'To S[idmouth] and C[astlereagh]' (p. 774).

8 *Seven bloodhounds*: Various references have been detected in the phrase: to the recurring number seven in Revelation, e.g. the beast with seven heads in 17:3; to the seven other European nations that joined Great Britain to postpone indefinitely the abolition of the slave trade in 1815; and to the pro-war party in Pitt's administration (1783–1801), who were known as 'bloodhounds'.

15 *Eldon*: The Lord Chancellor, John Scott, 1st Earl of Eldon (1751–1838), an uncompromising defender of the established order in Church and State, had in the Court of Chancery in March 1817 delivered the verdict that deprived PBS of the custody of his children by his first wife, Harriet. *ermined gown*: The mark of a peer of the realm and a judge.

16 *tears*: Eldon was known for weeping in court.

17 *mill-stones*: Cp. Matthew 18:6: 'But whoso shall offend one of these little ones which believe in me, it were better for him that a millstone were hanged about his neck, and that he were drowned in the depth of the sea.' See also Richard of Gloucester addressing the murderers he has

commissioned in *Richard III* I.iii.351: 'Your eyes drop millstones when fools' eyes fall tears.'

24 *Sidmouth*: See headnote to 'To S[idmouth] and C[astlereagh]' (p. 774). The pious Sidmouth supported the building of new churches to serve the growing population of industrial towns.

25 *crocodile*: In popular lore, the crocodile shed tears while devouring its victim. See 'To — [the Lord Chancellor]', ll. 47–8 (p. 447).

26 *Destructions*: Destroyers.

30–33 *Anarchy* is modelled upon the apparition in Revelation 6:8: 'And I looked, and behold a pale horse: and his name that sat on him was Death, and Hell followed with him. And power was given unto them over the fourth part of the earth, to kill with sword, and with hunger, and with death.' See the Dedication before *Laon and Cythna*, l. 86 (p. 150), and *The Triumph of Life*, ll. 285–6 (p. 579).

34–7 The lines borrow details from Revelation 19:11–16.

48–9 Alluding to the drunken 'Mother of Harlots' in Revelation 17:1–6 and to reports that the yeomanry who attacked the crowd at Manchester had been drinking or were drunk.

57 *triumph*: See note to 'To —' ('Corpses are cold in the tomb'), l. 19 (p. 779).

59 *blood and flame*: Recalling the red coats of the British army.

77 *ten millions*: The large allowances from the public purse granted to the seven sons of George III caused widespread offence. See 'England in 1819', ll. 2–3 (p. 405).

80 *globe*: 'A golden orb, emblem of sovereignty' (*OED*).

83 *Bank and Tower*: The Bank of England and the Tower of London, the latter both a fortress and an arsenal.

85 *pensioned*: In receipt of a stipend from government and so biased to support its policies and prerogatives.

115 *A planet, like the Morning's*: Venus as the morning star, emblem of love, one of the principal symbols in PBS's verse.

145 *accent*: Utterance.

151 The line adopts a traditional simile, as in Numbers 23:24: 'Behold, the people shall rise up as a great lion.'

169 *pine and peak*: Waste away.

176–83 The radical reformer William Cobbett (1763–1835), whom PBS cautiously admired, was persuaded that the necessity of paying the interest on the large national debt had led to two measures which weighed disproportionately on the poor: the issue of paper currency unbacked by gold, which depreciated in value; and the introduction of regressive commodity taxes. Together, these deprived of their just reward those whose labour was the ultimate source of wealth. See 'From *A Philosophical View of Reform*' (p. 636) and *Peter Bell the Third*, ll. 152–6 (p. 378).

205–8 Recalling Matthew 8:20: 'And Jesus saith unto him, The foxes have holes, and the birds of the air have nests; but the Son of man hath not where to lay his head.'

220 *Fame*: Rumour, gossip. In Ovid, *Metamorphoses* XII.39 ff., Rumour (Latin *fama*) lives in a house of echoing brass.

233 The flag of the American Minutemen militia in the Revolutionary War pictured a coiled rattlesnake and the words 'Don't tread on me'. See K. N. Cameron, *Shelley: The Golden Years* (Cambridge, Mass.: Havard University Press, 1974), p. 623.

238–41 PBS deplored the threat of eternal punishment by institutional religion as a means of enforcing political submission. In his letter protesting against the conviction of the bookseller Richard Carlile for 'blasphemous libel' for publishing Thomas Paine's *Age of Reason* (1793, 1796), PBS defended freedom of opinion on religious matters and castigated its misuse for political advantage: 'the prosecutors care little for religion, or care for it only as it is the mask & the garment by which they are invested with the symbols of worldly power' (*Letters* II, p. 143).

245 In 1793 Britain joined other European powers in a coalition against revolutionary France (Gaul).

250–53 The stanza draws upon Luke's Gospel, on which PBS made notes in late 1819: the episode of the woman who washed and kissed Jesus's feet and is forgiven her sins in 7:36–50; of Christ's advice to the rich man in 18:18–22; and of the charity of Zacchaeus the Publican in 19:1–10.

286 *tares*: Noxious weeds, alluding to the parable in Matthew 13:24–40.

305 *targes*: Light shields.

319 *scimitars*: Short curved swords used especially in the Near East and associated with proverbial Oriental brutality and despotism.

320 *sphereless stars*: Stars that have left their proper sphere in the heavens (as understood in older astronomy) and appear as meteors.

330 *phalanx*: Compact battle array; more generally, a body of people drawn closely together for a common purpose.

331–4 Cp. PBS's *A Declaration of Rights* (1812): 'No man has a right to disturb the public peace, by personally resisting the execution of a law however bad. He ought to acquiesce, using at the same time the utmost powers of his reason, to promote its repeal' (*Prose Works* I, p. 57).

335 *old laws of England*: Reformers appealed to such legal milestones as Magna Carta (1215) and the Bill of Rights (1689) as well as to the rule of law generally, as forming a native English tradition.

341 *sacred heralds in their state*: In the exercise of their duties as representatives of the sovereign, the safety of heralds was to be scrupulously respected.

344–67 PBS argued for passive resistance in *A Philosophical View of Reform*: 'not because active resistance is not justifiable when all other means shall have failed, but because in this instance temperance and courage would produce greater advantages than the most decisive victory' (*Prose*, p. 257).

360 *bold, true warriors*: Reports in *The Examiner* for 22 and 29 August contrasted the restrained conduct of the regular troops at Peterloo with the undisciplined force used by the yeomanry cavalry.

364–7 Volcanic vapours were thought to inspire those who delivered the prophecies of the ancient oracles. Volcanoes regularly figure in PBS's poetry as emblems of revolutionary change. See *Prometheus Unbound* II.iii.1–10 (p. 226) and *Hellas*, ll.587–90 (p. 533).

PETER BELL THE THIRD

In summer 1819 at Livorno, PBS read in *The Examiner* for 2 May Leigh Hunt's review of Wordsworth's *Peter Bell: A Tale in Verse*, which had been published towards the end of April. He would also have read in the previous week's *Examiner* Keats's anonymous review of J. H. Reynolds's parody *Peter Bell: A Lyrical Ballad*, which had appeared a week before Wordsworth's *Peter Bell*. (The publication of Wordsworth's poem, finished in 1798, was expected.) It is not certain whether PBS read either Wordsworth's *Peter Bell* or Reynolds's parody; his acquaintance with each may have been confined to Hunt's and Keats's reviews and the extracts from the poems that they included. However that may be, between the summer and autumn (by which time the Shelleys were living in Florence) PBS composed *Peter Bell the Third* (*PB III*), quite possibly in about a fortnight in October, and on 2 November sent it to Leigh Hunt in London with instructions for immediate anonymous publication by Charles Ollier (*Letters* II, pp. 134–5). Ollier chose not to publish it, however; it remained unpublished until MWS included it in *1840*.

Wordsworth's *Peter Bell* recounts, in a ballad-like stanza, a number of incidents in the life of the character of the title, an itinerant seller of earthenware pots. The last of these, his overhearing of a Methodist preacher urging repentance, has the effect of completing his conversion from a cruel, selfish and brutal life to be 'a good and honest man' (l. 1135). *Peter Bell the Third* (in the Prologue, Reynolds's is the first Peter, Wordsworth's only the second) counters this fable of conversion with another, in which *his* Peter mimics the display of orthodox religious convictions in Wordsworth's recent verse as well as his change from a reforming to a conservative political outlook. PBS learned in a letter of July 1818 that in the parliamentary elections for Westmorland Wordsworth had supported the successful candidates, the two sons of his patron the Earl of Lowther, against the liberal Whig Henry Brougham, prompting a disgusted reply: 'What a beastly and pitiful wretch that Wordsworth! That such a man should be such a poet!' (*Letters* II, p. 26). The barter of political integrity for personal advantage is in *PB III* the cardinal sin for a poet, and Peter reaps its inevitable reward of dullness.

This narrative provides PBS with a satirical perspective on what he regarded as deadening features of contemporary literary culture: a narrow religious outlook, sexual prudery, political patronage and partisan reviewing. From all of these he felt he had himself suffered, no more so than in the review of his *Laon and Cythna/The Revolt of Islam* (1817–18) in the *Quarterly Review* for April 1819 (it reached him in mid October), which combined a vituperative personal attack with the charge that he had imitated, and perverted, Wordsworth. The central figure of the metropolitan literary scene in which Peter is corrupted is his patron the Devil, who is no goat-like demon but 'what we are' (l. 81) – of this world and able to embody himself in any convenient human form. In *PB III*, PBS imagines this Devil for a rational age (see the extract from 'On the Devil, and Devils': p. 630) as a member of the 'new aristocracy' that he recognizes in the essay *A Philosophical View of Reform* (p. 644), one of the nouveaux riches whose wealth allows them to patronize learning and taste without title to either.

PB III's ballad-like stanza of five lines of three or four stresses rhyming *abaab* is a variant of both Wordsworth's and Reynolds's, which rhyme *abccb*. Two satirical influences are of particular note. With Pope's *Dunciad* (1743) *PB III* shares the conviction that bad writing and debased civilization go hand in hand. The apocalyptic triumph of dullness bringing the return of ancient chaos and darkness at the end of *The Dunciad* provides the model for the conclusion to PBS's poem. T. L. Peacock's burlesque *Sir Proteus: A Satirical Ballad* (1814) combines the mock-heroic narrative of a comic character based on the Poet Laureate, Robert Southey, with an attack on the political apostasy of the Lake Poets.

Critical comment includes: *Poems* III, pp. 70–81; Carlo M. Bajetta, *Peter Bell: The 1819 Texts*, rev. edn (Milan: Mursia, 2005); James Chandler, *England in 1819* (Chicago and London: University of Chicago Press, 1998), pp. 484–90, 515–24; Richard Cronin, 'Peter Bell, Peterloo, and the Politics of Cockney Poetry', *Essays and Studies* (1992), pp. 63–87, and *The Politics of Romantic Poetry* (Basingstoke: Macmillan, 2000), pp. 147–55; Steven E. Jones, *Shelley's Satire: Violence, Exhortation, and Authority* (DeKalb, Ill.: Northern Illinois University Press, 1994), pp. 38–69; and Michael Henry Scrivener, *Radical Shelley* (Princeton, NJ: Princeton University Press, 1982), pp. 218–24.

Our text is taken from MWS's press copy of the poem with additions and corrections by PBS, now in the Bodleian Library (MS Shelley adds. c. 5, ff. 50–99: see *BSM* I).

Title *Miching Mallecho*: Sneaking mischief. See second epigraph.

First epigraph The scene is a nocturnal fantasy of the terrified Peter Bell in Wordsworth's poem. The stanza was omitted in editions after 1819 to avoid offending 'the pious' (*Letters of William and Dorothy Wordsworth: The Later Years 1821–1853*, ed. E. de Selincourt, rev. Alan G. Hill, 4 vols (Oxford: Oxford University Press, 1978–88), I, p. 312).

Second epigraph From Shakespeare, *Hamlet* III.ii.130–31. Hamlet explains to Ophelia the meaning of the dumb show he has arranged to uncover the hidden guilt of Claudius the king.

DEDICATION

p. 369 *To Thomas Brown Esqr., the younger, H. F. &c. &c.*: A comic parody of Wordsworth's dedication of his *Peter Bell* to 'Robert Southey, Esq. P. L.' (i.e. Poet Laureate). 'Thomas Brown, the Younger' was the name adopted by the Irish poet Thomas Moore (1779–1852) for two popular verse satires, *The Twopenny Post-Bag* (1813) and *The Fudge Family in Paris* (1818). 'H. F.' has been decoded as 'Historian of Fudges' or as *Hiberniae Filius* (Latin for 'Son of Ireland') or as *Hiberniae Fidicen* ('Harpist of Ireland').

Fudges: A fictional Irish family who go on a fashionable tour to Paris after the restoration of the Bourbons in Thomas Moore's verse satire (see previous note), which mocks their opinions and behaviour. The father of the family, Phil Fudge, a radical in the 1790s, now serves the foreign secretary, Castlereagh (for whom see headnote to 'To S[idmouth] and C[astlereagh]': p. 774), as spy and informer.

the Rat and the Apostate: The targets intended are not entirely evident. In the early nineteenth century, a 'rat' was political slang for a turncoat; an 'apostate' is one who abandons his religion or principles or allegiances. Reynolds's and Wordsworth's 'Peter Bells' might qualify, the first as appearing in the disguise of another, the second as having undergone a conversion (the potter Peter Bell) and changed political loyalty for personal advantage (Wordsworth himself).

p. 370 *Mr. Examiner Hunt*: Leigh Hunt edited the liberal weekly *The Examiner* from 1808 to 1821.

the Quarterly: The *Quarterly Review* was edited by William Gifford (1756–1826) from an upper room at the establishment of its publisher, John Murray. The conservative Gifford and the liberal Leigh Hunt were bitter critical and political opponents.

eleutherophobia: A coinage from the Greek, 'fear of freedom'.

borrow colours: Find pretexts.

venerable canon . . . grandmother: The Book of Common Prayer included as the first entry in its table of the degrees of kinship and affinity within which marriage was forbidden: 'A man may not marry his grandmother.'

Proteus: A sea god who could change shape at will.

ultra-legitimate dullness: The phrase conjoins Wordsworth's shift to conservative opinions and the – in PBS's view – degeneration of his verse. 'Legitimacy', or the incontestable right of hereditary monarchy, was imposed by the victorious powers as the basis of the post-revolutionary settlement in Europe.

White Obi: Obi was a system of magic and sorcery of West African origin current among the transported slaves of the British West Indies. 'White Obi' evidently means Obi as practised by whites, i.e. Christianity. See l. 552.

p. 371 *the world . . . or not at all*: A slight misquotation of the final three lines of Wordsworth's poem 'French Revolution, As It Appeared to Enthusiasts at Its Commencement' (1809), republished in *Poems* (1815).

six or seven days . . . literature of my country: Mocking Wordsworth's statement in the Preface to *Peter Bell* that he had been revising the poem since 1798 with a view 'to fit it for filling *permanently* a station, however humble, in the Literature of my Country'.

cyclic poems: Heroic narrative poems based on a cycle of legends or myths.

bitterns: Large marshland birds.

Waterloo bridge: Originally, Strand Bridge, renamed and reopened on 18 June 1817, the anniversary of the victory at Waterloo.

Prologue

3 *antenatal*: Reynolds's *Peter Bell*, which appeared before Wordsworth's poem.

4 *weeds*: Clothes.

7–12 The passage combines logical and theological language to construct a mock argument on the relations that bind the three Peter Bells to each other. Wordsworth's poem is likened to the 'mean' or middle term of a syllogism: that is, an argument in three propositions, of which the first and last are the 'extremes'. To be valid these two must be properly linked by the mean. This prevents a 'schism', or break in the argument, because it is correctly ordered ('orthodoxal'), and also a doctrinal split because the mysterious threefold nature of Peter Bell is affirmed on an analogy with the orthodox Christian belief in the Holy Trinity – for which see the third paragraph of the Dedication.

10 *Aldric's*: The reference is to Henry Aldrich (1647–1710), whose *Artis Compendium Logicae* (1691) was used as a textbook for teaching logic at Oxford.

13–26 The 'first Peter' is Reynolds's poem, the second Wordsworth's, the third PBS's. An 'antitype' fulfils the prophecy implicit in the original type.

32 *Predevote*: Predestined.

35 *Cotter*: One who occupies a farm cottage in return for work on the farm.

36 *polygamic Potter . . . [Shelley's note]*: In the second edition of *Peter Bell*, Wordsworth explained that in northern dialect a 'potter' was 'a hawker of earthenware'. A 'scholiast' is an early commentator on a Classical text; 'dodecagamic' means 'having married twelve times' (as had Wordsworth's Peter Bell); 'megalophonous' is 'high-sounding'.

[Peter Bell the Third]

8 *oiled his hair . . . [Shelley's note]*: Both whale oil and Russia oil (extracted from birch bark) were used to dress hair.

15 *the gravel*: Stones in the urinary tract; painful urination generally.

22 *brimstone hue*: Sulphureous yellow; as in *The Witch of Atlas*, l. 43 (p. 449).

25 *The other*: i.e. 'brimstone hue' (l. 22).

27 *water gruel*: A thin porridge of meal and water.

32 *lake of Windermere*: Located to the south-east of 'Grasmere vale' (l. 60), where Wordsworth lived in the early nineteenth century and from which the Langdale Pikes, or Peaks, can be seen (l. 56).

40 To curse one or the other of one's parents is forbidden under pain of death in Leviticus 20:9.

56–60 See note to l. 32.

76 *The Devil*: PBS's essay 'On the Devil, and Devils' (p. 630) makes an illuminating commentary on the character introduced here.

82 Cp. Shakespeare, *King Lear* III.iv.134: 'The Prince of Darkness is a gentleman.'

83–4 The Poet Laureate traditionally received a butt of 'sack' (white wine from Spain or the Canaries) as part of his stipend. The Laureate at that time, Robert Southey (1774–1843), PBS regarded as having abandoned the progressive politics of his youth for a reactionary conservatism, like his fellow 'Lake Poet' Wordsworth.

86 Cp. 1 Thessalonians 5:2: 'the day of the Lord so cometh as a thief in the night.'

87 That is, with high boots and fashionable close-fitting trousers.

92 *slop-merchant from Wapping*: A seller of cheap clothing in this poor district of east London populated by sailors and others engaged in shipping.

94 *perk*: To act in a lively, jaunty manner; also assertively, impudently or with conceit.

96 *upper Benjamin*: A short coat suitable for wear when driving a carriage.

101 *corse*: Corpse.

116 *phiz*: Face, from 'phiznomy' (physiognomy).

120 Wordsworth attributes pride and joy to children in the 'Ode: Intimations of Immortality' (1807), l. 101, and in *The White Doe of Rylstone* (1815), l. 1810.

128 *Grosvenor square*: Completed in 1737, this square was a fashionable address and the location of many grand residences.

146 *bowled . . . chaise*: Driven in the Devil's carriage.

152–6 John Castles was a hired government informer and agent provocateur, a discredited witness for the prosecution in the trial (9–17 June 1817) of the leaders of the Spa Fields riots of 2 December 1816. George Canning (1770–1827), Tory politician and member of cabinet in the Earl of Liverpool's administration, spirited contributor to the weekly *Anti-Jacobin* (1797–8), foreign secretary (1807–9), succeeded Castlereagh in that office (1822) and became prime minister briefly in 1827. William Cobbett (1763–1835), reformist editor of the weekly *Political Register* (1802–35); fearing prosecution, he fled to America in 1817, returning in October 1819. PBS admired the vigour and clarity of Cobbett's writing, though regarded some of it as inflammatory and deplored Cobbett's appeal to the people to exact retribution for the wrongs they had suffered. See l. 239. For Robert Stewart, Viscount Castlereagh, see headnote to 'To S[idmouth] and C[astlereagh]' (p. 774).

154 *caitiff*: Base, wicked.

155 *cozening*: Cheating, trickery.
trepanning: Swindling.

157 The three asterisks were substituted in the press-copy MS for 'S—th—y'. The Laureate Southey (see note to ll. 83–4 above) had suffered a serious mental decline by the time the poem was published in *1840*, so ll. 157–8 would have been considered unacceptably offensive had his name been retained.

162 *Chancery Court*: The court that could be petitioned in cases of equity, presided over by the Lord Chancellor. See note to *The Mask of Anarchy*, l. 15 (p. 760).

163 *manufacturing*: Made up of industrial workers.

163–5 *set / Of thieves . . . Similar thieves*: The unreformed Parliament, elected by a small minority to represent its interests.

166 *An Army*: PBS and other liberals opposed the maintenance of a standing army in peacetime as a threat to freedom. See note to l. 173.
public debt: See note to *The Mask of Anarchy*, ll. 176–83 (p. 761).

173 *Despotism*: In four leading articles in *The Examiner* in April and May 1816, Leigh Hunt had warned of the dangers to civil authority of the increased presence of soldiers in London.

174 *German soldiers*: Large numbers of German troops served abroad in the British army in the Napoleonic Wars (1803–15), but their presence on British soil was regarded by many with apprehension. King George III (reigned 1760–1820) was also Elector of Hanover.

175 *lotteries*: From 1694 to 1826, lotteries were sponsored by the state as a means of raising revenue, but by the early nineteenth century were criticized as inefficient and subject to various sorts of fraud.

176 *suicide and Methodism*: In *An Attempt to Show the Folly and Danger of Methodism* (1809), Leigh Hunt claimed that the extreme emotions encouraged by Methodism had resulted in a growth in the number of suicides.

177 *Taxes*: Increases in commodity taxes (which fell most heavily on the poor), on items such as tea, coffee and tobacco, were voted by Parliament in June 1819.

183 *amant miserè . . . [Shelley's note]*: The Swedish naturalist Carl Linné (1707–78) had thus described the screeching and howling (*amant miserè* = 'they love dolefully') of the cat in the act of mating.

186 *Without which . . . [Shelley's note]*: The self-appointed Society for the Suppression of Vice, formed in 1802, campaigned against (among other things) prostitution, gambling and public drunkenness. 'Women of the Town' are prostitutes.

187 *hobnobbers*: Drinking companions, familiar friends.

190 *stock jobbers*: Members of the Stock Exchange who deal in stocks on their own account (*OED*); speculators.

197 *moiling*: Drudging at menial or dirty tasks.

202 *levees*: Receptions held by persons of eminence for men only.

207 *aldermanic*: Dinners given by aldermen, municipal officials, were traditionally sumptuous.

209 *Cretan-tongued*: St Paul (Titus 1:12) reports that 'Cretians [sic] are always liars'.

210 *Alemannic*: German.

212 *conversazioni*: Small assemblies for cultivated discussion of the arts and sciences.

213 *Conventicles*: Originally a meeting or place of meeting for illegal religious worship; more generally, a clandestine gathering.

222–3 *'God damns!' . . . [Shelley's note]*: One of the central themes of the poem, that it is not God who damns men but men who damn themselves, is illustrated in the stanzas that follow. 'Heaven's Attorney General' is the Devil: see the extract from 'On the Devil, and Devils' (p. 630).

224 *flams*: Falsehoods.

239 *Cobbett's snuff, revenge*: See note to ll. 152–6 above.

242 *some few*: PBS himself and other reform-minded individuals, such as Leigh Hunt, who strive for justice.

273–332 The strengths and limitations attributed to Peter in this passage are those that PBS, together with Leigh Hunt and the liberal critic, journalist and essayist William Hazlitt (1778–1830), considered characteristic of

Wordsworth: great poetic power; an egotism, or intense sense of self, that coloured all he wrote, and a restricted capacity for dealing with physical pleasure and erotic experience.

285 *trim*: Type.

287 *play*: Gambling.

320 *Diogenes*: Diogenes of Sinope (*c*.400–325 BC), Greek Cynic philosopher, taught that a radically simple life with the minimum of attachments was the condition of happiness.

328–9 'A kissed mouth loses nothing but renews itself like the moon.' PBS writes in a letter of 27 September 1819 that this maxim from Boccaccio's *Decameron* (end of the seventh tale of the second day) might stand against 'the common narrow-minded conception of love' (*Letters* II, p. 122).

341 *toadlike*: Alluding to Milton, *Paradise Lost* IV.799–809, in which Satan, 'Squat like a toad', tempts Eve.

346 *limes his lazy wing*: Becomes ensnared by the sticky substance birdlime.

348 *wight*: Individual.

349 *fixed aera*: Appointed time.

350 *turtle*: Turtle soup.

352 *East Indian Madeira*: Madeira wine that had improved in cask on the voyage to and from India.

373–97 PBS credits the guest who fascinates Peter with the exceptional mental and imaginative powers that he admired in S. T. Coleridge's poetry and criticism, but also with the tendency to obscurity in Coleridge's writings on philosophy and religion, which T. L. Peacock had burlesqued in the character of Moley Mystic in chapter 31 of the novel *Melincourt* (1817).

374 *petit soupers*: Late-evening private suppers for invited guests.

390–91 Alluding to John 3:8: 'The wind bloweth where it listeth, and thou hearest the sound thereof, but canst not tell whence it cometh, and whither it goeth: so is every one that is born of the Spirit.'

407 *heart of man*: A Wordsworthian phrase, e.g. in the poem 'Michael' (1800), l. 33.

425 *quickset fence*: A hedge, e.g. of hawthorn.

428–32 The Wanderer, a leading character in Wordsworth's *The Excursion* (1814), had previously been a pedlar. Books V–VIII of the poem are set in a churchyard where the character of the Pastor is one of the principal speakers. Most of Wordsworth's 'The Brothers' (1800) is narrated by the local priest in a churchyard.

447 *pipkins*: Small earthenware pots or pans.

448–9 Wordsworth and Coleridge were paid 30 guineas for *Lyrical Ballads* (1798) by the Bristol bookseller Joseph Cottle.

452 *warning*: Notice that he was leaving his position.

458–9 *'O, that . . . book'*: Cp. Job 31:35: 'Oh . . . that the Almighty would answer me, and that mine adversary had written a book' – the words of Job wishing his suffering to be accounted for.

463 *next new book*: Wordsworth's *Poems, in Two Volumes* (1807), *The Excursion* and *The White Doe of Rylstone* had all attracted adverse criticism.

468 *seriatim*: One after another.

470–72 Betty Foy is the mother of the title-character, Johnny, in 'The Idiot Boy' in *Lyrical Ballads* (1798). She has no daughter. PBS himself had been censured for abandoning his first wife, Harriet, who drowned herself in London in 1816. Ullswater is a large lake in the north-eastern part of the Lake District. In the copy of the poem sent to London for publication in November 1819, a stanza is cancelled at this point:

> Another—'Impious Libertine!
> That commits i——t with his sister
> In ruined Abbies—mighty fine
> To write odes on it!'—I opine
> Peter had never even kissed her.

473–4 Shaving the head was jokingly said to relieve manic excitement and was a preliminary to blistering the scalp as a treatment for mental disorder. Dr Francis Willis (1718–1807) and his sons, John (1751–1835) and Robert Darling Willis (1760–1821), treated George III's mental illness.

478–9 Accusations of adultery and incest had been made against both PBS and Leigh Hunt in reviews of their poetry. See note to ll. 470–72.

483 *WE*: Reviews in contemporary periodicals were written anonymously.

500 *Betty*: PBS's draft and fair-copy MS and *1840* all read 'Emma'. PBS asked Charles Ollier to alter the name to 'Betty', if he published the poem, in order to avoid offence, as he apparently thought that Wordsworth had a sister Emma (*Letters* II, p. 196).

514 *sad stuff in prose*: Wordsworth defended his verse from critical disapproval in the Preface and 'Essay, Supplementary to the Preface' of *Poems* (1815).

518–19 The Devil sends to the annual book fair at Leipzig for the four volumes of F. G. Born's translation into Latin (1796–8) of the works of Immanuel Kant (1724–1804).

524 *psychologics*: Science of the mind, psychology.

525 *furor verborum*: Rage for words.

532 *Sir William Drummond* (?1770–1828): The author of *Academical Questions* (1805), which is severely critical of Kant's philosophy.

534 *'P. Verbovale Esquire' . . . [Shelley's note]*: Verbovale, as the mock-learned Latin of PBS's note indicates, approximates an early pen name adopted by Wordsworth, 'Axiologus' – a compound from the Greek, signifying 'Worthword' or 'Wordworth'. The phrase 'a pure anticipated cognition' was used by Sir William Drummond (see previous note) to criticize the Kantian notion of a kind of knowledge arrived at by pure reason, as opposed to knowledge deriving from sense experience. The phrase became a joke in the Shelley circle: see, for example, *Letters* II, p. 438.

536 *Carlisle mail*: The coach carrying mail from London to Carlisle and the surrounding region.

538 *ex luce praebens fumum*: 'From light producing smoke', reversing the terms of Horace's praise of Homer's practice in *Ars Poetica* 143–4.

541 *subter humum*: 'Under ground'.

549 *hobby*: Both a smallish horse or pony and an obsession.

552 *White Obi*: See notes to the Dedication above.
555 *Flibbertigibbet*: The 'foul fiend' of *King Lear* III.iv.104.
566 *Deist*: A subscriber to 'natural' religion who accepts on rational grounds the existence of a supreme being, creator of the universe, but rejects such supernatural elements as miracles, revelation and the divinity of Christ.
574 *Calvin and Dominic*: Jean Calvin (1509–64), French theologian and religious reformer, and Dominic de Guzmán (*c.*1170–1221), founder of the Dominican Order, both notorious for zealous severity in suppressing heresy. See 'Letter to Maria Gisborne', ll. 25–6 (p. 438).
583 *Otter . . . [Shelley's note]*: Coleridge lived as a child in Devonshire near the river which he celebrates in the sonnet 'To the River Otter' (1796). The pompous phrase 'Dynastophilic Pantisocratists' mocks the support for hereditary European monarchies of Coleridge and Southey, who in their youth planned to establish in Pennsylvania a democratic agricultural community holding land in common ownership, a scheme known as Pantisocracy. The 'new Atlantis' refers to a utopian fiction by Francis Bacon published posthumously in 1627.
584–8 *In the death hues . . . [Shelley's note]*: PBS recalls ll. 556–71 of Wordsworth's *The Excursion* on the beauty of some trout that have been caught and are lying dead. He opposes to it ll. 568–71 of Wordsworth's 'Hart-leap Well' (1800).
602 *Sherry*: The familiar name of the dramatist and Whig MP Richard Brinsley Sheridan (1751–1816), who had been a friend and adviser to the Prince of Wales. When the latter became Prince Regent, he disappointed the expectations of Sheridan (and of liberals generally) and was accused of deserting his friend in his final years when ill and impoverished.
603 The line is the reply of Peter's soul.
615 The line alludes chiefly to *The Excursion* V–VIII.
616 George Colman the Younger (1762–1836) was a comic dramatist and wit noted for his affable disposition.
617 *male Molly*: The word 'Molly' ranged in meaning from a lower-class girl or woman to a prostitute; a 'male Molly' would appear to mean an effeminate or homosexual man.
618 *staves*: Stanzas.
636–52 The 'ode' parodies the address to 'Almighty God' in Wordsworth's 'Ode. The Morning of the Day Appointed for a General Thanksgiving. January 18, 1816' (1816), a hymn of gratitude for the victory at Waterloo. Lines 279–82 provoked widespread consternation: 'But thy most dreaded instrument, / In working out a pure intent, / Is Man – arrayed for mutual slaughter,— / Yea, Carnage is thy daughter!' Wordsworth altered the final couplet in subsequent editions of his poetry.
644–5 Alluding to the Peterloo Massacre of 16 August 1819, for which see the headnote to *The Mask of Anarchy* (p. 759), as well as to recent demonstrations for reform in other manufacturing towns.
650 *Moloch*: A deity of the Ammonites to whom children were sacrificed. See 2 Kings 23:10 and Leviticus 18:21.
652 *It was thou . . . [Shelley's note]*: See note to ll. 152–6 above.
655 *Lord McMurderchouse*: 'Chouse' can mean both cheat (as here) and dupe.

656 *interest in both houses*: Influence in both the House of Commons and the House of Lords.

658 *cure or sinecure*: In 1813 Wordsworth had accepted the salaried post of Distributor of Stamps (in effect a collector of revenue) for Westmorland and part of Cumberland through the patronage of William Lowther, 2nd Earl of Lonsdale, whose political interests he served following the appointment.

664 *boroughs*: Lord McMurderchouse controls several of these districts and so the member or members of Parliament that represent them.

665 *front*: Forehead.

671 *Oliver*: William Oliver was the pseudonym of a notorious government spy and agent provocateur. See *An Address to the People on the Death of the Princess Charlotte* (p. 605).

679 *pelf*: Money and property.

687 An additional stanza occurs at this point in PBS's draft:

> So in the luxury & the pride
> Which Tyrants wring from the oppressed;
> Peter's thought even now espied—
> A thought of pleasure & of pride
> Wherewith to 'feather his own nest'.

688 *a house*: Soon after his appointment as Distributor of Stamps (see note to l. 658 above), Wordsworth moved his family to a larger and more comfortable house, Rydal Mount, where he remained until his death in 1850.

705 *rehearsed*: Recited aloud.

711–12 In *Gulliver's Travels* (Part III, chapter 10) the Struldbruggs, a race of beings that never die, increase in infirmities and follies as they age, becoming intolerable to others.

721–2 Various accounts of the torture of the Aztec emperor Guatimozin by the Spanish under Hernán Cortés have been recorded, including that he was made to lie on a hot gridiron to force him to reveal the whereabouts of hidden treasure.

725 *famed seven*: The Seven Sleepers, Christian youths of Ephesus who under the persecution of the Roman emperor Decius in the third century were sealed up in a cavern where, according to legend, they slept for nearly two centuries only to awake without having aged. See Gibbon, *History of the Decline and Fall of the Roman Empire* (1776–88), chapter 33.

734 *pest*: Plague.

763 *bailiff*: The landowner's agent who collected rent.

Ode to the West Wind

PBS began and probably completed a draft of this, one of his best-known poems, in Florence in late October 1819. It was published in *1820*, from which we take our text. Punctuation and capitalization have been modified after consulting PBS's MSS (see *BSM* V and XVIII) and *1839*.

The 'Ode' addresses the West Wind as both the natural energy that drives the abrupt passage of autumn to winter in the Mediterranean region and as prophetic symbol in relation to what PBS perceived as converging public and personal crises in October 1819. In the political sphere he feared that social injustices in England would precipitate a 'bloody struggle' (*Letters* II, p. 149), in contrast to the non-violent revolutions he had imagined in *Laon and Cythna* (1817) and *The Mask of Anarchy* (p. 357), written the previous month. In mid October *Laon and Cythna*, which he had hoped would promote 'a happier condition of moral and political society' (*Poems* II, p. 32), was comprehensively denigrated and himself branded as cowardly and vicious in the *Quarterly Review* dated April 1819. His family life was also deeply troubled. All three children born to him and MWS in the past five years had died, the loss four months earlier of their three-year-old son, William, leaving them particularly disconsolate. That MWS was pregnant with their fourth child (who would be born on 12 November) is likely to have influenced l. 64 (see also note).

These circumstances inform the 'Ode', which, like 'Hymn to Intellectual Beauty' (p. 134), shares many features with prayer. The West Wind is invoked as a powerful deity and petitioned to aid the poet in a radical transformation that will confer on him the power of prophecy as well as a form of posthumous existence. Prosodically intricate and demanding, the poem's five divisions each consist of four groups of lines in *terza rima* (rare in English poetry of the period) – the Italian verse form of three-line stanzas rhyming *aba bcb cdc*, and so on – and a concluding couplet, which together compose a sonnet. Both Dante's *Divina Commedia* and Petrarch's *Trionfi* employ *terza rima*; the latter supplies the model for *The Triumph of Life* (p. 570).

Critical commentary includes: Andrew Bennett, *Romantic Poets and the Culture of Posterity* (Cambridge: Cambridge University Press, 1999), pp. 158–78; James Chandler, *England in 1819* (Chicago and London: University of Chicago Press, 1998), pp. 525–54; *Chernaik*, pp. 90–97; Richard Cronin, *Shelley's Poetic Thoughts* (London: Macmillan, 1981), pp. 23–42; Stuart Curran, *Shelley's Annus Mirabilis* (San Marino, Calif.: Huntington Library, 1975), pp. 156–72; Edward Duffy, 'Where Shelley Wrote and What He Wrote For', *SiR* 23 (1984), pp. 351–77 (360–71); and Paul H. Fry, *The Poet's Calling in the English Ode* (New Haven, Conn.: Yale University Press, 1980), pp. 203–17.

Footnote *temperature*: Attributes in combination.
Cisalpine: South of the Alps.

1 *Wind*: The wind is associated with creation and inspiration in Genesis 1:2 and Acts 2:2.

2 *leaves dead*: The comparison of the human dead to dead leaves is traditional in epic poetry: e.g. Homer, *Iliad* VI.146–9; Virgil, *Aeneid* VI.309–10; Dante, *Inferno* III.112–17; cp. also Milton, *Paradise Lost* III. 300–303 and *The Triumph of Life*, ll. 49–51 and 528–9 (pp. 571, 587).

4 *hectic*: Flushed, as if with a wasting fever.

9 *azure sister*: The gentle west wind of spring, called Zephyrus or Favonius in Classical literature, was traditionally represented as a young man rather than a woman.

14 *Destroyer and Preserver*: Attributes, respectively, of the Hindu deities Shiva and Vishnu.
hear, O hear: Cp. Psalm 61:1: 'Hear my cry, O God; attend unto my prayer.'
17 *tangled boughs*: The ocean provides moisture for the formation of clouds, which returns to the sea as rain.
18 *Angels*: Harbingers, forerunners: from the Greek *aggelos* = 'messenger'.
21 *Maenad*: A female follower of Dionysus, Greek god of wine and ecstasy, typically represented as dancing ecstatically. PBS saw a relief sculpture of Maenads at the Uffizi Gallery in Florence on 11 October 1819; in 'Notes on Sculptures' he describes their 'hair loose and floating [which] seems caught in the tempest of their own tumultuous motion' (*Ingpen and Peck* VI, p. 323). See also note to *Prometheus Unbound* II.iii.9–10 (p. 743).
32–6 *pumice isle . . . picturing them*: Pumice is porous rock formed from cooling lava. In December 1818, PBS made an excursion that included Baiae on the Bay of Naples (described in *Letters* II, p. 61), where from a boat he was able to see the sunken ruins of its ancient buildings.
54 Recalling Byron, *Childe Harold's Pilgrimage*, Canto IV (1818), ll. 88–9: 'The thorns which I have reaped are of the tree / I planted, – they have torn me, – and I bleed.'
57 *lyre*: See *A Defence of Poetry*: 'Man is an instrument over which a series of external and internal impressions are driven, like the alternations of an ever-changing wind over an Aeolian lyre' (p. 652). (See also *Alastor*, ll. 41–9 and note to l. 42: pp. 114, 710.)
63 *dead thoughts*: PBS's poems and prose writings, which had failed to find the readers he wished to influence.
64 *new birth*: PBS expanded on the idea in *A Philosophical View of Reform* (p. 636), begun in late 1819, in a passage that he later adapted in *A Defence of Poetry*: 'The literature of England, an energetic development of which has ever followed or preceded a great and free developement of the national will, has arisen, as it were, from a new birth' (p. 677).

To S[idmouth] and C[astlereagh]

Composed in autumn 1819, published under the title 'Similes' by Thomas Medwin in *The Athenaeum* for 25 August 1832 and by MWS in *1839*. In *1840* the title was expanded to 'Similes, For Two Political Characters of 1819'. Our text is from PBS's fair copy in Bodleian MS Shelley adds. e. 12, pp. 60–61 (see *BSM* XVIII).

The poem is addressed to two government ministers, Henry Addington, Viscount Sidmouth (1757–1844), and Robert Stewart, Viscount Castlereagh (1769–1822), pillars of the Tory administration of Lord Liverpool from 1812 to 1822. Steadfastly hostile to electoral reform, Sidmouth and Castlereagh were regarded as reactionary and repressive by liberal opinion. As home secretary, Sidmouth often dealt harshly with popular discontent following the Napoleonic Wars (1803–15), overseeing a network of government spies and informers. See headnote to *The Mask of Anarchy* (p. 759). Castlereagh, foreign secretary and Leader of the House of Commons, was accused of excessive severity in suppressing – in 1798 when chief secretary to the Lord Lieutenant of Ireland – a rising of United Irishmen, and was unresponsive to popular demands for relief and reform following the Napoleonic Wars.

2 *empty*: Hungry.
wind: Blow.
4 *smoke*: Vapour from rotting corpses.
9 *in a fit*: Hidden for a time.
11–13 *shark and dogfish . . . Negro ship*: The predators wait for a vessel transporting African slaves to the West Indies, anticipating that those among them who are dead or sick will be thrown overboard.
18 *bloodless*: Heartless, unfeeling.
19 *murrained*: Diseased.

Love's Philosophy

On 16 November 1819, PBS sent a copy of this playfully erotic lyric, probably just composed, from Florence to London, where Leigh Hunt published it in his literary weekly *The Indicator* on 22 December under the present title, which may be either his or PBS's. At the end of December, PBS presented a copy of the poem to Sophia Stacey, inscribed in *The Literary Pocket-Book* for 1819, also edited by Leigh Hunt – a combined calendar, memorandum book, compendium of miscellaneous information and anthology of contemporary writing – on her departure from Florence, where she had been lodging in the same house as the Shelleys. Miss Stacey, a year older than PBS and distantly related to him through a family marriage, was travelling in Italy with an older female companion. She and PBS spent much time together during her stay in Florence from 9 November to 29 December. The version of the poem presented to her, now in the library of Eton College, supplies our text. It is untitled and shows minor variations from the *Indicator* version. Another transcription, in a notebook (now Harvard MS Eng. 258.2: see *MYR (Shelley)* V), is entitled 'An Anacreontic' after the Greek poet (Anacreon) of the sixth century BC whose lyrics typically celebrate the pleasures of the senses.

7 The line is more explicitly erotic in both the Harvard and *Indicator* versions: 'In one another's being mingle.'

Goodnight

Probably composed in autumn 1819, 'Goodnight' was presented to Sophia Stacey in late December on her departure from Florence, inscribed in a copy of the *The Literary Pocket-Book* for 1819 (see previous headnote), which is now in the library of Eton College and which supplies our text. Another transcription of the poem, in a notebook (now Harvard MS Eng. 258.2: see *MYR (Shelley)* V), is entitled 'Song'. 'Goodnight' was first published in late 1821 in *The Literary Pocket-Book* for 1822. PBS made a free imitation of the poem in Italian in 1821, 'Buona Notte', for which see *Poems* IV, pp. 93–6.

Time Long Past

PBS inscribed this poem, together with 'Love's Philosophy' (p. 401) and 'Good-night' (p. 402), into a copy of *The Literary Pocket-Book* for 1819, which he gave to Sophia Stacey on her departure from Florence for Rome at the end of December 1819. It is now in the library of Eton College and supplies our text. (For Sophia Stacey and *The Literary Pocket-Book*, see headnote to 'Love's Philosophy': p. 775.) The poem could have been written towards the end of the period from early November to late December 1819, when Sophia was in Florence. If written earlier, it might have been inspired by the strained relations between PBS and MWS following the death in Rome in June 1819 of the Shelleys' three-year-old son, William, which is alluded to in ll. 15–18. It was first published in *Rossetti 1870*.

15 *corse*: Corpse.

On a Dead Violet: To —

In March 1820, PBS appended this lament for faded love to a letter sent from Pisa by MWS to Sophia Stacey (for whom see headnote to 'Love's Philosophy': p. 775) in Rome, enjoining her to keep its origin secret. In his accompanying note he refers to the poem as 'old stanzas', and they appear to have been drafted some months earlier, perhaps addressed to MWS. His relations with her had been severely strained since the death in Rome in June 1819 of their three-year-old son, William. PBS later sent a copy of the poem to Leigh Hunt in London, who published it in *The Literary Pocket-Book* (see headnote to 'Love's Philosophy': p. 775) for 1821 under the title 'Song. On a faded Violet'. Our text is from PBS's holograph on MWS's letter to Sophia Stacey of 7 March 1820, now in the Bibliotheca Bodmeriana, Cologny-Genève, Switzerland (see *MYR (Shelley)* VIII).

On the Medusa of Leonardo da Vinci, In the Florentine Gallery

PBS probably composed this poem on a painting in the Uffizi Gallery in Florence in November–December 1819. No holograph MS is known to exist. It was published by MWS in *1824* (from which our text is taken) in its present form, with ll. 18 and 37 incomplete. The painting, in oil on a wooden panel measuring 74 × 49cm, is now considered the work of an unidentified Flemish artist of the late sixteenth or early seventeenth century, though when PBS was in Florence it was attributed to Leonardo. The picture draws on two mythical traditions concerning the Medusa. According to one, she was a monster (a Gorgon – see l. 26) so hideous that to gaze on her (or to be gazed upon by her) was to be turned to stone. In his struggle with the Medusa, the hero Perseus avoided looking directly on her face, instead viewing her reflection in a polished shield, and was thus able to cut off her head. The other tradition represents the Medusa as a remarkable beauty whom Minerva punished by changing her hair into a knot of serpents. This combination of beauty and horror in art fascinated PBS, who wrote (disapprovingly) of Michelangelo in a letter of early 1819: 'What is terror without a contrast with & a connection with loveliness?' (*Letters* II, p. 80).

Mario Praz takes the poem as typical of a characteristically Romantic idea of beauty in the first chapter of *The Romantic Agony*, 2nd edn (Oxford: Oxford University Press, 1970). See also: Jerome McGann, 'The Beauty of the Medusa: A Study in Romantic Literary Iconology', *SiR* 11 (1972), pp. 3–25; and W. J. T. Mitchell, *Picture Theory* (Chicago and London: Chicago University Press, 1994), pp. 171–6.

3 *tremblingly*: As if blurred, perhaps by mist.
9–13 It is rather the grace than the terror of the Medusa's countenance that turns the spirit of 'the gazer' to stone on which her features are engraved and so assimilated.
16 *strain*: i.e. of music.
18 *watery*: Damp, moist; or perhaps located *in* water, such as a stream.
22 *mailed*: Covered with scales.
mock: Defy or mimic.
25 *eft*: A small lizard.
35 *inextricable error*: Convoluted winding that cannot be disentangled.
36 *thrilling*: Quivering.

To Night

PBS probably composed this lyric on a traditional theme (cp. 'Epithalamium' (p. 509) and Shakespeare, *Romeo and Juliet* III.ii.1–31) in late 1819. MWS published it in *1824*. In Greek myth, both Night (*Nyx*) and Day (*Hemera*) were goddesses. PBS alternates the gender of Day and Night in stanzas 2–4. Kurt Schlueter traces the poem's debt to the Classical hymn to a deity as well as to other Classical models in *SiR* 36/2 (1997), pp. 239–60; *Chernaik*, pp. 144–6, examines its character as a lyric of desire. The urgency of the address to Night is embodied in an intricate stanza of seven lines of eight, seven, four or three syllables rhyming *ababccb*.

Our text is from PBS's holograph fair copy in Harvard MS Eng. 258.2 (see *MYR (Shelley)* V). Some punctuation has been modified.

England in 1819

Not published until *1839*, though written in late 1819 and sent on 23 December in a letter to Leigh Hunt that includes PBS's lament 'What a state England is in!' and his instruction 'I do not expect you to publish it, but you may show it to whom you please' (*Letters* II, pp. 166–7). *Webb 1995* compares the liberal reformer Sir Francis Burdett's election address of 6 October 1812, published in *The Examiner* for 11 October 1812, pp. 654–6, on the condition of the nation: 'an army of spies and informers . . . a phantom for a King; a degraded Aristocracy; an oppressed People . . . irresponsible ministers; a corrupt and intimidated Press; pensioned Justices; packed Juries; vague and sanguinary Laws' (p. 655). The eighty-one-year-old King George III, who had reigned since 1760, had been diagnosed as incurably insane in 1810 and by late 1819 was blind, deaf and senile; he would die on 29 January 1820. His son, the unpopular Prince of Wales and future George IV, had exercised the office of regent from early 1811. The six other sons of George III, royal dukes supported from the public purse, were resented for their profligacy and extravagance. The first line invites comparison with Shakespeare, *King Lear* III.ii.20, in which the old former ruler of a kingdom in turmoil describes himself as 'A poor, infirm, weak and despised old man'. The play was not allowed to be performed during the Regency (Jonathan Bate, *Shakespeare and the English Romantic Imagination* (Oxford: Clarendon Press, 1986), pp. 204–5).

Our text is from PBS's fair copy in Bodleian MS Shelley adds. e. 12 (see *BSM* XVIII), which is untitled. MWS supplied the present title in *1839*.

7 An allusion to the killing and wounding of demonstrators for reform, many of them agricultural and industrial labourers who had suffered great hardship, by armed militia on 16 August 1819 at St Peter's Field, Manchester; see headnote to *The Mask of Anarchy* (p. 759).

8–9 An army maintained to oppress the people and extinguish liberty (the sense of 'liberticide') can turn against those who employ it.

10 Gold and blood (here 'sanguine' = 'sanguinary', 'bloody') are in PBS's poetry regularly presented as the foundations and instruments of tyranny. They 'tempt and slay' by bribery and corruption, and judicial murder.

11 *a book sealed*: Cp. Isaiah 29:11 – 'And the vision of all is become unto you as the words of a book that is sealed' – directed at those who refuse God's warnings.

12 *senate . . . unrepealed*: Parliament, for too long unrepresentative and in need of reform.

13–14 The lines borrow a symbolic figure from the conclusion to PBS's *An Address to the People on the Death of the Princess Charlotte*, written two years earlier: 'Let us follow the corpse of British Liberty slowly and reverentially to its tomb: and if some glorious Phantom should appear, and make its throne of broken swords and sceptres and royal crowns trampled in the dust, let us say that the Spirit of Liberty has arisen from its grave and left all that was gross and mortal there, and kneel down and worship it as our Queen' (p. 613). Cp. the similar apparition in *The Mask of Anarchy*, ll. 102–25 (pp. 360–61).

Song: To the Men of England

The text given here is from PBS's fair copy in Bodleian MS Shelley adds. c. 4, ff. 75v–76r (see *MYR (Shelley)* V). The 'Song' was probably written some time in early 1820; MWS published it in *1839*. On 1 May 1820, PBS wrote to Leigh Hunt: 'I wish to ask you if you know of any bookseller who would like to publish a little volume of *popular songs* wholly political, & destined to awaken & direct the imagination of the reformers. I see you smile but answer my question' (*Letters* II, p. 191). PBS never carried out his plan for such a collection; had he done so, this poem as well as a number of others that he wrote in late 1819 and early 1820 are likely to have figured in it, among those in the present selection: *The Mask of Anarchy* (p. 357), 'To S[idmouth] and C[astlereagh]' (p. 400), 'To —' ('Corpses are cold in the tomb') (p. 407) and 'God save the Queen!' (p. 423). MWS noted in *1839* (III, p. 307) that the reason none of them could appear in print until years later was that 'in those days of prosecution for libel' no bookseller would dare publish them. All of these poems emerge from the mixed outrage and apprehension that PBS felt following 'Peterloo', the killing of civilians by mounted militia at Manchester on 16 August 1819. See headnote to *The Mask of Anarchy* (p. 759).

10 *scourge*: Whip.

27–8 The sense of the couplet is: 'You yourselves have manufactured the chains and the steel that are now used against you.' The verb 'glance' can mean both 'flash' and 'strike a blow obliquely'.

To — ('Corpses are cold in the tomb')

Text from Harvard MS Eng. 822 (see *MYR (Shelley)* V). This bitterly defiant lament for the state of England was probably written in the early months of 1820 and may have been intended for a collection of political songs that PBS planned but never completed. See previous headnote. It was not published until 1832, in *The Athenaeum*, under the title 'Lines Written during the Castlereagh Administration'. The conspicuous absence of a name in the title suggests that some individual too dangerous to specify is being addressed as the 'Oppressor' of l. 11, perhaps Castlereagh himself or the home secretary, Sidmouth. See headnote to 'To S[idmouth] and C[astlereagh]' (p. 774).

3 *Abortions*: Lifeless foetuses.

5 *Albion*: England.

9 *travaileth*: Labours in childbirth; see note to l. 3.

12 *redressor*: One who puts right a wrong.

18 *crying 'havoc'*: To 'cry havoc' was to license a victorious army to plunder a defeated enemy.

19 *Bacchanal triumph*: In ancient Rome, the Bacchanalia was an orgiastic ritual, often disorderly, in honour of Bacchus (the god of wine and ecstasy); a 'triumph' was a public procession celebrating victory over a foreign foe.

20 *Epithalamium*: A wedding song; see 'Epithalamium' (p. 509).

24 *Hell*: PBS originally wrote 'God' before altering the word to the present reading.

The Sensitive-Plant

PBS composed 'The Sensitive-Plant' in Pisa in spring 1820, probably in March. It was published as one of the 'Miscellaneous Poems' in *1820*, which supplies our text, though we have adopted some features of MWS's fair copy in Harvard MS Eng. 258.2 (see *MYR (Shelley)* V). The plant of the title is the *Mimosa pudica*, popularly known as the 'humble plant' or 'shame plant', which shrinks from contact and closes its leaves at night. Its sensitivity to changes in light and temperature, as well as to touch – and hence the resemblance of its movements to animal reactions – had made its place in nature, on the border between animal and vegetable, the object of scientific interest. *Mimosa pudica* is an annual, a characteristic of importance for its representation in the poem. PBS's intriguing 'Conclusion' speculates on the existence of a transcendent dimension in which the features of the exquisite garden and its lovely custodian continue to exist in permanent perfection despite the seasonal alterations they have undergone. In creating the garden in which the plant grows, and the lady who tends it, PBS drew upon (and revised) a long tradition of fictional gardens presided over by a female attendant, including those in: Genesis 1–3; Dante, *Purgatorio* XXVIII; Spenser, *The Faerie Queene* III.vi.30–50; Milton, *Paradise Lost* IV and IX; and the botanical verses of Erasmus Darwin's *The Botanic Garden* (1791). William Cowper's brief moral fable in verse, 'The Poet, the Oyster, and the Sensitive Plant' (1782), makes a revealing contrast with PBS's poem.

The sparse commentary on 'The Sensitive-Plant' includes: Desmond King-Hele's chapter on Shelley in *Erasmus Darwin and the Romantic Poets* (Basingstoke: Macmillan, 1986); R. M. Maniquis, 'The Puzzling *Mimosa*: Sensitivity and Plant Symbols in Romanticism', *SiR* 8 (1969), pp. 129–55; and Michael O'Neill, '*The Sensitive-Plant*: Evaluation and the Self-Conscious Poem', in his *Romanticism and the Self-Conscious Poem* (Oxford: Clarendon Press, 1997).

PART FIRST

3–4 The mimosa 'Shuts her sweet eye-lids to approaching night; / And hails with freshen'd charms the rising light' in Erasmus Darwin, *The Botanic Garden* II.i.307–8.

17 *wind-flowers*: Anemones.

18–20 Alluding to the myth of Narcissus who, having scorned the love of the nymph Echo, pined away to death for love of his own reflection in a pool and was changed into a flower (Ovid, *Metamorphoses* III.344–511).

21 *Naiad-like*: In Greek mythology, Naiads were water nymphs.

24 *pavilions*: Coverings, canopies.

25 *hyacinth*: In Classical myth, Apollo loved the youth Hyacinth; when he died, the god caused a flower to spring from his blood.

27–8 The first of many examples of synaesthesia, representing one sense-impression in terms of another – a principal stylistic figure in the poem.

34 *Maenad*: See note to 'Ode to the West Wind', l. 21 (p. 774).

37 *jessamine*: Jasmine.

42 *prankt*: Ornamented, decorated.

54 *asphodels*: A plant of the lily family imagined by Homer as growing in the Elysian Fields (*Odyssey* XI.539) and by Milton in Paradise (*Paradise Lost* IX.1040).

63 *mine-lamps*: In 1815 Humphry Davy invented a miner's lamp which could be used safely underground.

76–7 Recalling Plato's *Symposium*, which PBS translated in July 1818: 'Love wants and does not possess beauty' (*Ingpen and Peck* VII, p. 195).

88 *spirits*: Angelic beings who guided the concentric spheres that made up the heavens, in older astronomy.

108 *Elysian*: Exquisitely delightful, as in Elysium, the abode of the blessed after death in Classical mythology.

PART SECOND

2 *grace*: In Classical myth, the Graces were three sisters, goddesses of beauty, ministers of joy and affection and sources of artistic inspiration.

10 *meteors*: Any luminous atmospheric phenomenon.

sublunar: Under the moon's influence, earthly, and so subject to change.

38 *ozier*: Willow.

43 *woof*: Woven material.

49 *ephemeris*: An insect (usually 'ephemerid') whose brief winged adult life may fill no more than a day.

53 *antenatal tomb*: The pupal case from which the adult butterfly emerges.

PART THIRD

3–4 Mount Vesuvius is visible from Baiae on the Bay of Naples, which PBS visited in December 1818 (*MWS Journal* I, p. 242).

34–41 The lines rework 'Ode to the West Wind', ll. 2–8 (p. 398).

48 *parasite bowers*: Bowers formed by climbing plants, not necessarily those that feed off a host.

54 *darnels*: Weeds, harmful grasses generally.

55 Dock is a weed with deep roots and broad leaves; henbane and hemlock are both poisonous and foul-smelling.

56 *shank*: The stem or footstalk.

62 *agarics*: A variety of fungi with gills on the underside, including edible mushrooms.

66–9 The fungi that emerge from the ground in the previous stanza are compared as they decay to the rotting corpse of an executed criminal exposed on a gibbet.

70 *Spawn*: The fibre-like filaments of a mushroom or other fungus.

72 *flags*: This perhaps designates a species of iris, though in older usage it could also signify a reed or rush.

78 *unctuous meteors*: Unctuous = 'inflammable' (cp. *OED* unctuous 3); for meteors, see note to II.10 above. The will-o'-the-wisp or marsh fire – glowing gases resulting from decaying vegetation – is here imagined as flitting from plant to plant spreading infection.

82 *forbid*: Accursed.

91 *choppy*: Chapped, cracked; cp. Shakespeare, *Macbeth* I.iii.42–3 describing the weird sisters: 'By each at once her choppy finger laying / Upon her skinny lips'.

113 *griff*: Claw.

116 *mandrakes*: Plants common in the Mediterranean area, having white flowers tinged with purple and traditionally thought to possess magical properties. Their large roots were supposed to resemble the human form and to shriek when plucked.

117 *charnels*: Places of burial, tombs.

CONCLUSION

9–12 Relevant antecedents for the life-dream comparison would be Shakespeare, *The Tempest* IV.i.156–7, 'We are such stuff / As dreams are made on', and Calderón's play *La vida es sueño* (Life is a Dream).

15 *own*: Acknowledge.

16 *mockery*: Illusion; PBS formulates this intuition more firmly in 'On Life': 'Whatever may be his [man's] true and final destination, there is a spirit within him at enmity with change and extinction' (p. 621).

21 PBS's first version was 'For love & thought there is not death' (Huntington Library HM 2176 f. 33[r] reverso: see *MYR (Shelley)* VI).

22–4 *their might . . . obscure*: The sense is that our limited organs of perception are inadequate to discern the permanent transcendent radiance of 'love, and beauty, and delight' (l. 21).

23 *Exceeds our organs*: PBS first wrote 'Outlives our feelings/visions' (see *MYR (Shelley)* VI).

An Exhortation

Composed between late 1819 and spring 1820, published in *1820*, which provides our copy-text; punctuation has been somewhat modified, taking into account the fair copy in Harvard MS Eng. 258.2 (see *MYR (Shelley)* V). PBS's remark in a letter of May 1820 to John and Maria Gisborne in London probably refers to the present poem: 'I send a little thing about Poets; which is itself a kind of an excuse for Wordsworth . . . You may shew it [Leigh] Hunt if you like' (*Letters* II, p. 195). This lyric handles lightly and deftly the theme of the poet's relation to 'wealth or power' (l. 19) which PBS had treated more seriously – with Wordsworth as case in point – in 'To Wordsworth' (p. 109) and *Peter Bell the Third* (p. 369). The chameleon's capacity to change colour in response to its environment made it an emblem of inconstancy, while its ability to exist for long periods without food gave rise to the belief that it fed on air.

7 *light*: Both the senses 'agile' and 'fickle' appear to be intended.

10–18 Just as an undersea cave would provide no light to bring about a change in the chameleon's colour, so the world cannot offer poets the love and fame they need. No wonder, then, that poets behave with inconstancy in their search for both.

Song of Apollo

PBS composed these lines and their companion piece, 'Song of Pan' (p. 419), in April–May 1820 for a scene in *Midas*, a mythological drama that MWS adapted from Ovid's *Metamorphoses.* Our texts are based on PBS's drafts in the Bodleian Library (MS Shelley adds e. 6: see *BSM* V) rather than the fair copies by MWS (*BSM* X), which differ from the drafts at a number of points. In MWS's play, as in her source (*Metamorphoses* XI.146–93), Midas attends a singing contest between Apollo and Pan which is judged by Tmolus, the local deity of the mountain of the same name. In Ovid, Pan sings first and is declared the victor by Midas; when Apollo's song is judged superior by Tmolus, Midas objects, provoking Apollo to punish him by causing ass's ears to grow on his head. MWS departs from Ovid by having Apollo sing first. In Greek myth and religion, Apollo was a god of music, poetry, healing, archery and prophecy (ll. 13–14, 33–4), and, as god of light (l. 35), was associated with the sun. Earl Wasserman, *Shelley: A Critical Reading* (Baltimore: Johns Hopkins University Press, 1971), pp. 46–56, makes an illuminating comparison of the two songs.

Title Neither of PBS's drafts is titled. In 1824 MWS supplied the titles 'Hymn of Apollo' and 'Hymn of Pan'.
22 *cinctured*: Encircled, girded.
27 *even*: Evening.
31–2 Wasserman, *Shelley: A Critical Reading*, p. 48, notices in these lines a reworking of the Sun's declaration in *Metamorphoses* IV.226–8: 'Lo, I am he who measure out the year, who behold all things, by whom the earth beholds all things – the world's eye.'

Song of Pan

For composition and context, see previous headnote. The god Pan was a rural deity, particularly of shepherds and flocks, who was reputed to haunt mountains and caves. His cult originated in Arcadia. Rough and shaggy in appearance, he was represented as half man and half goat and personified erotic energy, figuring in several myths of sexual pursuit. Because the Greek word *pan* means 'all', he was sometimes regarded as a universal deity.

Title See note to previous poem.
3 *river-girt*: Surrounded by rivers.
9 *cicadae*: Cicadas were traditionally imagined as blithe and carefree. See also note to *The Witch of Atlas*, l. 108 (p. 451).
11 *even old Tmolus*: The local deity presiding over the contest between Apollo and Pan (see previous headnote); 'even' – because Tmolus preferred Apollo's song.
13–15 The river Pineios (Peneus) flows through the valley of Tempe in north-eastern Thessaly, in Greece, and is overshadowed by the mountains of Pelion, Ossa and Olympus.
15 *[?]*: PBS first wrote then cancelled 'Ossa's', substituting an illegible word above the line. Editors have read this as 'Pelion' or 'Olympus'. See previous note.
18–19 *sileni . . . nymphs*: Minor demi-gods in Greek and Roman myth, often associated with particular localities or aspects of nature such as trees or streams.
26 *daedal*: Intricately formed; from Daedalus, the skilled inventor and father of Icarus. See 'Mont Blanc', l. 86 (p. 144), and 'Ode to Liberty', l. 18 (p. 427).
27 *the giant wars*: Pan sings of the archaic Greek myth of the battles for dominion over the world waged by the Olympian gods against the Giants, the offspring of Gaia (the Earth). The Olympians defeated the Giants with the aid of the mortal hero Heracles.
30–31 The nymph Syrinx, pursued by Pan, was transformed into a reed to escape him. Intrigued by the sound of the wind in the reeds, Pan joined several of different lengths together to make the musical pipes called *syrinx* traditionally associated with him. The Mainalo (Maenalus) Mountains are in northern Arcadia, a region sacred to Pan.
34 *both ye*: Apollo and Tmolus.

The Cloud

Composed in spring 1820, published in *1820*, which furnishes our copy-text. Partial drafts of a few lines and an autograph fair copy of ll. 35–84 have survived (see *BSM* V) and have been consulted. The punctuation of *1820* has been somewhat modified.

The two major literary precedents for PBS's poem are Aristophanes' comedy *The Clouds*, in which the chorus of female clouds points out the benefits they bring to the world by providing both rain and shade, and Leigh Hunt's poem 'The Nymphs' (published in *Foliage*, 1818), which gives voice to a group of 'Nepheliads', each of them a nymph-like spirit that guides a cloud as it travels through the heavens. PBS praised 'The Nymphs' as 'delightful' and 'truly *poetical*, in the intense and emphatic sense of the word' (*Letters* II, pp. 2–3). The poem also exhibits an understanding of the atmospheric cycle of evaporation–condensation–precipitation by which the earth is supplied with rain and which contemporary science had elucidated. Luke Howard's *On the Modifications of Clouds* (1803), for example, had established that the identifiable types of clouds were not fixed but that their existence involved constant transformation one into another. See Richard Hamblyn, *The Invention of Clouds* (New York: Farrar, Straus and Giroux, 2001), and Desmond King-Hele, *Shelley: His Thought and Work*, 2nd edn (London: Macmillan, 1971), pp. 219–27.

9 *flail*: A staff to which a freely swinging club is attached, used for threshing grain; also a weapon consisting of a handle to which a spiked ball is fastened by a chain.

17–30 The passage is influenced by the view of some contemporary scientists – no longer accepted by meteorologists – that the interaction of electrical charges in the atmosphere and in bodies of water on earth furnishes the energy for the production of clouds and rain. Adam Walker, who lectured at both Syon House Academy and Eton during PBS's time at each, held that 'water rises through the air, flying on the wings of electricity' (*A System of Familiar Philosophy* (London: 1799), p. 358). Equally important in these lines, however, is the analogy between cloud formation and erotic attraction.

23 *genii*: Spirits that preside in particular places.

31 *sanguine*: Blood-red.

33 *rack*: A mass of high clouds driven by the wind.

44 Echoing the apostrophe to the Holy Spirit in Milton, *Paradise Lost* I.20–21: '[thou] with mighty wings outspread / Dove-like sat'st brooding on the vast abyss.'

45–58 The stanza imagines the moon's footsteps as making gaps in the cloud through which the stars appear to 'whirl and flee' as it is driven along by the wind; thus exposed, the moon and stars are reflected in the waters below.

59–60 *zone* ... *girdle*: The halos of illuminated cloud round the sun and moon.

67–9 In ancient Rome, a triumphal arch was a monument commemorating a victory over a foreign foe. PBS had seen several examples in Rome. The victorious commander was typically represented in a chariot ('chair') and the foreign captives in chains. Cp. *The Triumph of Life*, l. 252, in which defeated prisoners are 'chained to the triumphal chair' (p. 578). The 'Powers of the Air' are atmospheric forces considered as celestial divinities. Cp. *Hellas*, l. 230 (p. 523).

71 *sphere-fire*: The sun.

75 *pores*: The moisture that forms the cloud has been drawn through the minute interstices between the particles that form the matter of sea and land.

78 *pavilion*: A large tent.

79 *convex*: 'The earth's atmosphere bends a ray of sunlight into a curve... convex to an observer in a cloud looking down' (King-Hele, *Shelley: His Thought and Work*, p. 225).

81 *cenotaph*: A funerary monument for one whose body rests elsewhere. Here it is the 'blue Dome of Air' (l. 80) which the winds and sunbeams have built for the cloud and which it destroys in ll. 83–4.

'God save the Queen!'

In *1840* MWS published without title six stanzas of this parody of the British national anthem, which PBS had drafted and left in a notebook, now Bodleian Shelley MS adds. e. 6 (see *BSM* V) and from which our text has been edited. Additional punctuation has been provided. The draft, which is rough and unfinished, appears to date from April–May 1820. The present title was supplied in *Rossetti 1870*. 'A New National Anthem' was the title given by Edward Dowden in his edition of the poem (1891) and has been followed by several twentieth-century editions. It is likely that the 'anthem' was intended for a collection of songs on political themes that PBS planned but never completed: see headnote to 'Song: To the Men of England' (p. 778).

Dating from the late seventeenth century, 'God Save the King' acquired something like its modern form in response to the Jacobite rising of 1745. Through the eighteenth century new stanzas were added in reference to royal events, and parodies of varying political colours were written, some sharply satirical. PBS's version avoids specific satire in favour of a generalized hymn of praise to Liberty expressed in a religious idiom adopted from biblical tradition.

3 *murdered Queen*: PBS introduces the figure of Liberty as murdered queen in *An Address to the People on the Death of the Princess Charlotte* (p. 605). See also 'England in 1819' (p. 405).

36 The line alludes to the conferring of prophetic power in Isaiah 6:6–7: 'Then flew one of the seraphims unto me, having a live coal in his hand... And he laid it upon my mouth, and said, Lo, this hath touched thy lips; and thine iniquity is taken away, and thy sin purged.'

40 The missing word, cancelled in the MS, is difficult to read: 'triumphal' and 'trumpet's' have been suggested.

Translation of Dante's Purgatorio, *Canto XXVIII, lines 1–51*

PBS drafted this translation from the *Purgatorio*, the second canticle of Dante's *Divina Commedia*, in late spring or summer 1820 in a notebook which is now Bodleian MS Shelley adds. e. 6 (see *BSM* V). Lines 1–9 and 22–51 were first published in Thomas Medwin, *The Angler in Wales* (London: Richard Bentley, 1834), the complete text in *Relics of Shelley*, ed. Richard Garnett (London: Edward Moxon, 1862). PBS's draft is incomplete and not always perfectly legible, so that the text offered below is necessarily conjectural in places. Some additional punctuation has been supplied.

Dante imagines Purgatory as a steep mountain which sinners must ascend in the afterlife in order gradually to purge their sins; the present passage is set in the earthly paradise at its summit. The woman that the pilgrim Dante encounters will later be named 'Matilda'; she, together with Beatrice, becomes his guide in the final six cantos of the *Purgatorio*. By mid 1820, PBS had come to hold Dante in the highest regard. The previous summer he had written that 'Matilda Gathering Flowers' was a representative specimen of 'all the exquisite tenderness & sensibility & ideal beauty, in which Dante excelled all poets except Shakespeare' (*Letters* II, p. 112). He felt both that no 'adequate translation' of the *Divina Commedia* existed (*Medwin 1913*, p. 244) and that Dante was 'the most untranslatable of all poets' (*Medwin's Conversations of Lord Byron*, ed. E. J. Lovell, Jnr (Princeton, NJ: Princeton University Press, 1966), p. 160). In *A Defence of Poetry* (p. 651), PBS defines the pivotal position he assigned to Dante in the development of European literature; while in *The Triumph of Life* (p. 570) he creates a Dantean visionary poem in the *terza rima* of the *Divina Commedia* – three-line stanzas rhyming *aba bcb cdc*, and so on – notoriously difficult to manage in English, which offers fewer possibilities for rhyme than Italian.

2 *woof*: The greenery of the wood is, as it were, woven closely together like fabric.

12 *That sacred hill*: The mountain of Purgatory.

15 *blithe quest*: Cheerful singing; 'quest' is a term for the baying of hounds in a hunt.

18 *roundelay*: A brief song with a 'burthen' (refrain).

20 *Chiassi*: Modern Classe on the Adriatic coast south of Ravenna.

21 *Aeolus* was the ancient god of the winds who released or restrained them. Sirocco is a hot wind from the south-east.

34–5 Dante's lines read, literally translated: 'I stopped with my feet and with my eyes passed across the streamlet, to gaze.'

42 *besprent*: Sprinkled, strewn.

48–51 In Classical myth, Proserpine, while gathering flowers, was taken away by Pluto to the underworld to rule there with him; distraught, her mother Ceres wandered over the entire world searching for her.

Evening. Ponte a Mare, Pisa

Our text is based on PBS's unfinished and untitled draft in Bodleian MS Shelley adds. e. 9, pp. 346–8 (see *BSM* XIV). Probably composed in summer 1820, possibly before the Shelleys left Pisa for Livorno on 15 June. In *1824*, where the lines were first published, MWS supplied the title and the date, 1821. There is little in the draft to suggest a specific location, although as *Poems* III, p. 421, observes, the windswept 'Town' described in ll. 10–12 would be apt for early nineteenth-century Pisa, where the population had been in decline for some time. The Ponte a Mare was the westernmost of the three bridges that then crossed the Arno at Pisa. The brief shift to the past tense in l. 14 would seem to be an inadvertence.

13–16 See note to ll. 63–4 of 'To Jane—The Recollection' (p. 843) and cp. 'Ode to Liberty', ll. 76–9 (p. 429).

15–16 Cp. Wordsworth, 'Elegaic Stanzas' (first published in *Poems, in Two Volumes* (1807)), ll. 7–8: 'thy Image still was there; / It trembled, but it never pass'd away.'

17–18 PBS cancelled 'Indies' and left l. 17 unfinished, but the sense is clear: you could go to the ends of the earth and return to find the city reflected in the river as always.

20 *cinereous*: Ashen, ash-coloured.

Ode to Liberty

PBS's draft is in the Bodleian Library (*BSM* V), as is a partial Italian translation by him of stanzas 1–13 and 19 (*BSM* III). A transcript of ll. 1–21 by MWS of a now-lost intermediate fair copy also survives, in the Houghton Library at Harvard University (see *MYR (Shelley)* V). PBS sent a copy of the poem, which was probably composed between early May and 12 July 1820 (see *Letters* II, pp. 213–14), to T. L. Peacock in London on the latter date with instructions to publish it with *Prometheus Unbound* (p. 184). It appeared as the final poem in *1820*, which supplies our copy-text.

'Ode to Liberty' (the 'Ode') is a free imitation of the odes of the ancient Greek poet Pindar (*c.*522–*c.*443 BC) in honour of the victors in athletic contests. In this case, the victory celebrated – or anticipated – is that of liberty over political oppression. The primary occasion of the poem was the military uprising in Spain in early 1820, which prompted King Ferdinand VII to grant a return to the broad reforms provided for in the liberal constitution of 1812, and which PBS saw as part of the growing advance of liberty across mainland Europe. The 'Ode' surveys the history of liberty from its origins in Classical Greece until the early nineteenth century, finishing with a glance at some national struggles for freedom and independence in contemporary Europe. In this respect, then, it retraces in concentrated poetic form the political history that PBS had charted in *A Philosophical View of Reform* (p. 636) and also anticipates the progress of artistic creation that he imagines in *A Defence of Poetry* (p. 651). As well as its debts to Classical sources, the 'Ode' had notable modern precedents in, for example, James Thomson's *Liberty* (1735–6), Thomas Gray's 'The Progress of Poesy' (1757), William Collins's 'Ode to Liberty' (1746) and Coleridge's 'France: An Ode' (1798).

On publication, the 'Ode' was attacked by the conservative reviews for its explicitly anti-religious and anti-monarchical stance. Interesting commentary is given in *Chernaik*, pp. 97–108, and William Keach, *Arbitrary Power: Romanticism, Language, Politics* (Princeton, NJ: Princeton University Press, 2004), pp. 151–8.

Epigraph From Byron, *Childe Harold's Pilgrimage*, Canto IV (1818), stanza 98, ll. 1–2. The stanza concludes Byron's own review of the history of political liberty.

1–2 PBS here compares Liberty to an electrical charge, which Spain now sends forth for a second time, the previous occasion having been the Spanish resistance to French occupation in 1807–8. Cp. PBS's Preface to *Prometheus Unbound*: 'The cloud of mind is discharging its collected lightning, and the equilibrium between institutions and opinions is now restoring, or is about to be restored' (p. 186).

6 *plumes*: Plumage, feathers. Images of the soul taking flight through poetry are common in Classical and Renaissance literature. In PBS's translation of Plato's *Ion* (1821) the souls of poets are 'arrayed in the plumes of rapid imagination' (*Ingpen and Peck*, VII, p. 238).

8 *a young eagle*: *Webb 1995* identifies an allusion to Pindar's *Nemean Odes* III.80–82, in which the poet compares his art to an eagle swooping on its prey.

11–15 The 'whirlwind' and the 'voice out of the deep' recall traditional figures for divine communication and inspiration: e.g. Job 38:1, Acts 9:4 and Revelation 1:10–12, 16:17. Cp. *The Mask of Anarchy*, ll. 1–3 (p. 357). The ship is a conventional figure for the poetic imagination, e.g. Dante, *Purgatorio* I.1–3.

11 *rapt it*: Carried it away; enraptured the poet's 'soul' (l. 5).

16 The words of the 'voice' of l. 15 are 'recorded' from here until l. 270.

18 *daedal*: Intricate, or cunningly made, after Daedalus, the master craftsman (and father of Icarus) in Greek mythology. Cp. 'Mont Blanc', l. 86 and note to ll. 84–95 (pp. 144, 721).

19 *the world*: i.e. the 'universe' (l. 21).

23 *thou*: Liberty.

28 *their violated nurse*: The earth.

41 *The sister-pest*: Institutional religion; 'pest' = 'plague', 'pestilence'.

42 *pinions*: Wings.

43 *Anarchs*: Tyrants who promote misrule; cp. 'Lines Written among the Euganean Hills, October, 1818', l. 152 (p. 157), and *The Triumph of Life*, l. 237 (p. 578).

45 *astonished*: Stunned, bewildered.

46 *nodding*: The sense is elusive: perhaps the image is of promontories covered with trees 'nodding' in the wind.

47 *dividuous*: The sense is not immediately clear. *OED* defines the word as 'divisible, characterized by division'; so PBS may have intended '(a large number of) individual waves'. *Webb 1995* suggests 'which break up'.

48–9 Perhaps referring to arguments made by, for example, the German classicist Johann Joachim Winckelmann (1717–68), on the climate and landscape of Greece and the flourishing of Classical Greek culture.

51 *unapprehensive*: Deficient in understanding.

53 *savage*: Uncultivated.

58 *Parian stone*: Fine white marble from the island of Paros, prized by ancient Greek sculptors.

73 *mock*: Imitate.

74 *that hill*: The Acropolis, the citadel on a rocky plateau dominating Athens which included the Parthenon and other magnificent temples built in the fifth century BC.

75 PBS identifies Athens as both the historical birthplace of liberty and an emblem of what mankind might achieve in the future.

76–9 Cp. 'Evening. Ponte a Mare, Pisa', ll. 13–16 (p. 426).

92 *Like a wolf-cub . . . [Shelley's note]*: A Maenad, in Greek myth, was a frenzied female follower of Dionysus, the god of wine and ecstasy (cp. l. 171). Dionysus was the son of Zeus and Semele, one of the daughters of Cadmus; in Euripides' play *The Bacchae*, the Maenads were Semele's sisters, the other daughters of Cadmus (hence 'Cadmaean'). PBS here blends the figures of Romulus and Remus, the mythical founders of Rome, supposed to have been suckled by a she-wolf, with the report of a Maenad suckling a wolf-cub in *The Bacchae*. On Maenads, see also *Prometheus Unbound* II.iii.7–10, IV.473–5 (pp. 226, 269).

93 *thy dearest*: Athens.

94 *Elysian*: From Elysium, the paradise of Greek and Roman myth.

95 *terrible*: Awe-inspiring.

98 Marcus Furius Camillus (*c.*446–365 BC) was a Roman statesman and military commander, sometimes known as the second founder of Rome after he returned from exile to defend the city from a besieging army of Gauls in 386 BC; PBS described Camillus as 'that most perfect & virtuous of men' (*Letters* II, p. 86). Marcus Atilius Regulus (consul 267 and 256 BC) led the Roman invasion of Africa during the First Punic War and was taken prisoner by the Carthaginians. Tradition had it that, sent to Rome to sue for peace, he instead advised the Romans to continue fighting, and then honourably returned to Carthage knowing he would be executed.

99 *thy robe . . . whiteness*: The Vestal Virgins, priestesses of the cult of Vesta, Roman goddess of the hearth, were charged with keeping alight a perpetual flame which guaranteed the safety of Rome.

100–105 PBS associates the Capitoline Hill in Rome with the founding of the Republic, and the Palatine Hill (l. 103) with the Empire.

104 *Ionian*: Here probably signifying the Greek, and specifically Athenian, attachment to political liberty celebrated in stanzas V and VI.

106 Traditionally wild and rugged, Hyrcania was a region south of the Caspian (Hyrcanian) Sea, in modern-day Iran and Turkmenistan.

111 *Naiad*: In Greek myth, Naiads were female spirits associated with particular rivers, lakes, or fountains.

115 *Scald . . . Druid*: Skalds were the court poets of Scandinavia and Iceland during the Viking era; Druids were priests in Celtic Britain, Ireland and France.

116 *shattered*: Some editors have emended to 'scattered', but 'shattered' could also mean 'dispersed' (*OED*).

119 *The Galilean serpent*: Christianity (as opposed to Jesus, whose teachings, PBS believed, had been perverted by the institutional Church).

123 *Alfred's olive-cinctured brow*: Alfred the Great (848–99), King of Wessex, repelled a Danish invasion and introduced legal and political reforms. In ancient Greece, an olive wreath was awarded to the victor in the Olympic Games and is a traditional symbol of peace ('cinctured' = 'encircled').

124–35 PBS compares the rise of the Italian city states in the Middle Ages and Renaissance, which maintained liberty in opposition to religious-political tyranny and created conditions which allowed the arts to flourish, to the rise of volcanic islands from the sea.

136 *huntress . . . Moon*: In Greek myth, Artemis was goddess of the hunt and of the moon.

141 In PBS's view, Martin Luther (1483–1546) inspired a religious awakening but did not go far enough in challenging ecclesiastical authority. See *A Defence of Poetry*: 'Dante was the first religious reformer, and Luther surpassed him rather in the rudeness and acrimony than in the boldness of his censures of papal usurpation' (pp. 669–70).

145 *England's prophets*: The writers and thinkers of the English Renaissance, including Shakespeare, Spenser and Milton. Cp. 'Letter to Maria Gisborne', ll. 31–2 (p. 438), and *A Philosophical View of Reform*: 'Shakespeare and Lord Bacon and the great writers of the age of Elizabeth and James the 1st were at once the effects of the new spirit in men's minds and the causes of its more complete development' (*Prose*, p. 231).

147–50 The restoration of the Stuart monarchy, a political calamity for the republican Milton, was a sombre circumstance beyond which his vision allowed him to see.

148–9 Contrasting Milton's prophetic powers with his physical blindness.

151–65 The stanza is a symbolic celebration of the progress of enlightened thought in Europe from the late seventeenth to the late eighteenth century, the period that included the American Revolution.

158 *the destroyer*: Death.

166–73 Centuries of oppression issued in the bloodshed that marred the French Revolution, the supporters of monarchy and the Church behaving like drunken revellers. For 'Bacchanals', see note to 'To —' ('Corpses are cold in the tomb'), l. 19 (p. 779).

174 *one*: Napoleon Bonaparte; for PBS's attitude to Napoleon, cp. 'Feelings of a Republican on the Fall of Bonaparte' (p. 110), 'Written on hearing the news of the death of Napoleon' (p. 508) and *The Triumph of Life*, ll. 215–31 (p. 577).

181–7 As Geoffrey Matthews was the first to point out ('A Volcano's Voice in Shelley', *ELH* 24 (1957), pp. 191–228), PBS deploys contemporary scientific investigations into the subterranean connections between volcanoes to symbolize the inevitable spread of revolution across Europe.

185–6 The Aeolian (or Lipari) Islands are a volcanic archipelago located off the north coast of Sicily. Pithecusa (Ischia) is south-west of Naples and Pelorus (Punta del Faro) lies at the north-eastern tip of Sicily.

188 The brilliant light diffused by the volcanic eruptions of Liberty obscures the heavenly bodies.

189–90 The interests of the wealthy, which England could easily shake off if it wished, contrast with the long traditions of absolutism in Spain which require a resolute struggle.

194 *West*: Referring to democratic developments in America, probably both North and South.

196 *Arminius* (*c.*18 BC–AD 21): A Germanic tribal chieftain who inflicted a defeat on the Romans in AD 9, effectively halting further Roman expansion into Germania.

201 While he was composing 'Ode to Liberty' PBS felt that a revolution in Germany was imminent. Cp. *A Philosophical View of Reform*: 'everything . . . wears in Germany the aspect of rapidly maturing revolution' (*Prose*, p. 237).

204 *lost Paradise*: In *Julian and Maddalo*, l. 57, Italy is described as 'Paradise of exiles' (p. 165).

212 KING: Replaced by four asterisks in *1820*; PBS authorized the substitution when he sent the poem to London in July 1820 (*Letters* II, pp. 213–14), because 'imagining or compassing the king's death' constituted high treason.

216 *Ye*: 'the free' (l. 211).

217–18 According to legend, Gordius, King of Phrygia, bound his chariot in a temple with a highly complicated knot; an oracle foretold that whoever untied the knot would become king of all Asia. Alexander the Great, having failed to undo it, simply sliced through it with his sword. Hence, 'gordian' = 'intricate', 'hard to solve'.

220 *irrefragably*: Obstinately, intractably.

221 *The axes and the rods*: The *fasces*, an axe tied in a bundle of rods, which was a symbol of public authority in ancient Rome, and became so again in fascist Italy.

224 *thou*: Liberty.

225 *reluctant*: 'Struggling, writhing' (*OED*).

231–3 Cp. PBS's characterization of those open to imaginative power in *A Philosophical View of Reform*: 'they are . . . compelled to serve, that which is seated on the throne of their own soul. And whatever systems <they> may professedly support, they actually advance the interests of Liberty' (p. 641). See also the final paragraph of *A Defence of Poetry* (p. 677).

233 *power unknown*: From *Queen Mab* (p. 23) onwards, PBS's work makes reference to a force which animates the natural world and which is distinct from the human mind and will. Cp., for example, 'Hymn to Intellectual Beauty' (p. 134) and 'Mont Blanc' (p. 140).

234–40 PBS evinces an acute awareness of the limitations and distortions of language, in e.g. 'On Life' (p. 619) and in his MS note to 'On Love': 'These words inefficient & metaphorical—Most words so—No help—' (p. 618).

240 In this secular version of the Last Judgement, words finally stand 'before their Lord', presumably the 'aweless soul' or 'power unknown' (l. 233).

241 *He*: Commentators have suggested that the antecedent is 'their Lord' in the previous line, or that 'He who' is used for 'Whoever'.

243–5 Cp. 'Sonnet: Political Greatness' (p. 470).

246–7 A challenge to Thomas Malthus's *Essay on the Principle of Population* (1798), which had identified famines and wars as necessary means of keeping in check a population whose growth threatened to exceed the increase of natural resources available to support it. Cp. l. 263 and note.

254 Cp. Coleridge, 'France: An Ode', l. 60: 'them that toil and groan'.

255 *thy . . . hers*: Liberty's and Nature's.

258 *Eoan*: Eastern; from 'Eos', the Greek goddess of the dawn.

259 *pennons*: Wings.

263 *life's ill-apportioned lot*: *Poems* III suggests a possible reference to Malthus's notorious phrase 'the unhappy persons who, in the great lottery of life, have drawn a blank' (*An Essay on the Principle of Population* (1798), chapter 10).

273 *a wild swan*: Cp. PBS's portrait of Byron as 'a tempest-cleaving Swan / Of the songs of Albion' in 'Lines Written among the Euganean Hills', ll. 174–5 (p. 158).

To a Sky-Lark

This well-known and much-anthologized lyric was composed at Livorno in late June 1820 and published in *1820*, which supplies our copy-text, though its punctuation and capitalization have been modified with reference to PBS's fair copy in Harvard MS Eng. 258.2 (see *MYR (Shelley)* V). MWS later recalled the occasion that provided the germ of the poem: 'It was on a beautiful summer evening, while wandering among the lanes whose myrtle hedges were the bowers of the fire-flies, that we heard the carolling of the sky-lark which inspired one of the most beautiful of his poems' (*1839* IV, p. 50). In the letter from Livorno to T. L. Peacock of 12 July 1820 that probably enclosed the press copy of the poem, PBS wrote: 'I wonder why I write verses, for nobody reads them' (*Letters* II, p. 213). Together with several other poems published in *1820* – 'The Sensitive-Plant' (p. 408), 'The Cloud' (p. 420), 'An Exhortation' (p. 418), 'Ode to the West Wind' (p. 398) – 'To a Sky-Lark' takes a closely observed aspect of the natural world as the starting place for a meditation on imaginative creation. Recent lyrics apostrophizing a bird, which PBS knew and which bear interesting comparison with his poem, include Wordsworth's 'To a Sky-Lark', 'To the Cuckoo' and 'The Green Linnet' – all in *Poems, in Two Volumes* (1807). The stanza of four lines of five or six syllables followed by an alexandrine of twelve syllables has been compared both to the lark's song and to its slowly rising flight and sudden fall.

5 *unpremeditated*: The word had come to describe genuine inspiration following Milton's allusion to his 'celestial' Muse Urania, who inspires his 'unpremeditated verse' in *Paradise Lost* IX.21–4.

8 *cloud of fire*: A cloud lit up by the setting sun, as in ll. 11–13 or, as G. M. Matthews suggests (*Shelley: Selected Poems and Prose* (Oxford: Oxford University Press, 1964)), a burst of smoke and flame sent up by a volcano.

22 *silver sphere*: The planet Venus as the morning star.

33–5 The 'Drops' are those that continue to fall from a cloud after the sun has appeared, creating a rainbow.

45 *bower*: Abode, or perhaps a chamber or bedroom (*OED* 2a).

64 *love or wine*: Themes traditionally associated with the Greek lyric poet Anacreon (born *c.*570 BC) and his imitators.

66 *Chorus Hymeneal*: Song sung at a wedding; Hymen was the Greek god invoked at marriage ceremonies.

86 Adapting Hamlet's words on human mental powers: 'he that made us with such large discourse, / Looking before and after, gave us not / That capability and god-like reason / To fust in us unused' (Shakespeare, *Hamlet*,

'Additional Passages' in Wells and Taylor OUP edition, p. 689; see headnote to Notes: p. 679).

103 *madness*: The traditional idea of the poet's inspiration as 'divine madness', without which he could not create true poetry whatever his technical skill, PBS will have encountered in Plato's *Phaedrus*, which he read in May 1819, and perhaps in Plato's *Ion*, which he was to translate in early 1821.

Letter to Maria Gisborne

Composed between late June and early July 1820, and probably sent to Maria Gisborne in London, with a letter from MWS, on 7 July. PBS's draft survives in the Bodleian Library (see *BSM* XIV). The fair copy he sent to Maria Gisborne has been lost, as has a transcript made of that copy by the Gisbornes in 1822, at MWS's request. MWS's transcript, now in the Huntington Library (MS 12338: see *MYR (Shelley)* III), probably derives from the copy made by the Gisbornes. A further copy, made by John Gisborne in 1831, presumably from the original sent by PBS, also survives in the Bodleian Library (MS Abinger d.19). Our text is based on the John Gisborne transcript, with some readings supplied from PBS's draft and MWS's transcript (see also note to ll. 272–3). First published in *1824*, the poem was given the present title in *1839*. MWS records in her 'Note on the Poems of 1820' in *1839*:

> We spent a week or two near Leghorn [actually 15 June–4 August], borrowing the house of some friends who were absent on a journey to England . . . [PBS] addressed the letter to Mrs. Gisborne from this house, which was hers: he had made his study of the workshop of her son, who was an engineer. Mrs. Gisborne had been a friend of my father in her younger days. She was a lady of great accomplishments, and charming from her frank and affectionate nature. She had the most intense love of knowledge, a delicate and trembling sensibility, and preserved freshness of mind after a life of considerable adversity. As a favourite friend of my father, we had sought her with eagerness; and the most open and cordial friendship was established between us. (IV, p. 50)

PBS first met Maria Gisborne, to whom William Godwin had proposed marriage in 1799 after Mary Wollstonecraft's death, her husband John, and son Henry, at Livorno (Leghorn) on 9 May 1818. A close friendship soon developed between the two families. PBS, in a letter to T. L. Peacock, described Maria Gisborne as 'a sufficiently amiable & a very accomplished woman' (*Letters* II, p. 114). She introduced him to the work of the Spanish playwright Pedro Calderón de la Barca (1600–1681) and began to tutor him in Spanish (see ll. 175–86). PBS, for his part, lent financial backing to Henry Reveley (her son by a previous marriage) for his (ultimately abandoned) plan to construct a steamboat to sail between Livorno and Marseilles (see ll. 15–21). MWS, in *1840 (ELTF)*, writes:

> He [PBS] set on foot the project of a steam-boat to ply between Marseilles and Leghorn, for their benefit, as far as pecuniary profit might accrue; at the same time that he took a fervent interest in the undertaking, for its own sake. It was not

> puerile vanity, but a nobler feeling of honest pride, that made him enjoy the idea of being the first to introduce steam navigation into the Gulf of Lyons, and to glory in the consciousness of being in this manner useful to his fellow-creatures. (I, pp. xxii–xxiii)

The light-hearted tone of the poem contrasts with the domestic difficulties facing the Shelleys in June 1820: the result of ongoing financial wrangling with Godwin, who was importuning PBS for yet another in a series of loans (see ll. 196–201), and of accusations that PBS had fathered an illegitimate child that was born in Naples during the winter of 1818–19 (*Bieri* II, pp. 102–15).

The verse epistle in rhyming couplets addressed to a friend or acquaintance was a form practised by Ben Jonson and Alexander Pope, and by Leigh Hunt, Thomas Moore and Keats among PBS's contemporaries. PBS's 'Letter', not intended for publication, encompasses private allusions, some acerbic personal opinions, and a range of literary references appropriate to the cultivated set of friends among whom it was intended to circulate. Relaxed and conversational in tone, its detailed observations and delighted attention to the ordinary contribute to its celebration of the varied pleasure of friendship.

For critical comment on the poem, see Ann Thompson, 'Shelley's "Letter to Maria Gisborne": Tact and Clutter', in *Essays on Shelley*, ed. Miriam Allott (Liverpool: Liverpool University Press, 1982), pp. 144–59; and Timothy Webb, 'Scratching at the Door of Absence: Writing and Reading "Letter to Maria Gisborne"', in *The Unfamiliar Shelley*, ed. Alan M. Weinberg and Timothy Webb (Farnham: Ashgate, 2009), pp. 119–36.

1 *The spider*: In *The Battle of the Books* (1704), Jonathan Swift contrasts the spider as an emblem of the modern writer, who spins his subjects out of his own entrails, with the bee representing the ancient writer, who seeks his subjects far and wide.

4 *His*: PBS's draft and John Gisborne's transcript both read 'Her'; 'His', the reading in MWS's transcript and *1824*, strengthens the identification of the 'silkworm' (l. 3) with PBS himself, but might not have his authority.

5 PBS refers to the attacks on his work and character made by *Quarterly Review* XXI (April 1819), in a review of *Laon and Cythna/The Revolt of Islam* (1817–18). See also ll. 106–14.

6–14 PBS spins words and ideas to make a cocoon from which when he is dead his winged verse will emerge to win fame and loving remembrance.

10 *that*: i.e. the 'decaying form' (l. 6) of PBS's body.

12 *asphodels*: Lily-like plants, in Greek myth growing in the Elysian Fields, immortal resting place of the heroic and the good after death.

15 *I wist*: I know.

16 *mighty mechanist*: One skilled in the construction of machines (but also, as *Poems* III observes, comprising the sense of one holding a mechanistic view of the universe), here associated with the Greek mathematician, scientist and inventor Archimedes of Syracuse (*c*.287–212 BC). A claim attributed to Archimedes – 'Give me a place to stand, and I will move the earth' – serves as epigraph to *Queen Mab* (p. 23) and *Laon and Cythna* (1817).

19–21 PBS alludes to the steamboat which Maria Gisborne's son, Henry Reveley, was planning to build, with his financial backing (see headnote). A 'gin' is an intricate or clever device (see *OED* n. 12).

23–4 *Vulcan . . . Titans*: Vulcan was the Classical god of the forge. On the orders of Jove (Jupiter), Vulcan constructed an ever-spinning wheel to which Ixion was bound in punishment for having committed parricide and for having attempted to seduce Juno, the wife of Jove. Vulcan also fashioned a number of the restraints with which Jove imprisoned the defeated Titans, including the chains which bound Prometheus to his mountain prison.

25 *St. Dominic* (*c.*1170–1221): The founder of the Dominican Order, which conducted the Spanish Inquisition, notorious for its severity in repressing heresy.

27–43 These lines allude to the disastrous fate of the Spanish Armada, which the Catholic Philip II of Spain and his council (ironically qualified as 'philanthropic'), sent against the Protestant England of Elizabeth I in 1588. After defeat by the English fleet, the Armada, in attempting to flee back to Spain, suffered heavy losses in storms off Scotland and Ireland.

33–4 *who now . . . Freedom's hearth*: After a military insurrection earlier in 1820, King Ferdinand VII of Spain had accepted demands for a constitutional government, inaugurating three years of liberal rule. See 'Ode to Liberty', ll. 1–5 (p. 427).

35 Instruments of torture associated with the Spanish Inquisition.

45 *Proteus*: In Greek myth, a sea god who could change shape at will.

51 *Tubal Cain*: In Genesis 4:22 'an instructer of every artificer in brass and iron'.

53 *what*: The planned steamboat.

55 *knacks and quips*: 'Ingenious contrivances' (*OED* 3) and 'curious objects' (*OED* 2), respectively.

56 *catalogize*: Make a catalogue of.

58 *quicksilver*: Mercury, which is liquid at room temperature.
gnomes: Diminutive goblin-like creatures dwelling underground, guardians of mines.

59 *swink*: Work.

60 *daemons of the earthquake*: Cp. 'Mont Blanc', l. 72 (p. 142).

65 *rouse*: A large or full cup, drunk as a toast (*OED* n. 21).

75 *A rude idealism*: A rough imitation of; PBS loved to make and sail paper boats.

83 *statical*: 'Of or relating to the science of statics' (*OED* 1b); that is, concerned with the effects of weight and the distribution of forces.

84 *rosin*: Resin.

95 Pierre-Simon Laplace (1749–1827) was a French mathematician and astronomer; PBS drew on his influential *Exposition du système du monde* (1796) in *Queen Mab* (p. 23). Nicholas Saunderson (1682–1739), professor of mathematics at Cambridge University and disciple of Isaac Newton, designed an abacus for complex calculations and published a treatise on algebra. Sims is usually identified as Robert Simson (1687–1768), whose textbook *Elements of Euclid* (1756) went through many editions.

98 *Baron de Tott's memoirs*: François Baron de Tott (1733–93), a French diplomat, served in Istanbul and the Crimea, and published his widely read *Mémoires sur les Turcs et les Tartares* in 1784.

103 *mo*: More; this form occurs in Spenser and other Renaissance writers, and in Byron, *Childe Harold's Pilgrimage*, Canto I (1812), stanza 93, l. 4, where the form is 'moe'.

104 *the pregnant womb of time*: Echoing Shakespeare, *Othello* I.iii.368–9: 'There are many events in the womb of time.'

106 *Archimage*: Chief 'mage' or magician, recalling 'Archimago', the evil enchanter in Spenser's *Faerie Queene*. See note to l. 186 of *The Witch of Atlas* (p. 802).

107–14 PBS likens the nautical steam engine Henry Reveley was planning to the mental mechanism of his own imagination which produces poetry that attracts abusive reviews. See notes to *Adonais*, 'Preface' (p. 815).

114 *Libeccio*: The south-west wind. On 12 July 1820, PBS wrote to Peacock: 'the Libecchio [sic] here howls like a chorus of fiends all day' (*Letters* II, p. 213).

129–30 *war / Of worms*: Cp. 'Ode to Liberty', l. 29 (p. 427)

132 *quaint*: Cunning, wise, insightful (*OED* 1).

137 *second-sighted*: Gifted with second sight, visionary, prophetic.

141 *sweet oracle*: i.e. 'Hope' (l. 139).

142 *the sad enchantress*: i.e. 'the quaint witch Memory' (l. 132).

149 *transverse lightning*: Lightning extending across the sky.

157–8 *or is . . . believe*: Cp. 'The flower that smiles today', ll. 3–7 (p. 554).

160 *anatomize*: Examine in minute detail.

164–6 'When we shall be as safe in death as we were before we were born' (G. M. Matthews, *Shelley: Selected Poems and Prose* (Oxford: Oxford University Press, 1964)).

168 *visionary rhyme*: *Poems* III suggests that PBS may refer to *Prometheus Unbound* (p. 184), which he read to the Gisbornes in the autumn of 1819. Cp. *The Witch of Atlas*, l. 8 (p. 448).

175–86 See headnote and note to ll. 33–4.

175 *indued*: 'Put on', as an article of clothing.

180 *'My name . . . Legion!'*: A demon in Mark 5:9 answers Jesus: 'My name is Legion: for we are many.'

181 *Calderon*: See headnote.

196–201 PBS describes his father-in-law, the novelist and political philosopher William Godwin (1756–1836), adapting Milton's description of himself in *Paradise Lost* VII.24–6: 'with mortal voice, unchanged / To hoarse or mute, though fallen on evil days, / On evil days though fallen'. In summer 1820, Godwin was causing MWS and PBS considerable distress with requests for money.

202–8 See note on Coleridge in *Peter Bell the Third*, ll. 373–97 (p. 769).

209–25 *Hunt*: James Henry (Leigh) Hunt (1784–1859) was a poet, journalist and editor of the liberal weekly *The Examiner*, which published some of PBS's poetry. PBS dedicated *The Cenci* (p. 273) to Hunt, one of his closest friends.

210 *the salt of the earth*: In Matthew 5:13, Jesus thus describes his followers.

213 *Shout*: Robert Shout (1764–1843), a London sculptor who made plaster copies of Classical statuary.
215 *coronals of bay*: Wreathes of laurel (bay) leaves, symbolic of literary achievement.
220 *duns*: Debt collectors.
226–32 Thomas Jefferson Hogg (1792–1862), PBS's friend since student days in Oxford, from which they were both expelled in March 1811. MWS characterizes Hogg in a letter to Leigh Hunt of 6 April 1819: 'You say that you *think* that he has a good heart – and so do I – but who can be sure of it – he wraps himself up in a triple veil – and places or appears to place a high wall between himself & his fellows' (*MWS Letters* I, p. 91).
232–47 Thomas Love Peacock (1785–1866), PBS's friend since 1812, married Jane Gryffydh from the mountainous Snowdonia region in north Wales on 22 March 1820, having become an employee of the British East India Company (hence 'Indian' and 'Hindoo' in ll. 235–6) the previous year. Poet, author of a number of satirical novels, including *Headlong Hall* (1815), *Melincourt* (1817) and *Nightmare Abbey* (1818), and of *The Four Ages of Poetry* (1820), which provoked PBS's reply in *A Defence of Poetry* (p. 651).
240 *cameleopard*: Giraffe.
250 *Horace Smith* (1779–1849): Poet, parodist (with his brother James), banker, friend and financial adviser to PBS since 1816.
257 *unpavilioned*: The sense seems to be 'without clouds'; cp. *Prometheus Unbound* IV.181–4 (p. 261).
260 Cp. 'Lines Written in the Bay of Lerici', ll. 8–9 (p. 589).
261 *the inverse deep*: The sky as counterpart to the sea.
266 *hackney-coaches*: Horse-drawn carriages available for hire.
267 *lordly*: MWS's transcript, *1824* and John Gisborne's transcript all read 'lonely', apparently the result of miscopying: PBS's draft has 'lordly'.
269–71 The night watchman acts as pimp for the drunken prostitute.
272–3 MWS wrote this couplet in the margin of PBS's draft; it was printed in *1840*, though not in *1824* or *1839*. Nor is it in MWS's transcript, though it is in John Gisborne's. Rather than PBS's, it may be the work of MWS or of Maria Gisborne. The allusion is to Apollonia (Pollonia) Ricci, the daughter of the Gisborne's landlord at Livorno, whose attraction to Henry Reveley (apparently reciprocated) is jokingly referred to by MWS in a letter to Maria Gisborne of 18 June 1820 (*MWS Letters* I, pp. 146–8).
274–7 PBS describes the garden of Casa Ricci, the Gisborne's house at Livorno.
278 *unsickled*: Not cut or harvested.
286 *contadino*: A countryman, peasant.
294 *low-thoughted care*: Echoing Milton, *Comus*, l. 6.
299–301 Replaced by lines of asterisks in *1824* and *1839*, to suppress the reference to PBS's estrangement from his father, Sir Timothy Shelley.
305 *syllabubs*: Flavoured mixtures of milk or cream to which wine has been added.
308 *Grand Duke*: Ferdinando III was Grand Duke of Tuscany from 1790 to 1801, and again from 1814 to 1824.

310–15 PBS says that, should his nerves become agitated during the Gisbornes' visit, he will settle them by studying geometry, avoiding altogether the excitement of composing poetry or falling in love.

312 *descant*: Discussion.

316 *laudanum*: Tincture of opium; prescribed for a variety of ailments.

317 *Helicon . . . [Shelley's note]*: The spring of Hippocrene on Mount Helicon was sacred to the Muses; the river Himera, in Sicily, gave its name to the Greek colony which grew up around it. (Himeros was a deity of erotic desire.)

318 *God*: Replaced by three asterisks in MWS's editions.

323 The last line of Milton's *Lycidas*.

To — [the Lord Chancellor]

As the MSS make clear, this exercise in sustained vituperation, written between summer and early autumn 1820 and published in part in *1839*, complete in *1840*, is addressed to John Scott, Earl of Eldon (1751–1838). In 1801–6 and 1807–27, Eldon held the office of Lord Chancellor; as such he was head of the judiciary and presided in the House of Lords. It was he who in March 1817 delivered the legal judgement that deprived PBS of the custody of the two children of his first marriage, to Harriet Westbrook, following her suicide the previous autumn. The court's decision cited the necessity of preventing PBS from inculcating in the children (what in its view were) the 'immoral and vicious' principles that his behaviour had demonstrated in leaving his first wife to cohabit with the then Mary Wollstonecraft Godwin. T. L. Peacock remembered that PBS spoke of Eldon with 'feelings of abhorrence' only equalled by his revulsion at the bullying he had suffered at Eton (*Life* II, pp. 312–13). The present poem may be compared to the curse which the Phantasm of Jupiter recalls Prometheus had directed against Jupiter in *Prometheus Unbound* I.262–301 (pp. 196–7). Our text is taken from MWS's transcription with corrections by PBS in the Houghton Library at Harvard University: the title 'To Lxxd Exxxn' is cancelled, suppressing the reference to one of the most powerful men in the country, and 'To —' substituted for it. In an earlier fair draft, 'Lord Chancellor' is scored through in the title (for both, see *MYR (Shelley)* V). Minor modifications to punctuation have been made.

2 *many-headed worm*: The mythical Hydra was a serpent with several heads.

3 *Priestly Pest*: Eldon was a devoted advocate of the Church of England's role in public life.

4 *buried form*: In *1839* MWS identifies this as the court of Star Chamber, abolished in 1641, which delivered arbitrary judgements in secret proceedings and was held to be politically motivated.

7 *fraud-accumulated gold*: Eldon grew wealthy in office.

14 *daughter's hope*: PBS's children with his first wife were Eliza Ianthe, born 23 June 1813, and Charles, whom he never knew, born 30 November 1814.

19 *prove*: Feel, experience.

21–4 This stanza was first cancelled then restored in the MS.

22 *were*: Were as.
stranger's hearth: Ianthe and Charles were in the care of guardians.
36 *why not fatherless*: *Poems* III glosses the phrase 'since they are to lose their father, why not execute him?'
40–41 Between these two stanzas another is cancelled in the copy-text:

By thy most impious Hell, and all its terror,
By all the grief, the madness, & the guilt
Which [*for* Of] thine impostures, which must be their error
That sand on which thy crumbling Power is built.

47–8 Eldon was known to weep in court. See *The Mask of Anarchy*, ll. 14–21 (p. 357).
48 *millstones*: Ironically recalling Christ's words in Matthew 18:6: 'But whoso shall offend one of these little ones which believe in me, it were better for him that a millstone were hanged about his neck, and that he were drowned in the depth of the sea.'

THE WITCH OF ATLAS

As he declares in l. 36, PBS composed the 672 lines of *The Witch of Atlas* (*WA*) in three days, 14–16 August 1820. This prodigious creative performance followed immediately upon his return from a two-day excursion from Bagni di San Giuliano near Pisa to Monte San Pellegrino (1,529 metres high) in the Apennines, where a shrine on the summit attracted pilgrims in the summer months. On 20 January 1821 the poem was posted to Charles Ollier in London, who chose not to publish it. MWS included it in *1824* without the dedication, the first three stanzas of which she supplied in *1839*, and the remaining three in *1840*. Our text is based on *1824* and, for the dedication, *1839* and *1840*. The punctuation of these editions has been modified and some readings have been adopted from PBS's fair copy in Bodleian MS Shelley d. 1 (see *BSM* IV).

Leigh Hunt astutely defined the scope of *WA* as encompassing both the 'fairy region' of imagination and the 'mortal strife' of the world as it is (*Lord Byron and Some of His Contemporaries*, 2nd edn, 2 vols (London: H. Colburn, 1828) I, p. 352). PBS's vehicle for bringing the fanciful and the real into critical relation is loosely constructed around major elements of story – birth, artistic creation and voyage of discovery – which he ends abruptly, conspicuously refusing to bring it to any narrative completion. For the details of *WA*'s episodes he drew upon a rich variety of sources in myth and poetry, history, philosophy and prose fiction. These range from Herodotus' *Histories* and Plato's dialogues through Spenser's *Faerie Queene* and Milton's *Paradise Lost* to the modern mythological poetry of T. L. Peacock's *Rhododaphne* (1818) and Robert Southey's *Thalaba the Destroyer* (1801) and *The Curse of Kehama* (1810). The *ottava rima* stanza of eight lines, rhyming *abababcc*, which PBS had adopted in July 1820 for his translation of the Homeric *Hymn to Mercury*, he had most recently encountered in the Italian comic epic *Il Ricciardetto*

(1738) by Niccolò Forteguerri, which he read aloud in that month, as well as in Byron's *Don Juan* I and II, which he read the previous January. *Poems* III, pp. 380–85, assesses the role of these and other sources.

WA celebrates the animation of nature to be found in 'the graceful religion of the Greeks' which PBS considered as having been deformed and rejected by Christianity (*Letters* II, p. 230) – and in particular the natural eroticism represented by Pan, together with his Sylvans and Fauns, beings originally imagined as embodying 'all that could enliven and delight' (see the extract from 'On the Devil, and Devils': p. 635). Poet that she is, the Witch is captivated by the beauty and strangeness of the world and creates from its materials with exhilaration, not neglecting on occasion to work the touch of mischief to which her powers tempt her. MWS found that the poem illustrated 'that sense of mystery that formed an essential portion of [PBS's] perception of life' (Preface to *1840*). Nevertheless, in the 'Note' on *WA* in *1840* she argues her conviction, playfully mocked in the dedication, that PBS would have taken 'his proper rank among the writers of the day' had he adopted 'subjects that would more suit the popular taste'.

Important readings of *WA* include: Harold Bloom, *Shelley's Mythmaking* (New Haven, Conn.: Yale University Press, 1959), pp. 165–204; Richard Cronin, *Shelley's Poetic Thoughts* (London: Macmillan, 1981), pp. 55–76; Michael O'Neill, *The Human Mind's Imaginings: Conflict and Achievement in Shelley's Poetry* (Oxford: Clarendon Press, 1989), pp. 126–56; and Stuart Sperry, *Shelley's Major Verse: The Narrative and Dramatic Poetry* (Cambridge, Mass.: Harvard University Press, 1988), pp. 143–57.

9 *fly*: The ephemerid or mayfly, one of an order of winged insects whose life lasts a day or less.

12 *swan . . . sun*: The swan, fabled to sing just before its death, was sacred to Apollo, god of the sun, poetry and music.

17–24 PBS dedicated his poem *Laon and Cythna* (1817), revised as *The Revolt of Islam* (1818), to MWS, laying it metaphorically 'at thy feet' (Dedication, l. 11: p. 148). It includes a scene in which 'a winged youth' appears in a dream (l. 500). The sales of the poem had been disappointing and it had been harshly reviewed. See the Dedication before *Laon and Cythna*' (p. 148) and the headnote to *Peter Bell the Third* (p. 763).

21 *watery bow*: Rainbow.

25–32 Wordsworth claimed in the Dedication before his *Peter Bell* (1819) that he had worked intermittently at improving the poem since finishing it in 1798. See headnote to *Peter Bell the Third* (p. 763).

34 *Ruth or Lucy*: Characters in Wordsworth's poems 'Ruth' and 'Lucy Gray' in *Lyrical Ballads* (1800).

37–8 Contrasting the 'Light' and 'flowing' verse that clothes his Witch with the 'stays' (as in a corset) that constrict Wordsworth's style.

40 The quotation is from Shakespeare, *King Lear* III.iv.31, in which Lear pities the poor whose tattered clothes offer no protection against the storm.

42–3 See *Peter Bell the Third*, ll. 21–5 (p. 374). In his review of *Peter Bell*, Leigh Hunt had accused Wordsworth of promoting fear of hell.

42 *hyperequatorial*: Hotter than at the equator.

44 *mark*: Target.

45 *Scaramouch*: A cowardly braggart in Italian farce.

47 *shrive you*: Absolve you.

55 *lady-witch*: Commentators have noted the resemblance of PBS's Witch to the Massylian priestess evoked in Virgil's *Aeneid* IV.480–91, guardian of the Hesperides' temple (see note to l. 57 below), who with her spells can bring ease or care to human minds and has the power to alter the course of nature and raise the dead.

Atlas' mountain: The highest peak of the Atlas range of mountains in present-day Morocco, Algeria and Tunisia is Toubkal in south-western Morocco. PBS here intends the mythical mountain into which the giant Atlas – forced by Zeus to bear the weight of the heavens on his shoulders – was transformed when shown the Medusa's head by Perseus.

57 *Atlantides*: Daughters of Atlas, also called the Hesperides; after their death they became the constellation Pleiades.

58–64 The stanza is indebted to Spenser's *Faerie Queene* III.vi.7 ff., recounting the conception and birth of the twin sisters Belphoebe and Amoret.

70 *in a fit*: Temporarily obscured; cp. 'To S[idmouth] and [Castlereagh]', l. 9 (p. 401).

73 *the Mother of the Months*: The moon.

74 *the folding-star*: Venus as the evening star, which appears at the time sheep are gathered into the fold.

89 *spotted cameleopard*: Giraffe.

92 *Of his own volumes intervolved*: Coiled in his own spirals.

93 *sanguine*: Bloody, carnivorous.

97 *brinded*: Brindled: tawny or brownish with differently tinted streaks or spots.

99 *pard*: Leopard or panther.

104 *imparadise*: Enrapture.

105 *Silenus*: A satyr-like minor woodland deity, a repository of wisdom and tutor to Dionysus – represented as fat, ugly, often drunk, and riding on an ass.

108 *Cicadae*: Cicadas were proverbially happy and carefree and supposed to drink dew, as in Anacreon, Ode 34.

109 *Dryope . . . Faunus:* In Ovid, *Metamorphoses* IX.329–93, Dryope is transformed into a lotus tree as punishment for having plucked one of its flowers, which shed the blood of a nymph who had herself been metamorphosed into the tree. She is mentioned as the mother of the warrior Tarquitus, fathered by Faunus, in *Aeneid* X.550–51. Originally a benevolent Roman god, Faunus was known as the protector of shepherds and flocks, associated with the forest demons known as fauns, who were half men and half goat. He was also revered as a legendary king of Latium before the founding of Rome.

110 *the God*: Silenus, who is teased to sing a song in Virgil, *Eclogues* VI.

113 *Universal Pan*: An Arcadian rural deity of shepherds and flocks, a satyr (half man and half goat), a follower of Dionysus and endowed with prodigious sexual energy. The Greek word *pan* means 'all', and in Greek religion of late antiquity Pan became known as a 'universal' god.

116 *want*: A mole (*Norton* 2002).

122 *every shepherdess of Ocean's flocks*: Oceanides, daughters of Oceanus (l. 124).

125 *quaint Priapus*: Priapus was a god of gardens, vineyards and orchards. Statues represent him as a small man with enormous genitalia – hence 'quaint' in the sense of 'strange' (*OED* III.8) or, perhaps ironically, 'cunningly contrived' (*OED* I.3a).

129–36 Commentators have traced the human and other creatures mentioned in this stanza to various Classical sources, especially Herodotus' *Histories* and Pliny's *Natural History*. See *Poems* III.

130 *Garamant*: A region in Libya said to be inhabited by a primitive people.

133 *Polyphemes*: One-eyed giants or Cyclopes such as Polyphemus in Homer, *Odyssey* IX.187 ff.

134 *Centaurs and Satyrs*: Centaurs were mythical creatures, half man and half horse. For Satyrs, see note to l. 113.

135 *clefts*: Crevices.

141 *betrayed*: Revealed.

156 *cells*: Small compartments as in a honeycomb.

161 *quaint:* see note to l. 125.

171 *Clipt*: Tightly enclosed.

174 *vans*: Wings.

185–95 Stored on scrolls in the Witch's cave, the wise spells of a benevolent sorcerer of the Age of Gold (when Saturn ruled the earth) could teach men how to recover the Golden Age by redeeming the vice they acquired as a birthright by being born in the Age of Iron. See Hesiod, *Works and Days*, ll. 109 ff., and Ovid, *Metamorphoses* I.89 ff.; ll. 189–91 clearly refer to the Age of Iron as described in *Metamorphoses* I.

186 *Archimage*: A chief or great enchanter, and the name of the wicked magician in Spenser's *Faerie Queene* whose books contain evil charms (I.i.36–8). See 'Letter to Maria Gisborne', ll. 106 ff. (p. 440).

199 *the prophane*: The uninitiated.

217–24 The nymphs specific to various natural locations ask the Witch if they might become immortal in her service. Hamadryades, Oreads and Naiads are nymphs, respectively, of trees, mountains and streams/rivers.

224 *satellite*: Attendant.

245 *knell*: A sound resembling a knell, i.e. the sound of a bell or other sound announcing a death (*OED* 3, citing this text).

247 *serene*: 'Unruffled expanse' (*OED* serene, adj. and n. B b).

253 *woof*: Woven fabric.

274 *that cold hill*: Mount Atlas.

276 *asphodel*: See note to 'The Sensitive-Plant', Part First, l. 54 (p. 780).

283 *bearded star*: A comet (with its following tail).

289–90 Vulcan, the blacksmith god of fire and husband of the goddess of love, makes a chariot in which the planet Venus, morning and evening star, travels across the sky.

292 *that sphere*: The third of the heavenly spheres, that of Venus. See note to 'The Sensitive-Plant', Part First, l. 88 (p. 780), and to l. 338 below.

294 *car*: Chariot.

297–9 Love is the first of the gods to be born, according to Plato's *Symposium*, which PBS translated in summer 1818 (*Ingpen and Peck* VII, p. 171). See also *Prometheus Unbound* II.iv.32–3 (p. 231).

301 *mould*: Soil as a growing medium.

302 *his mother's star*: The planet Venus.

312 *circumfluous*: Flowing around; in ancient geography the ocean was imagined as a stream surrounding the earth.

317 *Evans*: Evan was a name of Bacchus, often represented in a chariot drawn by panthers.

318 *Vesta*: The Roman goddess of the hearth in whose temple a perpetual flame, held to preserve the Roman state, was tended by the Vestal Virgins.

327–8 Pygmalion fell in love with an ivory statue of a beautiful woman he had sculpted and which Venus brought to life in response to his prayer.

329 *sexless thing*: Hermaphroditus (as the creature is addressed in l. 388), offspring of Hermes/Mercury and Aphrodite/Venus, was a youth desired so passionately by the nymph Salmacis that the gods answered her prayer and moulded them together into a single being uniting both sexes (*Metamorphoses* IV.285 ff.). According to Aristophanes' speech in Plato's *Symposium*, a third (androgynous and very powerful) sex originally existed but was divided into male and female as a punishment for challenging the gods. PBS's translation of the passage is in *Ingpen and Peck* VII, p. 183.

338 *the seventh sphere*: The sphere of Saturn, the seventh of the nine or ten concentric hollow globes that in the Ptolemaic astronomy made up the basic structure of the heavens. The first seven revolved round the earth, carrying the planets.

344 *with opposing feet*: i.e. she sat facing Hermaphroditus.

349 *pinnace*: Small boat.

369 *prone vale*: Descending valley.

382 *sunbows*: Miniature rainbows formed by sunlight on spray or mist.

399 *rime*: Frozen mist or fog.

401 *Elysian*: Exquisitely delightful, as in Elysium. See 'The Sensitive-Plant', Part First, l. 108 and note (pp. 411, 780).

417–18 *Or . . . Or*: Either . . . Or.

418 *interlunar*: Between the old and the new moon.

421 *amain*: 'At once and fully' (*Concordance*).

423 *Austral*: Of the southern hemisphere, southern generally.

424 *Thamondocana*: Timbuktu (Timbuctoo), in sub-Saharan Africa.

428 *Canopus*: The brightest star in the southern constellation, formerly known as Argo Navis, after the mythical ship in which Jason and the Argonauts sailed.

th' Austral lake: Probably the Ethiopian lake that is the source of both the Nile and the Niger (*Poems* III).

435 *solid vapours hoar*: Possibly glaciers, as *Poems* III suggests, or icebergs.

447–8 The haven reflects Heaven as if it were a jewel engraved with an image of it.

451 *Hydaspes*: The modern river Jhelum in north-eastern Pakistan, where Alexander the Great won an important victory before returning westward.

453 *quips and cranks*: Antics and pranks; the phrase occurs in Milton, *L'Allegro*, l. 27, where it signifies witty remarks and verbal play.

462 *meteor flags*: A recollection of Satan's ensign which 'Shone like a meteor streaming to the wind' in *Paradise Lost* I.537.

464 *mere*: Lake.

465–72 The lines recall the building of Pandemonium by the devils in *Paradise Lost* I.710–30.

466 *exhalations*: Mists.

467 *lambent*: Softly and mildly glowing.

469 *cressets*: Vessels containing fuel, such as oil, and mounted for illumination.

serene: The clear sky.

473 *throne*: The Witch's throne is to be compared with Satan's in *Paradise Lost* II.1 ff.

482 *crudded rack*: A mass of high cloud appearing as if curdled.

484 *Arion*: Herodotus, *Histories* I.23–4, recounts the legend of this supremely skilled musician who was travelling to Corinth in a ship when the crew attempted to rob and murder him. Having received their permission to play and sing one last time, Arion leapt into the sea, but one of the dolphins that had been charmed by his sweet music carried him safely to shore.

488 *fire-balls*: 'Certain large luminous meteors' or 'lightning in a globular form' (*OED* 1a).

498 *Nilus*: The Nile.

500 *Axumè*: Or Aksum, a city in the mountains of northern Ethiopia, once an important trading hub.

505 *Moeris . . . Mareotid lakes*: Lake Moeris lies some fifty miles south-west of Cairo, Lake Mareotis south and west of the city of Alexandria.

511 *the great Labyrinth*: An elaborate funerary and commemorative temple near Lake Moeris described in Herodotus, *Histories* II.148, and in Diodorus Siculus, *Library of History* I.lxvi.3–6.

512 *pomp*: Ceremonial display.

Osirian: Osiris was one of the principal Egyptian deities, brother and husband of Isis; patrons of male and female fertility and parents of the child-god Horus, they were imagined as ruling the underworld together. In religious myth, Osiris had been killed and cut to pieces by his brother Set but revived by Isis. As a god of regeneration and rebirth, Osiris was the object of a widespread cult which practised orgiastic rituals – as *Poems* III points out, citing Herodotus, *Histories* II.42, 144, and Diodorus Siculus, *Library of History* I.xi.3, xxii.6.

feast: Commemorative celebration of an event or personage of religious significance.

513–16 Cp. 'Evening. Ponte a Mare, Pisa', ll. 13–16 (p. 426).

519 *fanes*: Temples.

552 *weltering*: Tossing, tumbling.

577–84 Aurora, goddess of the dawn, counted the mortal Tithonus among her many lovers. She persuaded Jupiter to grant him immortality but neglected to ask also for perpetual youth; when Tithonus grew old and shrivelled, she shut him away. In some accounts he turns into a cicada. The myth of Adonis exists in various versions in which Proserpina detains the beautiful child or youth in Hades despite the pleas of Venus that he should be returned to her – until Jupiter decides that he should live part of the year with each of them. The Heliades were daughters of the Sun (Helios). The reference here ('The Heliad') appears to be to the Witch herself, who is also a daughter of the Sun (ll. 57–88). For further detail, see *Poems* III.

587–8 Diana, the virgin goddess of the moon, fell in love with the beautiful shepherd Endymion, whom she visited nightly, he having been granted the gift of eternal sleep and eternal youth by Jupiter.

589 *sexless*: Not restricted to a single sex, able to enjoy both sexes, as the next line makes clear. Hermaphroditus is described as 'sexless' in l. 329.

594 *panacea*: A medicine that heals all illness.

595 *wave*: The fluid medicine of the previous line.

623 *scribe*: The word can designate a public official generally but here retains something of the sense attached to it in the New Testament – of a severe and hypocritical interpreter of the law, as in Matthew 23.

626 The Rosetta Stone, with its texts of an official proclamation in three languages – hieroglyphics, demotic Egyptian and Greek – had been on display in the British Museum since 1802. For Shelley, Greek was the language par excellence of civilization and the arts, and 'in variety, in simplicity, in flexibility, and in copiousness excels every other language of the western world' (*Prose*, p. 217).

627–32 The pantheon of ancient Egyptian animal deities included Apis, the divine bull kept at Memphis. Hawks were sacred to Horus and cats to the goddess Bast; 'geese' (probably appropriating the sense of goose as 'a foolish person', as *Norton 2002* suggests) appears intended to ridicule the practice of animal worship.

641–4 The Cyclopes served as blacksmiths in the underground forge of Vulcan, god of fire (*Aeneid* VIII.416–53), where they helped fashion weapons for gods and heroic warriors.

645 Quoting Isaiah 2:4: 'they shall beat their swords into plowshares . . . nation shall not lift up sword against nation, neither shall they learn war any more.'

647–8 Amasis was a tyrannical king against whom the people revolted in Memphis, capital of ancient Egypt.

647 *I wis*: 'Iwis', i.e. certainly, truly. By the separation into 'I wis', the word came to mean 'I know'.

668 *slights*: i.e. 'sleights', cunning tricks, artifices, wiles.

670 *weird*: Strange, mysterious, fantastic.

671 *garish*: Extremely bright, glaring.

Sonnet: Political Greatness

First published in *1824*. Our copy-text is PBS's fair copy in the Bodleian Library (MS Shelley adds. c. 5: see *BSM* XXII). In *1839* MWS dates the poem to 1821, and it is probably the sonnet sent to Charles Ollier for publication in

February 1821 (*Letters* II, pp. 262, 269). However, another fair copy in PBS's hand (*MYR (Shelley)* V), entitled 'To the Republic of Benevento', suggests a likelier date of composition: late summer 1820, shortly after the declaration of independence from the Neapolitan monarchy by the small papal state of Benevento, near Naples. Michael Rossington, 'Shelley's Neapolitan-Tuscan Poetics: "Sonnet: Political Greatness" and the "Republic" of Benevento', provides a searching consideration of the sonnet's political contexts (*The Unfamiliar Shelley*, ed. Alan M. Weinberg and Timothy Webb (Farnham: Ashgate, 2009), pp. 137–56).

Title On the Bodleian fair copy PBS first wrote then cancelled 'Sonnet to Naples'. In his draft he had experimented with the titles 'The Republican', 'The True Republican' and 'Rex Sui' ('King of Himself').

1 *Nor . . . nor*: Neither . . . nor.

6 *glass*: Mirror (as PBS had first written in his draft).

7 *fleet*: Rush.

9 *numbers*: Verse.

10–14 The relation between civic and personal virtue asserted here is one of the central convictions of PBS's political writing; see e.g. *Prometheus Unbound* I.492 and III.iv.196–7 (pp. 205, 254); 'Ode to Liberty', ll. 241–5 (p. 433); and *The Triumph of Life*, ll. 209–15 (p. 577).

Sonnet ('Ye hasten to the grave')

First published in Leigh Hunt's *Literary Pocket-Book* (see headnote to 'Love's Philosophy': p. 775) for 1823. Two versions of the poem in PBS's hand are extant, a fair copy in the Houghton Library at Harvard University (see *MYR (Shelley)* V) and a neat press copy in the Morgan Library and Museum (see *MYR (Shelley)* VIII), which supplies our copy-text. MWS published the poem in *1824*, and in *1839* grouped it with 'Poems written in 1820'. The exact date of composition is uncertain, but the melancholy tone suggests that it might have formed part of the collection of PBS's 'saddest verses' which he gathered together in November 1820 and hoped to publish with *Julian and Maddalo* (p. 163) (*Letters* II, p. 246). A bitterly ironic challenge to the traditional *carpe diem* theme and an anticipation in brief of *The Triumph of Life* (p. 570), the sonnet varies the rhyme scheme but retains the final couplet characteristic of the English or Shakespearean form of the sonnet.

1 *grave*: PBS first wrote and cancelled 'dead', then substituted 'grave', which he also cancelled; his final choice is not clear. The Harvard MS and MWS's editions read 'dead'.

3 *livery*: Uniform, typically worn by a servant.

6–7 Cp. *The Triumph of Life*, l. 398: 'Shew whence I came, and where I am, and why' (p. 583). *Poems* III cites John 8:14: 'Jesus answered and said unto them, Though I bear record of myself, yet my record is true: for I know whence I came, and whither I go; but ye cannot tell whence I come, and whither I go.'

The Fugitives

Written between late 1820 and early 1821 and published in *1824* with the present title; in *1839* the poem is grouped by MWS with those written in 1821. An untitled draft survives in Bodleian MS Shelley adds. e. 8 (*BSM* VI). A fair copy in PBS's hand, also untitled, on which our text is based, is in the Rosenbach Museum and Library, Philadelphia (*MYR (Shelley)* VIII). PBS's draft continues for a further thirty-four lines beyond the end of the text given below; he did not transcribe these lines into the fair copy.

The poem's debts to the Gothic tradition (the 'mad weather', l. 54; the 'tyrant Father', l. 53; the rescued bride) recall some of PBS's earliest poetry, including 'Song' ('Fierce roars the midnight storm') and 'Fragment, or The Triumph of Conscience' in the present selection (pp. 5, 7). There are similarities to the narrative of escape in *Epipsychidion*, ll. 383 ff. (p. 485), which PBS drafted in the same notebook, as well as to poems by Walter Scott, Thomas Campbell and Thomas Moore, for which see *Poems* IV. Elements of 'The Fugitives' resonate with PBS and MWS's elopement in July 1814 and may also have been prompted by the situation of Teresa ('Emilia') Viviani, for whom PBS had developed an erotic and sentimental attachment at the time the poem was composed (see headnote to *Epipsychidion*: p. 808).

18–19 It would be a brave pilot who would follow us in these conditions.

18 *I trow*: I believe.

27 *beacon-cloud*: *Poems* IV gives the sense as 'signal-smoke'.

28 In the gales of the storm the sound of the cannon cannot be heard.

30 From the direction opposite the one from which the wind is blowing.

36 *boat-cloak*: 'A large cloak worn at sea' (*OED*).

47 *portress*: Gate-keeper; the feminine form preserves the rhyme. Cp. 'the portress of hell gate' in Milton, *Paradise Lost* II.746.

54 *To his*: Compared to his.

56–60 Recalling the old king's cursing of his youngest child, Cordelia, in Shakespeare, *King Lear* I.i.108–19, and Count Cenci's curse on his daughter Beatrice in *The Cenci* IV.i.114–36, 141–57 (pp. 322, 323).

58 *devotes*: Gives over to; cp. the sense of 'devote' as 'to invoke or pronounce a curse upon' (*OED* 3).

Memory ('Rose leaves, when the rose is dead')

Our text of this lyric is based on PBS's untitled draft in the Bodleian Library (Bodleian MS Shelley adds e. 8: see *BSM* VI), which probably dates from very late 1820 or very early 1821. Below the two stanzas given here is the opening line of what appears to be an abandoned third stanza: 'As desire when hope is cold'. MWS transcribed the draft, supplying the title 'Memory', but published it as 'To ——' in *1824*, where the order of the stanzas is reversed. Commentators have taken the latter title as an indication that the poem was addressed to Emilia Viviani (see note to l. 3 below and headnote to *Epipsychidion*: p. 808). There has been considerable debate on how to construct an accurate text from PBS's draft, for which see *BSM* VI and *Chernaik*, pp. 281–4.

3 *thy thoughts*: Perhaps the writings on love by Emilia Viviani (see headnote to *Epipsychidion*, below) are intended.

Dirge for the Year

Our text is based on PBS's unfinished and untitled draft in Bodleian MS Shelley adds. e. 9, pp. 176, 178–9, 201 (see *BSM* XIV), which he dated 'Jan 1. 1821'. MWS supplied the title and completed the fourth stanza in *1824* (see note to l. 23), where the poem was first published. The attempt to position the harshness of winter within a cycle of seasonal regeneration recalls the final lines of 'Ode to the West Wind': 'O Wind, / If Winter comes, can Spring be far behind?' (p. 400). Commentators have related this attempt both to PBS's own unhappiness and ill-health during the winter of 1820–21 and to his aspirations for political change.

1 *hours*: In Greek myth, the Hours (*Horai*) were three vegetation goddesses who ensured the growth of plants.

7 *corse*: Corpse.

14 *tree-swung*: Signifying both 'suspended from a tree' and 'swung by the motion of the tree'.

15 Cp. MWS's journal entry for 31 December 1820: 'it was a clear day with a bleak tramontano [wind]' (*MWS Journal* I, p. 344).

20 *sexton*: Employee of a parish church, responsible for bell-ringing, grave-digging and other tasks.

23 In *1824*, MWS completed this line and added another: 'but, O, ye hours, / Follow with May's fairest flowers.'

EPIPSYCHIDION

PBS sent *Epipsychidion* to his publisher, Charles Ollier, on 16 February 1821. It had probably been composed between that date and the beginning of the year, though drawing upon verse drafted some time earlier. PBS instructed Ollier to publish it anonymously and noted that 'indeed, in a certain sense, it is a production of a portion of me already dead; and in this sense the advertisement [see below] is no fiction' (*Letters* II, pp. 262–3). Our copy-text is the first edition of 1821, which Ollier published with the elaborate title that is given here.

The poem is addressed to Teresa (whom the Shelleys called 'Emilia') Viviani, to whom they were introduced in late November 1820 while she was confined in the convent of St Anna at Pisa, awaiting her marriage (Teresa was the daughter of the Governor of Pisa, and such a prenuptial arrangement was not altogether uncommon in Italy at the time for women of her social standing). The title is a compound from the Greek, apparently PBS's coinage, which combines three elements: *epi* (on, upon, above, concerning), *psyche* (soul) and a diminutive suffix. Deliberately enigmatic, it has been variously interpreted as meaning, for example, 'On the Subject of the Soul' (*Norton 2002*) and 'A little soul song' (*Webb 1995*). See l. 455 and *Poems* IV, pp. 125–6. The dozen occurrences of the word 'soul' in the poem repay close attention. In a letter to John

Gisborne of 18 June 1822 – in which PBS generally distances himself from the poem – he describes it as 'an idealized history of my life and feelings' (*Letters* II, p. 434). In this respect, the important visionary encounter of ll. 72–266 might be compared with similar episodes in *Alastor* (p. 112) as well as to Rousseau's encounter with the 'shape all light' in *The Triumph of Life*, ll. 352 ff. (p. 581). Despite its sentimental character (see, for example, note to ll. 267–383), however, *Epipsychidion* is also very much in the urbane, self-conscious and highly stylized tradition of writing about idealized love as transformative which was practised by Dante , to whose writings about his love for Beatrice in his *Vita Nuova* (1295) and *Convivio* (1304–7) PBS signals his debts in the 'Advertisement'. Cp. also Wordsworth's 'Ode: Intimations of Immortality' (1807), from which *Epipsychidion* makes a number of structural and conceptual borrowings.

PBS seems quite quickly to have distanced himself from the poem and asked Ollier to withdraw it from circulation except for that 'class of readers' (as he puts it in the 'Advertisement') who were able to appreciate its subtleties. PBS took this decision partly because, as he wrote to John Gisborne on 22 October 1821, the uninitiated were 'inclined to approximate me to the circle of a servant girl & her sweetheart', but presumably also because of the distress it must have caused to MWS (*Letters* II, p. 363). She for her part made no comment on *Epipsychidion* in any of her editions, dismissing PBS's involvement with Viviani, in a letter to Maria Gisborne of 7 March 1822, as 'Italian Platonics' (*MWS Letters* I, p. 223).

Epigraph 'The loving soul soars out of creation, and creates for itself in the infinite a world all its own, very different from this dark and fearful abyss', from Teresa Viviani's essay *Il Vero Amore*, which she allowed PBS to read.

ADVERTISEMENT

p. 474 *the Sporades*: Islands in the Aegean Sea.

the Vita Nuova of Dante: A sequence of sonnets (*c*.1292) with interlinked prose commentary, in which Dante explores his love for Beatrice. PBS read it to MWS on 31 January 1821.

gran … intendimento: PBS adapts Dante, *Vita Nuova* XXV: 'great embarrassment would come to one who, having written things in the dress of an image or rhetorical colouring, and then, having been asked, would not be able to strip his words of such dress in order to give them their true meaning' (trans. Mark Musa, *Dante's Vita Nuova* (Oxford: Oxford University Press, 1992)).

The stanza on the opposite page: PBS refers to the nine lines of verse following the Advertisement, the conclusion of the first canzone of Dante's *Il Convivio* (The Banquet; 1304–7), a work inspired by Plato's *Symposium*, on the subject of love. PBS translated the canzone, the first line of which, given here in Italian, has been rendered 'Ye who by intellection the third heaven move' (see *Poems* IV, p. 110). The injunction 'tell them that they are dull' is not in the original. Cp. ll. 116–19.

p. 475 *own* (l. 9 of 'The stanza'): Acknowledge.

Epipsychidion

1–2 Although the 'orphan one' has been understood as the spirit of either PBS himself or MWS, PBS's Italian version of these lines includes the phrase 'Il nome e la forma mia' (my name and form), suggesting that it is his own 'spirit'. See *Poems* IV, pp. 187–8.

4 *votive*: Offered as a sign of devotion.

21 *Seraph*: In the Christian tradition, a species of angel, associated with love.

44 *unvalued*: Extremely valuable, i.e. priceless.

45 Cp. Song of Solomon 8:1: 'O that thou wert as my brother, that sucked the breasts of my mother! When I should find thee without, I would kiss thee; yea, I should not be despised.'

58 Cp. Song of Solomon 4:12: 'A garden inclosed is my sister, my spouse; a spring shut up, a fountain sealed.'

60–61 *A Star . . . moving Heavens*: The pole star, around which the other stars seem to rotate.

67 *fond*: Doting, tender.

72 *Stranger*: 'Reader' in PBS's draft.

84 *honey-dew*: Perhaps an echo of Coleridge, 'Kubla Khan' (1816), l. 53, and *The Rime of the Ancient Mariner* (1798), ll. 400–401 (1805 version).

85 *the sense*: Both 'sensation' and 'understanding'.
stops: Notes.

85–6 *sweet . . . planetary music*: The so-called 'music of the spheres', the harmony produced by the planets in their orbits, a familiar trope of Classical and medieval literature. See *A Defence of Poetry* (p. 651).

90 *fathom-line*: A line bearing a weight, used to take depths at sea.

98 *unintermitted*: Uninterrupted (flow of).

100 *quiver*: The plural form of the verb with a singular subject ('pulse') may be an inadvertence on PBS's part, a deliberate solecism in the interest of rhyme, or (as *Forman 1876–7* suggests) an unusual subjunctive.

114 Cp. 'Lines Written in the Bay of Lerici', ll. 2–3, on the moon: 'To whom alone it has been given / To change and be adored for ever' (p. 589).

116–17 *a Splendour . . . pilotless*: Dante uses the term 'splendori' to refer to angels. In medieval astronomy, each of the spheres that composed the heavens was imagined as piloted by an angel; the 'third sphere' of heaven is the sphere of love (Venus).

122 *Anatomy*: Skeleton.

128–9 See the variant on these lines in 'Lines to —— [Sonnet to Byron]', ll. 13–14 (p. 557).

133 *the fields of immortality*: The Elysian Fields, where, according to Greek myth, souls exist before being born into the body and to which they can eventually return. Cp. l. 189.

139–40: Cp. Song of Solomon 8:6: 'Set me as a seal upon thine heart.'

162–73 *Major Works* suggests that PBS reworks in these lines Dante's explanation of the nature of divine love in *Purgatorio* XV.46–75.

167–9 Perhaps an allusion to the Greek myth of Python, the enormous serpent killed by the arrows of Apollo, god of the sun.

184–5 *This truth . . . hope*: The Greek philosopher Democritus was (incorrectly) supposed to have said that the truth lies hidden in a well.

213 *that best philosophy*: Convictions that find meaning and purpose in life despite cruelty and suffering, rather than any specific philosophical system.

219 *loadstar*: i.e. 'lodestar', a star by which one navigates; figuratively, 'an object of pursuit'.

221 *the owlet light*: Twilight, when owls hunt.

222 *Hesper*: The planet Venus, appearing as the evening star.

226 *winged planet*: i.e. a comet; cp. *Prometheus Unbound* IV.316–18 (p. 264).

228 *dreary cone*: The conical shadow which the earth casts, away from the sun, into space.

238 *Whither 'twas fled*: Cp. Wordsworth, 'Ode: Intimations of Immortality' (1807), l. 56: 'Whither is fled the visionary gleam?'
this soul out of my soul: Cp. 'On Love' (p. 619).

240 *sightless*: Invisible.

249 *wintry forest*: Dante uses the forest as an image of life in *Inferno* I.

253 *untaught foresters*: Those who have not shared the speaker's visionary experience.

256–66 These lines are commonly interpreted as referring to a youthful encounter with a prostitute and the resulting venereal disease. See Nora Crook and Derek Guiton, *Shelley's Venomed Melody* (Cambridge: Cambridge University Press, 1986), p. 148.

257 *night-shade*: A poisonous plant, sometimes known as belladonna.

265 *unblown*: Not yet in flower.

267–383 In an influential interpretation of this passage, Kenneth Neill Cameron associates the 'One' (l. 271) with PBS's first wife, Harriet Westbrook, who drowned herself in 1816 (cp. the 'Planet . . . quenched' in l. 313); the 'cold chaste Moon' (l. 281) with MWS; the 'Tempest' (l. 312) with the impact on PBS of Harriet's death and his unsuccessful attempt to secure custody of their two children, the 'twin babes' (l. 303), in a legal battle opposing him to Harriet's father and sister; the 'Sun' (l. 335) as Teresa Viviani; and the 'Comet' (l. 368) as Claire Clairmont. See 'The Planet-Tempest Passage in *Epipsychidion*', *PMLA* 63 (September 1948), pp. 950–72. As *Poems* IV notes, the 'One' of l. 271 is more likely to refer to PBS's cousin Harriet Grove, for whom see headnote to 'How eloquent are eyes!' (p. 684).

268 *that idol of my thought*: An image which is both 'an object of worship' and 'a creation' or 'personification'. Cp. PBS's letter to John Gisborne of 18 June 1822, in which he says of the 'idealized history of my life and feelings' contained in *Epipsychidion*: 'I think one is always in love with something or other; the error, and I confess it is not easy for spirits cased in flesh and blood to avoid it, consists in seeking in a mortal image the likeness of what is perhaps eternal' (*Letters* II, p. 434).

272–4 Recalling the Greek myth of Actaeon, transformed into a deer and killed by his own hounds after seeing Artemis, the virgin goddess of the hunt, bathing. PBS compares himself to Actaeon again in *Adonais*, ll. 274–9 (p. 501).

277 *One*: MWS.

286 *that sphere*: That of the moon, closest to the earth of the planetary spheres.

294 *Endymion*: In Greek myth, a shepherd beloved of Selene, goddess of the moon, who caused him to fall into an eternal sleep so that she should never be deprived of the sight of him. The myth is the subject of Keats's *Endymion* (1818).

308–19 The passage seems to refer to the suicides of Fanny Godwin in October 1816 and of Harriet Shelley in November and to the legal struggle for custody of Harriet's and PBS's two children. See note to ll. 267–383.

321 *the obscure Forest*: Alluding to the 'selva oscura' (dark wood) in Dante's *Inferno* I.2. See ll. 249, 253 and notes.

331 Perhaps recalling the 'still small voice' of God in 1 Kings 19:11–13.

334 *frore*: Freezing, frosty.

345 *Twin Spheres*: Emily (Teresa Viviani: the Sun) and MWS (the Moon).

355 *married lights*: The Sun and Moon (see previous note).

365 *sere*: Dry, withered.

368–83 Claire Clairmont, held by PBS in great affection but between whom and MWS there was much tension and strife, had gone to live in Florence in October 1820. See note to ll. 267–383.

374 *love's folding-star*: The planet Venus, evening star, when shepherds are returning their sheep to the fold.

379–80 *star of Death / And Birth*: The stars whose influence governs the life of an individual from beginning to end.

390 *vestal*: Virginal, from the virgin priestesses who tended the shrine of Vesta in ancient Rome.

405 *charnel*: See *Adonais*, l. 60 and note (pp. 495, 817).

412 *halcyons*: In ancient legend, the halcyon bird (now usually identified with the kingfisher) was able to calm the sea in order to nest on it for a period round the winter solstice. Cp. 'Far, far away, O ye / Halcyons of Memory' (p. 568).

416–17 Cp. 'Lines Written in the Bay of Lerici', ll. 10–14 (pp. 589–90).

422 The reference appears to be to the Aegean Islands off the west coast of Asiatic Turkey, an area known as Ionia in Classical times.

424 *for*: Because.

428 *the age of gold*: Hesiod, *Works and Days* 110–120, and Ovid, *Metamorphoses* I.89 ff., describe the first age of mankind, under the rule of Saturn, as a Golden Age of innocence, plenty and peace. See ll. 487–90.

445 Cp. Shakespeare, *The Tempest* III.ii.138–9: 'The isle is full of noises, / Sounds, and sweet airs, that give delight and hurt not.'

459 *Lucifer*: The name, which means 'light bearer', refers to the planet Venus as the morning star.

473 *zephyr*: The mild and gentle west wind.

492 *his sister . . . spouse*: Cp. Song of Solomon 4:9: 'Thou hast ravished my heart, my sister, my spouse.'

494 *Titanic*: In Greek myth, the Titans were giant gods who ruled the earth until they were deposed by Zeus and his allies.

501 *volumes*: Coils.

504 *woof*: Weave; i.e. the pattern formed by the bare branches in winter.

506 *serene*: Calm radiance.
507 *Parian floors*: The island of Paros was renowned in the Classical world as a source of white marble.
512 *call reality*: Indirectly affirming that there is a true reality underlying the mere appearances of nature which we commonly mistake for true – e.g. the permanent and intelligible ideas which, in Platonic philosophy, constitute the ultimate reality.
540 *Conscious*: 'Aware, but also "co-knowing", knowing as though they were one person' (*Major Works*).
545 *paramour*: Lover; here, the island.
557 *lights*: Eyes.
568–72 *Norton 2002* finds here an allusion to the myth of the nymph Arethusa, who was pursued by the river god Alpheus; when Arethusa was transformed into a fountain, Alpheus mingled his waters with hers.
571 *Confused*: Mingled.
577 *instinct with*: Animated by.
579 Cp. Exodus 3:2: 'the bush burned with fire, and the bush was not consumed.'
581 *unimbued*: Free from intermixture.
592–604 Dante often addresses his own verse directly in his *Vita Nuova* and *Convivio*, insisting on the inadequacy of words to express the experience of love.
601 *Marina, Vanna, Primus*: The names are usually taken to refer to MWS, Jane (in Italian 'Giovanna') Williams and Edward Williams (who became PBS's closest friend in Italy). See 'Sonnet. From the Italian of Dante' (p. 109).

ADONAIS

John Keats died in Rome on 23 February 1821 at the age of twenty-five. PBS (who was three years older) learned of his death on 11 April and began to compose this elegy on Keats shortly thereafter. Composition went on until mid June; by about mid July the poem had been printed in Pisa. Copies were quickly sent to Charles Ollier to be put on sale in London, where they sold poorly.

PBS and Keats were not close friends, though they were personally acquainted, having met on a number of occasions in London between 1816 and 1818. When, in July 1820, PBS learned that Keats was seriously ill, he immediately wrote to invite him to the warmer climate of Pisa for his health, an invitation that Keats provisionally accepted in August. Their exchange of letters includes a brief estimate by each of the poets of the other's verse. PBS praises *Endymion* (1818) for 'the treasures of poetry it contains' while regretting that they are 'treasures poured forth with indistinct profusion'. (PBS judged that Keats's powers had developed to quite another level upon reading 'Hyperion: A Fragment' in October 1820, three months after it was published.) For his part, Keats advises that 'you might curb your magnanimity and be more of an artist, and load every rift of your subject with ore' (*Letters* II, 220–22). Whatever their different taste and practice as poets, both had suffered from severe, vituperative and politically biased criticism in the *Quarterly Review*, where each was identified as an associate of Leigh Hunt, the editor of the liberal weekly *The Examiner*. Hunt had introduced them as promising young poets in an article of December 1816 and published some of their poems in his newspaper. In the Preface, PBS accuses the *Quarterly*'s article on *Endymion* of initiating a process of decline that issued in Keats's death. That he saw in this cruel handling of Keats a resemblance to the reception of his own *Laon and Cythna/The Revolt of Islam* in the April 1819 issue of the same periodical is clearly suggested in l. 300 of the elegy and was explicit in the drafts for the Preface, where PBS presents himself as the victim of calumny and despotic power as well as critical prejudice – traces of personal grievance which he removed from the final version.

As it was nearing completion, PBS described *Adonais* as 'a highly wrought *piece of art*, perhaps better in point of composition than any thing I have written' (*Letters* II, p. 294). Self-consciously literary and densely allusive, the poem borrows many of its features – invocation of the Muse, repeated formulaic lament, rhetorical questioning, the generalized grief of nature, the succession of mourners and profusion of symbolic flowers – from the Classical elegy, especially from two Greek examples of late antiquity: the 'Lament for Adonis' by Bion (*fl. c.*100 BC) and the 'Lament for Bion', attributed to Moschus (*fl. c.*150 BC). PBS translated parts of each of these (see *Poems* II, pp. 348–9, 697–700). The narrative of *Adonais* reworks the vegetation myth of Adonis, the young man beloved of Venus who, having been killed by a boar, was revived annually to spend part of the seasonal cycle in the world, the rest sleeping in the underworld. Keats had himself included a version of the myth in *Endymion* II.457–92. For the consolatory theme that is a feature of English elegies such as Spenser's *Astrophel* and Milton's *Lycidas*, PBS adopts a philosophical idiom which nuances the traditional claim for the immortality bestowed on true poets by the permanence of their verse.

The title has been interpreted as a conflation of 'Adonis' and of 'Adonai', the Hebrew word signifying 'Lord', and also (as *Poems* IV suggests) as a formation from a Greek word for nightingale, *aēdōn*, and so a learned allusion to Keats himself, who is recalled as the author of 'Ode to a Nightingale' (1819) in ll. 145 and 372. The Spenserian stanza, described by PBS as 'inexpressibly beautiful' and capable of 'brilliancy and magnificence of sound' in the Preface to the heroic poem *Laon and Cythna* (see headnote to the Dedication before *Laon and Cythna*: p. 721), lends an air of dignified seriousness to the memorializing of Keats.

Our text is that of the Pisa edition of 1821, though a few readings have been adopted from *1839*. The most important of these is in l. 72.

Epigraph This Greek epigram attributed to Plato was translated by PBS under the title 'To Stella' (see *Poems* III, pp. 721–2):

Thou wert the morning star among the living,
Ere thy fair light had fled;—
Now, having died, thou art as Hesperus, giving
New splendour to the dead.

Hesperus: The evening star.

PREFACE

Epigraph The Greek quotation from 'Lament for Bion', attributed to Moschus (see headnote), is translated by Anthony Holden, *Greek Pastoral Poetry* (Harmondsworth: Penguin Books, 1974), pp. 190–91:

> Poison, Bion, poison came to your lips,
> and you took it. How could it touch
> such lips without becoming nectar?
> And what man on earth could be so vicious
> as to mix poison and give it you
> when you asked? He has poisoned music.

p. 491 *London edition . . . highest genius*: PBS's plan for such an edition was never carried out.

twenty-fourth year: Actually his twenty-sixth year: Keats was born on 31 October 1795.

cemetery of the protestants: PBS described the 'English burying-place', the *cimetero acattolico*, in Rome in a letter of December 1818 as 'the most beautiful & solemn cemetery I ever beheld . . . one might, if one were to die, desire the sleep they [the dead buried there] seem to sleep' (*Letters* II, pp. 59–60). His and MWS's three-year-old son, William, who died on 7 June 1819, was buried there, as are the ashes of PBS himself.

Cestius: Gaius Cestius Epulo, a Roman senator whose tomb in the form of a pyramid (built between 18 and 12 BC) was incorporated into the ancient city walls bordering the cemetery. See ll. 444–7.

p. 492 *savage criticism . . . succeeding acknowledgements*: *Endymion* was reviewed with dismissive contempt by John Wilson Croker in the *Quarterly Review* XIX (April 1818) as an example of the 'Cockney poetry' whose leading exponent was Leigh Hunt. Francis Jeffrey, in the *Edinburgh Review* XXXIV (August 1820), while noting the 'extravagance' of *Endymion*, recognized its richly imaginative qualities as well as those of Keats's *Lamia, Isabella, the Eve of St Agnes, and Other Poems* (1820). In autumn 1820, PBS drafted a letter to the editor of the *Quarterly* protesting against its treatment of Keats (*Letters* II, pp. 251–3).

candid: Unbiased, impartial.

know not what they do: Appropriating the words of the crucified Christ on his executioners: 'Father, forgive them; for they know not what they do' (Luke 23:34).

penetrable stuff: From the Prince's words of accusation to his mother Gertrude in Shakespeare, *Hamlet* III.iv.34–5: 'let me wring your heart; for so I shall / If it be made of penetrable stuff.' Byron borrows the phrase in *English Bards and Scotch Reviewers* (1808), l. 1050, in a passage on hostile criticism of poets.

One of their associates . . . calumniator: PBS believed that the Laureate Robert Southey was the author of severely critical reviews both of Keats's *Endymion* and of his own *Laon and Cythna/The Revolt of Islam* in the *Quarterly Review*. But about the time he finished composing *Adonais* he 'discovered', he wrote on 11 June 1821 (*Letters* II, pp. 298–9), that his 'calumniator' in the *Quarterly* was the Reverend Henry Hart Milman, for whom see the following note.

Paris . . . and Lord Byron: The poem *Paris in 1815* (1817) by the conservative Church of England clergyman George Croly (1780–1860), the very popular *Woman: A Poem* (1810) by the satirist Eaton Stannard Barrett (1786–1820) and *Ilderim: A Syrian Tale* (1816, 1819) by the architectural historian Henry Gally Knight (1786–1846) had been reviewed with varying degrees of approbation in the *Quarterly Review*. The last-named was published by the *Quarterly*'s publisher John Murray. Alicia Lefanu (1791–*c*.1844) was an Irish poet and novelist. John Howard Payne (1791–1852) was an American actor and dramatist; his play *Brutus; or, The Fall of Tarquin, an Historical Tragedy* (1818) was successfully produced in London but unfavourably reviewed in the *Quarterly* XXII (January 1820). On MWS's return to England in 1823, Payne became her admirer and unsuccessful suitor. Henry Hart Milman (1791–1868) – a contemporary of PBS's at Eton and Oxford, Church of England clergyman, fellow of Brasenose College, Oxford (1814) – became Professor of Poetry at Oxford in 1821. Poet, dramatist and historian, his *Fall of Jerusalem: A Dramatic Poem* (1820) was approvingly reviewed as an orthodox antidote to Byron's pessimism in the *Quarterly* XXIII (May 1820).

gnat . . . camels: Recalling Christ's accusation of hypocrisy addressed to scribes and Pharisees: 'Ye blind guides, which strain at a gnat, and swallow a camel' (Matthew 23:24).

woman taken in adultery: In John 8:3–11, Jesus forgives an adulterous woman, confounding the scribes and Pharisees who wish to stone her, saying: 'He that is without sin among you, let him first cast a stone at her.'

spoken daggers, but used none: 'I will speak daggers to her, but use none' – Hamlet's words as he prepares to confront his mother Gertrude (*Hamlet* III.ii.385).

circumstances . . . Keats's life: PBS learned on 16 June that Keats felt he had been 'infamously treated' by some towards whom he had behaved generously, that his temper had become 'outrageously violent' towards the end of his life and that he had been selflessly attended by his friend the painter Joseph Severn (1793–1879) (*Letters* II, pp. 299–300).

p. 493 *'such stuff . . . made of'*: Quoting Shakespeare, *The Tempest* IV.i.156–8: 'We are such stuff / As dreams are made on, and our little life / Is rounded with a sleep.'

Adonais

1–2 A traditional opening and refrain of the Classical elegy, as in Moschus' 'Lament for Adonis': 'I weep for Adonis, cry, "Fair Adonis is dead."'

4–9 The hour of Adonais' death is urged to impart its grief to all past and future hours, which had not been specially chosen to mourn him.

5 *compeers*: Companions, equals.

10–12 *mighty Mother . . . Urania*: This complex figure, who functions as principal mourner of Adonais (as does the goddess Venus for Adonis), has multiple associations. Urania is the name of the Muse of Astronomy, as well as of the 'heavenly Muse' invoked by Milton in *Paradise Lost* VII. 1–39, and by Dante in *Purgatorio* XXIX.40–42 – hence she is 'Most musical' (ll. 28, 37). In Platonic tradition, Aphrodite Urania is the patroness of that love that rises above the merely physical to seek objects that are apprehended by the intellect, ultimately the good and the beautiful.

11–12 *the shaft which flies / In darkness*: The anonymous review of *Endymion* in the *Quarterly Review*. Cp. Psalm 91:5–6: 'Thou shalt not be afraid . . . for the arrow that flieth by day; Nor for the pestilence that walketh in darkness.'

14 *Paradise*: A park or garden; here a celestial retreat is probably intended.

15–18 The echo ('one') revives the poems of Adonais/Keats ('He').

17 *corse*: Corpse.

18 *bulk*: 'A body of great proportions' (*OED*).

29–36 *He . . . sons of light*: The post-Restoration political climate was dangerous for the republican John Milton (1608–74), who laments that he had then 'fallen on evil days' (*Paradise Lost* VII.25). PBS considered Milton 'the third Epic Poet', the voice of his age to succeeding ages, as Homer and Dante were of theirs (see *A Defence of Poetry*: p. 669). 'Hyperion', Keats's fragment of an epic poem in blank verse (see headnote), is decidedly Miltonic in subject and style.

38–43 Contrasting lesser poets who lived long enough to achieve a modest reputation with those of greater talent who were cut off at the height of their powers.

48 *pale flower . . . sad maiden*: Alluding to Keats's poem *Isabella; or, The Pot of Basil* (1818), in which a young woman buries the head of her murdered lover in a pot of basil and waters it with her tears.

51 *extreme*: Latest.

52 *blew*: Flowered.

55 *that high Capital*: Rome, the 'Eternal City'.

60 *charnel*: A mortuary chapel in which bones of the dead were piled.

63 *liquid*: Clear, bright, pure.

72 The reading in *1839*, no doubt originating with PBS. In *1821* the line read: 'Of mortal change, shall fill the grave which is her maw.'

73 *quick Dreams*: The living poems of Adonais/Keats.

94 *anadem*: A band for tying up the hair, a wreath or garland for the head.

99 *barbed fire*: The dream is likened to Cupid, whose arrows excite love.

100 *Another Splendour*: Another Dream; in Dante's *Paradiso* 'splendori' are radiant spirits.

107 *clips*: Embraces.

121 *hair unbound*: Loosened hair was a traditional sign of mourning.

123 *aerial eyes that kindle day*: The fading light of stars awakens daylight.

127 *Lost Echo*: The nymph Echo, disdained by Narcissus, pined away until only a sound remained of her.

140 *Phoebus . . . Hyacinth*: Apollo accidentally killed the beautiful youth Hyacinth, whom he loved.

141 *Narcissus*: For rejecting the love of the nymph Echo (see note to l. 127) Narcissus incurred divine vengeance, which caused him to fall in love with his own reflection.

142 *they*: The flowers into which both Hyacinth and Narcissus were metamorphosed.
sere: Withered.

144 *ruth*: Pity.

145 *Thy spirit's sister*: See penultimate paragraph of headnote.

147 *the eagle*: According to legend, every ten years the eagle soared into the region of the sun, then plunged into the sea, from which it emerged with its youth renewed.

151 *Albion*: England.
Cain: For slaying his brother Abel, Cain was cursed by God to become a wanderer over the earth bearing a mark upon him lest he be killed (Genesis 4:8–15).

159 *brake*: Thicket.

160 *brere*: Briar.

179 *sightless*: Invisible.

191 *childless Mother*: Urania.

198 *ambrosial*: 'Belonging to heaven or paradise' (*OED* 1b). Urania ('Splendour' – see note to l. 100) begins her journey from her 'secret Paradise' (l. 208).

204 *rapt*: Carried away.

212 *Palms*: Soles.

217–21 Urania's vitality causes Death to blush in shame and thereby momentarily restore signs of life to the pale corpse of Adonais.

222 Alluding to Keats's 'The Eve of St Agnes', ll. 311–15: 'How changed thou art! How pallid, chill, and drear! / Give me that voice again, my Porphyro, / Those looks immortal, those complainings dear! / Oh, leave me not in this eternal woe, / For if thou diest, my love, I know not where to go.'

234 As an inspiring Muse, Urania is implicated in the mortal world; as an immortal goddess, she cannot die.

236–8 Urania asks why Adonais/Keats abandoned the safety of the beaten track and courageously wrote the original poetry that stirred the wrath of conservative criticism.

238 *unpastured*: Unfed (and so hungry).

240 *mirrored shield*: Perseus slew the Medusa with the help of a polished shield which enabled him to avoid looking directly at her deadly image. See headnote to 'On the Medusa of Leonardo da Vinci, In the Florentine Gallery' (p. 403) and *A Defence of Poetry* (p. 651).
scorn the spear: The implication is that Keats was too good-natured to retaliate upon his critic.

242 *crescent*: Growing (like the moon).

245 *obscene*: Apparently combining the sense 'foul, loathsome' with the obsolete meaning 'ill-omened, inauspicious' (*OED*).

248 *wings rain contagion*: The raven was traditionally fabled to spread contagion from its wings.

250 *The Pythian of the age*: Byron responded to the adverse notice of his collection *Hours of Idleness* (1807) in the *Edinburgh Review* with his satirical *English Bards and Scotch Reviewers* (1808). He is here compared to Apollo, who slew with bow and arrows an enormous Python – hence his title of 'the Pythian' – then established athletic games in its honour.

261 *kindred lamps*: The stars, to which the sun, itself a star, is 'kindred'.

264 *Pilgrim of Eternity*: Byron, who in *Childe Harold's Pilgrimage*, Canto III (1816), stanza 70, contrasts those who strive in the world with 'wanderers o'er Eternity / Whose bark drives on and on, and anchored n'er shall be'.

266 The first two cantos of *Childe Harold's Pilgrimage* (1812) were phenomenally successful.

268–70 The Irish poet Thomas Moore (1779–1852), in effect the national poet of Ireland ('Ierne'), author of the very popular *Irish Melodies* (1808), many of which were set to music.

271 *one frail Form*: PBS himself.

276 *Actaeon-like*: In Greek myth, Actaeon the huntsman happened upon the virgin goddess Artemis as she was bathing; his punishment was to be turned into a stag and torn to pieces by his own hounds.

280 *pardlike*: Leopard-like; the god Bacchus was represented in a chariot drawn by leopards, as in Keats's 'Ode to a Nightingale', ll. 312–13: 'Not charioted by Bacchus and his pards, / But on the viewless wings of Poesy'.

283 *superincumbent*: Overhanging or lying upon; here used figuratively: 'weighty, oppressive' (*OED*).

289–95 The 'frail Form' (l. 271) and 'pardlike Spirit' (l. 280), a version of PBS himself, here appears as a follower of the god Bacchus carrying a spear, known as a *thyrsus*, wreathed with ivy and tipped with a 'cypress cone', associated respectively with poetry and mourning. Traditionally, poets were thought to create while in a frenzy of inspiration, like those who were possessed by Bacchus.

297 *herd-abandoned deer*: The poet William Cowper (1731–1800) described himself in well-known lines as 'a stricken deer that left the herd / Long since; with many an arrow deep infixt' (*The Task* (1785), III.108–9).

298 *aloof*: Apart.
partial moan: Lament expressing sympathetic attachment.

300 *Who*: PBS himself; see headnote.

301 *unknown land*: The phrase may indicate both that PBS is writing in English of a death in Italy and that the language and ideas of the poem are alien to most people.

305 *ensanguined:* Marked with blood.

306 *Cain's or Christ's*: The 'mark of Cain' (see note to l. 151 above) was traditionally thought to be on his forehead. Christ's brow was wounded by the crown of thorns (Matthew 27:29) placed upon it.

307 *softer voice*: That of Leigh Hunt, who had encouraged Keats's poetic ambitions and supported him in his illness. See headnote.

319 *nameless*: Reviews in the *Quarterly* and in other contemporary periodicals were anonymous.

325 *thou*: See Preface, 'One of their associates' (p. 492) and note.

332 *upon thy secret brow*: In private.

337 Echoing Satan's riposte to the guardian angels who surprise him as he tries to insinuate vain thoughts into Eve's ear in *Paradise Lost* IV.828–9: 'Ye knew me once no mate / For you, there sitting where ye durst not soar!'

338–40 *Dust to the dust . . . Eternal*: Adapting words from the Order for the Burial of the Dead in the Book of Common Prayer: 'earth to earth, ashes to ashes, dust to dust; in sure and certain hope of the Resurrection to eternal life'. The idea of an unquenchable spirit returning to the pure realm of its origin where it will exist permanently is found in Platonic and Neoplatonic philosophy.

352–60 This stanza alludes to and echoes the third stanza of Keats's 'Ode to a Nightingale', especially ll. 24–6: 'Here, where men sit and hear each other groan; / Where palsy shakes a few, sad, last grey hairs, / Where youth grows pale, and spectre-thin, and dies'.

375–9 PBS employs the non-theistic and rationalist term 'Power' to designate the force that animates nature and ensures its continuance, and with which Adonais has been reunited. See 'Hymn to Intellectual Beauty', ll. 1 and 78 (pp. 134, 138), and 'Mont Blanc', ll. 16, 96, 127–8 (pp. 140, 144, 146).

381–3 Variants on the idea of a creative 'Spirit' that moulds the undifferentiated mass of material nature into its various forms ('plastic' = 'shaping') are widely diffused, e.g. in the first chapter of Genesis. PBS will have encountered it (and the word 'plastic') in Coleridge, e.g. in 'The Eolian Harp' (1817 version), ll. 44–8, and *Religious Musings* (1796), which addresses spirits 'of plastic power, that interfused / Roll through the grosser and material mass / In organizing surge' (ll. 405–7).

384–5 The 'Greek philosophers . . . [supposed] that God, in making the world . . . moulded the reluctant and stubborn materials ready to his hand into the nearest arrangement possible to the perfect archetype existing in his contemplation.' See the extract from 'On the Devil, and Devils' (pp. 630–31).

388 *splendours*: Those great creators, now among 'the dead' (l. 395), who will permanently continue to inspire the living.

399 *the Unapparent*: PBS seems to have coined this noun from an adjective in order to designate a region of the heavens that cannot be seen from earth but from which the 'splendours' of l. 388 exercise their influence.

399–404 The three named poets died before fully realizing their early promise. Keats dedicated *Endymion* to Thomas Chatterton (1752–70). Sir Philip Sidney (1554–86) was a distant ancestor of PBS himself. The Roman poet Lucan, Marcus Annaeus Lucanus (AD 3–65), was the author of the epic poem *Pharsalia* on the civil war between Pompey and Caesar; it was a favourite of the young Shelley for its republican sympathies (*Letters* I, p. 432). Lucan's role in a plot to remove the emperor Nero having been discovered, he was forced to commit judicial suicide, which he carried out with courage and equanimity – hence he was 'approved' (justified, sanctioned) by his death.

414 *Vesper*: Hesperus, the evening star.

416 *Fond*: Foolish.

417 *pendulous*: Suspended, floating (in space).

439–41 *a slope . . . spread*: Describing the spot in the cemetery for non-Catholics where Shelley's son William was buried. See Preface, 'cemetery of the protestants' (p. 491) and note.

444 *one keen pyramid*: The pyramid that marks the tomb of the Roman official Caius Cestius, constructed at the end of the first century BC.

447 *flame*: The word 'pyramid' was formerly thought to derive from the Greek word for fire, *pur*. PBS describes a pyramid as 'sculptured flame' in *Laon and Cythna* (1817), l. 614.

454 *mourning mind*: PBS's own.

460–64 Cp. Dante, *Paradiso* XXIX.142–5: 'Look then how lofty and how huge in breadth / The' eternal might, which, broken and dispers'd / Over such countless mirrors, yet remains / Whole in itself and one as at the first' (trans. Henry Cary (London: Taylor and Hessey, 1814)). The idea of an enduring unity underlying the multiplicity of nature has been variously expressed in philosophy and notably by two philosophers that Shelley admired, Plato and Spinoza.

461 *Earth's shadows fly*: Cp. the Order for the Burial of the Dead in the Book of Common Prayer: 'Man that is born of woman hath but a short time to live . . . he fleeth as it were a shadow.'

466–8 The eternal splendour of 'The One' (l. 460) is inadequately expressed even by the full brilliance and variety of Roman culture.

477 Adapting the 'Form of Solemnization of Matrimony' in the Book of Common Prayer, from Matthew 19:6: 'Those whom God hath joined together let no man put asunder.'

478 Adapting the opening lines of Dante's *Paradiso*: 'His glory, by whose might all things are mov'd, / Pierces the universe, and in one part / Sheds more resplendence, elsewhere less' (trans. Henry Cary).

'When passion's trance is overpast'

PBS drafted this melancholy lyric, with its unusual stanza of eight-syllable lines rhyming *aabbb*, in a notebook, now Bodleian MS Shelley adds. e. 12 (see *BSM* XVIII), probably in late spring–summer 1821. MWS published it in *1824* with the title 'To ——', the third of five poems so titled in that volume. Our text is edited from adds. e. 12. Like several other of PBS's lyrics – such as 'Time Long Past' (p. 402), 'On a Dead Violet: To ——' (p. 403) and 'The flower that smiles today' (p. 554) – 'When passion's trance' laments what it affirms to be true on an analogy with other natural things, that love itself is subject to decay and death.

8 *dream the rest*: Echoing the words of Eloisa to her former lover Abelard, who has been castrated, in Pope's 'Eloisa to Abelard' (1717), l. 124: 'Give all thou canst – and let me dream the rest.'

Written on hearing the news of the death of Napoleon

A portion of PBS's draft survives in the Bodleian Library (see *BSM* XII). Our text is based on the press copy transcription by MWS which PBS sent to his publisher, Charles Ollier, on 11 November 1821, asking him to publish it 'at the end' of the volume containing *Hellas* (p. 512) (*Letters* II, p. 365). This transcription is now in the Huntington Library (HM 330: see *MYR (Shelley)* VIII); we have also consulted the first printing in *1822*. Napoleon Bonaparte died on 5 May 1821 on the island of St Helena in the South Atlantic where he had been held prisoner following his defeat at the Battle of Waterloo on 18 June 1815. PBS probably heard the news of Napoleon's death in July 1821 and composed the poem some time between then and 11 November. The title suggests an immediate response to the news which, Leigh Hunt wrote in *The Examiner* for 8 July

1821, 'fell upon the town, as if it had been a change in the natural world. And no wonder: for his life had been identified with a series of events so great and all-stirring, that they seemed to be connected with the very beating of his heart' (p. 417). In response to the prodigious nature of the subject, PBS constructed a technical tour de force, using three rhymes only, which deploys key words in a series of artful repetitions that subtly vary their sense and impact. PBS also considers Napoleon's career in 'Feelings of a Republican on the Fall of Bonaparte' (p. 110), 'To the Emperors of Russia and Austria' (not included in this selection), 'Ode to Liberty', ll. 174–80 (pp. 431–2), and *The Triumph of Life*, ll. 215–34 (p. 577). For further discussion, see Cian Duffy, ' "The Child of a Fierce Hour": Shelley and Napoleon Bonaparte', *SiR* 43 (2004), pp. 399–416.

5 *starry fold*: Echoing Milton, *Paradise Lost* V.708–10, on Lucifer and the fallen angels: 'His countenance, as the morning star that guides / The starry flock, allured them, and with lies / Drew after him the third part of heaven's host.' In a letter to Leigh Hunt of 6 October 1821, PBS compares himself to 'Lucifer who has seduced the third part of the starry flock' (*Letters* II, p. 356).

24 *the quick*: The living, as in the Creed of St Athanasius in the Book of Common Prayer: 'He ascended into heaven, he sitteth at the right hand of the Father, God Almighty: from whence he shall come to judge the quick and the dead.'

34–40 Cp. Leigh Hunt on Napoleon's career in *The Examiner*'s obituary:

> The torrent of wild enthusiasm and resentful passion,—which had rolled out from France, like a burning lava, and overwhelmed the despots who had tried to crush it in its earliest formation,—had long before [Waterloo] spent itself, and had produced by its recoil disappointment ... [Napoleon's] master-passion was a restless ambition, the impetuous tide of which bore him onward to his ends through many signal acts of injustice and violence. (pp. 418–19)

35 *blood, and gold*: PBS's work habitually associates tyranny with violence and wealth.

Epithalamium

In summer 1821, PBS inserted this antiphonal lyric into the MS of a play by his friend Edward Williams, now Bodleian MS Shelley adds. d. 3. The play, a romantic comedy entitled *The Promise; or, A Year, a Month, and a Day*, finishes with a wedding, and PBS's 'Epithalamium' was intended to be sung to the music which introduces the feast that follows the ceremony. MWS published a shorter version of the text in *1824* as 'A Bridal Song'; a somewhat garbled and inaccurate redaction was given by Thomas Medwin (*Medwin 1913*) under the present title, which is also the title adopted for the briefer variant in Williams's revised copy of the play. Our text has been edited with minor modifications from MS Shelley adds. d. 3.

The word 'epithalamium' derives from the Greek for 'at the nuptial chamber', and the poetic form of the wedding song that it designates has a long history in

Classical and Renaissance literature. Williams and PBS have followed the practice of seventeenth-century English dramatists by providing an epithalamium to accompany a wedding, as in Act I of Francis Beaumont and John Fletcher's *The Maid's Tragedy* (1619).

20 *Vesper*: Hesperus, the evening star, which was traditionally imagined as a boy holding a flaming torch.
car: The chariot in which the evening star is imagined as riding across the sky.

The Aziola

Probably composed in summer 1821, and first published posthumously in 1828 in the Christmas annual *The Keepsake for 1829*. PBS's partial and untitled draft is in the Bodleian Library (see *BSM* XXI), and there are three transcripts by MWS, which are reproduced in *BSM* II (first stanza only), *Massey* and *MYR (Shelley)* VIII. The third of these, under the present title, is in the Morgan Library and Museum (MA 406.15) and furnishes our copy-text. G. M. Matthews pointed out that the poem may be unfinished and that the reading of the other MS copies raises the possibility that MWS altered the final word to 'cry' in order to make a rhyme (*Shelley: Selected Poems and Prose* (Oxford: Oxford University Press, 1964)). The aziola (Italian *assiolo*) is a scops owl, small and brownish with a shrill cry.

9 *No mockery of myself*: No resemblance to myself as a human being.

HELLAS

PBS began work on *Hellas: A Lyrical Drama* (Hellas is the original name for Greece) in late September or early October 1821, in response to the Greek rebellion against Ottoman rule which began in March of that year. Much of PBS's draft survives in the Bodleian Library (see *BSM* XXI). Our text is based on the fair copy made by Edward Williams, with corrections by PBS, which PBS sent to his publisher, Charles Ollier, on 11 November 1821, insisting that 'what little interest this poem may ever excite, depends upon its *immediate* publication' (*Letters* II, p. 365; PBS's emphasis). This fair copy is now in the Huntington Library (*MYR (Shelley)* III). *Hellas* was first published in *1822*, with some of its more controversial religious and political passages expurgated. PBS had indicated, in his letter of 11 November, that Ollier was 'at liberty to suppress' anything that alarmed him in the Notes, anticipating the publisher's fear of prosecution for sedition or blasphemy (*Letters* II, p. 365). Ollier also printed a limited number of unexpurgated copies for private circulation. PBS wrote to him on 11 April 1822, the day after he received a copy of *Hellas*, sending a list of errata: we have consulted this list (which is now in the Huntington Library: see *MYR (Shelley)* III) in preparing our text.

In a letter to John Gisborne of 22 October 1821, PBS described *Hellas* as 'a sort of imitation of the *Persae* of Aeschylus' (*Letters* II, p. 364), a Greek play of the fifth century BC about the failed Persian invasion of Greece in 480–479 BC.

Hellas borrows a number of dramatic and narrative features from Aeschylus, including the use of messengers to relay information from disparate sources and locations, the appearance of a vision to the main character, and graphic accounts of battles on land and sea. However, while Aeschylus presents the defeat of the Persian invasion of Greece as a direct result of the hubris of the Persian leader Xerxes, PBS imagines the Greek rebellion and predicts the collapse of the Ottoman Empire as consequences of an unjust political system of which both the oppressed and the oppressors are the victims: unlike Aeschylus' critical portrayal of Xerxes, PBS offers a strikingly sympathetic portrait of the Ottoman sultan Mahmud II (see note to 'Dramatis Personae'), who was known to PBS's contemporaries as a moderate and a reformer.

Subtitled 'A Lyrical Drama', *Hellas* combines both choral lyrics and dramatic sequences in blank verse. In the main, the choral lyrics offer generalized reflections on the Greek struggle as part of the wider history of political liberty (similar to the conspectus offered in 'Ode to Liberty': p. 427), while the dramatic passages focus more on the specific historical incidents and human interest of the Greek cause. In his Preface, PBS apologizes to the reader for what he calls a 'display of newspaper erudition' (p. 513). While this overstates the case somewhat, the dramatic parts of *Hellas* are indeed much indebted to contemporary reports on the progress of the Greek struggle in newspapers like *The Examiner* and *Galignani's Messenger*, on which the Shelleys relied for much of their information about current affairs while living in Italy. Edward Gibbon's *History of the Decline and Fall of the Roman Empire* (1776–88) is another important source, and Shelley also makes reference to a broad range of Greek myth, literature and historiography.

1822 was the last volume of PBS's poetry to be published during his lifetime. In a letter to Horace Smith of 11 April of that year, PBS told his friend that he had 'just dropped [ano]ther mite into his [Time's] treasury, called *Hellas* which [I] know not how to send to you, but I dare say some fury of the Hades of authors will bring one to Paris' (*Letters* II, p. 411). Contemporary notices of *Hellas* were few and not, in the main, particularly flattering. The *General Weekly Register of News* for 30 June 1822 (No. 13), for example, found

> much to censure and but little to admire; the ideas are neither original nor poetical, the language obscure and frequently unpolished, and although the poem undoubtedly possesses some beauties, yet its defects as certainly predominate . . . upon the whole, though not entirely devoid of merit, [it] is but a bad specimen of Mr. Shelley's powers, and but ill calculated to increase the former fame of its author. (pp. 501–3)

Such comments should be seen within the context of the hostility towards PBS in much of the conservative press.

For a work of its substance by a canonical poet, *Hellas* has received comparatively little critical attention. Studies of significance include: Kenneth Neill Cameron, *Shelley: The Golden Years* (Cambridge, Mass.: Harvard University Press, 1974), pp. 375–93; Michael Erkelenz, 'Inspecting the Tragedy of Empire: Shelley's *Hellas* and Aeschylus' *Persians*', *Philological Quarterly* 76/3 (1997), pp. 313–37; Mark Kipperman, 'History and Ideality: The Politics of Shelley's *Hellas*', *SiR* 30/2 (Summer 1991), pp. 147–68; Jerome J. McGann, '"The Secrets of an Elder Day": Shelley after *Hellas*', *KSJ* 15 (Winter 1966), pp. 25–41; Constance Walker, '"The Urn of Bitter Prophecy": Antithetical Patterns in *Hellas*', *KSJ* 33 (1982), pp. 36–48; William A. Ulmer, '*Hellas* and the Historical Uncanny', *ELH* 58/3 (1991), pp. 611–32; and Jennifer Wallace, *Shelley and Greece* (Basingstoke: Macmillan, 1997), *passim*.

Epigraph 'I predict victorious struggles', Sophocles, *Oedipus at Colonus*, l. 1078. In a letter of 21 March 1821, PBS asked T. L. Peacock to have two letter-seals engraved with the same phrase (*Letters* II, pp. 276–7). Cp. *Hellas*, l. 664.

Dedication Alexandros Mavrokordatos (1791–1865), to whom the Shelleys had been introduced at Pisa during the winter of 1820–21, was the nephew of the Hospodar (Governor) of Wallachia, an Ottoman province in Eastern Europe. Mavrokordatos joined the Greek struggle in June 1821 and later served four times as prime minister of independent Greece.

PREFACE

p. 513 *The drama . . . goat*: According to tradition, Thespis, the Greek dramatist of the sixth century BC and reputed founder of Greek tragedy, used to travel with his actors in a cart which doubled as a stage. The Greek word for tragedy is thought to derive from 'goat song' because a goat was awarded as a prize for the best tragedy in the competitions which were held during the festival of Dionysus at Athens. PBS says his drama is too inartistic ('inartificial') to have won.

the Aristarchi of the hour: The Greek literary critic Aristarchus of Samothrace (*c.*220–*c.*143 BC) was known for the severity of his judgements.

The only goat-song: PBS's tragedy *The Cenci* (p. 273).

fame: Rumour.

their defeat in Wallachia: On 19 June 1821, Greek forces led by Alexandros Ypsilantis (1792–1828) suffered a heavy defeat by the Ottoman army at the Battle of Drăgăşani (in present-day Romania). This marked the formal end of Ypsilantis's attempted invasion of the so-called 'Danubian Principalities' (Moldavia and Wallachia) of the Ottoman Empire. See also notes to ll. 287–94, 361–2, 373–452.

We are all Greeks: PBS is indebted here to Leigh Hunt's estimation of the debt owed by European civilization to Classical Greece in *The Examiner* for 7 October 1821 (No. 718), pp. 626–7.

p. 514 *Anastasius*: Thomas Hope's novel *Anastasius; or, Memoirs of a Greek* (1819) describes the rise and fall of an adventurous and cunning Greek convert to Islam in the Ottoman Empire. In a letter to MWS of 11 August 1821, PBS described the novel as 'a faithful picture they say of modern Greek manners' (*Letters* II, p. 332).

The wise and generous . . . just: PBS may reply, here, to an editorial from the *New Times* reprinted in *Galignani's Messenger* on 29 October 1821, which asserted that Greece could not support itself as an independent nation, and argued against British support for Greek independence, on the grounds that it would constitute a betrayal of the Ottoman Empire, which had aided the British campaign against Napoleon in Egypt. PBS shares the view of Leigh Hunt in *The Examiner* for 2 September 1821 (No. 713): 'the interest as well as moral duty of England we consider then to consist in a prompt declaration in favour of Greek independence, and such aid as its own exhausted condition could reasonably afford' (p. 545).

pp. 514–15 *Should . . . dread*: Ollier omitted this paragraph from *1822*.

p. 515 *Of this holy alliance*: The Holy Alliance, a treaty signed by Russia, Austria and Prussia in September 1815 (following Napoleon's defeat at Waterloo), had the ostensible aim of establishing Christianity as the basis for international relations. For liberals, the Holy Alliance epitomized the reactionary climate of post-Napoleonic Europe.

Well do these . . . rest of Europe: Cp. Leigh Hunt on 'the Governments of Europe' in *The Examiner* for 7 October 1821 (No. 718): 'They see the Greek insurrection forerunning a Prussian insurrection, an Italian insurrection, insurrection everywhere' (p. 625).

DRAMATIS PERSONAE

The characters in PBS's 'Lyrical Drama' exemplify its mixture of the actual and the imagined. Mahmud is a representation of the historical Mahmud II (1785–1839), who ruled the Ottoman Empire from 1808. Ahasuerus, or the Wandering Jew, is a legendary figure who appears elsewhere in PBS's work; see notes to *Queen Mab* VII.67, 170–72 (p. 698), and to *Alastor*, ll. 675–81 (p. 713). Hassan, a not uncommon Turkish name, might mean to recall the celebrated Grand Admiral Cezayirli Gazi Hasan, who commanded the Ottoman navy 1774–89, subdued Egypt and served as Grand Vizier from 1789 until his death in 1790.

[Hellas]

Scene *Constantinople*: The name by which Istanbul was known from AD 330, after the emperor Constantine the Great (*c.* AD 272–337), who changed it from 'Byzantium'.

Stage direction *Seraglio*: In PBS's day, the term 'seraglio' usually referred to 'a palace, especially the palace of the Sultan at Constantinople' (*OED*).

16 *Samian*: From the Greek island of Samos, in the Aegean Sea near the coast of Turkey.

38 *charnel*: A repository for corpses and bones in a cemetery.

48 *The flag of Freedom*: Cp. PBS's epigraph to 'Ode to Liberty' (p. 427), taken from Byron, *Childe Harold's Pilgrimage*, Canto IV (1818), stanza 98, ll. 1–2: 'Yet, Freedom! yet thy banner, torn, but flying, / Streams like the thunder-storm *against* the wind.'

49 *banded Anarchs*: Allied tyrants; cp. ll. 318–19, where the reference is extended to comprise priests as well as political rulers.

50 In Classical literature, Imaus variously appears as both a mountain and a mountain range in Central Asia, and most probably refers to the western range of the Himalayas. In Milton, *Paradise Lost* III.431, Satan is described as 'a vulture on Imaus bred'.

54 *Thermopylae and Marathon*: The sites of two celebrated battles in the long-running war between Greece and Persia which forms the backdrop to Aeschylus' *Persians*.

57 *Philippi*: A city founded by Philip of Macedon where, in 42 BC, the armies of Mark Antony and Octavius Caesar defeated Brutus and Cassius, effectively ending the power of the Roman Senate.

60 See PBS's Note 1. Milan was the chief city in the Lombard League, an alliance of northern Italian city states established in 1167 to repel the Holy Roman Emperor Frederick I (called 'Barbarossa'). Sacked in 1162, the city was gradually rebuilt and played a leading role in the League's final victory over the emperor at the Battle of Legnano in 1176.

63 The Florentine republic, which, in *A Philosophical View of Reform*, PBS praised as the 'citadel' which 'long balanced, divided, and weakened the strength of the [Holy Roman] Empire and the Popedom' (p. 637); the consolidation of parliamentary government in England (Albion) by the Glorious Revolution of 1688 and the Bill of Rights of 1689; and the 'consolidation' and 'union' of the Swiss cantons, which PBS traced to the same 'progress of philosophy and civilization' that produced the Reformation.

70 *far Atlantis*: America; adapting Plato's myth of a powerful island kingdom, located to the west of the Pillars of Hercules (the Straits of Gibraltar), and now sunk into the Atlantic Ocean.

72 Referring to the French Revolution, the Reign of Terror and the French Revolutionary and Napoleonic Wars.

116 *the Bosphorus*: The narrow strait between the Black Sea and the Sea of Marmara ('Marmora' in l. 177) on which Istanbul is situated.

124–7 *The times . . . of them*: Cp. Shakespeare, *Macbeth* I.iii.77–8: 'The earth hath bubbles, as the water has, / And these are of them.'

143–4 *instinct / With*: Charged with, imbued with.

152 *Enoch*: Old Testament patriarch; said not to have died in Genesis 5:23–4: 'And all the days of Enoch were three hundred sixty and five years: And Enoch walked with God: and he was not; for God took him.'

153 *preadamite*: One of a legendary race that lived before Adam.

159 *science*: Acquired knowledge.

164 *the Demonesi*: The Prince (or Princes) Islands just south of Istanbul in the Sea of Marmara.

168 *westering*: Setting in the west.

171 *Erebinthus*: An older name for one of the Princes Islands. See l. 164 and note.

195–6 *Norton 2002* cites Francis Bacon, 'Of Empire' (1612): 'Princes are like to Heavenly Bodies, which . . . have much Veneration, but no Rest.'

197–238 See PBS's Note 2. This chorus narrates the rise of Christianity and Islam (ll. 211–24), and the concomitant decline in worship of the gods of Classical Greece (ll. 225–38). Cp. Byron, *Childe Harold's Pilgrimage*, Canto II (1812), ll. 23–6: 'Even gods must yield – religions take their turn: / 'Twas Jove's – 'tis Mahomet's – and other creeds / Will rise with other years, till man shall learn / Vainly his incense soars, his victim bleeds.'

197–210 These lines bear an analogy to the Platonic doctrine of the transmigration of souls from one body to another, as in *Phaedo* 87–8.

211 *A Power*: Jesus Christ. For 'the unknown God', see St Paul's address to the Athenians in Acts 17:22–3.

212 *A Promethean Conqueror*: The conflation of Prometheus and Christ entails another, between an oppressive Jupiter and the God of the Old Testament. Cp. PBS's Note 8.

217 *the orient planet*: Venus, seen in the eastern sky as the morning star.

221–4 The crescent moon is an important emblem of Islam. *Norton 2002* identifies an allusion to the vision of the Cross seen in the noontide sky by the Roman emperor Constantine before his victory in a decisive battle in AD 312 which led to his conversion to Christianity.

225–38 Cp. Milton's account of the decline of the Classical gods ('The Powers of earth and air') after the coming of Christ in 'On the Morning of Christ's Nativity' (1645).

227 *fond*: Foolish; cp. l. 909.

231 *folding star*: A star in the evening sky at the time when sheep return to their fold; specifically, the star that led the wise men to the newborn Jesus in Bethlehem in Matthew 2.

238 *the golden years*: See note to l. 1061 below.

240 *The Janizars*: The Janissary Corps was the elite section of the Ottoman army; because of its strength and influence, the Ottoman government often found the Corps difficult to manage and Mahmud II eventually disbanded it in 1826.

245 *Patriarch*: See PBS's Note 3 and editorial note on it.

252 *victorious Solyman*: Suleiman I ('the Magnificent') brought the Ottoman Empire to the height of its power and extent during his reign (1520–66); he was also an important patron of the arts and sciences and presided over many of the Empire's greatest cultural achievements.

267 *Caucasus* ... *Ceraunia*: Mountain ranges at the eastern and western extremities of the Ottoman Empire in the early nineteenth century. The Caucasus range stretches between the Black Sea and the Caspian Sea. The Ceraunian (Kanalit) range runs along the coast of Epirus and Albania; it is rich in marble, hence 'white'.

275 *Four hundred thousand*: *Galignani's Messenger* for 18 April 1821 estimates the Ottoman army at 406,400 soldiers.

277 *the Sirocco*: A hot wind which blows from North Africa towards the Mediterranean and southern Europe.

281–3 *Phrygian* ... *arms*: Mountainous regions in the west and north-west of Asiatic Turkey (Asia Minor), whose inhabitants are being levied to fight against the Greeks.

283 *horrent*: Bristling (*OED* 1). Cp. *Paradise Lost* II.512–13: 'enclosed / With bright emblazonry, and horrent arms.'

285–7 *Scala* ... *blood*: *Galignani's Messenger* for 10 September 1821 reported that the unsuccessful assault on Samos by the Ottoman navy was launched from Scala Nuova (Kuşadası), a port on the west coast of Turkey. The inhabitants of Samos had rebelled against the Ottoman administration in April–May 1821.

287–94 On 19 June 1821, the attempt by Alexandros Ypsilantis to invade the Danubian Principalities (Moldavia and Wallachia) of the Ottoman Empire was decisively repulsed at the Battle of Drăgăşani. European newspapers attributed Ypsilantis's defeat to the fact that he had been abandoned by his former allies in those provinces, hence Hassan's reference to the 'false Moldavian serfs' ('serfs' = people 'in a condition of servitude or modified slavery' (*OED*)) who fled from the Ottoman armies. See also notes to ll. 361–2, 367–8, 373–452 below.

290 *Allah-illah-Allah*: 'There is no god but God', Islamic declaration of faith, sometimes used as a battle-cry.

299 *The Anarchies of Africa*: The North African states of Algiers, Tripoli and Tunis, all (loosely) governed by the Ottoman Empire; *Galignani's Messenger* for 31 July 1821 reported that Ottoman ambassadors had sought naval assistance and had been granted it by Tunis.

303–4 *the Queen / Of Ocean*: Britain.

312 *recreant*: Cowardly.

319 *the key of gold*: The coat of arms of the papacy features two crossed keys, one of gold and one of silver.

330 *the Tartar chivalry*: Cavalry from Central Asia, known as 'Tartary' in PBS's day.

333 Cp. the 'mark' on Anarchy's 'brow' in *The Mask of Anarchy*, l. 37: 'I AM GOD, AND KING, AND LAW' (p. 358).

344 *One star*: The planet Venus, as the evening star.

355 *Abel*: Echoing God's reproach of Cain for murdering Abel in Genesis 4:10: 'What hast thou done? the voice of thy brother's blood crieth unto me from the ground.'

356 *the inheritors of the earth*: Ironically recalling Matthew 5:5: 'Blessed are the meek: for they shall inherit the earth.'

361–3 The reference is unclear: Drăgăşani, where Ypsilantis was defeated on 19 June 1821 (see note to ll. 287–94), is about sixty miles west of Bucharest. The fort has not been identified, but PBS might have been thinking of Baba Vida, an Ottoman stronghold in the town of Vidin, although it lies about sixty miles south-west of Drăgăşani. It has never been 'Islanded in the Danube', but was one of the principal strongholds of the Danubian Principalities of the Ottoman Empire.

363 *Ibrahim's scymitar*: *Galignani's Messenger* for 9 September identifies Ibrahim Paşa as the commander of the Ottoman forces in Wallachia (in the Ottoman Empire, *paşa* ('Pacha', l. 385) was an honorary title given to generals, governors and other officials of similar rank). For 'scymitar', see note to *The Mask of Anarchy*, l. 319 (p. 762).

367–8 *The light Wallachians . . . Albanian allies*: It was widely reported in British and European newspapers that Ypsilantis's defeat was triggered by the desertion of his allies in the Danubian Principalities of the Ottoman Empire (Wallachia and Moldavia) and Eastern Europe. Here 'light' means 'light infantry'; 'Arnaut' is an Ottoman Turkish word for mercenaries from the Ottoman possessions in Eastern Europe and the Balkans; 'Servian' means 'Serbian'. Hassan reports that Ypsilantis's allies fled from the Ottoman artillery, leaving him with only a core band of volunteers.

373–452 *Islanded . . . died*: PBS here expands upon reports of the destruction of the so-called Sacred Band of volunteers who made a last stand with

Ypsilantis at the Battle of Drăgăşani (see note to ll. 287–94). *Galignani's Messenger* for 20 July 1821 reported that 'this battalion was entirely annihilated' by the Ottoman army.

385 *Pacha*: See note to l. 363.

386 *Render*: Surrender.

414 *sanguine*: Bloodthirsty.

422 *Ascribe to*: Enrol among.

427 *pensioners*: Mercenaries.

446 *Genius*: Guardian spirit.

448 *A seraph-winged Victory*: Nike, the Greek personification of victory, was usually represented as a winged female.

459–527 PBS's account of the destruction of the Ottoman fleet draws both upon Aeschylus' *Persians* and upon contemporary newspaper reports of two significant Greek victories over the Ottoman navy, the first in June 1821 in the Strait of Mytilini and the second in July following the failed Ottoman assault on Samos.

470–71 Latmos is the highest peak in the Beşparmak Mountains, near the south-west coast of Turkey; Ampelos is a mountainous promontory on the island of Samos, facing Ikaria; Phanae is a harbour on the island of Chios; the 'Icarian isles' lie west of Samos and south of Chios.

482 *Nauplia*: A port city on the east coast of the Peloponnese.

485 *Hydriote*: From the island of Hydra.

500 *Naxos*: The largest island of the Cyclades.

519 *weltering*: Both 'tumbling on the waves' and 'decaying'.

523 *the voiceless . . . sea*: Marine creatures.

526 *Patmos*: An island north-east of Naxos.

528–9 *the Muscovite Ambassador . . . the city*: The Russian ambassador to the Ottoman court, Baron Grigory Aleksandrovich Stroganov (1769–1857), left Istanbul in June 1821, following a dual crisis over the arrest of the embassy's banker and the ongoing Ottoman refusal to allow Russian shipping to pass through the Dardanelles, the narrow channel linking the Sea of Marmara to the Aegean.

531 *the hippodrome*: Although no longer an arena for horse or chariot racing, the site of the Hippodrome in the centre of Ottoman Istanbul remained in use as a public square.

533 *planet-struck*: 'Panic-stricken' or 'bewildered' – as if by 'the supposed malign influence of a planet' (*OED*).

535 *Stamboul*: In western European usage, an older form of 'Istanbul'.

546–8 *Nauplia . . . Thebes*: Cities and towns across Greece; the Second Messenger is reporting widespread Ottoman defeats.

550 *Galilean*: Christian; the childhood home of Christ and scene of much of his ministry was in Galilee.

551–5 *the lust . . . light*: Ottoman and Greek atrocities were widely reported in European newspapers, and PBS alludes to them in his correspondence.

555–7 *The Examiner* for 6 May 1821 (No. 696) carried reports that Greek forces were besieging the Turkish fortress in the city of Patras (Pátra) on the north coast of the Peloponnese. *Galignani's Messenger* for 19 July reported that a Greek naval blockade was in place, following the capture of some Ottoman supply ships. The nearby Ionian Islands were a British Protectorate, hence the Second Messenger's reference to 'the Briton'.

560 *the oaths broke in Genoa and in Norway*: Sir William Bentinck (1774–1839) occupied Genoa at the end of the Napoleonic Wars, having promised British support for the restoration of the Genoese Republic, without knowing that the Treaty of Paris (1814) had already granted Genoa to the Kingdom of Sardinia; in December 1814, British troops administered the transfer of authority, which the Congress of Vienna ratified in January 1815. The Treaty of Kiel (1814), also ratified by the Congress of Vienna, forced the cession of Norway from Denmark, a former ally of France, to Sweden. Although the Norwegians drew up a constitution and declared their independence in May 1814, neither Britain nor the Holy Alliance supported them and Swedish control was ratified by the Swedish–Norwegian Act of Union in 1815 (although Norway retained much of its new constitution).

563–5 See PBS's Note 4.

564 *Attica*: The region surrounding Athens.

565 *Negropont*: Euboea, a large island off the coast of Attica.

566–78 The 'aged Ali' – Ali Paşa ('the Lion of Ioánnina') – controlled the western section of the Ottoman province of Rumelia (now the south Balkans) from his fortress at Ioánnina (Yanina), on the shore of Lake Pamvotis. He was something of a household name in Britain, not least because Byron had given an extended account of their meeting in Canto II of *Childe Harold's Pilgrimage*. Originally an Ottoman appointee, Ali had grown largely independent, and Mahmud II had been attempting to depose him since 1820. Ali's ongoing resistance to repeated Ottoman assaults was widely reported. Rumours (unfounded) of an alliance between Ali and Ypsilantis were also widespread.

578 *Indian gold*: Gold bullion (rather than currency) from India or, perhaps, South America; possibly a popular term for opium.

578–617 *The Christian tribes . . . Have sickened*: In the Third Messenger's account of the spread of revolt across the Ottoman Empire, PBS draws on but also exaggerates contemporary reports.

581 *the Arab menaces Medina*: PBS would have read in *The Examiner* (e.g. 15 April 1821), that the Wahabi – a radical fundamentalist sect of Islam – were mustering an army in Arabia; Medina, in present-day Saudia Arabia, is the destination of the *hijrah* of Muhammad and his followers and the site of the Prophet's tomb.

582–5 *The Ethiop . . . aid*: Mehmet Ali Paşa, the Ottoman governor of Egypt, launched an invasion of neighbouring Sudan ('Senaar') in 1821 which initially met with stiff resistance, although it eventually succeeded. Ali's relationship with the central Ottoman government was notoriously fractious (hence 'the Egyptian rebel' who 'claims investiture', i.e. formal establishment as an independent ruler of Egypt, in return for his assistance). *Galignani's Messenger* for 27 July 1821 carried an (unfounded) report that he had allied himself with the Greeks.

586–7 *the Georgians / Refuse . . . tribute*: Georgia, in the Caucasus, sent an annual tribute of women to the Sultan's harem at Istanbul.

591 *Santons*: An order of Islamic ascetics; cp. 'Dervise' in l. 595.

592 *prophesyings horrible*: Cp. *Macbeth* II.iii.56: 'prophesying with accents terrible'.

595–7 *Galignani's Messenger* for 5 September 1821 reported: 'on the 28th [of August], an old man appeared in the streets [of Istanbul], who gave himself out for a prophet, and by an explication of some passages in the Koran, foretold the demise of the Ottoman Empire.'

595 *Dervise*: Or Dervish, a Muslim holy man vowed to poverty and austerity of life.

598–601 See PBS's Note 5. Cp. Mark 13:26 on the second coming of Christ: 'And then shall they see the Son of man coming in the clouds with great power and glory.'

601–12 *Ominous signs . . . from among the stars*: Cp. Shakespeare, *Julius Caesar* II.ii.17–24.

606 *the Cydaris*: Classical name of the Alibey, one of the two streams which join together at the northern end of the Golden Horn, the estuary of the Bosphorus which divides northern and southern Istanbul.

620–22 *Chelonite's / Promontory . . . Briton's frown*: Akra Kyllinis, the westernmost point of the Peloponnese, overlooks the Ionian Islands, a British protectorate since 1814.

634–7 The Ottoman admiral Kara Ali Paşa was killed in 1822, along with around fifteen hundred sailors, when his flagship was destroyed off Chios by Constantinos Kanaris. The Fourth Messenger's vague report of his defeat ('reverse') near the Ionian Islands is not based in fact.

644–6 Cp. *Macbeth* V.v.18–25.

661 *battle paean*: War song.

672 *The rack*: 'Clouds, or mass of cloud, driven before the wind in the upper air' (*OED*).

682 *Let there be light*: Cp. Genesis 1:3.

688–9 The rivers Thermae and Asopus are near the sites of the battles of Thermopylae and Plataea, two decisive Greek actions in the defeat of the Persian invasion, led by Xerxes, in 480–479 BC.

690–92 The deluges are the successive blows to Greek liberty after the defeat of the Persian invasion. They include the Peloponnesian War (431–404 BC) between Athens and Sparta ('Discord'); the decline of the Greek city states in the fourth century BC, under the rule of Philip of Macedon and his son Alexander the Great ('Macedon'); and the subjugation of Greece by the Roman Empire ('Rome') and, most recently, by the Ottoman Empire ('Thou').

704 *Orphic*: In Greek myth, Orpheus was the first poet; his verse and music had supernatural power to charm and subdue.

705 *Titanian*: Of the earliest, giant, generation of the gods, the Titans; hence both 'ancient' and 'of immense size'.

707 On 10 June 1821, *The Examiner* reported that the city of Argos (once, like Corinth, one of the most powerful city states in ancient Greece) had been liberated from the Ottomans.

709 In Greek myth, daemons were spirits intermediary between gods and men; nymphs were localized, semi-goddesses, often associated with specific natural objects.

711–14 Cp. the blindfolded 'Shape' driving the chariot of 'Life' in *The Triumph of Life*, ll. 86–106 (p. 573).

715–16 *What eagle-winged . . . right hand*: Cp. *Paradise Lost* VI.762–3: 'at his right hand Victory / Sat eagle-winged.'

728 In 1 Kings 19:12, God speaks to the prophet Elijah not through violent and destructive natural phenomena but rather in 'a still small voice'.

728–32 Cp. Aeschylus, *Agamemnon* 758–60: 'It is the impious deed / that breeds more to follow, / resembling their progenitors.' PBS quotes from the same passage in a letter to MWS of 8 August 1821 (*Letters* II, p. 325).

733–5 For 'the unknown God', see l. 211 and note. There is no record of an altar to Pity in the Parthenon ('the fane [temple] / Of Wisdom') on the Acropolis, the spiritual centre of Athens. However, Pausanias, *Description of Greece* I.xvii.1, records seeing one in the nearby marketplace. Cp. Leigh Hunt praising the (supposed) forbearance of the Greeks towards their Ottoman prisoners in *The Examiner* for 4 November 1821: 'With delight the enlightened mind recognises in this conduct the descendants of those who raised temples to Pity' (p. 691).

742 *Frank*: Western European; the term originally designated the Germanic peoples who conquered Gaul and from whom 'France' derives.

761 Cp. *Prometheus Unbound* IV.483–7 (p. 269).

763–4 Cp. Shakespeare, *Hamlet* I.v.168–9: 'There are more things in heaven and earth, Horatio, / Than are dreamt of in our philosophy.'

773 *cressets*: Torches set on a pole or attached to or suspended from a high place, to provide illumination.

776 *Calpe*: The original Latin name for the Rock of Gibraltar.

776–81 Alluding to Prospero's speech on illusion and transience in Shakespeare, *The Tempest* IV.i.148–58. Cp. also *The Triumph of Life*, ll. 248–51 (p. 578).

781 *motes of a sick eye*: Cp. *Hamlet*: 'A mote it is to trouble the mind's eye' (see 'Additional Passages' in Wells and Taylor OUP edition, p. 688).

785 Cp. 'On Life': 'nothing exists but as it is perceived' (p. 620); and *A Defence of Poetry*: 'All things exist as they are perceived; at least in relation to the percipient' (p. 675).

793 *Dodona's forest*: The oak grove outside the city of Dodona in Epirus, in north-west Greece, surrounded a famous oracle of Zeus.

803–4 Cp. Matthew 7:7: 'Ask, and it shall be given you; seek, and ye shall find; knock, and it shall be opened unto you.'

807–8 Mehmet II ('the Conqueror'), who ruled the Ottoman Empire from AD 1451 until his death in 1481, captured Constantinople and made it his capital on 29 May 1453.

814–15 See PBS's Note 6. As PBS acknowledges, much of the detail and imagery of Mahmud's vision is drawn from Gibbon's account of Mehmet II's conquest of the city, in chapter 68 of his *History of the Decline and Fall of the Roman Empire* (1776–88).

822 *adamantine*: Unbreakable.

829 *'Ev τούτῳ νίκη*: The Greek battle-cry – 'In this sign [the Cross] you shall conquer' – from a legendary incident in the life of the emperor Constantine. See notes to ll. 221–4, 290.

838 *a Tartarian barb*: Horses from both Tartary (Central Asia) and Barbary (North Africa) were noted for their speed and endurance.

862–3 Cp. the ghost of Darius in Aeschylus, *Persians* 688–91: 'not with ease the way / Leads to this upper air; and the stern gods, / Prompt to admit, yield not a passage back / But with reluctance.'

865–6 *the power . . . I arose*: The Eastern Roman (Byzantine) Empire, overthrown when Mehmet II captured Constantinople (see note to ll. 807–8); for the previous three centuries, the city had been ruled by the Palaeologan Dynasty.

903 In legal terminology, 'reversion' is the process by which a loaned or granted estate returns to the grantor at the end of a set period of time, typically on the death of the grantee.

927 *Elysian*: Elysium was the abode of blessed souls in ancient Greek and Roman myth.

936 From the farthest north to the equator; Thule is a semi-legendary, northern land mass in ancient Greek and Roman literature. See also Shakespeare, *A Midsummer Night's Dream*: II.i.175: 'I'll put a girdle round about the earth.'

939 *eat, drink and die*: Cp. Isaiah 22:13: 'let us eat and drink; for to morrow we shall die.'

943 *pyramid of night*: The conical shadow cast by the earth into space, in the direction opposite the sun. PBS uses the same phrase in *Prometheus Unbound* IV.444 (p. 268).

948–9 'The flag of Russia under the Romanov czars featured a double-headed eagle; the Turkish flag, a crescent moon' (*Norton 2002*).

984–6 Cp. *Epipsychidion*, ll. 164–8 (p. 479); the mirror-like shield in Spenser, *The Faerie Queene* I.vii.33–4, viii.20; and note 36 to *A Defence of Poetry* (p. 874).

987 *Image of the Above*: The sense appears to be that if Truth covers its mirror so that it no longer reflects things as they are, then we should lament for it as we do for Liberty, Virtue and Love – all subject to the attrition of the world.

988–91 Xenophon, *Anabasis* (IV.vii) tells of 'the Ten Thousand', Greek mercenaries, Xenophon among them, who, after the failure of their attempt to overthrow the King of Persia, fought their way back through hostile territory to the Black Sea.

993 *young Atlantis*: The United States of America.

1006 *Amphionic music*: Amphion, the son of Zeus and Antiope, charmed the walls of Thebes into place with the sound of his lyre.

1008 Alluding to the celebrated comment attributed to the British leader Galgacus in Tacitus, *Life of Agricola* 30: 'Plunder, butchery, rape, these things they [the Romans] misname empire: they make a desolation and call it peace.'

1016–20 *The bought Briton . . . Victory*: PBS imagines that the British navy will not intervene on behalf of the Greeks. *Galignani's Messenger* for 18 August 1821 carried a report that five Turkish vessels off Lepanto were saved from the Greeks by British ships, while the issue for 13 September claimed that many of the sailors in the fleet sent by the Egyptian governor Mehmet Ali Paşa to Mahmud's aid were Europeans.

1030 *the Evening-land*: The west, where the sun sets; here, America.
1038 *Hesperus*: Venus, as evening star.
1049 *Prankt*: 'Set, like a gem' (*OED*); i.e. the 'mountains and islands' (l. 1048) are like jewels in the sea.
1053 *cope*: Canopy.
1060 See PBS's Note 7.
1061 *The golden years*: Or golden age, the peaceful and plenteous reign of Saturn, as described for example in Ovid, *Metamorphoses* I. Cp. Wordsworth, *The Excursion* (1814) III.756–8: 'I sang Saturnian rule / Returned, – a progeny of golden years / Permitted to descend, and bless mankind.'
1063 *weeds*: Clothes.
1068–70 The river Peneus (Pineios) flows into the Aegean Sea through the valley of Tempe in the northern Greek region of Thessaly; the river flows east, hence 'Against the morning-star' (i.e. the planet Venus), which rises in the east (see ll. 217, 231, 344, 1029, 1038). Tempe, renowned for its beauty, was a legendary haunt of the gods.
1071 *Cyclads*: The Cyclades, a group of islands in the Aegean south-east of Athens.
1072–3 Cp. Virgil, *Eclogues* IV.34–6: 'a second Tiphys shall then arise, and a second Argo to carry chosen heroes; a second warfare, too, shall there be, and again shall a great Achilles be sent to Troy.' Apollonius of Rhodes' *Argonautica* tells how Jason sailed to Colchis in quest of the Golden Fleece in a ship called *Argo*.
1074–5 The mythical poet Orpheus tried and failed to rescue his wife Eurydice from the underworld and was subsequently torn to pieces by jealous Thracian women or, in another tradition, by intoxicated women followers of Dionysus.
1076–7 In Homer, *Odyssey* IV and V, Ulysses is shipwrecked on the island home of the nymph Calypso, who falls in love with him and imprisons him for seven years before permitting him to continue his journey.
1078 *the tale of Troy*: Homer's *Iliad* and Virgil's *Aeneid* recount incidents in the siege and destruction of Troy by Greek armies.
1080–83 King Laius of Thebes, warned by an oracle that his son Oedipus would kill him, ordered the infant's death. Spared by the servant who was to expose him to die, Oedipus, grown to manhood, unwittingly killed his father. The Sphinx, a monster who ravaged a district near Thebes, would pose a riddle to travellers, devouring those who gave a wrong answer. Oedipus solved the riddle, at which the Sphinx leapt to her death from a high rock; he became King of Thebes and (again unwittingly) married his father's widow, and his mother, Iocasta.
1090–91 See PBS's Note 8.
1091–3 *more bright . . . unsubdued*: Ollier omitted these two and a half lines from *1822*, evidently to remove the reference to Christ ('One who rose').
1094 The devotions in honour of the gods of reawakened peace and love will require neither blood sacrifice nor riches; 'dowers' = 'furnishes', 'endows'.

[SHELLEY'S] NOTES

Note 1 [l. 60]

The quenchless ashes of Milan

p. 550 *Sismondi's Histoire des Républiques Italiennes*: See note to *The Cenci* II.ii.49 (p. 753).

Note 2 [l. 197]

The Chorus

p. 550 *Gordian knot*: An indecipherably complex problem only to be solved by radical action, after the intricate knot with which, according to legend, the chariot of King Gordias was tied in the temple of Zeus in the city of Gordium in Phrygia – and which had defeated all attempts to undo it. Alexander the Great is supposed to have cut the knot with his sword in 333 BC, thereby fulfilling the prophecy that whoever released it would rule Asia.

Note 3 [l. 245]

No hoary priests after that Patriarch

Gregorios V, head of the Eastern Orthodox Church, was hanged, along with three archbishops, outside Istanbul's Cathedral of St George, on Easter Sunday (22 April), 1821. Like most papers, *Galignani's Messenger* for 5 May 1821 recorded that Gregorios had been forced before his execution to excommunicate, or pronounce an 'anathema' against, the Greek revolutionaries. Mount Athos, on the easternmost promontory of the Chalkidiki peninsula, in PBS's day was the site of some twenty monasteries.

Note 4 [l. 563]

The freedman of a western poet chief

Demetrios Zographos had been Byron's servant in Greece and England 1809–1812: see Leslie Marchand (ed.), *Byron's Letters and Journals*, 12 vols (Cambridge, Mass./London: Harvard University Press/John Murray, 1973–82), IX, p. 23.

Note 5 [l. 598]

The Greeks expect a Saviour from the West

PBS probably derived this story from a report in *Galignani's Messenger* for 5 August 1821, which contains all the details given here.

Note 6 [ll. 814–15]

The sound as of the assault of an imperial city

p. 551 *1453*: Both PBS's draft and the fair copy give the date, incorrectly, as 1445.

Note 7 [l. 1060]

The Chorus

p. 552 *'magno nec proximus intervallo'*: PBS is altering a phrase from Virgil, *Aeneid* V.320, 'longo sed proximus intervallo' (next but by a long way), which describes a runner who is in the second position in a race but far behind the leader. PBS's formulation may be translated 'next but not by a long way'. His meaning is not perfectly unambiguous but appears to be that the reader of the prophecy in the chorus will find it not so very different from the prophecies in Isaiah and Virgil which he goes on to quote from, and which had been interpreted in Christian tradition as foreshadowing the birth of Christ.

'lion . . . lamb': Misquoting Isaiah 11:6: 'The wolf also shall dwell with the lamb, and the leopard shall lie down with the kid.'

'omnis . . . tellus': Quoting Virgil, *Eclogues* IV.39: 'every land shall bear all fruits.'

Note 8 [ll. 1090–91]

Saturn and Love their long repose shall burst

p. 552 *the One . . . worship*: Ollier omitted this clause from *1822*.

amerced: Forcibly deprived of.

p. 553 *The sublime . . . torture*: Ollier omitted this sentence from *1822*.

'The flower that smiles today'

PBS's untitled fair copy in the Bodleian Library (MS Shelley adds. e. 7: see *BSM* XVI) supplies our copy-text. First published without date in *1824*, where MWS gave it the title 'Mutability'. Probably composed in October 1821, while PBS was working on *Hellas* (p. 512), many of the drafts for which occupy the same notebook. The opening lines might have been suggested by letters containing dried flowers which PBS and T. J. Hogg exchanged in October (*Letters* II, p. 360 and note and p. 361). G. M. Matthews suggested that PBS had intended the lines as a dramatic lyric for *Hellas*, 'to be sung by a favourite slave, who loves him, to the literally sleeping [Sultan] Mahmud before he awakens to find his imperial pleasures slipping from his grasp' ('Shelley's Lyrics', in D. W. Jefferson (ed.), *The Morality of Art* (London: Routledge & Kegan Paul, 1969), p. 204). Whether or not this was PBS's intention seems impossible to determine certainly, but the melancholy tone of the lyric is consistent with much of his writing in the winter–spring of 1821–2, such as in 'When the lamp is shattered' (p. 563).

6–7 Recalling Juliet's misgivings at the suddenness of her and Romeo's love in Shakespeare, *Romeo and Juliet* II.i.161–2: 'Too like the lightning which doth cease to be / Ere one can say it lightens.'

13 *Survive their joy*: Persist, though without the gladness that once accompanied them.

21 *wake to weep*: Cp. Caliban's words in Shakespeare, *The Tempest* III.ii.143–6: 'and then in dreaming / The clouds methought would open and show riches / Ready to drop upon me, that when I waked / I cried to dream again.'

The Indian Girl's Song

This lyric was first published after PBS's death by Leigh Hunt in the second number of *The Liberal* (1823) under the title 'Song written for an Indian Air'. MWS included it in *1824* as 'Lines to an Indian Air'; in *1839* she grouped it with 'Poems written in *1821*'. It was probably composed late in that year (see *BSM* XII, pp. lii–liii, and *BSM* XVI, pp. l–liii). PBS's drafts are in the Bodleian Library (*BSM* XVI and *BSM* XII). A fair copy in MWS's hand (*MYR (Shelley)* V) is entitled 'The Indian Serenade', as is another autograph fair copy which was salvaged from the wreck of the *Don Juan*, the boat in which PBS had been sailing when he drowned (*MYR (Shelley)* VIII). Our text is from PBS's fair copy now in the Bibliotheca Bodmeriana, Cologny-Genève, Switzerland (*MYR (Shelley)* VIII). According to Thomas Medwin, PBS wrote the lines, which are imagined as being sung by the Indian girl of the title, for Jane Williams to sing (*Medwin 1913*, pp. 317–18). See headnote to 'To —' ('The serpent is shut out from Paradise') (p. 840).

11 *champak*: Or 'champac' or 'champaka': an evergreen of the magnolia family bearing fragrant yellow-orange-coloured blossoms.

'Rough wind that moanest loud'

Our text of these stanzas is based on MWS's transcription in the Bodleian Library (MS Shelley adds. d. 7: see *BSM* II), the only recorded MS. MWS transcribed the stanzas – the second is incomplete – as separate poems, but close similarities of theme, metre and rhyme suggest that they may well be parts of the same draft (see *BSM* II). In the 1847 edition of PBS's *Works*, MWS included the first stanza with 'Poems written in 1822'. Both stanzas probably date from late winter 1821 or spring 1822. The first may have been inspired by the severe storms which struck Pisa in the last week of December 1821 (*Letters* II, pp. 370, 374), while the second seems to look back from spring on the previous winter. The sparse punctuation of MWS's transcript has been modified and supplemented. Lines 1–8 were first published in *1824*, as 'A Dirge', but omitted 'by an unaccountable oversight' from *1839* and *1840* (*MWS Letters* III, p. 17). Lines 9–15 were first published in *Rossetti 1870*.

6 *stain*: The sense is unclear; *Rosetti 1870* thought that MWS, in making her transcription, might have misread 'strain' as 'stain', but notes that 'stain' could refer 'to the tints which come off on hands that touch soppy sprays of foliage' (II, p. 577).

7 *main*: Ocean.

To the Moon

MWS published these lines, providing them with the present title, in the 'Fragments' section of *1824*. She had transcribed them from PBS's notebook (Bodleian MS Shelley adds. e. 17, our copy-text; see *BSM* XII) containing a draft for his unfinished play *Charles the First*, for which, Nora Crook suggests in *BSM* XII, pp. xlviii–xlix, they may have been intended as a dramatic lyric. They were probably composed in January 1822 as PBS was working on the play, and not in 1820, the date assigned by MWS in *1839* and adopted by subsequent editors. After a space left on the MS page, a draft of two further lines follows:

> Thou chosen sister of the spirit
> That gazes on thee till in thee it pities.

Remembrance

Three autograph versions of this lyric are recorded: an untitled draft (probably composed in the latter half of 1821) in the Huntington Library (see *MYR (Shelley)* VII); a fair copy, also untitled, on the endpapers of a copy of *Adonais* (p. 491), now in the Firestone Library, Princeton University (see *MYR (Shelley)* VIII); and another fair copy, entitled 'Remembrance', now in Eton College Library (see *MYR (Shelley)* VIII). There is also a transcript, entitled 'Song', in MWS's hand, in the Houghton Library, Harvard University (see *MYR (Shelley)* V). These copies display a number of variants, of which the most important is signalled in the note to l. 20. Our text is based on the Eton fair copy, apparently PBS's latest version, which he sent to Jane Williams (see headnote to 'To ——' ('The serpent is shut out from Paradise': p. 840) in mid to late January 1822 with the following note inscribed at the end of the poem:

> if this melancholy old song suits any of your tunes or any that humour of the moment may dictate you are welcome to it.—Do not say it is mine to any one even if you think so;—indeed it is from the torn leaf of a book out of date. How are you to day? & how is Williams? Tell him that I dreamed of nothing but sailing & fishing up coral. Your ever affectionate PBS.— (See *Letters* II, pp. 386–7, for a transcription of this note)

The 'book out of date' may refer to the copy of *Adonais* in which PBS inscribed the poem: see note to l. 20. In any case, the phrase suggests an interval of time between first composition and the copy sent to Jane Williams. 'Remembrance' shares the melancholy tone of much of the other poetry that PBS composed during the winter–spring of 1821–2, in particular 'To ——' ('The serpent is shut out from Paradise') (p. 557). First published in *1824* as 'A Lament', it is the first of two poems in the volume with that title.

20 'Pansies let my flowers be' is the reading of PBS's draft, his fair copy in *Adonais*, MWS's transcript and *1824*. In a letter of 26 July 1822 to her friend the Irish painter Amelia Curran (1775–1847), shortly after PBS's death, MWS wrote of her intention to wear a locket with an image of a pansy in memory of him: 'In a little poem of his are these words—*pansies let my flowers be* pansies are hearts ease—and in another ['An Ode, Written, October, 1819', not included in this selection] he says that pansies mean memory' (*MWS Letters* I, pp. 240–41). See *Adonais*, ll. 289–90 (p. 501). The pansy (or heartsease) was an emblem of remembrance.

Lines to —— [Sonnet to Byron]

Our text of this sonnet is taken from PBS's autograph fair copy (now British Library MS Zweig 188: see *MYR (Shelley)* VIII), which is entitled simply 'To ——' and dated 'Jan 22'. The poem was probably composed in January 1822, perhaps on the twenty-second of the month, which was Byron's thirty-fourth birthday. MWS did not publish it in any of her editions. A variant, complete in fourteen lines, but deriving from an earlier draft as well as from inaccurate transcriptions by Thomas Medwin, was first published in *Rossetti 1870*, where it is given the title 'Sonnet to Byron', by which it has become known. Between the title and first line Rossetti prints an incomplete sentence from PBS's draft – 'I am afraid these verses will not please you but' – and later editors have followed this practice. The sentence seems likely to be the beginning of an apologetic address to Byron; Medwin reported that Byron never saw the poem (*Medwin 1913*, p. 258).

By January 1821, PBS had become acutely despondent about the failure of his poetry to win either critical acclaim or popular success. By contrast, Byron's *Don Juan* III–V (1821) and his theological drama *Cain* (1821), which PBS had recently read, had reaffirmed his conviction that Byron was the pre-eminent writer of the age, worthy of comparison with the greatest English poets. PBS's letters of late 1821 and early 1822 record his feelings on his own and Byron's powers, fame and prospects. The unusual rhyme scheme (*abababab cddcee*) conforms to neither the Italian (*abbaabba cdecde*) nor the English (*abab cdcd efef gg*) model of the sonnet.

7 *worlds*: Planets or other celestial bodies (*OED*).

8 *godhead*: Divine nature, or the quality of divinity.

9–12 PBS's draft of these lines in Bodleian MS Shelley adds. e. 17 (see *BSM* XII) reads:

But such is my regard, that nor your power
To soar, above the heights where others
Nor fame, that shadow of the [unborn] hour
Cast from the envious future on the time

To —— ('The serpent is shut out from Paradise')

In January 1821, Thomas Medwin introduced PBS to his friends Jane and Edward Williams. Though married to another, Jane lived with Edward as his wife and had taken his name; the couple had just arrived in Pisa. PBS and

Edward ('one of the best fellows in the world' (*Letters* II, p. 438)) remained close friends until their deaths on 8 July 1822, when their boat the *Don Juan* sank in the Gulf of Spezia, off the north-west coast of Italy. During the last six months of his life, PBS developed an intense attachment to Jane, whom he described in a letter of 12 January 1822 as 'amiable and beautiful . . . a sort of spirit of embodied peace in our circle of tempests' (*Letters* II, p. 376; see also pp. 342, 435). The nature of PBS's involvement with Jane Williams has prompted much speculation (for an overview, see *Bieri* II, pp. 281–347), though few facts have been established with certainty. Between January and July 1822, PBS composed a number of poems either addressed to Jane or variously informed by his feelings for her, including 'To Jane. The Invitation' (p. 559), 'To Jane—The Recollection' (p. 561), 'The Magnetic lady to her patient' (p. 565), 'With a Guitar. To Jane' (p. 566), 'To Jane' ('The keen stars were twinkling') (p. 589) and 'Lines Written in the Bay of Lerici' (p. 589). Although the present poem has often been titled 'To Edward Williams', PBS addresses both the Williamses as well as one of them, in particular, in l. 18. The stanza form, apparently of PBS's own contriving, follows the rhyme scheme (*abababcc*) of the Italian *ottava rima* while varying the usual ten-syllable iambic line customary in English adaptations – such as his own *The Witch of Atlas* (p. 448) and Byron's *Don Juan* (1819–24) – to six syllables in ll. 3 and 6 and eight in l. 7.

No draft of the poem is known to survive. Our text is based on the fair copy, now in Edinburgh University Library (MS Dc.1.100[4]: see *MYR (Shelley)* VIII), which PBS sent to Edward Williams on 26 January 1822 with a note enjoining him to show it to no one but Jane and preferably not even to her. Williams's journal entry for that date records that 'S sent us some beautiful but too melancholy lines' (*Gisborne Journal*, p. 127). The 'serpent' of the opening line is PBS himself, so nicknamed by Byron after the tempter Serpent of Genesis (*Letters* II, pp. 368–9). The melancholy tone of the poem can be accounted for not only by PBS's conflicted feelings for Jane Williams, but also by his ill-health, faltering marriage and sense of failure as an author (*Letters* II, pp. 367–8).

The poem was first published (in an inaccurate text) in *Fraser's Magazine for Town and Country* (November 1832), pp. 599–600; *Rossetti 1870* published a version with corrections from the fair copy sent to Edward Williams.

2–3 Cp. *Adonais*, l. 297 (p. 501), where PBS portrays himself as 'A herd-abandoned deer struck by the hunter's dart'. In traditional animal lore, the deer seeks medicinal herbs when wounded. Cp. Wordsworth, *The Excursion* (1814) VI.107–12.

16 *its evil, good*: Cp. Satan in Milton, *Paradise Lost* IV.109–10: 'Farewell remorse: all good to me is lost; / Evil be thou my good.'

18 *dear friend*: Deliberately ambiguous: either Edward or Jane Williams could be intended.

28–31 Adapting the Shakespearean conceit that 'All the world's a stage, / And all the men and women merely players' (*As You Like It* II.vii.139–40).

36 *Vision long since fled*: A recurrent motif in PBS's verse: cp. *Alastor*, ll. 149–91 (pp. 117–18); *Epipsychidion*, ll. 190–255 (pp. 480–81); and 'The Magnetic lady to her patient', ll. 24–5 (p. 565). The formulation is Wordsworthian: see 'Ode: Intimations of Immortality' (1807), ll. 56–7.

49 *her*: Apparently MWS.
54–5 *were . . . but*: Would have been . . . except.

To Jane. The Invitation

On 2 February 1822, PBS, MWS and Jane Williams (see previous headnote) walked out in fine weather from Pisa 'through the Pine Forest to the sea' (*MWS Journal* I, p. 393). This poem and its companion piece, 'To Jane—The Recollection' (p. 561), commemorate the occasion. Our text is based on the fair copy which PBS gave to Jane Williams, now in the Cambridge University Library (MS ADD 4444: see *MYR (Shelley)* VIII). Together the poems share with a number of other pieces that PBS composed in the spring of 1822 a concern with the role of memory, and of poetry itself, in reconstituting and preserving intense and valued moments. In *1824* MWS published a combined text entitled 'The Pine Forest of the Cascine, near Pisa', based on her transcript of PBS's drafts of this poem and of 'The Recollection', which suggests that he may originally have composed the two poems as one. In *1840* she published a separate text of each from his fair copies.

6 *brake*: A thicket or clump of bushes.
9 *halcyon*: Calm; the legendary halcyon (kingfisher) was able to quieten the waves and nest at sea. Cp. 'Far, far away, O ye / Halcyons of Memory' (p. 568).
10 *hoar*: White (with frost and with age).
35–7 Cp. Byron, *Don Juan* (1819–24), X.xxxviii.5–7: 'Care, like a housekeeper, brings every week / His bills in, and however we may storm, / They must be paid.' Byron is unlikely to have known PBS's poem, and it is possible that the similarity points to a common source.
38 *stave*: A stanza of a poem or song.
55 *lawns*: Grassy glades in the forest.
57 *hoar-frost*: Frozen dew.
59 *wind-flowers*: Wood anemones.
65–6 *the multitudinous / Billows*: The numerous waves (of the sea); cp. Shakespeare, *Macbeth* II.ii.59–60: 'No, this my hand will rather / The multitudinous seas incarnadine.'

To Jane—The Recollection

Composed and given to Jane Williams (see headnote to 'To —' ('The serpent is shut out from Paradise'): p. 840) in early February 1822, as the companion piece of 'To Jane. The Invitation' (see previous headnote). Only a few lines of draft have survived (see *BSM* XXI). Our text is based on the fair copy that PBS transcribed for Jane, now in the British Library (BL Add. MS 37538: see *MYR (Shelley)* VIII). Beneath the title the MS bears the date 2 February 1822. On this day PBS, MWS and Jane took the walk through the pine forest to the sea that is recalled in this poem and in 'The Invitation'. 'The Recollection' was first published in combination with 'The Invitation' in *1824* and as a separate poem in *1840*. The first (unnumbered) stanza, an invocation to memory, serves as a prologue to the four succeeding stanzas.

5 *wonted*: Accustomed, usual.

6 *fled*: PBS's fair copy reads 'dead', presumably inadvertently copied from l. 3. MWS's transcription from PBS's draft in Bodleian MS Shelley adds. d. 7 and *1824* both read 'fled'.

10 *skirts*: Borders.

29–32 PBS's note to 'Ode to the West Wind' cites a 'phenomenon . . . well known to naturalists. The vegetation at the bottom of the sea, of rivers, and of lakes, sympathizes with that of the land' (p. 398).

41–2 *the remotest* . . . *waste*: The snow-capped peaks of the Apennines, visible from Pisa.

45 Cp. Wordsworth, 'Tintern Abbey' (1798), ll. 96–7: 'a sense sublime / Of something far more deeply interfused'.

51 *one fair form*: Jane Williams; see headnote to 'To ——' ('The serpent is shut out from Paradise') (p. 840).

63–4 Cp. PBS's observation in a working notebook (Bodleian MS Shelley adds. e. 7: see *BSM* XVI), probably made in 1821: 'Why is the reflexion in that canal far more beautiful than the objects it reflects. The colours are more vivid, & yet blended with more harmony & the openings from within into the soft & tender colours of the distant wood & the intersection of the mountain line surpass & misrepresent truth.'

65 *lawn*: A grassy clearing in a forest.

74 *Elysian*: Heavenly; from Elysium, the mythical abode of blessed souls after death.

79 *lineament*: Feature.

81–4 An analogy is suggested between the image in the pool erased by the wind and the memory of MWS, who, although present on the walk, is not addressed or represented in the poem.

85 *thou*: Jane Williams.

87 *——'s*: The missing word invites the name 'Shelley'.

88 Below this line PBS has written the numeral 5 followed by a line of x's. *Norton 2002* suggests that these might signal to Jane Williams that he has omitted as too intimate a further stanza which he had written or might write.

'When the lamp is shattered'

Probably composed in spring 1822. The position of the draft (Bodleian MS Shelley adds. e. 18: see *BSM* XIX) suggests that it may have been intended for a play that PBS was then attempting to write in the same notebook for the members of his circle at Pisa. In *1839* MWS described PBS's idea for the surviving 'Fragments of an Unfinished Drama':

> An Enchantress, living in one of the islands of the Indian Archipelago, saves the life of a Pirate, a man of savage but noble nature. She becomes enamoured of him; and he, inconstant to his mortal love, for a while returns her passion; but at length, recalling the memory of her whom he left, and who laments his loss, he escapes from the Enchanted Island and returns to his lady. His mode of life makes him go again to sea, and the Enchantress seizes the opportunity to bring him, by a spirit-brewed tempest, back to her Island. (IV, pp. 168–9)

There is an incomplete fair copy in Glasgow University Library (MS Gen. 505/34: see *MYR (Shelley)* VIII) and a complete fair copy in the British Library (Add. MS 37232: see *MYR (Shelley)* VIII), which provides our copy-text. The lyric shares, with a number of other poems that PBS composed in late 1821 and early 1822, a melancholy insistence on the impermanence of love. Published in *1824* as 'Lines', it is the first of four poems in the volume with that title.

17 In the Glasgow fair copy, which appears to have preceded our copy-text, stanzas 3 and 4 are headed 'second part', suggesting that at that point PBS intended the lines for a dramatic or musical arrangement.

19–20 Love departs first from the stronger of two hearts that have come together, leaving the weaker heart to suffer the love it once enjoyed.

'One word is too often prophaned'

Our text is based on the sole recorded MS, a transcription by MWS into her copy-book, now in the Bodleian Library (MS Shelley adds. d. 7: see *BSM* II). She published the poem in *1824* as 'To ——', the second of five poems with that title, and in *1839* grouped it with those 'written in 1821', although it probably dates from the spring of 1822, possibly April. Geoffrey Matthews suggested that the lyric might be connected with the drama (the immediately preceding transcription in MWS's copy-book) which PBS was attempting to compose for the members of his circle at Pisa in the spring of 1822, and which contains parts for a number of disconsolate lovers (see *BSM* II and *BSM* XIX, pp. xlix–l). See headnote to 'When the lamp is shattered' (p. 843). The situation of poet and beloved bears comparison with that of practitioner and sufferer in 'The Magnetic lady to her patient' (p. 565), and other poems given to Jane Williams (see headnote to 'To ——' ('The serpent is shut out from Paradise'): p. 840).

3 *falsely*: *1824* reads thus, presumably MWS's correction of 'often', which is the reading of her transcription.

The Magnetic lady to her patient

Probably composed in spring 1822, this poem is an imaginative portrayal of an occasion, which may actually have occurred, on which PBS was hypnotized ('magnetized' or 'mesmerized', in contemporary parlance) by Jane Williams, who is identified in l. 42. For PBS's relationship with Edward and Jane Williams, see headnote to 'To ——' ('The serpent is shut out from Paradise') (p. 840). No draft has been recorded. Our text is based on the fair copy which PBS gave to Jane Williams, now in Aberdeen University Library (MS 937: see *MYR (Shelley)* VIII). On the cover sheet, PBS wrote 'To Jane. Not to be opened unless you are alone, or with Williams', and above the poem itself 'For Jane and Williams alone to see'.

'Animal magnetism', based on the theories and practice of the Austrian physician Franz Anton Mesmer (1734–1815), posited the existence of an invisible 'magnetic fluid', a sort of vital energy present in all beings and able to pass from one to the other by a force analogous to magnetism. Adepts varied in their understanding of the phenomenon and its therapeutic application. The practitioner might, as in the present poem, lay hands on a patient, inducing a hypnotic state. The aim was to provoke an improved circulation of the fluid in the sufferer until a state of equilibrium conducive to health was achieved.

In the last eighteen months of his life, PBS was 'magnetized' on a number of occasions in order to alleviate the pain in his side (l. 41) and abdomen, which he believed to be a symptom of kidney stones. The first to do this was Thomas Medwin, in December 1820 (*MWS Journal* I, p. 342, and *Medwin 1913*, pp. 269–70), but the practice was later continued by MWS and, so this poem suggests, by Jane Williams. PBS here displays little interest in the cosmic aspect of mesmerism or its physiological basis; his focus is on the interchange between patient and therapist.

A text (inaccurate) was first published in *The Athenaeum* (11 August 1832), pp. 522–23; it was reprinted in *1839* and (corrected) in *1840*.

6 *sign*: Protective mark, like the Christian 'sign of the cross'. Cp. the 'Incantation' of the female spirit of Manfred's dead beloved in Byron, *Manfred* (1817), I.i. 200–201: 'Shall my soul be upon thine, / With a power and with a sign.'

11 *he*: Edward Williams.

19–20 *the slumber . . . unborn*: Alluding to the Pythagorean doctrine of the antenatal and post-mortal existence of the soul.

28–30 In a letter of 19 June 1822 to Leigh Hunt, PBS compares Jane Williams to the Lady who tends the mimosa in 'The Sensitive-Plant', while, in a letter to Claire Clairmont of 11 December 1821, he acknowledges Claire's nickname for him, 'The Exotic [plant]' (*Letters* II, pp. 438, 367).

35–6 Cp. *Epipsychidion*, ll. 51–2: 'How beyond refuge I am thine. Ah me! / I am not thine: I am a part of *thee*' (p. 476).

42–5 Commentators have variously proposed that these lines were influenced by PBS's fear of the dangerous surgery to remove kidney stones, by suicidal thoughts, by his troubled marriage with MWS. The name *Jane* first appeared in *Rossetti 1870*.

With a Guitar. To Jane

PBS wrote these lines to accompany a guitar that he purchased for Jane Williams (see headnote to 'To ––' ('The serpent is shut out from Paradise'): p. 840) probably in March or early April 1822 (*Letters* II, p. 412; and see 'To Jane' ('The keen stars were twinkling'): p. 589). A draft of ll. 1–12 is in the Bodleian Library (see *BSM* XIX), as is the guitar itself (for a photograph and description see Bruce Barker-Benfield, *Shelley's Guitar* (Oxford: Bodleian Library, 1992)). Our text is based on the copy given to Jane, also in the Bodleian (MS Shelley adds. e.3: see *BSM* XXI). The poem is in octosyllabic couplets which PBS employed in other poems inspired by Jane: 'To Jane. The Invitation' (p. 559) and 'Lines Written in the Bay of Lerici' (p. 589). As the first line indicates, the poet assumes the character and voice of Prospero's servant, the 'airy spirit' Ariel, in Shakespeare's *The Tempest*, imagining Jane and Edward Williams (see headnote to 'To ––' ('The serpent is shut out from Paradise'): p. 840) as Prospero's daughter Miranda and her beloved '*prince Ferdinand*' (l. 10). Light and playful in tone, the poem nevertheless raises serious questions about the role of impersonation, tradition, formal harmony, performance and audience response in art.

First published in *The Athenaeum* for 20 October 1832 (ll. 43–90), and in *Fraser's Magazine* for January 1833 (ll. 1–42); a full and corrected text appeared in *1840*.

13–15 The immortal 'guardian spirit Ariel' promotes Jane's happiness through successive existences. See note to ll. 23–30.

17–22 At the conclusion of *The Tempest* (Shakespeare's 'mighty verses'), Prospero instructs Ariel to guide Ferdinand, Miranda, King Alonso and his retinue safely back across the sea to Naples.

23–30 A whimsical reference to the doctrine of the transmigration of souls or reincarnation.

23–6 *the silent Moon . . . Ariel*: A footnote in *Fraser's Magazine* compares these lines with Milton, *Samson Agonistes*, ll. 87–9: 'silent as the moon, / When she deserts the night / Hid in her vacant interlunar cave'; 'interlunar' describes the period between the old and new moons.

28 *Star of birth*: Traditional astrology held that the star or planet under which an individual was born influenced his disposition and later life.

36 *remembered not*: Because the reincarnated soul's memory of its previous lives is erased on rebirth. See note to ll. 23–30.

39 Shakespeare's Ariel had been imprisoned by a witch in a cloven pine tree until released by Prospero (*The Tempest* I.ii.270–94).

43 *idol*: Image, likeness – alluding to the tree in which Ariel was imprisoned (see previous note) and looking forward to the one from which the guitar is fashioned (ll. 53–8).

48 *Apennine*: The Apennine range runs down the centre of the Italian peninsula.

57 *Heaven's fairest star*: The planet Venus, the morning and evening star.

75–8 The revolving earth participates in the 'music of the spheres', which expresses the cosmic harmony of the planets in motion.

76 *diurnal*: Daily.

'Far, far away, O ye / Halcyons of Memory'

Our text is taken from the draft, revised by PBS, in a notebook now in the Huntington Library (MS HM 2111: see *MYR (Shelley)* VII), which he used between the latter half of 1821 and his death in July 1822. In *1839* MWS dated the poem 1820 but *MYR (Shelley)* VII adduces MS evidence for composition between January and June 1822. Two words, 'Ye birds', on the page following the draft of the second stanza, suggest that PBS at first thought of continuing the poem. The scope and limitations of memory are also addressed in other poems of late 1821 to early 1822, such as 'To Jane—The Recollection' (p. 561) and 'Remembrance' (p. 556). First published in *1824* as 'Lines', the fourth poem of that title in the volume. Both the *1824* text and MWS's transcript (see *Massey*) lack ll. 11–12, evidently a deliberate omission on her part.

2 *Halcyons*: Legendary birds, 'usually identified with a species of kingfisher' (*OED*), which were supposed to nest on the ocean in a period of

calm around the winter solstice. 'Halcyons' also signifies 'Halcyon days', a period of fourteen days of tranquil seas during which the halcyon could nest.

13 *Wrecked*: Both MWS's fair copy and *1824* read 'Withered'.

'Tell me star, whose wings of light'

Composed sometime between January 1822 and PBS's death in July of that year. The rough and unfinished draft, which supplies our copy-text, closely follows the draft for 'Far, far away, O ye / Halcyons of Memory' (p. 568) in PBS's notebook, now in the Huntington Library (MS HM 2111: see *MYR (Shelley)* VII). The three stanzas were published without date in *1824*, as 'The World's Wanderers'.

4 *pinions*: Wings.

9–12 Cp. 'To ——' ('The serpent is shut out from Paradise'), ll. 41–8 (p. 558); 'When the lamp is shattered', ll. 17–18 (p. 564); and 'Far, far away, O ye / Halcyons of Memory', ll. 3–4 (p. 568).

12 This line is cancelled in PBS's draft. There follow two cancelled lines and part of a third:

> Restless Life, whose spirit flies
> From birth to death without repose
> And from

THE TRIUMPH OF LIFE

PBS began *The Triumph of Life* (*TofL*) in late May 1822, while he was living at San Terenzo on the north-west coast of Italy, and left the poem unfinished at his death on 8 July. Our text is based on PBS's unfinished and in places very rough and unresolved draft, now in the Bodleian Library (MS Shelley adds. c. 4: see *BSM* I). A text derived from it was first published in *1824*, where MWS noted that it 'was left in so unfinished a state, that I arranged it in its present form with great difficulty' (p. vii).

TofL offers a bleak assessment of the human condition, in which 'life' in the form of a blind and brutal juggernaut is perceived to ride in 'triumph' over almost every form of human aspiration and endeavour. In particular, the poem interrogates the recent cultural history of Europe, leading up to and including the French Revolutionary and Napoleonic Wars, 'the times that were / And scarce have ceased to be' (ll. 233–4).

The most important of the poem's debts to its two principal precursor texts, Dante's *Divina Commedia* and Petrarch's *Trionfi*, are recorded in the notes. Like those two poems, *TofL* is composed in *terza rima*, the Italian verse form of three-line stanzas with interlocking rhymes. The narrative device of a guide interpreting objects, characters and events as they are encountered in a visionary landscape PBS borrows from the *Divina Commedia*, in which the poet is guided through Hell and part of Purgatory by the figure of the Roman poet

Virgil. The successive victories in the *Trionfi* of love over man, chastity over love, death over chastity, fame over death, time over fame, and God over time, have led some commentators to suggest that PBS might have developed *TofL* towards an affirmative conclusion.

Many analogues for the triumphal pageant at the heart of *TofL* have been suggested, including: the relief sculptures on the triumphal arches of Titus and Constantine at Rome (see note to ll. 111–20); Buonamico Buffalmacco's fresco *The Triumph of Death* in the Campo Santo at Pisa; the procession of the chariot of the Hindu deity Jagannath during the festival of Ratha Yatra (to which PBS refers in *Queen Mab* VII.33–6: p. 64); and the 'infamous triumph' of 6 October 1789, luridly represented by Edmund Burke in his *Reflections on the Revolution in France* (1790), when the French royal family were forced to leave the palace at Versailles and escorted by an angry mob to the Tuileries Palace in Paris.

The extensive critical discussion of the poem includes: Paul de Man, 'Shelley Disfigured', in Harold Bloom (ed.), *Deconstruction and Criticism* (New York: Continuum, 1979), pp. 39–73; Cian Duffy, *Shelley and the Revolutionary Sublime* (Cambridge: Cambridge University Press, 2005), pp. 187–201; Edward Duffy, *Rousseau in England: The Context for Shelley's Critique of the Enlightenment* (Berkeley, Calif.: University of California Press, 1979); John Hodgson, '"The World's Mysterious Doom": Shelley's *The Triumph of Life*', *ELH* 42 (1975), pp. 595–622; Geoffrey Matthews, 'Shelley and Jane Williams', *RES* 45 (1961), pp. 40–48; and Donald Reiman, 'Shelley's *The Triumph of Life*: The Biographical Problem', *PMLA* 78 (1963), pp. 536–50, and *Shelley's 'The Triumph of Life': A Critical Study* (Urbana, Ill.: University of Illinois Press, 1979).

7 *orison*: A prayer.
8 *matin lay*: A song or hymn at daybreak.
11 *censers*: Vessels for burning incense.
the element: The air.
15–20 *And in . . . them*: Cp. *Prometheus Unbound* IV.394–9 (p. 267).
21 *thoughts . . . untold*: Cp. 'Lines Written in the Bay of Lerici', ll. 35–6: 'I dare not speak / My thoughts' (p. 590).
23 *The cone of night*: The conical shadow that the earth casts away from the sun into space.
32–3 *As clear . . . glimmer*: As clearly as the evening hills shine when bathed in the light of the setting sun.
35–6 In *Purgatorio* I.121–9, Virgil washes Dante's face with morning dew.
42 *tenour*: Theme, substance.
43 *public way*: This emblem for the course of life is also used by Dante and Petrarch.
44–6 *a great stream . . . gleam*: Recalling Dante's first glimpse of the myriad damned in *Inferno* III.55–7.
49–51 *yet so . . . bier*: The analogy between the dead and autumn leaves is an epic commonplace: e.g. Homer, *Iliad* VI.146–9; Virgil, *Aeneid* VI.309–10; Dante, *Inferno* III.112–17. Cp. also 'Ode to the West Wind', l. 2 (p. 398).
78 *with [ ] light*: PBS cancelled the word 'fascinating' in the draft but provided no substitute.

79–85 *Like ... chair*: Cp. Coleridge, 'Dejection: An Ode' (1802): epigraph, from the 'Ballad of Sir Patrick Spence' ('I saw the new Moon, / With the old Moon in her arms; / and I fear, I fear, my Master dear! / We shall have a deadly storm'), and ll. 9–14. The new crescent moon with the outline of the old full moon form the natural basis of the image of the triumphal chariot.

91–3 PBS's draft of these lines is unpunctuated apart from a semicolon after 'light'. The present edition takes 'cloud' as the subject of 'Was bent', but other constructions are possible.

94 *Janus-visaged*: Janus, the Roman god of beginnings, transitions and endings, was typically represented with two, or, as here, four faces.

100 *banded*: Covered with a blindfold.

101 *the van*: The front.

102 *the beams ... Sun*: The 'cold glare' in l. 77.

105 *car*: Chariot.

111–20 *such seemed ... driven*: The narrator compares the spectacle before him to the triumphs of imperial Rome, when a victorious commander would pass through the streets of the city with the spoils of victory, often comprising bound captives, in train behind his chariot. PBS saw representations of such spectacles on the arches of Constantine and Titus at Rome (*Letters* II, pp. 86, 89–90), which he described as 'that mixture of energy & error which is called a triumph'.

123 *in weal or woe*: In prosperity or misfortune.

126 *the great winter*: The end of the world. In a letter to Peacock from Chamonix of 22 July 1816, PBS outlines the French naturalist Buffon's 'sublime but gloomy theory, that the earth which we inhabit will at some future period be changed into a mass of frost' (*Letters* I, p. 499).

128 *the sacred few*: The leading figures of the Hellenic and Judaeo-Christian traditions; 'they of Athens and Jerusalem' in l. 134 would include Socrates and Jesus, whom PBS greatly admired.

143–6 *They ... begun*: In *Inferno* V.27–45, the damned who have yielded to lust are swept about in a whirlwind.

175 Cp. Milton, *Paradise Lost* II.594–5: 'the parching air / Burns frore, and cold performs the effect of fire.'

187–8 *the holes ... eyes*: Cp. Shakespeare, *Antony and Cleopatra* II.vii.15–17.

190 *grim Feature*: The phrase used to describe the monstrous figure of Death in *Paradise Lost* X.279. 'Feature' = 'form' or 'shape'.

204 *Rousseau*: Jean-Jacques Rousseau (1712–78). PBS's opinions of Rousseau varied over time. In *TofL* he considers him not as political theorist and inspirer of the French Revolution but as an author who, by representing his personal longings and afflictions, whether fictionalized in the novel *Julie; ou La Nouvelle Héloïse* (1761) or directly in his *Confessions* (1781–8), introduced a powerful and infectious strain of sentiment into literature – as the figure of Rousseau himself indicates in ll. 240–43, 274–81.

206–7 These lines are cancelled in PBS's draft. Cp. 'Ode to the West Wind', ll. 66–8 (p. 400).

210–11 *Mitres ... thought*: The first three ('Mitres and helms and crowns') are worn by religious leaders, military commanders and monarchs respectively;

'wreathes of light' distinguish thinkers and artists, combining the laurel wreath of the poet and the halo (as *Webb 1995* points out).

211 *lore*: Learning, knowledge.

217 *The Child . . . hour*: Napoleon Bonaparte. See 'Written on hearing the news of the death of Napoleon' (p. 508).

222 *pinion*: Wing.

227 *every pigmy*: May signify the monarchies restored by the Treaty of the Holy Alliance after the defeat of Napoleon.

228–31 Cp. *Prometheus Unbound* I.625–8 (pp. 209–10).

235–6 François-Marie Arouet, known as Voltaire (1694–1778), whose works, along with those of Rousseau, were widely held by PBS's contemporaries to have provided intellectual stimulus for the French Revolution. Frederick II ('the Great') of Prussia (1712–86), Catherine II ('the Great') of Russia (1729–96), and Leopold II, Grand Duke of Tuscany, Archduke of Austria and Holy Roman Emperor (1747–92), were three proponents of so-called 'enlightened absolutism'. The reclusive German philosopher Immanuel Kant (1724–1804) developed the transcendental idealist philosophy which PBS mocks in *Peter Bell the Third*, ll. 518–32 (p. 389). PBS's draft of this passage also mentions 'Pitt', a reference to either William Pitt the Elder (1708–78) or (more likely) the Younger (1759–1806), both of whom had served as prime minister of Great Britain.

237 *anarch*: An absolute ruler who by definition promotes misrule. Cp. 'Ode to Liberty', l. 43 (p. 428), and 'Lines Written among the Euganean Hills, October, 1818', l. 152 (p. 157).

254–9 Usually taken as a reference to Aster (the Greek word for 'star'), a youth with whom Plato, disciple of Socrates ('his master'), is reputed to have been in love. See epigraph to *Adonais* (p. 491). Socrates and Plato also appear together in *Inferno* IV.134.

260 PBS's draft of this line is incomplete.

261 *The tutor and his pupil*: Aristotle (384–322 BC) and Alexander the Great (356–323 BC), who was the philosopher's pupil until the age of sixteen. Aristotle is honoured as pre-eminent among philosophers in *Inferno* IV.130–33.

269 *Bacon's spirit*: Francis Bacon (1561–1626), an early advocate of empirical scientific method, i.e. induction based on experimentation and evidence rather than deduction from first principles.

271 *The Proteus shape*: Proteus, a Greek god of the sea, could change his shape at will. Bacon's empirical method began an orderly consideration of the varying phenomena of the natural world, just as in Homer, *Odyssey* IV, Menelaus compels Proteus to reveal the truth by holding him fast.

274 *the great bards of old*: A cancelled draft for this line reads 'Homer & his brethren'.

278–9 PBS struggled with this portion of the draft and there is a line missing in this stanza. In *1824*, MWS noted 'there is a chasm here in the MS which it is impossible to fill up. It appears from the context, that other shapes pass, and that Rousseau still stood beside the dreamer.'

280 *my words . . . misery*: Recalling Ugolino's speech in *Inferno* XXXIII.7–8: 'if my words will be seed to bear the fruit of infamy for the traitor'.

283–4 *the heirs / Of Caesar's ... Constantine*: The Roman emperors, from Julius Caesar, who transformed the Republic into an empire, to Constantine I ('the Great'), who made Christianity its official religion.

288 *Gregory and John*: Commentators have identified these as Gregory I, 'the Great' (Pope 590–604), or Gregory VII, 'Hildebrand' (Pope 1073–85), and John XXII (Pope 1316–34) but many popes took the name 'Gregory' or 'John'.

288–92 Theologians and the church hierarchy created a dogmatic institutional Christianity which obscured true divinity.

289 *Man and god*: 'The manuscript capital and lower-case reinforce S.'s heterodox meaning' (*Major Works*).

299 *one sad thought*: Cp. l. 21.

331 *the oblivious spell*: The 'spell' that obliterates all memory.

336–9 Recalling Wordsworth's lament, in 'Ode: Intimations of Immortality' (1807), for the fading of the 'vision splendid' of youth into 'the light of common day' (ll. 73–6).

354 PBS made a number of cancelled attempts at this line, and the present text is conjectural.

357 *Iris*: Goddess who personified the rainbow; a messenger of the gods to humans, she is often represented as a winged female.

358–9 The glass froths ('Mantling') with nepenthe, a drug that banishes sorrow and grief, given by Helen of Troy to Telemachus in *Odyssey* IV.219–32; cp. also Milton, *Comus*, ll. 63–6, 674–7.

361 *palms*: The soles of the feet; cp. *Adonais*, l. 212 (p. 499).

386 *As if the gazer's mind*: PBS's draft of ll. 386–8 is very heavily worked and the present text is conjectural.

392–405 PBS's draft of these lines has been lost and the present text is based on *1824*, which remains the sole textual witness.

398 The questions Rousseau asks of the Shape here parallel those which the narrator asks of Rousseau in l. 296. Cp. Eve's account of Eden in *Paradise Lost* IV.449–52.

404 *Touched with faint lips the cup*: As a number of commentators have observed, this phrase might imply that Rousseau does not actually drink from the cup.

414–15 'Lucifer' is here the planet Venus, 'that fairest planet' (l. 416), seen amid the yellowish-green (the colour of 'chrysolite', i.e. the precious stone olivine) sky just before dawn.

417–19 *one who ... smile*: Although Classical authors often have Venus appearing as morning and evening star on the same day, this is not actually possible.

420 *jonquil*: A type of narcissus, known for its intense fragrance.

422–3 Brescia is a province and a city in northern Italy. In *1824*, MWS added a note explaining that 'The favourite song, "Stanco di pascolar le peccorelle" [I am tired of grazing my sheep], is a Brescian national air'.

432 *tenour*: Course or direction.

446 *atomies*: Tiny particles.

463 *Lethean song*: In Greek myth, the waters of Lethe, one of the five rivers of the underworld, induced forgetfulness in those who drank them. See *Purgatorio* XXXI, where Mathilda compels Dante to drink from Lethe.

471–6 The *Divina Commedia* is a visionary journey through Hell, Purgatory and Paradise in which the pilgrim Dante comes to understand that all human love has its source in transcendent Divine Love. The phrase 'Behold a wonder' echoes *Paradise Lost* I.777.

473 *Through every Paradise*: In the *Divina Commedia* Paradise is imagined as made up of nine concentric celestial spheres plus the immaterial region of the Empyrean.

477–548 Some commentators have found in these lines PBS's adaptation of the *simulacra* of *De Rerum Natura* IV.30–468, in which Lucretius accounts for visual perception, but also for dreams and visions of ghosts ('phantoms'), on the hypothesis that thin, film-like replicas of things detach themselves from their surfaces and move about in the atmosphere.

479 The Third Sphere of Heaven in Dante's *Paradiso*, the sphere of Venus.

494 PBS's draft of this line is unresolved; his latest intentions for the second phrase can only be conjectured.

496–7 *tiar / Of pontiffs*: The tiara or triple crown worn by popes.

499 *A baby's . . . brow*: Perhaps recalling Thomas Paine's critique of hereditary monarchy, in *Rights of Man*, Part II (1792), as 'an office which any child or idiot may fill' (ed. Eric Foner and Henry Collins (Harmondsworth: Penguin Books, 1984), p. 174). PBS may also allude to the mental incapacity of George III. Cp. also the 'Embryos and idiots' consigned to Limbo in *Paradise Lost* III.474.

500 *anatomies*: Skeletons.

505 *charnel*: A house for storing the bones of the dead or corpses.

544–8 These lines were first published in *Locock*.

544 *the cripple cast*: These words are cancelled in PBS's draft.

548 *Of*: The MS breaks off at this point.

To Jane ('The keen stars were twinkling')

PBS's draft is now in the Bodleian Library (MS Shelley adds. c. 4: see *BSM* I). Our text is based on the fair copy (Box A, Special Collections, in the John Rylands University Library of Manchester: see *MYR (Shelley)* VIII). PBS gave this copy to Jane Williams (see headnote to 'To —' ('The serpent is shut out from Paradise'): p. 840) in June 1822, with the following note:

> I sate down to write some words for an ariette [a brief song] which might be profane—. but it was in vain to struggle with the ruling spirit, who compelled me to speak of things sacred to yours & Wilhelmeister's [Edward Williams's, playfully nicknamed after the hero of Goethe's *Wilhelm Meisters Lehrjahre* (1795–6)] indulgence—. I commit them to your secrecy & your mercy & will try & do better another time.

The skilfully varied line-lengths and the deft use of single and double rhymes create a verbal and formal analogy for the musical occasion which the poem evokes and which, it suggests, had the power to intimate a reality beyond the pleasures of the moment. Lines 7–24 were published in *The Athenaeum* for 17 November 1832 as 'An Ariette for Music' and the complete poem in *1840*, where it was entitled simply 'To —'.

4 *guitar*: See headnote to 'With a Guitar. To Jane' (p. 845).
22–4 PBS describes an evening's sailing with the Williamses in a letter of 18 June 1822: 'we drive along this delightful bay in the evening wind, under the summer moon, until earth appears another world' (*Letters* II, p. 435).
23–4 Cp. 'To Jane. The Invitation', ll. 47–68 (pp. 560–61).

Lines Written in the Bay of Lerici

PBS drafted these lines while composing *The Triumph of Life* (*TofL*), evidently in mid to late June 1822. His much-cancelled and untitled draft interrupts the draft of *TofL* (see headnote thereto (p. 847) and *BSM* I); it is uncertain whether he meant to add further lines (see *BSM* I). The details of time and place suggest that the poem had its origin in an evening spent in the company of Jane Williams near the village of San Terenzo on the Bay of Lerici, on the north-west coast of Italy, where the Shelleys were sharing a house for the summer with Jane and her common-law husband Edward. (For PBS's relationship with the Williamses, see headnote to 'To —' ('The serpent is shut out from Paradise'): p. 840.) In common with *TofL* the lines question the nature and significance of fleeting moments of pleasure. Cp. PBS's letter to John Gisborne of 18 June 1822, in which he says of an evening's sailing with Edward and Jane: 'if the past and the future could be obliterated, the present would content me so well that I could say with Faust to the passing moment, "Remain, thou, thou art so beautiful"' (*Letters* II, pp. 435–6, alluding to Goethe, *Faust* (1808), I.vii.1699–706). Richard Garnett published ll. 7–58 in *Macmillan's Magazine* for June 1862, under the present title, by which the poem has become known; he included the full text in *Relics of Shelley* (1862) later that year.

10–11 The albatross was supposed to sleep in flight because of the long distances it travels over the sea.
21–4 Cp. 'The Magnetic lady to her patient', l. 2 (p. 565).
32 *As they*: As if they.
57–8 PBS's draft of ll. 57–8 is not resolved. There is no word after 'pleasure' in l. 57; in l. 58 'Destroying' is cancelled; 'Seeking' is written below it, and 'alone' above the line; 'not peace' is underlined. Various readings of the final line have been conjectured: 'Destroying life alone not peace' (*Norton 2002*); 'Seeking life not peace' (*Chernaik*); 'Seeking Life alone *not peace*' (G. M. Matthews (ed.), *Shelley: Selected Poems and Prose* (Oxford: Oxford University Press, 1964)).

THE PROSE

From *History of a Six Weeks' Tour*

In August 1816, PBS sent from Geneva to T. L. Peacock in England a long journal-letter recounting the excursion to Chamonix ('Chamouni') and Mont Blanc which he, MWS and Claire Clairmont had made between 21 and 27 July

(*Letters* I, pp. 495–502). The following year a somewhat modified version of the letter, the text given here, was published in *1817*, where it immediately precedes 'Mont Blanc' (p. 140). The present extract excludes the first four paragraphs.

1 *woof*: Texture.
2 *an exhalation*: A mist or cloud.
3 *Bethgelert*: Beddgelert, a village in the Snowdonia region of north Wales.
4 *aiguilles*: Peaks.
5 *awful*: Terrifying, inspiring awe and reverence.
6 *Saussure . . . increase and decay*: The Genevan meteorologist, geologist, botanist and progressive political reformer Horace-Bénédict de Saussure (1740–99) was rector of the University of Geneva 1774–6. In 1787 he led a party to the summit of Mont Blanc; his was the second ascent, Jacques Balmat and Michel-Gabriel Paccard having made the first the previous year. Saussure spent four and a half hours on the summit making scientific observations and measurements. He collected his extensive researches in the four volumes of *Voyages dans les Alpes* (1779–96).
7 *Buffon's . . . points of the earth*: PBS had read (*MWS Journal* I, p. 100) the *Théorie de la Terre* in the first volume of *Histoire naturelle, générale et particulière* (1749–1804) by the French naturalist Georges-Louis Leclerc, Comte de Buffon (1707–88), which advanced the hypothesis that the earth had been progressively cooling since its separation from the sun.
8 *Ahriman*: T. L. Peacock, to whom the original letter was addressed, had begun *Ahrimanes*, a mythological narrative in verse which he never completed or published. The poem adopts the ancient Zoroastrian belief in the supreme dominion over the world of two opposed divinities, one good (Oromaze), the other evil (Ahrimanes).
9 *adamantine*: Unbreakable.
10 *toises*: A *toise* measured nearly two metres.
11 *mauvais pas*: A particularly difficult part of a mountain route.
12 *god of the Stoics*: The ancient Stoic philosophers held that God was immanent as the active principle in nature, which they conceived of as a single, continuous being composed of directing spirit and passive matter.
13 *aubergistes*: Innkeepers.
14 *the Celandine*: See 'Verses written on receiving a Celandine in a letter from England' and notes (pp. 132, 714).

From *Preface to LAON AND CYTHNA*

PBS devoted the period from mid March to late September 1817 to the composition of the epic-romance *Laon and Cythna; or, The Revolution of the Golden City: A Vision of the Nineteenth Century. In the Stanza of Spenser*, which was published in December and is the source of our text. The poem's 4,818 lines, of which we include only the verse Dedication (p. 148), in effect address the nation in what he intended to be a major literary statement at a time of national crisis. In England the year 1817 was one of unrest and apprehension. The economic depression following the defeat of Napoleon had resulted in extensive unemployment, while a poor harvest and commodity taxes sharply increased the cost of living. Unrest at the consequent hardship, especially for the labouring classes, as well as a widespread conviction that only reform of a narrow parliamentary representation would bring any substantial improvement, provoked riots and demonstrations in several parts of the country, which were met with repressive measures on the part of government. In this tense atmosphere the poem stages 'such a Revolution as might be supposed to take place in an European nation' (*Letters* I, p. 563) – a bloodless rising of modern Greeks against their Ottoman masters which is crushed by a treacherous international alliance of royal power sanctioned by established religion. PBS makes it clear that his narrative looks back to the French Revolution as well as forward to an idealized version of it at some future date. The poem was also highly adventurous in the sphere of personal morality. As first published in late 1817, it places at its centre, as an instance of the love it recommends as supreme moral principle, sexual consummation between the revolutionary leaders, the brother and sister Laon and Cythna. Following the objections of the publisher, the poem was revised so as to alter their blood kinship and to temper the most uncompromising of its anti-religious sentiments, then reissued in early 1818 under a new title, *The Revolt of Islam*. *Laon and Cythna* was a daring, provocative and very risky intervention in the febrile literary-political climate of the day, and was to prompt a comprehensive and unrelenting attack on both poem and author in the *Quarterly Review* for April 1819. Aware of the danger of publishing such a work at such a time, when prosecution for blasphemous libel was a real possibility, PBS takes exceptional pains in the Preface to explain his aims and to present himself, then a little-known author, as a serious commentator on matters of urgent public concern.

1 *tempests . . . we live*: The French Revolutionary (1792–1802) and Napoleonic Wars (1803–15) and their reverberations throughout Europe.

2 *celebrated productions . . . human mind*: The works of the great imaginative writers, such as Homer and Shakespeare (see *Letters* I, p. 507).

3 *accidental education*: The experiences that form the mind independently of any formal instruction or public coercion.

4 *Alps . . . Mont Blanc*: PBS's visit to Switzerland in spring and summer 1816 proved to be a rich creative period: see 'Hymn to Intellectual Beauty' (p. 134), 'Mont Blanc' (p. 140) and the extract from *1817* (p. 595).

5 *sailed . . . mighty rivers*: In late summer 1814, PBS, MWS and Claire Clairmont sailed from Lake Lucerne down the Reuss and the Rhine to Bonn, a journey described in *1817*, pp. 55–71.

6 *ravages of tyranny . . . desolated thresholds*: PBS, MWS and Claire Clairmont had observed such scenes in France in August 1814 (see *1817*, pp. 19–28).

7 *I have conversed . . . men of genius*: PBS had both spoken and corresponded with William Godwin (from December 1816 his father-in-law) and Lord Byron, who are chiefly intended here.

8 *[Shelley's note]*: PBS advances the hypothesis that poetry, considered broadly as imaginative creation, may like science be advancing towards perfection.

9 *a resemblance . . . between all the writers of any particular age*: This paragraph is PBS's first formulation of the idea of the 'spirit of the age',

which he refines upon in the Preface to *Prometheus Unbound* (p. 184), and to which he gives central importance in the final paragraph of *A Defence of Poetry* (p. 678).

10 *tragic Poets of the age of Pericles*: The ancient Greek tragedians Aeschylus, Sophocles and Euripides, who flourished in Athens in the fifth century BC. Pericles (*c*.495–429 BC) was the chief statesman of Athens.

11 *[Shelley's note]*: PBS considered the literature of the period in which Milton's major poems were published, beginning with the restoration of Charles II in 1660, as vitiated by the restored monarchy. See *A Defence of Poetry* (p. 651).

Lord Bacon: Francis Bacon, Baron Verulam and Viscount St Albans (1561–1626), held several high political offices as well as writing widely on philosophical, legal and scientific subjects.

12 *Ford*: The dramatist John Ford (1586–*c*.1640) was Shakespeare's younger contemporary.

An Address to the People on the Death of the Princess Charlotte

Princess Charlotte, daughter and only child of the Prince Regent and Princess Caroline of Brunswick, and wife since the previous year of Prince Leopold of Saxe-Coburg, died on 6 November 1817, at the age of twenty-one, having given birth to a stillborn boy two days previously. The two deaths left the British throne without a direct heir and occasioned extraordinary public demonstrations of grief. Unlike her unpopular father and her mentally disabled grandfather George III, the princess was widely held in affection; and hopes were entertained that, on acceding to the throne, she would be favourable to political reform. Her funeral was scheduled for 19 November, the intervening fortnight having been declared a period of national mourning. The day after the princess's death, three men, Jeremiah Brandreth, William Turner and Isaac Ludlam, were executed at Derby for their part in the 'Pentridge Rising' of 9 and 10 June 1817, a poorly planned and ineptly executed insurrection in the form of an armed march on Nottingham by about two hundred artisans and workers desperate at the widespread hardship resulting from unemployment, high prices and an unrepresentative electoral system. At Nottingham the group was quickly dispersed by a small detachment of mounted troops. The coincidence of the royal death and the execution of the working men PBS took as the occasion of *An Address*, which he began in the evening of 11 November 1817 and finished the following day (*Letters* I, p. 566; *MWS Journal* I, p. 184). No MS is known to survive. Modern texts, including this one, derive from an edition published in 1843 by the bookseller Thomas Rodd, who described it as a 'fac-simile reprint' of an original that was limited to only twenty copies. If Rodd was correct, it may be that Charles Ollier and/or the publisher Thomas Hookham, both of whom PBS visited on 15 November, declined to offer the pamphlet for sale for fear of prosecution, and that only twenty copies were run off for private circulation. No date or publisher's name appears on the title-page of Rodd's edition, where the author is identified only as 'The Hermit of Marlow', the nom de plume that PBS had assumed for *A Proposal for Putting*

Reform to the Vote throughout the Kingdom, his pamphlet recommending an extension of the suffrage and annual parliaments, which Ollier had published in March 1817. That assumed name and a reference to *An Address* as PBS's by his cousin Thomas Medwin in *The Shelley Papers* (1833), together with similarities to other poems and prose by PBS, form the basis for accepting his authorship.

Stephen C. Behrendt, *Royal Mourning and Regency Culture: Elegies and Memorials of Princess Charlotte* (London: Macmillan, 1997), examines literary responses to the death of the princess in the arts and popular culture. E. P. Thompson provides an account of the Pentridge Rising in *The Making of the English Working Class* (Harmondsworth: Penguin Books, 1980), pp. 723–34.

1 *The Hermit of Marlow*: PBS resided at Marlow in Buckinghamshire for a year from March 1817. The nom de plume suggests the retired sage, a role that he regularly imagined for himself.

2 *'We Pity . . . Dying Bird'*: In *Rights of Man* (1791) Thomas Paine wrote of Edmund Burke's *Reflections on the Revolution in France* (1790) that 'He pities the plumage but forgets the dying bird' as a challenge to Burke, who had lamented the disdain of the French revolutionaries for the traditional graces and virtues of the aristocracy while disregarding the plight of the people, who had suffered under arbitrary aristocratic power.

3 *illustrated it with their genius*: Rendered it illustrious.

4 *'that bourne . . . returns'*: Quoting Shakespeare, *Hamlet* III.i.80–82: 'death, / The undiscovered country from whose bourn / No traveller returns'.

5 *Horne Tooke and Hardy . . . high treason*: In the repressive political atmosphere following the declaration of war against France in 1793, several of those calling for constitutional reform were arrested and imprisoned before being tried for treason in autumn 1794 – among them the philologist and veteran activist John Horne Tooke (1736–1812) and Thomas Hardy (1752–1832), a shoemaker who was the founding secretary and treasurer of the London Corresponding Society, which advocated a broadening of the suffrage and annual parliaments as a condition for reforming the country's economic and social ills. After celebrated trials, both were acquitted to widespread public rejoicing.

6 *hurdle*: 'A frame or sledge on which a traitor was drawn through the streets to execution' (*OED*).

7 *[Shelley's note]*: PBS misquotes Shakespeare, *Cymbeline* V.v.272–3: 'Your death has eyes in 's head, then. I have not seen him so pictured.'

8 *depending on*: Suggested by, related to.

9 *a check*: *Prose Works* I suggests that this is the 'Sinking Fund', into which state revenue was paid in order to reduce the size of the national debt. See note 12 below.

10 *fundamental defect*: An unrepresentative parliament.

11 *pensioners . . . placemen*: Those in receipt of state funds as a salary, reward for services or loyalty, and those appointed to public sinecures.

12 *The effect . . . civilized life*: In common with many liberals, PBS deplored the size of the national debt which had grown to fund the wars

against the American colonies and against revolutionary France and which required an increase in taxation, falling most heavily on the poor, merely to pay the interest on the large sums borrowed.

13 *double aristocracy*: PBS elaborates on the character of this 'new aristocracy' in *A Philosophical View of Reform* (p. 636).

14 *sans peur et sans tache*: 'Without fear or stain'; the qualities of bravery and upright conduct proper to a knight.

15 *gambling in the funds*: Investing for gain in the stock of the national debt; in effect, lending to the state.

16 *'Corinthian capital of polished society'*: Edmund Burke's characterization of aristocracy in *Reflections on the Revolution in France* (1790), which was derided by Thomas Paine in *Rights of Man*, Part II (1792).

17 *two chasms*: Those of anarchy and misrule.

18 *manufacturers, the helots*: Factory-workers as serfs.

19 *spies were sent forth*: Cp. Luke 20:20: 'And they [chief priests and scribes] watched him [Jesus], and sent forth spies, which should feign themselves just men, that they might take hold of his words, that so they might deliver him unto the power and authority of the governor.'

20 *extraordinary powers*: In March 1817, Parliament suspended Habeas Corpus and granted magistrates the power to disperse meetings of more than fifty persons which they judged to be seditious.

21 *OLIVER*: The paid government informer who had acted as an agent provocateur in the Pentridge affair.

22 *chaplain prevented . . . observations*: So forestalling the traditional right of the condemned man to speak his last words, which might have embarrassed the government.

23 *[Shelley's note]*: The liberal weekly *The Examiner*, edited by PBS's friend Leigh Hunt, carried a report to which *An Address* is indebted for its account of the executions.

24 *glorious Phantom*: PBS introduces similar emblematic figures in 'England in 1819' (p. 405), *The Mask of Anarchy*, ll. 102 ff. (p. 360), and 'God save the Queen!' (p. 423).

From *On Christianity*

PBS set down this untitled series of reflections on the teachings of Jesus in late 1817 in a notebook containing other writings and notes on religion (Bodleian MS Shelley e. 4; see *BSM* III). They were not published until after his death: in *Shelley Memorials*, edited by Jane, Lady Shelley (1859). The complete text, which includes some pages from a separate MS (Bodleian MS Shelley adds. c. 4; see *BSM* XXI), is included in *Prose Works*; the whole makes a substantial essay of over ten thousand words, of which about one-fifth is excerpted here.

PBS had an abiding interest in the Christian religion and writings. He regarded the essential moral message of the Gospels as of great potential benefit to the age, provided it was purged of its supernatural elements (the report of miracles, for example) as well as freed from the accreted distortions and perversions of institutional Christianity. To this end he prepared 'Biblical Extracts', a little volume featuring Christ's 'moral sayings' which in late 1812 he attempted unsuccessfully to have published (*Letters* I, pp. 265, 332, 348). Then in late 1819 he made notes on Luke's Gospel 1–20 which identify passages relevant to contemporary social and political concerns (see *BSM* XIV). 'On Christianity' proposes a rational and benevolent interpretation of Christ's doctrines, insisting on their revolutionary character, in three broad divisions: the nature of God, the iniquity of revenge and the equality of humankind. Each of these is represented by one of the three extracts offered here.

Bodleian MS Shelley e. 4, our copy-text, is unfinished: the argument sometimes breaks off abruptly, and PBS has left blank spaces for words or phrases to be filled in later. The punctuation of the MS has been supplemented, ampersands and abbreviations expanded. Summaries are provided in the notes for substantial editorial omissions.

Examination of PBS's views on Christianity and the Gospels can be found in: David Fuller, 'Shelley and Jesus', *Durham University Journal* 85.54 (2) (1993), pp. 211–23; Michael O'Neill, '"A Double Face of False and True": Religion in Shelley', *Literature and Theology* 25/1 (March 2011), pp. 32–46; Bryan Shelley, *Shelley and Scripture: The Interpreting Angel* (Oxford: Clarendon Press, 1994), chapter 3; and Timothy Webb, *Shelley: A Voice Not Understood* (Manchester: Manchester University Press, 1977), chapter 6.

1 *[imbued by their Spirit]*: A conjectural reading of a passage left unresolved in PBS's MS.

2 *Utter darkness . . . mountains*: See Matthew 27:45–53.

3 *Universal Pan*: Pan was a proverbially amorous deity who ensured the fertility of flocks; represented as half goat and half man, he frequented mountains, caves and wildernesses and was sometimes regarded as a universal god. Cp. *The Witch of Atlas*, l. 113 (p. 451).

4 *who*: PBS's draft breaks off at this point.

5 *Vesta*: In this list of Roman deities, Vesta was the goddess of fire in the domestic hearth.

6 *Proteus*: Proteus was a sea god who had the power to change his shape.

7 *capable*: PBS's draft breaks off at this point.

8 *Blessed . . . God*: One of the Christian 'Beatitudes'; see, for example, Matthew 5:8.

9 *motionless lyre*: An Aeolian harp, whose strings respond to the motions of the wind. See *Alastor*, ll. 41–9 (p. 114), and cp. Coleridge, 'The Eolian Harp' (1796).

10 *consentaneity:* A state of accordance.

11 *There is a power . . . over their frame*: PBS explores similar intuitions in 'Hymn to Intellectual Beauty' (p. 134) and in *Alastor*, ll. 37–49 (p. 114).

12 *it*: PBS's draft breaks off at this point.

13 *be perfect . . . various shapes*: See Matthew 5:39–48: 'Be ye therefore perfect, even as your Father which is in heaven is perfect' (48); 'whosoever shall smite thee on thy right cheek, turn to him the other also' (39).

14 *[. . .]*: In the MS, PBS concludes this paragraph by quoting in Greek from Diogenes Laërtius' 'Life of Diogenes', in *The Lives and Opinions of Eminent Philosophers* (third century AD). The quotation derides fame

and distinctions of birth and asserts that the only true nation is the universe.

15 *Rousseau*: In his *Discours sur l'origine et les fondements de l'inégalité parmi les hommes* (1754), Jean-Jacques Rousseau argued that the natural state of human equality had been obscured by modern civil society and recommended the order of nature as a standard for social reform.

16 *No man . . . masters*: Quoting Matthew 6:24: 'No man can serve two masters: for either he will hate the one, and love the other; or else he will hold to the one, and despise the other. Ye cannot serve God and mammon.' In the remainder of the essay, PBS further interprets Christ's doctrines, stressing the need to minimize bodily wants and to pursue the virtue and knowledge that promote universal love, justice and equality.

On Love

PBS appears to have drafted these remarks on the psychology of love between 20 and 25 July 1818 after translating Plato's *Symposium* and before drafting what he refers to as a 'prefatory essay' (*Letters* II, p. 26) to his translation, 'A Discourse on the manners of the Antient Greeks relative to the subject of Love'. In the 'Discourse' he examines the differences between ancient Greek and modern notions and practices in the domain of sexual behaviour, taking special care to explain the social circumstances in which male homosexuality became the model of erotic love that figures centrally in the *Symposium*. He also affirms his conviction that the innate human impulse to love another being increases in complexity, depth, intensity and duration as civilization advances, is indeed an index of its advance. 'On Love' takes inspiration from the lyrical praise of love in the *Symposium* while maintaining its own reservations on the possibility of erotic fulfilment. Among other important explorations of love in PBS's work which amplify, vary, test and alter the ideas of the essay are: *Alastor* (Preface, p. 112, and ll. 149–91, pp. 117–18), *Laon and Cythna* (Dedication, p. 148, and ll. 2587–2712), *Epipsychidion* (p. 474) and *A Defence of Poetry* (p. 651).

The text is taken from PBS's untitled MS draft in Bodleian MS Shelley adds. e. 11 (see *BSM* XV). The title 'On Love' was supplied by MWS when she published the essay for the first time in *The Keepsake for 1829*.

1 *proof*: Test or trial.

2 *what is Love*: PBS first wrote then cancelled the response: 'It is the sweet chalice of life whose dregs are bitterer than wormwood.'

3 *This is Love*: Followed in PBS's draft by the cancelled sentence: 'All else is vanity.'

4 *prototype*: 'The first or primary type of a person or thing; an original on which something is modelled' (*OED*). See note 7 below.

5 *soul within our soul*: PBS introduces the figure of a 'soul out of my soul' into his affective autobiography in *Epipsychidion*, l. 238 (p. 481).

6 *Paradise . . . overleap*: Alluding to Satan's entry into Paradise by leaping over the boundary surrounding it in Milton's *Paradise Lost* IV.179–83.

7 *antitype*: A person or thing foreshadowed by and conforming to the prototype. See note 4 above.
8 *inconceivable*: Incomprehensible.
9 *Sterne says . . . some cypress*: 'Was I in a desart, I would find out wherewith in it to call forth my affections—if I could not do better, I would fasten them upon some sweet myrtle, or seek some melancholy cypress to connect myself to' (Laurence Sterne, *A Sentimental Journey*, ed. Paul Goring (London: Penguin Books, 2001), p. 28).

On Life

PBS drafted this untitled prose fragment in late 1819 in the notebook that contains his draft of *A Philosophical View of Reform*. It was later removed from the notebook and is now in the Morgan Library and Museum (MA 408) and supplies our text. Thomas Medwin published a version in 1832 in *The Athenaeum* and again the following year in *The Shelley Papers*. MWS included a more accurate text in *1840 (ELTF)* under the present title.

Beginning as an expression of wonder and astonishment, 'On Life' develops a series of metaphysical and epistemological reflections which encapsulate PBS's thinking on a range of philosophical questions. Both materialism and the 'popular' dualism of mind and matter (together with the dogmatic theism such dualism has underpinned) are deemed inadequate to account for our experience of 'life'. Instead PBS subscribes to the 'intellectual system', a sceptical idealism derived from the empiricist philosophers David Hume (1711–76) and William Drummond (?1770–1828). Drummond's *Academical Questions* (1805), a major source for 'On Life', defended Hume against the attacks of Scottish 'Common Sense' philosophers like Thomas Reid (1710–96) and Dugald Stewart (1753–1828). In a letter of November 1819, PBS cited Drummond as 'the most acute metaphysical critic of the age' (*Letters* II, p. 142). The central tenet of the 'intellectual system' is that we can have no knowledge of things independent of the ideas that we form of them, or, as PBS puts it, that 'nothing exists but as it is perceived'. This position is to be distinguished from the 'immaterialism' which PBS rejected in a letter to Godwin in July 1812 (*Letters* I, p. 316). Although MWS wrote in her Preface to *1840 (ELTF)* that PBS was 'a disciple of the Immaterial Philosophy of Berkeley', PBS does not accept the conclusion of George Berkeley (1685–1753) that the ideas that form the world have been created and are maintained in existence by an act of divine perception. 'Mind', PBS writes, 'as far as we have any experience of its properties . . . cannot create, it can only perceive', a position he reaffirmed in September 1819 (*Letters* II, p. 122–3). Hence things, according to PBS's understanding of the 'science of mind', exist: it is just that we can have no objective knowledge of them. Compare 'Mont Blanc', ll. 142–4 (p. 146), where PBS interrogates the relationship between the mountain and 'the human mind's imaginings'.

For critical consideration of PBS's engagement with the 'intellectual philosophy', see: Timothy Clark, *Embodying Revolution: The Figure of the Poet in Shelley* (Oxford: Clarendon Press, 1989), pp. 13–43; Cian Duffy, *Shelley and the Revolutionary Sublime* (Cambridge: Cambridge University Press, 2005), pp. 61–72; C. E. Pulos, *The Deep Truth: A Study of Shelley's Skepticism* (Lincoln, Nebr.: University of Nebraska Press, 1962), pp. 24–41; and Earl Wasserman, *Shelley: A Critical Reading* (Baltimore: Johns Hopkins University Press, 1971), pp. 131–53.

1 *of*: The draft possibly reads 'by'.
2 *'Non merita . . . il Poeta'*: 'None but God and the Poet deserve the name of creator.' See *A Defence of Poetry* (p. 675).
3 *'such stuff . . . made of'*: Quoting Shakespeare, *The Tempest* IV.i.156–8: 'We are such stuff / As dreams are made on, and our little life / Is rounded with a sleep.'
4 *'looking both before and after'*: Shakespeare, *Hamlet*: 'Sure, he that made us with such large discourse, / Looking before and after, gave us not / That capability and god-like reason / To fust in us unused' (see 'Additional Passages' in Wells and Taylor OUP edition, p. 689).
5 *'thoughts . . . eternity'*: In Milton's *Paradise Lost* II.142–51, Belial fears lest he and the other rebel angels might be annihilated if they exasperate God further and so lose their 'thoughts that wander through eternity' (l. 148).
6 *change and extinction*: PBS first wrote 'nothingness and dissolution'. Neither phrase is cancelled.
7 *pioneer*: An infantryman whose task was 'to clear terrain in readiness for the main body of troops' (*OED*).
8 *the state called reverie*: In the fifth *Promenade* of his *Rêveries du promeneur solitaire* (Reveries of a Solitary Walker; 1782) Rousseau gives just such an account of this 'state'.
9 *blunted*: The word is ambiguously formed in the MS. MWS and some later editors read 'planted'. *Norton 2002* prefers 'blunted', citing the identical phrase 'impressions blunted by re-iteration' in *A Defence of Poetry* (p. 675).
10 *preceded*: MWS in *1840 (ELTF)* gives the word as 'produced'.
11 *basis of*: Written above 'cause of' in the MS; neither phrase is cancelled.
12 *thoughts*: Written above 'things' in the MS; neither word is cancelled.

The Coliseum

PBS began this unfinished story on 25 November 1818, after he, MWS and Claire Clairmont had been in Rome for four days and had made daily visits to the ruined amphitheatre (*MWS Journal* I, p. 239). It is impossible now to tell when he gave up working on it, but the Colosseum was still on his mind in mid December 1818, when he sent T. L. Peacock an enthusiastic description of it from Naples, some two weeks after leaving Rome (*Letters* II, pp. 58–9). PBS might have taken the story up again during his second visit to the city, from March to June 1819, when the celebrations of the Easter season ('The Coliseum' is set on Easter Day), and the Shelleys' renewed visits to the amphitheatre, will have rekindled his interest.

A partial first draft survives in Bodleian MS Shelley adds. e. 12 (see *BSM* XVIII). Our text is based on the fair draft in MWS's hand, with corrections by PBS, in Bodleian MS Shelley adds. c. 5 (see *BSM* XXII), and on the continuation of this draft in PBS's own hand now in Bodleian MS Shelley adds. c. 4 (see *BSM* XXI). A number of gaps in MWS's transcription have been supplied from PBS's first draft, which we have also preferred on some points of punctuation and spelling. In a few instances where the fair draft is unresolved, a conjectural reading has been necessary. Thomas Medwin published a partial text in *The Shelley Papers* (1833), where he described it as 'the first scene of a tale which promised to rival, if not to surpass, "Corinne"' (*Shelley Papers*, pp. 51–2), Mme de Staël's romance (1807) set principally in Rome and Naples. Medwin says that PBS 'allowed me to copy' this 'exquisite fragment', but editors have found his text unreliable. MWS published a complete text in *1840 (ELTF)*, where she drew comparison in her Preface with PBS's essay 'On Love':

> 'The Coliseum' is a continuation to a great degree of the same subject. Shelley had something of the idea of a story in this. The stranger was a Greek,—nurtured from infancy exclusively in the literature of his progenitors,—and brought up as a child of Pericles might have been; and the greater the resemblance, since Shelley conceived the idea of a woman, whom he named Diotima, who was his instructress and guide. In speaking of his plan, this was the sort of development he sketched; but no word more was written than appears in these pages. (I, p. x)

The similarity that MWS notes to PBS's essay 'On Love' (p. 618) is pronounced but other interpretative contexts are possible. For example, it may be that PBS conceived his story as a response to Byron's treatment of the Colosseum in his much-anticipated and widely read Canto IV of *Childe Harold's Pilgrimage* (1818), where the ancient ruin is presented as a symbol of the frailty of human nature and the futility of human endeavour. In December 1819, PBS wrote to Charles Ollier of *Julian and Maddalo* (p. 163), composed in 1818, that he meant 'to write three other poems [like it], the scenes of which will be laid at Rome, Florence, and Naples, but the subjects of which will all be drawn from dreadful or beautiful realities, as that of this was' (*Letters* II, p. 164), and it may be that he had conceived 'The Coliseum' as part of a series of prose (rather than verse) pieces to be set in different Italian cities. Medwin claimed that 'like Byron in "Childe Harold", or Madame De Staël, [PBS] meant to have idealised himself in the principal character', i.e. the stranger who accosts the old man and his daughter in the amphitheatre (*Shelley Papers*, p. 52).

The place of the Colosseum in the cultural history of Romantic-period Europe is considered by Carolyn Springer, *The Marble Wilderness: Ruins and Representation in Italian Romanticism, 1775–1850* (Cambridge: Cambridge University Press, 1987). For detailed critical commentary, see Kevin Binfield, '"May They Be Divided Never": Ethics, History, and the Rhetorical Imagination in Shelley's "The Coliseum"', *KSJ* 46 (1997), pp. 125–47; Timothy Clark, 'Shelley's *The Coliseum* and the Sublime', *Durham University Journal* 85 (July 1993), pp. 225–35; Cian Duffy, *Shelley and the Revolutionary Sublime* (Cambridge: Cambridge University Press, 2005), pp. 163–73; and Charles E. Robinson, *Shelley and Byron: The Snake and Eagle Wreathed in Fight* (Baltimore: Johns Hopkins University Press, 1976), pp. 76–80.

1 *The Coliseum*: PBS's first draft is entitled 'Diotima' (the name of a woman in Plato's *Symposium* who instructs Socrates on the true nature of love).

The fair draft is untitled; the title 'The Coliseum' first appeared in Medwin's *Shelley Papers* (1833).

2 *Praxitelean . . . greatest of poets*: Praxiteles (born *c.*390 BC) was one of the leading sculptors of Classical Greece. The 'greatest of poets' is Homer, traditionally held to have been blind.

3 *awful*: Awe-inspiring.

4 *the Forum*: An area at the heart of ancient Rome which enclosed the city's most important public buildings; also known in the eighteenth and early nineteenth century as the *Campo Vaccino* (literally 'cow pasture') because of its overgrown condition.

5 *clamys*: Usually spelled *chlamys*: 'A short mantle or cloak worn by men in ancient Greece' (*OED*).

6 *Antinous*: A Greek youth, famed for beauty and the favourite of the Roman emperor Hadrian (reigned AD 117–38).

7 *Over all . . . form and gestures*: In *Shelley Papers*, Medwin glossed this description of the stranger: 'There never was drawn a more perfect portrait of Shelley himself' (p. 129n.).

8 *obtrusions*: Unwelcome intrusions or advances.

9 *Il Diavolo di Bruto*: 'Brutus' Devil'; Plutarch recounts, in the *Life of Julius Caesar* and the *Life of Marcus Brutus*, the appearance of an evil spirit to Brutus on two occasions, at Sardis and before the Battle of Philippi, the second occasion portending Brutus' death. Shakespeare's *Julius Caesar* (IV.ii.326–39) gives the apparition the form of Caesar's ghost, which Brutus questions – 'Art thou some god, some angel or some devil?' – receiving the reply: 'Thy evil spirit'. Brutus interprets the ghost as a sign that his 'hour is come' (V.v.20).

10 *its clear . . . universe*: Cp. *Epipsychidion*, ll. 164–9 (p. 479).

11 *'Are they . . . chambers?'*: As Timothy Clark observes, the old man's question recalls the fact that in ancient Rome elephants were kept in the Colosseum to kill and be killed during the games, and that the amphitheatre could be partly flooded to stage mock sea battles ('Shelley's *The Coliseum*', p. 233).

12 *its craggy summit*: The Colosseum is not nearly high enough to intercept the clouds.

13 *the condition of life*: Cp. this and the following sentence with PBS's description of love in his essay 'On Love' (p. 618).

14 *with tingling joy*: Perhaps to be replaced by 'with extas[y]', which is written in a minute hand above this line.

15 *[?have been sought by them]*: PBS's draft is difficult to decipher and our text is conjectural.

16 *Heraclitus . . . so sour a disposition*: Greek philosopher (*c.*535–*c.*475 BC), author of the treatise *On Nature*, and noted for his melancholic and sometimes misanthropic disposition.

17 *Democritus . . . her request*: The Greek philosopher Democritus (*c.*460–*c.*370 BC) was one of the founders of the 'atomist' school, which maintained that the universe was composed of space and tiny, indivisible particles. The story of his sister and the festival of Ceres (goddess of agriculture) is told in Diogenes Laërtius' 'Life of Democritus', in *The Lives and Opinions of Eminent Philosophers* (third century AD).

18 *The men . . . wisdom*: The ancient Romans and the Greeks from whom they acquired philosophy.
19 *my limbs*: An uncancelled word below the line, perhaps 'person', may be intended as a replacement.
20 *and*: PBS's draft ends here, in mid sentence.

Related Passage

In *1840 (ELTF)* MWS printed this passage without title as a footnote keyed to the phrase 'It was such itself'; later editors have followed her example. However, apart from the reflections on the remains of ancient Rome which figure in both the 'Related Passage' and the story, there does not appear to be any specific connection between them. Placing the passage in a footnote, as MWS has done, suggests that she recognized a general similarity to 'The Coliseum' but did not regard it as integral to the text. The passage was drafted separately from the body of the story in PBS's MS notebook and there is no indication that it should figure as part of the narrative. Moreover, unlike the story, the passage describes a broader scene, such as might be found in the Roman Forum. It has more in common with PBS's draft of 1819 on 'The Arch of Titus' than with the 'The Coliseum' (see *BSM* XXI and *Letters* II, pp. 89–90). The Arch of Titus is located near the Roman Forum; neither is visible from within the Colosseum, where PBS's story is set. PBS might have intended the passage for a part of 'The Coliseum' which is now missing from the MS or which he planned but never wrote, or for another purpose altogether.

1 *[?palaces]*: PBS's draft is difficult to decipher and might read 'places'.
2 *a human . . . solemn joy*: PBS alludes to the Roman 'triumphs', processions of troops, captives and booty, organized to celebrate military victories abroad and sometimes passing under triumphal arches constructed to memorialize the occasion.

From *On the Devil, and Devils*

Our text is based on PBS's draft, now Bodleian MS Shelley adds. e. 9 (see *BSM* XIV), which was composed in late 1819–early 1820. MWS planned to include a version in *1840 (ELTF)*, but withdrew it shortly before publication of that volume, having presumably decided that the content was too controversial (a printer's proof with corrections by MWS survives in the Bodleian Library).

'On the Devil, and Devils' was first published in *The Prose Works of Percy Bysshe Shelley* (1880), edited by Harry Buxton Forman. PBS's leading purpose in this witty piece seems to be to poke fun at the Christian religion by drawing attention to the problematic nature of one of its chief figures: the Devil. He was almost certainly referring to 'On the Devil' in his letter of 20 January 1821, to his publisher Charles Ollier, in which he remarks that he 'had written a Lucianic essay' (after the ancient Greek satirist Lucian) concerning how 'the popular faith is destroyed—first the Devil, then the Holy Ghost, then God the

Father' (*Letters* II, p. 258). However, PBS also takes his disquisition as an occasion covertly to attack the use, by the British government, of informers and agents provocateurs to repress political dissent. *Peter Bell the Third* (p. 369) features PBS's serio-comic creation of a Devil for the contemporary world.

1 *the European mythology*: PBS here uses 'mythology' to mean 'the study of myth' rather than the myths themselves.
2 *The Manichaean philosophy*: A system of belief, founded by Mani, a Persian religious teacher and writer of the third century AD, which held that the cosmos is governed by a good and an evil divinity of equal power in perpetual struggle.
3 *Chaldaean ... captivity*: The Chaldean (Neo-Babylonian) civilization flourished in Mesopotamia (comprising parts of modern-day Iraq, Iran, Turkey and Syria) during the sixth century BC. The Jewish people were exiled in Babylonia from 587 to 538 BC. Chaldeans were known for their study of astrology and the occult sciences.
4 *[...]*: We omit some sentences in which PBS considers the authorship of the biblical Book of Job.
5 *[...]*: We omit a brief discussion of ancient Greek ideas about 'the author or superintendent of the world'.
6 *the Platonic scheme*: The idea that the imperfection of the material world compared to the realm of ideal forms is a consequence of the defective matter from which the world is fashioned.
7 *the reversion ... little*: Reversion is the legal process by which an estate or title is inherited after the death of its owner ('incumbent'); PBS quips that such a prospective inheritance is worth little when the incumbent will never die.
8 *alledged design:* Declared purpose; an allusion to Milton, *Paradise Lost* I. 213–20, which explains that God has 'Left him [Satan] at large to his own dark designs, / That with reiterated crimes he might / Heap on himself damnation ... Treble confusion, wrath and vengeance'.
9 *[...]*: We omit a brief discussion of 'the laws of epic truth'.
10 *[...]*: Some sentences are omitted in which PBS speculates about Milton's religious opinions.
11 *one more superstition*: Christianity itself.
12 *Dante and Tasso*: Two Italian poets who wrote extensively on religion and love: Dante Alighieri (*c.*1265–1321) in his *Vita Nuova* (1295), *Convivio* (1304–7) and *Divina Commedia* (1308–20); and Torquato Tasso (1544–95) in his *Gerusalemme liberata* (1581) and *Rime* (1567–93).
13 *diocesans*: The clergy or people of a diocese.
14 *coquetting*: Trifling.
15 *'local ... name'*: PBS quotes from Shakespeare, *A Midsummer Night's Dream* V.i.14–17: 'And as imagination bodies forth / The forms of things unknown, the poet's pen / Turns them to shapes, and gives to airy nothing / A local habitation and a name.'
16 *to scout*: 'To mock at, deride' (*OED*).
17 *torments of ... ever*: In Mark 9:44 and 9:46, the damned are condemned to Hell, 'Where their worm dieth not, and the fire is not quenched'.
18 *[...]*: A passage is omitted in which PBS expands on the means by which questions about the Devil can lead to 'disbelief'.

19 *Διάβολος*: Greek, *Diabolos*: 'slanderer', 'false accuser'.
20 *[. . .]*: We omit a brief discussion of the role of the Devil in the Book of Job.
21 *delators*: Paid informers.
22 *[. . .]*: A partly cancelled and unresolved sentence is omitted here.
23 *irritate*: Excite, stimulate.
24 *Tiberius, or Bonaparte or Lord Castlereagh*: Tiberius Julius Caesar Augustus (42 BC–AD 37) was the third Roman emperor; Napoleon Bonaparte (1769–1821) was First Consul and then Emperor of France; Robert Stewart, Lord Castlereagh (1769–1822), was foreign secretary and Leader of the House of Commons, and associated with the brutal repression of dissent in both Britain and Ireland. See *The Mask of Anarchy*, ll. 5–6 (p. 357), and headnote to 'To S[idmouth] and C[astlereagh]' (p. 774).
25 *anatomising . . . alive*: Vivisecting, i.e. dissecting a living animal.
26 *[. . .]*: A number of paragraphs are omitted here in which PBS considers the extent of the Devil's 'sphere of operation' in the light of the immense universe being revealed by new astronomical instruments. PBS wonders whether the Devil is to be understood, by Christians, as having dominion over a potential 'multitude' of other worlds whose putative 'inhabitants' he is also responsible for tempting, and whether, if so, the Devil performs this function in person or through agents, i.e. whether the Devil partakes of the omnipresence of God.
27 *A droll story . . . were drowned*: In Mark 5:1–20, Matthew 8:28–34 and Luke 8:26–39.
28 *Gadarean Ichthyophagists*: 'Fish eaters of Gadara', site of the events here described. The fish was an early Christian symbol.
29 *I should . . . consumers*: PBS was no doubt aware of the Jewish prohibition on the eating of pork.
30 *[. . .]*: A passage is omitted in which PBS considers the subject of possession by demons, and the supposed location of Hell.
31 *[. . .]*: A passage is omitted in which PBS considers the origins of the name Lucifer, meaning 'the light bearer'.
32 *antient Gods of the Woods*: The fauns and satyrs of Greek myth, of whom Pan (mentioned later) was the leader.
33 *by its sight*: By the sight of it.
34 *Aesculapius and Apollo*: Gods associated in Greek mythology with medicine and healing.
35 *the Serpent . . . hieroglyph of eternity*: PBS refers to the ouroboros: the image of a serpent devouring its own tail, the earliest appearance of which is in ancient Egyptian funerary texts.
36 *propitiation*: Atonement, expiation; i.e. for the sin of Adam and Eve which devolved upon humankind. PBS's draft ends here.

From *A Philosophical View of Reform*

PBS began work on *A Philosophical View of Reform* (*PVR*) towards the end of 1819, perhaps around 6 November, when he wrote to Maria Gisborne that he had 'deserted the odorous gardens of literature to journey across the great sandy desert of politics' (*Letters* II, p. 150). Composition seems to have continued until at least late December, and perhaps into 1820. Our extracts are taken from PBS's unfinished and in places rather rough draft (as transcribed in *SC* VI), which survives in the Carl H. Pforzheimer Library; a transcript by MWS is now Bodleian MS Shelley adds. d. 6 (see *BSM* XXII). PBS sought to have the essay published in 1820, so as to address the crisis in English political life that followed the 'Peterloo Massacre' of August 1819 (see *The Mask of Anarchy*, p. 357), recommending it to his publisher Charles Ollier, in a letter of 15 December 1819, as 'an instructive and readable book, appealing from the passions to the reason of men' (*Letters* II, p. 164); and in a letter of 26 May 1820 to Leigh Hunt as 'boldly but temperately written—& I think readable—It is intended for a kind of standard book for the philosophical reformers' (*Letters* II, p. 201). MWS considered publishing *PVR* after PBS's death but it was not published until 1920. PBS did, however, recycle some material from *PVR* in *A Defence of Poetry*, including his assertion that 'poets . . . are the unacknowledged legislators of the world'.

Summaries are provided in the notes for significant editorial omissions.

1 *two recent wars*: Presumably the American War of Independence (1775–83), and the French Revolutionary (1792–1802) and Napoleonic Wars (1803–15).

2 *The Republics . . . its enemy*: The northern Italian city states whose alliance as the Lombard League defeated the Holy Roman Emperor Frederick Barbarossa in 1176, thereby ensuring their freedom. The Medici were one of the leading families in the Republic of Florence (part of the Lombard League), whose power kept the authority of the popes in check. In his characterization of the Medici, it is possible that PBS meant 'polished tyrants' to replace rather than augment 'flattered traitors'.

3 *Raphael and Michelangelo*: Raphael (1483–1520) and Michelangelo (1475–1564) were two of the leading artists of the Italian Renaissance.

4 *nursling of this Republic*: Giovanni Boccaccio (*c*.1313–75), whose writings were a major source of and influence on the work of Geoffrey Chaucer (*c*.1343–1400).

5 *[. . .]*: Three paragraphs are omitted in which PBS discusses the spread of liberty and religious reform across Europe, culminating in the English Renaissance and the beginning of the Enlightenment ('This new epoch' of the following paragraph). Cp. similar histories in 'Ode to Liberty' (p. 427) and *Hellas* (p. 512).

6 *Lord Bacon . . . Montaigne*: Francis Bacon (1561–1626), Baruch Spinoza (1632–77), Thomas Hobbes (1588–1679), Pierre Bayle (1647–1706) and Michel de Montaigne (1533–92): founding thinkers of the European Enlightenment, who promoted humanist ideals, rational enquiry and empirical method.

7 *Locke*: John Locke (1632–1704), another Enlightenment thinker of central importance: a defining figure of British empiricism and classical liberalism.

8 *Europe*: Followed in PBS's draft by: 'Philosophy went forth into the enchanted forest of the daemons of worldly power, as the pioneer of the

overgrowth of ages.' PBS excluded this sentence, part of which is incorporated into his essay 'On Life' (p. 621), which is drafted in the same notebook.

9 *Hartley, Berkeley and Hume*: David Hartley (1705–57) developed an associationist theory of the operations of the mind, George Berkeley (1685–1753) was the leading British proponent of idealist philosophy and David Hume (1711–76) practised a rigorously sceptical strain of empirical argument. For PBS, their systematic reasoning established the limits of human knowledge, so undermining the pretensions of theology to possess transcendent truth by faith.

10 *A crowd of writers in France*: In a cancelled version of this passage, PBS mentions the French philosopher Montesquieu (1689–1755), and the English philosophers Algernon Sidney (see next note) and James Harrington (1611–77). In the revised version, PBS probably intends, in addition to Montesquieu, French critical and materialist thinkers such as Voltaire (1694–1778) and Holbach (1723–89), whose work he also examines in 'On Life' (p. 619).

11 *Swift ... Bentham*: The political satirist Jonathan Swift (1667–1745); Henry St John, Viscount Bolingbroke (1678–1751), Tory politician, sceptical essayist, journalist, political philosopher and controversialist; Algernon Sidney (1622–83), republican soldier, politician and political writer; Jean-Jacques Rousseau (1712–78), novelist, essayist and political philosopher, author of *The Social Contract* (1762), a major figure of the French Enlightenment; William Godwin (1756–1836), novelist, essayist and political philosopher, author of *An Enquiry Concerning Political Justice* (1793); and Jeremy Bentham (1748–1832), legal reformer, moral philosopher, political theorist, best known for elaborating the principle of utility, for which see note 13 below.

12 *inartificial*: Based on authority rather than evidence and reason.

13 *the principle of Utility*: The foundation of Jeremy Bentham's utilitarian ethics in his *Introduction to the Principles of Morals and Legislation* (1789), and one of the fundamentals of William Godwin's political thought. The principle might be paraphrased: 'In any given situation, the right action is that which promotes the happiness of the greatest number of people.' See also note 11 above.

14 *[. . .]*: A passage is omitted in which PBS discusses 'the system of government' and the political situation in America.

15 *[. . .]*: A lengthy passage is omitted in which PBS reflects further on the history of political liberty in Europe and its colonies.

16 *The literature . . . new birth*: Cp. this paragraph with PBS's similar assessment in his Preface to *Prometheus Unbound* (p. 184) and in *A Defence of Poetry* (p. 651), where he reworked much of this passage.

17 *low-thoughted*: Mean, small-minded.

18 *[. . .]*: We have omitted a sentence which PBS appears to have intended as a note rather than as part of the main text: 'In this sense, Religion may be called Poetry, though distorted from the beautiful simplicity of its truth—Coleridge has said that every poet was religious; the converse, that every religious man must be a poet was more true—.'

19 *[. . .]*: A passage is omitted in which PBS considers the reign of William III and Mary II of England (see next note) 'as a compromise between liberty and despotism'.

20 *the epoch adverted to*: The reign of William and Mary, which began in 1689; after Mary's death in 1694, William continued on the throne until 1702.

21 *[. . .]*: We omit PBS's account of the role of public credit (i.e. of a national debt) in government policy. Together with other reformers, and notably William Cobbett in his *Paper Against Gold* (1815), PBS considered that the necessity of paying the interest on the huge national debt (greatly increased to fund the American and Napoleonic wars) to the well-off who invested in government funds entailed a depreciating currency and increased regressive taxation – thus perpetuating an unequal distribution of national wealth and resulting in widespread and unjust hardship for the majority of people, who were obliged to work longer hours for less reward in order indirectly to service the debt.

22 *they*: The 'modern rulers of England'.

23 *excisemen*: Tax collectors, specifically of duty on manufactured goods.

24 *stock jobbers*: Traders in stocks and shares; stock brokers.

25 *pelting*: Petty, worthless.

26 *the substantial merchant*: PBS may have intended the following as a note to this sentence: 'As usual the first persons deceived are those who are the instruments of the fraud, and the merchant and the country gentleman may be excused for believing that their existence is connected with the permanence of the best practicable forms of social order.'

27 *antitype*: Example, instance of the type.

28 *idealisms*: Creations of the imagination.

29 *[. . .]*: A passage is omitted in which PBS contrasts the privileged lives of the aristocracy with the 'miseries' of the general population.

30 *A writer . . . excess of population*: Thomas Malthus (1766–1834), whose *Essay on the Principle of Population* (1798) offered a significant challenge to progressive accounts of the perfectibility of human society by arguing that, as the number of humans increased more rapidly than the means of subsistence, factors such as disease, famine, poverty and war were necessary to check the growth of population. William Godwin responded to Malthus in his *Of Population* (1820).

31 *the mark of Cain*: In Genesis 4:14–15, Cain, who is condemned to be 'a fugitive and a vagabond' after murdering his brother Abel, is marked by God with a sign lest he be slain by those whom he encounters.

32 *[is]*: PBS's draft reads 'being'.

33 *as they please*: In PBS's draft, this sentence is followed by another which he seems to have intended as a note rather than part of the main text: 'The rights of all men are intrinsically and originally equal and they forgo the assertion of all of them only that they may the more securely enjoy a portion.'

34 *sinecures*: Salaried positions demanding little work and yielding profit or bestowing status on the office-holder.

35 *tithes*: Taxes (traditionally one-tenth of income) paid to the Church.

36 *liberticide*: The destruction (literally 'killing') of liberty. Cp. 'England in 1819' (p. 405).

37 *must be paid*: Followed in PBS's draft by an incomplete sentence, set off from the main text: 'This sum cannot have amounted to less than two thousand millions; it would be a curious problem in political economy to calculate the precise degree of comfort and of ornament . . .'

38 *[. . .]*: A passage is omitted in which PBS assesses the advantages and disadvantages of repaying the national debt.

39 *of Hampden, of Lor[ ]*: John Hampden (*c.*1594–1643), one of the most active and influential of the English parliamentarians who challenged the authority of Charles I. There is a gap after 'Lor' in PBS's draft and MWS's transcript; editors have suggested 'Lor[d Bacon]'.

40 *then*: The MS breaks off here.

41 *[. . .]*: A lengthy passage is omitted in which PBS reflects on the process by which a gradual reform of Parliament might be achieved and the dangers of revolutionary violence ('the last resort of resistance') should it be denied.

42 *Robespierre to Louis 18*: Maximilien Robespierre (1758–94), one of the principal figures of the French Revolution, urged the execution of Louis XVI and oversaw much of the Reign of Terror in his role as head of the Committee of Public Safety. Louis XVIII (1755–1824) became King of France in 1814 when the Bourbon dynasty was restored after the first abdication of Napoleon Bonaparte.

43 *[. . .]*: PBS's draft continues for two further paragraphs, which consider the possibility and the nature of future political change.

A Defence of Poetry

The first and only number of *Ollier's Literary Miscellany*, a magazine launched in 1820 by PBS's publisher, Charles Ollier, included an essay by T. L. Peacock entitled 'The Four Ages of Poetry'. In this wittily mischievous piece, Peacock ridicules trends among contemporary poets that he regarded as affected and backward-looking by proposing a grand scheme according to which the character of poetry alters through time in response to historical circumstances, in four stages. In the iron age 'rude bards celebrate in rough numbers the exploits of ruder chiefs'; the succeeding golden age sees poetry attain its perfection, only to decline thereafter through a silver age of 'civilized life' and cultivated verse, which encompasses comic and satiric forms, to finish in an age of brass where it takes 'a retrograde stride to the barbarisms and crude traditions of the age of iron' in an attempt 'to return to nature and revive the age of gold'. Such a pattern, Peacock argues, can be discerned in the poetry of ancient Greece and Rome as well as in that of modern Europe. In England, the age of the medieval romance preceded the golden age of Shakespeare and Milton and was followed by a silver age typified by the polished style of Dryden, Pope, Gray and Collins, finally issuing in the present age of brass in which Scott, Byron, Wordsworth, Coleridge and Southey mimic primitive bards by taking as subject the actions of outlaws, country folk and remote figures of history and legend. These examples,

Peacock maintains, illustrate the law that poetry progressively falls away from its earliest role of civilizing and instructing to become at last a mere vehicle of amusement, with no claim to advance either knowledge or well-being, these having become the province of practical sciences such as mathematics, chemistry, history and political economy.

PBS received his friend Peacock's essay at Pisa in January 1821. It 'excited [his] polemical faculties so violently' (*Letters* II, p. 258) that he determined to make a response, which he began in February and sent to Ollier on 20 March for publication in the second number of the *Literary Miscellany*, which never appeared. Nor was a second or third part of the *Defence*, which he planned to add to the first, ever written (*Letters* II, pp. 258, 275). MWS eventually included it, without its references to Peacock's essay, in *1840 (ELTF)*. Our text is based on the press copy transcribed by MWS and corrected by PBS, now Bodleian MS Shelley e. 6, which was sent to Ollier, though some features have been adopted from PBS's draft and his intermediate fair copy (see *BSM* IV (Part Two), VII, XX and XXII).

Wide-ranging and closely argued, the *Defence* draws largely upon the European critical tradition reaching back to Plato and Aristotle, on the Renaissance reinterpretation of that tradition in Sir Philip Sidney's *The Defence of Poesy* (1595), and on the empirical philosophy of John Locke, George Berkeley and David Hume. PBS considers poetry historically as well as from perspectives offered by contemporary science, ethics and psychology. He engages with recent writing on the nature and uses of poetry such as Wordsworth's Preface to *Lyrical Ballads* (1802) and Coleridge's *Biographia Literaria* (1817). And he displays the eloquent partisanship of an enthusiastic reader and practitioner of the art he is defending.

The relation to Peacock's 'Four Ages' is explored in H. F. B. Brett-Smith's edition, *Peacock's Four Ages of Poetry, Shelley's Defence of Poetry, Browning's Essay on Shelley* (Oxford: Blackwell, 1921; hereafter *Brett-Smith*), and in Jean Hall, 'The Divine and the Dispassionate Selves: Shelley's *Defence* and Peacock's *The Four Ages of Poetry*', *KSJ* 41 (1992), pp. 139–63. General studies of the *Defence* include: M. H. Abrams, *The Mirror and the Lamp: Romantic Theory and the Critical Tradition* (Oxford: Oxford University Press, 1953), pp. 125–32; Kenneth Neill Cameron, *Shelley: The Golden Years* (Cambridge, Mass.: Harvard University Press, 1974), pp. 188–215; David Duff, 'Shelley and the "Great Poem"', in his *Romanticism and the Uses of Genre* (Oxford: Oxford University Press, 2009), pp. 191–200; Paul Hamilton, 'Poetics', in *The Oxford Handbook of Percy Bysshe Shelley*, ed. Michael O'Neill and Anthony Howe (Oxford: Oxford University Press, 2013), pp. 177–92; and Earl Wasserman, *Shelley: A Critical Reading* (Baltimore: Johns Hopkins University Press, 1971), pp. 204–20.

1 *A Defence of Poetry*: PBS originally wrote on the press copy sent to Ollier: 'A Defence of Poetry. or Remarks suggested by an Essay entitled "The four ages of Poetry Part I."'.

2 *τὸ ποιειν . . . τὸ λογιζειν*: The Greek words (*to poiein, to logizein*) signify respectively 'making' and 'reasoning'.

3 *connate*: Born at the same time.

4 *Aeolian lyre*: A wind-harp; see *Alastor*, l. 42 and note (pp. 114, 710).
5 *antitype*: Here, the word appears to carry the sense 'the original of what is represented', but see note to ll. 13–26 in the Prologue to *Peter Bell the Third* (p. 766) and note 7 to 'On Love' (p. 860).
6 *pencil*: A fine paintbrush.
7 *mimetic*: Imitative.
8 *Lord Bacon . . . world*: PBS supplies a reference to Francis Bacon's *De Dignitate et Augmentis Scientiarum* (Of the Dignity and Advancement of Learning; 1623), Book 3, chapter 1, in which Bacon affirms that similar observations made by different arts and sciences, some of which he has noted, are not mere figures of speech but real correspondences: 'clearly the same footsteps or signs of nature impressed upon different matters or subjects' (*The Works of Francis Bacon*, ed. James Spedding, Robert Leslie Ellis and Douglas Denon Heath, 15 vols (Boston: Houghton Mifflin, 1900), V, pp. 256–7, VIII, pp. 474–5).
9 *the chaos of a cyclic poem*: The unsystematized matter which has yet to be formed into a poem or series of poems based upon a cycle of myths. See pp. 658–9 and the Dedication before *Peter Bell the Third* (p. 369).
10 *copiousness of lexicography*: The ample linguistic resources provided by dictionaries.
11 *institutors . . . civil society*: The earliest poets were 'not only historians but theologians, moralists, and legislators' ('The Four Ages of Poetry', *Brett-Smith*, p. 5).
12 *Janus*: The Roman god of entrances and beginnings who was represented with two faces looking in opposite directions.
13 *prophets*: 'Among the Romans a poet was called *vates*, which is as much as a diviner, foreseer, or prophet': Sir Philip Sidney, *The Defence of Poesy*, in *Sir Philip Sidney*, ed. Katherine Duncan-Jones, 'The Oxford Authors' (Oxford: Oxford University Press, 1989), p. 214.
14 *germs*: Seeds.
15 *curse of Babel*: In Genesis 11:1–9, God punishes the overweening ambition of the inhabitants of Babel by introducing heterogeneous languages among them and scattering them over the earth.
16 *measure*: Appropriate metre.
17 *Cicero*: Marcus Tullius Cicero (106–43 BC), Roman statesman, orator, philosopher and essayist.
18 *periods*: A series of sentences composing a group.
19 *Lord Bacon was a poet*: PBS provides references to two of Bacon's essays, 'Filum Labyrinthi' (The Thread of the Labyrinth; before *c.*1607), which considers inductive reasoning, and the essay 'Of Death' (1612), which counsels against fear of dying.
20 *eternal music*: See note 24 below.
21 *epitomes . . . moths of just history*: The metaphor is Bacon's in *The Advancement of Learning* (1605), Book 2: 'As for the corruptions and moths of history, which are Epitomes, the use of them deserveth to be banished'. 'Epitomes' are summaries.
22 *Herodotus, Plutarch, Livy*: Herodotus (*c.*490–*c.*425 BC) was the first Greek historian properly so called; he later came to be regarded as the 'father of

history'. Plutarch, Greek biographer, historian, moralist and philosopher (*c.* AD 46–*c.*120), was best known for his *Parallel Lives* of eminent Greek and Roman public figures. Titus Livius (59 BC–AD 17), known as 'Livy' in English, was a Roman historian, author of a history of Rome from its beginnings to his own time in 142 books, of which about a quarter survive.

23 *Achilles, Hector and Ulysses*: Heroes of Homer's *Iliad* and *Odyssey*.

24 *planetary music . . . mortal ears*: The so-called 'music of the spheres', harmonious sounds supposed to be produced by the motion of the planets in their orbits and, in Christian tradition, inaudible to human ears since the Fall.

25 *Elysian*: Delightful, heavenly. Elysium in Classical myth was the dwelling place of virtuous souls after death.

26 *The great secret . . . not our own*: PBS develops more amply his theory of love in 'On Love' (p. 618).

27 *intervals and interstices*: Gaps and crevices.

28 *imperfections*: In 'A Discourse on the manners of the Antient Greeks relative to the subject of Love' (1818) PBS refers to the shortcomings of ancient Greek political institutions as well as to personal slavery and the inferior position of women (*Prose*, pp. 218, 220).

29 *the century . . . Socrates*: The fifth century BC.

30 *constant conjunction of events*: PBS adopted this principle from David Hume: 'Hume has shewn . . . that the only idea which we can form of causation is <derivable> from the constant conjunction of objects, and the consequent inference of one from the other' (*Prose Works* I, p. 121).

31 *idealisms*: Imaginative representations.

32 *actor's face . . . mask*: Actors in ancient Greek tragedy wore masks.

33 *trilogies*: Three plays of Sophocles – *Antigone*, *Oedipus the King* and *Oedipus at Colonus* – treat myths to do with the city of Thebes and Athens but were not written as a trilogy. Aeschylus' 'Oresteian' trilogy consists of *Agamemnon*, *The Libation-Bearers* and *The Eumenides*.

34 *Calderón . . . Autos*: PBS greatly admired the plays of the Spaniard Pedro Calderón de la Barca (1600–1681); he translated part of one, *El Mágico Prodigioso* (The Mighty Magician; 1637). An *auto sacramental* is a short allegorical drama on a religious theme.

35 *rigidly-defined . . . distorted superstition*: PBS's estimate of Calderón's religious dogmatism.

36 *the knight . . . necromancers and pagans*: PBS had written to Peacock on 15 February 1821 that he wished to 'break a lance with you, within the lists of a magazine' (*Letters* II, p. 261). Continuing the same idiom, he here imagines himself and Peacock as jousting knights, his own shield bearing the title of a great tragedy by Sophocles or Aeschylus or Shakespeare. In Tasso's romance *Gerusalemme liberata* (1581) XVI.29–31, the knight Rinaldo is freed from thraldom to the enchantress Armida with the help of a polished shield in which his true situation is reflected. In Spenser's *Faerie Queene* I.vii.33–4, Prince Arthur's diamond shield is described as being brighter than the sun; it dazzles his foes, a giant and a dragon (I.viii.19–20). Here 'Paladins' are knights errant; 'necromancers' are wizards who communicate with the dead.

37 *Addison's Cato*: A tragedy (1713) by Joseph Addison (1672–1719), based on the death of the Roman statesman of the title.
38 *Machiavelli*: Niccolò Machiavelli (1469–1527), Florentine historian and political theorist, author of *The Prince* (1532).
39 *bucolic writers*: The Greek poets Theocritus (first half of the third century BC), Bion (end of the second century BC) and Moschus (mid second century BC) are principally intended. PBS translated from the latter two. See *Poems* I, p. 450, II, pp. 348–9, 695–700.
40 *Astraea*: In Ovid's *Metamorphoses* I.149–50, Astraea, the maiden goddess of justice, was the last of the immortals to leave the earth, after the violent and bloody age of iron had succeeded to those of gold, silver and bronze. She was identified with the constellation Virgo.
41 *sacred links . . . life of all*: PBS has borrowed an analogy from the *Ion* of Plato, which he translated (*Notopoulos*, pp. 462–85) and in which Socrates explains to Ion (a rhapsode or public reciter of verses) that the divine influence of poetry resembles a magnetic force that passes from the inspiring Muse through the poet and the performer of poetry to each member of the audience, binding one to the other like links in a chain (pp. 472–3).
42 *Ennius, Varro, Pacuvius and Accius*: Early Roman poets (third to first century BC) in a range of genres and styles, including drama, epic, didactic poetry and satire. Fragments only of their poems and plays survive.
43 *Camillus . . . Cannae*: PBS recalls four examples of conspicuous civic virtue in the public life of ancient Rome. Marcus Furius Camillus was a general and statesman of the early fourth century BC renowned for probity; he returned from exile (unmerited, according to tradition) to defeat the Gauls who had captured Rome in 390 BC, becoming known as the second founder of the city. See *Ode to Liberty*, ll. 97–8 (p. 429). Captured by the Carthaginians during the First Punic War around the middle of the third century BC, Marcus Atilius Regulus was sent to Rome to negotiate peace, promising to return should his mission fail. He advised the Romans to continue the war and, true to his word, returned to Carthage, where he died in captivity, after, it was said, being tortured (Horace, *Odes* III.v). When the victorious Gauls entered Rome in 390 BC, the Roman patricians, who were about to be slaughtered, awaited them with such lofty demeanour and dignified composure, seated in formal dress before their magnificent houses, that the Gauls gazed on them as if they were statues (Livy, *History of Rome* V.xli). After the heavy defeat inflicted on the Roman army at Cannae in 216 BC by the Carthaginians under Hannibal, some of Rome's allies switched their allegiance; the Roman Republic refused to do so, eventually overcoming Carthage in 202.
44 *quia carent vate sacro*: 'Because they lack a sacred poet' (Horace, *Odes* IV.ix.28).
45 *rhapsodist*: A performer of poetry in ancient Greece. See note 41 above.
46 *Moses, Job . . . Jesus and his disciples*: PBS considers at greater length the effect of the poetry of the Old Testament on the mind of Jesus in 'On Christianity' (*Prose Works* I, pp. 249–50).
47 *the three forms . . . faculties of mind*: *Brett-Smith* (p. 95) cites Plato's *Timaeus*, where the 'faculties of mind' are divided into three, which have been implanted in human beings from creation. An immortal soul that

partakes of the divine is located in the skull and governs the mortal soul, which is subdivided into a higher mortal soul in the breast, source of the nobler passions such as courage and ambition, and in the abdomen a lower mortal soul, seat of the physical appetites (69–72). In Plato's *Phaedrus* the three divisions of the soul are likened to a charioteer and the two unruly horses that he guides (253d–255).

48 *Light . . . rouze*: Shakespeare, *Macbeth* III.ii.51–4.

49 *Celtic*: Here used to designate tribes from lands to the north of Rome, such as the Gauls; more generally, peoples to the north of ancient Greece and Rome.

50 *Plato in his Republic*: Plato has Socrates set out ideas on a just society as co-operative community in the *Republic* 369 ff. In 'On Christianity', PBS considers that the legal scheme of the Republic promoted equality (*Prose Works* I, p. 263).

51 *Timaeus and Pythagoras*: Timaeus of Locris is a principal character in Plato's dialogue *Timaeus*, where he is said to be an eminent Pythagorean philosopher. Pythagoras (*c.*570–*c.*495 BC) lived chiefly in the Greek colony of Crotona in southern Italy, where he established a religious and philosophical community governed by strict ethical principles and dedicated to the investigation of nature. Pythagoreans were notable for their contributions to the sciences of mathematics and music.

52 *exoteric . . . esoteric*: Respectively, 'available to all' and 'restricted to the initiated'. Jesus preached to all what the ancient philosophers taught only to a small number.

53 *'Galeotto . . . scrisse'*: 'Galeotto was the book and he who wrote it' (Dante, *Inferno* V.137). In *Inferno* V.118–42, Francesca recounts how she and her lover Paolo first kissed while reading the story of Lancelot and Guinevere, who were brought together by Galeotto (Galahad), so that the book and its author performed the office of go-between for them that Galeotto had for the knight and the queen.

54 *trouveurs . . . Petrarch*: The *trouveurs*, or *trouvères*, were medieval poets of northern France known chiefly for epic and narrative poetry; the *troubadours* of southern France developed love lyrics especially. It is evidently these latter to whom PBS refers. Francesco Petrarca (1304–74), 'Petrarch' in English, was the author of the *Canzoniere*, a series of love poems which profoundly influenced later European literature. PBS admired the 'tender & solemn enthusiasm' (*Letters* II, p. 20) of Petrarch, whom he celebrates in 'Lines Written among the Euganean Hills, October, 1818', ll. 200–205 (p. 158), and whose *Trionfi* he takes as model in *The Triumph of Life* (p. 570).

55 *Vita Nuova*: Dante's account (1295) in verse and prose of his youthful love for Beatrice which marked the beginning of his 'new life'.

56 *Beatrice in Paradise . . . modern poetry*: In the *Paradiso* Beatrice is Dante's companion and guide as they ascend through the heavens to the Divine presence.

57 *'Divine Drama'*: Dante's *Divina Commedia*.

58 *Love, which found a worthy poet in Plato*: Notably in the *Symposium*, which consists of a series of speeches on the nature of, and in praise of, love; and in the *Phaedrus*.

59 *Ariosto . . . Rousseau*: Ludovico Ariosto (1474–1533), author of the verse romance *Orlando Furioso* (1516–32), which includes a variety of amorous episodes. For Tasso see note 12 to the extract from 'On the Devil, and Devils' (p. 866) and for Calderón see note 34 above. Jean-Jacques Rousseau (see note 11 to 'From *A Philosophical View of Reform*': p. 869), the only writer of prose in PBS's list, is included for his novel *Julie; ou, La Nouvelle Héloïse* (1761), which PBS described as a work of 'sublimest genius' in summer 1816 when visiting the Swiss locations where some episodes of the novel are laid (*Letters* II, p. 485). PBS introduces Rousseau as guide in *The Triumph of Life* (p. 570).

60 *trophies*: Tokens (enemy arms or armour) set up on a field of battle to mark a victory, in honour of the god who had brought it about.

61 *Riphaeus . . . justissimus unus*: In Virgil's *Aeneid* II.426–7, the slain warrior Riphaeus is called 'one most just [*justissimus unus*] and zealous for the right among the Trojans'. Dante imagines him among the just in Paradise, departing from strict Christian doctrine in thus rewarding a pagan who lived before Christ (*Paradiso* XX.67–72).

62 *Milton's poem*: The commentary on *Paradise Lost* that PBS develops here is anticipated, in greater detail and in bolder terms, in 'On the Devil, and Devils' (p. 630), and also in the Preface to *Prometheus Unbound* (p. 184).

63 *alledged design*: Declared purpose; see *Paradise Lost* I.213–20.

64 *modern mythology*: The narratives deriving from the Bible and other sources of the Judaeo-Christian tradition.

65 *Lucretius . . . sensible world*: The Roman poet Titus Lucretius Carus (98–*c*.55 BC) was the author of the scientific and philosophical poem *De Rerum Natura* (On the Nature of Things), which proposes a materialist metaphysics, in which all natural phenomena are accounted for as combinations of atoms moving in space, and recommends an ethical system aiming to liberate humans from fear of the gods and of punishment after death. PBS judged him to be 'wise and lofty-minded' in the Preface to *Laon and Cythna* (1817) but here suggests that his attachment to the material limits the appeal of his philosophy. He is 'limed' – trapped, as with the sticky substance 'birdlime' – in the 'sensible world', i.e. the world as perceived by the senses.

66 *mock-birds*: Birds that imitate the calls of other birds.

67 *Apollonius Rhodius . . . Claudian*: The list comprises ancient authors of epics generally regarded as lesser achievements than those of Homer and Virgil. In Greek: the *Argonautica* by Apollonius Rhodius (*c*.295–215 BC), the *Posthomerica* by Quintus Smyrnaeus (late fourth century AD), the *Dionysiaca* by Nonnus (fifth century AD); in Latin: the *Pharsalia* by Lucan (Marcus Annaeus Lucanus, AD 39–65), the *Thebiad* by Publius Papinius Statius (*c*. AD 45–96), *The Rape of Proserpine* by Claudian (Claudius Claudianus, late fourth–early fifth century AD).

68 *Orlando Furioso . . . Fairy Queen*: Sixteenth-century epics by the Italians Ludovico Ariosto (1474–1533) and Torquato Tasso (1544–95), the Portuguese Luís de Camões (*c*.1524–80), and Edmund Spenser (*c*.1552–99).

69 *a language . . . inharmonious barbarisms*: Dante's *Divina Commedia* (*c*. 1308–20) represented a decisive advance in the use of the Italian language

for literary purposes. In his *De Vulgari Eloquentia* (On Eloquence in the Vernacular; *c.*1304–7) he distinguishes between the numerous dialects of Italian in his day and an elevated idiom, distinct from any one of them, which could serve as the vehicle of a vernacular literature.

70 *Lucifer . . . starry flock*: Lucifer ('light-bearer') is Venus as the morning star, which (like a shepherd) guides the other stars to their fold at day-break. Traditionally, Lucifer was identified with Satan before the Fall, as in *Paradise Lost* V.708–9: 'His countenance, as the morning star that guides / The starry flock, allured them.'

71 *republican Italy*: PBS specifies the medieval republics of Florence and Pisa as fostering masterpieces of Italian literature and painting in *Letters* II, p. 122.

72 *instinct with*: Imbued with, animated by; the phrase occurs in *Paradise Lost* VI.752.

73 *Boccaccio*: Giovanni Boccaccio (*c.*1313–75), author of the prose stories collected in the *Decameron*. PBS describes him as 'in the high sense of the word a poet' in *Letters* II, p. 122.

74 *mechanists*: Advocates of a 'mechanical theory of the universe' (*OED*). PBS seems to intend those who aim to improve the conditions of life solely by promoting 'useful art and science' ('The Four Ages of Poetry', *Brett-Smith*, p. 19).

75 *mechanist*: Machine-maker.

76 *combines, labour*: Organizes specialized kinds of work for efficiency.

77 *'To him . . . taken away'*: PBS's version of a saying of Jesus in three of the Gospels, e.g. Matthew 13:12.

78 *Scylla and Charybdis*: Respectively, a six-headed monster living in a cave overlooking the ocean and a deadly whirlpool opposite; tradition located them in the straits of Messina between Sicily and the Italian mainland. Paired, they became an emblem of dangerous extremes: avoiding one entailed risking the other. See *Odyssey* XII.94 ff.

79 *'It is better . . . house of mirth'*: Cp. Ecclesiastes 7:2–4: 'It is better to go to the house of mourning, than to go to the house of feasting . . . The heart of the wise is in the house of mourning; but the heart of fools is in the house of mirth.'

80 *[Shelley's note]*: See note 59 above. In the 'Four Ages' Peacock cites Hume, Gibbon, Rousseau and Voltaire as 'deep and elaborate thinkers' who challenged 'every portion of the reign of authority' (*Brett-Smith*, p. 13).

81 *Inquisition in Spain*: Established in 1478, the Spanish Inquisition was abolished for the three years of Liberal government that followed the Revolution of 1820; restored in 1823, it was finally abolished in 1834.

82 *Raphael and Michael Angelo*: Raphael (1483–1520) and Michelangelo (1475–1564) were two of the leading artists of the Italian Renaissance.

83 *Hebrew poetry*: Of the Old Testament, e.g. Job, Psalms, Isaiah.

84 *'let I dare not . . . adage'*: Quoting *Macbeth* I.vii.44–5.

85 *the abuse . . . inequality of mankind*: The effect of mechanization and the specialization of labour in the industrial system has been to increase rather than reduce inequality.

86 *curse imposed on Adam*: In Genesis 3:19, God afflicts Adam for his disobedience: 'In the sweat of thy face shalt thou eat bread, till thou return unto the ground.'

87 *God and Mammon*: See Matthew 6:24: 'No man can serve two masters: for either he will hate the one, and love the other; or else he will hold to the one, and despise the other. Ye cannot serve God and mammon.' 'Mammon' derives from the Hebrew for 'money', 'wealth'.

88 *Poetry is . . . knowledge*: Cp. Wordsworth, Preface to *Lyrical Ballads* (1802): 'Poetry is the breath and finer spirit of all knowledge . . . the first and last of all knowledge' (ed. Michael Mason (Harlow: Longman, 1992), pp. 76–7).

89 *the intertexture*: The weaving-in.

90 *'dictated . . . song'*: See *Paradise Lost* IX.21–4: 'my celestial patroness, who deigns / Her nightly visitation unimplored, / And dictates to me slumbering, or inspires / Easy my unpremeditated verse'. Cp. 'To a Sky-Lark', ll. 1–5 (pp. 434–5).

91 *alledge*: Place in evidence.

92 *interlunations*: Periods of about four days between the old and the new moon when no moon is visible in the sky.

93 *All things . . . perceived*: PBS elaborates on this principle in 'On Life' (p. 619).

94 *'The mind . . . Hell of Heaven'*: Satan thus challenges the reality of his damnation in *Paradise Lost* I.254–5.

95 *film of familiarity*: PBS is echoing Coleridge's account of Wordsworth's purpose in *Lyrical Ballads* (1798): 'to give the charm of novelty to things of every day, and to excite a feeling analogous to the supernatural, by awakening the mind's attention from the lethargy of custom, and directing it to the loveliness and the wonders of the world before us; an inexhaustible treasure, but for which in consequence of the film of familiarity and selfish solicitude we have eyes, yet see not, ears that hear not, and hearts that neither feel nor understand' (*Biographia Literaria* (1817), chapter 14: ed. James Engel and W. Jackson Bate, 2 vols (Princeton, NJ: Princeton University Press, 1983), II, p. 7).

96 *Non merita . . . il Poeta*: 'None deserves the name of creator but God and the Poet.' PBS cites Tasso's dictum in *Letters* II, p. 30, and in 'On Life' (p. 620), and he recalls in *Letters* II, p. 29, Socrates' claim in Plato's *Phaedrus* 245a, 265b that the inspired poet experiences a kind of divine madness. See also PBS's translation of Plato's *Ion* (*Notopoulos*, pp. 472–3).

97 *institutor*: Teacher, instructor.

98 *arbitration of popular breath*: The casual judgement of common opinion.

99 *'there . . . soar'*: 'there sitting where ye durst not soar': Satan's recollection of his former eminence (*Paradise Lost* IV.829).

100 *Homer . . . poet laureate*: This catalogue of charges laid against poets, and one painter, ranges from the fanciful (Homer) to the established (Bacon) through various traditional imputations. A 'peculator' is an embezzler. Spenser was not Poet Laureate but had celebrated monarchy by creating an idealized figure of Elizabeth I in the *Faerie Queene*. PBS deplored the conservative political views of the current Poet Laureate, Robert Southey, whom he had accused of slandering him, anonymously, in print. See Preface to *Adonais* (p. 491) and note 102 below.

101 *Their errors . . . redeemer Time*: The biblical language of the passage derives from: Isaiah 40:15: 'the nations . . . are counted as the small dust of

the balance'; Isaiah 1:18: 'though your sins be as scarlet, they shall be as white as snow'; Revelation 7:14: 'these . . . have washed their robes, and made them white in the blood of the Lamb.' The lamb was a traditional emblem of Christ the Redeemer.

102 *contemporary calumnies . . . poets*: PBS was himself the object of such 'calumnies'. See note to *Peter Bell the Third*, Dedication (p. 369).

103 *judge not . . . judged*: Cp. Matthew 7:1: 'Judge not, that ye be not judged.'

104 *a Poet becomes a man*: PBS insisted on this distinction in a letter of 19 July 1821: 'The poet & the man are two different natures: though they exist together they may be unconscious of each other, & incapable of deciding upon each other's powers & effects by any reflex act' (*Letters* II, p. 310).

105 *obnoxious to*: Subject to.

106 *Theseids . . . Maevius*: Juvenal (Satire I) complains of the tedious epic *Theseid* by Codrus; Bavius and Maevius were Roman poets castigated for their dull and inferior verses by Virgil (Eclogue III); Horace urges the winds and tide to shipwreck Maevius (Epode X).

107 *For the literature of England*: In his peroration to the *Defence*, PBS borrows from the Preface to *Prometheus Unbound* (p. 184), where the principal topics are more amply considered, and from *A Philosophical View of Reform*, then unpublished, which contains an earlier version of this passage (pp. 640–41). A comparison of the three texts reveals a number of important differences as well as providing a comprehensive view of PBS's thinking on the topics he considers.

108 *low-thoughted*: Mean, small-minded.

109 *spirit of the age*: PBS defines this spirit as 'the new springs of thought and feeling, which the great events of our age have exposed to view' in a letter of 15 October 1819 (*Letters* II, p. 127).

110 *hierophants of an unapprehended inspiration*: Poets act as interpreters of truths which they intuit rather than grasp rationally.

111 *legislators of the World*: In chapter 10 of Samuel Johnson's *The History of Rasselas: Prince of Abissinia* (1759), the sage and poet Imlac declares that the poet 'must write as the interpreter of nature, and the legislator of mankind, and consider himself as presiding over the thoughts and manners of future generations' (ed. J. P. Hardy (Oxford: Oxford University Press, 1968), p. 27). See 'institutors . . . civil society' (p. 654) and note 11 above.

Appendix

The Contents of Shelley's Volumes of Verse Published in His Lifetime

Original Poetry; by Victor and Cazire by Shelley and his sister Elizabeth (London: J. J. Stockdale, 1810)
Letter ('Here I sit with my paper, my pen and my ink')
Letter: To Miss —— —— From Miss —— ——
Song ('Cold, cold is the blast when December is howling')
Song ('Come ——! sweet is the hour')
Song: Despair
Song: Sorrow
Song: Hope
Song: Translated from the Italian
Song: Translated from the German
The Irishman's Song
Song ('Fierce roars the midnight storm')
Song: To —— ('Ah! sweet is the moonbeam that sleeps on yon fountain')
Song: To —— ('Stern, stern is the voice of fates fearfull command')
Saint Edmond's Eve [The discovery that this poem was plagiarized from Matthew ('Monk') Lewis, *Tales of Terror* (1801), caused the volume to be withdrawn]
Revenge
Ghasta; or, The Avenging Demon!!!
Fragment, or The Triumph of Conscience

Posthumous Fragments of Margaret Nicholson; Being Poems found amongst the Papers of that Noted Female who attempted the Life of the King in 1786, edited by John Fitzvictor (Oxford: J. Munday, 1810)
'Ambition, power, and avarice, now have hurl'd'
Fragment. Supposed to be an Epithalamium of Francis Ravaillac and Charlotte Cordé
Despair ('And can'st thou mock mine agony, thus calm')
Fragment ('Yes! all is past—swift time has fled away')
The Spectral Horseman
Melody to a Scene of Former Times

Queen Mab; A Philosophical Poem: With Notes (printed privately, 1813; first unauthorized edition: London: William Clark, 1821)
Dedication: To Harriet*****
Queen Mab

Alastor; or, The Spirit of Solitude: and Other Poems (London: Baldwin, Cradock and Joy and Carpenter and Son, 1816)
Alastor; or, The Spirit of Solitude
O! there are spirits of the air
Stanzas.—April, 1814
Mutability
'The pale, the cold, and the moony smile'
A Summer-Evening Church-Yard, Lechlade, Gloucestershire
To Wordsworth
Feelings of a Republican on the Fall of Bonaparte
Superstition
Sonnet. From the Italian of Dante
Translated from the Greek of Moschus
The Daemon of the World. A Fragment

Laon and Cythna; or, The Revolution of the Golden City: A Vision of the Nineteenth Century. In the Stanza of Spenser (London: Sherwood, Neely & Jones and C. and J. Ollier, 1817), withdrawn and reissued as *The Revolt of Islam; A Poem, in Twelve Cantos* (London: C. and J. Ollier, 1818)
Dedication: To Mary —— ——
Laon and Cyntha
[or]
Dedication: To Mary —— ——
The Revolt of Islam

Rosalind and Helen, A Modern Eclogue; With Other Poems (London: C. and J. Ollier, 1819)
Rosalind and Helen
Lines Written among the Euganean Hills, October, 1818
Hymn to Intellectual Beauty
Sonnet. Ozymandias

The Cenci. A Tragedy, in Five Acts, [printed in] Italy (London: C. and J. Ollier, 1819)
The Cenci

Prometheus Unbound: A Lyrical Drama in Four Acts, With Other Poems (London: C. and J. Ollier, 1820)
Prometheus Unbound
The Sensitive-Plant
A Vision of the Sea
Ode to Heaven
An Exhortation
Ode to the West Wind
An Ode [Written, October, 1819, before the Spaniards had recovered their Liberty]
The Cloud
To a Sky-Lark
Ode to Liberty

Oedipus Tyrannus; or, Swellfoot the Tyrant. A Tragedy. In Two Acts. Translated from the Original Doric (London: J. Johnston, 1820)
Oedipus Tyrannus

Epipsychidion: Verses Addressed to the Noble and Unfortunate Lady Emilia V——, Now Imprisoned in the Convent of —— (London: C. and J. Ollier, 1821)
Epipsychidion

Adonais: An Elegy on the Death of John Keats, Author of Endymion, Hyperion Etc. (Pisa: 'With the types of Didot', 1821)
Adonais

Hellas: A Lyrical Drama (London: C. and J. Ollier, 1822)
Hellas: A Lyrical Drama
Written on hearing the news of the death of Napoleon

Acknowledgements

Any editor working on Shelley's texts at present necessarily owes a large debt to two series of manuscript facsimiles with commentary: *The Bodleian Shelley Manuscripts* and the volumes containing material by Shelley in *The Manuscripts of the Younger Romantics*, both under the general editorship of Donald H. Reiman. In addition, we have benefitted particularly from the documents and commentaries in the volumes of *Shelley and His Circle 1773–1822*, edited (successively) by Kenneth Neill Cameron, Donald H. Reiman and Doucet Devin Fisher, as well as several recent editions of Shelley's work: by Donald H. Reiman, Neil Fraistat and Nora Crook for Johns Hopkins University Press; Geoffrey Matthews, Kelvin Everest and others for the Longman Annotated English Poets series; Timothy Webb for Dent; Donald H. Reiman and Neil Fraistat for Norton; and Michael O'Neill and Zachary Leader for OUP World's Classics.

For valuable advice and help over many years the editors wish to thank especially Bruce Barker-Benfield, John Barnard, John Birtwhistle, Nora Crook, Elizabeth Denlinger, Kelvin Everest, Doucet Devin Fisher, Michael O'Neill, Michael Rossington, Timothy Webb and Alan Weinberg.

Kate Parker's meticulous and patient copy-editing has been exemplary.

The following institutions have kindly allowed us to take manuscripts in their possession as the basis of our texts, for which detailed references are supplied in the notes to the relevant poems and prose: the Pierpont Morgan Library, New York; the British Library; the Houghton Library, Harvard University; Edinburgh University Library; the Provost and fellows of Eton College; Special Collections Centre, University of Aberdeen; the Bodleian Libraries, University of Oxford; the Carl H. Pforzheimer Collection of Shelley and His Circle, New York Public Library; the Carl and Lily Pforzheimer

Foundation, Inc.; the Library of Congress; the Syndics of Cambridge University Library; the Rosenbach of the Free Library of Philadelphia; the Bibliotheca Bodmeriana, Cologny-Genève, Switzerland; the Henry E. Huntington Library, San Marino, California; and the John Rylands University Library of Manchester.

Index of Titles

Page numbers in italics refer to the relevant endnotes for each work.

Index of First Lines of Verse

Page numbers in italics refer to the relevant endnotes for each work.

Penguin Classics

THE COMPLETE POEMS
JOHN MILTON

'I may assert Eternal Providence
And justify the ways of God to men'

John Milton was a master of almost every type of verse, from the classical to the religious and from the lyrical to the epic. His early poems include the devotional 'On the Morning of Christ's Nativity', 'Comus', a masque, and the pastoral elegy 'Lycidas'. After Cromwell's death and the dashing of Milton's political hopes, he began composing *Paradise Lost*, which reflects his profound understanding of politics and power. Written when Milton was at the height of his abilities, this great masterpiece fuses the Christian with the classical in its description of the Fall of Man. In *Samson Agonistes*, Milton's last work, the poet draws a parallel with his own life in the hero's struggle to renew his faith in God.

In this edition of the *Complete Poems*, John Leonard draws attention to words coined by Milton and those that have changed their meaning since his time. He also provides full notes to elucidate biblical, classical and historical allusions and has modernized spelling, capitalization and punctuation.

Edited with a preface and notes by John Leonard

read more 

PENGUIN CLASSICS

THE COMPLETE POEMS
ANDREW MARVELL

'Thus, though we cannot make our sun
Stand still, yet we will make him run'

Member of Parliament, tutor to Oliver Cromwell's ward, satirist and friend of John Milton, Andrew Marvell was one of the most significant poets of the seventeenth century. *The Complete Poems* demonstrates his unique skill and immense diversity, and includes lyrical love-poetry, religious works and biting satire. From the passionately erotic 'To his Coy Mistress', to the astutely political Cromwellian poems and the prescient 'Garden' and 'Mower' poems, which consider humankind's relationship with the environment, these works are masterpieces of clarity and metaphysical imagery. Eloquent and compelling, they remain among the most vital and profound works of the era – works by a figure who, in the words of T. S. Eliot, 'speaks clearly and unequivocally with the voice of his literary age'.

This edition of Marvell's complete poems is based on a detailed study of the extant manuscripts, with modern translations provided for Marvell's Greek and Latin poems. This edition also includes a chronology, further reading, appendices, notes and indexes of titles and first lines, with a new introduction by Jonathan Bate.

Edited by Elizabeth Story Donno

With an introduction by Jonathan Bate

THE NEW PENGUIN BOOK OF ROMANTIC POETRY

'And what if all of animated Nature
Be but organic harps, diversely framed'

The Romanticism that emerged after the American and French revolutions of 1776 and 1789 represented a new flowering of the imagination and the spirit, and a celebration of the soul of humanity with its capacity for love. This extraordinary collection sets the acknowledged genius of poems such as Blake's 'Tyger', Coleridge's 'Khubla Khan' and Shelley's 'Ozymandias' alongside verse from less familiar figures and women poets such as Charlotte Smith and Mary Robinson. We also see familiar poets in an unaccustomed light, as Blake, Wordsworth and Shelley demonstrate their comic skills, while Coleridge, Keats and Clare explore the Gothic and surreal.

This volume is arranged by theme and genre, revealing unexpected connections between the poets. In their introduction Jonathan and Jessica Wordsworth explore Romanticism as a way of responding to the world, and they begin each section with a helpful preface, notes and bibliography.

'An absolutely fascinating selection – notable for its women poets, its intriguing thematic categories and its helpful mini biographies' Richard Holmes

Edited with an introduction by Jonathan and Jessica Wordsworth

Penguin Classics

DON JUAN
LORD BYRON

'Let us have wine and women's mirth and laughter,
Sermons and soda water the day after'

Byron's exuberant parody involves the adventures of a youth named Don Juan. His exploits include an adulterous liaison in Spain, an affair on a Greek island with a pirate's daughter, a stay in a Sultan's harem, a bloody battle in Turkey and a sojourn in Russia as the lover of Catherine the Great – all described by a narrator who frequently digresses from his hero in order to converse with his readers about war, society and convention. A revolutionary experiment in epic, Don Juan blends high drama with earthy humour, outrageous satire of Byron's contemporaries (in particular Wordsworth and Southey) and mockery of Western culture, with England under particular attack.

This edition represents a significant contribution to Byron scholarship and the editors have drawn on their authoritative edition of the poem published by the University of Texas Press. Their extensive annotation covers points of interest, selected variant readings and historical allusions Byron wove into his poem. This edition also includes an illuminating new introduction by Susan J. Wolfson and Peter J. Manning, and updated further reading.

Edited by T. G. Steffan, E. Steffan and W. W. Pratt

With a new introduction by Susan J. Wolfson and Peter J. Manning

PENGUIN CLASSICS

PERCY BYSSHE SHELLEY: SELECTED POEMS AND PROSE

The eldest child of a family of landed gentry in West Sussex, PERCY BYSSHE SHELLEY (1792–1822) was heir to a considerable fortune and, from 1806, to a baronetcy. The major directions of his thought and writings were formed early. At Eton (1804–10), where he was teased and bullied by the other boys, he developed (encouraged by the enlightened physician Dr James Lind) an enthusiasm for contemporary science, began to read radical writers, published a short Gothic novel and, on leaving school, collaborated with his sister on his first volume of verse. Matriculating at University College, Oxford, in autumn 1810, he became a close friend of Thomas Jefferson Hogg, with whom he wrote and distributed the pamphlet *The Necessity of Atheism*, leading to their joint expulsion from the university in March 1811. In August of that year Shelley eloped with the sixteen-year-old Harriet Westbrook, precipitating a rupture of relations with his family. During a visit to Ireland in February–March 1812 he agitated for Catholic emancipation and repeal of the Union with England and distributed political pamphlets he had written for the purpose, an early instance of a life-long engagement with liberal politics. Shelley's first major poem, the radical, anti-religious and visionary *Queen Mab* (1813), was printed and distributed privately. In July 1814 he left London to travel in France and Switzerland with his future wife Mary Godwin and her step-sister, Claire Clairmont.

Following his grandfather's death in 1815, Shelley inherited a substantial sum and was provided with a regular income, both of which he shared generously. The following summer he spent with Byron in Switzerland, beginning a complex and challenging friendship that lasted until Shelley's death. Another lasting friendship, with the poet, essayist and editor Leigh Hunt, introduced him to a group of writers that included John Keats and William Hazlitt. After leaving England in March 1818, the Shelleys travelled widely in Italy before settling at Pisa. During these final years of his life he produced a series of masterpieces which include *Prometheus Unbound*, *Adonais*, *The Triumph of*

Life and *A Defence of Poetry*. Shelley drowned off the north-west coast of Italy in July 1822.

JACK DONOVAN was formerly Reader in English at the University of York (UK), having previously taught at universities in the United States and France. He has written on French and English Sentimental and Romantic literature and is currently one of the editorial team preparing a complete annotated edition of Shelley's poetry.

CIAN DUFFY is Professor of English Literature at Lund University, Sweden. He has written on various aspects of British Romantic-period literature and is currently working on the relationship between romanticisms and romantic nationalisms in Britain and the Nordic countries.